Vegetation and the terrestrial carbon cycle
Modelling the first 400 million years

Plants have colonised and modified the World's surface for the last 400 million years. In this book the authors demonstrate that an understanding of the role of vegetation in the terrestrial carbon cycle during this time can be gained by linking the key mechanistic elements of present day vegetation processes to models of the global climate during different geological eras. The resulting simulations of climate and vegetation processes tie in with observable geological data, such as the distributions of coals and evaporites, supporting the validity of the authors' approach. Simulation of possible conditions in future centuries are also presented, providing valuable predictions of the status of the earth's vegetation and carbon cycle at a time of global warming.

DAVID BEERLING is a Royal Society University Research Fellow and Honorary Reader in the Department of Animal and Plant Sciences at the University of Sheffield. He is holder of a 2001 Philip Leverhulme Prize for his work in the earth sciences.

IAN WOODWARD is Professor of Plant Ecology in the Department of Animal and Plant Sciences at the University of Sheffield. He is author of *Climate and Plant Distribution* (1987) and co-editor of *Plant Functional Types* (1997).

Vegetation and the terrestrial carbon cycle:

Modelling the first 400 million years

D. J. BEERLING & F. I. WOODWARD
Department of Animal and Plant Sciences, University of Sheffield, Sheffield S10 2TN, U.K.

CAMBRIDGE
UNIVERSITY PRESS

PUBLISHED BY THE PRESS SYNDICATE OF THE UNIVERSITY OF CAMBRIDGE
The Pitt Building, Trumpington Street, Cambridge, United Kingdom

CAMBRIDGE UNIVERSITY PRESS
The Edinburgh Building, Cambridge CB2 2RU, UK
40 West 20th Street, New York, NY 10011–4211, USA
10 Stamford Road, Oakleigh, VIC 3166, Australia
Ruiz de Alarcón 13, 28014 Madrid, Spain
Dock House, The Waterfront, Cape Town 8001, South Africa

http://www.cambridge.org

First published 2001

Printed in the United Kingdom at the University Press, Cambridge

Typeface TEFF Lexicon 10/14 pt   *System* QuarkXPress®   [SE]

A catalogue record for this book is available from the British Library

Library of Congress Cataloguing in Publication data

Beerling, D. J.
    Vegetation and the terrestrial carbon cycle : modelling the first 400 million years /
D. J. Beerling & F. I. Woodward.
      p. cm.
    Includes bibliographical references (p.   ).
    ISBN 0 521 80196 6
      1. Carbon cycle (Biogeochemistry)–Mathematical models. 2. Plant
    ecology–Mathematical models. 3. Paleoclimatology–Mathematical models.
    I. Woodward, F. I. II. Title.
    QH344. B43 2001   577′.144′015118–dc21

ISBN 0 521 80196 6 hardback

Contents

Preface

The study of plant distributions is a continuous feature of ecology. These studies may range from a small area of ground to the whole of the terrestrial biosphere. The information from such studies underpins our current understanding of the terrestrial biosphere. Unfortunately this information, on its own, is not sufficient to answer large questions, such as what controls the current distribution of plants, or how will the current distribution and behaviour of plants respond to global environmental change? These are important questions and ones which are presented increasingly in order to satisfy human knowledge and decision making. Indeed the question, put to ecologists in the 1980s, of how will terrestrial vegetation respond to global warming could not be answered then and only now, 20 years later, is there some hope that we understand some of the major mechanisms involved and their likely outcomes. There is also no doubt that such questions are good for the development of ecology, in contrast to likely serious consequences for mankind.

A feature of long-term studies in ecology is that there is nothing really new, most things have happened before, if only we could have seen them. There is current concern over the rapid increase in atmospheric CO_2 concentrations but in geological times the atmospheric CO_2 concentrations, and the Earth's temperature have frequently been higher than the present. No doubt plants and vegetation will respond and adapt to future change, however mankind requires a more improbable outcome, that nothing should change, even though atmospheric composition and climate are changing rapidly. An outcome as likely as that expected from the actions of Svein Forkbeard's son. A more serious question is how much will vegetation change and how much will ecosystem services change, such as water supply, the provision of biomass and the capacity of the biosphere to sequester anthropogenic releases of CO_2. These are difficult questions to answer and any approach which makes predictions must have mechanistic underpinning to have any chance of approaching reality.

One approach taken in the area of climate change research has been to make predictions back in time, when the environment was different from the present. Predictions can then be made and tested against data collected at the appropriate time. Previous warm periods, such as 6000 years before present, have been a favourite for investigation and have proved useful for testing models developed for the contemporary world. A problem in going further back in time to geological eras is that the information about the climate and the biosphere is much more limited. However the relatively recent application of general circulation models to simulating past climates has provided a useful source of past climatic data. These GCM runs are constrained by proxy estimates of ocean temperatures and are probably reasonable estimates of past climates, although there are limited opportunities for testing their validity. The value of these simulations is that their data can be used to drive vegetation models and the outputs of the vegetation models can be compared with fossil data which have not been used to constrain the GCMs.

This approach of looking at past vegetation behaviour, and the carbon cycle in particular, is a new endeavour which implies a number of critical features. In particular it assumes that the contemporary understanding of the carbon cycle applies equally well at any other time. It also assumes that associated processes, for instance the water cycle and vegetation processes, such as succession and responses to climate and atmospheric CO_2 have also operated in essentially the same manner as the present. The fact that photosynthesis drives vegetation processes suggests that contemporary understanding will have geological relevance. This book describes approaches to testing quantitatively how much this relevance amounts to and how we can deal with uncertainty in both vegetation and climate models. It is axiomatic that models are wrong, the question is how wrong and how much does this matter. These features will be tested for a wide range of eras before finally modelling the responses of vegetation to one particular scenario of future climatic change. Not all eras during the life of terrestrial vegetation have been covered, because GCMs are not currently available but those which have been completed have been periods when vegetation has been challenged by a wide variety of unusual conditions. Our final hope is that we can show a range of responses by vegetation and the carbon cycle which stimulate further interest and enquiry, before our predictions of the future become the predictions of the present.

D. J. Beerling
F. I. Woodward

Acknowledgements

Numerous scientific friends and colleagues gave generously of their time and hard-won data during the course of writing this book. In particular, we are indebted to Paul Valdes (University of Reading) for providing the global palaeoclimatic datasets from the Universities Global Atmospheric Modelling Programme (UGAMP) which constitute the core portion of the global simulations presented here, and Bette Otto-Bliesner (National Center for Atmospheric Research, Boulder, Colorado) and Gary Upchurch (Southwest Texas State University, Texas) for providing the global climatic simulation of the latest Cretaceous used in Chapter 7 as the basis for our analysis of the effects of the Cretaceous–Tertiary boundary impact event. This book would not have been possible without Mark Lomas whose mathematical, programming and mapping skills apparently know no bounds. Bill Chaloner provided much unwitting encouragement over the past three years and brought an even greater amount of sanity to bear on some of our wilder excursions, and we are both extremely grateful for his input. Jayne Young is thanked for the arduous task of diligently checking and pointing up errors in citations and the reference list throughout the entire text.

For critically reviewing and commenting upon various parts of the text, and in some cases unselfishly providing unpublished data, we thank (in alphabetical order): Pat Behling, Richard Betts, Bill Chaloner, Chris Cleal, Geoff Creber, Jane Francis, Colin Osborne, Andrew Scott, Paul Valdes, Paul Wignall and Jack Williams. Various discussions along the way with Bob Berner, Bill Emanuel, Jane Francis, Tim Lenton, Barry Lomax, Martin Heimann, Colin Osborne, Paul Quick, Hank Shugart, Andrew Watson and Gary Upchurch further helped shape our ideas on different parts of the text. Any remaining errors are, of course, our own responsibility.

DJB gratefully acknowledges funding through a Royal Society University Fellowship and, for some of the research reported here, through grants from the Natural Environment Research Council, the European Commission and the Leverhulme Trust. FIW gratefully acknowledges support from the Natural Environment Research Council and the European Commission.

Finally, we thank our families and friends for providing that all-important quality rest and relaxation time. DJB thanks Mum & Malcolm, Dad & Sue, Julie & Simon (& little Sophie), and Juliette for love and support. I also thank the many friends who have put up with me during the various stages of writing of this book especially Colin, Jarrod, Dan, Simon, Maria, Liz, Phil, Vicky, Charlotte, Helen, Steve and Mark A. FIW thanks Pearl, Helen and David and his wood-turning lathe for unpredictable but enjoyable pointers to another life.

1

Introduction

Overview

This book considers the operation of the terrestrial carbon cycle across a range of spatial and temporal scales, with special emphasis on the photosynthetic carbon metabolism of land plants over the last 400 million years. Chapters 2 and 3 outline some of the fundamental approaches used in attempting to predict the operation of plants in the past from a knowledge of present-day processes, possible means of testing these approaches, and detailed consideration of the nature of the relationship between vegetation, soils and climate in a contemporary climatic setting. The later chapters consider a number of 'globally-averaged' responses of plant processes to changes in global mean temperature and atmospheric composition throughout much of the Phanerozoic. In taking this approach, our view has been to open up investigation and discussion of how predictions of geochemical models impinge on the processes governing the regulation of carbon gain and water loss in leaves of plants, following earlier work of this sort (Beerling, 1994).

Consideration of the global view is initiated in Chapter 4 with a detailed discussion of global climate simulations using computers and examining how these simulations can be modified to predict ancient climates. The discussion is then extended to deal with the development of a model representing the various above- and below-ground processes of the terrestrial carbon cycle. After extensive satisfactory testing of several key model outputs against a variety of ground truth data, including observations from satellites, the stage is set to bring these two global-scale approaches together and investigate changes in the operation of the terrestrial biosphere through geological time.

The following series of chapters (Chapters 5 to 9) consider, at the global

1

scale, the effects of several computer climate simulations, representing particular averaged 'slices' of geological time, on terrestrial ecosystem properties
and function. The selection of a particular interval for detailed global investigation was constrained by the availability of palaeoclimate simulations from
the climate modelling community. In taking this approach it has been
assumed, we hope not unreasonably, that what constitutes an interesting
interval for climate modellers to test and apply their models represents a correspondingly interesting time to investigate the impact of the modelled climates on plants, vegetation and terrestrial ecosystem carbon cycling.

The geological timescale

Studies of a geological nature necessarily, by definition, deal with
intervals of time typically ranging from thousands to millions of years. These
timescales are difficult for the human mind to appreciate yet are those
required for considering the gradual processes operating to shape the Earth's
climate and the course and pattern of evolution. Indeed, it is interesting to
note that amongst other political reasons, the very difficulty humans have of
comprehending and accepting a time span of thousands to millions of years
bedevilled our ability to formulate the concept of so-called 'deep time' in the
first place. The first realisation that the Earth was in fact millions of years old
was made by James Hutton in his *Theory of the Earth* (1780s) and was subsequently refined and developed further by Charles Lyell in his *Principles of
Geology* (1830–1833). With this advancement in hand, Charles Darwin was
able to proceed with the development of his theory of evolution by the accumulation of small gradual changes, via natural selection, over millions of
years.

A basic appreciation of the geological time span and the names of the key
geological eras, periods and epochs is required for this book. For simplicity, we
have refrained from adopting detailed geological names and stratigraphic
nomenclature and used only those more widely agreed upon (Table 1.1). Table
1.1 provides diagrammatic representation of the geological column, note that
it is not scaled equidistantly through time. The Phanerozoic era extends from
544 Ma (million years ago). Its first three periods, the Cambrian, Ordovician
and Silurian encompass the time before the evolution of vascular land plants,
the focus of this text, and have been omitted from Table 1.1. Several global
simulations deal with the Mesozoic era ('middle life' or the Age of Dinosaurs),
which encompasses the Triassic, Jurassic and Cretaceous periods. The name
Cretaceous derives from the latin 'creta' meaning chalk (widely deposited in
shallow seas during the later stages of the Mesozoic). Following the Mesozoic

Table 1.1. *The geological timetable and key names used in this text*

Time in millions of years ago (Ma)	Eon	Era	Period		Significant biotic events
⇑0			Quaternary		Ice ages.
1.8		Cenozoic	Tertiary	Neogene	Establishment of regional differences in floras, including temperate floras and grasslands.
24				Palaeogene	First grasses, first horses, rapid diversification of mammals.
65	Phanerozoic	Mesozoic	Cretaceous		Origin and diversification of angiosperms. Extinction of dinosaurs at the Cretaceous–Tertiary boundary.
144			Jurassic		Rise of modern ferns, diversification of conifers.
205			Triassic		Cycads and Ginkgos dominant. Massive biotic extinction at the Permian–Triassic boundary.
248		Palaeozoic	Permian		Spread of upland floras into lowlands, demise of lowland swamps.
295			Carboniferous		Major interval of coal formations, forest dominance by arborescent lycopods. First land winged insects, first land vertebrates.
354			Devonian		First seed plants, first sharks. Diversification of plants.
⇓ to 416					

Source: After Haq *et al.* (1998).

is the Cenozoic era ('recent life' or the Age of Mammals) which includes the Tertiary, a term remnant from when Earth history was divided into four intervals: primary, secondary, tertiary and quaternary. The first two are now out of use whilst the name Tertiary is used to define the time between the end of the Cretaceous and the beginning of the most recent succession of ice ages, the Quaternary. The boundary between the Cretaceous and the Tertiary is termed the K/T boundary, K from the German word for chalk ('Kriede') and T to indicate the Tertiary.

Chapters 8 and 9 deal with changes in biospheric operation during intervals represented by subdivisions of the Tertiary and Quaternary periods, respectively, and since these require some familiarity with the timing and names of the different periods and epochs within, these are given in Table 1.2.

The global-scale studies in Chapters 5 to 10 recognise the Earth operating in, broadly, either an ice age or a greenhouse mode.

Ice age Earth

The Earth has experienced four major phases of glaciation over the last billion years (Crowley & North, 1991): the late Precambrian (800–600 Ma), Late Ordovician (440 Ma), Permo-Carboniferous (330–275 Ma) and the late Cenozoic (40–0 Ma). We consider the impacts of two of these ice age episodes on the terrestrial carbon cycle at times of widely differing continental configurations: the late Carboniferous (300 Ma) (Chapter 5), and during the last glacial maximum (LGM) at 18 000 years (18 ka) (Chapter 9). During the Carboniferous several of the continents sutured to form three major land masses (Gondwana, Eurasia and Kazakhstan). These were configured in very different locations from the present day, with the land masses cutting across many parts of zonal circulation, a large portion of land exposed in the low mid-latitudes, and the presence of a warm seaway (Tethys). All of these features combined to exert major effects on the operation of the global climate system with a resultant marked difference between Palaeozoic and contemporary climates (Parrish, 1993).

A further and important difference between the late Quaternary ice ages and those of the Permo-Carboniferous lies in the atmospheric composition. Late Quaternary ice core records indicate that the LGM was characterised by low concentrations of atmospheric CO_2 (180–200 ppm); and geochemical modelling of the long-term carbon cycle, as well as stomatal-based palaeo-CO_2 estimates, suggest a low value for the Carboniferous (300 ppm) (reviewed in Berner, 1998). So both glaciations are likely to have resulted in part from

Table 1.2. *Summarised geological timetable of the Cenozoic era*

Time in millions of years ago (Ma)	Era	Period	Epoch	Climatic comments
⇑0.0			Holocene	The last 10 000 years before present (ka BP), including a climatic optimum around 6 ka BP.
0.01		Quaternary	Pliestocene	Interval of repeated glacial–interglacial cycles
1.8			Pliocene	Closure of Panamanian seaway, with profound changes in deep Atlantic circulation at *c.* 4.6 Ma.
4.9	Cenozoic		Miocene	Interval of global warmth without evidence of high atmospheric CO_2 content. Global expansion of grasslands with the C_4 photosynthetic pathway in the late Miocene.
24.0		Tertiary	Oligocene	Episodes of large fluctuations in global sea level and polar ice sheet growth and retreat.
34.0			Eocene	Onset of the formation of Antarctic bottom water. India collides with Asia.
54.0			Palaeocene	Abrupt climatic warming at the Palaeocene–Eocene boundary.
⇓65.0				

Source: After Haq *et al.* (1998).

the same mechanism, a lowered greenhouse effect. What differs between them, however, are the processes involved in sequestering carbon from the atmospheric reservoir and the subsequent effects on the atmospheric O_2 content. In the Carboniferous, the massive organic carbon burial, as witnessed by the vast coal swamps of the Carboniferous and early Permian (330–260 Ma), removed CO_2 from the atmosphere, and was calculated to have been accompanied by a rise in atmospheric O_2 content (Berner & Canfield, 1989). During the Quaternary ice ages, CO_2 removal from the atmosphere was mainly driven through changes in Milankovitch orbital insolation lowering global temperatures (Hays *et al.*, 1976) thereby increasing CO_2 solubility into the oceans, but with little effect on their O_2 content since oxygen is relatively insoluble in water. Milankovitch insolation variations probably also operated in the Carboniferous, as revealed by high frequency cyclical sea level variations in sediments of that age (Wanless & Shepard, 1936), but the effects of organic carbon burial dominated atmospheric CO_2 changes at that time. Indeed, it is possible to reasonably predict ice sheet location and growth in the Carboniferous using the same model as that capable of predicting ice sheet occurrence during Quaternary glacial stages (Hyde *et al.*, 1999). The low ice-age atmospheric CO_2 concentrations place severe constraints on the efficiency of the photosynthetic metabolism of plants, constraints further exacerbated by a high Carboniferous O_2 content. The underlying reasons for these constraints in the different periods are discussed in detail in Chapters 5 and 9.

Greenhouse Earth

Three chapters investigate the impact of the Earth's climate in periods of what might broadly be described as a greenhouse mode: the Jurassic (Chapter 6), Cretaceous (Chapter 7) and Eocene (Chapter 8). Chapter 10 deals with vegetation-climate interactions in a future greenhouse Earth, driven by CO_2 accumulation in the atmosphere following the anthropogenic activities of fossil fuel burning and deforestation.

There has been a long-standing interest in assessing the major determinants regulating global climate in the distant past, especially at times when sedimentary rocks and fossilised biota indicate much warmer climates than now. General circulation models of the Earth's climate provide a means of exploring this sensitivity and separating out the relative importance of continental configuration, oceanic circulation and greenhouse gases (e.g. Barron *et al.*, 1995). There has also been the motivation that simulations of these ancient greenhouse climates together with similar models used to make predictions of future global change, offer a means of testing the underlying physics and other mathematical representations of the Earth's climate system. However, it is doubtful (Chapter 8) that any past greenhouse climate provides a realistic representation for a future greenhouse world.

By analogy, these warm greenhouse climates offer us a means of examining the productivity of the terrestrial biosphere under such conditions, and

Chapter 8 gives an explicit comparison between the impacts of the most recent of the 'ancient' greenhouse climate episodes, of the Eocene (50 Ma), and those modelled for the future. Limitations in our knowledge of how the processes represented within the terrestrial carbon cycle model described in Chapter 4 acclimate, or become modified by long-term exposure to a warm climate and/or a high CO_2 environment, have to be conceded in making these model predictions. However, meta-analyses of the responses of photosynthesis to elevated CO_2 generally indicate that a large and continuing stimulation of photosynthesis is well described by the Farquhar *et al.* (1980) photosynthesis sub-model (Medlyn *et al.*, 1999; Peterson *et al.*, 1999) and so this core process might be regarded as somewhat robust. Further discussion of the issue of acclimation by the photosynthetic apparatus can be found in Chapter 6, in which the first global simulation with a higher-than-present CO_2 atmosphere is presented.

Catastrophic climatic change: the end-Cretaceous mass extinction

Abundant and globally-widespread geochemical, morphological, marine and terrestrial evidence has increasingly accumulated, supporting the idea, first proposed by Alvarez *et al.* (1980), that a large extraterrestrial bolide hit the Earth at the end of the Cretaceous. This represents a major perturbation of the global climate system with a correspondingly large expected effect on the functioning of the biosphere. Terrestrial carbon cycle sensitivity studies, with modified global late Cretaceous climate datasets, provide one means of assessing such effects. Therefore, Chapter 7 presents global simulations of vegetation properties and carbon cycling near the end of the Cretaceous (66 Ma) to establish 'baseline' conditions from which to explore the effects of different climatic change scenarios resulting from the impact of a large bolide. The post-impact scenarios contrast the effects of the possible resulting short-term (global darkness, climatic cooling, high atmospheric CO_2 concentrations) and long-term (high CO_2, global warming) climatic change that may have arisen owing to the impact.

Conclusions

The various global simulations described in this book provide representations of contrasting past and future climates and allow us to ask how the physical and chemical nature of the Earth has influenced the functioning of biological systems, with specific emphasis on terrestrial plant photosynthesis and the cycling of carbon through ecosystems. Some aspects of this work point to the importance of climatic feedback on vegetation, its role in determining other geochemical processes, and the possible responses of the terrestrial biosphere to abrupt environmental perturbations at the global scale.

We readily acknowledge that specific gaps exist in geological time which remain to be investigated with a modelling approach and that some of these gaps represent interesting intervals during the course of Earth history and plant evolution. Among these, two in particular stand out: the late Silurian and early Devonian, when the land became colonised by terrestrial plants; and the end of the Permian (*c.* 249 Ma), recognised as the greatest mass extinction in the history of life. The role played by large Devonian vascular land plants in the cycling of carbon was probably substantial, with deep root penetration into soils, and colonisation of drier upland and primary successional areas significantly enhancing rates of chemical weathering and atmospheric CO_2 draw-down (Algeo & Scheckler, 1998; Elick *et al.*, 1998).

In contrast to the early Devonian situation, the end-Permian mass extinctions would have severely altered the global carbon cycle through very different processes. Extinction of many groups of marine organisms would have limited oceanic primary production whilst a major and sudden mass extinction of terrestrial floras, clearly evident in the high southern palaeolatitudes (Retallack, 1995) and elsewhere, would have severely curtailed the terrestrial carbon cycle. This 'bottleneck' in carbon cycling was probably further increased by an extensive insect extinction at this time. As a result, decomposition was probably largely rate-limited by fungal activity, a feature evident in the fossil record by the extraordinarily widespread occurrence of fungal spores at the Permian–Triassic boundary (Visscher *et al.*, 1996).

The development of more flexible and easier-to-use global climate models should in the future allow model-based assessments of some of these intriguing issues. Preliminary palaeoclimate modelling studies for the late Permian (Kutzbach & Ziegler, 1993), and general circulation climate modelling studies with different Palaeozoic continental configurations (e.g. Crowley *et al.*, 1993), offer promise for investigating how significant changes in biological systems influenced biogeochemical cycles, particularly terrestrial carbon cycle dynamics.

2

Investigating the past from the present

Introduction

The time frame of this book is rather less than 500 million years, the time over which the Earth's terrestrial surface became first colonised and subsequently dominated by land plants. Land plants now constitute over 90% of the world's biomass, a true measure of their quantitative dominance in the biosphere. The fossil evidence of this takeover (e.g. Niklas *et al.*, 1983) is sporadic and incomplete, often frustratingly so. However, the sequence from the first miniature vascular land plant, *Cooksonia*, of the Silurian period, about 430 Ma (Edwards *et al.*, 1983), to the massive *Lepidodendron* tree of the Carboniferous period (300 Ma; DiMichele & DeMaris, 1987) indicates that the evolution of complex and large plant structures was very rapid, whilst communities of different species of plants would have been the rule as early as the Devonian period (395 Ma; Chaloner & Sheerin, 1979; Banks, 1981; Edwards, 1996).

The prospect of predicting or modelling the activities of land plants over 400 million years ago appears a task doomed to failure. However, we know that all land plants have derived the carbon for their structures from organic molecules constructed in the process of photosynthesis. The process of photosynthesis is very ancient and the ubiquitous CO_2-fixing enzyme, ribulose 1,5-bisphosphate carboxylase/oxygenase (rubisco), which may reach as much as 50% of the soluble protein in leaves, is thought to have a marine origin along with chemo-lithotrophs at about 3500 Ma (Badger & Andrews, 1987). Therefore, the period of occurrence of plants on land (500 Ma) extends for only the last 14% of the period of occurrence of rubisco. We also know (Bowes, 1993) that marine algae and cyanobacteria, of ancient origin, have evolved the same complexities of the photosynthetic system, such as carbon concentrating mechanisms, as the very modern-day plant species with the C_4 mechanism of photosynthesis.

It appears, therefore, that there is a rather restricted potential for the evolutionary improvement of rubisco activity (Roy & Nierzwicki-Bauer, 1991), a feature which greatly enhances our capacity to predict its historical activity. Other critical features of the photosynthetic system, such as the light reactions, are discussed in Chapters 3 and 4. This apparent overemphasis of the process of photosynthesis has been made because it underlies all processes of growth and therefore evolutionary development. Its ubiquity through time ensures a moderate degree of success in predicting its historical activity. In contrast, the processes and rates of plant morphogenesis, growth and all aspects of reproduction will have changed markedly through time, but with very restricted information on the processes concerned and therefore no strong evidence to support the notion that we can use present-day understanding to investigate the past. Therefore the whole tenor of this book will be to investigate the likely changes in basic and well-understood processes of global-scale terrestrial plant physiology over the last 500 Ma, and which can be reliably understood from the present day.

A critical feature of this book will be to make predictions of past plant processes and then to find different approaches, from fossil evidence, which can be used to assess the validity of the predictions. The basic plant physiological processes which will be addressed are photosynthesis, respiration and stomatal transpiration. The manner in which ecosystem processes, such as nutrient uptake and litter decomposition, also play a part is detailed in Chapter 4.

Rubisco

The rubisco of all plants has the same three biochemical characteristics (Keys, 1986; Walker *et al.*, 1986; Bowes, 1993; Lawlor, 1993):

1. For high CO_2-fixing capacity as a carboxylase, rubisco requires a high concentration of dissolved CO_2 in the water of the chloroplast stroma, compared to what is available in the environment.
2. CO_2 fixation by rubisco is competitively inhibited by oxygen.
3. In the presence of oxygen, rubisco also acts as an oxygenase in the process of photorespiration.

All three properties of rubisco are active in the present-day atmospheric composition of 350 ppm (35 Pa or 350 μmol mol^{-1}) of CO_2 and 21% O_2. However, at the time of the origin of life itself and even at the time of the spread of land plants, the atmospheric composition was very different, with CO_2 concentrations at 420 Ma being perhaps 16 times higher than at the present day (Yapp & Poths, 1992), with O_2 much lower at *c.* 2–10% (Budyko *et al.*, 1987). Under such conditions, the rate of photorespiration would have been small, with little inhibition of carboxylation by O_2 and moderate concentrations of CO_2 in the chloroplast. Under the present-day atmosphere, all three characteristics cause the rate of carboxylation to be about 60–70% of its full potential (Bowes, 1993). Photorespiration causes the release of CO_2 and so it offsets CO_2 assimilation by carboxylation, causing this decreased net photosynthetic capacity.

Rubisco characteristics

Rubisco, and all enzymes, have similar operational constraints and employ similar methods of quantifying their activity. There must be a substrate for the enzyme, which in turn has a maximum rate and a rate which is determined by the substrate concentration. For example the rate of carboxylation, v_c, of rubisco can be defined by Michaelis–Menten characteristics as:

$$v_c = \frac{V_c^{max}[C]}{K_c + [C]} \tag{2.1}$$

where $[C]$ is the concentration of CO_2 in the water of the chloroplast stroma, K_c is the substrate concentration at which v_c reaches one half of its maximum rate, V_c^{max}. Under the present-day atmosphere $[C]$ is about 8 μM (Keys, 1986), while K_c ranges between 8 and 25 μM (Bowes, 1993) for terrestrial plants with the C_3 pathway of photosynthesis. The higher the value of K_c the lower the affinity of rubisco for CO_2. A typical value of V_c^{max} is about 50 μmol m^{-2} s^{-1} (Wullschleger, 1993). Given these quantities it is then easy to apply equation 2.1 to investigate the sensitivity of carboxylation to its different controlling variables (Fig. 2.1).

A number of features emerge from the rubisco characteristics. At a present-day CO_2 concentration of 350 ppm, the CO_2 concentration in the intercellular air spaces of the leaf will be about 240 ppm, which equilibrates with a concentration of free CO_2 in solution at the chloroplast stroma of about 8 μM at 25 °C (Keys, 1986).

At the CO_2 concentration of 8 μM, rubisco is well below its maximum capacity for carboxylation, and equal to or less than the typical values of K_c, the half maximum rate of carboxylation. Therefore, under current atmospheric CO_2 concentrations, the carboxylase activity of rubisco is markedly limited by the availability of CO_2. At the CO_2 concentration of 8 μM a three-fold variation in K_c leads to a two-fold variation in the rate of carboxylation.

It is difficult to envisage the impact of variations in atmospheric CO_2 concentration on the carboxylation rate, as Figure 2.1 relates variations in CO_2 concentration in the chloroplast to the rate of carboxylation. However, it is

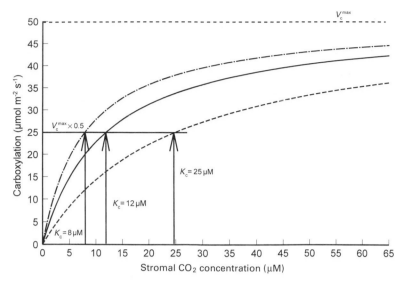

Figure 2.1. The responses of carboxylation to changes in stromal CO_2 concentration and for three different values of K_c and a V_c^{max} of 50 μmol m^{-2} s^{-1}. (---) $K_c = 25$ μm, (——) $K_c = 12$ μm, (—·—·—) $K_c = 8$ μm.

possible to estimate roughly the external ambient CO_2 concentration, as follows. Ambient CO_2 diffuses through the stomata of leaves into the intercellular spaces and then to the chloroplasts, where CO_2 passes into solution. Many observations of photosynthetic rates and the ratio of intercellular to external ambient concentration of CO_2, c_i/c_a, have demonstrated this ratio to be $c.$ 0.7 (Lawlor, 1993). The concentration of CO_2 in chloroplast water, $[C]$, will be close to equilibrium with the c_i, and so according to Henry's Law (Woodward & Sheehy, 1983):

$$[C] = \frac{0.7 c_a n_w}{k} \tag{2.2}$$

where c_a is the external CO_2 concentration, n_w is the number of moles of water in 1 kg water and k is the solubility coefficient of CO_2 in water (0.17×10^9 Pa at 25 °C). Equation 2.2 can then be rearranged to solve for c_a as:

$$c_a = \frac{[C]k}{0.7 n_w} \tag{2.3}$$

Figure 2.2 is therefore redrafted, using equation 2.3, to show the relationship between the approximate external ambient CO_2 concentration and the rate of carboxylation. It is notable that even at CO_2 concentrations of 3000 ppm, the rate of carboxylation is still only 70–90% of saturation.

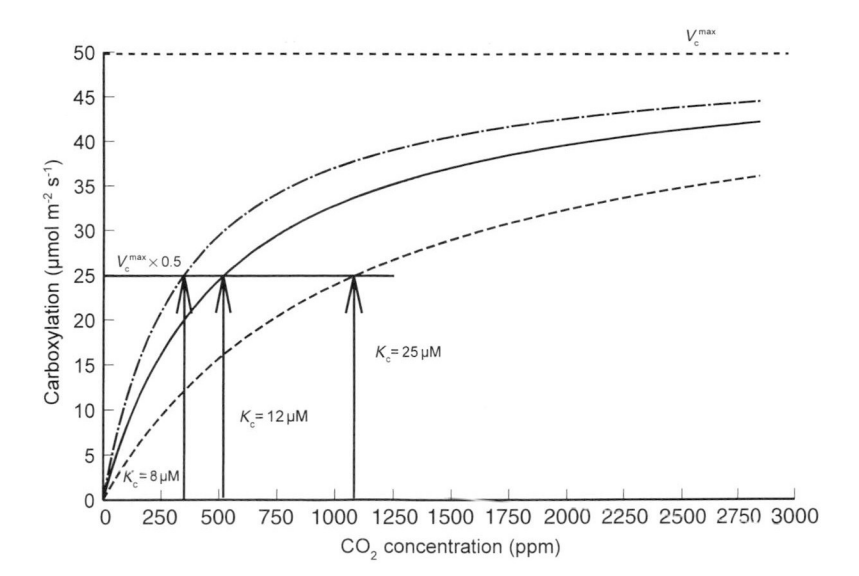

Figure 2.2. The rate of carboxylation, for different values of K_c, as for Fig. 2.1, but in terms of the external ambient CO_2 concentration.

Photorespiration

So far, the effects of the rival process to carboxylation – photorespiration or oxygenation – have not been considered. At this stage, it is assumed that the first acceptor molecule for CO_2, ribulose bisphosphate (RuBP), is in excess for all conditions. This does not change the importance of the oxygen effect, but it simplifies an additional treatment when RuBP is in limited supply. This limitation is considered in Chapters 3 and 4. Both CO_2 and O_2 compete for RuBP at their binding sites on rubisco, and so CO_2 and O_2 are mutually competitive inhibitors. When this competitive inhibition occurs, the rate of carboxylation, v_c, is defined (Farquhar *et al.*, 1980) as:

$$v_c = \frac{V_c^{max}[C]}{[C] + K_c\left(1 + \dfrac{[O]}{K_o}\right)} \qquad (2.4)$$

where $[O]$ is the concentration of O_2 in the stroma (typically 260 μM with an external ambient O_2 concentration of 21%) and K_o is the concentration of O_2 in the stroma at which the oxygenation reaction reaches one half of its maximum value. Current observations show a range in K_o from about 360 to 650 μM (Keys, 1986), indicating a much lower affinity of rubisco for O_2 rather than CO_2 as a substrate. The impact of the competitive inhibition by oxygen on carboxylation is shown for two ambient O_2 concentrations, representing

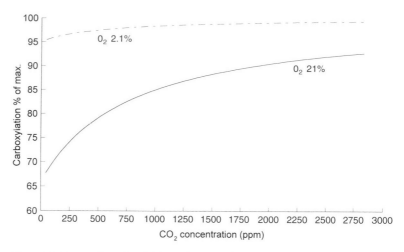

Figure 2.3. Competitive inhibition of carboxylation at two ambient oxygen concentrations, 2.1% and 21%, calculated using eq. 2.4, with all rubisco and CO_2 characteristics as for Fig. 2.1 and 2.2 but with ambient O_2 concentrations of 2.1% and 21%, (chloroplast concentrations of 25.8 and 258 μM respectively, calculated using eq. 2), a K_c of 12 μM and a K_o of 500 μM.

the present day (21%) and 400 Ma (2.1%; Fig. 2.3). The inhibitory effect is displayed as the percentage of the carboxylation-only rate at all CO_2 concentrations, as shown in Figures 2.1 and 2.2.

Under present-day O_2 concentrations (21%), the competitive inhibition of carboxylase is greater than 20% when the external ambient CO_2 concentration is 350 ppm (Fig. 2.3). Clearly, any increase in atmospheric CO_2 concentration should stimulate the rate of photosynthesis. Under the low O_2 concentrations which may have typified the late Silurian and early Devonian periods, the inhibitory effect of O_2 is small at all CO_2 concentrations, and so it follows that photorespiration will have been of negligible importance at this time.

The final consideration of the effect of O_2 on the rate of carboxylation must account for the fact that oxygenation consumes O_2 and releases CO_2. For every two oxygenations of rubisco one molecule of CO_2 is released by photorespiration, reducing the rate of carboxylation. Therefore, the net rate of carboxylation, A_n, is defined (from Farquhar *et al.*, 1980) as:

$$A_n = v_c - 0.5v_o \tag{2.5}$$

where v_o is the rate of oxygenation by rubisco. The rate of oxygenation, including competitive inhibition by CO_2, can be predicted in a similar fashion to the rate of carboxylation (eq. 2.4) as:

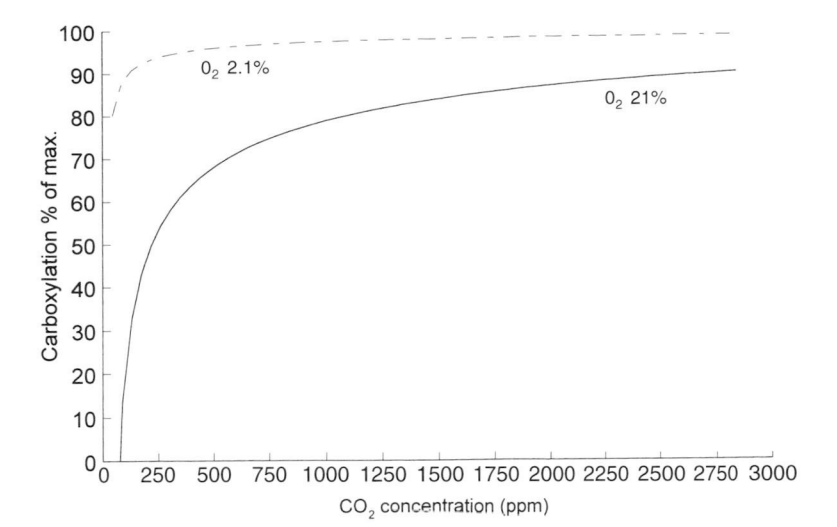

Figure 2.4. The combined effects of oxygen on the rate of carboxylation. Values as for Fig. 2.3 and with a V_c^{max} of 26 μmol m^{-2} s^{-1}. The degree of oxygen inhibition is calculated as the net rate of photosynthesis, A_n, in eq. 2.5 divided by the rate of carboxylation calculated with eq. 2.1 (Fig. 2.1).

$$v_o = \frac{V_o^{max}[O]}{[O] + K_o\left(1 + \dfrac{[C]}{K_c}\right)} \tag{2.6}$$

where V_o^{max} is the maximum rate of oxygenation. The rates of oxygenation (eq. 2.6) and carboxylation (eq. 2.4) may then be incorporated into equation 2.5 to determine the net rate of carboxylation, including the three limitations to rubisco activity outlined earlier (i.e. low substrate concentration of CO_2, competitive inhibition between CO_2 and O_2 for a rubisco binding site and the photorespiratory release of CO_2).

The final impacts of the latter two effects are shown on Figure 2.4, which indicates that under current CO_2 and O_2 concentrations the negative impacts of O_2 amount to a c. 35% reduction in the rate of carboxylation, for the particular values used in equations 2.4 and 2.6. Any excursions of atmospheric CO_2 below the current concentration, such as have been recorded for the last glaciation (see Chapter 9), will have had very marked inhibitory effects on carboxylation. Indeed, it is considered likely that periods of low atmospheric CO_2 concentration at the end of the Cretaceous (65 Ma) and at the start of the Miocene (25 Ma) may have been the selective force for the evolution of the C_4 pathway of photosynthesis (Ehleringer *et al.*, 1991).

The C_4 pathway of photosynthesis is a CO_2 concentrating mechanism which leads to CO_2 concentrations around rubisco, in the bundle sheath, at least 12 to 15 times greater than in plants with the C_3 pathway of photosynthesis (Hatch, 1992). This mechanism is interesting in that it parallels observations in the evolutionary ancient photosynthetic bacteria and cyanobacteria, where carbon concentrating mechanisms raise concentrations of dissolved inorganic carbon within the cells to as much as 1000 times higher than the external medium (Bowes, 1993). This appears to be necessary in these organisms where rubisco has a low affinity for CO_2 (K_c between 80 and 300 μM; Jordan & Ogren, 1983) and at times of low dissolved inorganic carbon in the marine environment, such as during the day (Bowes, 1993), the rate of carboxylation would have been very low without the concentrating mechanism. It is again notable (Fig. 2.4) that under conditions of low O_2 there is little impact of photorespiration on the rate of carboxylation.

Rubisco evolution

The quantitative descriptions of carboxylation (eqs. 2.1, 2.4 and 2.5) and oxygenation (eq. 2.6) indicate that the rate of carboxylation by rubisco, in the presence of CO_2 and O_2, is dependent on various kinetic properties of rubisco and also on the concentrations of CO_2 and O_2 dissolved in the chloroplast stroma. It is actually more simple, when considering the capacity for evolution to change the kinetic characteristics of rubisco, to consider an integrated measure of these characteristics. This characteristic is known as the rubisco specificity factor, S_r, which is defined (Jordan & Ogren, 1983) as follows. Dividing equation 2.4 by equation 2.6:

$$\frac{v_c}{v_o} = \frac{V_c^{max}K_o[C]}{V_o^{max}K_c[O]} \tag{2.7}$$

then the specificity factor, S_r, of carboxylation to oxygenation is defined as:

$$S_r = \frac{V_c^{max}K_o}{V_o^{max}K_c} \tag{2.8}$$

A number of measurements of the specificity factor has been made, for organisms with different ages of evolutionary origin (Jordan & Ogren, 1983).

It has to be assumed that calculations of the specificity factor made at the present day for extant organisms of ancient plant groups provide a measure of the specificity factor for the ancestral groups. This is not possible to validate. Observations of the specificity factor (Fig. 2.5), however, suggest a rather small range of specificities between vascular plants of different ancestral origins. The photosynthetic bacteria and cyanobacteria, with low specificities are

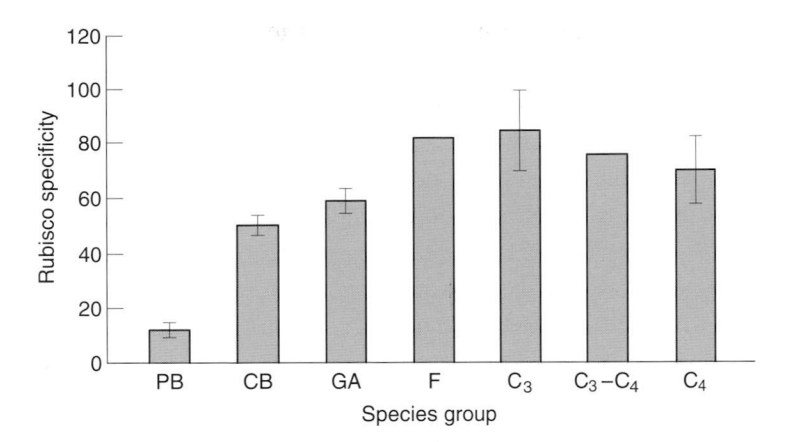

Figure 2.5. Rubisco specificity factor for different plant groups (from Jordan & Ogren, 1983). PB, photosynthetic bacteria; CB, cyanobacteria; GA, green algae; F, fern; C3, other vascular plants with the C_3 pathway of photosynthesis; C3–C4, species with C_3–C_4 intermediate photosynthesis; C4 species with C_4 pathway of photosynthesis. Standard errors shown.

known to possess carbon concentrating mechanisms which circumvent the problems of poor CO_2 acquisition (Bowes, 1993). The photosynthetic bacteria (PB; Fig. 2.5) have a low rubisco specificity, but also a simpler rubisco structure than the other plant groups (McFadden *et al.*, 1986), perhaps suiting them to anaerobic environments and suggesting a direct descent from ancient photosynthetic bacteria (McFadden & Tabita, 1974). Rubisco of organisms other than the photosynthetic bacteria is encoded by genes present in both nuclear and chloroplast DNA (Ellis, 1984). The *rbc*L gene, for example, is located in the chloroplast and encodes the large subunit of rubisco. Although there is much similarity between species from groups as diverse as the cyanobacteria and the higher plants (Lawlor, 1993), there are sufficient differences in the *rbc*L gene sequences to suggest that this provides an example of a molecular clock. This slowly accumulates mutational changes in the gene sequence, estimated to be at a rate of <1% in the base pairs of the gene over 20 million years (Soltis *et al.*, 1993; Savard *et al.*, 1994), with an inbuilt record of elapsed evolutionary time (Golenberg *et al.*, 1990; Bousquet *et al.*, 1992). Another important consequence of this finding is that changes in rubisco structure and the gene sequences coding for rubisco do occur, but this has a rather small impact on the physiological efficiency of rubisco, except for some photosynthetic bacteria.

This molecular information, in addition to the range of data on rubisco activity in diverse plant groups, implies that physiological functions have changed rather little as a consequence of genetic change, at least over the last 450 Ma. Therefore the responses of rubisco to a range of natural and simulated environments at the present day will be very similar to the responses that would have occurred at any time over the last 450 Ma, increasing the confidence in our capability to model ancient physiological responses to climate and environment.

Stomata

Although rubisco from 450 million years ago has probably changed little from present-day rubisco, under the same range of *in vitro* conditions, it is very possible that *in vivo* rubisco may operate in quite different endogenous environments. For example, the stomatal densities of the Lower Devonian (395 Ma) *Aglaophyton major* and *Sawdonia ornata* were about 4 mm^{-2} (McElwain & Chaloner, 1995). By contrast, the stomatal density of present-day *Quercus robur* may reach 400 mm^{-2}. The stomatal density, together with the stomatal aperture, controls the resistance (or conductance, which is the inverse of resistance) to diffusion for CO_2 from outside a leaf or stem to the intercellular air spaces inside the plant. This intercellular CO_2 concentration then reaches equilibrium with the CO_2 concentration dissolved in the chloroplast stroma and therefore the subsequent rate of carboxylation (eqs. 2.1 and 2.4). In these two extreme cases of stomatal density it is possible that rubisco may have significant effects on the intercellular concentration within the leaf or stem, which exerts a negative feedback on the rate of carboxylation, or net photosynthesis (eq. 2.5). The interesting feature is that this proposal can be tested using fossil plant material, specifically by analysing the ratio of the two stable isotopes of carbon in plants, which is influenced by physiological activity.

Stable isotopes of carbon

The stable isotopes of carbon, ^{12}C and ^{13}C, have always been present in the atmosphere, and the current (taken as 1988; see p. 48) molar abundance ratio of $^{13}C:^{12}C$ is about 0.01115 (Jones, 1992). In general use, particularly for fossil material, the $^{13}C:^{12}C$ ratio of plant tissue, or of an air sample, is usually expressed as a composition relative to a fossil belemnite standard (Pee Dee Belemnite, PDB), where:

$$\delta^{13}C = \left[\frac{(^{13}C:^{12}C)_{sample}}{(^{13}C:^{12}C)_{standard}} - 1 \right] \times 10^3 \qquad (2.9)$$

Atmospheric CO_2 (1988) has a $\delta^{13}C$ value of -7.7 parts per thousand (‰), which is equivalent to a molar abundance ratio of 0.01115 for $^{13}C:^{12}C$. By contrast, photosynthetic tissue, in plants with the C_3 pathway of photosynthesis, has a typical isotopic composition of -20 to $-35\permil$, indicating that the process of photosynthesis discriminates against the rarer and heavier isotope, $^{13}CO_2$. Farquhar *et al.* (1982) have explained the processes by which this discrimination occurs and define the interrelationship between plant $\delta^{13}C$ and the processes of CO_2 diffusion into the leaf and CO_2 fixation of by rubisco as follows:

$$\delta^{13}C_p = \delta^{13}C_a - a - (b-a)\frac{c_i}{c_a} \tag{2.10}$$

where $\delta^{13}C_p$ is the isotopic carbon composition of the plant material and $\delta^{13}C_a$ is the isotopic composition of the air. The constant a is the discrimination of $4.4\permil$ against ^{13}C due to diffusion in air (the diffusivity of $^{13}CO_2$ is $4.4\permil$ less than that of $^{12}CO_2$ in air; Craig, 1953). The constant b is the discrimination of between 27 and $30\permil$ against $^{13}CO_2$ by rubisco (Farquhar *et al.*, 1982), c_i is the CO_2 concentration in the intercellular spaces of the plant and c_a is the external ambient CO_2 concentration. The intercellular CO_2 concentration, c_i, is an important variable for considering plant function, as it is determined by the balance between the rate of diffusional supply of CO_2 through the stomata and the boundary layer of the photosynthetic organ and the rate of CO_2 fixation by rubisco.

An important feature of $\delta^{13}C_p$ is its stability in fossil material and so it is possible to measure long time-series of this plant composition using fossils, such as for the whole of the Phanerozoic period of 450 Ma (e.g. Beerling & Woodward, 1997). The important feature of the relationship described in equation 2.10 is that the mean ratio of the intercellular to external ambient CO_2 concentrations can be extracted for the period in which the plant fossil was actually growing. This ratio provides an important quantitative measure of the *in situ* activity of rubisco, also taking into account the resistance to CO_2 diffusion into the plant, through the stomata and the boundary layer. Therefore, the isotopic composition of living and fossil plant material can be used to test whether the present-day understanding of rubisco and stomatal behaviour is equally applicable in the past. The approach to this end is as follows, building on the earlier discussions about the controls of carboxylation and oxygenation by rubisco and, again, taking the special case which assumes that RuBP is in saturating supply for carboxylation.

The net rate of carboxylation, A_n, has already been defined (eq. 2.5) in terms of the rates of carboxylation and oxygenation, in essence a description of the biochemical sink for CO_2. The net rate can also be defined in terms of the diffusional source of CO_2:

Table 2.1. *Predictions of $\delta^{13}C_p$ (eq. 2.10, a is 4.4‰, b is 27‰, $\delta^{13}C_a$ is −7‰) using equation 2.12 and observations of $\delta^{13}C_p$ for the Devonian period (high CO_2 concentrations and low stomatal density) and for the present day*

Stomatal density (mm^{-2})	g (mol/m²/s)	CO_2 (ppm)	$V_c{}^{max}$ (μmol/m²/s)	$V_o{}^{max}$ (μmol/m²/s)	c_i/c_a	$\delta^{13}C_p$ predicted (‰)	observed (‰)
4	0.005	3500	50	26	0.05	−13	−27
400	0.204	350	50	26	0.7	−27	−27

Source: From Beerling & Woodward (1997).

$$A_n = (c_a - c_i)g \tag{2.11}$$

Where g is the combined conductance for CO_2 through the stomata and the boundary layer and c_a and c_i are defined as parts per million (ppm). In subsequent chapters, the measure of CO_2 may also be in partial pressures (units of Pa), which is the partial pressure of CO_2 divided by the total atmospheric pressure.

Equations 2.4, 2.5, 2.6 and 2.9 can then be combined, and with some modification:

$$(c_a - c_i)g = \frac{V_c{}^{max}c_i}{c_i + K_c\left(1 + \dfrac{o}{K_o}\right)} - 0.5\frac{V_o{}^{max}o}{o + K_o\left(1 + \dfrac{c_i}{K_c}\right)} \tag{2.12}$$

The necessary modification is to consider the mole fractions of CO_2 and O_2 in the intercellular air spaces, rather than dissolved in the stroma. This modification causes the values of K_o and K_c to be higher than shown on Figure 2.1 where the CO_2 and O_2 concentrations were in solution (eqs. 2.2 and 2.3) and therefore of a much lower mole fraction.

In equation 2.12, all variables except c_i and g are known from earlier discussions. The combined stomatal and boundary layer conductance, g, can be estimated for stomatal densities of 4 and 400 mm^{-2} using the approach described in Chapter 3 and also by Beerling & Woodward (1997). The intercellular CO_2 concentration, c_i, can then be solved from equation 2.12, as the positive root of a quadratic equation.

The characteristic variables for equation 2.12 are shown in Table 2.1, where it has been assumed that the plants with low stomatal density occur in a high CO_2 environment, 10 times greater than the present day; the O_2 concentration is taken, for simplicity, to be equal to the present day. The variables for the high stomatal density case are taken from observations at the present day (e.g.

Table 2.2. *Details as for Table 2.1, except that* V_c^{max} *and* V_o^{max} *have been allowed to vary until* c_i/c_a *reaches a value of 0.7*

Stomatal density (mm^{-2})	g (mol/m²/s)	CO_2 (ppm)	V_c^{max} (μmol/m²/s)	V_o^{max} (μmol/m²/s)	c_i/c_a	$\delta^{13}C_p$ predicted (‰)	observed (‰)
4	0.005	3500	6	3	0.7	−27	−27
400	0.204	350	50	26	0.7	−27	−27

Wullschleger, 1993) and the same values for V_c^{max} and V_o^{max} have been applied to both cases. The K_c referenced to the gaseous intercellular CO_2 concentration is 200 μM and the K_o is 500 mM.

Assuming the same activity of rubisco (V_c^{max} and V_o^{max}) leads to an anomalous prediction of $\delta^{13}C_p$ for the Devonian period because this high activity causes a very large draw-down of the intercellular CO_2 concentration (c_i/c_a).

By contrast, if the rubisco activities are allowed to vary until the c_i/c_a is the same as for the present day (0.7), then the predicted $\delta^{13}C_p$ closely matches the observation of fossil material from the Devonian (Table 2.2) (Woodward & Beerling, 1997).

This simple analysis indicates a number of interesting features. The first is that there appears to be some feedback between the diffusion capacity of the stomata (stomatal conductance) and the activity of rubisco, such that the two are positively correlated, a feature often noted but still poorly understood (Wong et al., 1979; Farquhar & Wong, 1984; Raven, 1993). The second point, the aim of this exercise, is that this analysis clearly indicates that the present-day understanding of stomata/rubisco relationships can be successfully applied to plants at the beginning of their arrival on land.

Conclusions

This chapter has introduced some of the basic aspects of rubisco and stomatal operation, which will be expanded in the subsequent chapters. The reason for this treatment was to assess the validity of applying present-day understanding of photosynthetic physiology to past plants and environments. Photosynthesis figures in this exploration because it is and has been the major source, at least 95%, of the carbon building blocks of all organisms and must therefore have a central position in any considerations of past and present-day ecology. The analysis presented here indicates that, although there has been some phylogenetic variation in the nucleotides of the rubisco genes, once embedded in terrestrial organisms there is rather little evidence for significant differences in carboxylation and oxygenation capacity (Raven, 1996). What differences there are will also be muted by the modifying influence of CO_2 diffusion through stomata. Therefore, it will now be assumed that photosynthesis in fossil plants can be understood in terms of the present-day understanding of rubisco and stomatal operation.

3

Climate and terrestrial vegetation

Introduction

Assemblages of species of plants constitute vegetation. At any location, the type of vegetation, in terms of its structure and its functioning, is dependent on both the constituent species and the environment of the vegetation. The natural environment can be considered to encompass the long-term climate and the underlying soil conditions. Increasingly, we see that the present-day environment of vegetation is being influenced by human-controlled disturbances. These disturbances, such as vegetation clearance for food and fuel, for urbanisation and for agriculture constitute the total environment of vegetation. Human impacts on the carbon cycle are considered in Chapter 10.

The primary emphasis of this book is on the effects of changes in climate on the distribution and functioning of vegetation, since the first emergence of land plants about 450 million years ago. The two components needed to investigate the functioning of vegetation over the last 450 Ma are the climatic constraints on plant and vegetation functioning and the climatic conditions in which plants occur. In addition, it is important to recognise that investigating and modelling the activity of past vegetation assumes that the basic plant processes, as we understand them for the present day, such as photosynthesis, respiration, transpiration and nutrient uptake, are equally valid for earlier times, an issue already discussed in Chapter 2.

Palaeoclimatic records are not like simple mercury thermometers but depend on sophisticated analyses of fossil plant and rock material. Chapter 4 discusses the ways in which the global climate is simulated by computer for different past eras, using palaeoclimatic information as a constraint on climatic predictions.

This chapter discusses the climatic constraints on plants and vegetation and provides a general overview of the functioning of vegetation over the last 450 Ma.

The climatic limits of vegetation

Plants have two suites of climatic limits. Most obvious and most frequently detected are the limits on growth. Equally important, but perhaps less frequently realised, are the absolute limits of survival. For plants in seasonal climates there may be one or more periods of the year in which growth is not possible, generally because of limiting temperatures or precipitation. At high latitudes there are periods of the year in which the sun does not appear above the horizon and so photosynthesis would be impossible, even if temperatures were appropriate for growth. Plants may either endure or avoid such periods. Endurance is characterised by plants showing little growth or activity but retaining all obvious productive characters such as green leaves and living roots. Avoidance is characterised by very marked changes in plants, seen particularly as leaf abscission and the death of fine roots. Once the environment again becomes suitable for growth, plants will develop new and active leaves and roots. Even plants which are evergreen endurers tend to progress through periods of new development and repair at this transition to the growing season (Larcher, 1995).

Often, but not always, during the periods of growth inactivity plants may have to endure climatic extremes for survival – truly a case of life or death. These limits are typically those of temperature, particularly low temperatures (Sakai & Larcher, 1987; Woodward, 1987a), and of water supply, usually drought (Larcher, 1995) but also waterlogging. These limits tend to occur in conditions which are far from suitable for growth, so that the plants have reduced growth and may have been through active processes of hardening, which generally occurs in advance of extreme climatic conditions. Plants undergoing active growth tend to be much less able to endure extreme climatic conditions (Larcher, 1995).

The extreme limits for plant survival have been extensively investigated and it is possible to recognise cardinal limits for the survival of different species of plants (Fig. 3.1) (Woodward, 1987a; Larcher, 1995). Significant low temperature limits are 10 °C, below which chilling damage can occur, 0 °C, below which freezing can occur and −40 °C, the point of spontaneous freezing of pure supercooled water. Broad-leaved evergreen species of trees only survive temperatures greater than about −15 °C. Broad-leaved deciduous trees survive to −40 °C, whilst boreal coniferous species survive all low temperatures to which they are naturally exposed.

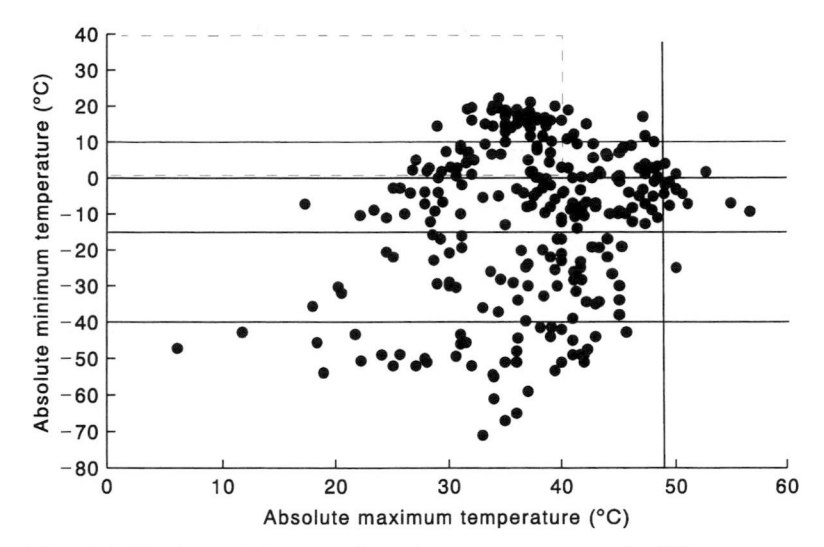

Figure 3.1. Absolute minimum and maximum temperatures for 281 meteorological stations (from Müller, 1982) selected for a global terrestrial coverage. Continuous lines indicate different survival ranges, indicated in the text, box in broken lines indicates the range of temperatures for active plant growth (see text, p. 24).

In contrast to the wide range of low temperature tolerances, plants are much more conservative in terms of their high temperature limits. The observations of Gauslaa (1984), Nobel (1988) and Larcher (1995) indicate a mean upper temperature limit of 49 °C for non-succulent plants and to *c.* 64 °C for some very hardy succulent species.

The range of temperatures for plant growth is defined within the rectangular box in Figure 3.1. It is clear that the temperature range for growth is much smaller than for survival and that for the large majority of the sites there are periods during the year and between years when only survival and not growth is possible.

Plants consist of at least 80% water and so a continued supply of water is essential for survival. Globally, there is a range of about four orders of magnitude in annual precipitation (Fig. 3.2). Plants growing in warmer climates require more precipitation than those in cool climates because with increasing temperature the air holds more water vapour and this property represents an increasing sink size, with temperature, for transpired water from plants.

It is possible to calculate the minimum precipitation required to support the growth of a plant through its whole life cycle. The extreme life cycle is that of a so-called annual plant which can complete the cycle from seed to seed in as little as a couple of weeks (Woodward, 1987a, 1988). The time to complete the life cycle decreases with temperature, because growth has a positive

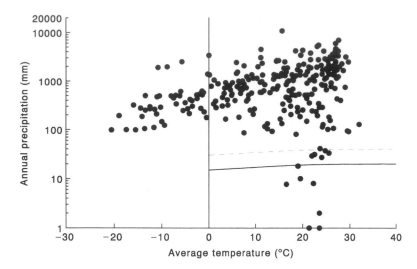

Figure 3.2. Annual precipitation for meteorological stations shown in Fig. 3.1. The average temperature is calculated as the mean of the absolute maximum and minimum temperatures in Fig. 3.1. The two curves indicate calculations of total plant transpiration for an annual life cycle (35 days at 20 °C) with a mean relative humidity of 90% (solid line) and 80% (broken line).

temperature coefficient. The temperature coefficient, the Q_{10}, is calculated as follows:

$$Q_{10} = e^{\frac{10}{t_2 - t_1} \log_e \left(\frac{r_2}{r_1} \right)} \tag{3.1}$$

where the Q_{10} is the proportional increase in the rate of the process r_2 following an increase in temperature from t_1 (°C), with a rate r_1, to t_2. $Q_{10} = 2$ for a doubling in the rate with a 10 °C increase in temperature. Plant processes have values of Q_{10} within the range 1.4–2.0 (Larcher, 1995).

Typical life cycles of annual plants may be completed within about 80 days, when the mean temperature is 5 °C. This period may be reduced to as little as 35 days, when the mean temperature is 20 °C. The Q_{10} for this life cycle is then calculated to be 1.7. Using this crude estimate of Q_{10} it is then possible to calculate the rate of the life cycle, r_2, at a range of temperatures, t_2, where the rate of the life cycle is the inverse of the period of the life cycle:

$$r_2 = Q_{10}^{\left(\frac{t_2 - t_1}{10} \right)} r_1 \tag{3.2}$$

where r_1 is 1/80 at a temperature t_1 of 5 °C. Calculated in this way, the life cycle decreases from 105 days at 0 °C to 35 days at 20 °C and 20 days at 30 °C.

The necessary opening of the stomata for CO_2 to diffuse into the leaf and to the chloroplasts also entails a necessary loss of water by transpiration. The total transpiration, E_2 (mm), for the life cycle, $1/r_2$, of the plant at a temperature t_2 can be calculated as follows:

$$E_2 = \frac{e_2\left(1 - \dfrac{RH}{100}\right)}{P} gmsd\frac{1}{r_2} \tag{3.3}$$

where e_2 is the saturation water vapour pressure of the air at temperature t_2 and the vapour pressure deficit of the air – the sink for transpiration – is $e_2(1 - RH/100)$ where RH is the relative humidity of the air (%). The constant m (0.018, mm mol^{-1}) converts moles of transpired water vapour to mm, P is atmospheric pressure (Pa), s is the number of seconds in one hour and d is daylength (hours). The capacity for water vapour to diffuse through the stomata is represented by g, the stomatal conductance (the inverse of resistance), with units of mol m^{-2} s^{-1}. For simplicity it has been assumed that g does not vary with temperature or vapour pressure deficit, although this is not the case and that g has a typical value of 0.3 mol m^{-2} s^{-1}. Multiplying the equation by $1/r_2$ (the length of the life cycle in days) provides a calculation for the estimated water loss by transpiration for the whole life cycle.

In Figure 3.2 it is assumed that the daylength is constant at 12 hours. When the relative humidity is 90%, about the maximum which will occur in regional climates, then the total transpiration loss for the complete life cycle increases from 15 to 20 mm as the temperature increases from 0 °C to 40 °C. This is not a large increase with temperature because the life cycle becomes markedly shorter with increasing temperatures, decreasing the time for transpiration. When relative humidity is 80%, total transpiration for the life cycle ranges from 30 to 40 mm.

These calculations provide estimates of the minimal water requirements for plant growth. The calculation ignores water evaporated from soil independently of transpiration, which may double the precipitation requirements of a site. However, this is strongly dependent on soil characteristics, in particular wetness, surface temperature and the occurrence of cracks.

The range of limits for growth and survival are calculated for plants and climates of the present day. The aim of this book is to investigate how plant–climate interactions have changed since the arrival and subsequent evolution of vascular plants on the Earth's surface. One important feature of plant evolution may have been the extension of the hard climatic limits shown on Figures 3.1 and 3.2. The possibility of such changes will be determined by comparisons between predicted distributions and functioning of vegetation during previous times, and observations from the fossil record.

500 million years of changing global climate

The temperature of the Earth and the photosynthetic rates of plants are both primarily dependent on solar irradiance (Crowley & North, 1991). The secondary control of global temperature occurs through changes in atmospheric composition and the albedo (reflectivity) of both the Earth's surface and the atmosphere (North *et al.*, 1981, 1983; Kuhn *et al.*, 1989). These controls can be contained within a zero-dimensional statement – i.e. latitude, longitude and altitude are not considered – of the global climate (North, 1988; Kiehl, 1992; Schneider, 1992):

$$\frac{S_c}{4}(1 - \alpha) = \epsilon \sigma T^4 \tag{3.4}$$

where S_c is the solar constant (1367 W m^{-2} at the present day), α is the planetary albedo (viewed from the top of the atmosphere), ε is the planetary emissivity, i.e. the capacity to emit long-wave radiation, σ is the Stefan–Boltzmann constant (5.67×10^{-8} W m^{-2} K^{-4}) and T is the planetary temperature (K). The division of the solar constant by the factor 4 accounts for the fact that the Earth absorbs radiation like a two-dimensional disc of area πr^2, but in fact this radiation is spread over the surface area of a sphere, which has four times the area of a disc. The solar constant has been increasing throughout the life of the Earth. The change is a result of the gradual conversion of hydrogen to helium, which increases the density of the sun; as a consequence the sun's core temperature increases which leads to greater rates of fusion reactions and luminosity (Kasting & Grinspoon, 1991). Over the last 500 million years the solar constant is calculated to have increased by about 5% (Caldeira & Kasting, 1992). According to equation 3.4, with no other changes in planetary characteristics the increase in the solar constant should have led to continuous global warming. At the present day, equation 3.4 balances for a mean planetary temperature of 255 K, with a current planetary albedo of 0.31.

Although it is of interest to determine the mean planetary temperature, it is more relevant for terrestrial ecology to calculate the mean terrestrial surface temperature. This is more difficult to calculate because of the exchanges of water vapour between the Earth's surface and the atmosphere (Raval & Ramanathan, 1989), and through changes in cloudiness (Ramanathan & Collins, 1991) and natural concentrations of other greenhouse gases, notably CO_2. However, a range of satellite and observational data has been used to relate the outward flux of long-wave radiation from the top of the atmosphere (the right-hand side of equation 3.4) to the Earth's surface temperature (North, 1975; Ramanathan & Coakley, 1978; Kiehl, 1992). Equation 3.4 can therefore be changed to relate the surface temperature, T_s, and incoming solar radiation as:

$$\frac{S_c}{4}(1 - \alpha) = 1.55 T_s - 212 \tag{3.5}$$

Using this equation, the Earth's mean surface temperature is calculated as 288.9 K. A reduction in the solar constant by 5%, simulating the period of 500 Ma and with no other changes in equation 3.5, would lead to a world which is 7.6 K cooler than the present day, a temperature which would be characteristic of a significant glacial climate – a feature not supported by the fossil evidence, for this time, of a warm climate (Crowell, 1982; Stanley, 1986; Crowley & North, 1991). One explanation for this divergence is the presence in the atmosphere of higher concentrations of greenhouse gases, primarily CO_2 (Kasting & Grinspoon, 1991; Berner, 1993).

Increasing the atmospheric CO_2 concentration reduces the loss of long-wave radiation from the top of the atmosphere. Using the radiative forcing calculated for changes in CO_2 concentration (Hansen *et al.*, 1988), it is possible to modify equation 3.5 so that the temperature of past times can be calculated, given information about the changing solar constant and the atmospheric concentration of CO_2:

$$\frac{S_c l}{4}(1 - \alpha_T) = 1.55 T_s - 212 - 6.3 \log_e \left(\frac{280 + c}{280}\right) \tag{3.6}$$

where l is the solar luminosity as a fraction of the present day, α_T, is the temperature-sensitive global albedo and c is the CO_2 concentration (ppm) difference from a threshold of 280 ppm, the CO_2 concentration of the atmosphere calculated for the onset of the industrial revolution.

The global albedo is calculated by the methods described by North *et al* (1981, 1983) and Kiehl (1992). This approach assumes that the albedo can fall into three temperature-dependent regions, as seen in Figure 3.3. At temperatures below 230 K the planetary albedo is very high, indicating a highly reflective and ice-bound Earth. The albedo is assumed to be at a minimum when temperatures are >270 K. Between these two extremes, albedo is linearly dependent on temperature, decreasing as temperature increases.

The global surface temperature can be calculated graphically using equations 3.5 and 3.6. The present-day plot (Fig. 3.4) shows three possible equilibrium climates, indicated as the intersections of the solar and long-wave radiation curves. The highest temperature equilibrium represents the present day.

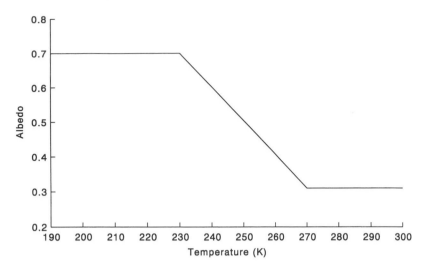

Figure 3.3. The temperature-dependence of the planetary albedo.

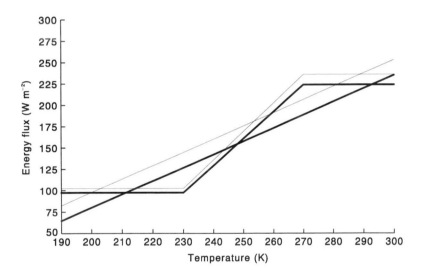

Figure 3.4. Plots of energy fluxes with global surface temperature. Straight lines, long-wave radiation emitted from the top of the atmosphere to outer space: faint line, present day; bold line, 500 Ma, with an atmospheric CO_2 concentration of 4800 ppm. Reverse Z-shaped lines, solar irradiance: faint line, for present day; bold line, for 500 Ma, when the solar constant was 5% less than the present day.

The central equilibrium is unstable because any small changes in solar irradiance, or planetary albedo, for example, would lead to further changes in temperature, until a stable plateau is reached. At this point changes in temperature have little impact on albedo or energy fluxes and so a stable climate is reached. The lowest temperature, for example, represents a stable glacial

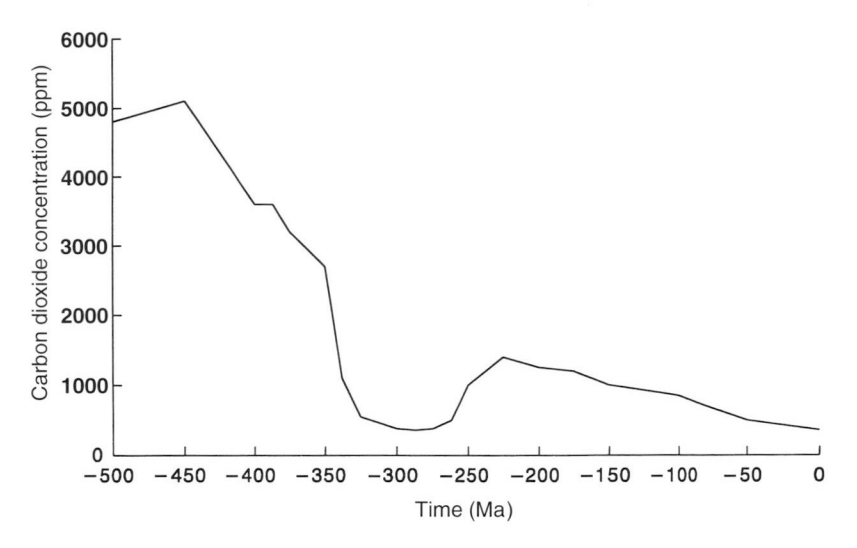

Figure 3.5. Postulated change in atmospheric CO_2 concentration over the last 500 Ma, simplified trends (from Graham *et al.*, 1995).

world. When solar irradiance is reduced, simulating a 5% weaker sun at 500 Ma, then with no changes in long-wave emission patterns (the faint present-day line on Fig. 3.4) the world is predicted to be 7.6 K cooler than the present day. In contrast, if the atmospheric concentration is increased substantially to 4800 ppm, in line with calculations and predictions of Berner (1993, 1994), then the Earth is predicted to have been 3 K warmer than the present.

The world has clearly enjoyed constant change through variations in the natural greenhouse effect – the changing downward fluxes of long-wave radiation to the Earth's surface as a consequence of changes in atmospheric CO_2 concentrations. Long-term assessment of vegetation responses to climate must therefore consider changes in atmospheric CO_2 concentration, a feature which will also affect global photosynthetic rates. A general trend in atmospheric CO_2 concentration (Fig. 3.5) has been extracted from Graham *et al* (1995) and will be used to predict global temperatures, using equation 3.5. This approach assumes that only changes in the solar constant and radiative forcing by changes in the atmospheric concentrations of CO_2 control global temperatures. Other factors which may play a critical role in controlling global climate, such as changes in the global patterns of ocean circulation (Broecker, 1989) and the consequences of plate tectonic activity (Crowley & North, 1991) are not considered. A final problem lies in the uncertainty of the trends in CO_2 themselves (Crowley & North, 1991; Berner, 1993; Graham *et al.*, 1995).

The uncertainty is difficult to resolve, but the best current estimates (Graham *et al.*, 1995) fall within the range of errors from independent geological sources (Berner, 1993, 1994).

The general decline in CO_2 concentration over the whole time period is thought to be due to the slow accumulation of carbonate sediments in the oceans. The carbonates are derived on land by the weathering of silicate rocks, followed by the deposition of precipitated carbonates in the oceans (Urey, 1952; Berner, 1993):

$$CO_2 + CaSiO_3 \rightarrow CaCO_3 + SiO_2 \tag{3.7}$$

$$CO_2 + MgSiO_3 \rightarrow MgCO_3 + SiO_2 \tag{3.8}$$

The rates of weathering are dependent on global temperatures and also on the presence of terrestrial vegetation. Vegetation enhances the rates of weathering, and therefore the removal of atmospheric CO_2, through respiratory enrichment of CO_2 concentrations in the soils, and also by the secretion or loss of organic acids from the roots into the soil (Volk, 1989; Kasting & Grinspoon, 1991; Berner, 1993). The reverse of the weathering and carbonate deposition occurs primarily through tectonic activity on ocean sediments, a process which re-forms the silicates and reverses equations 3.7 and 3.8, causing CO_2 release into the atmosphere (Walker *et al.*, 1981; Volk, 1987).

Changes in atmospheric CO_2 concentration (Fig. 3.5) can be used with equation 3.6 to calculate approximate trends in global temperatures over the last 500 Ma. The reconstructions (Fig. 3.6) may only be approximate as the trends in CO_2 concentration are also uncertain. It is also assumed that no other greenhouse gases have influenced climate and that the sensitivity of long-wave energy transfer (eqs. 3.5 and 3.6) to changes in surface temperature has not changed over this period.

In spite of a continual increase in the solar constant there is an apparent downward trend in global surface temperature (Fig. 3.6), a feature which is positively correlated with the gradual decline in atmospheric CO_2 concentration. The simple model used here has good agreement with temperature predictions from more complex models and moderate agreement with global temperatures reconstructed from fossil and other geological evidence. The latter is globally patchy in its distribution and, as a consequence all of the temperatures estimated from geological evidence, will have large estimates of error. Errors of prediction from the model used here could also be presented, using the errors associated with the estimates of atmospheric CO_2 concentration. However, this is not the aim of the current exercise, which is to indicate that global temperatures can be predicted with moderate accuracy using a simple zero-dimensional model. This moderate accuracy then

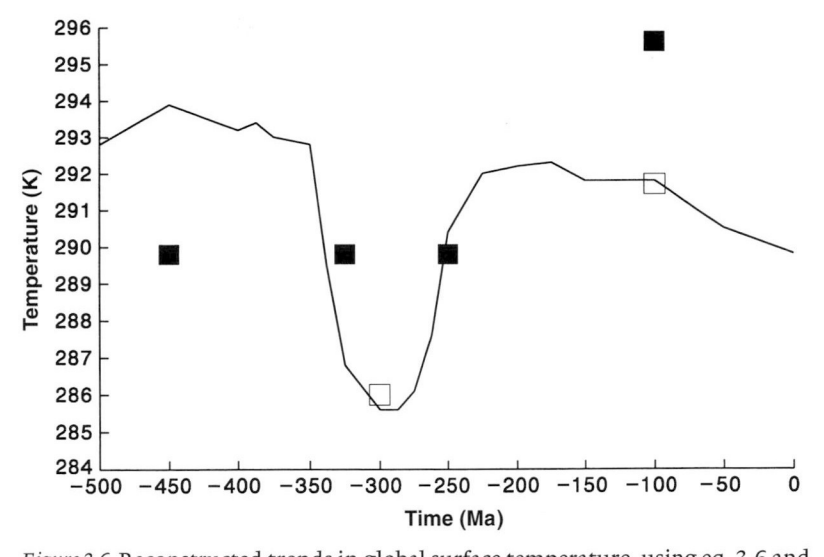

Figure 3.6. Reconstructed trends in global surface temperature, using eq. 3.6 and the CO_2 trends from Fig. 3.5. ($\square$), global temperatures estimated from climate modelling exercises (Barron, 1983; Crowley and Baum, 1994); ($\blacksquare$), global temperatures estimated from the composition of stable isotopes of oxygen in forams of ocean sediments (Barron, 1983; Frakes, *et al* 1992).

allows discussion of the relevance to vegetation of the trends in CO_2 and temperature.

A particularly marked reduction in temperature (7.5 K) is predicted between about 350 and 250 Ma. This prediction is in keeping with strong fossil evidence for a period of marked global cooling and glaciations (Parrish *et al.*, 1986; Crowley & Baum, 1991). In addition, the climate modelling experiment by Crowley and Baum (1994) for 305 Ma is in close agreement with the predictions presented here. The agreement may be somewhat fortuitous, as the model run may be too cool because the transfer of heat by ocean currents is not addressed.

The Carboniferous period is one of very significant accumulation of coal measures, indicating that photosynthetic production by terrestrial ecosystems exceeds the rate of litter decomposition (Berner, 1987). This positive rate of net ecosystem production (i.e. vegetation photosynthesis minus vegetation respiration minus heterotrophic respiration) will have removed CO_2 from the atmosphere, purely by litter accumulation. If decomposition rates are very low, particularly when soils are waterlogged, oxygen use and carbon dioxide release by heterotrophic respiration will both be reduced (Berner, 1987). In addition, the rate of weathering (eqs. 3.7 and 3.8) will also have been strongly stimulated by the active vegetation, increasing rates of CO_2 removal (eqs. 3.7 and 3.8; Berner, 1993). Given these considerations, it is difficult to avoid the

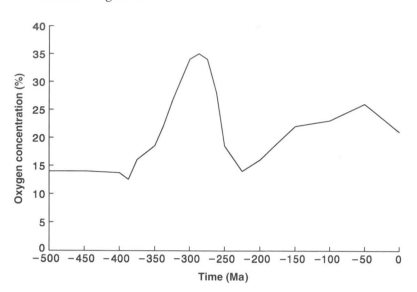

Figure 3.7. Simplified trend in atmospheric oxygen concentration (from Graham *et al.*, 1995).

conclusion that terrestrial vegetation played a major part in the inception and control of this period of low temperatures and active glaciation (Berner, 1993).

Removal of plant litter into non-decomposing material will reduce heterotrophic respiration and increase atmospheric oxygen concentrations. This prediction is supported by the modelled trends in atmospheric oxygen (Fig. 3.7) reviewed by Graham *et al* (1995).

500 million years of terrestrial photosynthesis

The decreases in CO_2 concentration and temperature and the increase in oxygen concentration during the Carboniferous and Permian periods (350–250 Ma) will all have acted to reduce the photosynthetic potential of terrestrial vegetation. This reduced vegetation activity may have led to a reversal of the climatic conditions and atmospheric concentrations of oxygen and CO_2 during this period. It is particularly interesting to note, using molecular clock techniques (Savard *et al.*, 1994), that present-day seed plants (cycads, conifers, *Ginkgo*, Gnetales and the angiosperms) shared a common ancestor till *c.* 285 Ma, towards the end of the low CO_2, low temperature and high oxygen period. This clearly suggests that not only was the vegetation likely to have driven the large changes in climate: it also led to marked subsequent evolutionary divergence. These probably interlinked issues can be investigated further by determining the trend of the primary photosynthetic process during this whole period, based on the current understanding of the mechanisms of photosynthesis.

Farquhar *et al.* (1980) have described a mechanistic model of photosynthesis, which has been extensively validated for the present day and is now widely used for plant and vegetation modelling. The photosynthetic rate is considered to be controlled by either the concentration, activation state and kinetic properties of the primary enzyme for fixing CO_2 (rubisco) – W_c, or by the rate of ribulose bisphosphate (RuBP) regeneration through electron transport – W_j. Rubisco catalyses the processes of both carboxylation and oxygenation, which compete for the action of rubisco. Under conditions of high oxygen concentration, as in the Carboniferous period, the oxygenation process of photorespiration will have been favoured more than in subsequent periods of lower oxygen concentration, with the effect of reducing overall photosynthetic carboxylation. The following equations describe the processes of photosynthesis. The explicit description of this well-validated model allows its use under a wide range of conditions with considerable confidence (Woodward *et al.*, 1995). The basic equations are described here; further amplification of the use of the equations, their temperature sensitivities and the use of the model for vegetation simulation at a global scale, can all be found in Woodward *et al.* (1995).

The net rate of photosynthesis, A (mol m^{-2} s^{-1}) is defined as follows:

$$A = V_c \left(1 - \frac{0.5o}{\tau c_i} \right) - R_d \qquad (3.9)$$

where V_c, the rate of carboxylation (mol m^{-2} s^{-1}), is the minimum of either W_c or W_j. The oxygen and CO_2 partial pressures, within a photosynthetic organ such as a leaf or stem, are o and c_i respectively (Pa). τ is the specificity factor (J mol^{-1}) of rubisco for CO_2 relative to O_2 and R_d is the rate of respiration in the light (mol m^{-2} s^{-1}) attributed to processes other than photorespiration.

When the rate of photosynthesis is primarily controlled by rubisco – W_c – then the rate is defined as:

$$W_c = \frac{V_c{}^{max}c_i}{c_i + K_c(1 + o/K_o)} \qquad (3.10)$$

where $V_c{}^{max}$ is the maximum rate of carboxylation by rubisco and K_c and K_o are the Michaelis coefficients for carboxylation and oxygenation by rubisco.

The rate of RuBP regeneration, W_j – depends on the rate of electron transport, J (mol electrons m^{-2} s^{-1}) as:

$$W_j = \frac{Jc_i}{4(c_i + o/\tau)} \qquad (3.11)$$

The rate of electron transport, J, is dependent on irradiance, S (mol m^{-2} s^{-1}) and on the light-saturated rate of electron transport J_{max} as:

$$J = \frac{\alpha_p S}{\left(1 + \frac{\alpha^2_p S^2}{J_{max}^2}\right)^{0.5}} \tag{3.12}$$

where α_p is the efficiency of light conversion (0.24 mol electrons/mol photons, Harley *et al.*, 1992).

For general modelling purposes in which J_{max} is not known, it may be calculated from a robust but empirical relationship with a specified V_c^{max} as follows, based on a review by Wullschleger (1993):

$$J_{max} = 2.91 \times 10^{-5} + 1.64 V_c^{max} \tag{3.13}$$

The photosynthetic rate, as defined by equations 3.9 to 3.13, is described as a demand function, in which the rates of carboxylation and electron transfer demand a supply of CO_2 to the intercellular spaces and chloroplasts of the photosynthetic organ. The intercellular CO_2 partial pressure, c_i, is also controlled by the rate of CO_2 diffusion through the boundary layer of air surrounding the organ and through the stomata. The photosynthetic rate can then be defined by a supply function:

$$A = \left(\frac{c_a - c_i}{P}\right)g - R_d \tag{3.14}$$

in which c_a is the CO_2 partial pressure beyond the boundary layer and g is the conductance to CO_2 diffusion through the boundary layer and the stomata.

The impacts of the demand and supply functions on the realised rate of photosynthesis can be most easily shown graphically (Fig. 3.8).

The lowest rate of carboxylation, i.e. the most limiting, is taken as the photosynthetic rate (eq. 3.9), and is dependent on the intercellular CO_2 partial pressure (Fig. 3.8). At low partial pressures rubisco activity dominates the control, while at higher CO_2 partial pressures electron transport and RuBP regeneration limit photosynthesis. The lines describing the supply functions (Fig. 3.8, lines 1 and 2) are drawn from the x-axis, with the intercept at 35 Pa, the CO_2 partial pressure external to the boundary layer (c_a). The intersections with the carboxylation curves are drawn for the values of intercellular CO_2 partial pressure (c_i) at which the photosynthetic rate from equation 3.9 (demand) is equal to the photosynthetic rate from equation 3.14 (supply). It is clear that the different slopes of lines 1 and 2 (Fig. 3.8) lead to different photosynthetic rates and that as the stomatal plus boundary layer conductances decrease then the intercellular CO_2 partial pressure is drawn down by photosynthesis.

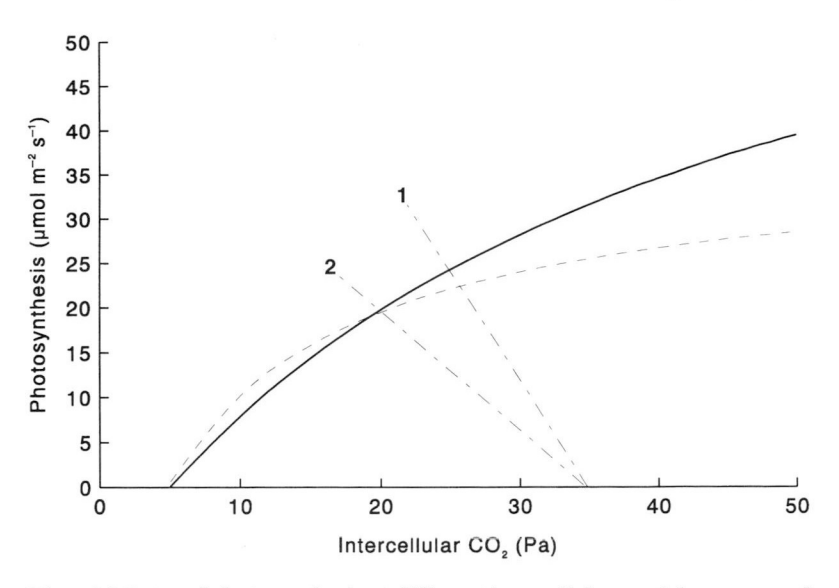

Figure 3.8. Rates of photosynthesis, at different intercellular partial pressures of CO_2, calculated using eq. 3.9, in which W_c is the rubisco limited rate (——) and W_j the RuBP regeneration limited rate, (– – – – –). The supply function curves (— ·— ·— ·—) are calculated from eq. 3.14, for (1) high and (2) low conductances to CO_2 diffusion.

Analyses of the DNA sequence for the *rbcL* gene, which encodes part of the rubisco molecule (Soltis *et al.*, 1993; Savard *et al.*, 1994), indicate that over the last 20 million years there have been fewer than 1% changes in the base pairs of the gene. This indicates that the enzyme rubisco has probably changed little in its molecular structure and presumably its biochemical activity and therefore it should be acceptable to use the current understanding of photosynthesis for investigating past changes in photosynthetic activity (Beerling 1994). Therefore equations 3.9 to 3.13 have been used to predict likely changes in photosynthesis over the last 500 Ma using calculations of past concentrations of carbon dioxide (Fig. 3.5) and oxygen (Fig. 3.7) and of past temperature (Fig. 3.6). The approach can only resolve the photosynthetic rates at the mean global temperature. The effects of temperature on photosynthesis are taken into account by established methods and the impacts on τ, V_c^{max}, K_c, K_0 and J_c^{max} (Harley *et al.*, 1992; Woodward *et al.*, 1995).

The rate of photosynthesis is dependent on W_c (equation 3.10) and W_j (equation 3.11). In addition W_c and W_j are dependent on the maximum rate of rubisco carboxylation, V_c^{max} and the light-saturated rate of electron transport, J_{max}. In the first investigations of the trends in photosynthesis, V_c^{max} is not known and so a range of values is used. In addition to the above requirements for calculating photosynthetic rate, there is also a need to know the CO_2

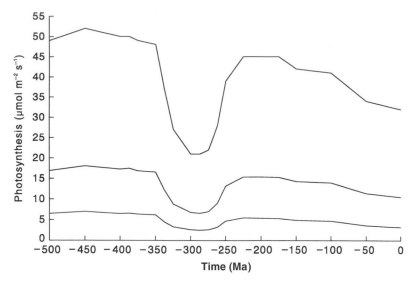

Figure 3.9. Estimated photosynthetic rates for three values of maximum rubisco carboxylation rate, V_c^{max} in eq. 3.10. In order of increasing photosynthetic rate the values of V_c^{max} are 10, 40 and 160 μmol m^{-2} s^{-1}.

partial pressure within the photosynthetic organ. This concentration is dependent on both the photosynthetic rate, which tends to draw down this partial pressure with increasing rate, and the degree of opening and number of stomata. In the latter case high stomatal density and large stomatal opening allow a maximum rate of CO_2 diffusion into the photosynthetic organ and so these characteristics will tend to cause the internal CO_2 partial pressure to increase. In this first step, it is assumed that the atmospheric partial pressure of CO_2 is equal to the internal partial pressure. Subsequent steps will then introduce the stomatal diffusional limitation and it then becomes possible to calculate the internal CO_2 partial pressure.

The estimated and light-saturated photosynthetic rates for three different values of V_c^{max} (Fig. 3.9) indicate marked reductions in photosynthetic capacity during the Carboniferous and Permian periods (350 to 250 Ma). The highest predicted rates of photosynthesis are for the earliest period from 500 to 350 Ma, the time of arrival and spread of the first vascular land plants. A quadrupling of V_c^{max} from 40 to 160 μmol m^{-2} s^{-1} has a much larger impact on photosynthetic rate than a quadrupling from 10 to 40 μmol m^{-2} s^{-1}.

The degree of stomatal opening is CO_2-sensitive, increasing with a reduction in CO_2 concentration (Beerling & Woodward, 1993). As the process of photosynthesis tends to reduce the internal CO_2 concentration below the external ambient air (Fig. 3.8), then photosynthesis can also cause stomata to open. These interactions have been combined into an empirical relationship between photosynthesis and stomatal conductance (Ball *et al.*, 1987; Aphalo & Jarvis, 1993), which also accounts for the fact that increasingly dry air causes stomata to close. The combined influence of differences in stomatal density and the opening of the stomata is characterised as the stomatal conductance (see also equation 3.14), the inverse of stomatal resistance to diffusion. The stomatal conductance, g (mol m^{-2} s^{-1}), is then defined as:

$$g = g_0 + g_1 A \frac{RH}{c_s} \tag{3.15}$$

where g_0 and g_1 are temperature-sensitive constants, A is the photosynthetic rate, RH is relative humidity (%) and c_s is the CO_2 partial pressure beneath the boundary layer of the photosynthetic organ, but external to the stomata. The relative humidity is calculated from air temperature and is based on the present-day relationship between temperature and relative humidity where $RH = 116 - 0.14T$. The surface partial pressure of CO_2, c_s, is less than the ambient CO_2 partial pressure and is calculated from the following equation:

$$A = \left(\frac{c_a - c_s}{P} \right) g_a - R_d \tag{3.16}$$

in which g_a is the boundary layer conductance to CO_2. The boundary layer conductance can be calculated from the wind speed and a knowledge of the size of the photosynthetic organ (Jones, 1992). For these long-term simulations, in which wind speed is unknown, g_a is given a typical value of 2 mol m^{-2} s^{-1}.

All of the photosynthetic equations – 3.9 to 3.16 – are subsequently calculated as a looped iteration, in which the equations are first seeded with a calculated intercellular CO_2 partial pressure as 0.75 c_a, and then the equations are calculated as a repeated loop, with changing values of A, c_i and g calculated from the various equations. The iteration is continued until equilibrium values of all of the variables are achieved: this typically takes about 10 cycles. In all cases it is assumed that the solar irradiance is saturating for photosynthesis.

The calculated stomatal conductances (Fig. 3.10) for the three values of V_c^{max} used in Figure 3.9 indicate a general increase in conductance to the present day, with marked and increasing excursions during the Carboniferous and Permian periods. The trends in stomatal conductance are inversely related to the photosynthetic rates, the highest conductances being predicted for the periods of lowest CO_2 concentration (Fig. 3.5). The high stomatal conductances are first predicted for the Carboniferous and Permian periods and associated with this high capacity to lose water by transpiration will be a high rate

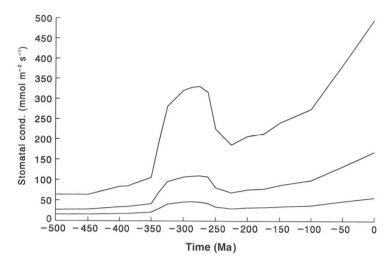

Figure 3.10. Predicted trends in maximum stomatal conductance, using eq. 3.14, a relative humidity of 80% and the photosynthetic rates from Fig. 3.9. The $V_c{}^{max}$ values (see Fig. 3.9) increase up the y-axis.

of water transport and supply through the xylem. It is interesting to note that the first fossil occurrence of high transport rate xylem vessels, with perforated end walls, as opposed to the slow transport rate tracheid predecessors (Edwards, 1993) with end walls, was in the late Permian (270–250 Ma; Li *et al.*, 1996), a time of high potential stomatal conductances and transpiration rates.

Although the Carboniferous period and the present day have very similar atmospheric CO_2 concentrations, both the photosynthetic rates (Fig. 3.9) and the stomatal conductances (Fig. 3.10), at the same values of $V_c{}^{max}$, are predicted to be higher for the present day. This results from the dual impacts of the higher oxygen concentrations in the Carboniferous, which lead to lower photosynthetic rates and higher rates of photorespiration, and the lower temperatures, which also lead to reduced rates of photosynthesis.

During the period 450 to 350 Ma it is predicted that stomatal conductance will have been very low and with a rather small absolute sensitivity to changes in $V_c{}^{max}$. It is known that stomatal density is also sensitive to CO_2 concentration, decreasing as CO_2 concentration increases (Woodward, 1987b, 1998; Beerling & Chaloner, 1993) and so it is likely that species evolving and growing in different CO_2 concentrations will possess different stomatal densities (Beerling & Woodward, 1996). This prediction is supported by fossil evidence, in both the long and the short term (Stubblefield & Banks, 1978; Edwards, 1993; Beerling, 1993; Van de Water *et al.*, 1994; McElwain & Chaloner, 1996). As the stomata limit CO_2 diffusion to the sites of photosyn-

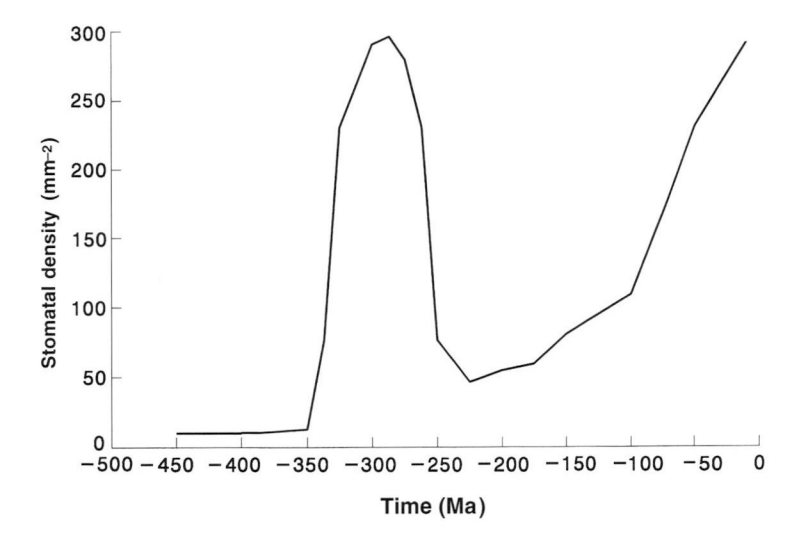

Figure 3.11. Predicted stomatal densities of plants over the last 450 Ma, based on eq. 3.17.

thesis, it must be that the CO_2-controlled stomatal densities will also exert controls on maximum rates of photosynthesis.

The likely impact of the stomatal density response to CO_2 on photosynthesis has been investigated by the following sequence of responses.

$$s_c = s_{max} e^{-0.02c_a} + 10 \times 10^{-6} \tag{3.17}$$

Equation 3.17 predicts the influence of ambient CO_2 concentration, c_a (Pa), on stomatal density, s_c (m^{-2}), where s_{max} is the maximum stomatal density on fresh leaf material (taken as 600×10^{-6} m^{-2}) and the minimum value of 10×10^{-6} m^{-2} is the mean of the lowest stomatal densities observed in fossil material (Edwards, 1993; Beerling & Woodward, 1997). This equation is based on data summarised in Beerling & Woodward (1997).

The trend in stomatal density indicates a very high peak during the Carboniferous period and another rise up to the present day (Fig. 3.11). The trend is based on stomatal density responses to CO_2 over the last 150 000 years and on observations of stomatal densities for fossil plants of the Devonian (400 Ma) and Carboniferous periods (reviewed in Beerling & Woodward, 1997).

The impact on photosynthesis of the marked variations in stomatal density with time can be predicted by converting the changes in density to changes in stomatal conductance. The following equation (Beerling & Woodward, 1993), modified from that of Van Gardingen *et al.* (1989), calculates stomatal conductance from data on stomatal density, s_c (m^{-2}) and the maximum length, l (m), width, w (m) and depth, d_s(m), of the stomatal pore.

$$G = \frac{s_c DP}{RT\left(\dfrac{d_s}{\pi l w} + \dfrac{\log_e\left(4\dfrac{l}{w}\right)}{\pi l}\right) \times 10^{-12}} \tag{3.18}$$

where R is the gas constant, T is temperature (K), D is the diffusion coefficient for water vapour (m^2 s^{-1}) and P is atmospheric pressure (Pa).

The characteristic dimensions of the stomatal pore have to be calculated from microscopic observations on fossil and extant material. For the purposes of this simulation the length and stomatal pore depth are held constant at 10 and 15 μm, respectively and the maximum width of the stomatal pore is 7 μm. The width of the stomatal pore is sensitive to the relative humidity and water vapour pressure deficit of the air, as follows (Beerling & Woodward, 1995, 1997):

$$w_w = w\exp\left(-0.003\left(614\exp\left(\frac{17.5t}{241+t}\right)\right)\left(1-\frac{RH}{100}\right)\right) \tag{3.19}$$

where w_w is the stomatal width, after accounting for the effect of the water vapour pressure deficit. The historical trends in relative humidity, RH, are not known and so a constant value of 80%, typical of moist terrestrial habitats is used. The use of a constant value of RH is supported by growing season observations from meteorological stations world-wide (Müller, 1982) and may be taken as a reasonable representation of past climates. The constant relative humidity does mean that with increasing temperatures the drying capacity of the air – the water vapour pressure deficit – will increase (Woodward & Sheehy, 1983).

Finally, the combined direct effects on pore width by temperature and intercellular CO_2 are accounted for by the following empirical relationship (from Beerling & Woodward, 1995):

$$w_t = w_w\left(0.37 - 5.7 \times 10^{-4}t^2 + 3.45\,10^{-2}t\right)\left(1 - 0.116\log_e(c_a 10)\right) \tag{3.20}$$

where t is temperature (°C) and c_a is the atmospheric CO_2 partial pressure (Pa).

This approach assumes that the environmental responses of the stomata (equations 3.17 to 3.20) operated in the past in the same way as the present day. This is the most simple assumption but it can not be verified directly. However, the predictions of all past gas exchange responses will be used to provide characteristics which can be observed in fossil plant material, and

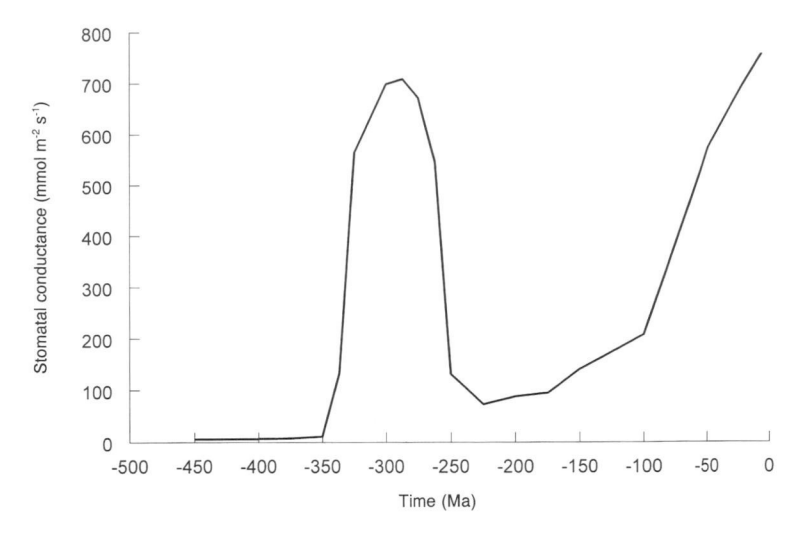

Figure 3.12. Calculated maximum stomatal conductances of plants, using eqs. 3.17 to 3.20 and estimates of atmospheric CO_2 concentrations (Fig. 3.5) and mean global temperatures (Fig. 3.6).

which can then be used to provide an overall assessment of the validity of the approach.

The maximum stomatal conductance can now be estimated for the last 450 million years, based on equations 3.17 to 3.20 and estimates of atmospheric CO_2 concentrations (Fig. 3.5) and mean global temperatures (Fig. 3.6).

The trend in stomatal conductance closely mirrors that of stomatal density (Fig. 3.9). The value is that the estimation of stomatal conductance makes it suitable for use in the photosynthetic equations and so the stomatal supply limitation on photosynthesis can be calculated. In addition, it is now possible to calculate the mean value of V_c^{max} based on the simple notion that the CO_2-diffusion supply function (Fig. 3.8; eq. 3.14) sets a maximum value of photosynthetic rate, which must in turn be satisfied by a maximum value of V_c^{max}, as described by equations 3.9 and 3.10. The photosynthetic rate estimated from equation 3.14 is then substituted into equations 3.9 and 3.10. The equations are then rearranged to solve for V_c^{max} (Beerling & Quick, 1995).

As suspected, the trend in V_c^{max} closely follows the trends in stomatal density (Fig. 3.11) and conductance (Fig. 3.12) and is inversely related to the trend in atmospheric CO_2 concentration (Fig. 3.5). The latter case clearly indicates some form of selection for improvements in rubisco activity as CO_2 concentration decreases and photorespiration rate increases. The most interesting feature is that the stomata, in particular stomatal density, appear to exert such a major control over photosynthetic development. The degree of

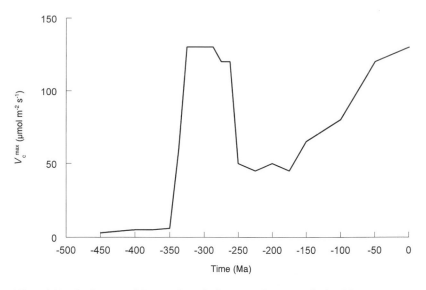

Figure 3.13. Maximum rubisco carboxylation capacity, V_c^{max}, derived from estimates of maximum stomatal conductance (Fig. 3.12) and by the use of eqs. 3.9, 3.10 and 3.14.

this control can be seen by comparing Figure 3.9, where with constant V_c^{max} there is a general decline in photosynthetic rate to the present day, with a marked decline during the Carboniferous and Permian periods, with Figure 3.13 which is virtually opposite in all trends.

The combined limitations of CO_2 supply and demand (equations 3.9 to 3.16) can now be used to estimate the maximum rate of photosynthesis over the last 450 million years (Fig. 3.14).

The maximum rates of photosynthesis (Fig. 3.14) follow a similar trend to those of V_c^{max} except that the rates of photosynthesis are relatively greater in periods of high and moderately high CO_2 partial pressures, i.e. 400–350 Ma and 250–100 Ma. This indicates that the stomatal supply limitation can be overridden to some degree by high absolute concentrations of atmospheric CO_2. It is important to note that these simulations are for undivided, well-illuminated leaves, with no limitations due to nutrient and water supply.

Testing the predictions of the photosynthetic models

The process of photosynthesis appears not only to construct new plant material but, when of sufficient global magnitude, also influences the concentration of CO_2 in the atmospheric reservoir and consequently exerts an effect on global climate. Figures 3.9 to 3.14 indicate likely trends in the

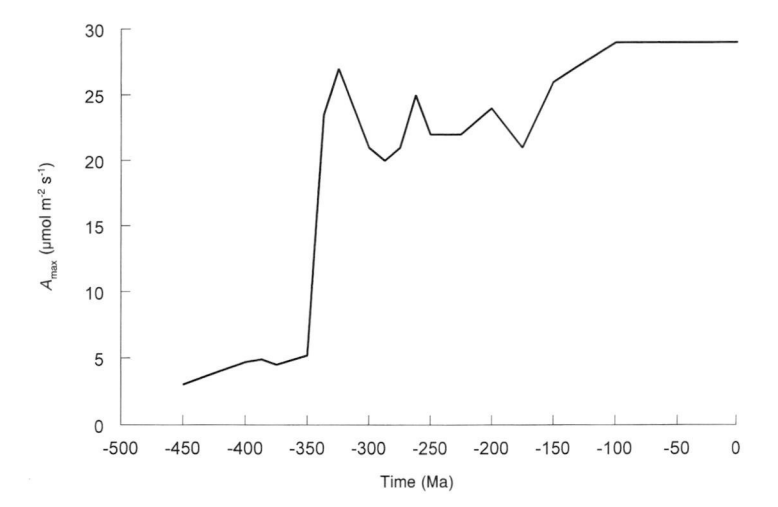

Figure 3.14. Calculated maximum rates of photosynthesis, A_{max}, using values of V_c^{max} from Fig. 3.13 and eqs. 3.9 to 3.16.

photosynthetic capacity of well-illuminated individual leaves and fronds. However, a more quantitative test of the photosynthetic predictions is required. This can be achieved by using and calculating plant discrimination against the two stable isotopes of carbon, ^{13}C and ^{12}C. Plants discriminate against ^{13}C during photosynthesis, such that the ratio of ^{13}C to ^{12}C is different for CO_2 in the atmosphere and for plant carbohydrates (Farquhar *et al.*, 1982). The $^{13}C:^{12}C$ ratio, in plants which carry out photosynthesis by the C_3 pathway, is influenced by the rate of photosynthesis and also by the stomatal conductance in a manner which, when simplified, is described as follows (from Farquhar *et al* 1982; Farquhar & Richards 1984):

$$\Delta = \left(4.4 + 22.6 \frac{c_i}{c_a}\right) \times 10^{-3} \qquad (3.21)$$

where Δ is the degree of discrimination against ^{13}C in units of per mil, or per thousand, c_i is the intercellular CO_2 partial pressure, c_a is the ambient CO_2 partial pressure, 4.4 is the per thousand discrimination against ^{13}C by the process of diffusion into the intercellular spaces and 22.6 is the discrimination by rubisco against ^{13}C, after discounting for the effect of discrimination by diffusion.

When plant leaves fall from the plant, they contain carbohydrates which have a value of Δ determined by the photosynthetic and stomatal activities of the leaf. In addition to the effect of discrimination during gas exchange, the $^{13}C:^{12}C$ ratio in the leaf is also influenced by the $^{13}C:^{12}C$ ratio in the

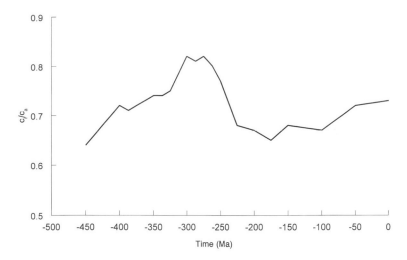

Figure 3.15. The ratio of the intercellular to ambient CO_2 partial pressures, calculated for mean daily (12 h) rates of photosynthesis.

atmosphere. Thus discrimination Δ is more completely described as follows (Farquhar & Richards, 1984):

$$\Delta = \frac{\delta^{13}C_a - \delta^{13}C_p}{1 + \delta^{13}C_p \times 10^{-3}} \tag{3.22}$$

where $\delta^{13}C$ indicates the carbon isotope composition by reference to a standard carbonate source (units of per thousand), and the subscripts a and p indicate atmosphere and plant respectively. Therefore it is necessary to know the $\delta^{13}C_a$ in order to calculate the discrimination due to the activity of the plant. The $\delta^{13}C$ is defined (Craig, 1957) as:

$$\delta^{13}C = \left(\frac{(^{13}C:^{12}C)_{\text{sample}}}{(^{13}C:^{12}C)_{\text{standard}}} - 1 \right) \times 10^{-3} \tag{3.23}$$

According to equation 3.21, the ratio c_i/c_a determines plant discrimination, Δ. This ratio needs to be calculated for the whole period in which photosynthetic activity produces carbohydrates and also relative to the rate of photosynthesis itself. This is because average Δ of the plant material is influenced in direct proportion to the amount of material accumulated with a particular value of Δ. For this calculation it is assumed that the daily activity of photosynthesis during the growing season of any era is only dependent on the daily trend in solar radiation and for a period of 12 hours (Fig. 3.15).

The degree of the reduction in the c_i/c_a ratio below unity indicates the degree to which photosynthesis is limited by the supply of CO_2 by diffusion.

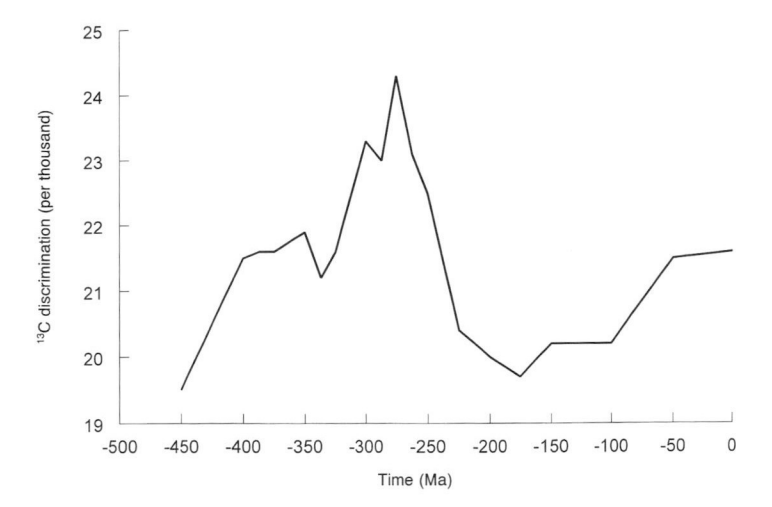

Figure 3.16. ^{13}C discrimination (per thousand), calculated from eq. 3.21.

Consequently the periods of lowest atmospheric CO_2 concentration are also the periods with the highest c_i/c_a ratios, when stomatal conductances are at a maximum (Fig. 3.12). Such a response indicates that, when the CO_2 concentration was low and the O_2 concentration was high, the rate of CO_2 supply through the stomata to the chloroplasts was less limiting than the photosynthetic capacity.

The trend in discrimination follows that of the c_i/c_a ratio (eq. 3.21) and also indicates the reduced discrimination by plants during periods of low atmospheric partial pressures of CO_2. In order for these predictions of discrimination to be tested against observations, it is necessary to provide some calculation of the stable isotope composition of the atmosphere. This has been achieved (Fig. 3.16) by using smoothed trends of the δ^{13}C composition of carbonates (reviewed in Frakes *et al.*, 1992), which have been calibrated against estimates of atmospheric δ^{13}C from soil carbonates (Mora *et al.*, 1996) and from the current, pre-industrial atmospheric δ^{13}C composition (-7.0 per thousand; Friedli *et al.*, 1986). The δ^{13}C composition of fossil plant material is then calculated by adding the estimated atmospheric δ^{13}C composition (Fig. 3.17) to equation 3.22 and then solving for $\delta^{13}C_p$, using the values of Δ from Figure 3.16.

The predicted values of leaf δ^{13}C composition (Fig. 3.18) indicate that the Carboniferous and Permian periods should have fossil leaves with the lowest ^{13}C discrimination, with a continuous increase from the earliest terrestrial vascular plants in the Silurian (*c.* 430 Ma; Edwards, 1993) to the end of the Carboniferous period (285 Ma). The peak of δ^{13}C is predicted for about 350

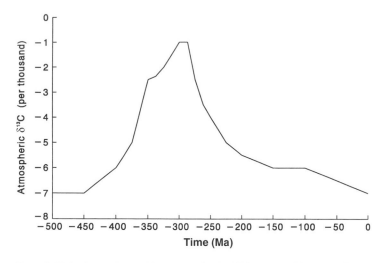

Figure 3.17. Estimated trend in atmospheric $\delta^{13}C$ composition (per thousand).

Ma, after which a decline continues to the mid-Triassic, followed by little change to the present day.

The predictions of $\delta^{13}C$ can be tested against $\delta^{13}C$ measured for a range of source materials. Leaves from the present day (Körner *et al.*, 1991) have been extensively sampled and provide an excellent estimate of the mean global $\delta^{13}C$ composition and also the typical range of values. Fossil $\delta^{13}C$ composition has been measured for soils (Mora *et al.*, 1996), plants (Bocherens *et al.*, 1994; Jones, 1994) and coals (Holmes & Brownfield, 1992). There is good agreement between the predictions of $\delta^{13}C$ composition and observations (Fig. 3.18), although the effects of diagenetic changes cannot be discounted. Nevertheless, this suggests that the stomatal-photosynthesis model of the last 450 Ma is a reasonable representation of historical plant physiological responses to atmospheric composition and climate. In addition, the reasonable agreement also indicates that the simple zero-dimensional climate model (Fig. 3.6) and the trends in atmospheric CO_2 concentration (Fig. 3.5) provide reasonable estimates of historical change.

No explicit account is taken of variations in precipitation. Very dry conditions over time would tend to cause stomatal closure and therefore $\delta^{13}C$ would become less negative. The less negative fossil $\delta^{13}C$ for 200–100 Ma may result from such an effect, and this will be investigated further (see Chapter 7). With the aim of maintaining the simplest interpretation of past events – applying Occam's razor – there is no strong need to invoke marked changes in precipitation to explain the trends in $\delta^{13}C$, particularly as the global ranges of $\delta^{13}C$ (Fig. 3.18) are most likely to overlap the predicted trends in $\delta^{13}C$. The

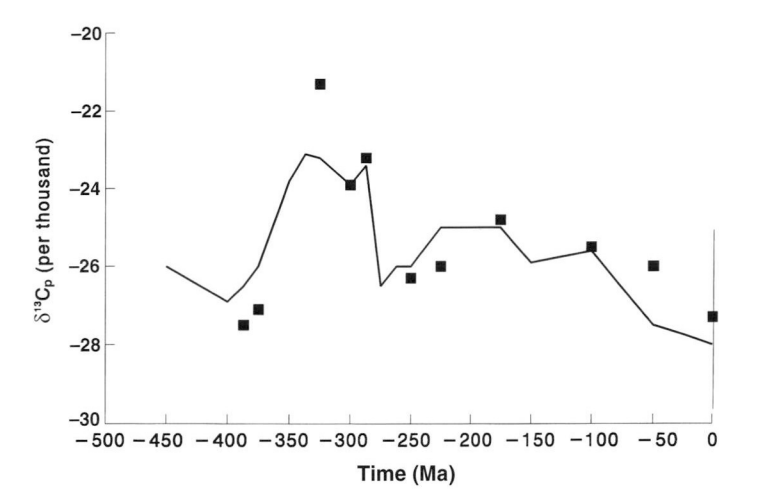

Figure 3.18. Calculated isotopic composition (per thousand) of fossil leaves, using eq. 3.22. (■),$\delta^{13}C$ of fossil soils and coals and from living plants (indicated with the maximum range of observations) at the present day.

apparent and low contribution of likely past variations in precipitation (Crowley & North, 1991) to plant $\delta^{13}C$ occurs because the observed $\delta^{13}C$ is weighted by productivity. Therefore when plants are photosynthesising most rapidly, when the stomata are fully open, and by implication the plant is well-supplied with water, the rapidly accumulating carbohydrates will have a particular $\delta^{13}C$ signal mirroring the relative controls of photosynthesis and stomatal conductance on ^{13}C discrimination. As the water supply declines then so also will the rate of carbohydrate accumulation and the impact on the overall tissue $\delta^{13}C$ will also decrease. The observation of $\delta^{13}C$ is therefore likely to be rather insensitive to variations in precipitation and their subsequent effects on plant photosynthesis.

Conclusions

Over the timescales considered here, geochemical cycles play the major role in controlling the atmospheric composition of CO_2 and O_2. The CO_2 concentration of the atmosphere is determined by the balance between weathering rates and precipitation rates on a timescale of millions of years (François *et al.*, 1993; Walker, 1994). The evidence presented here, and discussed elsewhere (Berner, 1993; Mora *et al.*, 1996) strongly supports the notion that the vegetation plays a major part in these long-term weathering processes and tends to cause the atmospheric CO_2 concentration to decrease, as seen in the Carboniferous and Permian periods. A decrease in the atmospheric CO_2 concentration to the similarly low concentrations of the

Carboniferous period, as well as the present pre-industrial revolution and the last ice age, will exert a major negative feedback on plant processes by decreasing the rate of photosynthetic carboxylation in favour of photorespiratory oxidation. In addition the oxygen concentration probably increased during the Carboniferous (Fig. 3.7), a feature which will also have stimulated photorespiration. Although this negative effect on CO_2 fixation will have occurred, there will have been some benefits for plants. In particular photoinhibition of photosynthetic chlorophyll (photosystem II) will have been protected under stimulatory conditions of bright sunlight and low CO_2 concentrations (Lawlor, 1993). The cooler conditions of the Carboniferous will have reduced the rate of photorespiration more than photosynthesis (Lawlor, 1993); however, at the high oxygen concentration of 35%, CO_2 fixation would have been reduced by about 45%, compared with a 25% reduction at the current oxygen concentration of 21% (Ogren, 1994).

The increase in stomatal density in the Carboniferous is predicted to have played a major part in increasing photosynthetic capacity. This same increase will also have exerted an effect on the rate of photorespiration. The rate of photorespiration increases as the CO_2 concentration decreases. Within a photosynthetically active leaf the CO_2 concentration will tend to decrease as the rate of photosynthesis increases. For plants with low stomatal densities and therefore low rates of CO_2 diffusion into the leaf the intercellular CO_2 concentration will be much lower than for plants with high stomatal densities. As a consequence rates of photorespiration will be much greater for plants with low stomatal densities and so the rate of photosynthesis will also have been lower (Robinson, 1994a). These critical effects will have driven genetic selection for plants with higher stomatal densities, which would lead to higher intercellular CO_2 concentrations and therefore relatively higher rates of photosynthesis and growth. This particular response is implicit in the differences between rubisco-limited photosynthesis (Fig. 3.9) and the combined influences of CO_2 supply and demand (Fig. 3.14).

The restricting influence of low stomatal density on maximum rates of photosynthesis is easily seen (Fig. 3.19) for three examples of increasing stomatal density. At the lowest density, typical of Devonian plants (Edwards, 1993), V_c^{max} can only operate within a small range. At the highest value the photosynthetic rate rapidly decreases to zero, due to low rates of CO_2 diffusion, in addition to an increase in the relative rate of photosynthesis. Increasing the stomatal density by quite small absolute densities has a marked influence on the photosynthetic potential and also on the operating range of V_c^{max} (Fig. 3.19).

Given the large potential increase in photosynthetic rate with increasing

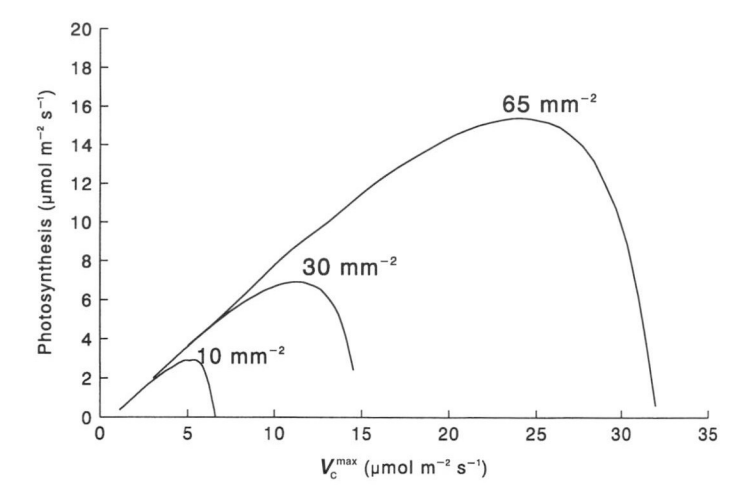

Figure 3.19. Predicted maximum rates of photosynthesis (using eqs. 3.9 to 3.20) for three different stomatal densities, at high O_2 (30%) and low CO_2 concentrations that may be characteristic of the Carboniferous period.

stomatal density, it seems rather surprising that plants should show any reductions in stomatal density with increasing CO_2 concentration, as described by equation 3.17. The likely explanation may be tied more with water conservation. Decreasing stomatal density at times of high CO_2 concentration, as evident through the Cretaceous period, will have had only a small impact on photosynthetic rate as photorespiratory rate will be reduced under the high CO_2 atmosphere. However, the rate of transpiration will be diminished, a feature which will reduce the impact of excessive drought and also reduce the likelihood of xylem cavitation on the column of water through the xylem (Tyree & Sperry, 1989). As a consequence the plant will also be more water-use efficient.

An increase in stomatal density with decreasing CO_2 concentration will maximise CO_2 diffusion to the chloroplasts and will tend to reduce the stimulation of photorespiration by low intercellular CO_2 concentrations (i.e. by maximising the CO_2 concentration at the chloroplast), as described in the previous paragraphs. Under present-day low CO_2 concentrations there is a general tendency to find plants with low stomatal densities in shaded habitats, a situation of low irradiance and limited likelihood of photosynthetic photoinhibition. With low photosynthetic rates, these species will show rather limited reductions in intercellular CO_2 concentrations. In contrast, plants growing in high irradiances tend to have higher stomatal densities, a feature which will enhance CO_2 diffusion into the leaf and diminish photorespiratory rates.

The basic processes of climatic change, vegetation feedbacks on climate and the photosynthetic and stomatal responses to climate and changing atmospheric composition, are the major themes of this chapter. The following chapters will provide explicit treatments of the spatial and temporal responses of terrestrial vegetation, at the global scale, to climatic change.

4

Climate and terrestrial vegetation of the present

Introduction

Climate drives particular vegetation processes from the short term, such as photosynthesis from minute to minute, to the long term, such as the gradual accumulation of plant litter in the soil, over periods up to millennia. Terrestrial vegetation can also influence climate though variations in its structural characteristics, such as surface reflectivity and roughness length, and functional characteristics, such as evapotranspiration (Bonan *et al.*, 1992; Lean & Rowntree, 1993; Betts *et al.*, 1997). These features are not considered here as this intimate coupling of vegetation and climate is not yet a standard feature of the General Circulation Models (GCMs) which are used throughout this book for predicting past and present climates.

In order to appreciate the predictions of terrestrial vegetation activity and climate it is necessary to provide a general introduction to the two areas of modelling. Aspects of vegetation modelling have already been covered in Chapters 2 and 3. This chapter will provide a fuller description of the vegetation model which is used in all of the simulations in this book. A general introduction to GCMs will also be provided, although details of these complex models must be found elsewhere (e.g. Washington & Parkinson, 1986; Trenberth, 1992; McGuffie & Henderson-Sellers, 1997). In addition, considerable information can be gleaned about GCMs, and other climate models, on the World Wide Web (e.g. Kevin's Numerical Model page, www.erols.com/klc9986, with details of over 200 models; full details of the National Centre for Atmospheric Research, NCAR, Community Climate Change Model, CCM3 can also be found on the Web page, www.ucar.edu/rs.html).

General Circulation Model description

GCMs were developed as a method for understanding the various mechanisms, interactions and feedbacks which control the global climate. As their name indicates, these models explicitly model circulation, which includes motions of the atmosphere and the oceans. These motions are influenced strongly by exchanges of momentum, mass and energy between the atmosphere, the oceans, the cryosphere and the land surface/biosphere. In the model itself, these processes are defined and solved from equations which satisfy the principles of the conservation of momentum, mass, energy and the state of water in the atmosphere and oceans (Peixoto & Oort, 1992).

GCMs model these different equations at defined time steps, typically of about 30 minutes, and thus have the potential to model short-term variations of climate – weather – or synoptic-scale climate. The spatial scale of such events is typically a few kilometres (McGuffie & Henderson-Sellers, 1997), which is too fine a scale for current GCMs for which the smallest horizontal spatial unit is 2° to 3° of latitude and longitude. To this horizontal grid must be added a vertical resolution of between six and 50 levels in the atmosphere and a range of depths within the ocean. The relatively coarse horizontal scale is therefore one consequence of the considerable computing time required to run these models with high atmospheric vertical resolution, which is considered a necessity for appropriate model operation (McGuffie & Henderson-Sellers, 1997). The limited horizontal resolution requires that a number of important finer-scale processes, such as those arising through variations in altitude, or the occurrence of thunderstorms, have to be added to the appropriate grid cell by a scheme known as sub-grid-scale parameterisation, which can appear to be more an art than a science.

Each GCM is usually constructed as an interacting set of component GCMs, namely an atmospheric GCM (AGCM) and an ocean GCM (OGCM), with a coupling model between the two systems. Also, the Earth's surface consists of areas of ice – the cryosphere – and the terrestrial surface, with and without vegetation. GCMs are not derived for these components but, rather, they are modelled as modifications of the ocean surface by land surface models, which simulate various vegetation, soil and cryosphere processes. The nature of the various processes and their interactions and feedbacks is shown rather simply in Figure 4.1. It should be noted that all of these processes (at least) influence and determine climate. In addition, though this is not shown in Figure 4.1, the strength of the coupling between the different sub-components varies with latitude. For example, at high latitudes the atmosphere is most tightly coupled to ocean activity by changes in salinity and the formation of deep

ATMOSPHERE

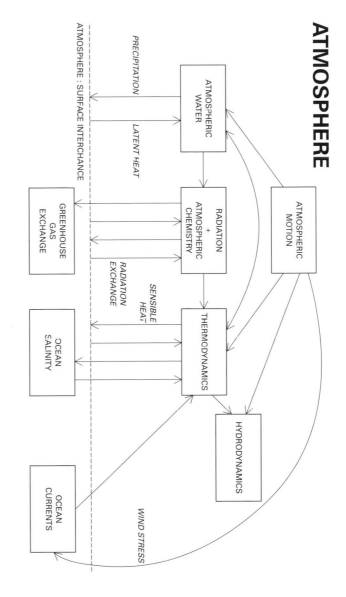

OCEANS + BIOSPHERE + CRYOSPHERE

Figure 4.1. A greatly simplified representation of some of the major component processes and interactions in a General Circulation Model of climate.

ocean bottom water. By contrast, in the tropics the ocean and atmosphere are most closely coupled through processes associated with temperature, e.g. thermodynamics, hydrodynamics and atmospheric water. In addition, at high latitudes the presence of ice, in particular sea ice, decouples the ocean and atmosphere which therefore undergo somewhat independent developments, although ocean circulations always reduce the independence.

A major issue, when GCMs are used to investigate the consequences of changes in atmospheric constituents and chemistry, is the impact of relatively small changes in long-wave and short-wave radiation exchange, brought about by changes in atmospheric concentrations of 'greenhouse gases', e.g. CO_2, chlorofluorocarbons and methane, and the impacts of the oceans and their biota, and terrestrial vegetation, on these gases.

GCM initialisation and operation

The different sub-systems of a GCM have very different response times to change. For example, the free atmosphere takes about 11 days to reach an equilibrium response to an imposed change in temperature, whilst the response of deep ocean is considerably slower reaching about 300 years (Saltzman, 1983). Such a marked contrast makes considerable difficulties for running a GCM. The ocean will change slowly in response to some perturbation and to track this equilibrium would typically carry a very significant burden if the atmospheric model, with a 30 minute time step, had to run for the model equivalent of centuries for the ocean deep water temperature to reach the correct level. Modellers have therefore developed a range of schemes to reduce this computational load. In some cases the GCMs were run prematurely, i.e. before the period of relevance, at least in terms of the oceans reaching initial equilibrium and, as a consequence, during the runs of relevance there may be an unwanted climatic drift, as the whole system still moves to an equilibrium state. In general, the optimal approach to such a mismatch of response times is to develop an asynchronous coupling in which the atmospheric model may be run initially to equilibrium with the ocean model, and then the various atmospheric conditions are stored and used as constant inputs to an evolving ocean, with the atmospheric model, with its very heavy computational demands, turned off. After a certain time period the atmospheric model is turned on again, and the system repeated. This approach allows a more rapid evolution of an equilibrium ocean, in terms of the necessary computer time, with other modifications which may temporarily speed up the ocean physics (Manabe *et al.*, 1991). In the application of GCMs to climate change issues, it is the case that some short-cut approaches are generally used in order that the whole GCM reaches some satisfactory representation of a stipulated starting time or date, often the present day or the onset of the industrial revolution.

Often, GCM simulations of climates have used atmospheric GCMs constrained by prescribed sea surface temperatures (modern, or derived from geological evidence, depending on the time frame of the model experiments), avoiding the need to run the time-intensive ocean GCMs for initialisation (Washington & Meehl, 1989). The subsequent GCM run may then be partially immune from the problems of climatic drift, at least for century-long simulations (Meehl, 1992). The ocean GCM also needs to be constrained by surface fluxes of energy, freshwater and momentum (Gates *et al.*, 1996). In addition, flux correction techniques may be employed to cancel drift. These techniques are variants on establishing the flux differences associated between the initially prescribed temperature fields and those derived from the model with some inherent drift (Meehl, 1989).

GCM simulations of palaeoclimates

Model drift and initialisation continue to create problems in all current GCM simulations. Drift and the various methods employed to counteract it will also affect the accuracy or reasonableness of the GCM simulations of the period under question, although experience is gradually indicating the types and ranges of the problems (Meehl, 1992). Other problems arise when GCMs are used to simulate past climates. In such situations, the prescribed initialisation fields may not be known with great precision, as they have to be extracted and inferred from fossil evidence, such as found in marine sediments, and from isotopic measurements (Barron & Peterson, 1990; Berger *et al.*, 1990; Crowley & North, 1991; Kutzbach, 1992). The most effective approach must be to prescribe as many boundary conditions of the GCM as possible so that drift is counteracted to some degree. One interesting approach is to tune the boundary conditions of the GCM until it runs and predicts the more or less established distribution of fossil evidence; for example, Pollard and Shulz (1994), ran a GCM to model the geographical distribution of evaporites during the Triassic period (225 Ma). Evaporites, which include minerals such as gypsum and rock salt, occur near ocean boundaries and in shallow basins which periodically flood and dry out. The GCM can then be run until the observed distribution of evaporites matches climatic predictions of areas where evaporation exceeds precipitation. A good match will then imply that the boundary conditions of the GCM, including sea surface temperatures and ocean salinity, are a good approximation to the average climate of the modelled era.

GCM reliability and accuracy

GCMs have a solid theoretical underpinning to their operation, suggesting that continued improvements in predictive accuracy are likely, particularly as continued advances in computing power will allow finer-scale processes, currently parameterised, to be included. However, the question remains about the general accuracy of these models of climate. The models are efficient at predicting the present-day seasonal cycle of temperature, at the global scale (Schneider, 1992; Gates *et al.*, 1996), and are also now effective at predicting large-scale distributions of temperature, salinity and sea ice in the oceans (Gates *et al.*, 1996). The major limitation of the GCMs lies in predicting clouds, which in turn influence the radiation balance and the hydrological cycle, particularly over the land surface (Gates *et al.*, 1996). However, coupled GCMs are now quite successful in simulating the broad-scale structure and magnitude of precipitation (Gates *et al.*, 1996), which is particularly important for this book in which we investigate the responses of vegetation to climate, and in which precipitation is particularly critical.

The basic operational flow of the vegetation model

The introduction to the general details of GCMs indicate that they are powerful but not fully accurate models of climate. Their accuracies can be controlled by the various boundary conditions which are imposed and so they are at a state of development which is particularly useful for investigating impacts of past, present and future climates on vegetation.

The impacts of GCM-derived climates on vegetation are determined with a vegetation model, the operation of parts of which has been discussed independently, and with some detail, in Chapters 2 and 3. However, it is necessary to discuss how all the various processes interrelate in order to provide a full model description. The details of an early version of the model can be found in Woodward *et al.* (1995); a more integrated and updated description is provided here. The modules of the overall vegetation model connect as lines of either control or feedback (Fig. 4.2). Climate and CO_2 concentration are variables which are exogenous to vegetation and control the basic plant-level processes of photosynthesis, respiration and stomatal conductance. In addition, climate controls soil water, through water inputs by rain and snow and by variations in the gradient for soil evaporation.

The operation of the plant is controlled by the collective photosynthetic, respiratory and stomatal activities of individual plants. Therefore canopy leaf area index (LAI) is controlled by the overall net primary productivity (NPP) of

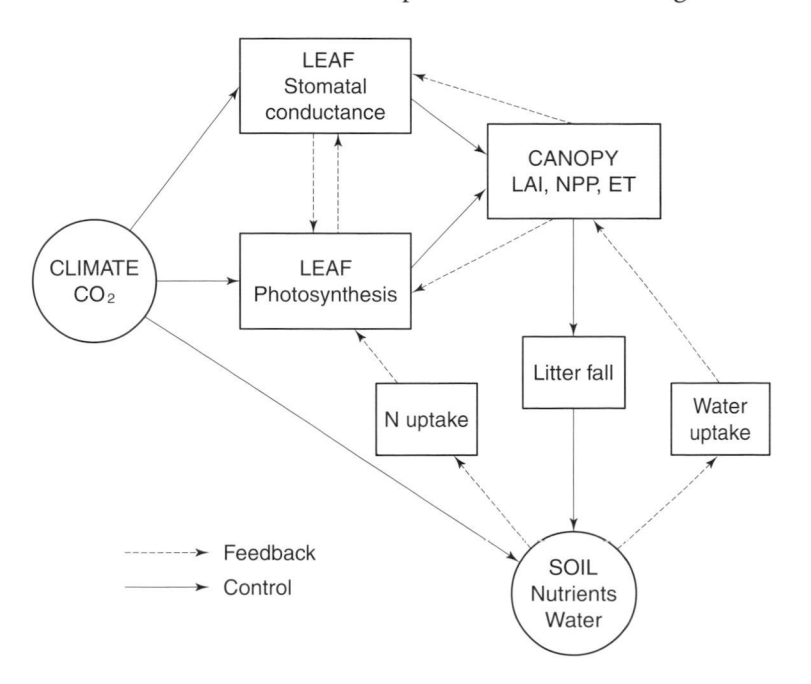

Figure 4.2. General description of the vegetation model, which is directly controlled by climate and soil characteristics (control) and by feedbacks between plant and canopy processes (LAI, leaf area index; NPP, net primary productivity; ET, evapotranspiration) and with the soil.

all plants in the canopy and a balance between water uptake from the soil, evaporation from the soil and precipitation supply. The influence of soil on plants and canopies of plants is indicated entirely as feedbacks (Fig. 4.2). Water uptake continues, at a canopy rate determined by stomatal conductance and LAI, until the soil water content reaches wilting point. The potential photosynthetic rates of the plants are controlled by the rate of nitrogen uptake from the soil, which is a feedback control, through variations in nitrogen mineralisation rate, which is in turn controlled by climate and the rate and nutrient quality of litter fall (Parton *et al.*, 1993).

Other feedbacks occur between photosynthesis and stomatal conductance, as already described in Chapter 2. If canopy water loss exceeds water supply from the soil then there is a feedback to reduce stomatal conductance, which then reduces the rate of photosynthesis. If the soil water status remains below wilting point then some leaves may abscise, immediately reducing plant photosynthesis, stomatal conductance and LAI.

Module descriptions

Leaf responses

The plant photosynthesis and stomatal conductance modules, and their interactions, are described fully in Chapter 3. To reiterate, the net rate of photosynthesis, A (mol m^{-2} s^{-1}) is defined as follows:

$$A = V_c \left(1 - \frac{0.5o}{\tau c_i}\right) - R_d \tag{4.1}$$

where o is the partial pressure of oxygen in the leaf, c_i is the partial pressure of intercellular CO_2, τ is the specificity factor of rubisco for CO_2 relative to O_2 and R_d is the rate of non-photorespiratory leaf respiration in the light; V_c, the maximum potential rate of carboxylation, is determined either by the maximum rate of rubisco activity, V_c^{max}, or on the light-saturated rate of electron transport, J_{max}. These rates of rubisco activity and electron transport need to be calculated for every site for which the vegetation model operates. From the work of Wullschleger (1993) it follows that V_c^{max} and J_{max} are closely related as:

$$J_{max} = 2.91 \times 10^{-5} \, 1.64 V_c^{max} \tag{4.2}$$

therefore it is only necessary to be able to determine V_c^{max}. The approach to determine V_c^{max} is based on an empirical analysis by Woodward and Smith (1994b), in which it was found that the maximum rate of leaf photosynthesis, A_{max}, was determined by the rate of nitrogen uptake into the leaf, N. They defined A_{max} as equal to V_c^{max} and then solved for V_c^{max} as follows:

$$A_{max} = \frac{190N}{360 + N} \tag{4.3}$$

The rate of uptake was defined in terms of the nitrogen and carbon contents of the soil and is sensitive to both temperature (Woodward *et al.* 1995) and precipitation.

$$V_c^{max} = \frac{(A_{max} + R_d)\left[o + K_c\left(1 + \dfrac{o}{K_o}\right)\right]}{c_i - 0.5\dfrac{o}{\tau}} \tag{4.4}$$

where K_c and K_o are the Michaelis–Menten coefficients for carboxylation and oxygenation by rubisco. Once V_c^{max} is calculated in this way, J_{max} can be determined from equation 4.2 and the effects of ambient temperature are then accounted for using the general function described by McMurtrie & Wang

(1993). This approach defines the photosynthetic demand capacity of the leaf. Nitrogen taken up from the soil is allocated to the different leaf layers within a plant canopy according to their mean irradiance, a feature which simulates closely observations in the field (Hirose & Werger, 1987):

$$N_l = N\frac{I_l}{I_o} \tag{4.5}$$

where N_l is the nitrogen allocated to leaf layer l with an irradiance I_l and an irradiance at the top of the canopy I_o. In addition to determining the photosynthetic capacity of a particular leaf layer, the allocated nitrogen also influences the dark respiration rate, R, of a leaf (Woodward et al. 1995):

$$R = \frac{N_l}{50} e^{r_1 - \frac{r_2}{8.3144 T_k}} \tag{4.6}$$

where r_1 and r_2 are functions of temperature (Woodward et al., 1995) and T_k is temperature (K).

In addition to the demand control of photosynthesis, the realised rate of photosynthesis is also dependent on the supply rate of CO_2 into the leaf, which is shown graphically in Chapter 3 (Fig. 3.8). The rate of photosynthesis, in terms of supply, is defined as:

$$A = \left(\frac{c_a - c_i}{P}\right) g - R_d \tag{4.7}$$

where c_a is the partial pressure of CO_2 surrounding the leaf, P is the atmospheric pressure and g is the CO_2 diffusion conductance into the leaf, through both the boundary layer and the stomata of the leaf. The controls of stomatal conductance, in terms of stomatal opening has already been defined in detail in Chapter 3. The water content of the soil is a further limitation to stomatal conductance and this is introduced as a multiplier of stomatal conductance, k_s, which has previously been defined, such as by equation 3.15 (p. 39). The multiplier, k_s, has a value between unity (soil water at maximum water-holding capacity) and zero (wilting point) and is defined (Woodward et al., 1995) as:

$$k_s = \frac{s_1(w - s_0)}{w - 2s_0 + s_2} \tag{4.8}$$

where w is the soil water content, s_0 is the soil water content when stomatal conductance is zero, s_1 defines the slope of the response of stomatal conductance to increases in w above s_0, and s_2 is the rate at which the stomatal conductance response to w flattens as soil water content reaches saturation.

Canopy responses

Canopy processes are the sum of the activities of all leaves (Fig. 4.2). For example, soil water content controls the stomatal conductance of plants (eq. 4.8), but is itself controlled by the total uptake and loss of water of all of the plants constituting a canopy. The transpiration rate, E_t, of a canopy of plants is defined by the well-established Penman–Monteith equation (Monteith, 1981):

$$E_t = \frac{sR_n + c_p\rho g_a D}{\lambda\left(s + \gamma\left(1 + \dfrac{g_a}{g_s}\right)\right)}$$ (4.9)

where s is the slope of the curve between saturation water vapour pressure and temperature, R_n is the net radiant balance of the canopy (less the flux of heat into the soil), c_p is the specific heat capacity of air, ρ is the density of air, g_a is the boundary layer conductance of the canopy, D is the water vapour pressure deficit, λ is the latent heat of vaporisation of water, γ is the psychrometer constant and g_s is the canopy stomatal conductance. Further details on this wide range of variables may be found elsewhere, e.g. Monteith & Unsworth, 1990; Jones, 1992.

In equation 4.9, the canopy stomatal conductance is essentially the mean plant stomatal conductance multiplied by the canopy leaf area index. The canopy boundary layer conductance is difficult to measure at the global scale, and a fixed value may be given to vegetation of a particular type, e.g. forest, shrub, or grassland. However, if wind speed measurements above the vegetation, are available and vegetation height is known, then the boundary layer conductance may be determined (Jones, 1992):

$$g_a = \frac{k^2 u}{\left\{\log_e\left[\dfrac{z - d}{z_0}\right]\right\}^2}$$ (4.10)

where k is von Karman's constant (0.41), u is the wind speed measured at some height, z, above the canopy of height, h, where the roughness length, z_0, can often be approximated as $0.13h$ and the zero-plane displacement, d, can be approximated as $0.64h$ (Campbell, 1977). Unfortunately the equation provides somewhat incorrect estimates of the boundary layer when there is an inversion layer of air above the canopy, or when the temperature decreases with height more rapidly than the standard neutral condition (0.01 °C m^{-1}). As a consequence, boundary layer estimates of canopies are generally associated with a degree of error.

At any particular location, or climate, the canopy leaf area index, net primary productivity and transpiration rate are all interconnected (Woodward et al., 1995). Canopy photosynthesis increases with LAI, although self-shading of lower leaves by those higher in the canopy reduces the photosynthetic potential through the canopy. The LAI increases until the NPP (photosynthesis less dark respiration) of the lowest layer of leaves is zero, then the model assumes that no further leaf layers can be supported. If the annual transpiration of this LAI exceeds the annual supply of precipitation which reaches the soil (precipitation less evaporated canopy-intercepted water), then LAI is reduced until precipitation reaching the soil at least equals canopy transpiration. Finally, the canopy NPP must be sufficient to supply the construction costs of new leaves and roots. If the NPP is too low, then the LAI is reduced until the situation is satisfied.

Soil interactions

The uptake of mineralised nitrogen from the soil is a critical determinant of both photosynthesis and respiration (eqs. 4.3 and 4.6) and is therefore an important process to model. The supply of phosphorus may also be critical, particularly on soils which have not been rejuvenated by ice ages. For ease of computing and the reduction of complexity, phosphorus supply is not included in the vegetation model described here. Instead, it is assumed that the strong relationship and stoichiometry between soil carbon, soil nitrogen and mycorrhizal activity and occurrence (Woodward & Smith, 1994a,b) also applies to phosphorus (Read, 1991). There is much evidence for these interconnections (Schlesinger, 1997). For example, the photosynthetic rate is dependent on both N and P, and in bacterial systems when N is in short supply, any increases in P stimulate N fixation (Stock et al., 1990), restoring the N levels in the system. Therefore, adequate consideration of carbon and nitrogen cycles will tend to carry along the influences through the natural phosphorus cycle. However, if P availability increases, for example by human activity, the model may prove somewhat inaccurate in its predictions.

When plant litter reaches the soil surface (surface litter), or is detached from living roots (root litter), the process of decomposition converts some of the carbon in the litter to CO_2 (heterotrophic respiration) and the remainder to notional pools of carbon with differing longevities (Fig. 4.3).

The longevity of the carbon pools is broadly related to the chemical nature of the carbon component of the litter. If it is cellulose, then its decomposition rate is rapid; if it is primarily lignin, then the rate is very slow. These processes are generally described in Figure 4.3 and were developed for the Century

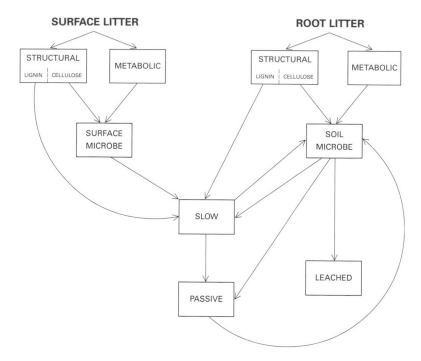

Figure 4.3. Structure and pathways for carbon in the Century model. Each arrow *from* the boxes entails a loss of CO_2 to the atmosphere and the probability of the release of nitrogen for uptake by plant roots.

model of soil nutrient cycling (Parton *et al.*, 1993). The active pools of carbon are the microbial pools, whilst the 'slow' and 'passive' pools can have turnover rates of decades to millennia (Schlesinger, 1997). As the microbial decomposers utilise the carbon in the litter, the N in the soil may become mineralised and available for uptake by roots. The C:N ratio of soils averages about 15 to 20 (Schlesinger, 1997), although in wood (C:N average 160) and leaves (20–80) the ratios tend to be higher. This ratio indicates the potential for N mineralisation, the high ratio litter being very slowly mineralised. The fact that both plants and soils have rather restricted ranges of C:N ratio supports the earlier proposal that, with respect to the utilisation of nutrients by plants, the cycling of C and N (and also P) is intimately linked.

The basic equations of the carbon and nitrogen cycle for the vegetation and the soil are linked as follows. For the carbon cycle:

$$C_v = NPP - (L_c + P_c) \qquad (4.11)$$

$$C_s = L_c - (R_l + S_c) \qquad (4.12)$$

where C_v is carbon in vegetation available for growth, *NPP* is net primary productivity, L_c is carbon in litter and P_c is carbon stored in vegetation biomass (all units in t C ha^{-1}). The availability of carbon for biological activity in the soil, C_s, is determined by the input of litter carbon, the loss of carbon by heterotrophic respiration of the litter, R_l, and carbon storage in the soil, S_c. The nitrogen cycle may be similarly defined as:

$$N_v = N_m - (L_n + P_n) \tag{4.13}$$

$$N_s = L_n - (M_m + S_n) \tag{4.14}$$

where the subscript n indicates nitrogen, rather than carbon as in equations 4.11 and 4.12, and N_m is mineralised N which is taken up by the plant. Therefore, the loss of litter from vegetation to the soil depletes the carbon stock of the vegetation, but adds nitrogen to the soil which can be made available for plant uptake following microbial breakdown of the carbon associated with litter N. This mineralised N constitutes part of N_m, which might be supplemented by N from N-fixing organisms, from atmospheric sources of inorganic N and from any fertilisers used by humans.

Defining vegetation structure

Vegetation structure, here considered simply in terms of forest, grassland, or a mixture of the two, is predicted within the vegetation model in dynamic fashion. In this context, 'dynamic' signifies that the vegetation at any particular point, or area, is always changing: in terms of growing, in terms of competitive interactions between species and in terms of the occurrence of disturbances, in particular fire, which may completely disrupt the existing vegetation. This dynamic component to the model is used to define the model as a Dynamic Global Vegetation Model (DGVM; Steffen *et al.*, 1992). DGVMs are different from the more typical equilibrium or static vegetation models often used for assessing climatic impacts on vegetation (Watson *et al.*, 1995), which include no disturbance or vegetation dynamics, therefore limiting their value (Woodward & Beerling, 1997) when considering the trends of vegetation change in response to transient changes in climate (Mitchell *et al.* 1995).

Perhaps the easiest way to understand a DGVM (Fig. 4.4) is to consider that it consists of patch models of interacting species (Shugart, 1984) at every grid cell (smallest spatial unit) of the whole area under consideration, in this case the whole Earth. Patch models, of small spatial extent, simulate the life, death and interactions of individual plants within a larger area of vegetation, such as a forest. Within the DGVM (the Sheffield DGVM, SDGVM; Fig. 4.4) the

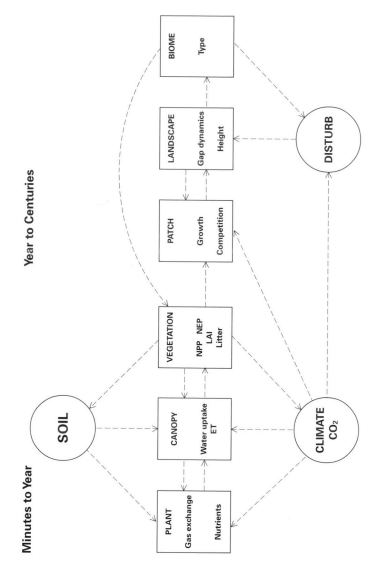

Minutes to Year

Year to Centuries

- - - - - - - - ▷ **Feedbacks**

No vegetation Initialisation

Figure 4.4. Diagram of the basic structure of the Sheffield Dynamic Global Vegetation Model (SDGVM). The model scales from the short-term processes (to the left) to the long-term (to the right). Long-term processes are concerned with the dynamics of functional types of species and of vegetation structure; short-term processes are concerned, in general, with fluxes of energy and materials.

growth, development, death and disturbance of individuals in the patch are driven by information such as NPP, LAI, the amount of soil and surface litter, and water status, from the overarching model, already described. As individual plants within the patch start to dominate, information is fed to the overarching model, where there may be impacts on energy and momentum transfer (Fig. 4.4).

A major difference between the typical patch model (Shugart, 1984) and the patch-type model employed in the SDGVM is that the dynamic and life-history characteristics of all the local and potential species which might occur in a typical patch model are defined initially. At the global scale this might reach the scale of defining the characteristics of all flowering plants of the world (*c.* 250 000), an impossible task as only a very small proportion of the species are sufficiently well understood for such a task. Therefore functional groupings or types of species are used, such as evergreen broad-leaved trees, or grasses with the C4 pathway of photosynthesis, and the groupings are defined in a number of different ways to suit the vegetation model which is being used (Box, 1996; Woodward & Cramer, 1996; Smith *et al.*, 1997).

Defining functional types

The first filter employed to discriminate between groupings of species – functional types – is based on the capacity to survive the lowest temperatures, defined as the absolute minimum temperatures which often show return times of 20 to 30 years at a particular site, i.e. they do not recur annually. Woodward (1987a) reviewed a wide range of experimental and observational data on the survival capacity of different species exposed to chilling and freezing temperatures. Functional types emerged from this dataset as groups of species with particular low temperature tolerances. These were also readily recognisable groups in terms of physiognomy and included evergreen and deciduous broad-leaved species, and evergreen and deciduous needle-leaved species, the majority being trees.

Woodward (1996) extended and refined the analysis of low temperature tolerances by including an explicit description of abundance (Fig. 4.5). This modification is necessary to explain why the lowest temperatures may limit the survival of a species although there is no obvious mechanism for an upper temperature limit; yet there is an obvious geographical limit in that a cold-climate functional type is not found in a warmer climate. Competitive exclusion of the cold-climate type by the more vigorous warm-climate type is usually taken to be the explanation, often defined explicitly in models (Neilson *et al.*, 1992; Prentice *et al.*, 1992), but there is little evidence for such a process (Woodward,

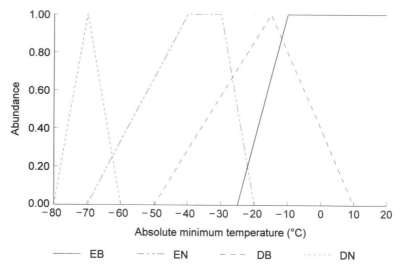

Figure 4.5. Relative abundance of different functional groups of species in relation to absolute minimum temperature. EB, evergreen broad-leaved species; EN, evergreen needle-leaved species; DB, deciduous broad-leaved species; DN, deciduous needle-leaved species (based on data in Woodward, 1987a, 1996).

1996). Therefore the high-temperature declines in species abundance (Fig. 4.5) are based on present-day occurrences of the species.

Under a scenario of climate warming it will be possible for a particular functional type to exist in a climate which is beyond the limits defined in Figure 4.5. Within the SDGVM this occurs, but the fraction of this functional type will gradually decline with time through mortality and replacement by more rapidly-growing functional types following vegetation disturbance. In the model, the growth of the functional types already described, and also grasses with the C_3 and C_4 pathways of photosynthesis, are simulated within a patch and the most rapidly-growing functional types dominate the patch with time. The growth of the functional types is driven by the NPP values described earlier, including NPP values for C_4 functional types (Collatz *et al.*, 1992).

For trees, growth to a maximum tree height is determined from the NPP allocated to the stem, calculated as the remainder after the costs of leaves and roots are removed. The cost of leaves is simply the product of the LAI and the specific leaf area of the leaves (m^2 leaf area/gC). The cost of roots is determined as a function of the yearly total of transpiration as:

$$NPP_r = Tk_t \tag{4.15}$$

where NPP_r is root NPP, T is the annual total of transpiration (mm) and k_t is the root mass necessary to support the annual transpiration rate. This constant is determined for different species and biomes from observational data of root growth and plant transpiration (Cannell, 1982).

The maximum height, h, of a tree is defined (Beerling *et al.*, 1996) as follows:

$$h = \frac{\sqrt{\Delta\psi}}{\sqrt{T_m}} \frac{\sqrt{x}}{\sqrt{w}} NPP_s \qquad (4.16)$$

where $\Delta\psi$ is the maximum drop in water potential from the roots to the top of the stem or trunk, T_m is the maximum transpiration rate of the canopy, x is the xylem water conductivity, w is stem or wood density and NPP_s is the stem net primary productivity. The above-ground biomass, b, at the maximum canopy height, h, is determined as follows:

$$b = \left[\pi\left(\frac{d}{2}\right)^2 h \right] w \qquad (4.17)$$

where d is the stem or trunk diameter at breast height, which can be calculated by one of the methods described in Niklas (1992).

The time taken to reach the maximum canopy height is then determined as b/NPP_s. The different functional types of tree species will grow at different rates, dependent on $\Delta\psi$, x, w and d. The fraction of each functional type will then be a direct function of height growth and time elapsed since a canopy-removing disturbance, such as fire. In the SDGVM the frequency of fires (see Chapter 5), for a particular pixel, is determined by the availability and water content of plant litter, an approach which provides a positive correlation with actual observations of fire (Woodward *et al.*, 2001).

Model runs of LAI and NPP for the present day

The previous section completed the general description of the vegetation model which will be used throughout this book. The proof of all models is their capacity to simulate some aspect of the real world. In this chapter, the aims are to simulate (i) the global-scale patterns of vegetation LAI and NPP and see if these maps bear close resemblances to observations and (ii) the distribution of basic vegetation types, defined in terms of mixtures of the functional types listed above.

The year 1988 has been chosen as a representative of the present day because of the easy availability of climate and remotely-sensed data, for that year, for running and testing the model. The first initiative of the International Satellite Land Surface Climatology Project (ISLSCP) was to collate global datasets for the years 1987 and 1988 onto CD-ROMs, covering the Earth's surface at a common resolution and grid of $1° \times 1°$ (Meeson *et al.*, 1995). The datasets are organised into five groups: vegetation; hydrology and soils; snow, ice and oceans; radiation and clouds; and near-surface meteorology.

The global-scale near-surface meteorology and soil texture datasets in the ISLSCP CD-ROM are used to drive the SDGVM (Figs. 4.2 and 4.4). The year 1988 has been selected for coverage here and the predictions of vegetation LAI and NPP can be compared with satellite measurements of reflected red and far-red radiation from the vegetation surface. The reflected data are converted to an index, the Normalized Difference Vegetation Index (NDVI), which is positively correlated with vegetation leafiness (Goward *et al.*, 1985; Justice *et al.*, 1985). However, the correlation between NDVI values is non-linear, with NDVI being rather insensitive to differences in high leaf area indices (Nemani & Running, 1996).

The vegetation model has to be spun-up before it can be used to predict the LAI and NPP for 1988. This is achieved by initially solving analytically for the soil pools of carbon and nitrogen. Finally vegetation equilibrium is achieved over a 400-year spin-up. Another climate database (Leemans & Cramer, 1991) is used for this spin-up, following which the SDGVM is run with the ISLSCP data for 1987 and 1988. A further model run has also been made with the United Kingdom Meteorological Office (UKMO) Unified Forecast and Climate Model. This is a fully-coupled ocean–atmosphere GCM and the particular version used is the 2nd Hadley Centre Coupled Model (HadCM2). This model, which has a lower resolution than the ISLSCP data at $2.5° \times 3.75°$, is used to predict global climate from 1860 to the year 2100 and, with the inclusion of atmospheric components such as sulphate aerosols, provides a good prediction of climate to the present day (Johns *et al.*, 1997). It will be used in Chapter 10 to make predictions of future changes in vegetation in a greenhouse climate. Initial assessments of the HadCM2 climate dataset showed that it gave an imperfect match for the established global climate dataset for 1931 to 1960 (Leemans & Cramer, 1991; modified version CLIMATE). As a consequence, temperature and precipitation corrections have been applied to the HadCM2 data (W. Cramer, personal communication) so that they match closely with the Leemans and Cramer modified dataset, based on observations between 1931 and 1960. These corrections have been applied to all other time periods of the HadCM2 run. Therefore it is incorrect to say that these are simply HadCM2 climate data; however, this is taken as the meaning of the term HadCM2 climate data in this and subsequent chapters. Note also that although the HadCM2 climate dataset is produced as a time series with actual dates, this in no way implies that the model attempts to predict the climate of a particular year. However, the CO_2 concentration is appropriate for a particular year.

The aim of running the SDGVM with both datasets of climate is to look not only for similarities of predicted vegetation responses but also differences, which will most probably reflect differences in the simulation of climate. It should be pointed out that the climate data in the ISLSCP CD-ROM are also model-derived, in this case from the European Centre for Medium-Range Weather Forecasting (ECMWF). The data produced by this model are for forecasting purposes, and so it is more appropriately described as a weather prediction model. The data in the ISLSCP CD-ROM result from a combination of atmospheric observations and model runs. However, no surface data are actually included in the runs, but previously recorded observations are used to constrain the model predictions (Brankovic & Van Maanen, 1985; Betts *et al.*, 1993).

Global patterns of LAI for the year 1988

Model predictions of LAI can take a number of forms; in this case, global maps of the mean LAI for the growing season and the mean annual LAI have been derived. The mean LAI for the growing season using the ISLSCP data (Fig. 4.6) is shown at the highest resolution of $1° \times 1°$. The LAI for the growing season derived from the HadCM2 model (Fig. 4.7) is shown at the lower GCM resolution of $2.5° \times 3.75°$ (Fig. 4.7).

The overall spatial patterns of LAI appear rather similar for both sets of predictions, with high LAI (up to 8) for tropical and equatorial rainforests, intermediate values (3–5) for deciduous forests and evergreen needle-leaved boreal forests, and low values (<2) for grasslands and semi-arid regions. The annual mean LAI has been determined for the ISLSCP (Fig. 4.8) and the HadCM2 (Fig. 4.9) data. The resolution of the ISLSCP predictions has also been reduced to be equal to that of the HadCM2 grid. This downgrade has been carried out so that inter-comparisons can be made with the same resolution, and therefore numbers of grid cells (1631), such as in Figure 4.10.

Comparisons between the maps of annual mean and growing season LAI indicate areas of cold- and drought-deciduous vegetation, such as in Africa, North and South America, Europe and Siberia. Differences between the two simulations are more evident, such as the lack of a forest fringe along the east coast of Australia and the Pacific North West coast of the USA, in the HadCM2 runs (Fig. 4.9). By contrast, the ISLSCP runs suggest too much ingression of vegetation into the southern Sahara (Figs. 4.6 and 4.8) and an underestimate of vegetation LAI in the high latitudes. These differences will become more

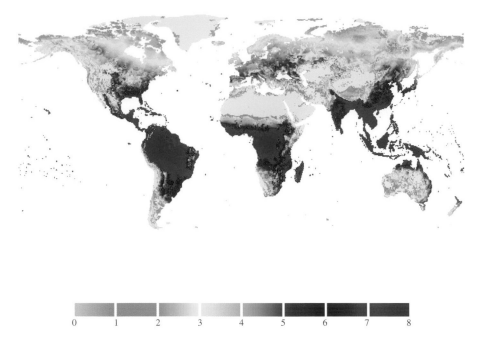

Figure 4.6. Mean growing season leaf area index for 1988, using climate data from the ISLSCP CD-ROM.

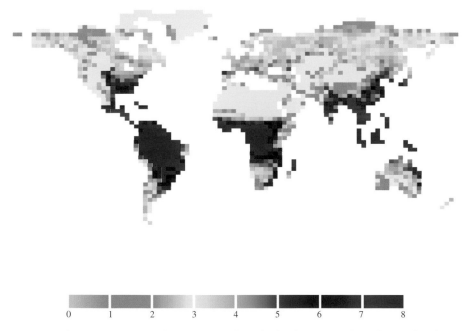

Figure 4.7. Mean growing season leaf area index for 1988, using climate data from the HadCM2 model.

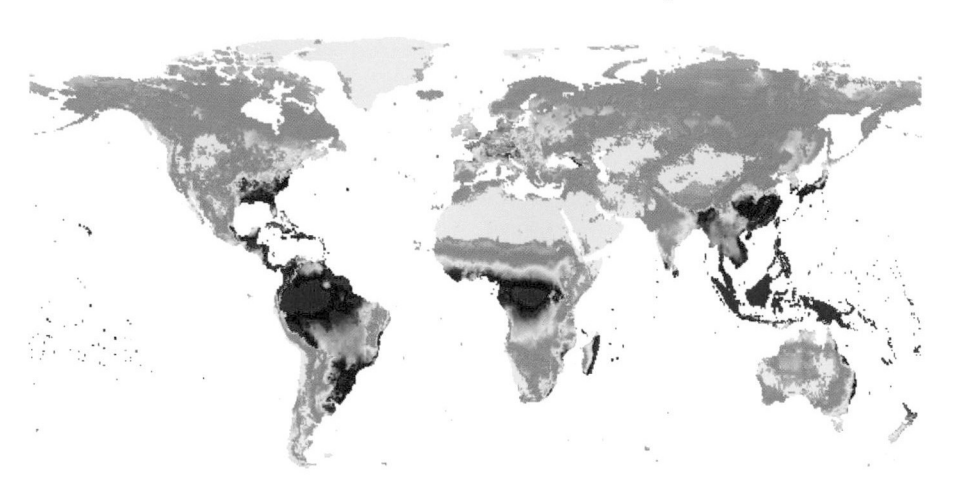

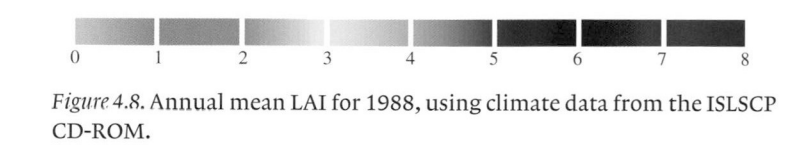

Figure 4.8. Annual mean LAI for 1988, using climate data from the ISLSCP CD-ROM.

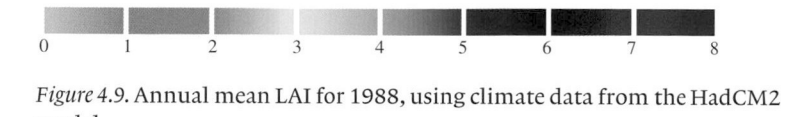

Figure 4.9. Annual mean LAI for 1988, using climate data from the HadCM2 model.

evident when the maps of LAI are later compared with a satellite image map for 1988.

The first test of the two model outputs is by a regression between the mean annual values of LAI (Fig. 4.10). A perfect agreement would place all points along a line of one-to-one agreement with an intercept at zero. None of these features is precisely realised, although the intercept is close to zero and the slope of the regression line is close to unity (Fig. 4.10).

Mitchell (1997) clearly indicates that the use of regression analysis is not an ideal tool for testing model predictions. Regression analysis is primarily designed for predicting values of y from values of x. However, in Figure 4.10 the aim is not to predict the LAI for the HadCM2 runs from the ISLSCP runs. The difference of the slope of the regression line from a one-to-one relationship might also be employed; however, with such a large number of points and scatter as seen in Figure 4.10 it is clear that many points do straddle the one-to-one line and so the slope will have a significant error term, or confidence limit. The actual arithmetic of the regression line is generally of no value for validation, it is not part of the model and it is not output from the model and so is not a direct indication of performance. A much improved approach to testing the models is to look at the difference between the two output sets, in this case LAI(HadCM2) minus LAI(ISLSCP) (Fig. 4.11). When this difference is then plotted against the LAI, from either model, it will indicate any biases, and can also be used as an estimate of the range of accuracy of prediction. This approach cannot detect whether both models are equally incorrect and this must be done by reference to an independent standard, which will be addressed from Figure 4.14 onwards.

The plot of the differences in LAI shows no trend with LAI, therefore there is no obvious bias in the model outputs, except for the ramps in the lower left and upper right sectors of the graph. The ramps arise from the fixed lower (zero) and upper (8) limits of LAI derived by the model and which restrict the range of possible differences that can occur at or near the limits. The final test is to convert the LAI differences to a frequency histogram of the differences (Fig. 4.12), which provides a quantitative picture of the distribution of differences and also a measure of the confidence in applying the regression technique, which should produce a normal distribution of these residual values.

The histogram (Fig. 4.12) indeed indicates a close agreement in the predictions of LAI using the HadCM2 and ISLSCP data and a normal distribution of residual values. Over 75% of the predictions agree within a range of LAI of ± 1 and 95% within an LAI range of ± 2. Some differences might be expected between the two climate models as the ECMWF model is designed to address

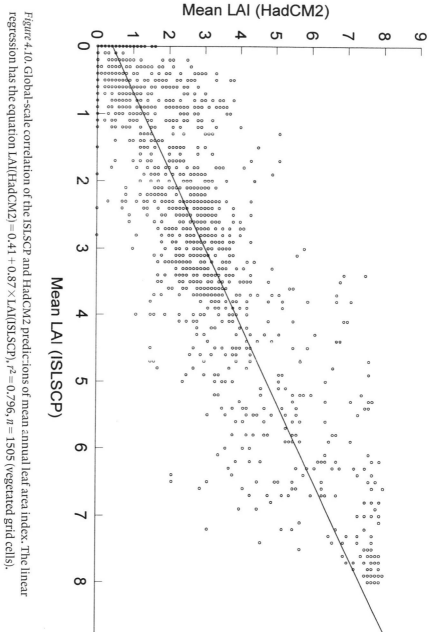

Figure 4.10. Global-scale correlation of the ISLSCP and HadCM2 predictions of mean annual leaf area index. The linear regression has the equation LAI(HadCM2) = 0.41 + 0.87 × LAI(ISLSCP), $r^2 = 0.796$, $n = 1505$ (vegetated grid cells).

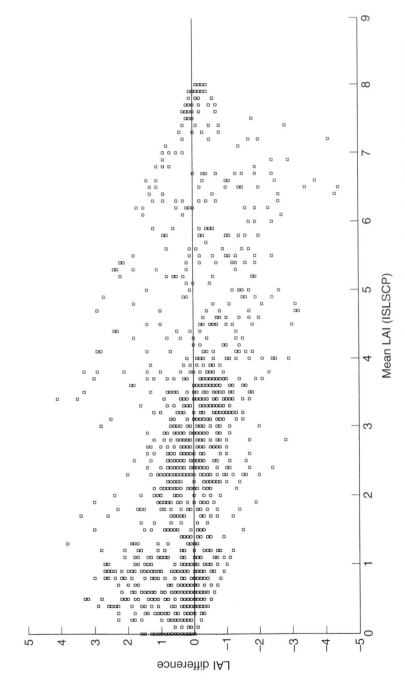

Figure 4.11. Plot of LAI differences (LAI(HadCM2) − LAI(ISLSCP)) against annual mean LAI projected from the ISLSCP CD-ROM. There is no statistically detectable trend in the differences, with LAI.

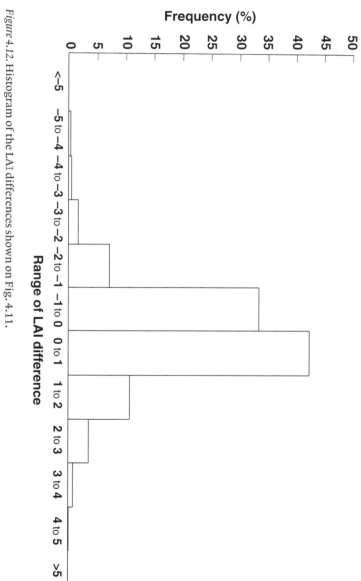

Figure 4.12. Histogram of the LAI differences shown on Fig. 4.11.

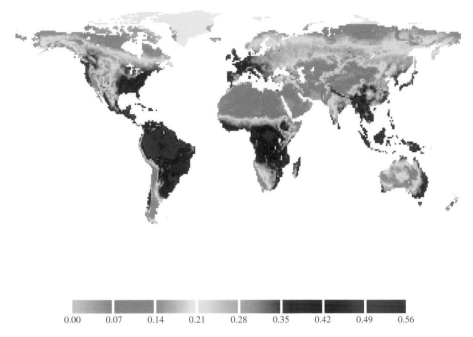

0.00   0.07   0.14   0.21   0.28   0.35   0.42   0.49   0.56

Figure 4.13. Mean annual average NDVI for 1988. NDVI generally increases with LAI.

interannual differences, such as during and following El Niño events (Diaz & Markgraf, 1992).

The second test of the model predictions of LAI is against observations of vegetation made by satellites, which detect reflected radiation in the red (strongly absorbed by chlorophyll in leaves) and far-red wavebands (not absorbed by chlorophyll). These data are converted to a normalised index, the NDVI, which is related in a non-linear, saturating fashion with LAI (Los *et al.*, 1994; Nemani & Running, 1996). NDVI, the normalised difference vegetation index, is calculated as the ratio $(L2 - L1)/(L2 + L1)$, where L1 is the flux density of red light reflected by vegetation to the satellite and L2 is the flux density of far-red light.

The ISLSCP CD-ROM includes NDVI data for the year 1988 and the mean annual NDVI (Fig. 4.13) can be compared directly with the annual averages of predicted LAI (Figs. 4.8 and 4.9). The NDVI is based on actual vegetation, which includes, for example, areas where forests have been converted to arable agriculture and where urban sprawl has engulfed natural vegetation. Therefore it cannot be expected that there will be perfect agreement between the NDVI and the predictions of LAI. In addition, the NDVI is sensitive to differences in bare soil characteristics, and these are included in an unknown fashion in the annual index. Finally, the index is used only as a correlative tool: a better approach would be for the vegetation model to predict the reflected fluxes of radiation, in the different wavebands, and then to compare these values with fluxes actually measured by the satellites. A further problem is the fact that the reflected fluxes must pass through the atmosphere, with its varying amounts of clouds and atmospheric aerosols, causing problems in defining the precise impact of vegetation on the reflected fluxes.

Visual comparison of the three maps (Figs. 4.8, 4.9 and 4.13) indicates areas of close agreement, such as the areas of high LAI in equatorial and tropical rainforests, the gradient of decreasing LAI with increasing latitude in the eastern USA, the transitions from drought-deciduous forest to desert in southern Africa, and the prairie boundary in the USA. Areas where the models differ are in eastern and south-west Australia, where the HadCM2 predictions (Fig. 4.9) fail to predict high LAI. Both models fail to predict the high leafiness of the forests of the Pacific North West and southern Chile, while the ISLSCP data shows better the transition from boreal forest to tundra in Canada. There are unusual patterns from the map of NDVI, such as the very high values in Ireland and south-west England (Fig. 4.13). These areas are dominated by intensive agriculture and pasture lands. These are areas of high and regular rainfall throughout the year; this shows that a continuously green canopy of grasses, such as in these sites, can produce as high an NDVI return as the equatorial rainforests, indicating that NDVI will not be an ideal indicator of LAI. In general, however, it is noted that NDVI and LAI are correlated in a non-linear fashion (Nemani & Running, 1996) and this relationship can, therefore, be used to provide an independent method for testing the modelling predictions.

Rather than convert NDVI to LAI using empirical relationships, and thus introducing a new source of error on each point, a general relationship has been derived between NDVI and LAI using the independent approach of Hunt et al. (1996). The annual values of NDVI on the ISLSCP CD-ROM have been used to recalculate and average the relationships between LAI and NDVI reported by Hunt et al. (1996) for 1987, but in this case by recalculating and averaging their equations for mean annual NDVI, compared with the maximum values originally used, and for the year 1987 of ISLSCP climatic and NDVI data. An analysis can then be made for the deviation of the global-scale model projections of annual mean LAI from the mean LAI/NDVI relationship. There is much scatter between NDVI and LAI projected from the ISLSCP climatic data (Fig. 4.14). However, the expected asymptotic relationship between NDVI and LAI is apparent.

The non-linear regression line of LAI on NDVI, derived from Hunt et al.

(1996) and the ISLSCP data, is subtracted from the individual points on Figure 4.14 to derive a plot of the residuals of the relationship (Fig. 4.15), in the same manner as for Figure 4.11. The residual LAI differences are scattered round the zero line with no obvious bias and, as for Figure 4.11, there are ramps at the lowest and highest values of NDVI, which arise from fixed upper and lower limits to LAI. Within the vegetation model the maximum LAI is determined, in the absence of all other climatic constraints, by the predicted capacity of the lowest leaf layer in the canopy to maintain an annual NPP equal to or greater than zero. The data presented here and on Figure 4.14 suggest that this may not be true for all canopies and that higher values of LAI than $c.$ 8 might be expected.

The histogram of the LAI differences (Fig. 4.16) indicates that the great majority of LAI projections fall within a narrow range of the mean regression line of LAI and NDVI; 63% of the residual values fall within a range of ± 1 LAI units and just over 90% fall within the range of ± 2 LAI units.

The same analysis as for the ISLSCP data has also been carried out for the predictions using the HadCM2 data. In this case only the histogram of the differences (Fig. 4.17) has been shown as the other plots are very similar to Figures 4.15 and 4.16. For the HadCM2 projections, 61% of the observations are within an LAI range of ± 1 and 86% fall within an LAI range of ± 2 of the regression line.

Overall, therefore, there is global-scale agreement between the model projections of LAI and LAI inferred from NDVI with about 90% of the residual errors, around the general regression of LAI on NDVI, within ± 2 LAI units. This is not an ideal test of the vegetation model, as its predictions have been tested against another, albeit empirical, model of LAI on NDVI. This has been an important exercise as only satellite monitoring can provide a global coverage. However, it is important to test both the vegetation and NDVI models against actual observations of LAI. Data for this test have been collected from Woodward (1987a) and also from the European Union funded project EURO-FLUX (courtesy of R. Valentini). Well-established forested and grassland sites, with only the dominant native species, have been chosen for this test and examples have been taken from Africa, Australia, south-east Asia, Europe, Japan and USA. The latitude and longitude of the field sites have been used to locate the nearest observation of annual NDVI (1988) and projection of annual mean LAI, using the ISLSCP data for 1988.

The linear regression of observed on predicted LAI (Fig. 4.18) indicates a strong correlation between the two, although the slope is less than unity and indicates that, overall, the model appears to underestimate LAI, although for these few observations the largest errors appear to be associated only with mid-range values of LAI.

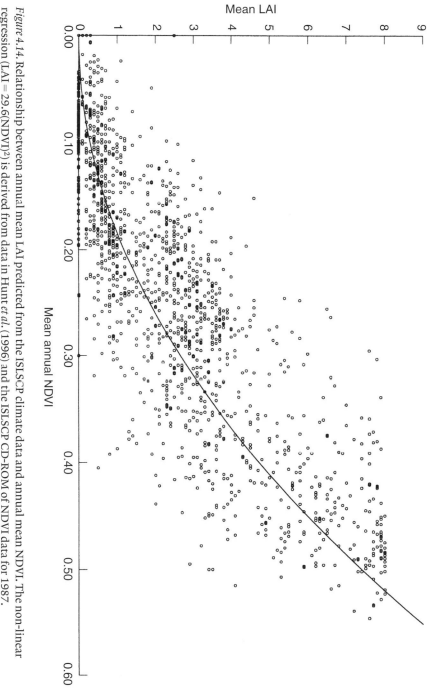

Figure 4.14. Relationship between annual mean LAI predicted from the ISLSCP climate data and annual mean NDVI. The non-linear regression (LAI = 29.6(NDVI)^2) is derived from data in Hunt *et al.* (1996) and the ISLSCP CD-ROM of NDVI data for 1987.

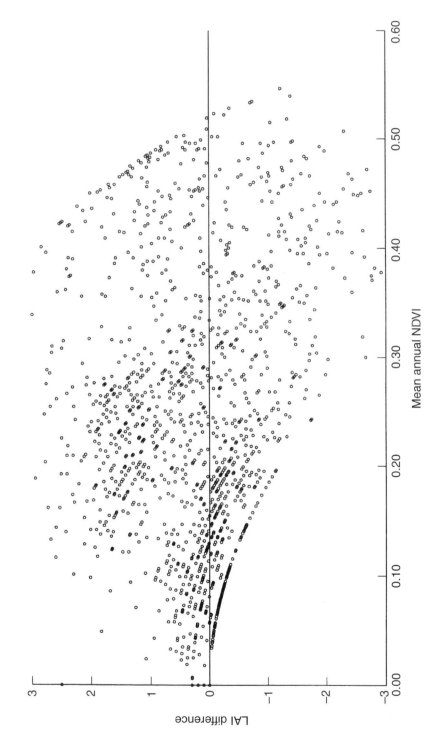

Figure 4.15. Plot of residual LAI differences against mean annual NDVI, for the predictions using the ISLSCP climate data.

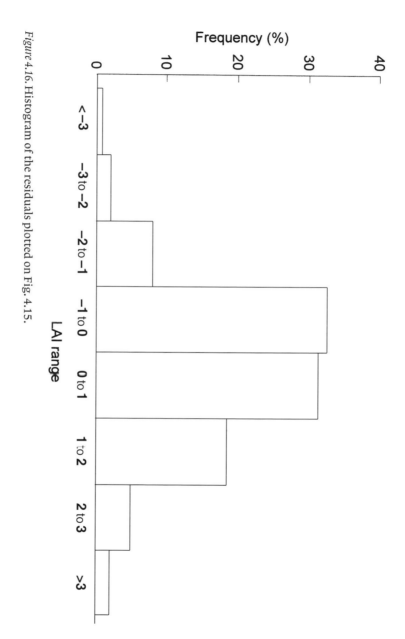

Figure 4.16. Histogram of the residuals plotted on Fig. 4.15.

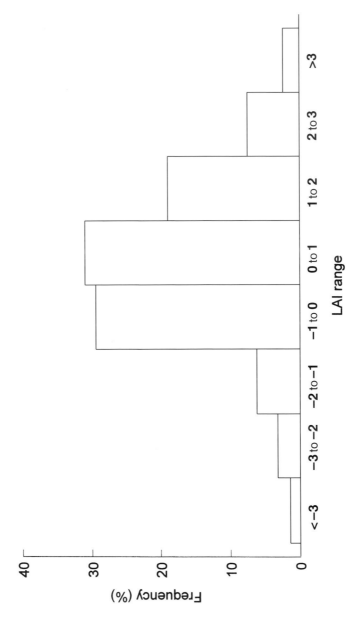

Figure 4.17. Histogram of the residuals calculated as for Fig. 4.15, but for the LAI projections by the HadCM2 model.

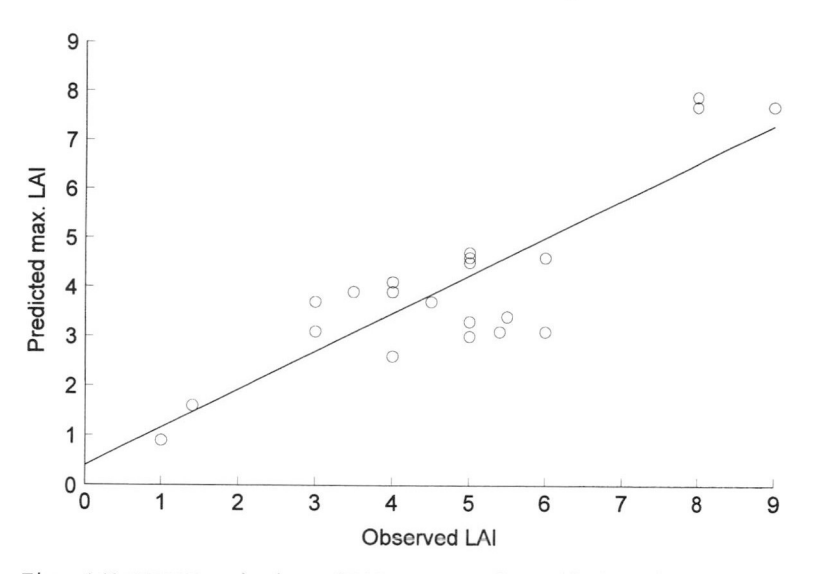

Figure 4.18. ISLSCP projections of LAI corresponding with sites of LAI observation.

The deviations of the predicted values of LAI, i.e. LAI(ISLSCP) − LAI(Observed), demonstrate (Fig. 4.19) that the model underestimates at moderate values of LAI: 64% of the observations are within ± 1 unit of LAI and 86% are within ± 2 units of LAI. It is not possible to explain these but part of the problem may be in the use of the ISLSCP climatic data for the chosen year of 1988, whose features may have been very different from the years in which LAI was actually measured. Even for these tests against observations, the field observation of LAI is a spot event and is not a measure over the whole growing season or year. The climate for the site of collection is taken from the ISLSCP modelled climate data, which also produces imprecision in the model projections. When climate station averages are used and then interpolated between climate stations (as, for example, employed by Leemans & Cramer, 1991) the model predictions of LAI and NPP (Woodward *et al.*, 1995) are more in error, when compared with observations, than when using the recorded data from the climate stations.

It is interesting to note that when the HadCM2 data are used, the vegetation model produces a smaller range of estimates of LAI than the ISLSCP data (Fig. 4.20). In this case 59% of the deviations are within ± 1 unit of LAI but all observations are within ± 2 units of LAI. The greater confidence in the model projections using HadCM2 suggests that the ISLSCP climate data for the year 1988 are different from the general trend in climate at this time, such as is projected by the Hadley Centre GCM.

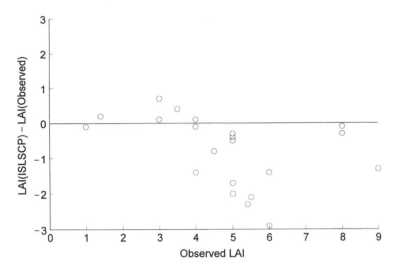

Figure 4.19. LAI differences, calculated as LAI(model predictions with ISLSCP data) less observed values of LAI, plotted against observed values of LAI.

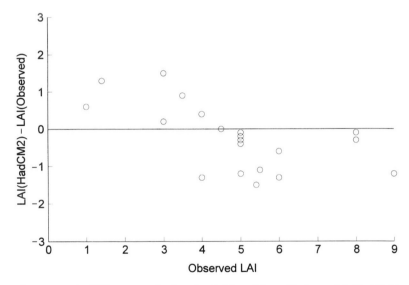

Figure 4.20. LAI differences, calculated as LAI(model predictions with HadCM2 data) less observed values of LAI, plotted against observed values of LAI.

It is also possible to test the accuracy of the general LAI/NDVI empirical relationship used for the tests shown on Figures 4.14 to 4.17. Here the NDVI data for both 1987 and 1988 have been averaged to reduce some of the problems of inter-annual fluctuations in climate. The NDVI-derived estimates of LAI (Fig. 4.21) show considerably more scatter than those from the vegetation model predictions. In addition there is a trend of increasing underestimation

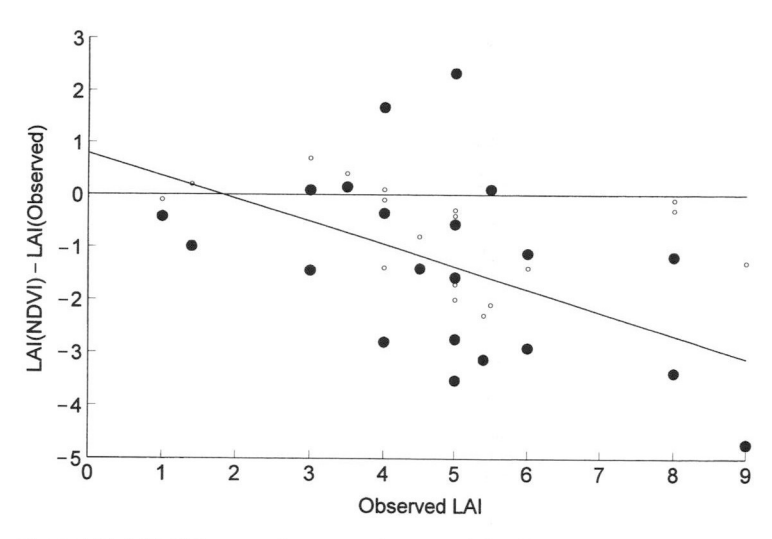

Figure 4.21. LAI differences between those modelled from NDVI, according to the relationship described on Fig. 4.14, and those observed. The line of linear regression indicates that the NDVI model of LAI underestimates LAI by 0.43 units per unit increase in observed LAI ($r^2 = 0.24$, $n = 22$). ●, NDVI comparison, ○, data from Fig. 4.19.

with increasing LAI, indicating that the general relationship between NDVI and LAI (Fig. 4.14) is inaccurate, particularly at high values of LAI. This may be because the relationship between NDVI and LAI is species or vegetation-type specific (Nemani & Running, 1996), a feature which was deliberately excluded in the earlier analysis (Fig. 4.14) because vegetation type was not identified.

Global patterns of NPP for the year 1988

The global patterns of LAI show good agreement between the vegetation model runs using the two sources of modelled climate. In addition, the global-scale projections of LAI match quite closely with observations based on NDVI. In all cases there are differences, some of which are attributable to differences in the modelled climate (e.g. Figs. 4.12 and 4.18) and some of which are due to the combined errors in the vegetation model itself and to other methods of testing the model, such as NDVI (Figs. 4.16, 4.17 and 4.19). Overall, these errors combine to limit the global-scale precision of LAI, using the present vegetation model and model-simulated climate to *c.* ±1 to ±1.5 units of LAI.

Although vegetation LAI and NPP are closely correlated (e.g. Woodward *et al.*, 1995), it is not thought desirable, for two reasons, to use NDVI data for testing the vegetation outputs of NPP. First, the NDVI data have already been used to test the predictions of LAI. Second, radiation which is reflected from vegetation, and used to calculate NDVI, can only be related to the presence of leaves and chlorophyll. If, for reasons such as drought, the stomata of leaves are closed, even though the chlorophyll content is quite unchanged, then in this short term NPP will be either zero or negative, while the satellite will detect an unchanging reflection characteristic of a fully-watered canopy of leaves. In addition, as CO_2 concentrations change then so also may NPP, but in some cases, at least, without any changes in the optical characteristics of the canopy. These features will then tend to reduce the capacity of NDVI to indicate NPP, as a correlate of LAI. Therefore another approach is necessary for testing the NPP data from the vegetation model.

A substantial dataset of NPP observations exists (Esser *et al.*, 1997; Parton *et al.*, 1993; Long *et al.*, 1992) which may be used for testing the vegetation model. However, it should be borne in mind that considerable errors may be involved when measuring the net annual productivity of vegetation, these are well described by Long *et al.* (1992), and it seems likely that the error involved in an individual annual measurement is likely to be in the order of 10 to 20%. The large database of Esser *et al.* (1997) includes all recorded observations of NPP from 1869 to 1982. As the aim is to test these observations against the vegetation models, using data from 1987 and 1988, the most recent observations of NPP have been taken. In addition, only data with observations of above- and below-ground productivity and an indication of the species composition of the vegetation, including the latitude and longitude of location, have been used for testing.

The global-scale predictions of NPP for 1988 using the ISLSCP climate data (Fig. 4.22) and the HadCM2 data (Fig. 4.23) indicate very similar spatial patterns, from high productivity in the tropical and equatorial rainforests, through the lower productivities of the mid-latitude forests to the low productivities of the high latitude boreal forests and tundra.

The linear regression of NPP predictions against observations, for a range of vegetation types (Fig. 4.24), indicates a close correlation between the two; like the predictions for LAI (Fig. 4.18), the vegetation model underestimates NPP.

The differences between the predictions and observations of NPP increase with NPP (Fig. 4.25) with a *c.* 20% underestimate of the highest values of NPP. Including the lower 15% error on the estimates of observed NPP indicates that the model underestimation of NPP is probably not detectable.

A histogram of the NPP differences (Fig. 4.26) indicates that, although there is a bias to model underestimates of NPP, 60% of the model predictions are ± 1 t C ha^{-1} yr^{-1} and 88% are ± 2 t C ha^{-1} yr^{-1}.

The predictions of NPP using the HadCM2 climate data are very similar to

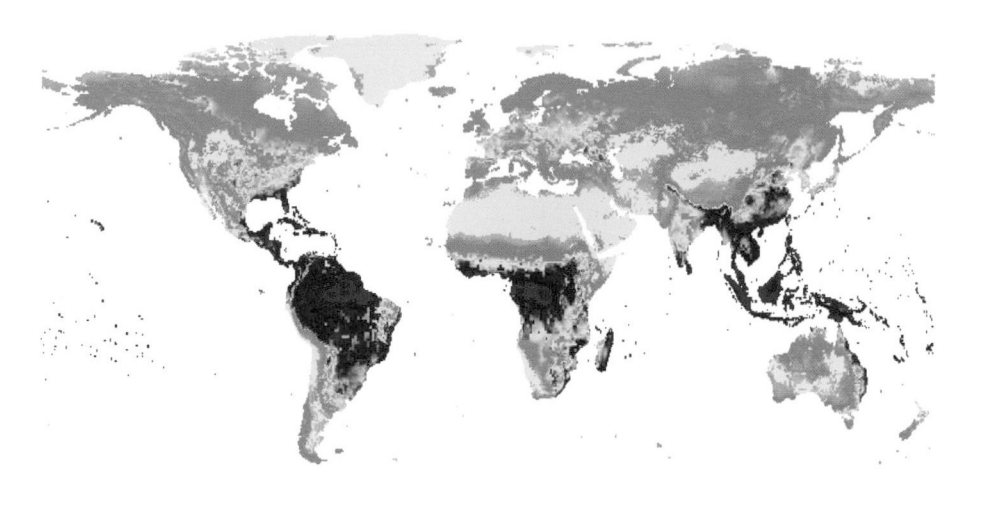

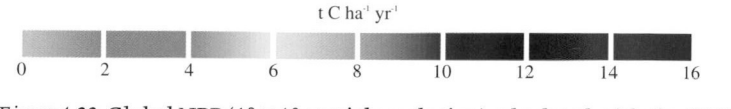

t C ha⁻¹ yr⁻¹

Figure 4.22. Global NPP (1° × 1° spatial resolution) calculated with the ISLSCP climate data for 1988.

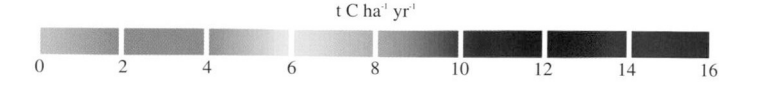

t C ha⁻¹ yr⁻¹

Figure 4.23. Global NPP calculated with the HadCM2 climate data for 1988.

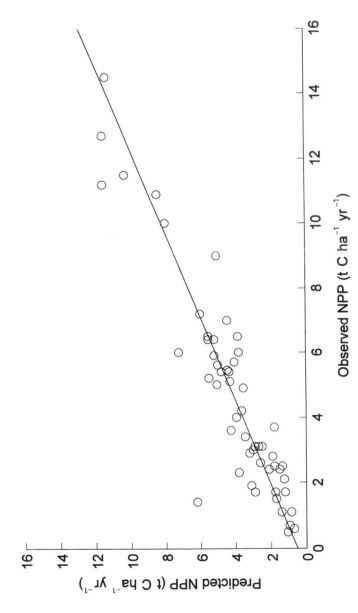

Figure 4.24. Regression of predicted NPP, using the ISLSCP 1988 climate data against observations of NPP. The predictions of NPP underestimate NPP (Predictions = $0.51 + 0.77 \times$ Observations, $r^2 = 0.84$, $n = 55$).

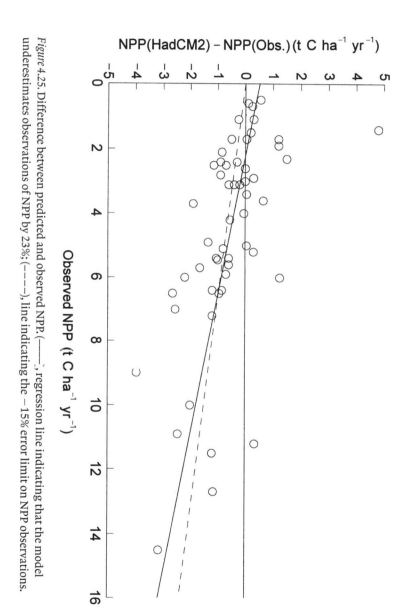

Figure 4.25. Difference between predicted and observed NPP. (——), regression line indicating that the model underestimates observations of NPP by 23%; (– – –), line indicating the −15% error limit on NPP observations.

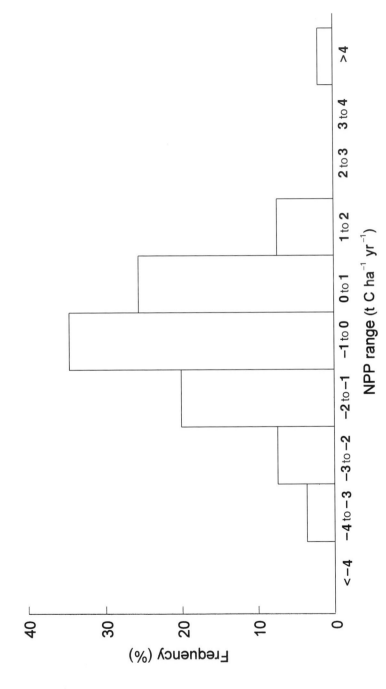

Figure 4.26. Histogram of the differences between NPP calculated using ISLSCP climate data and NPP observations.

those achieved with the ISLSCP data. The same underestimation of NPP is observed, indicating that climatic differences between the two climate sources are secondary in influencing the NPP test. For the HadCM2 simulations, 56% of the observations are within ± 1 t C ha^{-1} yr^{-1} and 82% are ± 2 t C ha^{-1} yr^{-1}. The problem for both tests is that it is not possible to ascribe errors to either the model or the observation set, as both sets are likely to include significant error. However, the precision of the NPP estimations appears to be about ± 1.5 to 2.5 t C ha^{-1} yr^{-1}, based on the whole dataset. The contemporary global total of NPP is 52 Gt C yr^{-1}. This compares well with a total of 56.4 Gt C yr^{-1} (Field *et al.*, 1998), derived using satellite data.

Predicting the present-day distribution of dominant functional types

The approach employed in the SDGVM to predict functional types has already been described. The number of functional types is only six (four tree types based on low temperature survival [Fig. 4.5] and two grass types with either C$_3$ or C$_4$ pathways of photosynthesis) but this provides a coarse description of the global vegetation types of the world. The functional types of species which have been predicted are evergreen broad-leaved tree species, evergreen needle-leaved tree species, deciduous broad-leaved tree species, deciduous needle-leaved tree species, grasses and herbs with the C$_3$ pathway of photosynthesis and those with the C$_4$ pathway of photosynthesis. Most sites are predicted to develop with mixtures of functional types and for the purposes of this demonstration, only the dominant functional types, in terms of ground cover, are described.

Any map of vegetation which is predicted should be compared with a map of observed vegetation. The production of an actual vegetation map is not without its own problems of recognition and classification. A number of vegetation maps are available (Küchler, 1983; Matthews, 1983; Olson *et al.*, 1983; Wilson & Henderson-Sellers, 1985; Prentice *et al.*, 1992; Haxeltine & Prentice, 1996). However, this analysis will use the land cover map in the ISLSCP CD-ROM (Meeson *et al.*, 1995). The land cover map is primarily determined from the annual variations in the NDVI for each $1° \times 1°$ pixel of the terrestrial surface. The approach (DeFries & Townshend, 1994) builds on previously established techniques of analysis and classification of NDVI data (Los *et al.*, 1994; Sellers *et al.*, 1994). In addition, the classifications based on the NDVI data have been trained, and therefore constrained to some degree, by established vegetation maps, such as those by Matthews (1983), Olson *et al.* (1983) and Wilson & Henderson-Sellers (1985). Only the HadCM2 simulations are used as the ISLSCP climate data may be used in classifying vegetation.

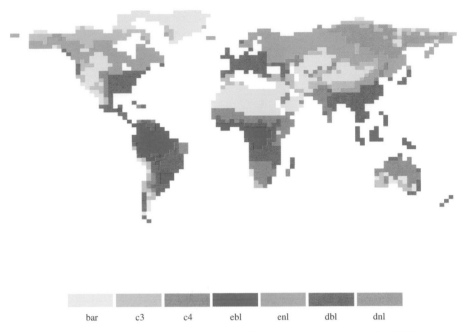

Figure 4.27. Dominant functional types (fts) in terms of cover for the 1990s, derived from the HadCM2 climate data, using the SDGVM. dbl, deciduous broad-leaved tree; dnl, deciduous needle-leaved tree; ebl, evergreen broad-leaved tree; enl, evergreen needle-leaved tree; c3, grass and herb with C3 photosynthetic metabolism; c4, grass and herb with C4 photosynthetic metabolism; bar, bare ground.

The land cover classification, from the ISLSCP CD-ROM, also includes land cover modified for agriculture, and so is an attempt at predicting actual vegetation. The map derived by the SDGVM is for potential vegetation, i.e. it does not take into account any human impacts on vegetation.

A general comparison of the two vegetation maps (Figs. 4.27 and 4.28) indicates a wide range of agreement in terms of the geographical distribution of the functional types. The broad bands of evergreen and deciduous needle-leaved boreal forests have similar distributions between the two maps, which also agree quite well in the distribution of evergreen broad-leaved forests in the tropics, and deciduous broad-leaved forests (both cold and drought deciduous) in eastern USA, South America, Africa, south-east Asia and east Australia. The long extension of the cold deciduous forest into Russia on the ISLSCP land cover classification (Fig. 4.28) is partly an artefact of simplifying the two maps, so that no areas of mixed dominant functional types are included. The ISLSCP and the SDGVM data both predict areas of mixed deciduous broad-leaved and evergreen needle-leaved forests in this area. The mixed C3 and C4 grasslands of the prairies, the Asian steppes and in Africa are also in

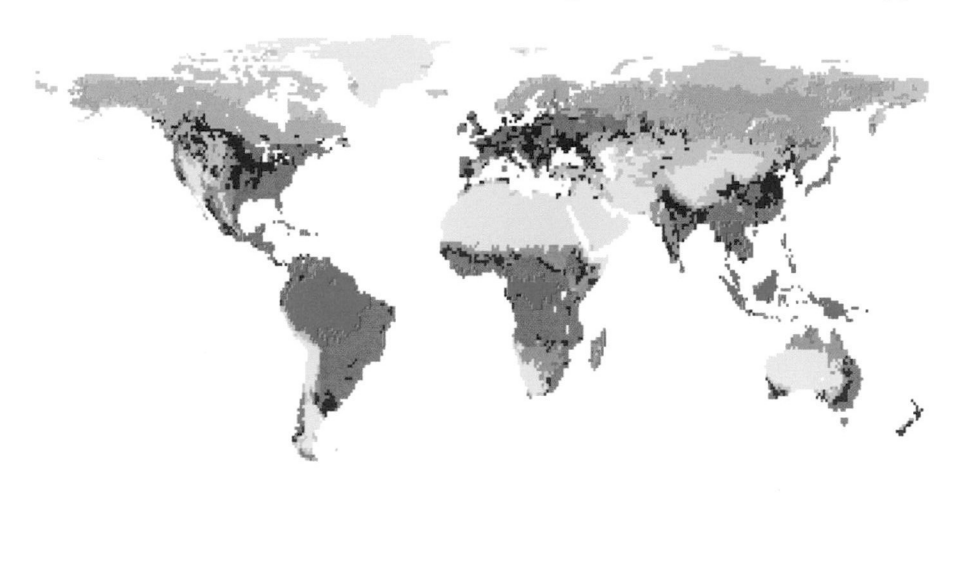

bar   c3   c4   ebl   cnl   dbl   dnl   crp

Figure 4.28. Dominant functional types derived from the ISLSCP land cover classification. The original classification has been simplified for comparison with the SDGVM simulations. Symbols as for Fig. 4.27, with the addition of crp, for areas of agricultural crops.

agreement. In both cases, however, the shrub functional type has not been explicitly defined either in the SDGVM or in this version of the land cover classification. Therefore the area of tundra, on both maps, is classified as C_3 grassland. The SDGVM appears to underestimate the area of tundra in Russia but provides a reasonable agreement with the ISLSCP classification for North America.

Areas of more obvious disagreement include central Australia, the Middle East, south-west South America and southern Africa, where the SDGVM predicts grassland (albeit rather sparse), while the ISLSCP indicates significant areas of desert. Another area of notable disagreement is north-west China, where the SDGVM predicts evergreen needle-leaved forest, while the ISLSCP classification indicates either C_3 grassland or broad-leaved deciduous forest. However, Haxeltine and Prentice (1996) suggest the presence of evergreen needle-leaved forest mixed with deciduous broad-leaved forest in this area, with some areas of grassland. So it is possible that this simplified version of the land cover classification, in addition to the original classification, is in some degree of error in this area. The ISLSCP classification also includes areas

Table 4.1. *Matrix of dominant functional type classifications by the SDGVM and the ISLSCP land cover classification. Functional type abbreviations as for Fig. 4.27, excluding the areas classified as crops from Fig 4.28 (10% of the 2.5° × 3.75° grid cells). The figures in bold, along the diagonal, are for the numbers of exact agreements in the two classifications*

SDGVM PREDICTIONS

ISLSCP ↓	dbl	dnl	ebl	enl	C3	C4	bare
dbl	**204**	0	46	46	2	3	0
dnl	2	**46**	0	55	2	0	0
ebl	21	0	**94**	0	0	0	0
enl	8	19	0	**169**	8	2	2
C3	23	52	0	102	**76**	13	16
C4	49	0	1	2	5	**25**	1
bare	6	0	0	8	60	73	**202**

of agriculture (*c.* 10% on Fig. 4.28). These are not included in the SDGVM but this is clearly a necessary task for investigating the dynamics of actual vegetation.

The matrix of the classifications by the SDGVM and provided in the ISLSCP CD-ROM have been made at the coarser grid cell resolution of the SDGVM (Table 4.1). Overall 57% of the grid cells are classified in the same manner (the diagonals of Table 4.1). In the vegetated areas, the deciduous broad-leaved forests and the evergreen needle-leaved forests are predicted most frequently. This agreement somewhat underplays the effectiveness of the SDGVM which usually predicts mixes of functional types where they were originally presented in the ISLSCP CD-ROM. The areas of greatest disagreement are in semi-arid areas, where there is a tendency for the SDGVM, and the HadCM2 climate model, to make the areas sufficiently wet to support some grasses.

Overall, therefore, there is reasonable agreement between the two maps, but some of the differences in climate, described earlier in the discussions of the LAI and NPP comparisons, are also seen here, particularly, according to the SDGVM, in increasing the vegetation cover in desert areas beyond that observed by NDVI (Fig. 4.13).

Conclusions

This chapter has provided a general background to the climate, vegetation and soil models which will be used in the following chapters, in order to investigate the impacts of changes in climate and atmospheric CO_2 concentration on vegetation function and structure. This chapter has addressed the present day and so is best suited to testing the capacity of the combination of a modelled climate, from a GCM, and a model of terrestrial vegetation to predict observations. The capacity to interpret data collected from satellite observations of radiation reflected from the Earth's surface and to use this as a global-scale test of the vegetation model has proved valuable. No other technique has the capacity to scan rapidly the whole surface of the Earth, as a regular event. However, the satellite data are subject to a range of perturbations from the atmosphere, from changes in the calibration of on-board radiometers and the problems of the different angles of 'look' towards the vegetation. In addition, the conversion of actual radiometric data to simple normalised indices tends to reduce the quality of the data, particularly as its final use tends to be in a correlative mode with different output from the vegetation model. The ideal test of a model is that it should provide the same output as the data against which it is tested. This would entail two changes, the inclusion of a radiative transfer model in the vegetation model, therefore predicting the reflected solar radiation into space and the use of radiation data from the satellites. These approaches are still in their infancy for global-scale modelling (Sellers *et al.*, 1996).

Therefore the potentially ideal standard of the satellite data is, in reality, less than ideal. Similar problems may be raised for all of the test data, including measurements of LAI and NPP, both of which – particularly NPP – are inherently imprecise measurements (Hall & Scurlock, 1991). In addition these are taken as essentially point measures and so do not provide estimates of the mean LAI or NPP at the landscape scale, which is the finest scale of resolution of the vegetation models. On the other hand, vegetation models such as the SDGVM are designed to be driven by climatic data, and observational data of climate are not available at the landscape scale. Therefore interpolation techniques are necessary to give a global coverage, but these inevitably downgrade the accuracy of the climatic data (Woodward *et al.*, 1995).

So all of the tests of the SDGVM and the climate data from HadCM2 and ISLSCP have errors in both the predictions and the independent measures. On a positive note, the errors in estimating vegetation NPP and LAI are sufficiently low to permit quite precise and accurate global-scale predictions and are based on a model which scales up from well-characterised plant, canopy and soil processes at, in effect, the point scale to the full global scale. In experimental studies, results are usually quoted with confidence limits in the data which define the limits within which some fraction, say 90 or 95% of the observations are included. This approach could be applied to vegetation models but the error limits would be very large, in part because of uncertainties in the necessary input data (on climate and soils), in part due to uncertainties in the testing or calibration of the vegetation models and in part due to the inevitable problems within the model itself. This chapter has indicated that about 60% of model predictions of both LAI and NPP are within ± 1 unit of LAI and ± 1 t C ha^{-1} yr^{-1}, with $c.$ 80–90% of the observations within about 1.5 to 2 units. It does not seem useful to push these error limits any further, given the errors of observation and clearly particular uses of model outputs will have differing requirements of both accuracy and precision.

The quantitative estimation of error on a particular prediction of LAI or NPP is one use of the vegetation model; perhaps more important is the use of the model to describe the spatial distributions of these values and also plant functional types. The global-scale patterns of NPP have no robust comparison for testing and calibration; however, the satellite-derived NDVI can be used for testing the spatial patterns of LAI. When the NDVI and climate data for running the vegetation model are from the same year, then this should be a useful test. At present the ISLSCP CD-ROM of data provides such a possibility and analyses indicate (Figs. 4.14 to 4.17) the same range of errors as described above for the spot tests of the model predictions.

An alternative approach for comparing maps is the use of the kappa statistic (Monserud & Leemans, 1992; Prentice *et al.*, 1992). This statistic compares two maps, grid cell by grid cell, and assesses the fraction of agreement, such that the kappa statistic has a maximum value of unity and a minimum of zero. Such a comparison will always produce some agreements purely by chance and the derivation of the kappa statistic also takes this into account. Unfortunately, observations indicate that any two maps with many grid cells will always show some highly significant level of disagreement, producing a low value of kappa. The suggestion then appears to convert kappa quantities to kappa qualities, such as poor, fair, good, very good and excellent (Prentice *et al.*, 1992). An earlier version of the SDGVM, when used to predict the potential vegetation (no agricultural conversion) of the USA, produced a kappa statistic of 0.72 or very good (VEMAP, 1995), which was similar to other vegetation models (Neilson, 1995; Haxeltine *et al.*, 1996).

Unfortunately, therefore, the kappa statistic is not ideal for comparing maps. A further difficulty arises when comparing the ISLSCP NDVI and LAI projections for the same year. In this case NDVI needs to be converted to LAI, but analyses indicate (Fig. 4.21) that this conversion can inject significant error. This leads to the general conclusion that vegetation models can be tested, but only so far before the method of testing, be it point comparisons with data or spatial comparisons of maps, fails to resolve any further problems of accuracy and precision. However, it is clear that the SDGVM has, in qualitative terms, good or very good precision and accuracy and certainly sufficient for addressing past and future climates, when the driving variables, in particular climate, will be a greater source of inaccuracies of simulation than the vegetation model itself.

5

The late Carboniferous

Introduction

One of the fundamental aims of interpreting and analysing the fossil record of land plants is to understand the patterns and processes underlying their evolution. This may best be achieved through palaeobotanical interpretations of the plant fossil record, and through modelling. This book is primarily concerned with the use of core physiological models, based on a knowledge of present-day processes, to address the impacts of past atmospheres and climates on plant function. The approach is offered as complementary to analyses of the fossil record of plant life itself. In some cases a modelling approach can be achieved rather simply, at least at the scale of individual leaves (Beerling, 1994; Beerling & Woodward, 1997), by considering the mathematical relationships between leaf CO_2 assimilation and the stoichiometry of the biochemistry of leaf photosynthesis (Farquhar *et al.*, 1980; von Caemmerer & Farquhar, 1981) and the composition of ancient atmospheres. In other cases, features characteristic of the Carboniferous period, such as the role played by fire in shaping the development of terrestrial ecosystems (Cope & Chaloner, 1980; Chaloner, 1989; Robinson, 1989; Jones & Chaloner, 1991; Scott & Jones, 1994) are important to consider but more difficult to represent.

The Berner & Canfield (1989) geochemical model of atmospheric O_2 variations predicts that the highest O_2 values (35%) over the past 570 million years probably occurred in the Carboniferous – compared with the present atmospheric level (PAL) of 21%. A value of 35% is widely regarded to be the most extreme upper bound, especially since some experimental data suggest this would result in frequent and intense wildfires ('forest fire') (Watson *et al.*, 1978; Chaloner, 1989). When taken at face value and viewed from a plant physiological perspective, it is surprising that relatively few studies have attempted to investigate, either through modelling or by experiment (Raven *et al.*, 1994), the impact of high O_2 events on plant function.

The low CO_2/O_2 ratio of the Carboniferous created unique conditions for the operation of terrestrial vegetation, which bears on a number of interesting features of Palaeozoic plant physiology and ecology. This chapter begins by considering the likely effects of a low CO_2/high O_2 ratio, at the scale of individual leaves, on the basic plant processes of photorespiration and photosynthesis. The approach is extended with a simple growth model to consider how photosynthetic O_2 effects translate into canopy growth responses (Lloyd & Farquhar, 1996). Where possible, the growth predictions have been tested against data reported from the limited number of plant growth experiments conducted in a high O_2 environment. Included in the leaf-scale consideration is a quantitative assessment of the influence of changes in stomatal density, in the context of values recorded on fossil Carboniferous leaves, on photorespiration and photosynthesis (Beerling *et al.*, 1998).

At the global scale, the vegetation model described in Chapter 4 has been driven with the 'Carboniferous climate' simulated by the Universities Global Atmospheric Modelling Programme (UGAMP) GCM to predict global patterns of terrestrial net primary productivity (NPP), leaf area index (LAI) and soil carbon (C) concentration. However, the impacts of changing stomata development with CO_2 (Chapter 3) have not been included, due to the lack of a global quantification response. The impact of 35% O_2, relative to the present-day value of 21% O_2, on the productivity and structure of terrestrial vegetation has also been quantified at the global scale; in effect this represents an assessment of scaling from leaf photosynthetic impacts to productivity. The vegetation predictions, including analyses of site water balance (Moore, 1995), have been compared with the global distribution of Carboniferous coals (Crowley & Baum, 1994).

Storage of organic carbon in soils, and its subsequent incorporation into the sedimentary record as coal, in the late Carboniferous, is the focus of much economic interest and has led to the development of conceptual non-quantitative models of coal formation (DiMichele & Philips, 1994) combining palaeobotanical data with information from petrography, sedimentology and geochemistry. Quantitative estimates of carbon storage in soils are particularly well suited to global-scale modelling investigations and have been considered in relation to decomposition rates of surface and root litters. Reduced rates of organic matter decomposition, resulting from the increased dominance of plant groups with a high lignin content, may have contributed to increased carbon burial and coal accumulation in the Carboniferous because of the inferred relative paucity of lignolytic organisms in the late Palaeozoic (Robinson, 1990a,b). The impact of this suggestion on soil C storage is investigated by varying the rates of organic matter decomposition within the Century (Chapter 4) biogeochemistry model.

Several workers have noted that the low atmospheric CO_2/O_2 ratio of the Carboniferous might have favoured the evolution and development of plants with the C_4 photosynthetic pathway (Moore, 1983; Wright & Vanstone, 1991; Raven *et al.*, 1994) and possibly even crassulacean acid metabolism (CAM) (Raven & Spicer, 1996). The suggestions arise because plants with the C_4 photosynthetic pathway possess structural properties and use the enzyme phosphoenol pyruvate (PEP) carboxylase. PEP has a higher affinity for CO_2 than rubisco, and so C_4 plants might be expected to show smaller reductions in photosynthetic productivity under a high O_2 atmosphere than C_3 plants using rubisco. Therefore the costs, in terms of water loss (transpiration), might also be reduced in C_4 and CAM plants operating in the Carboniferous atmosphere. CAM plants, typically succulents, represent an intermediate between C_3 and C_4 plants because they assimilate small amounts of CO_2 during the day via the C_3 pathway and operate in CAM mode with the C_4 pathway at night, when the stomata tend to remain closed. In view of these considerations, the functional type model described in Chapter 4 has been used to predict the possible distribution of C_3 and C_4 plants at the global scale in the late Carboniferous. These simulations represent a test of the suggestion that the climate and atmosphere of the Carboniferous may have been favourable for C_4 species thereby allowing the evolution of this photosynthetic pathway more than once since the Silurian (Spicer, 1989a; Wright & Vanstone, 1991).

In the final section, the possible role of fire is considered by combining climatic data with predictions of litter and surface soil water content, and experimental data on the effect of O_2 on ignition probabilities for cellulose (Watson *et al.*, 1978; Beerling *et al.*, 1998). The abundance of fossil charcoal plant remains in Carboniferous sediments is testament to the existence of wildfire in Palaeozoic terrestrial ecosystem ecology (Cope & Chaloner, 1980; Chaloner, 1989; Robinson, 1989; Jones & Chaloner, 1991; Scott & Jones, 1994; Falcon-Lang, 2000; Falcon-Lang & Scott, 2000) and underscores the necessity of making some first predictions of its frequency and effects on ecosystem structure, even if based on a rather simplified approach (Beerling *et al.*, 1998).

Effects of the late Carboniferous atmosphere on photorespiration

As described in Chapters 2 and 3, rubisco is the primary carbon-fixing enzyme in terrestrial vegetation. It catalyses two reactions, the fixation of CO_2 by photosynthesis and the release of CO_2, when O_2 binds with the acceptor molecule RuBP, by photorespiration. The extent to which photosynthesis and photorespiration occur depends crucially on the relative concentrations of the two substrates of the reactions (CO_2 and O_2), and on temperature. Over the Phanerozoic the ratio of these two gases shows a dramatic trend (Fig. 5.1a), in addition to changes in climate (Chapter 2), with clear implications for changes in the functioning of plants in the late Palaeozoic (360–250 Ma). The effects of changing CO_2 and O_2 on the processes of photosynthesis and photorespiration have been investigated at a fixed temperature (25 °C) and at the temperatures predicted for the past 400 Ma by the zero-dimensional climate model described in Chapter 2. The rate of photorespiration can be calculated from the Farquhar *et al.* (1980) model of leaf CO_2 assimilation as follows. The net photosynthetic rate of a leaf, A (mol m^{-2} s^{-1}), can be defined as (Farquhar *et al.*, 1980):

$$A = v_c - 0.5 v_o - R_d \tag{5.1}$$

where v_c is the rate of photosynthetic CO_2 fixation (carboxylation, mol m^{-2} s^{-1}), v_o is the rate of photorespiratory O_2 fixation (oxygenation, mol m^{-2} s^{-1}) and R_d is the rate of respiration other than photorespiration (mol m^{-2} s^{-1}). The rate of carboxylation is given by:

$$v_c = \frac{(A + R_d)}{\left(1 - \dfrac{0.5o}{\tau c_i}\right)} \tag{5.2}$$

where c_i is the intercellular CO_2 partial pressure (Pa), which is typically 70% of the ambient CO_2 partial pressure (von Caemmerer & Evans, 1991), o is the partial pressure of oxygen (Pa) and τ is the specificity factor of rubisco for CO_2 relative to O_2. Substituting equation 5.2 into equation 5.1 and solving for v_o gives:

$$v_o = 2o \frac{(A + R_d)}{(2\tau c_i - o)} \tag{5.3}$$

Since one CO_2 molecule is released for every two oxygenations, the rate of photorespiration is then calculated as $0.5 v_o$. To estimate the rate of photorespiration, and the ratio of photorespiration to photosynthesis in the following simulations, equation 5.3 has been used with predictions of leaf photosynthesis from the Farquhar *et al.* (1980) biochemical model of leaf carbon assimilation. Temperature sensitivities of each parameter are as given in previous chapters.

The resulting predictions highlight a physiological difficulty, represented by high photorespiratory rates, faced by plants in growing in the Carboniferous (Fig. 5.1b). Associated with this is the additional consideration

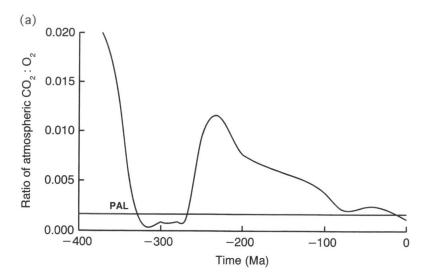

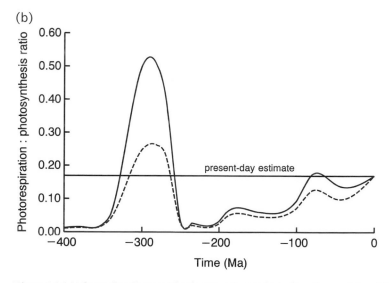

Figure 5.1. (a) The ratio of atmospheric $CO_2 : O_2$ predicted by the models of Berner (1994) and Berner & Canfield (1989) respectively (PAL = present atmospheric level) and (b) effects of these gases on the ratio of photorespiration to photosynthesis, modelled using the Farquhar *et al.* (1980) model of photosynthesis and eqs. 5.1–5.3, with J_{max} and V_{max} values of 210 and 105 μmol m^{-2} s^{-1}, a saturating irradiance of 1000 μmol m^{-2} s^{-1} at 25 °C (solid line) and at the temperatures calculated by the zero-dimensional climate model (broken line).

of the energy costs associated with repairing damage caused by the production of toxic O species (Raven et $al.$, 1994). From 350 to 300 Ma terrestrial vegetation is predicted to have experienced dramatically increasing photorespiratory demands (Fig. 5.1b), as the concentration of atmospheric CO_2 declined and that of O_2 increased – both reducing the efficiency of carboxylation. At higher temperatures photorespiration increases (Sharkey, 1988), therefore cooling below the baseline temperature of $25\,°C$ in the Carboniferous leads to lower estimates of photorespiration (Fig. 5.1b).

It is particularly intriguing that the combination of CO_2 and O_2 concentrations arising in the Carboniferous, possibly through the activities of land plants, caused the greatest increase in photorespiration, and a subsequent reduction in photosynthesis (Fig. 5.2a). Indeed, this simple modelling exercise predicts that $c.$ 30–40% of carbon fixed by photosynthesis in a Carboniferous atmosphere will be lost through photorespiration (Fig. 5.2b, as also shown on Fig. 3.14). If these calculations are realistic, the biological control of the Carboniferous atmospheric composition appears to be a clear case of the failure, at least in the short term, of biotic systems to regulate their abiotic environment in a manner consistent with the Gaia hypothesis (Lovelock, 1979). Robinson (1991) went further and suggested that strict regulatory control is unlikely, in the Gaian sense, where geochemical cycling of elements (C and O) introduces time lags of 100 Ma over-printed on biological evolution. On a longer timescale, however, after the Carboniferous the decrease in photosynthetic activity of terrestrial vegetation and the possible evolution of new degradation pathways for bacterially-resistant organic matter perhaps enabled the atmospheric composition to recover to conditions more favourable for growth (Robinson, 1991; Berner, 1993, 1994). One interesting feature of the current and future continued increases in atmospheric CO_2 concentration, under a relatively constant O_2 concentration (on a geological timescale), is that the photorespiration burden on terrestrial C_3 plants is likely to be reduced (Fig. 5.2).

Effects of the late Carboniferous atmosphere on leaf gas exchange

Chapter 3 proposed that plants may combat the problem of high photorespiration by the development of leaves with high stomatal densities, thereby raising the intercellular CO_2 concentration. A first experimental test of this suggestion, by growing plants in 35% and 21% O_2, indicated that O_2 influences stomatal index (Beerling et $al.$, 1998) implying that the mechanism controlling stomatal initiation is regulated by light intensity, O_2 and CO_2

(a)

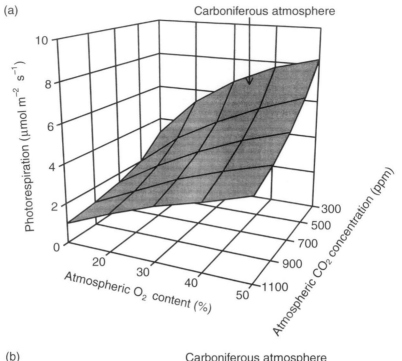

(b)

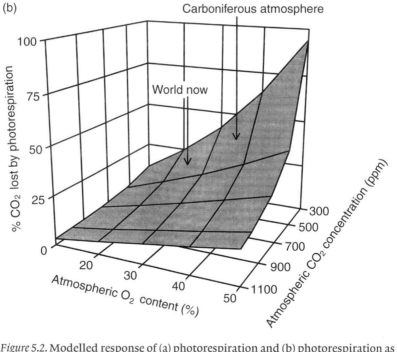

Figure 5.2. Modelled response of (a) photorespiration and (b) photorespiration as a percentage of net CO₂ fixed by photosynthesis, in response to changes in the concentration of atmospheric CO₂ and O₂ at 25 °C. Photosynthetic and environmental variables as in Fig. 5.1.

concentrations. Regardless of the mechanism, the functional consequences of this change in leaf structure for plants operating in the late Carboniferous are now explored in greater detail.

The analysis begins by investigating the effect of increasing leaf stomatal densities on photosynthesis and intercellular CO_2 concentrations (Fig. 5.3) at an atmospheric CO_2 partial pressure of 30 Pa (Berner, 1994) and at present-day (21%) and Carboniferous (35%) O_2 concentrations. These simulations show that as leaf stomatal density increases, the corresponding increase in photosynthesis is asymptotic (Fig. 5.3a), a response similar to that reported from experimental studies (Woodward & Bazzaz, 1988). Assuming the modelling to be realistic, there appears to be little advantage to be gained by plants, in terms of photosynthetic CO_2 fixation, in developing leaves with a stomatal density above 300 mm^{-2} given the stomatal pore lengths, widths and diffusion depths used here (Fig. 5.3). Information on the stomatal densities of Carboniferous vegetation, reviewed by Beerling & Woodward (1997), supports this prediction, the most common densities being between 100 and 300 mm^{-2}. Stomatal density measurements of Carboniferous plants have mostly been reported from pteridosperm leaves, representing only a small proportion of forests, and additional fossil data would be useful.

A consideration of the high O_2/low CO_2 impact of the Carboniferous on plant function must include the processes of both stomatal conductance and photosynthesis to gain some measure of their influence on the carbon and water balance of leaves. Leaves with high stomatal densities have proportionally higher photosynthetic rates and intercellular CO_2 partial pressures (Fig. 5.4a), the latter helping to reduce photorespiration. However, the penalty of increasing leaf stomatal density is a c. 75% increase in stomatal conductance to water vapour, assuming no concomitant changes in pore length with density (Fig. 5.4b). On calculating the instantaneous leaf water-use efficiency (photosynthesis divided by stomatal conductance) (Fig. 5.4c) it becomes clear that plants in a Carboniferous atmosphere must have operated at times with a rather poor water economy, depending on the regulation of transpiration by stomatal responses to the environment and the aerodynamic coupling between the canopy and the atmosphere. Water supply to the roots is unlikely to be limiting for vegetation which grew in mire conditions, but the ability of the water-conducting tissues to deliver that water to actively photosynthesising tissues in arborescent lycopods, sometimes over 40 m in height, must have been critical. Measurements of xylem conductivity and the ratio of xylem to non-xylem tissue (i.e. number of xylem strands) in fossil plants show an increase in conductivity from the late Silurian into the Devonian (Knoll & Niklas, 1987). No further increases have been found, moving from the

(a)

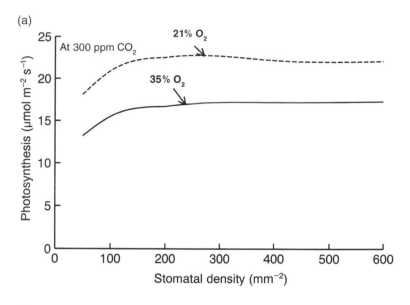

(b)

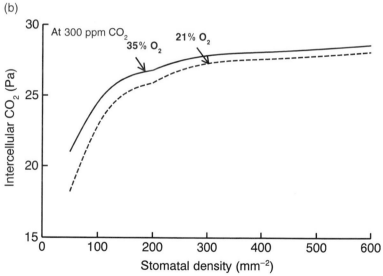

Figure 5.3. Effect of increasing stomatal density on (a) the rate of leaf photosynthesis and (b) leaf intercellular CO_2 concentrations at two concentrations of O_2. Photosynthetic and environmental conditions were as given in Fig. 5.1, but with 50% relative humidity and assuming a stomatal pore length of 10 μm, maximum aperture width of 5 μm and diffusion depth pathway of 15 μm. Simulations were made using the model described by Beerling & Woodward (1997).

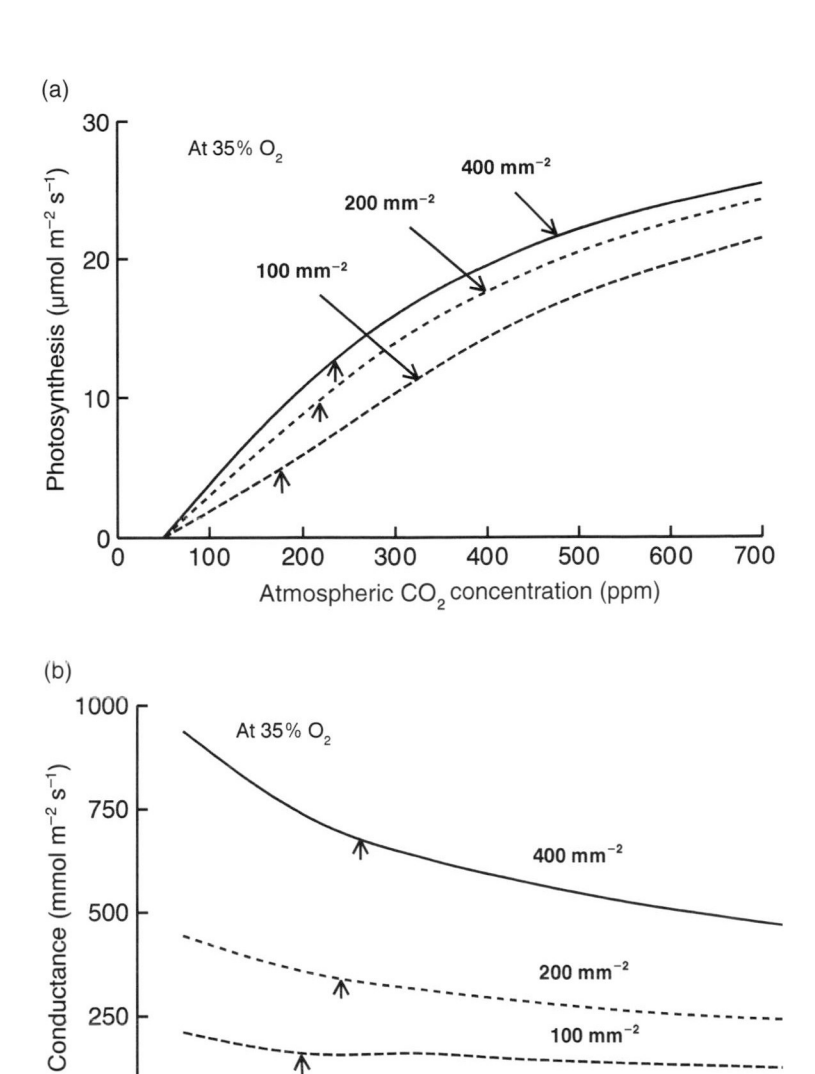

Figure 5.4. The impact of stomatal density on (a) the net rate of photosynthesis, (b) stomatal conductance and (c) instantaneous water-use efficiency (photosynthesis/stomatal conductance) across a range of atmospheric CO_2 concentrations. The photosynthetic and environmental conditions are as given in Fig. 5.3. Vertical arrows indicate intercellular CO_2 concentrations.

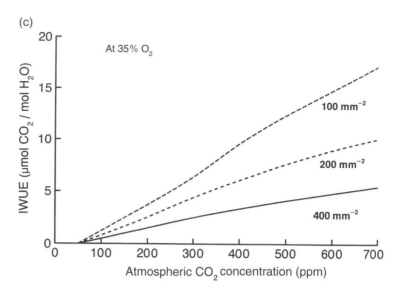

Figure 5.4. (cont.)

Devonian into the Carboniferous and through the Jurassic, based on xylomet-ric analyses of fossils (Cichan, 1986; Niklas, 1985). Therefore, a combination of limited xylem conductivity and high stomatal density may have resulted in strong selection pressure for xeromorphic structures (linear rather than broad leaves, cuticularised leaves, sunken stomata with over-arching papillae) recorded from Carboniferous plant fossils (Spicer, 1989a).

Photosynthesis and plant growth in the late Carboniferous

Figures 5.3 and 5.4 demonstrate a depression of C_3 photosynthesis by *c.* 30–40% by the high O_2 of the late Carboniferous atmosphere compared with the present-day. Simulations of the response of photosynthesis to a range of intercellular CO_2 concentrations (the A/c_i response) confirm this suggestion (Fig. 5.5). Whilst the atmospheric O_2 content is predicted to have been higher than present at other times in the geological history of land plants (Berner & Canfield, 1989), the impact of the Carboniferous high O_2 event would have been exacerbated by the low atmospheric CO_2 concentration at the time. This effect is illustrated in Fig. 5.5 which denotes by vertical arrows the calculated intercellular CO_2 concentrations for the atmospheric values representative of several geological intervals. With an atmospheric CO_2 concentration of 300 ppm, the leaf intercellular CO_2 concentration is still on the ascending portion

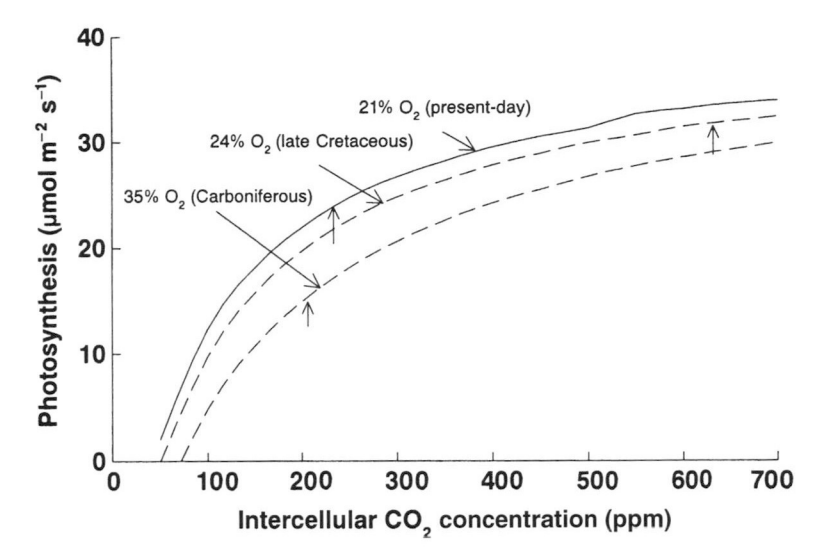

Figure 5.5. Effect of O_2 on the response of photosynthesis to a range of intercellular CO_2 concentrations. Vertical arrows indicate calculated intercellular CO_2 values from the atmospheric CO_2 concentrations predicted for each of three different time periods. Model and conditions as given in Fig. 5.1.

of the curve, i.e. the system is not yet saturated, so the effects are expected to be greater than, for example, in the late Cretaceous, where atmospheric CO_2 concentration is thought to have been higher.

Photosynthesis and growth are linked but growth responses cannot be simply modelled as a function of the response of photosynthesis. The relationship between the two can be examined by considering a simple expression linking the rate of photosynthesis to growth (Lloyd & Farquhar, 1996):

$$\frac{dM}{dt} = A(1 - \phi) \tag{5.4}$$

where M is the moles of C in the plant, t is time, A is the photosynthetic rate of the whole plant (mol C day^{-1}) and ϕ is the proportion of A lost in respiration (typically 0.3; Lloyd & Farquhar, 1996). Respiratory losses can be divided into those associated with the growth and maintenance of the existing plant biomass:

$$\phi = \phi_0 + \frac{mM}{A} \tag{5.5}$$

where ϕ_0 is the proportion of carbon lost when converting recently fixed carbon into structural biomass (0.2; Penning de Vries, 1975) and m is the maintenance respiration coefficient (mol C mol^{-1} C day^{-1}). Combining equations

5.4 and 5.5 provides a simple description of plant growth based on photosynthesis (Masle *et al.*, 1990):

$$\frac{dM}{dt} = A(1 - \phi_o)\, mM \tag{5.6}$$

Application of this equation using the photosynthetic response given in Fig. 5.5 requires a conversion from a unit leaf area basis in μmol m^{-2} s^{-1} to a plant canopy basis in mol C per canopy C day^{-1}. Here, equation 5.4 has been used to predict the growth response of a forest canopy with a leaf area index (LAI) of 5. Photosynthetic rates were calculated in response to simulated hourly values of irradiance and temperature, at a latitude of 45°, using standard meteorological equations (Jones, 1992) and integrated for a six-hour day. Each layer in the canopy is then summed to obtain mols C day^{-1}. The mean irradiance, I (mol m^{-2} s^{-1}), beneath each canopy layer was calculated from Beer's Law:

$$I = I_o e^{-k.\mathrm{LAI}} \tag{5.7}$$

where I_o is the irradiance incident on the canopy and k is the extinction coefficient (typically 0.5; Woodward, 1987a). The maintenance respiratory term in equation 5.5, mM, has then been calculated by solving equation 5.4 for mM with a ϕ_o value of 0.2 and the calculated value of A.

Adopting this procedure enables the effects of a Carboniferous atmosphere on leaf photosynthetic rates to be translated into canopy growth rates. The translation is a rather crude one, especially given that lycophytes were probably only 'leaf poles' producing a crown on reaching maturity. The resulting simulations show that a 40% lower photosynthetic rate at 35% O_2 and 30 Pa CO_2 (compared with the present-day) is translated into a 30% decrease in growth for a canopy with an LAI of 5 (Fig. 5.6a). Experimental data from growth experiments with the C_3 species *Panicum bisulcatum* grown at high O_2 (40%) show the same decrease in vegetative dry matter production (30%) (Quebedaux & Chollet, 1977) in agreement with these predictions. For this simulation, O_2 effects were calculated for a canopy with an LAI value of 5. It is not, however, clear at this stage, whether this is a realistic LAI for vegetation in the Carboniferous. Therefore, to investigate further the significance of canopy structure, the growth responses have been modelled as a function of LAI and atmospheric CO_2 (Fig. 5.6b).

It emerges from this analysis that increasing LAI above c. 3 has little effect on growth at 30 Pa. The situation improves at higher CO_2 concentrations (Fig. 5.6b), canopy growth rate increasing as LAI increases. Therefore, for plants developing leaves with high stomatal densities, and which tend to have a rather high transpiration demand, one obvious adaptation besides xeromorphy is to

(a)

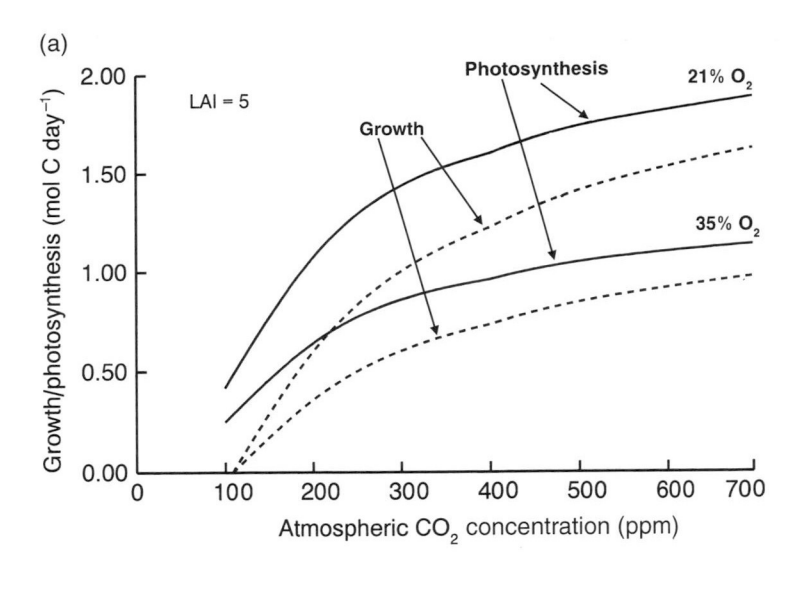

(b)

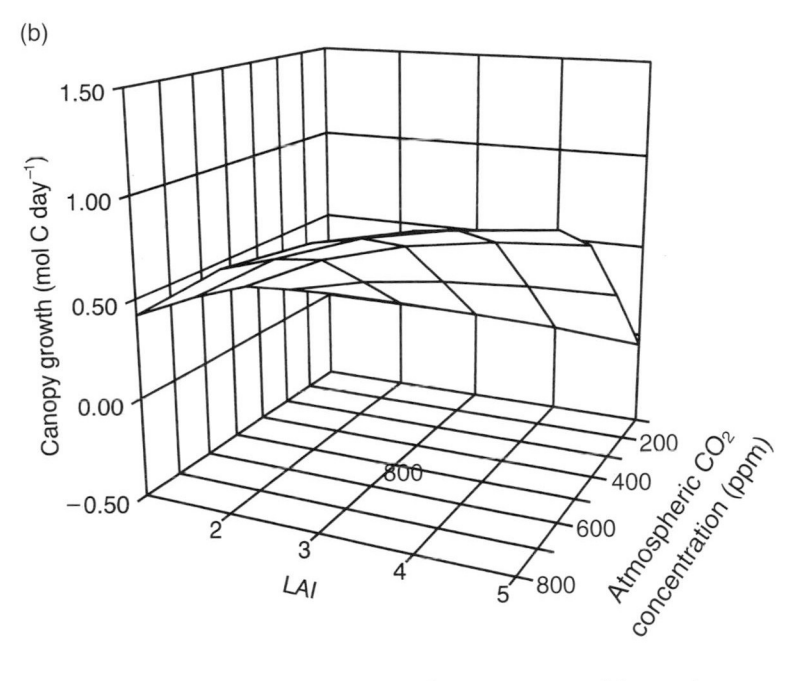

Figure 5.6. (a) Effect of O_2 on canopy growth responses at ambient and Carboniferous O_2 contents across a range of atmospheric CO_2 concentrations. Modelled using the photosynthetic responses in Fig. 5.5 and eqs. 5.4 to 5.7, (b) response of canopy growth rate to canopy structure and atmospheric CO_2 concentrations at 35% O_2.

reduce the LAI of the canopy particularly since there appears to be little expense incurred in terms of growth rate. The model results provide a physiological explanation for the idea of a rather sparse canopy. We next consider how these leaf and canopy scale responses to the unusual high O_2/low CO_2 ratio of late Carboniferous atmosphere interact with seasonal variations in climate to influence ecosystem structure and productivity at this time.

The late Carboniferous global climate

Major differences from the present in the position of the land masses existed at 300 Ma (Fig. 5.7) and for some of them movement has continued through geological time. Three key terms require definition to aid interpretation of subsequent discussions. Gondwana is taken to be the major land mass or 'super-continent' in the southern hemisphere consisting of Antarctica, Australia, South America, Africa, Madagascar, India, Arabia, Malaya and the East Indies, before their separation. The northern hemisphere 'super-continent' equivalent is Laurasia, consisting of North America, Europe, and Asia north of the Himalayas prior to their separation (Fig. 5.7). Together both Laurasia and Gondwana make up the 'super-continent' Pangaea (Whitten & Brooks, 1972). Reconstruction and analysis of the movements of land masses in the Carboniferous (Scotese & McKerrow, 1990) indicate a progressive compression from NE to SW of the major plates as Gondwana rotated clockwise; Kazakhstan had collided with Siberia but northern China continued its isolation (Fig. 5.7). The shifting position of Gondwana and the presence of the Pangaean land mass both exerted major influences on the prevailing climate in the Carboniferous (Parrish, 1993).

The Universities Global Atmospheric Modelling Programme (UGAMP) climate model (Valdes & Sellwood, 1992) simulated the global Westphalian (c. 305 Ma) Carboniferous climate with a spatial resolution of 3.75° × 3.75° (Valdes, 1993; Valdes & Crowley, 1998). This interval was near the peak of the late Carboniferous glaciation, although there is sedimentary evidence for glacial–interglacial fluctuations (Witzke, 1990). Continental positions were those used by Crowley & Baum (1994); other significant boundary conditions were a 3% lower solar luminosity, an atmospheric CO_2 partial pressure of 30 Pa (Berner, 1994) and orbital configurations of the Pleistocene interglacials (Berger, 1978). The UGAMP model does not explicitly model the oceans but instead uses prescribed sea surface temperatures based on simple energy balance model results. These sea surface temperatures are energetically consistent with the choice of CO_2 and solar constant. The model was integrated for five years, and the last two years were averaged to produce the 'Carboniferous

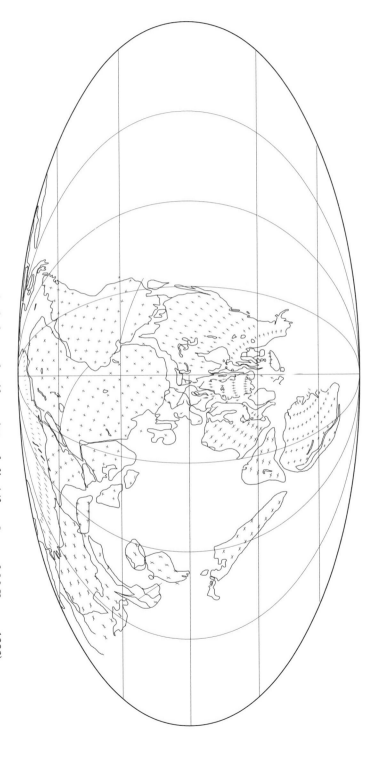

Figure 5.7. Reconstructed world map of the landmasses in the late Carboniferous (Westphalian) (from Scotese & McKerrow, 1990).

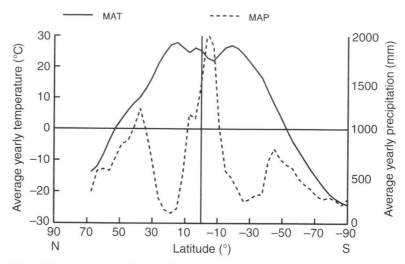

Figure 5.8. Area-weighted latitudinal averages of mean annual temperature (MAT) and mean annual precipitation (MAP) simulated by the UGAMP GCM for the late Carboniferous.

climate' consisting of monthly values of precipitation, temperature and humidity.

The resulting global climate (temperature and precipitation) datasets used for driving the SDGVM are summarised in Figures 5.8 and 5.9, which show warm mean monthly temperatures and bands of high precipitation over the northern extension of Gondwana. Where precipitation is low, there is rapid drying of the soil and negligible evaporative cooling resulting in very hot conditions. In addition, low moisture content lowers cloud cover, which results in large absorption of solar radiation and enhancement of surface temperatures (Figs. 5.8 and 5.9). Note that these maps represent a summary of the climatic datasets and give no indication of seasonality. Valdes and Crowley (1998) consider in detail a comparison of the Carboniferous climates simulated by the UGAMP model and that by the GENESIS model at the National Center for Atmospheric Research (NCAR) in Boulder, Colorado, USA. The principal differences are higher southern hemisphere summer temperatures and greater seasonal distribution in precipitation predicted by the UGAMP model compared with the GENESIS model. Nevertheless both models support the basic idea that a super-continent experienced a highly seasonal climate and, with a hot summer orbit, summer temperatures sufficient to prevent the initiation of ice sheets. Unfortunately the quality of the geological evidence for comparison with the climate model outputs, in terms of continental reconstructions, dating and interpretation of the geological indicators, precludes a rigorous evaluation of the simulated climates at this stage.

(a)

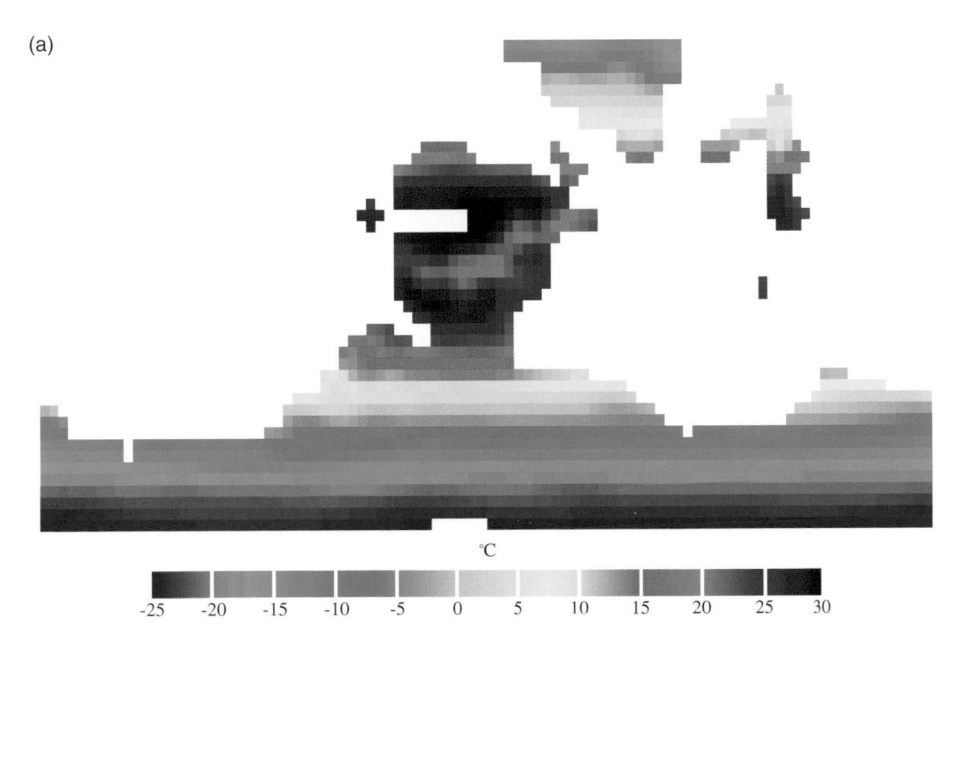

(b)

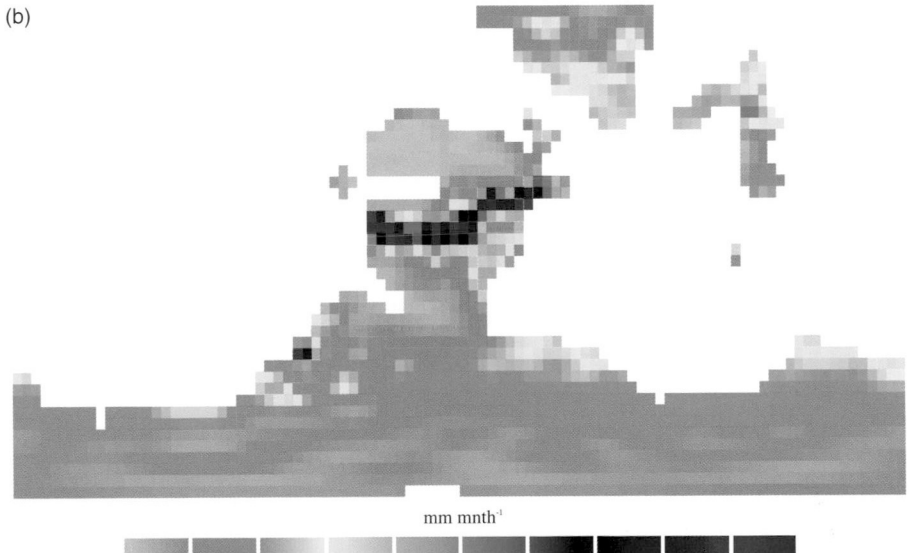

Figure 5.9. Global patterns of mean annual temperature (a) and precipitation (b) over the terrestrial grid squares for the late Carboniferous.

Global terrestrial productivity in the late Carboniferous

The modelled leaf and canopy responses to the late Carboniferous atmosphere have so far been considered in isolation from edaphic effects (i.e. soil nutrient status and soil water availability). Nevertheless, the approaches represent a useful starting point for analysing the impact of a high O_2/low CO_2 atmospheric composition on plant function and for deriving a functional interpretation of the evolution of vegetation with high stomatal densities. A global-scale analysis requires consideration of soil nutrient status and leaf area index, the latter determined from the annual carbon and hydrological budgets, and the extent to which canopy conductance feeds-back and moderates photosynthesis via soil moisture.

The equilibrium model solutions for NPP and LAI under the Carboniferous climate track the driving climatic dataset, particularly precipitation (Fig. 5.9). The global distribution of NPP shows a band of higher values than elsewhere in the land surface (Fig. 5.10b) in the central region of the northern land mass extension of Gondwana (northern Pangaea). Areas of high NPP are also predicted along the southern edge of Siberia/Kazakhstan and in parts of northern China. A similar pattern is evident for the distribution of LAI (Fig. 5.10a), vegetation biomass (Fig. 5.10b) and soils with a high carbon concentration (Fig. 5.10d). All of these areas occur in regions predicted by the climate model to have high temperatures and abundant precipitation (cf. Figs. 5.8 and 5.9). Total global NPP is 38.2 Gt C yr^{-1}, which, in comparison with the present-day situation, is rather low (see Chapter 4). Comparison of the NPP map (Fig. 5.10b) with an earlier simulation, made using a different version of the vegetation model in which the treatment of seasonality of growth and the allocation of photosynthate to roots, stems and leaves differed, shows a similar spatial distribution but different absolute values (Beerling & Woodward, 1998; Beerling *et al.*, 1998).

Comparison of model results with the geological record

The problems (dating of sediments and their climatic interpretation) encountered when attempting to test the SDGVM predictions against the geological record are similar to those encountered when testing the driving climatic dataset itself. Nevertheless, despite these reservations, the global maps of vegetation structure and function and soil C can be compared with global datasets of climatically-sensitive sediments for the late Carboniferous assembled previously (Crowley & North, 1991) (Fig. 5.11). These comparisons indicate that a band of coal deposits across northern Pangaea, throughout

Siberia/Kazakhstan and in parts of northern China, largely matches the areas of high NPP and soil carbon concentrations predicted by the modelling (Fig. 5.10). The coincidence of bands of coal and high soil C concentration patterns suggests that coal accumulation in the Carboniferous resulted from moderate productivity and slow decomposition rates.

Other lithic palaeoclimatic indicators also show several areas of agreement. Witzke (1990) recorded thick and abundant evaporites, providing clear evidence of an arid belt through northern Pangaea above the equator. Here, the vegetation modelling indicates zero potential for plant growth, in agreement with the geological record and therefore providing some support for the suggestion that the climate and vegetation simulations are adequate representations for this period, as least at the broad spatial scale considered here.

If it is assumed that modern peat-forming processes are of relevance to coal formation in the Palaeozoic and Mesozoic (Moore, 1995), then information for predicting coal distribution might be obtained from the extent of waterlogging in late Carboniferous soils. This is because modern peat-forming systems require an excess of precipitation over transpiration (i.e. waterlogging) for incomplete decomposition and the accumulation of residual organic material (Moore, 1995). Therefore, a general approach to predicting coal formation, in tandem with model estimates of soil C concentration, has been to examine site water balance, defined as the difference between the annual totals of incoming precipitation and outgoing evapotranspiration (water loss from soils and vegetation surfaces) (Beerling, 2000b). The results (Fig. 5.12) show a considerable reduction in the possible geographical extent of coal formation, and predict almost exclusively areas of coal formation matching those recorded in the geological record (compare Figs. 5.11 and 5.12), providing further support for the model simulations.

As an additional quantitative test of the modelled soil C estimates, the total soil C predicted for Euramerica (north land mass of Pangaea) has been calculated and compared with calculations based on coal reserves for this region (A.C. Scott, personal communication). Total soil C storage for this region is modelled to be 108 Gt C yr^{-1} (Fig. 5.10). A.C. Scott estimates that the Upper Carboniferous coal reserves for Euramerica are between 400 and 4000 Gt C and that *c.* 20% of this material is probably of Westphalian B age, based on commercial figures from oil companies. Since coals are typically *c.* 70% C, this gives a calculated soil C storage for Euramerica of 56–560 Gt C. Although the errors are necessarily large, the predicted soil C storage lies within this range.

Extensive glaciogenic sediments record evidence for a southern hemisphere ice sheet extending from Argentina across south-central Africa to Madagascar, India, Antarctica and Australia, although the spatial extent is uncertain

(a)

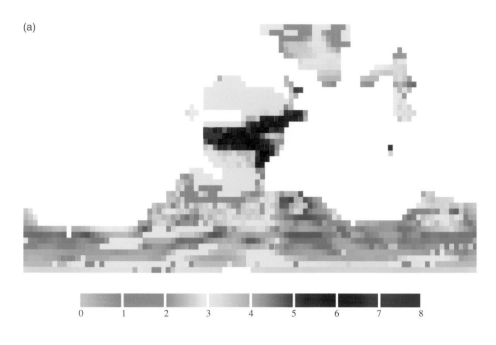

(b)

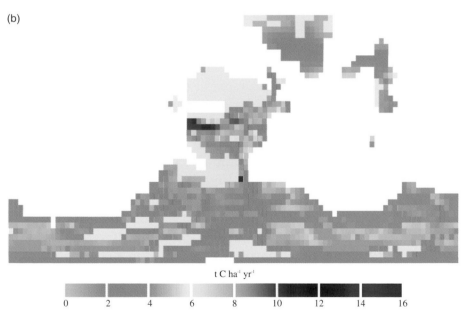

t C ha⁻¹ yr⁻¹

Figure 5.10. Modelled global patterns of (a) leaf area index (LAI), (b) net primary productivity (NPP), (c) vegetation biomass and (d) soil C concentration in the late Carboniferous.

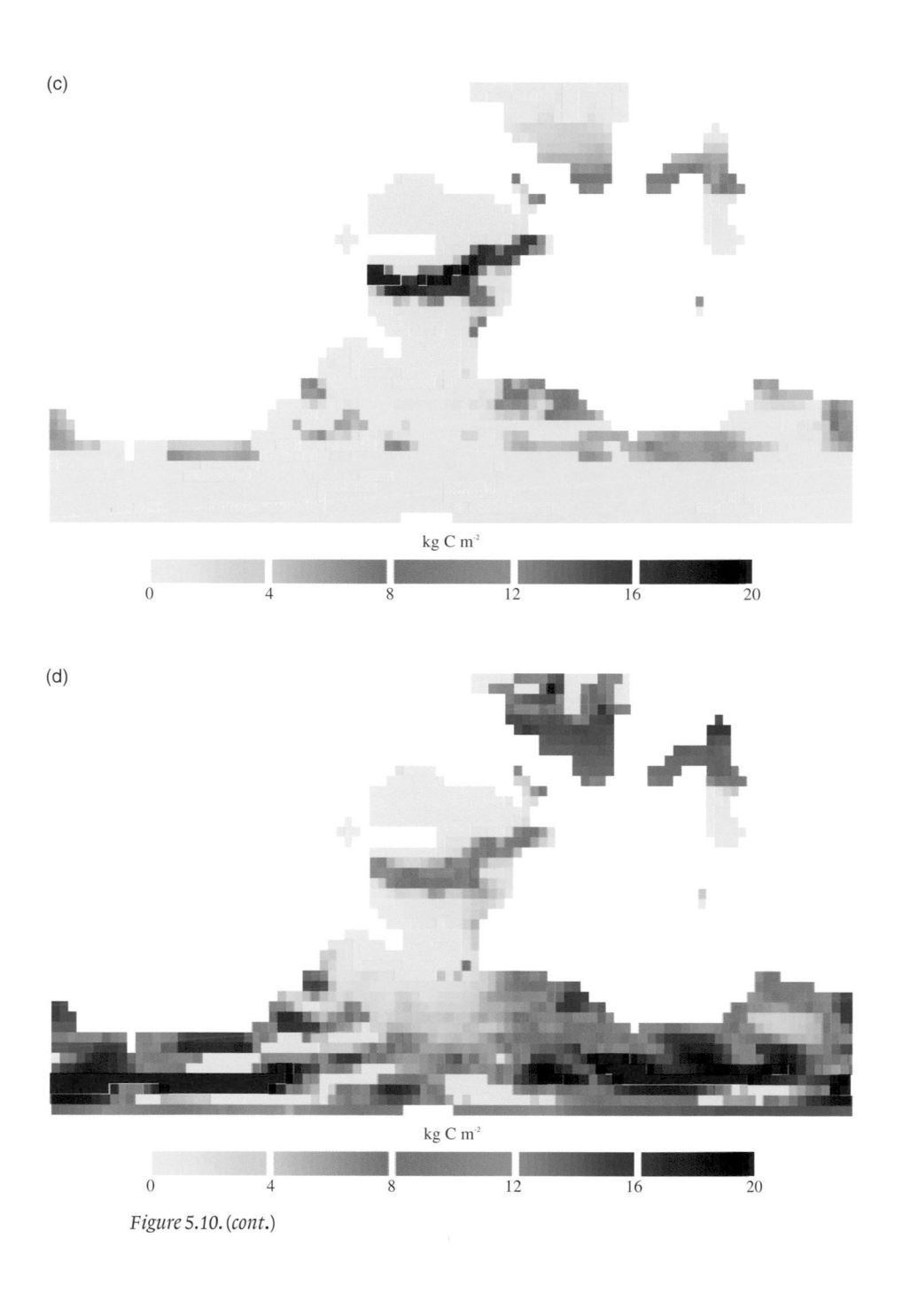

Figure 5.10. (cont.)

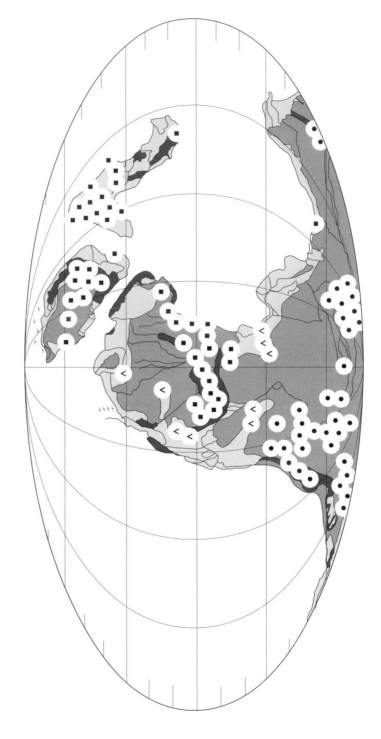

Figure 5.11. Global distribution of climatically-sensitive sediments in the late Carboniferous (from Crowley & Baum, 1994). ●, tillites (glacial deposits); ■, coal deposits (high moisture regions); Λ, evaporites (low moisture regions); dark shading, highlands; medium shading, lowlands; light shading, continental shelf.

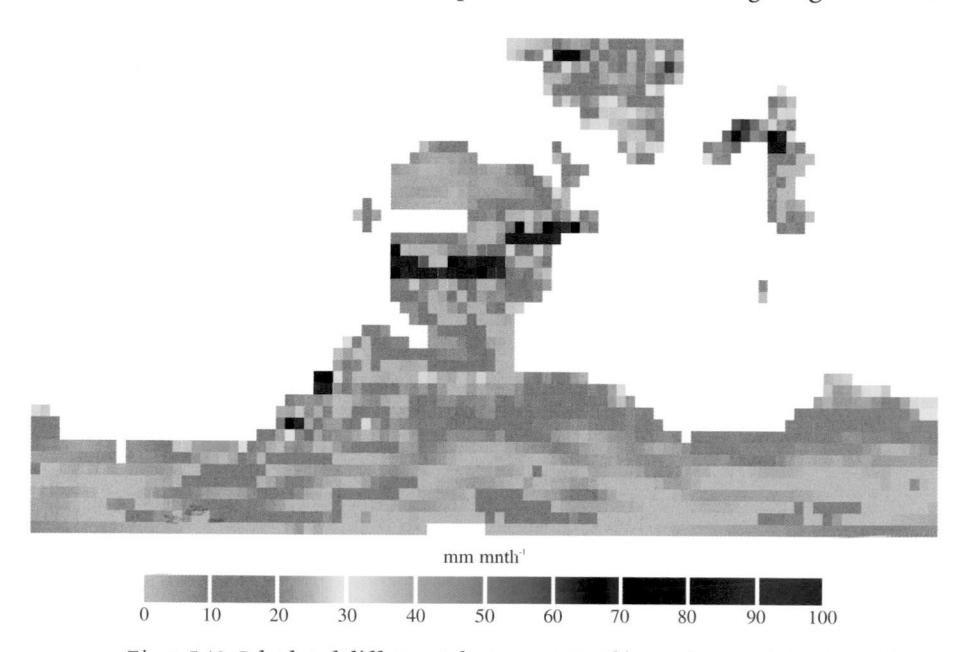

mm mnth⁻¹

| 0 | 10 | 20 | 30 | 40 | 50 | 60 | 70 | 80 | 90 | 100 |

Figure 5.12. Calculated differences between annual incoming precipitation and outgoing water loss from soils and vegetation surfaces (evapotranspiration).

(Crowley & Baum, 1991). Therefore, the simulated low productivity (1–2 t C ha⁻¹ yr⁻¹) of these regions is unlikely to have been realised (Fig. 5.10). This discrepancy between the predictions of models and data may indicate one area where the GCM and/or vegetation model is not simulating realistic climates or responses at high latitudes in the southern hemisphere. Some of the largest differences between climate model simulations of Carboniferous climates occur in the polar regions of the southern hemisphere, indicating potential difficulties with the climate models (Valdes & Crowley, 1998). However, in support of the NPP predictions for the southern hemisphere, Chaloner and Lacey (1973) reported the general coincidence of late Carboniferous/early Permian *Glossopteris* floras over high latitudes previously covered by ice, particularly around the margins of Antarctica and South America, indicating the occurrence of small regions of positive terrestrial productivity. There have also been reports of *Botrychiopsis* tundra, a type of low diversity scrub in parts of Australia and South America (C. Cleal, personal communication).

An alternative physiology-based approach to model testing is to compare ecophysiological attributes of the plants predicted by the model with those calculated and constrained by evidence from the fossil record. In this case, maximum rates of carboxylation (V_{max}) have been compared with two estimates based on the stable carbon isotope composition ($\delta^{13}C_p$) of fossil plant materials. V_{max} estimates for two localities (UK and USA) have been obtained from the fossil $\delta^{13}C_p$ values by solving equation 2.10 (Chapter 2) for intercellular CO_2 concentration (c_i) using an estimate of the atmospheric CO_2 concentration at the time the fossils grew (300 ppm), an estimate of its isotopic composition from the ocean carbonate record ($-1‰$) and an estimate of A_{max} taken from the calculated photosynthetic rate for a leaf with a stomatal density of c. 200 mm^{-2} (mean of all available observations on Carboniferous fossil leaves) at 35% O_2 and 300 ppm CO_2 (15 μmol CO_2 m^{-2} s^{-1}). The Farquhar *et al.* model of photosynthesis can then be solved for V_{max} (Beerling & Quick, 1995), and although the approach is not entirely independent of the model calculations it nevertheless offers a means of testing the predictions of vegetation activity initialised by the fossil record. This approach provides estimates of V_{max} representing the mean of vegetation activity over the growing season and is corrected for growing season temperatures. Given isotopic values of organic matter from the UK (Jones, 1994) and the USA (Mora *et al.*, 1996) of $-24.1‰$ and $-23.6‰$ (see Fig. 5.7), this approach gives V_{max} values of 52 and 54 μmol m^{-2} s^{-1} – similar to those computed independently of the fossil evidence for these regions (Fig. 5.13).

The impact of O_2 on global terrestrial productivity and C storage

The impact of 35% O_2 on NPP, LAI and soil C was assessed with a second model run using the same Carboniferous climate dataset but with the present-day O_2 content of 21%. The difference between the 21% and 35% O_2 runs represents the effects of O_2 on the structural and/or functional attribute under investigation. A positive difference indicates a limitation at 35% O_2. In general, the globally mapped differences are positive, indicating that the high O_2 content was limiting LAI, NPP and soil C (Fig. 5.14). Higher NPP, in this case, leads to greater storage of C in the biomass of vegetation (Table 5.1). The limitation on NPP and LAI occurs mainly through the representation of the effects of O_2 on rubisco function in the leaf gas exchange sub-model. Any change in LAI results from changes in the seasonal course of rates of CO_2 fixation and loss of water via transpiration in a high O_2 atmosphere.

At 21% O_2, canopy conductance is typically higher than at 35% O_2, because of higher photosynthetic rates and lower intercellular CO_2 partial pressure. Higher canopy conductances lead to higher rates of canopy transpiration under the same climate, but as long as this is less than or balances the available precipitation, the LAI increases in concert with CO_2 assimilation. This response is most typical (Fig. 5.14). In some areas LAI and NPP show small decreases at 21% O_2 relative to 35% O_2 (Fig. 5.14), owing to increases in evapotranspiration.

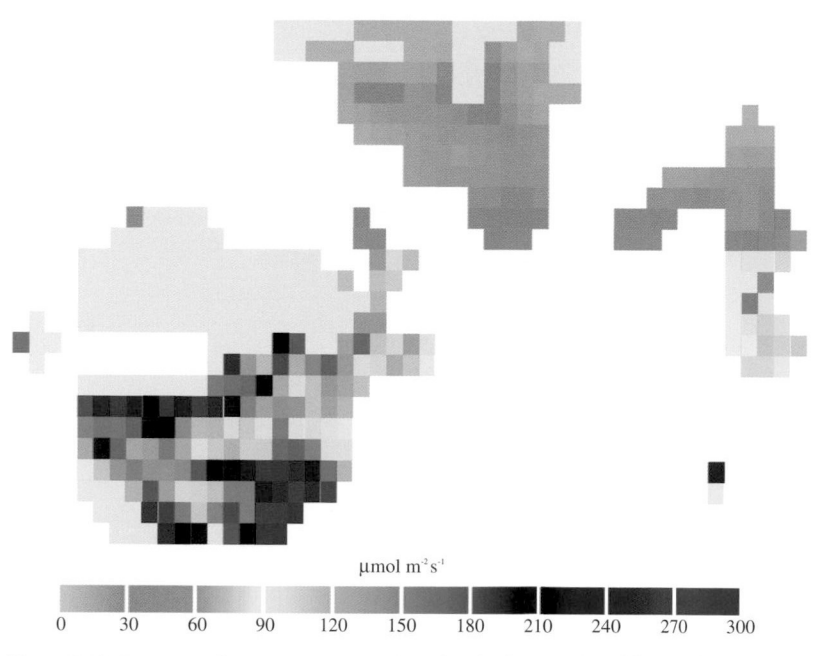

μmol m⁻²s⁻¹

0   30   60   90   120   150   180   210   240   270   300

Figure 5.13. Patterns of growing season V_{max} for the late Carboniferous landmasses of Euramerica, Laurasia and Kazakhstan.

Global NPP at 21% O_2 was *c.* 20% greater than under the Carboniferous maximum of 35% O_2 (Table 5.1). Generally, higher soil C concentrations at 21% O_2 concentration occur (Fig. 5.14d, Table 5.1) because of the greater accumulation of litter from vegetation with higher productivity. Analysis on a pixel by pixel basis shows that the magnitude of the NPP changes at 21% O_2 was climatically dependent (i.e. sites with a favourable climate show the greatest response to a decrease in O_2 content). The predicted carbon storage in live vegetation biomass at 35% O_2 (Table 5.1) is less than half the speculative estimate of Moore (1983), based on present-day figures of global biomass in swamp forests (1148 Gt) projected back into the past using reconstructions of the areal extent of swamp forests in the late Carboniferous. However, his tentative first estimates took no account of O_2 effects on rubisco, an important feature to include quantitatively in such calculations (Table 5.1). Nevertheless is it important to remember, in the context of earlier discussions, that the operation of rubisco is dependent upon the CO_2 to O_2 ratio of the atmosphere and climate. Uncertainty in the background CO_2 concentration will necessarily lead to uncertainty in the predicted response of the terrestrial biosphere to a high O_2 excursion (Beerling & Berner, 2000). If, for example, the background late Carboniferous CO_2 concentration was towards the upper limit predicted by geochemical models (600 ppm), high O_2 effects on NPP and carbon storage in vegetation become strongly attenuated (Beerling & Berner, 2000).

(a)

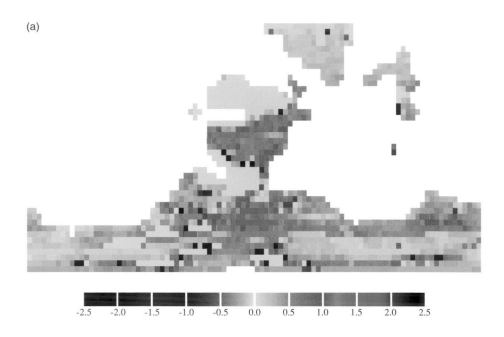

(b)

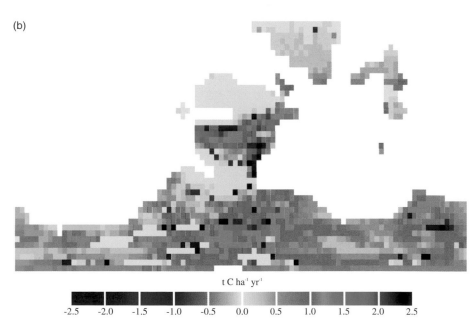

t C ha⁻¹ yr⁻¹

Figure 5.14. Difference maps of the effects of a rise in atmospheric O_2 content from 21% to 35% on (a) LAI, (b) NPP, (c) vegetation biomass, and (d) soil C concentration.

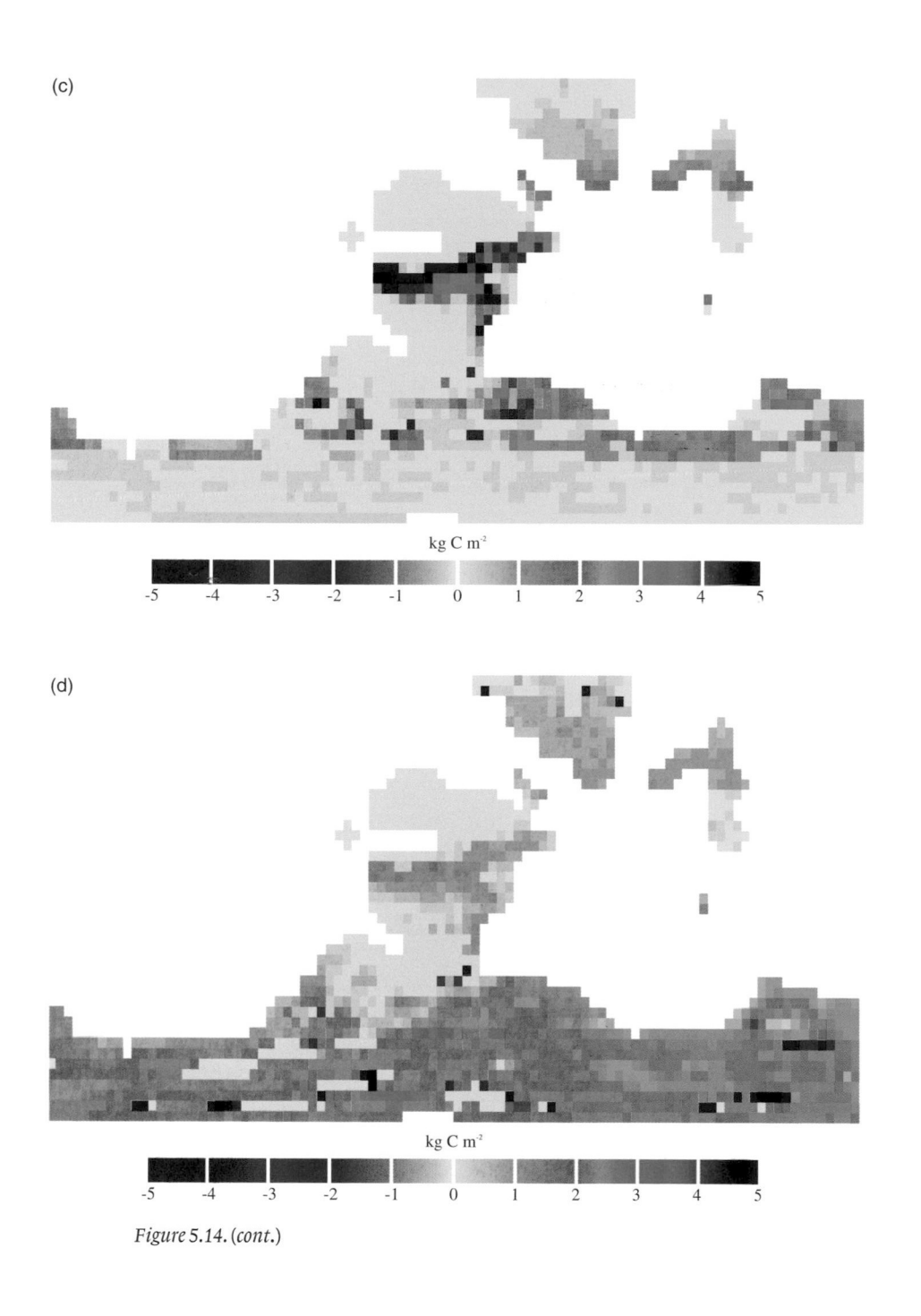

Figure 5.14. (cont.)

Table 5.1. *Net and gross terrestrial primary productivity (NPP and GPP) and carbon storage in vegetation and soils in the late Carboniferous*

Global totals (Gt yr^{-1})	Atmospheric oxygen content	
	35% O_2	21% O_2
Terrestrial NPP	38.2	45.8
Terrestrial GPP	92.5	111.9
Soil carbon	887.9	1026.9
Vegetation carbon	365.2	512.7

Decomposition rates and C storage in terrestrial ecosystems

Robinson (1990a,b) suggested that the increased dominance of taxa with a high lignin content resulted in a 'bottleneck' of the decomposition of refractory organic compounds, based on extensive Palaeozoic records of fungal spores showing low numbers of basidiomycete species in the Carboniferous and their relative proliferation in later geological periods. Taken at face value, it seems unlikely that micro-organisms would have been unable to evolve the complex biochemical pathways required for lignin degradation, especially given their short generation times and the time interval concerned (several million years). Nevertheless, the effect of this potential 'bottleneck' has been specifically investigated by reducing the rate of decomposition of both the surface litter and root litter components of the Century soil nutrient cycling model (Chapter 4) by 50% and 75% of the unchanged rates, respectively.

As might be expected, reductions in surface and root litter decomposition rates increase soil C storage (Table 5.2). There is also an associated decrease in NPP because as the soils become more C-rich the rate of nitrogen uptake to the plant is reduced thereby limiting growth (Chapter 3). Neither simulation showed any changes in the geographical pattern of soil C concentrations. The conclusion from this simple modelling exercise is that Robinson's (1990a,b) hypothesis, according to our simulations, is not essential for obtaining high carbon burial rates or global patterns consistent with the distribution of late Carboniferous coals. However, quantitative tests of the results beyond those described earlier are difficult since figures of global coal reserves are not available because coals are classified by type, rather than age, in the coal industry.

Table 5.2. *The impact of reduced surface and root litter decomposition rates on net and gross terrestrial primary productivity (NPP and GPP) and carbon storage in vegetation and soils for the late Carboniferous*

Global totals (Gt yr^{-1})	Decomposition rates (% of unchanged rate)	
	75%	50%
Terrestrial NPP	37.8	36.8
Terrestrial GPP	91.4	89.7
Soil carbon	921.6	986.9
Vegetation carbon	351.6	331.3

C$_3$ and C$_4$ plant distribution in the Carboniferous

The paucity of the fossil record makes it difficult to trace the possible evolutionary origins of the C$_4$ photosynthetic pathway (Moore, 1983; Wright & Vanstone, 1991; Raven & Spicer, 1996). Nevertheless, the kinetic characteristics of PEP versus rubisco clearly indicate the potential for 35% O$_2$ to impact less on rates of leaf photosynthesis for plants with the C$_4$ photosynthetic pathway compared with those with the C$_3$ pathway (Collatz *et al.*, 1992, 1998). This potential occurs because leaf photosynthesis with the C$_4$ pathway saturates at a much lower concentration of CO$_2$ than that of C$_3$ plants, becauses of the higher affinity of PEP carboxylase for CO$_2$. Based on these core physiological mechanisms, the functional type model (Chapter 4) has been used to predict the potential distribution of C$_3$ and C$_4$ plants at the global scale in the Carboniferous (Fig. 5.15).

The resulting distribution patterns, based on percentage cover of a given pixel, indicate that regions of highest productivity are associated with stands of near 100% C$_3$ plants, particularly in Laurasia and through central Gondwana (compare Fig. 5.15 with Fig. 5.10b). The potential for C$_4$ plants to exist and out-compete C$_3$ plants occurs at low latitudes of southern Gondwana in parallel with strong climatic seasonality, expressed as several months of sub-zero temperatures followed by two months of high summer temperatures. In these regions, the GCM simulates a short but hot (monthly temperatures in excess of 27 °C) growing season favouring the development of plants with C$_4$ photosynthesis (Collatz *et al.*, 1998) over C$_3$ shrubs and trees. It is interesting to speculate whether these regions represent early sites of C$_4$ evolution and Fig. 5.15 indicates the potential for the evolution of C$_4$ photosynthesis before its oldest-dated discovery in Miocene plant fossil record (Thomasson *et al.*, 1988). An important

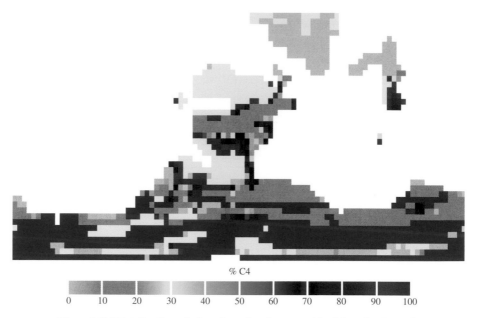

% C4

| 0 | 10 | 20 | 30 | 40 | 50 | 60 | 70 | 80 | 90 | 100 |

Figure 5.15. Distribution of plant functional types with either the C₃ or the C₄ pathway of photosynthesis in the late Carboniferous, expressed as a percentage of C₄ in a given pixel after a simulation for 400 years.

caveat relating to this map is that the continued sub-zero temperatures of southern Gondwana may have led to the development of extensive ice sheets (Crowley & Baum, 1991), the physical presence of which would have diminished, but not removed entirely, the extent of land area favouring C₄ plants.

Fire and late Carboniferous terrestrial ecosystems

As indicated earlier, an atmospheric O_2 concentration of 35% for the Carboniferous is not readily reconcilable with the current available experimental evidence for O_2 effects on the combustion of plant material. The experiments of Watson *et al.* (1978), determining the minimum energy required to ignite plant fuel, suggest that atmospheric O_2 levels between 25 and 35% may be incompatible with the existence of land-based vegetation (Chaloner, 1989), indicating some discrepancy between the experimental and observational data. Wildfire, initiated by both lightning strikes and volcanic activity, was frequent in the Carboniferous, as shown by the abundance of fusian (now more or less accepted to be fossil charcoal and so the product of wildfire; Chaloner, 1989) in Carboniferous coals and sediments of Euramerica (Scott & Jones, 1994; Falcon-Lang, 1998), yet they were evidently not as common or as widespread as would be predicted by the data of Watson *et al.* (1978). A further, as yet untested, possibility is that plant growth under high

O_2 may alter the chemical and/or structural nature of the tissues, and that this altered structure may be more resistant to burning and decay, a parallel example being the growth of plants at high CO_2 altering the C:N ratio of leaves. Experiments on plant growth and the combustion of plant tissues which developed at high O_2 concentrations are now warranted to investigate the incompatibility between fossil and current data.

In the absence of these high O_2 experiments and burning trials, a final global-scale analysis is described where the relative water content of the surface litter and soils layer is used to predict the annual probability of fires. Two key features, in conjunction with climate, are critical in determining the occurrence of fires: litter dryness and litter quantity (Johnson & Gutsell, 1994). A very simple approach has been taken to modelling fires in the SDGVM, based on previous work (Beerling et al., 1998).

First, an empirical fire climatic index (fci) is computed from monthly rainfall, temperature and litter water content. The values of this index were tuned to closely match fire return intervals (fri) observed under the present-day climate and CO_2 concentration. The relationship between fci and fri has next been determined, for the present-day climate and atmospheric composition, by correlating model predictions at particular sites and regions for which there are published data (Archibold, 1995), and is given by:

$$fri = 7.24182e^{(4.937 fci)} - 9.4399 \qquad (5.8)$$

The probability of fire (fprob) is given by modification of a previously described fire probability function (Beerling et al., 1998):

$$fprob = 1.0 - e^{\left(\frac{-1}{fri}\right)} \qquad (5.9)$$

Global-scale predictions of fire return intervals have then been made over the period 1970–1980 and successfully tested against observations from a separate source (Olson, 1981), providing some support for the empirical approach adopted here.

A further consideration is the impact of high atmospheric O_2 content on ignition probabilities (Watson et al., 1978.) Therefore equation 5.9 has been modified to include the effects of 35% O_2 (fprob(35% O_2)) using the data of Watson et al. (1978) giving a new relationship:

$$fprob\ (35\%\ O_2) = 1.261 \times fprob1^{0.314} \qquad (5.10)$$

Using this approach, it is possible to model, at the global scale, the annual probability of fire in the litter layer of soils for the late Carboniferous, with and without the direct effects of high O_2 on combustion (Fig. 5.16). When O_2 effects are excluded (eq. 5.9), fire probabilities are uniformly rather low, with a 10 to

20% chance of fire almost everywhere; equivalent to a fire once every $c.$ 5–10 years. Although such a probability is difficult to estimate it is also difficult to test against palaeodata. Nevertheless, fire return intervals have been estimated for the upper Carboniferous based on the repeated occurrence of fossil charcoal in sediments of this age. Given an assumed sedimentation rate for this site, estimates of fire return intervals are 6–70 years for the upper Carboniferous in Nova Scotia, Canada – a value compatible with Fig. 5.16a (Falcon-Lang, 2000).

Inclusion of the direct effects of O_2 considerably increases the probability of fire (Fig. 5.16b), some regions showing a 60% chance of fire within a year. Note that the model only predicts fires in the soil litter layer; lightning ignition of foliage, rather than leaf litter, is not considered, neither are predictions made of the proportion of a given pixel which would burn or the duration and intensity of a fire. The rather high probability of fire in this case, however, does seem incompatible with the development of large mature arborescent lycopods in Carboniferous swamp ecosystems (Scott, 1978, 1979; DiMichele & Hook, 1992; Falcon-Lang & Scott, 2000). Because charcoal is abundant in European and North American Carboniferous deposits it has been possible to estimate the fire return intervals for some tropical plant communities at this time by examining the vertical spacing of charcoal layers in coals, assuming a rate of peat accumalation and degree of compaction (Falcon-Lang, 2000). Estimated in this way, early Carboniferous gymnosperms of tropical climates were subjected to quite high fire frequency events (3–35 yr) and may represent ecosystems analogous to modern seasonal tropical savannas. In the late Carboniferous, however, the dense lowland lepidodendrid forests experienced infrequent fires, with return times of around 105 to 1085 years, a situation similar to that of forest fires in modern rainforests (with fire return times of 389 to 1540 years) (Falcon-Lang, 2000).

The inclusion of O_2 on fire probability also impacts directly on ecosystem structure by changing the dominance of different plant functional types. Increased fire frequency removes tall long-lived trees and shrubs and allows their replacement by shorter shrubs. In this case, C_4 shrubs have a higher productivity than C_3 trees and shrubs and consequently increase in dominance. This shift in functional types is reflected by a marked reduction in global totals of C storage in live vegetation biomass from 365 Gt C yr^{-1} with the unadjusted fire routines to just 47 Gt C yr^{-1} with the increased O_2 probabilities.

It should be recognised that our predictions of fire return interval say nothing about the probability of a fire spreading (i.e. fire behaviour) and leaving significant charcoal deposits in the fossil record. Besides fire frequency, taphonomic considerations will also be important in this context as well as the potential for evolutionary selection of characteristics that retard ignition. The O_2 experiments on burning, that we have attempted to use as a basis for our

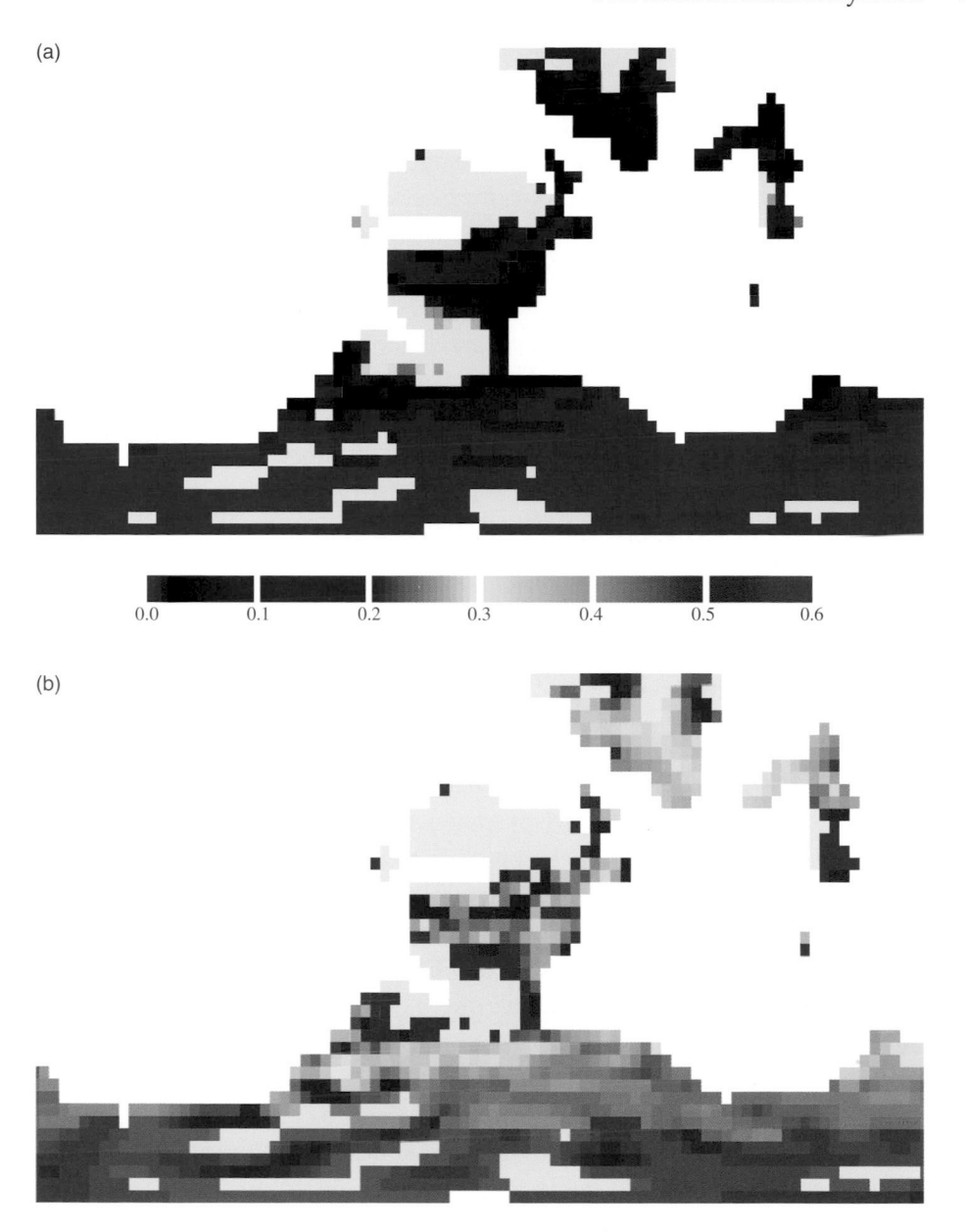

Figure 5.16. Global patterns of annual fire probability in the late Carboniferous (a) made without any inclusion of high O_2 effects (eq. 5.9) and (b) with the modifications allowing inclusion of 35% O_2 effects.

numerical simulations, considered the probability of fuel (paper strips) igniting under different levels of O_2 (Watson *et al.*, 1978). How representative this type of fuel is for actual forest fires has been strongly questioned (Robinson, 1989). In fact, besides appropriate controls on fuel type, critical to the development of forest fires is whether, at O_2 levels above a given value, a fire is uncontrollable (i.e. easily spread). Quantifying realistically the relationship between atmosphere O_2 and fire dynamics (ignition, spread, etc.) is important and a goal that has not yet been adequately achieved. The importance is two-fold. First, because fire–climate–vegetation dynamics strongly influence the development of ecosystem structure at this time, our interpretation of processes leading to the vegetation of Carboniferous (and indeed throughout much of the Mesozoic) is limited. Second, because fire has been proposed, on the basis of earlier burning experiments with paper strips, to regulate atmospheric O_2 over millions of years (Lenton & Watson, 2000). The negative feedback regulation of Lenton & Watson (2000) operates so that as the atmospheric O_2 content exceeds present-day levels, fire frequency increases, suppressing vegetation cover and reducing carbon burial on land. In addition, the loss of vegetation reduces plant-mediated phosphorus weathering of rocks thereby reducing nutrient input to the oceans and carbon burial there. Testing of this hypothesised feedback mechanism requires improved empirical data describing O_2–fire interactions. Clearly this is an area of study worthy of further investigation.

Conclusions

This chapter has investigated the likely impact of the late Carboniferous atmosphere and climate on the functioning of terrestrial plants and vegetation at a variety of spatial scales. Molecular-scale effects are considered through the competition of CO_2 and O_2 molecules for rubisco binding sites and how this competitive interaction influences the extent of photorespiration, canopy growth and, ultimately, terrestrial net primary productivity. Global productivity in the late Carboniferous was probably lower than the present day as a consequence of the high atmospheric O_2 concentration, rather than climate (Table 5.1).

The global simulations of vegetation structure and function show some compatibility with the limited palaeodata for the late Carboniferous, supporting the adequacy of the global climate model and the SDGVM to operate in the distant past. Coal accumulation in the Carboniferous resulted from markedly waterlogged conditions, particularly in equatorial regions, but with low net primary productivity (Fig. 5.10). We find no need to invoke a reduction in decomposition rates to account for high C burial rates in the late Carboniferous (Table 5.2). There was some suggestion from the models that plants with the C_4 photosynthetic pathway could dominate areas of the southern hemisphere (Fig. 5.15), depending on the extent of the glaciation, supporting palaeobotanical arguments that plants may have had this pathway since the Silurian. The inclusion of fire in the vegetation model remains a difficult issue requiring further experimental data.

6

The Jurassic

Introduction

By the late Jurassic, present-day plant groups had begun to appear and terrestrial floras were composed predominantly of woody gymnosperm groups and herbaceous pteridophytes (Wing & Sues, 1992). Generally, the climate was warm and equable, in the sense of an Earth with a more even latitudinal distribution of temperatures, and ice-free poles (Valdes *et al.*, 1996) with high latitude floras. Seasonal aridity occurred at middle to low latitudes, particularly in southern Eurasia (Hallam, 1984, 1985, 1993) and parts of northern Europe (Parrish, 1993). The geochemical models considered previously predict an atmospheric CO_2 concentration of 1800 ppm (Berner, 1994) and an O_2 content of 22% (Berner & Canfield, 1989), a combination that would be expected to produce very low rates of photorespiration and high photosynthetic productivity. There is, however, some uncertainty surrounding the changes in the concentration of atmospheric CO_2 at the boundary between the Triassic and Jurassic (T–J boundary) (Hallam & Wignall, 1997) and this represents a time suitable for investigation by the study of stomatal characters of fossil leaves (McElwain *et al.*, 1999). These authors studied the fossilised remains of terrestrial vegetation spanning the T–J boundary from plant beds in Sweden and Greenland, with the aim of reconstructing past changes in atmospheric CO_2. Given the importance of palaeo-CO_2 reconstructions, especially for the T–J boundary with its absence of oceanic sedimentary geochemical records, this chapter begins by illustrating in more detail the palaeo-CO_2 estimation from fossil leaves and its implications for the survival of different taxa, based on ecophysiological considerations.

The late Jurassic represents the first of several periods described in this book where simulations of vegetation activity are required at CO_2 concentrations above present (cf. Berner, 1994, 1997). Therefore, before considering global-scale analyses of late Jurassic climatic effects on vegetation, the

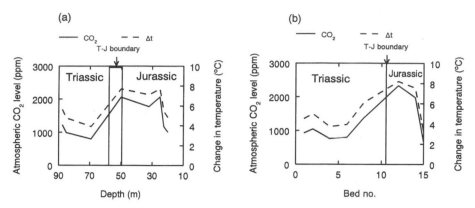

Figure 6.1. Reconstructed changes in atmospheric CO_2 and global mean temperature across the Triassic–Jurassic boundary, based on ecophysiological analyses of fossil leaves from plant beds in (a) Sweden and (b) Greenland (after McElwain *et al.*, 1999).

importance of plant acclimation to a high CO_2 environment (Drake *et al.*, 1997) is discussed. This theme is then extended to consider how increasing the atmospheric CO_2 concentration from the present day (350 ppm) to that of the late Jurassic (1800 ppm) influences the biochemical control of CO_2 assimilation rates in leaves (Wullschleger, 1993) at the global scale. Analyses of this sort make an interesting case study for the potential physiological responses of vegetation in a future high CO_2 'greenhouse world'.

Next, global predictions of vegetation structure and function in a late Jurassic atmosphere and climate on vegetation are considered, using the UGAMP GCM late Jurassic 'climate' (Valdes & Sellwood, 1992; Valdes, 1993; Price *et al.*, 1995) and the vegetation model described earlier (Chapter 4). Included in this section is a sensitivity analysis of responses of vegetation productivity and structure to CO_2, both of which exert an influence on the Earth's surface energy balance. Several key land surface energy exchange parameters required by climate models require an estimation of leaf area index (LAI) (Sellers, 1985; Betts *et al.*, 1997). If LAI is sensitive to atmospheric CO_2 concentration, then vegetation represented within climate models with a fixed LAI, based on values of modern vegetation types extrapolated back to those of the past (i.e. the modern analogue approach; e.g. Otto-Bliesner & Upchurch, 1997), will introduce errors into the climate model predictions. Consequently, the sensitivity studies provide an assessment of CO_2 impacts on vegetation structure relevant for more accurate modelling of vegetation feedbacks on climate.

As in Chapter 5, the simulated patterns of vegetation and edaphic properties are compared with the global distribution of the sedimentary climatic indicators, evaporites and coals (Parrish *et al.*, 1982; Rees *et al.*, 2000). Predicted vegetation activity, characterised here by the maximum rate of carboxylation (V_{max}), is compared with estimates reconstructed from the fossil record of the isotope composition of Jurassic leaves (Bocherens *et al.*, 1994). Finally, the geographical patterns of the main plant function groups have been predicted for comparison with detailed reconstructions of the distribution of major vegetation types for the late Jurassic, based on palaeobotanical and sedimentary data (Rees *et al.*, 2000). This provides an important model test under high CO_2 concentrations relevant to simulations in a future 'greenhouse world' and, if reasonably accurate, a more secure foundation for the interpretation of carbon storage figures in vegetation biomass.

Atmospheric CO₂ and climatic change across the Triassic–Jurassic boundary

The T–J boundary marks one of the most severe mass extinctions in Earth history (Raup & Sepkoski, 1982), with a loss of 30% of marine genera, 50% of tetrapod species and marked shifts in the floral composition of Europe and North America. Despite this, little is known about the environmental changes surrounding these biotic events because of a marked paucity of geochemical records documenting environmental changes across the T–J boundary, much less records of possible variations in atmospheric CO_2 partial pressure (Berner, 1994; Yapp & Poths, 1996). The former is mainly attributable to the lack of suitable continuous, unaltered pelagic sediments for geochemical analysis (Hallam, 1997). In addition, geochemical records from existing terrestrial sections are considered to be compromised by diagenesis (Morante & Hallam, 1996; McRoberts *et al.*, 1997). One of the best available means for reconstructing environmental changes at this time is through the analysis and interpretation of the fossilised remains (leaves) of land plants.

Measurements of stomatal index from fossil leaves of the rich plant beds of southern Sweden and eastern Greenland have been used for detecting possible perturbations of the global carbon cycle at the T–J boundary. The approach utilises the inverse relationship between atmospheric CO_2 and stomatal index (McElwain & Chaloner, 1996; Beerling & Woodward, 1997). Semi-quantitative palaeo-CO_2 estimates can be obtained by calculating the stomatal ratio (SR), the stomatal index (SI) of a fossil taxon divided by the SI of its nearest ecological equivalent (McElwain & Chaloner, 1995), where one SR unit = 300 ppm CO_2. Taking this approach, McElwain *et al.* (1999)

reconstructed past atmospheric CO_2 partial pressures across the T–J boundary, together with estimates of changes in mean global temperature (ΔT), based on the simple greenhouse formulation:

$$\Delta T = 4 \ln \left(\frac{P_{atm}}{P_{atmo}} \right)$$

where P_{atmo} is the pre-industrial CO_2 concentration (280 ppm) and P_{atm} is the reconstructed atmospheric CO_2 concentration (Kothavala *et al.*, 1999).

The results from fossil leaves in both Greenland and Sweden indicate a consistent increase in the global atmospheric CO_2 concentration and temperature across the T–J boundary (Fig. 6.1). Quantified using stomatal ratios, the atmospheric CO_2 concentration is estimated to have increased from 600 to 2400 ppm, a more conservative increase than that suggested by Yapp & Poths (1996) for the same interval (900–4800 ppm), based on geochemical analyses of geothites. This rise in CO_2 is most plausibly explained by increased volcanic degassing from the Earth's mantle to the atmosphere during the rifting of Africa and North America, in conjunction with rapid sea level changes (Hallam, 1997). Furthermore, since the solubility of CO_2 in seawater decreases by 4% for every 1 °C increase in temperature (DeBoer, 1986), with higher sea temperatures this mechanism would have resulted in a positive feedback of the oceans on the greenhouse effect.

Consequences for plant adaptation and survival

The calculated increases in mean global surface air temperatures (Fig. 6.1) would be over and above summer temperatures of *c.* 35 °C at 60–70° N, estimated by GCM modelling for the end-Triassic (Wilson *et al.*, 1994). Reconstructed leaf temperatures for these conditions, based on a range of eco-physiological measurements made on the fossils themselves (stable carbon isotope composition and stomatal characters), suggest that leaves in the upper canopy (or for taxa on open ground) exceeded the heat limit for CO_2 uptake in tropical plants (Larcher, 1994), even at quite high latitudes (60–75° N). The range of this limit (48–52 °C) is highly conserved across a wide range of plant taxa (Larcher, 1994). High CO_2 would have limited transpirational cooling of leaves by reducing stomatal index and inducing partial stomatal closure, the latter exacerbated by high leaf-to-air vapour pressure deficits associated with high temperatures. The exceptionally long duration of repeated seasonally high temperatures, particularly at low wind speeds, may have led to severe and irreversible damage to leaf photosynthetic and protein synthesis systems

(Larcher, 1994), particularly in the upper canopy, possibly leading to death of the individual through its inability to regulate carbon fixation and water loss.

Thermal damage of this sort might be avoided, in the short term (i.e. millennia), through a phenotypic reduction in leaf size, leading to increased boundary layer conductance and heat dissipation. Energy budgets, computed as described in Beerling & Woodward (1997), and based on stomatal and isotope characters of the fossils themselves, predict marked reductions in leaf width, *c.* 50% of the maximum, are required to avoid leaf temperatures reaching the lethal limit for CO_2 uptake. Therefore the prediction, based on modelling initialised by the fossil record, is that smaller and/or more dissected leaves might be selected for across the T–J boundary (Fig. 6.2). Indeed, the fossil record in east Greenland indicates that selection for increased dissection/narrow leaves did actually occur (Fig. 6.2). The key point here is that we would only expect to observe a reduction in leaf size if both CO_2 increases and warming occurred at the T–J boundary.

The impacts of large and small leaves, operating in either a 'constant' or a 'variable' climate, on gas exchange processes show that when leaf width is small, e.g. 1 cm, photosynthetic rates increase relative to larger leaves (Fig. 6.3). With large leaves, temperatures reach a near lethal threshold which disrupts stomatal functioning and photosynthetic CO_2 uptake. Photosynthetic metabolism in this situation would be further disrupted by photoinhibition at such high temperatures (Long *et al.*, 1994). In contrast to the photosynthetic effects, there are no marked effects of leaf size on rates of transpiration (Fig. 6.4). Therefore, small-leaved taxa would have higher photosynthetic productivity and moderate rates of transpiration leading to a greater water-use efficiency (important during hot–dry summers) than large-leaved taxa with lower photosynthetic rates. These conclusions remain unchanged whether or not plants change from being hypostomatous (stomata on the lower side of leaves only) to being amphistomatous (stomata on the upper and lower leaf surfaces) (Fig. 6.5). However, both photosynthetic and transpiration rates of hypostomatous leaves would have been lower than in amphistomatous leaves.

The use of fossilised terrestrial plant remains in this example provides a unique environmental record spanning the T–J boundary mass extinction events. Furthermore, the reconstructed palaeoenvironmental changes of CO_2 and temperature lead to a testable prediction (leaf size should decrease), supported by independent observations from the fossil record of a shift to taxa with smaller leaves after the boundary. Whilst plants have physiological mechanisms to help survive short-lived high temperature events, particularly

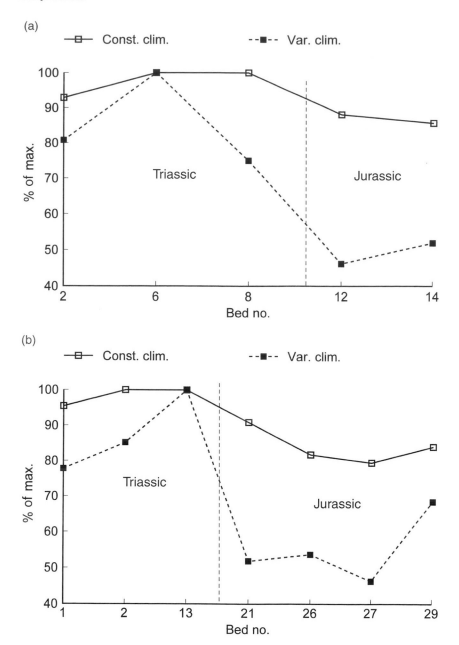

Figure 6.2. Calculated reductions in leaf width for plants operating in an end-Triassic climate, but with the imposition of increased CO_2 and temperatures shown in Fig. 6.1, required for plants to avoid the lethal limit for uptake, based on data from leaves in (a) Sweden and (b) Greenland. Const. clim. and Var. clim. refer to a constant climate across the T–J boundary and a climate with the additional warming reconstructed in Fig. 6.1. (From McElwain *et al.*, 1999.)

(a)

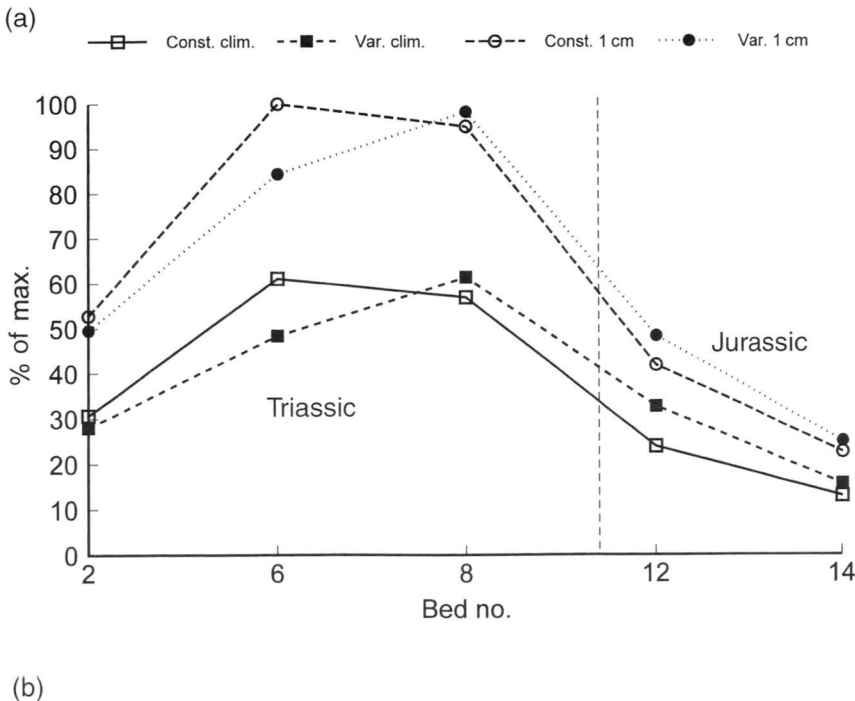

(b)

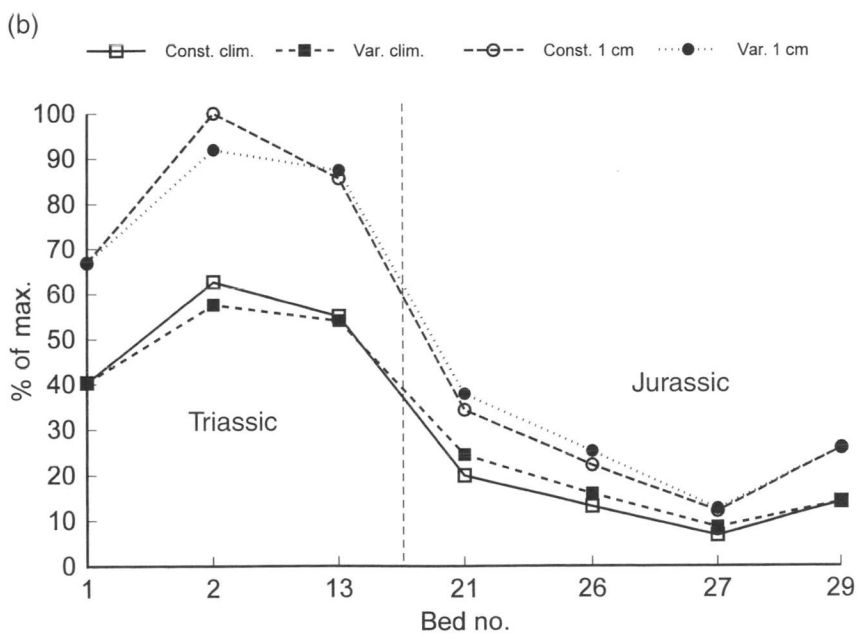

Figure 6.3. Reconstructed rates of photosynthesis for leaves from (a) Sweden and (b) Greenland with diameters of 1 cm and 4 cm, based on stomatal and isotopic characters of the fossils (McElwain *et al.*, 1999), and using both a variable and constant climate as in Fig. 6.2. Note that narrow leaves achieve rates of photosynthesis closer to the maximum than broader leaves.

(a)

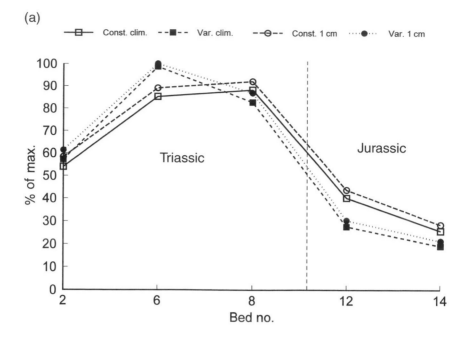

(b)

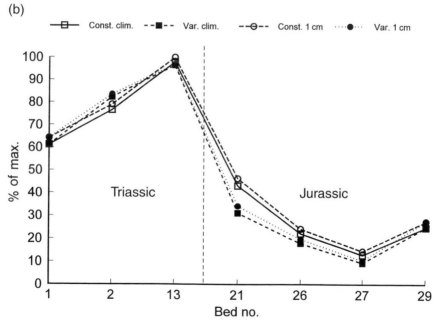

Figure 6.4. Reconstructed rates of transpiration using the model described in Chapter 2, for leaves from (a) Sweden and (b) Greenland with diameters of 1 cm and 4 cm, based on stomatal and isotopic characters of the fossils (McElwain *et al.*, 1999), and using both a variable and constant climate as in Fig. 6.2.

synthesis of heat shock proteins (Downs *et al.*, 1998) and isoprene (Singsaas *et al.*, 1997), these were evidently insufficient to cool leaves and prevent extinction of larger-leaved taxa.

These considerations provide a basic mechanism for interpreting selective plant extinctions at this time. Moreover, because increased CO_2 and land air temperatures, together with changes in sea level, characterise several other mass extinction events of the past, e.g. the Cenomanian–Turonian boundary (90.4 Ma; Kerr, 1998) and the Cretaceous–Tertiary boundary (65 Ma; Wolfe, 1990; O'Keefe & Ahrens, 1989), selective thermal damage to taxa (depending on leaf size) may represent an environmental means for selective plant extinctions at these times as well. We note that the energetic considerations discussed here apply only to those taxa dominating the upper canopy (of plants growing in open habitats) and that thermal damage might only be sustained on hot, sunny days with low wind speeds.

This section has considered the use of fossil plants for reconstructing palaeoenvironments with an emphasis on ecophysiological considerations. Plants and vegetation were exposed to CO_2 partial pressures above present in the early Jurassic and this continued into the late Jurassic with further ecophysiological implications. The next section considers the issues surrounding plant responses to high CO_2 and its impacts on the modelling results.

Plant acclimation to high CO_2 concentration

Before considering global-scale analyses in the late Jurassic, the issue of whether plants acclimate (in the sense of a down-regulation of photosynthetic activity) to a high CO_2 atmosphere, and how this may modify the modelled responses of photosynthetic productivity, requires discussion. Exposure of current genotypes to CO_2-enriched atmospheres increases leaf net photosynthetic rates (Drake *et al.*, 1997). The increase in photosynthesis, however, can be transient, declining with time, depending on how soil nitrogen supply and other environmental factors influence plant source–sink balance (Sage *et al.*, 1989; Sage, 1994; Gunderson & Wullschleger, 1994), leading to so called 'acclimation'. The mechanism underlying this down-regulation is thought to concern accumulation of sugars in leaves repressing gene transcription of enzymes involved in photosynthesis (Sheen, 1990; Webber *et al.*, 1994; Drake *et al.*, 1997), and experiments with *Arabidopsis* grown with CO_2 enrichment confirm this suggestion (Chen *et al.*, 1998). However, these experiments also showed that repression of photosynthetic gene transcription cannot fully explain decreases in rubisco protein content and that it is under multiple

(a)

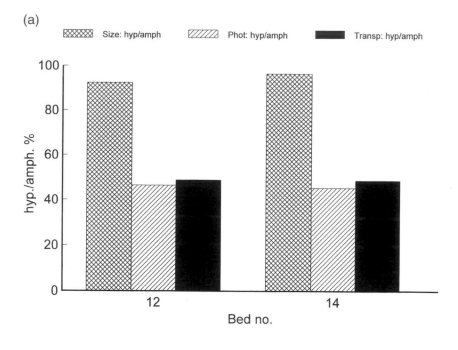

(b)

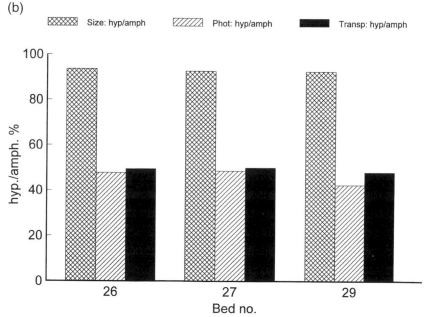

Figure 6.5. The simulated impact of hypostomaty and amphistomaty on leaf size, photosynthetic rate and transpiration rate at different times for leaves from (a) Sweden and (b) Greenland in the early Jurassic. It has been assumed that the fossil stomatal densities (McElwain *et al.*, 1999) were either present equally on both leaf surfaces, or present on only the one surface. The ordinate shows the ratio of the simulated response of the hypostomatous to the amphistomatous case.

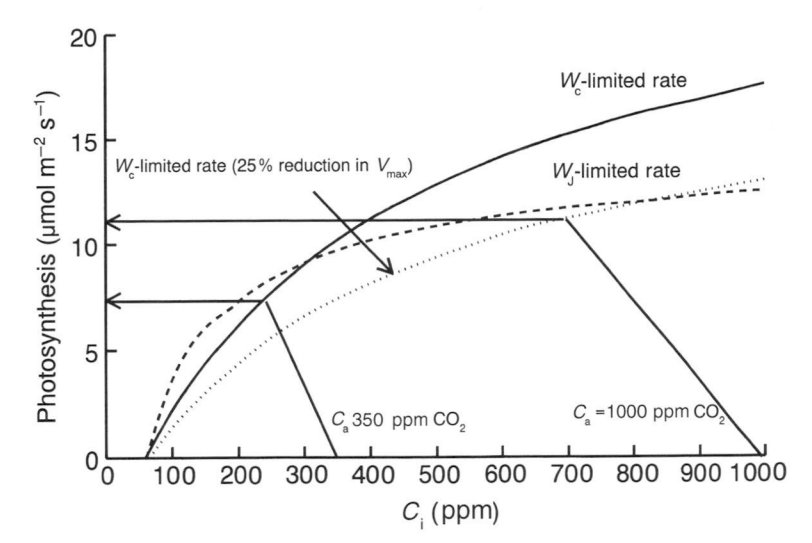

Figure 6.6. Modelled A/C_i responses for a typical leaf growing at 35 Pa CO_2 and 100 Pa CO_2 with a 25% reduction in V_{max}, simulating an acclimatory response to elevated CO_2. The slopes of the angled lines represent stomatal conductances, their intercepts are calculated as $0.7 \times C_a$. A/C_i curves were calculated with $V_{max} = 27$ μmol m⁻² s⁻¹ and $J_{max} = 63$ μmol m⁻² s⁻¹ at 25 °C, PAR 900 μmol m⁻² s⁻¹. Definitions of W_c and W_j, p. 35.

control at a variety of molecular levels (Chen *et al.*, 1998). In some cases down-regulation of CO_2 assimilation represents a restricted capacity to assimilate the extra carbon, so that acclimation represents the reallocation of resources (predominantly nitrogen) away from non-limiting components (carbon acquisition) to more limiting (e.g. light harvesting) components in the photosynthetic system, i.e. an optimisation response (Bowes, 1996).

The optimisation suggestion can be investigated by constructing A/C_i response curves (Fig. 6.6). The curves indicate that reductions in rubisco activity/amount in elevated CO_2-grown plants do not necessarily lead to a reduction in net CO_2 assimilation (Fig. 6.6). At an atmospheric CO_2 concentration (C_a) of 350 ppm, the net rate of photosynthesis is lower than for leaves operating at 1000 ppm CO_2 but with a 25% reduction in rubisco activity (Fig. 6.6). The situation occurs because at the higher CO_2 level, stomatal conductance (the CO_2 supply function) decreases and the leaf operates at a higher C_i, compensating for any loss of rubisco activity. In this example (Fig. 6.6) it emerges that the W_c-limited (V_{max}-controlled) photosynthetic rate at 1000 ppm is close to the W_j-limited rate (J_{max}-controlled) supporting the notion that plants can re-invest nitrogen away from rubisco and into the light harvesting proteins, i.e. increasing nitrogen-use efficiency, without loss of photosynthetic activity in a high CO_2 atmosphere. Further discussion of optimisation of photosynthesis, as a process operating at the co-limiting point between W_c and W_j rates, is described later in this chapter (p. 152).

It is clear that when acclimation of the photosynthetic proteins occurs, it probably relates to optimisation of resources. However, *a priori* predictions of which species might show acclimation to CO_2 enrichment are not currently possible and no correlation has been found with plant growth rates (Stirling *et al.*, 1997). Growth rates provide a measure of 'sink' strength with, for example, slow-growing species more likely to reflect a limited capacity to utilise additional photosynthate and thus a tendency to down-regulate photosynthesis. Indeed, in their review of measurements of V_{max} (rubisco activity) and J_{max} (electron transport), made on a wide range of woody species grown in elevated CO_2, Gunderson and Wullschleger (1994) reported no marked changes in either capacity as a result of CO_2 enrichment (Fig. 6.7). Measurements on field-grown woody plants exposed to elevated CO_2 generally show a lack of acclimation (e.g. Ellsworth *et al.*, 1995; Beerling, 1999a). The magnitude of the photosynthetic response to CO_2 enrichment has been reported in a recent synthesis of the literature to be around 66% (Norby *et al.*, 1999), a value greater than that found by Gunderson & Wullschleger (1994) (44%). The study of Norby *et al.* (1999) supports the notion that in experiments with trees rooted in the ground, no major losses in CO_2 enhancement of photosynthesises are the norm, with little evidence for the loss of sensitivity to CO_2.

One possible explanation for the lack of acclimation is that the length of exposure to CO_2 enrichment is critical for plants to show acclimation. This idea has been tested with gas exchange measurements made on vegetation growing naturally around geothermal springs in a high CO_2 environment. Studies of these species assume such environments are analogues for the longer-term responses of plants to naturally high concentrations of CO_2, and where contamination by sulphurous gases can be excluded (Miglietta *et al.*, 1993; Körner & Miglietta, 1994; Fordham *et al.*, 1997). The results indicate that long-term adaptation to growth in elevated CO_2 increases potential for growth but without changes in the photosynthetic enzymes (Fordham *et al.*, 1997).

Given the variability in which species might show acclimation of the photosynthetic enzymes, the influence of exposure time and the lack of understanding for a precise mechanism, the inclusion of this phenomenon in vegetation models is not yet possible, although empirical formulations have been attempted (Sellers *et al.*, 1996). Until these uncertainties become more fully understood, we have not explicitly accounted for the influence of accli-

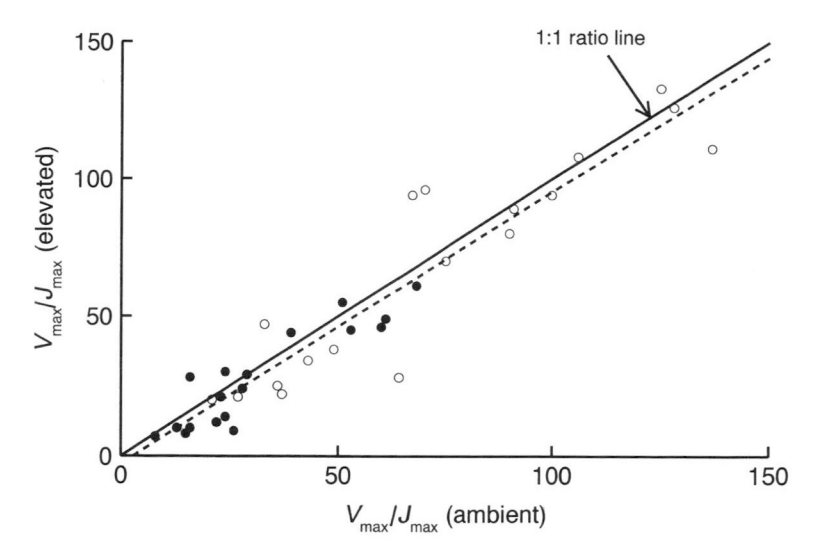

Figure 6.7. Comparison of V_{max} ($\bullet$) and J_{max} ($\bigcirc$) measurements made on woody taxa grown at ambient and elevated CO_2 concentrations (data from Gunderson & Wullschleger (1994)). The solid line indicates perfect correlation between ambient and elevated measurements, the broken line is fitted to the data. Regression details: intercept $= 0.98$, slope $= -2.789$, $r = 0.94$.

mation in this book. Consequently, the equilibrium model solutions of terrestrial NPP for those time intervals where the CO_2 concentration is above present (Chapters 7, 8 and 10) should be taken to represent upper estimates. Nevertheless, the SDGVM has been successfully tested against measurements obtained from plants and vegetation within an entire ecosystem exposed to increased CO_2 and temperature (Beerling *et al.*, 1997). Predictions of leaf gas exchange, run-off, and soil nutrient concentrations, chosen as time-integrators of a wide range of ecosystem processes, all showed favourable comparisons with observations, implying that the processes and scaling procedures are adequately represented in the model and that it provides realistic ecosystem responses under elevated CO_2 and temperature (Beerling *et al.*, 1997). The stage is now set for considering the global situation in the Jurassic environment.

The late Jurassic global climate

The UGAMP GCM uses a close approximation to the land surface distribution at 150 Ma, as reconstructed by Smith *et al.* (1994), when sea level was relatively high (Hallam, 1992), with Tethys (the seaway between Gondwana

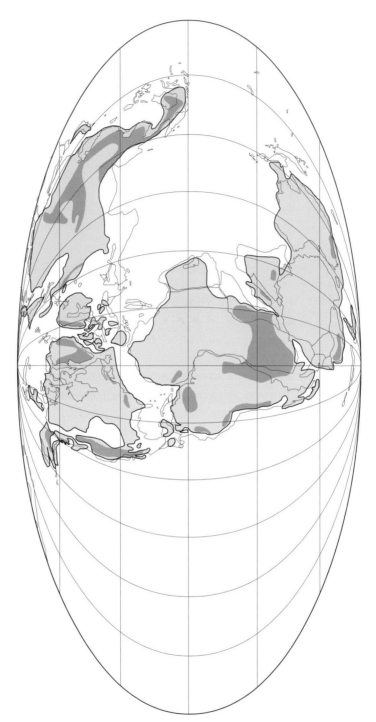

Figure 6.8. Reconstructed land mass positions during the Kimmeridgian stage of the Jurassic (150 Ma) (from Smith *et al.*, 1994). Dark grey indicates upland regions.

and Laurasia) and the central Atlantic forming a continuous seaway (Fig. 6.8). The late Jurassic climate was simulated as described in Chapter 5 (fixed sea surface temperatures) and with a spatial resolution of 3.75° × 3.75° (Valdes & Sellwood, 1992; Valdes, 1993; Price *et al.*, 1995). The UGAMP late Jurassic palaeoclimate simulation has been extensively and favourably compared with the geological data (Valdes & Sellwood, 1992; Valdes, 1993; Sellwood & Price, 1994; Price *et al.*, 1995; Rees *et al.*, 2000), including a good match between modelled sites of coastal upwelling and the distribution of petroleum source rocks. It should be noted that the UGAMP simulation of the late Jurassic climate differs from that of the NCAR GCM (Moore *et al.*, 1992a,b), probably due to the treatment of the oceans (Valdes, 1993).

The climatic data used to drive the SDGVM are summarised in Figures 6.9 and 6.10. The SDGVM was run using CO_2 and O_2 estimates of 1800 ppm and 15%, respectively (Berner & Canfield, 1989; Berner, 1997). Yearly average temperatures in the tropics were warm (up to 30 °C), and polar regions experienced extremely mild temperatures (Figs. 6.9 and 6.10). The climate simulation predicts no permanent ice cover near either pole, arid conditions over the south-western USA and seasonally arid climate over southern Europe (Fig. 6.9). Winter storminess over Europe and Australasia is also predicted. Land surface temperatures over Siberia and south-eastern Gondwana drop below 0°C for a significant part of the winter. Precipitation patterns are broadly consistent with the geological evidence (Valdes, 1993), although the location of bands of tropical precipitation is one of the most uncertain features of climate models.

Global patterns of photosynthesis in the late Jurassic

Before considering the productivity of vegetation in the late Jurassic, the impact of the high CO_2 concentration (1800 ppm) on canopy photosynthesis is considered since it obviously underpins productivity and is also relevant to plant behaviour in a high CO_2 future 'greenhouse' world. According to the Farquhar *et al.* (1980) model, photosynthetic rates are controlled either by the concentration, activation state and kinetic properties of rubisco (W_c), or the rate of RuBP regeneration through electron transport (W_j), depending upon the environmental conditions. Under the current CO_2 concentration, C_3 plants tend to optimise resource distribution, particularly nitrogen, within the photosynthetic apparatus, such that the capacity for carboxylation and RuBP regeneration are balanced (Nie *et al.*, 1995; Lloyd & Farquhar, 1996), i.e. that the maximum photosynthetic rate is on the boundary between W_c and W_j limitation (Chapter 3). Even leaves growing under conditions of low

(a)

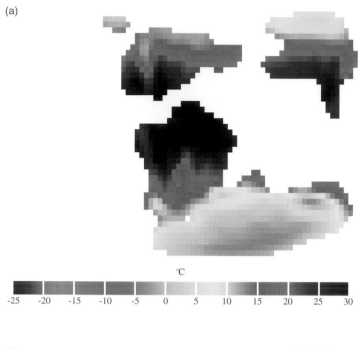

°C

(b)

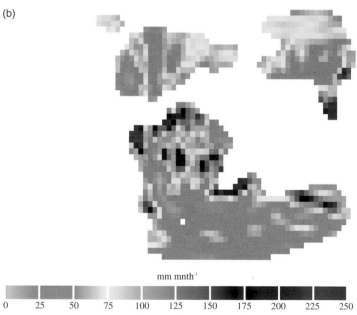

mm mnth⁻¹

Figure 6.9. Global patterns of yearly mean (a) temperature and (b) precipitation simulated by the UGAMP GCM for the late Jurassic.

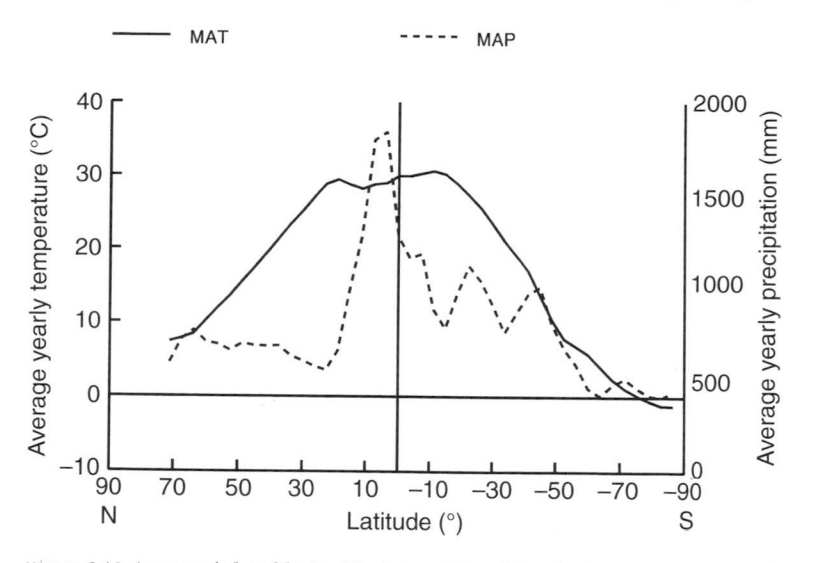

Figure 6.10. Area-weighted latitudinal averages of yearly mean temperature (MAT) and precipitation (MAP), for the late Jurassic.

irradiance, e.g. canopy shade leaves, tend to adjust their nitrogen partitioning to maintain the balance between electron transport and rubisco activity (Evans & Terashima, 1988). Over the course of the growing season, as canopy development and climate vary, plants experience seasonal adjustments in resource partitioning to maintain the balance of photosynthetic control between the two processes of W_c and W_j in an attempt to maximise carbon gain with respect to canopy nitrogen content (Chen *et al.*, 1993; Lloyd & Farquhar, 1996).

For plants growing in the high CO_2 conditions of the Mesozoic atmosphere, the control of photosynthesis may well have differed from the present-day situation, to an extent dependent on climate. Theoretically, W_j control should operate, in the absence of any stomatal acclimation (Fig. 6.6), because high CO_2 leads to higher CO_2 concentrations inside the leaves (C_i) so that RuBP generation is most limiting. Gas exchange measurements made on a range of boreal woody shrubs and trees growing in an experimentally CO_2 enriched atmosphere for three years show such a response (Beerling, 1998).

Nitrogen partitioning down through the canopy is included in the vegetation model, together with the Farquhar *et al.* model of CO_2 assimilation and the feedbacks between soil water, canopy conductance and photosynthesis (Chapter 4). Therefore, it is instructive to extract information from the global simulations at the current (350 ppm) and late Jurassic concentrations of CO_2 (1800 ppm) to investigate how it alters the governing process over the growing season (i.e. mainly W_c or W_j limitation). To aid interpretation, only leaves at the top of the canopy are considered.

At the present day CO_2 concentration, but with a late Jurassic climate, photosynthetic rates of leaves at the top of the canopy are controlled in hot regions predominantly by W_j throughout the growing season (Fig. 6.11). In cooler regions, where rubisco activity is temperature limited, photosynthesis is controlled for a greater proportion of the growing season by W_c (Fig. 6.11). These two differences largely reflect the temperature sensitivities of the maximum rates of carboxylation and electron transport (DePury & Farquhar, 1997). At 1800 ppm, however, the situation is quite complex and it emerges that the control processes governing photosynthesis depend upon temperature and the responses of LAI. In hot regions at 1800 ppm, with minimal changes in LAI, biochemical control of photosynthesis during the growing season by W_j is extended (Fig. 6.11b). However, in cooler regions control by W_c is increased (Fig. 6.11b). This occurs because these are the same regions showing quite large increases in LAI (see next section). An increase in LAI reduces the nitrogen content of leaves in the canopy, because the N available from the soil is partitioned through more layers, and the litter produced under high CO_2 has a higher C:N ratio, thereby releasing less N to the soil via decomposition processes. Therefore, cool conditions and low leaf N concentrations reduce rubisco activity and amount, moving the control of photosynthesis towards W_c (Fig. 6.11).

The maximum rate at which photosynthesis proceeds under either W_c and W_j control is limited by the maximum rate of carboxylation by rubisco, V_{max}, and the maximum rate of carboxylation limited by electron transport, J_{max}, respectively. Because V_{max} is linearly related to J_{max}, only a consideration of V_{max} is described here. Both V_{max} and J_{max} are dependent upon nutrient status, irradiance and temperature (Long, 1991; McMurtie & Wang, 1993; Woodward *et al.*, 1995). Calculated average growing-season V_{max} values in the late Jurassic show rather high values in hot, equatorial regions (Fig. 6.12) compared with those observed for present-day vegetation (Table 6.1), an effect due to the warm late Jurassic temperatures. As a consequence, one factor limiting W_c-limited photosynthetic rates is relaxed and a similar effect would also be expected for J_{max} and the W_j-limited rates of photosynthesis. Therefore, the warmer climate and relatively high V_{max} and J_{max} values allow corresponding high leaf photosynthetic rates (Fig. 6.13).

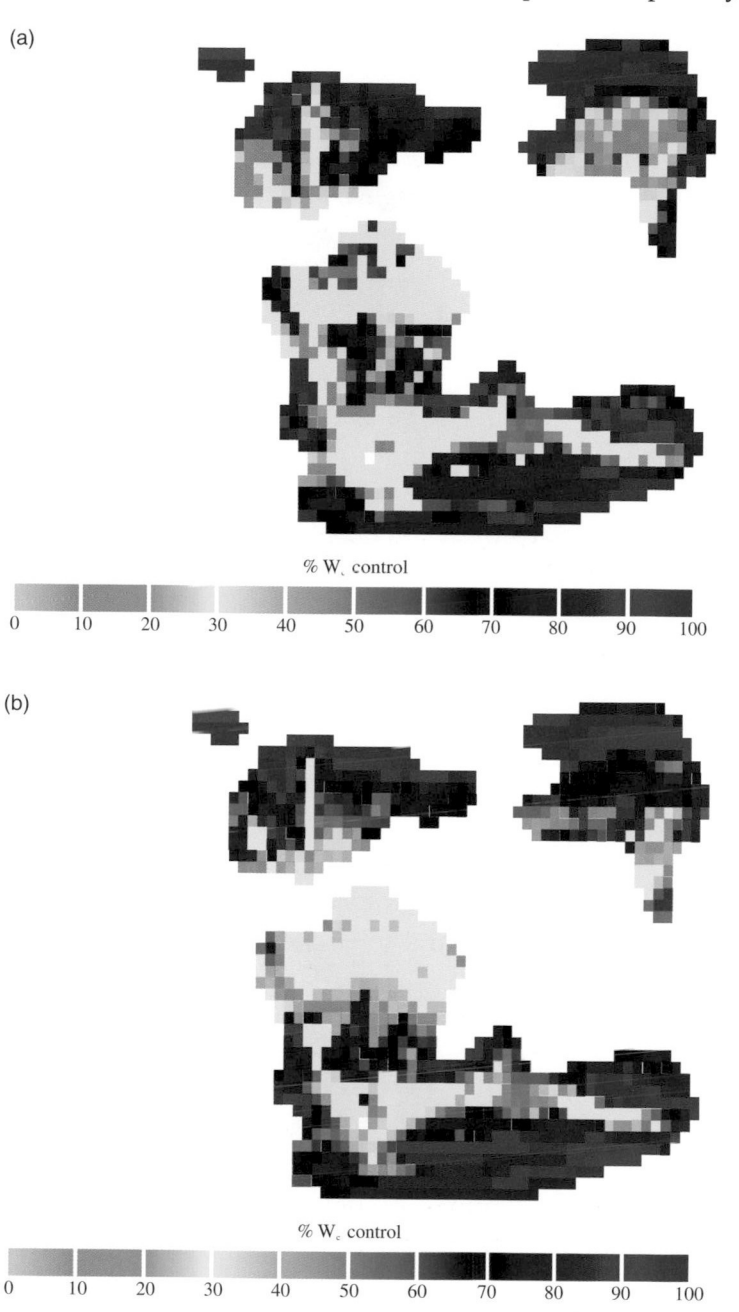

Figure 6.11. Proportion of the growing season that photosynthesis by leaves at the top of the canopy is controlled by W_c or W_j in the late Jurassic at (a) 350 ppm CO_2 and (b) 1800 ppm CO_2.

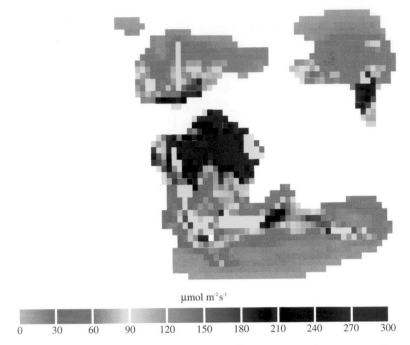

μmol m^{-2} s^{-1}

0   30   60   90   120   150   180   210   240   270   300

Figure 6.12. Global patterns of the mean growing-season maximum rates of carboxylation (V_{max}) simulated for the late Jurassic.

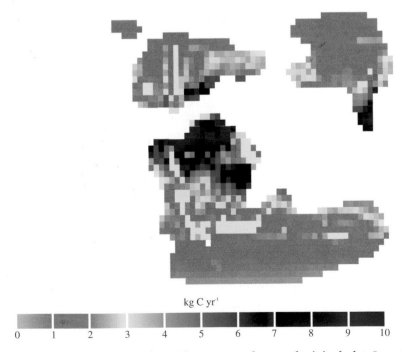

kg C yr^{-1}

0   1   2   3   4   5   6   7   8   9   10

Figure 6.13. Global patterns of annual net canopy photosynthesis in the late Jurassic.

Table 6.1. *Estimated average values of* V_{max} *and* J_{max} *for different types of vegetation under the current climate*

Plant category	V_{max} (μmol m^{-2} s^{-1})		J_{max} (μmol m^{-2} s^{-1})	
	Mean	Range	Mean	Range
Tropical forest[a]	51 ± 31	9–126	107 ± 53	30–222
Tropical rainforest[b]	62.4		120.6	
Tropical seasonal forest[b]	94.1		183.1	
Temperate forests				
Conifers[a]	25 ± 12	6–46	40 ± 32	17–121
Cool/cold deciduous forest[b]	36.1		71.4	
Cool/cold mixed forest[b]	46.9		89.6	
Cool/cold conifer forest[b]	30.6		53.8	
Sclerophyllous shrubs[a]	53 ± 15	35–71	122 ± 31	94–167
Xerophytic woods and scrub[b]	171.4		276.9	

Notes:
[a]Data from Wullschleger (1993); [b]data from Beerling & Quick (1995).

Comparison of modelled vegetation activity with palaeodata

One approach to testing the vegetation model, introduced in the previous chapter, has been to compare predicted growing season maximum carboxylation rates with those derived from the stable carbon isotope composition ($\delta^{13}C_p$) of fossil leaves. For the Carboniferous (Chapter 5), no measurements were available for fossil leaves and instead $\delta^{13}C$ values of bulk terrestrial organic matter were used. There is a similar paucity of isotopic measurements on late Jurassic fossil plant materials, but measurements have been made on fossil leaves of several well-identified taxa of middle Jurassic age (Bocherens *et al.*, 1994). Therefore, V_{max} has been calculated for these leaves from the $\delta^{13}C_p$ measurements and an estimate of the maximum rates of photosynthesis (A_{max}), taken from previous calculations initialised in the fossil record of stomatal characters (Beerling & Woodward, 1997).

The test is imperfect because stomatal and isotope data from the same leaves of late Jurassic age are not available to estimate C_i and A_{max} for each set of leaves. Nevertheless, it offers an approach for checking the modelled vegetation activity against estimates based on the fossil record. Calculated in this way, V_{max} values for a range of middle Jurassic fossil leaves (Table 6.2) are similar to those of modern conifers (Table 6.1). All of the isotope measurements were made from sites within the UK (Bocherens *et al.*, 1994), and these

Table 6.2. *Average growing season* V_{max} *values estimated from stable carbon isotope measurements of Jurassic fossil leaves*

Sample	$\delta^{13}C_p{}^a$ (‰)	$C_i{}^b$ (ppm)	$V_{max}{}^c$ (μmol m^{-2} s^{-1})
Cycadales			
Ctenozamites cycadea	−24.0	108.3	30.0
Ctenozamites leckenbyi	−25.7	121.8	29.0
Taeniopteris tenuinervis	−26.2	125.8	28.7
Bennettales			
Dictyozamites johnstrupii	−24.5	112.3	29.7
Nilssoniopteris vitatae	−23.8	106.7	30.2
Ptilophyllum pecten	−23.4	103.5	30.4
Weltrichia spectabilis	−24.3	110.7	29.8
Ginkgoales			
Baiera furcata	−26.4	127.4	28.7
Baiera gracilis	−23.5	104.3	30.4
Ginkgoites regnellii	−23.8	106.7	30.2
Ginkgo huttonii	−24.1	109.1	29.9
Czekanowskiales			
Solonites vimineus	−23.7	105.9	30.2

Notes:
[a]Stable carbon isotope values of fossil leaves from Bocherens *et al.* (1994).
[b]Isotopic composition of atmospheric CO_2 at 200–150 Ma is estimated from the ocean carbonate record but with values 7‰ more negative (see Fig. 3.17, p. 48), giving a value of −6‰. C_i is then estimated by solving equation 2.10 (p. 19) for the given values of $\delta^{13}C_p$, $\delta^{13}C_a$ and an estimated C_a of 1800 ppm (Berner, 1994).
[c]V_{max} calculated by solving the Farquhar CO_2 assimilation model using the estimated C_i value and an estimate of A_{max} from the fossil stomata data for 200–150 Ma, giving a value of 22 μmol m^{-2} s^{-1} (Beerling & Woodward, 1997) at 25 °C (from Fig. 6.10).

compare well with the model estimates of V_{max} for this region (see Fig. 6.8 for location of the UK in the late Jurassic), which gave values of 30–40 μmol m^{-2} s^{-1}. Although an imperfect test, the agreement between the palaeodata and modelled vegetation activity suggests that despite acclimation issues the model simulates appropriate rates of this key photosynthetic process.

Global terrestrial productivity in the late Jurassic

Global-scale predictions of the net primary productivity (NPP) indicate that the late Jurassic climate, in combination with the high atmospheric CO_2 content, was suitable for high terrestrial productivity (Fig. 6.14). A much

Table 6.3. *Net and gross terrestrial primary productivity (NPP and GPP) and carbon storage in vegetation and soils in the late Jurassic at ambient and 'best guess' CO_2 concentrations*

Global totals	Atmospheric CO_2 concentration	
	1800 ppm	350 ppm
Terrestrial NPP (Gt yr^{-1})	108.3	62.9
Terrestrial GPP (Gt yr^{-1})	376.1	199.7
Soil carbon (Gt)	1451.0	807.9
Vegetation carbon (Gt)	1670.1	785.0

greater proportion of the available land surface area is highly productive relative to the Carboniferous, a time when productive regions were confined to narrow equatorial regions of Gondwana (see Chapter 5). Global terrestrial productivity at this time is estimated to be 108 Gt carbon (Table 6.3), over double that modelled for the present-day biosphere. Both the LAI and NPP show several strong climatic gradients severely limiting canopy structure and productivity, particularly through western Gondwana, in parts of southern Laurasia and in southern China (Fig. 6.14). Given the rather warm temperatures and the high CO_2 concentration, these areas are likely to result from the low precipitation regime simulated by the GCM, and correspond to the geological data (Parrish *et al.*, 1982).

In some areas of the equatorial regions, terrestrial NPP is very high (*c.* 20 t C ha^{-1} yr^{-1}) (Fig. 6.14), a value approximately double that of tropical evergreen forests in Brazil, which in today's climate and CO_2 is *c.* 6.8–10 t C ha^{-1} yr^{-1} (McGuire *et al.*, 1992; Lloyd & Farquhar, 1996). This strong stimulation of tropical forest productivity in the late Jurassic supports previous suggestions that vegetation in the tropics should be a strong responder to CO_2 increases in the future (Lloyd & Farquhar, 1996). We note however that the taxonomic composition of tropical forests in the past relative to the present was very different (Wing & Sues, 1992). The simulations also confirm previous calculations (Creber & Chaloner, 1985) that the climate and short growing season (owing to the very rapid shortening of daylength from summer to winter) at high latitude regions in the Mesozoic were suitable for quite productive vegetation (Fig. 6.14), and are in line with the occurrence of high latitude fossil floras from Siberia (Hallam, 1984; Vakhrameev, 1991).

(a)

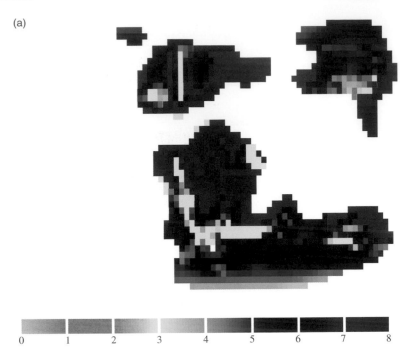

(b)

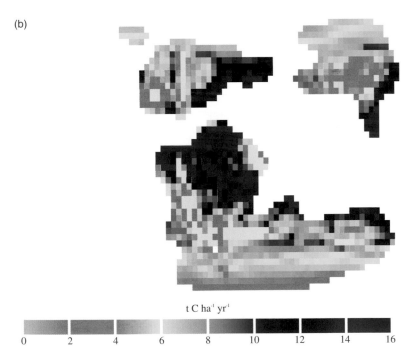

t C ha⁻¹ yr⁻¹

Figure 6.14. Global patterns of (a) LAI, (b) NPP, (c) vegetation carbon concentration and (d) soil carbon concentration simulated for the late Jurassic.

(c)

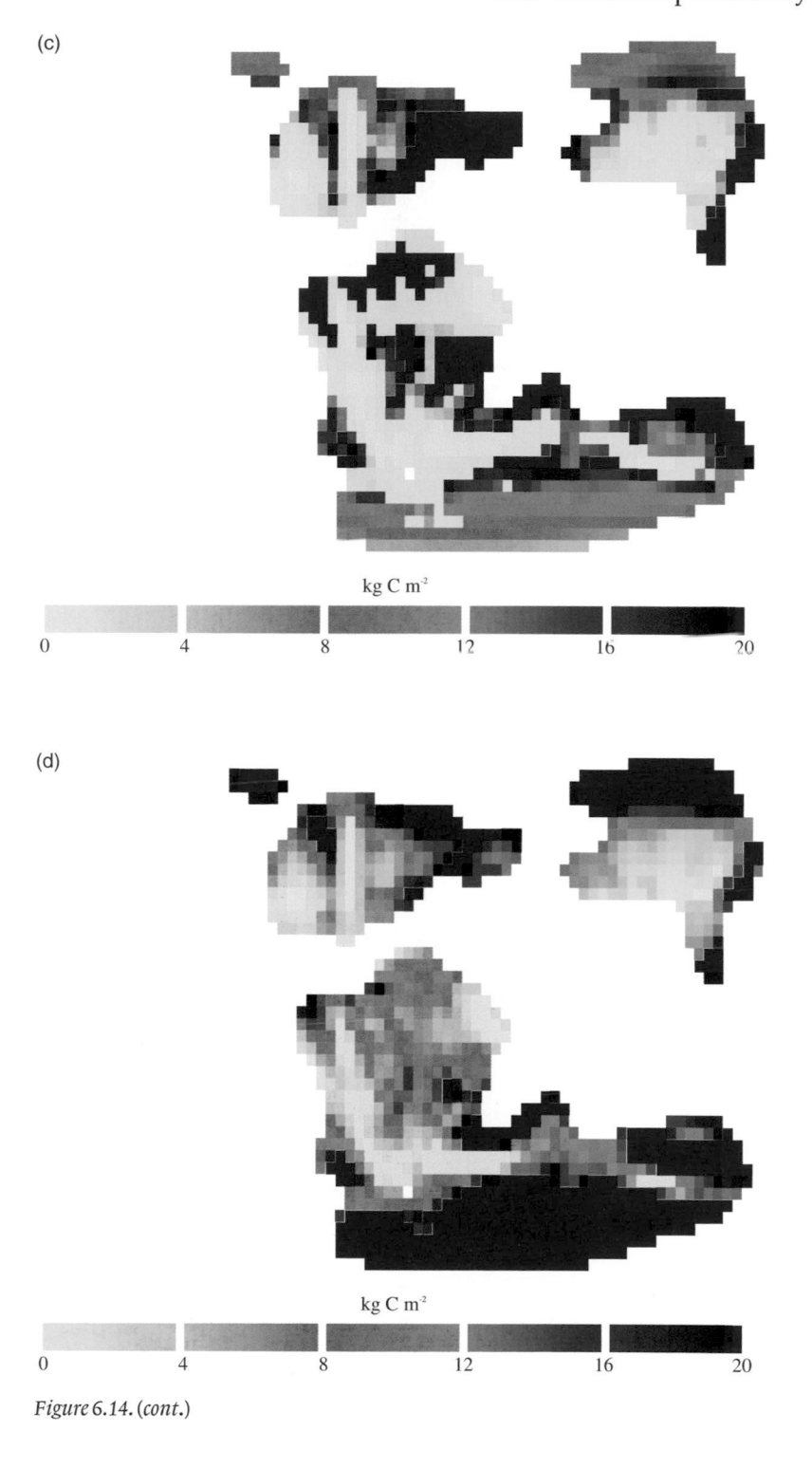

(d)

Figure 6.14. (cont.)

It has been suggested, based on the habits of nearest living relatives, that the major groups of late Jurassic vegetation, comprising araucariacean and cheirolepidiacean conifers, cycads, bennettitales and ginkgoalean plant groups had rather low rates of productivity and did not produce large quantities of foliage (Wing & Sues, 1992). However, simulations of NPP and LAI for the late Jurassic suggest that the situation was very different from that of the present day (Fig. 6.14b), with the potential for deeper, more productive canopies. Late Jurassic herbivorous dinosaurs presumably required substantial terrestrial productivity to sustain their populations. Wing & Sues (1992) suggest this may have come, in part, from the low-stature herbaceous pteridophytes but acknowledge a significant difficulty in reconciling their conclusions regarding the supposed low productivity of woody plants. The modelling simulations show that in contrast to these interpretations of the fossil record, the atmospheric composition and climate were suitable for a highly productive land surface (Fig. 6.14, Table 6.3). This seems to apply even in regions with seasonal aridity, possibly because of the high water-use efficiency of plant growth in a high CO_2 environment. Such an environment would also be important for the preservation of fossil plant materials. For example, well-preserved Jurassic plant fossils are predominantly found in sediments that represent dry climates.

Carbon storage in vegetation and soils in the late Jurassic is predicted to be large (Table 6.3), a situation very different from the present day and the Carboniferous (Chapter 5). Nevertheless, the storage of a large amount of carbon in vegetation biomass implies the establishment of long-lived trees of large above- and below-ground biomass. Such a prediction is supported by evidence from 'fossil forests' of the Purbeck formation (Francis, 1983) and from north-western China where large trees, with trunks some 2.5 m in diameter, have been recorded (McKnight et al., 1990).

Quantitative data from the geological record of carbon storage figures in late Jurassic coals is lacking, although there is now good geographical coverage of localities of late Jurassic coals (Parrish et al., 1982; Fawcett et al., 1994; Rees et al., 2000) and this is compared with model predictions later in the chapter. Given that not all soil C is incorporated in the geological record as coal (Cobb & Cecil, 1993), it is interesting to note that the data show increased coal deposition in the late Jurassic relative to the Triassic in Australia (Fawcett et al., 1994) and the formation of thick (670 m) Upper Jurassic–Lower Cretaceous Mist Mountain formations in the southern Rocky Mountains and Foothills of British Columbia (Bustin & Dunlop, 1992), is testament to high C burial rates in these regions at least.

CO₂ impacts on vegetation function

Sensitivity analyses of the model results to high CO_2 concentrations indicate large increases in the global totals of gross and net primary productivity, as well as in the storage of C in vegetation and soils (Table 6.3). These changes occur because CO_2 directly stimulates CO_2 assimilation via its action on rubisco at the leaf and canopy scale (Chapter 2) and through improved resource use efficiencies. This suggests that productivity estimates made using present-day correlations, as opposed to processes, between climate and NPP for vegetation under the present concentrations of CO_2 will be in error when applied to ancient environments with greater CO_2 concentrations (Creber & Francis, 1987; Ziegler *et al.*, 1987; Lottes & Ziegler, 1994).

The spatial changes in LAI, NPP, vegetation and soil C, due to an increase in CO_2 concentration, show a geographically heterogeneous pattern (Fig. 6.15). The magnitude of the difference in NPP between 1800 and 350 ppm CO_2 increases when moving from polar to equatorial regions, whereas the effect of increased CO_2 on LAI is greatest at mid- to low latitudes (Fig. 6.15a) (Beerling, 1999b). For NPP, the increases towards the equator reflect a reduction in the limitations of nutrient and water use due to high CO_2, the additional CO_2 being converted to biomass, as typically observed in field experiments (Lloyd & Farquhar, 1996). In addition, the high CO_2 and high temperatures also reduce photorespiration with higher net photosynthetic rates (Long, 1991).

For LAI, the CO_2 effect is not simply a function of higher air temperatures with decreasing latitude (Fig. 6.15). The relatively smaller increase in LAI at the equator compared with 50° N, for example, occurs because a high LAI already exists in these regions (Fig. 6.14a). Despite the high CO_2, the addition of another layer to the canopy cannot be supported because insufficient light penetrates to that canopy depth to support the maintenance and structural costs of making that leaf layer. This effect occurs despite a reduction in the light compensation point with CO_2 enrichment (Long & Drake, 1991). Some support for this idea comes from CO_2-enriched growth experiments with *Trifolium repens* which show the strongest biomass increases at low LAIs (Schenk *et al.*, 1995). In contrast, at lower latitudes where the LAI is lower, high CO_2 effectively allows increased growth for the same amount of precipitation due to higher water-use efficiency. The greatest increases in LAI occur in regions of highest rainfall. The implication of this is that palaeo-methods relying on extrapolating LAI estimates of present-day vegetation back to the past are unlikely to be correct. For example, Kojima *et al.* (1998) proposed that the accumulation rates of Eocene lignites from the Canadian Arctic could be

(a)

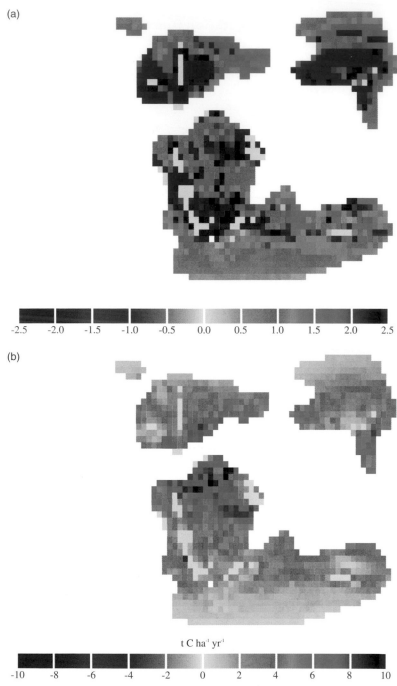

t C ha^{-1} yr^{-1}

Figure 6.15. CO$_2$ effects on (a) LAI, (b) NPP, (c) vegetation biomass carbon and (d) soil carbon storage. The difference maps were computed by running the vegetation model with the late Jurassic climate but at 1800 ppm CO$_2$ and 350 ppm CO$_2$. A positive value indicates a stimulatory effect of CO$_2$.

(c)

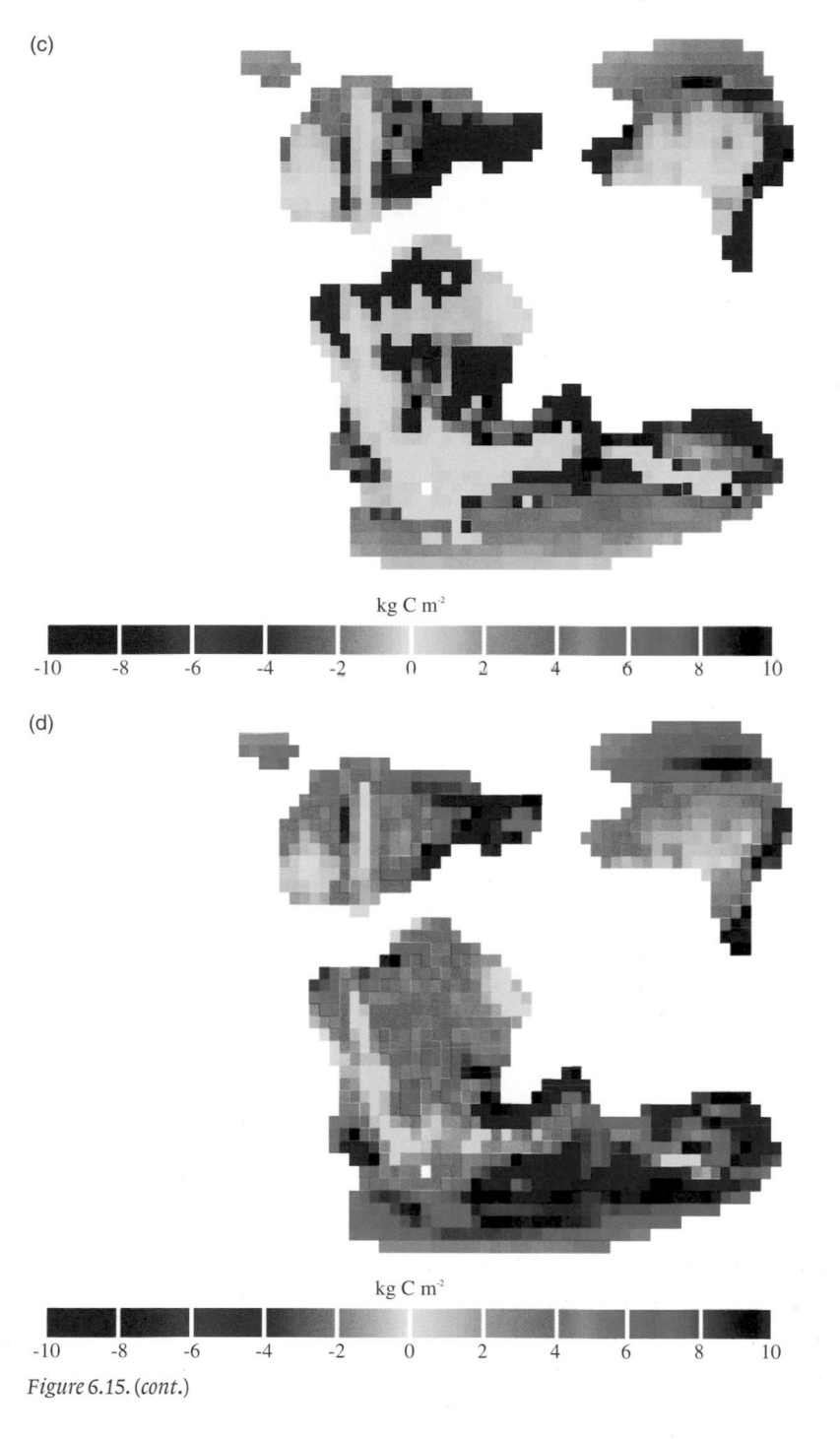

kg C m⁻²

(d)

Figure 6.15. (cont.)

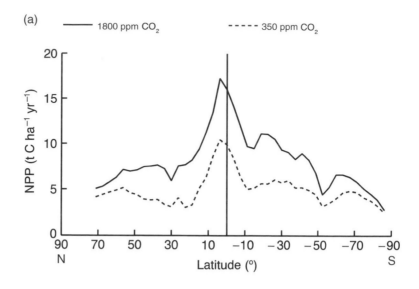

(a)

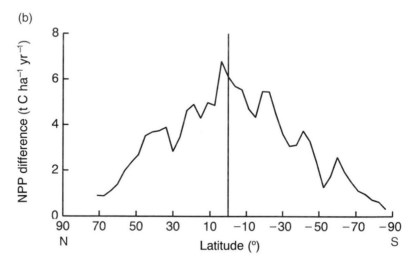

(b)

Figure 6.16. Area-weighted latitudinal averages of (a) NPP and (c) LAI and the difference between values at the high and low CO_2 concentration for (b) NPP and (d) LAI. Calculated from the model simulations described in Fig. 6.15.

calculated based on the assumption that the LAI of the dominant taxon *Metasequoia occidentalis* will be equivalent to those of modern deciduous conifers. The simulations described here, and the experimental observation summarised in Table 6.4, indicate this type of modern analogue approach to palaeoenvironmental reconstructions will introduce errors because of neglected CO_2 effects.

Spatial changes in LAI, as a result of an increase in the concentration of

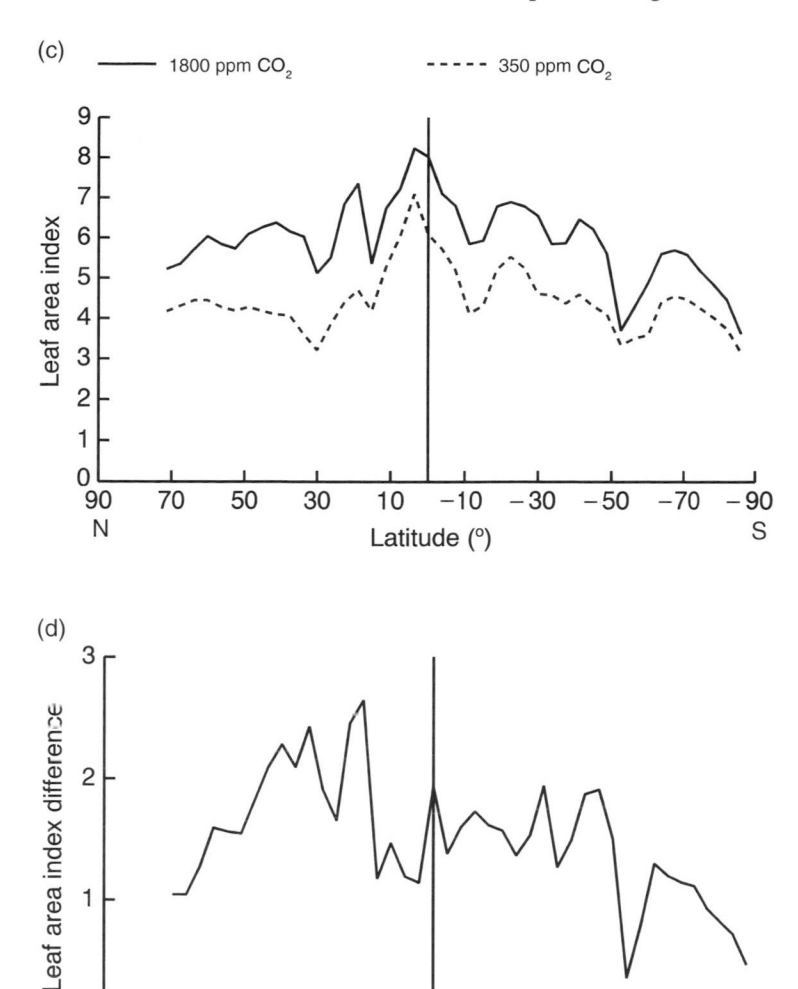

Figure 6.16. (cont.)

atmospheric CO_2, indicate it typically increases (Fig. 6.15), to an extent dependent upon climate (which determines soil nutrient status) and the original LAI at a particular site. Data from plant growth experiments have been used to investigate the likelihood of this response. CO_2 enrichment experiments on crops and native species show that LAI was rather insensitive to CO_2, with a 3% increase across observed all studies (summarised by Drake *et al.*, 1997). An updated analysis, based on more recent experimental results (Table 6.4) supports this conclusion, with only modest increases occurring at elevated CO_2 (Fig. 6.17). More detailed inspection of Figure 6.17 reveals that individual

Table 6.4. *The effect of growth in different CO_2 concentrations on leaf area index (LAI)*

Species	Atmospheric CO_2 (ppm) and duration of exposure to CO_2	Leaf area index (LAI) (in order of growth conditions)	Reference
Trees			
Populus trichocarpa × *P. deltoides*	350, 700 for 1 year	1.0, 1.2	Ceulemans et al. (1996)
	350, 700 for 2nd year	3.2, 4.7	
Populus trichocarpa × *P. euramericana*	350, 700 for 1 year	0.5, 0.6	Ceulemans et al. (1996)
	350, 700 for 2nd year	4.0, 4.5	
Pinus ponderosa	360, 540, 710 for 3 years	4.2, 4.2, 6.6	Tingey et al. (1996)
Herbs/crops			
Abutilon theophrasti	360, 700 for 53 days	0.76, 2.3	Hirose et al. (1996)
Ambrosia artemisifolia	360, 700 for 53 days	1.0, 2.3	
Andropogon gerardii (C$_4$ species)	350, 700 for 1 year	0.32, 0.65	Oswensby et al. (1993)
	350, 700 for 2 years	1.1, 1.15	
Poa pratensis	350, 700 for 1 year	0.3, 0.25	Oswensby et al. (1993)
	350, 700 for 2 years	0.4, 0.4	
Lolium perenne	350, 700 for 1 year	9.1, 10.7	Schapendonk et al. (1997)
	350, 700 for 2 years	3.4, 3.6	
Triticum aestivum	350, 550, 680 for 100 days	2.8, 3.2, 4.1	Mulholland et al. (1998)
Oryza sativa	350, 700 for 56 days	1.6, 1.7	Ziska et al. (1996)
+90 kg ha^{-1} N	350, 700 for 56 days	3.4, 2.8	
+200 kg ha^{-1} N	350, 700 for 56 days	4.6, 5.2	
Glycine max cv. Bragg	160, 220, 280, 330, 660, 990 for 34 days	1.6, 1.6, 2.4; 2.5, 2.4, 3.3	Campbell et al. (1990)
Glycine max cv. Clark	350, 700 for 21 days	3.8, 6.9	Ziska & Bunce (1997)
Solanum tuberosum	350, 460, 560, 650 for 193 days	3.6, 3.4, 4.0, 3.7	Miglietta et al. (1998)

Ecosystems			
Model spruce eocsystems	280, 420, 560 for 1.5 years	3.7, 3.0, 2.9	Hättenschwiler & Körner (1996)
+ 30 kg N ha^{-1} yr^{-1}	280, 420, 560 for 1.5 years	3.5, 3.1, 2.8	
+ 60 kg N ha^{-1} yr^{-1}	280, 420, 560 for 1.5 years	3.6, 3.1, 3.0	
Model spruce ecosystems	280, 420, 560 for 3 years	5.0, 4.0, 3.6	Hättenschwiler & Körner (1998)
Alpine grassland	360, 680 for 4 years	1.2, 1.1	Körner et al. (1997)
Tallgrass prairie (all species)	350, 700 for 1 year	1.4, 1.7	Owensby et al. (1993)
	350, 700 for 2 years	3.1, 3.0	
Forbs only	350, 700 for 1 year	0.2, 0.3	
	350, 700 for 2 years	0.3, 0.8	
Quercus woodlands Rapolano, Italy	350, 700 >30 years	4.0, 4.0	Hättenschwiler et al. (1997)
Quercus woodlands Laiatico, Italy	350, 700 >30 years	4.0, 4.0 350, 700 >30 years 3.5, 3.5	Hättenschwiler et al. (1997)

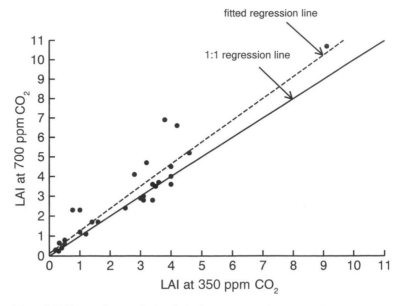

Figure 6.17. Regression analysis of LAI data measured at 350 and 700 ppm CO_2 (from Table 6.4). Regression details of the fitted line: $r = 0.93$, slope $= 1.124$, intercept $= 0.135$, $P < 0.001$.

plants and communities with an LAI of 1–5 at ambient CO_2 can show increases of up to 3 LAI units. These observations, however, provide rather little information on the potential effect of CO_2 on LAI in a closed-canopy forest where it is constrained by nutrients, light and water. Further problems exist in extrapolating from experiments to validate model predictions. Experimental CO_2 enrichment studies must be of sufficient duration to allow trees to grow a mature canopy (i.e. over several years) and, so far, no studies have achieved this long-term response. It is interesting to note that theoretically a higher light compensation point of photosynthesis under elevated CO_2, as observed in field experiments (Osborne *et al.*, 1997), would allow leaves to operate deeper in the canopy, potentially increasing LAI in the long term. We note that these experiments typically enrich the CO_2 concentration to 700 ppm, considerably lower than the late Jurassic atmosphere (1800 ppm), suggesting that the experimental data are indicative only of the direction of the response rather than its absolute magnitude for the late Jurassic.

Changes in LAI driven by CO_2 increases are intimately linked with canopy carbon and water balance and therefore canopy water-use efficiency. Increasing the concentration of CO_2 from 350 to 1800 ppm stimulates canopy photosynthesis, most strongly in equatorial regions (Fig. 6.18a). The response of canopy

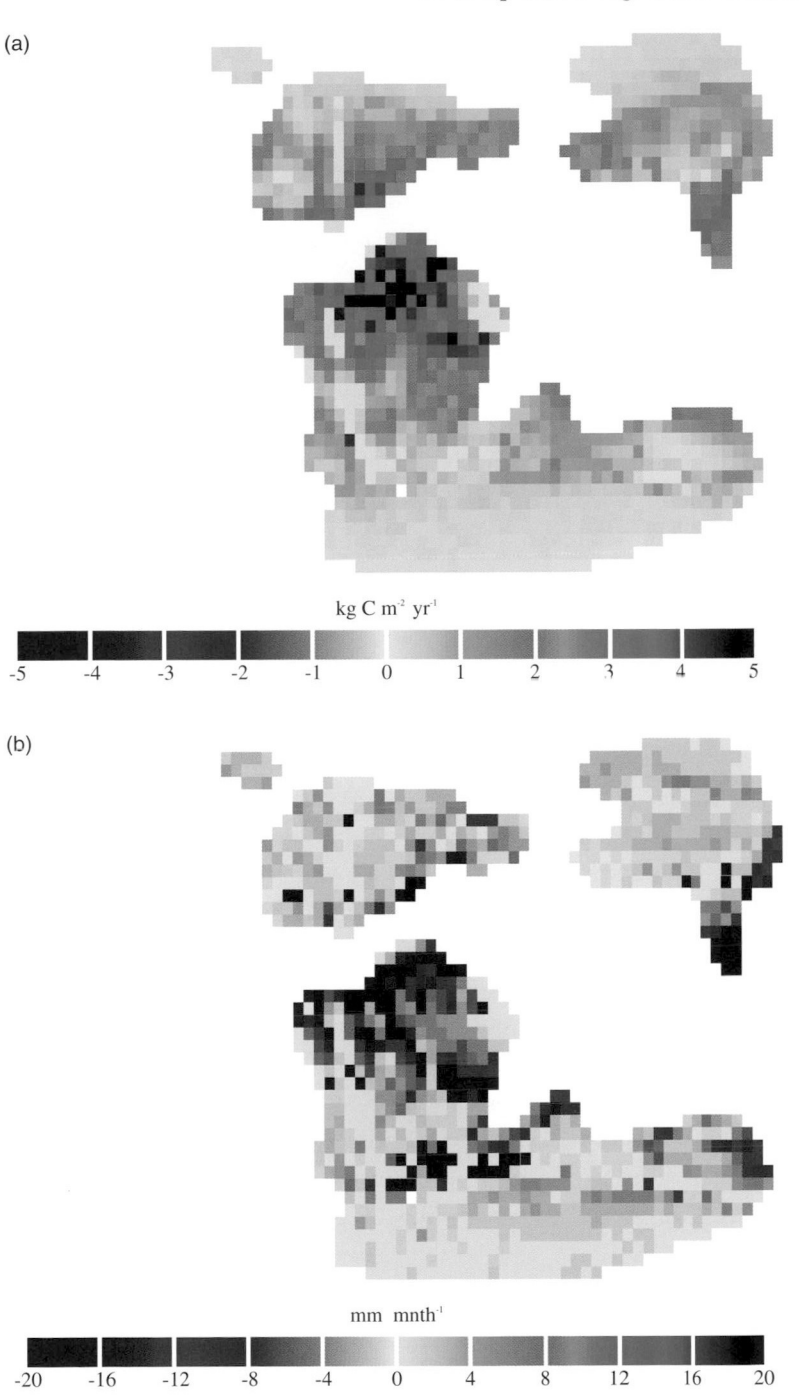

(a)

kg C m⁻² yr⁻¹

-5   -4   -3   -2   -1   0   1   2   3   4   5

(b)

mm mnth⁻¹

-20   -16   -12   -8   -4   0   4   8   12   16   20

Figure 6.18. The effect of CO₂ on (a) annual canopy C fixation and (b) transpiration for the late Jurassic. The values represent the difference between elevated late Jurassic (1800 ppm) and ambient modern (350 ppm) CO₂ concentrations.

transpiration is more variable, but is most commonly reduced in the CO_2 sensitivity simulations (Fig. 6.18b) because of a CO_2-induced reduction in the stomatal conductance to water vapour in individual leaf layers within the canopy. In support of this response, a reduction in canopy transpiration has been reported for CO_2 enrichment experiments on a range of different ecosystems (reviewed by Drake *et al.*, 1997). In certain mid-latitude regions, canopy transpiration increases because the relative effect of CO_2 on LAI is greater than that on stomatal conductance. A CO_2-related drop in canopy transpiration and an increase in canopy productivity will influence the plant–soil hydraulic conductance, with an effect on the maximum height that Mesozoic (including Jurassic) forests and could attain (Osborne & Beerling, 2001). According to the 'hydraulic limitation hypothesis' of tree height (Ryan & Yoder, 1997), the progressive increase in tree height is associated with a similarly progressive restriction in flow rates of water from the soil to the leaves. This effect, in turn, reduces stomatal opening, photosynthesis and hence growth as the trees approach their maximum height. Direct consideration of CO_2 influences on predictions of forest height, based on these hydraulic considerations, has shown that high CO_2 in the past was probably a key factor allowing the development of gigantic Mesozoic forests across much of the globe (Osborne & Beerling, 2001).

The impact of CO_2 effects on all of the processes controlling LAI has implications for the representation of vegetation within GCMs since it is used to define several structural land surface parameters required for calculating surface energy partitioning and exchange (Chen *et al.*, 1997). The effects of CO_2 on LAI in the Jurassic have been calculated for two such parameters, the vegetated fraction and surface roughness length, to illustrate its potential to influence the land surface energy balance characteristics. The vegetated fraction (v) is the fractional ground area covered by vegetation and determines the relative weighting of values appropriate to vegetation and soil for other variables, and is calculated as (Sellers, 1985):

$$v = 1 - \exp\left(\frac{-LAI}{LAI^*}\right) \tag{6.1}$$

where LAI^* is a reference LAI, taken as 2.0. Calculated in this way, the impact of the Jurassic CO_2 concentration on LAI has a substantial effect on v (Fig. 6.19a), with LAI calculated at modern CO_2 concentrations underestimating the vegetated fraction obtained if the late Jurassic CO_2 concentration is included.

Surface roughness length influences the depth of boundary layer of the land surface and so the heat and mass transfer simulated by the GCM. It therefore represents an important parameter contributing to vegetation feedbacks

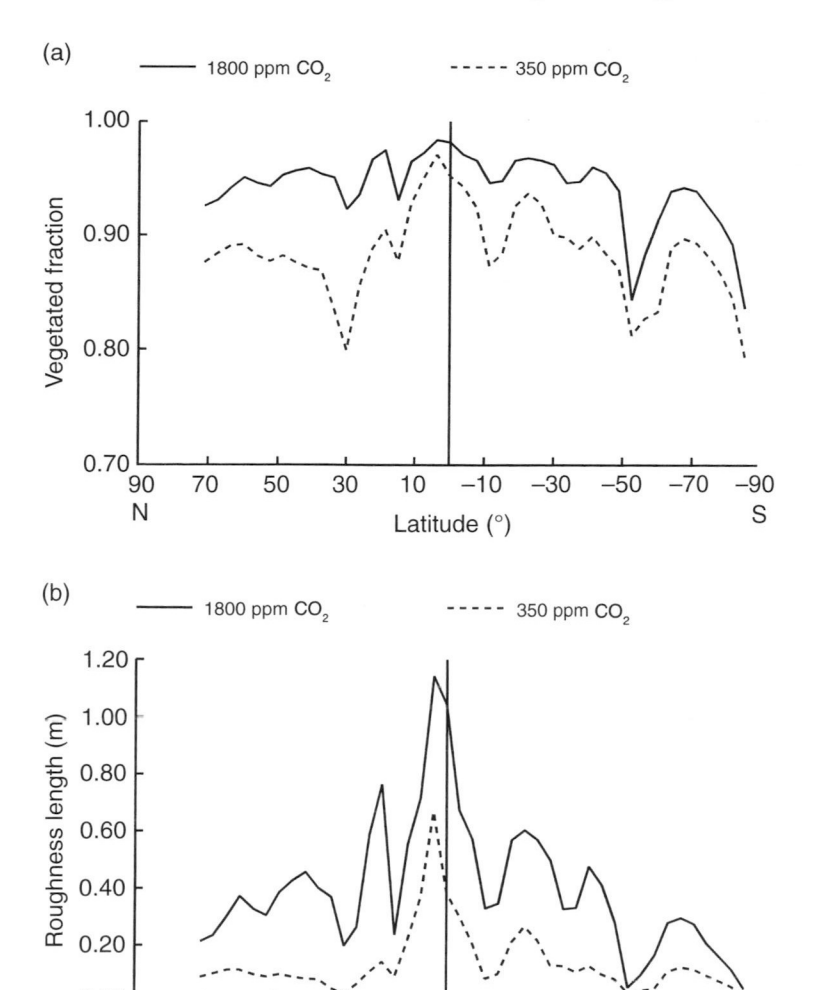

Figure 6.19. Calculated impact of CO₂ effects on latitudinal average of LAI on (a) the vegetated fraction and (b) surface roughness length. Both variables are required by GCMs to model land–atmosphere energy exchange.

on climate. Using the latitudinal LAI profiles for modern and late Jurassic concentrations of CO₂, roughness length, z (m), can be estimated from (Sellers, 1985):

$$z = \frac{1}{\left(\dfrac{\ln(l_b)}{z_{ov}}\right)^2} + \frac{1 - v}{\left(\dfrac{\ln(l_b)}{z_{os}}\right)^2} \qquad (6.2)$$

where l_b is the 'blending height', z_{os} is the roughness length of bare soil (0.0003 m) or ice (0.0001 m) and z_{ov} is the roughness length of the vegetation

(Shaw & Pereira, 1982). z_{ov} is dependent upon height, h (m), and the LAI of vegetation, both are related through (Woodward *et al.*, 1995):

$$h = 0.807LAI^{2.137} \tag{6.3}$$

z_{ov} can then be estimated, after Shaw & Pereira (1982) and Shuttleworth & Gurney (1990), from:

$$z_{ov} = z_{os} + 0.3hx^{\frac{1}{2}} \qquad \text{for } 0 < x < 0.2 \tag{6.4}$$

and

$$z_{ov} = 0.3h\left(1 - \frac{d}{h}\right) \qquad \text{for } 0.2 < x < 1.5 \tag{6.5}$$

where $x = c_d \times LAI$, with c_d as the effective mean drag coefficient for individual vegetative elements making up the canopy, typically 0.07 (Shuttleworth & Gurney, 1990), and d is the zero plane displacement of the vegetation, given by:

$$d = 1.1h\ln\left(1 + x^{\frac{1}{4}}\right) \tag{6.6}$$

The resulting roughness lengths, calculated for latitudinal averages of the two LAI profiles at two different CO_2 concentrations, show considerable differences (Fig. 6.19b). A higher roughness length increases the boundary layer conductance and the transfer of heat by moving air resulting in greater mixing of air temperatures between the lower atmospheric layer and the vegetation canopy. The net effect on air temperatures is not so easily predicted. Simulations with the SDGVM in a future climate with a CO_2 concentration of 700 ppm (Betts *et al.*, 1997) indicated in that regions with increased LAI the land surface tends to be cooled via increased albedo, but counteracting this is a warming effect resulting from decreased transpiration (cf. Fig. 6.18b). It seems likely, though, that if the vegetation cover is sparse the albedo effects dominate, whereas with dense cover the transpiration 'warming' effect dominates. Simple application of modern analogues, with a fixed LAI everywhere a given vegetation type occurs, are unlikely to capture accurately the spatial detail of vegetation impacts on climate (e.g. Otto-Bliesner & Upchurch, 1997).

Distribution of plant functional types in the late Jurassic

There is a problem in using contemporary ecological data, first to define functional types of plants and then to apply them to past eras, when such functional types as deciduous broad-leaved trees may not have existed. However, it is an interesting exercise to compare predictions using modern

(a)

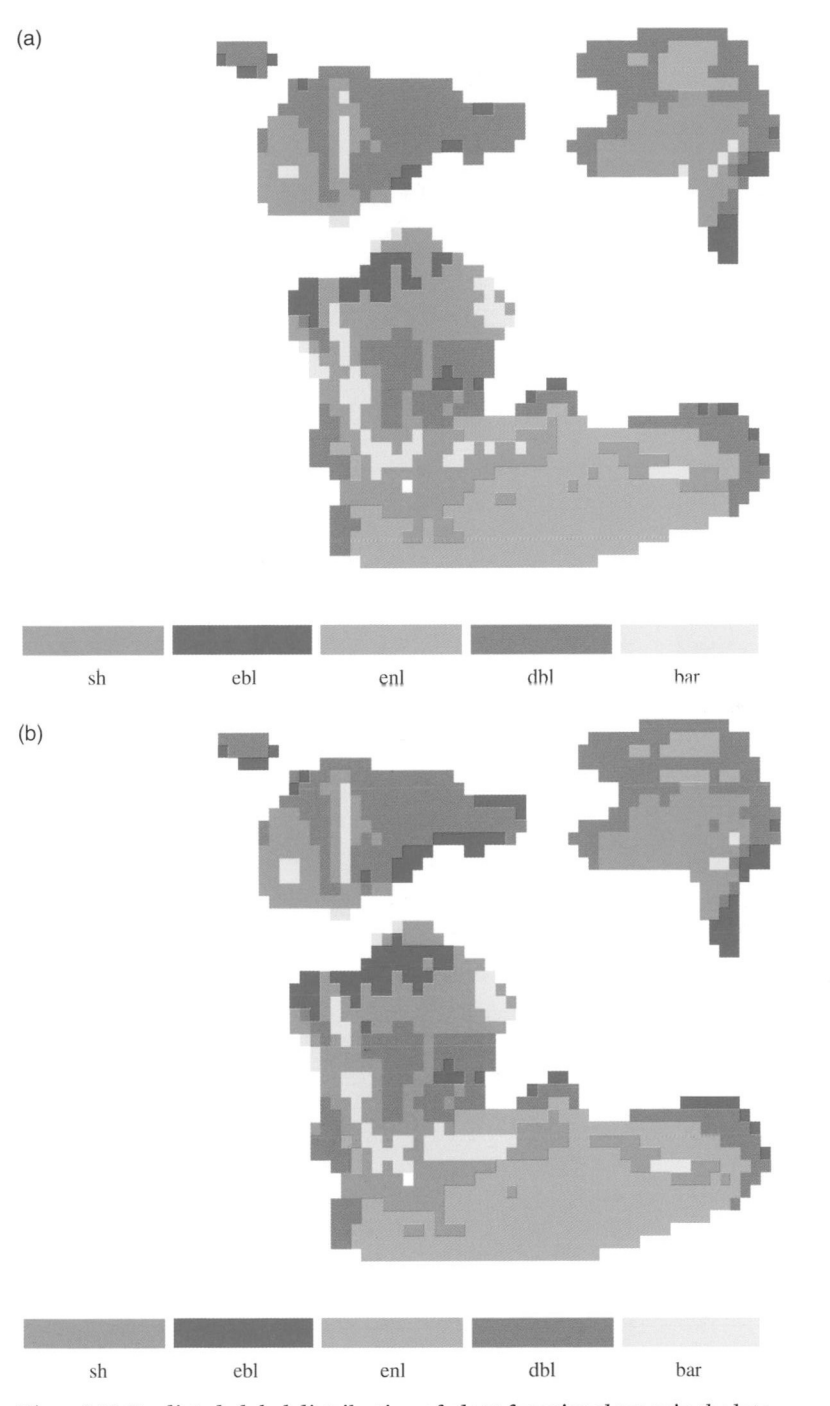

(b)

Figure 6.20. Predicted global distribution of plant functional types in the late Jurassic at (a) 350 ppm CO₂ and (b) 1800 ppm CO₂. Key to functional types: sh, shrubs; ebl, evergreen broad-leaved; enl, evergreen needle-leaved; dbl, deciduous broad-leaved; bar, bare-ground

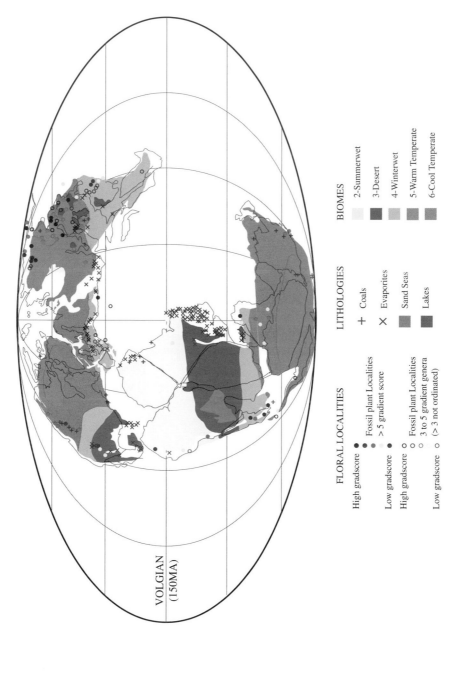

VOLGIAN
(150MA)

FLORAL LOCALITIES

High gradscore
●●● Fossil plant Localities
  ●●● > 5 gradient score

High gradscore
○○○ Fossil plant Localities
  ○○○ 3 to 5 gradient genera
  ○ (> 3 not ordinated)

Low gradscore

LITHOLOGIES

+ Coals

× Evaporites

▨ Sand Seas

▨ Lakes

BIOMES

2-Summerwet

3-Desert

4-Winterwet

5- Warm Temperate

6-Cool Temperate

Figure 6.21. Global patterns of floral provinces and lithological indicators based on data from fossils (from Rees *et al.*, 2000).

analogues with fossil reconstructions. The global distribution of plant functional types in the late Jurassic at 1800 ppm CO_2 can be compared with the reconstruction distribution of vegetation types for the same interval based on analyses of fossil plants (Figs. 6.20b and 6.21). The simulation indicates that in the southern hemisphere, evergreen needle-leaved forests dominated Antarctica and Australia, and these forests correspond to the distribution of the cool temperate biome of Rees *et al.* (2000). In these areas, podocarpous conifers were thought to be an important component of the floras (Wing & Sues, 1992).

At lower latitudes, shrub distribution is widespread (Fig. 6.20b) and corresponds with areas reconstructed as the winter-wet biome and, in some places, desert (Fig. 6.21). The prediction of shrubs agrees with the suggestion (Crane, 1987) that the Jurassic bennettitaleans distributed at low latitudes were shrubby plants occupying open habitats, with some members of the group thought to be deciduous and closely analogous to extant shrubs (Wing & Sues, 1992). Note that shrubs are not classified into broad-leaved and needle-leaved categories and could represent either leaf form. The distribution of the warm temperate biome of Rees *et al.* (2000) most closely matches the simulated distribution of the deciduous broad-leaved forests in the northern hemisphere. Evergreen broad-leaved trees are severely limited in spatial extent and generally confined to regions at low (near equatorial) latitudes, overlapping with areas of summer-wet and warm temperate biomes.

The model does not reproduce the large areas designated 'desert' by Rees *et al.* (2000). Since these areas are evidently suitable for positive NPP (Fig. 6.14b), although quite restricted in some areas, it suggests that either the underlying GCM climate is too wet, and/or the vegetation model is too sensitive to the seasonal distribution of precipitation. Alternatively, the extrapolation of such large desert areas based on relatively few palaeodata points by Rees *et al.* (2000) may not be warranted (Fig. 6.21). The deciduous habit is predicted to be quite widespread, particularly in the northern hemisphere (Fig. 6.20), and fossil evidence suggests some genera of the late Jurassic Cheirolepidaceae conifers were deciduous, based on shoot morphology and the accumulation of foliage in bedding planes (Alvin *et al.*, 1981).

Comparisons of predicted and observed distributions of different types of vegetation at 150 Ma are limited by the global abundance of fossilised plant remains, according to reports and descriptions of such finds in the literature as well as uncertainties in interpretation. Nevertheless, at a very broad scale, the comparison between observed and predicted distributions produces many areas of agreement, indicating that the approach taken to modelling the distribution of functional types operates reasonably.

The impact of the low CO_2 concentration of the present day (350 ppm) on the distribution of functional types in the late Jurassic is rather small. The most notable difference is the decrease in the geographical extent of shrubs in the northern hemisphere and their replacement by deciduous broad-leaved forests. The replacement occurs because the deciduous habit allows a longer growing season, so that soil water is not depleted. There is also a small increase in the extent of evergreen broad-leaved forests in low latitudes at 350 compared with 1800 ppm CO_2.

Comparison with the Jurassic geological record

This chapter has outlined some rather specific approaches to testing the model predictions, all based on the use of the plant fossil record. Here, the comparisons are extended further by examining global and latitudinal patterns of the vegetation properties for comparison with global compilations of the distribution of evaporites and coals (Parrish *et al.*, 1982; Rees *et al.*, 2000). The observed distributions of evaporites and coals are particularly valuable and update those of Parrish *et al.* (1982) with new dates, stratigraphy and palaeolatitudes of the source sites. Simulated productivities will be tested against reconstructions using fossil tree ring data.

Comparing the observed global distribution of coals (Fig. 6.21) with modelled soil C concentration (Fig. 6.14c) indicates areas of correspondence between high soil C and the presence of coals, in Australia and on the eastern and western edges of Antarctica. There is some correspondence along the northern and eastern edges of the land mass comprising Russia, central Europe and China. Similarly good correspondence is evident when comparing Figs. 6.14c and Fig. 6.22, the latter showing the original reconstruction of Parrish *et al.* (1982) for the late Jurassic. Calculated as area-weighted latitudinal averages, the soil C values track the number of coal deposits (Fig. 6.23; Crowley & North, 1991). In the Volgian (*c.* 150 Ma), coal deposits were concentrated around 50° N, near the equator and below 50° S and the latitudinally averaged pattern of soil C reflects this feature of the geological record (Fig. 6.23). Since soil C integrates the ecosystem properties of productivity, litter production and the nutrient and water cycling through vegetation and soils, the similarity between observed and predicted latitudinal bands provides broad support for the global-scale approach to our palaeo-biogeochemical modelling efforts.

Comparisons between the distribution of evaporites, typical of seasonally arid conditions, with LAI predictions, indicates areas of similarity and differences. Areas of agreement extend along the eastern coast of Africa and in eastern areas of northern America, evaporite deposits are abundant (Figs. 6.21 and 6.22) which correspond to very low (0–3) LAI values (Fig. 6.14a). There is

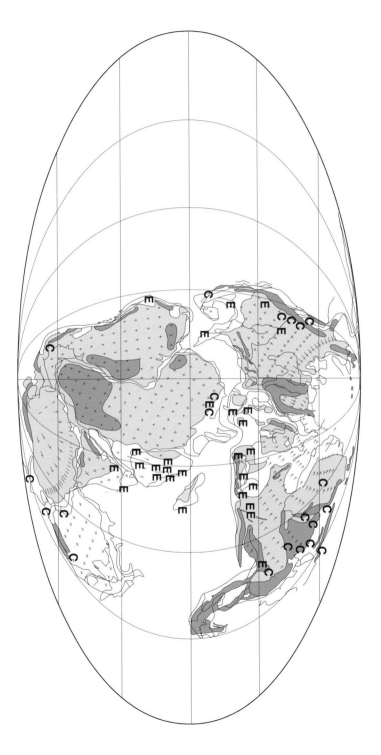

Figure 6.22. Global distribution of evaporites (E) and coals (C) in the late Jurassic (from Parrish *et al.*, 1982). Dark grey regions represent uplands.

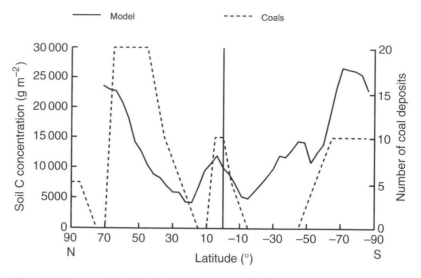

Figure 6.23. Area-weighted latitudinal averages of soil C concentration and the number of coal deposits for the Volgian stage of the Jurassic. Coal deposit data from Crowley & North (1991).

also a large area towards the central interior of the Kazakhstan land mass where evaporites occur and LAI is low. The reconstructed desert region through central South America and Africa (Rees et al., 2000), although predicted to be vegetation (Fig. 6.19), corresponds to regions of low or zero LAI, albeit of small geographical extent, suggesting the potential for the existence of sparse cover. One significant area of mismatch between model predictions and the geological record is along the southern edge of central Europe where evaporites are abundant but LAI is high, c. 11–12.

Interestingly, the reconstructed global distribution of evaporites shows a pattern most strongly reflected in terrestrial productivity rather than LAI (Fig. 6.14b). When both LAI and NPP are expressed as area-weighted latitudinal averages and compared with the latitudinal distribution of evaporite deposits (Crowley & North, 1991; Fig. 6.24), the low LAI values are not confined to latitudes with a high frequency of deposits, whereas for NPP there is a stronger correspondence (Fig. 6.24b).

The final test of the model results has been to compare estimates of terrestrial NPP with estimates derived from tree ring data obtained from fossilised Upper Jurassic woods (Creber & Chaloner, 1985). Following previous approaches (Creber & Chaloner, 1985; Creber & Francis, 1987; Chaloner & Creber, 1989), NPP is calculated from observations on fossil woods by first assuming that annual increases in trunk wood can be conveniently regarded as the volume of a rotation paraboloid (Gray, 1956), so that the annual volume of wood (m³) produced in a year is given by:

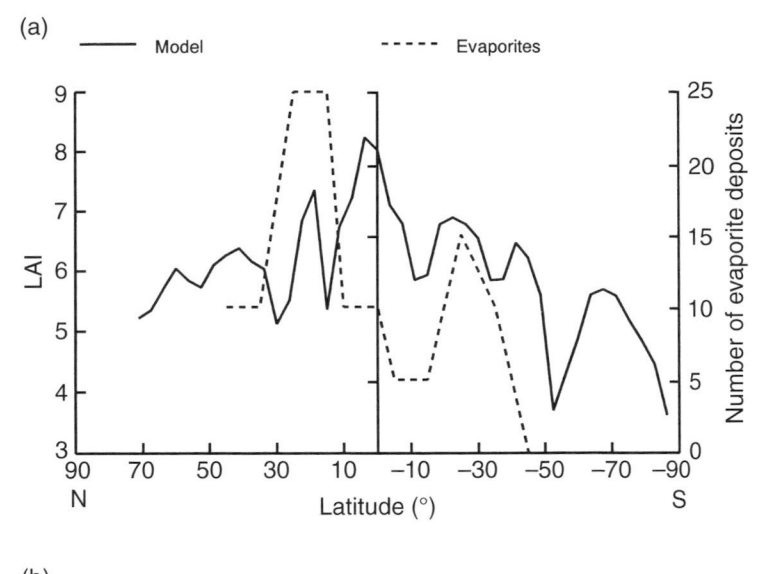

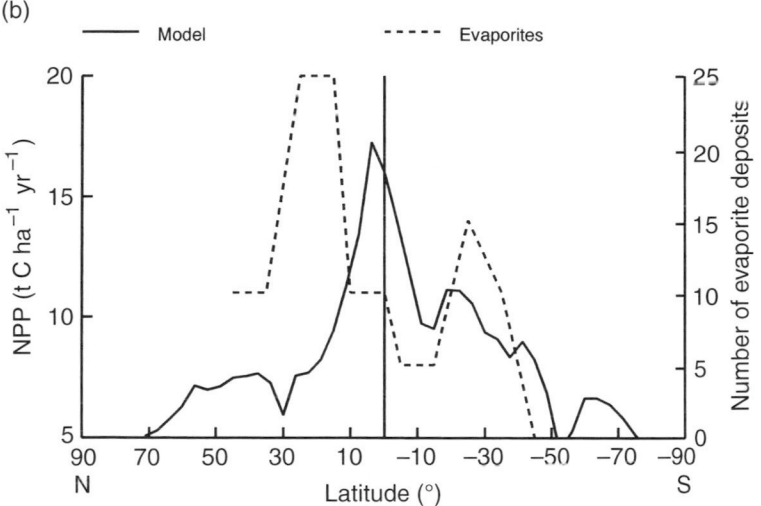

Figure 6.24. Area-weighted latitudinal averages of (a) leaf area index and (b) net primary productivity compared with the frequency of evaporite deposits recorded in the geological record. Evaporite deposit data from Crowley & North (1991).

$$\text{Annual wood volume} = \left(\pi(r+x)^2\, \frac{h}{2} \right) - \left(\pi r^2\, \frac{h}{2} \right) \tag{6.7}$$

where r is the radius of the trunk base (m), h is height (m) and x is tree ring width (m). The left-hand side of equation 6.7 describes the wood volume after one year's growth whilst the right-hand side gives it before one year's trunk wood is laid down. The height of a gymnosperm tree, h (m), can be estimated from measurements of fossil trunk diameter, d (m), assuming that the

Table 6.5. *Estimates of tree ring widths from fossil woods of Upper and Middle Jurassic ages and corresponding net primary productivities (NPP) for two different tree densities and model productivities*[c]

Age/Locality[a]	Latitude	Ring width (mm)	NPP[b] (t C ha^{-1} yr^{-1}) Tree density (ha^{-1})		Modelled NPP (t C ha^{-1} yr^{-1})
			50	100	
Upper Jurassic					
Dorset, England	36 °N	3.7	9.4	18.1	10–12
Hopeh, China	37 °N	5.0	12.2	24.5	10–12
Koryak, Russia	72 °N	3.0	7.3	14.6	8–9
Koti-ken, Japan	36 °N	3.0	7.3	14.6	8–10
Santa Cruz, Argentina	53 °S	2.5	6.1	12.6	12–14
Middle Jurassic					
Bihar, India	40 °S	1.2	2.9	5.9	10–12
New Zealand, South Island	70 °S	1.1	2.7	5.4	7–8

[a]Data from the summary of Creber & Chaloner (1985).
[b]Net primary productivty (NPP) was estimated, unless stated otherwise, for all trees using an average trunk diameter of 1.8 m for Jurassic forest trees (Francis, 1983; McKnight *et al.*, 1990). The density of forest trees is less secure so NPP has been estimated for two values.
[c]Model estimates taken from Fig. 6.14b.

contemporary empirical relationship with the diameter was true for the past, using (Niklas, 1993):

$$h = 27.8d^{0.43} \tag{6.8}$$

The volume of trunk wood in a year is then converted to weight by multiplying with the gravimetric density (ρ) of wood, taken for conifer wood as 4.6×10^5 g m^{-3} (G. Creber and J. Francis, personal communication), converted for the equivalent mass (*em*) of C for organic matter (42%) (Larcher, 1994) and finally multiplied by the density of trees per unit area (*td*). Calculated in this way, tree rings provide a crude estimate of annual trunk wood productivity. This can then be extended to calculate forest NPP based on the estimate that trunk or bole wood is *c.* 40% of the net primary productivity of modern trees Creber & Francis (1987). Combining equations 6.7 and 6.8 and simplifying, this yields the following term for NPP (t C ha^{-1}):

$$NPP = \frac{1}{8 \times 10^5} \pi(2r + x)\rho.em.td \tag{6.9}$$

Some of the assumptions used in each of the above steps are probably undermined by the effects of high atmospheric CO_2 on tree growth, and consequently are likely to be in error (Beerling, 1998). We note that this approach is

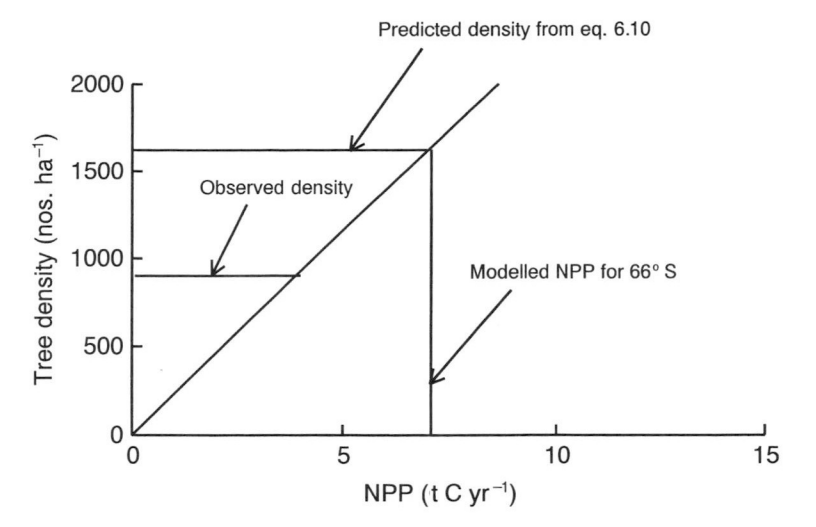

Figure 6.25. Calculated relationship between modelled net primary production and observed tree density for the middle Jurassic fossil forest in Curio Bay, New Zealand, observed density from Pole (1999).

correlative, but use it nevertheless since it provides the only basis of extrapolating productivity estimates back in time, based on the plant fossil record. Therefore, with these reservations, the approach has been applied to tree rings of fossil woods, summarised by Creber & Chaloner (1985). Table 6.5 includes data from mid- to high latitudes in the northern and southern hemispheres where a strong seasonal climatic regime results in regular wood growth, i.e. distinct growth rings. In fossil woods from low latitudes, growth rings are either absent or very faint, reflecting the lack of seasonality in these regions; consequently these are of limited value for calculating NPP in the method given above.

The density-dependent range of NPP estimates calculated from tree rings of Upper Jurassic fossil woods are within those estimated by the model for all five sites for which tree ring data are available (Table 6.5). Comparison of the model with middle Jurassic fossil wood data suggests that the climate at this time was different from that modelled for the late Jurassic. Although the comparison with Upper Jurassic woods is encouraging, there are several uncertainties with this approach to calculating NPP in the past. Not least of these uncertainties is the tree (plant) density of the original forests, and whether the proportion of NPP allocated to stem tissue under elevated CO_2 is the same as for ambient CO_2 partial pressures. For trees with a diameter of 1.8 m, the predictions of NPP do not support the idea of very high densities of trees, i.e. much above *c.* 100 mature trees ha^{-1} (Table 6.5).

For smaller diameter trees (0.1–0.16 m diameter) much higher densities have been reported (up to 850 ha^{-1}) for a middle Jurassic forest in New Zealand, at a palaeolatitude of 66° S (Pole, 1999). In this case, it is possible to rearrange equation 6.9, using the modelled NPP (c. 7 Gt C yr^{-1}; Fig. 6.14) to predict the equivalent tree density (td, ha^{-1}), given measurements of mean tree diameter (0.16 m), ring width (r, 2.5 mm), and tree height (14 m) (Pole, 1999):

$$td = 8 \times 10^5 \frac{NPP}{[\pi hr\rho(2x + r)]} \tag{6.10}$$

Calculated with these figures, it can be seen (Fig. 6.25) that there is an overestimation of tree density from the model estimate of 7 Gt C by about double compared with the observed density. As with the previous middle Jurassic estimates (Table 6.5), these differences would seem to indicate differences in polar climate between the middle and late Jurassic. It is, however, difficult to isolate the exact causal nature of any such differences with any degree of certainty and further work on the allometry of tree growth and stem wood production under elevated CO_2 concentrations would be useful in this respect.

Conclusions

At the global scale, the late Jurassic was a far more productive period than the Carboniferous (Table 6.3), despite evidence for arid continental zones. Vegetation in a high CO_2 environment is predicted to experience shifts in the metabolic control of photosynthesis, mostly dependent upon temperature, relative to ambient CO_2. Sensitivity analyses of these CO_2 effects indicate a marked influence on net primary productivity and leaf area index. Globally, for example, total terrestrial NPP increases some 70% from 63 to 109 Gt C yr^{-1} with CO_2 concentrations from 350 to 1800 ppm (Table 6.3). Some point estimates of NPP based on calculations using ring widths of fossil woods overlap those predicted by the vegetation model, providing support for our modelling approach. LAI is modelled to be strongly influenced by the increase in CO_2, but this response has not yet been adequately tested in a manner consistent with experimental data by plant growth experiments with CO_2 enrichment (Table 6.4, Fig. 6.17). Moreover, this has a number of important implications for accurate modelling the effect of feedback of vegetation on climate.

7

The Cretaceous

Introduction

The Cretaceous period (140–65 Ma) is generally considered to represent the Earth in an extreme 'greenhouse' mode (Frakes *et al.*, 1992), most obviously manifested in the plant fossil record by the high latitude occurrence of substantial polar forests. Increased global warmth is thought to have been derived, in part, from the configuration of the continents (Barron & Washington, 1985), allowing significant poleward heat transport (Herman & Spicer, 1996), and also from the high partial pressure of atmospheric CO_2 (Berner, 1994). The mid-Cretaceous in particular has received considerable research attention as a period for evaluating the extent to which it provides a possible analogue for a greenhouse Earth warmed by a high atmospheric CO_2 content (Barron, 1982, 1983; Barron *et al.*, 1993, 1995; Price *et al.*, 1995, 1997, 1998). It is unlikely, however, that the mid-Cretaceous greenhouse world, or indeed any other period in Earth history, represents a robust analogy for a future globally-warmed Earth, because of the large number of differences between the past and now, particularly geography, orography and oceanic boundary conditions (Crowley, 1990, 1993; Barron, 1994). Nevertheless, this suggestion has not been addressed for vegetation and the terrestrial carbon cycle. Therefore the future relevance of the most geologically recent episode of extreme 'greenhouse' warmth in the mid-Eocene is explored in further detail in Chapter 8.

Although described as a warm 'greenhouse' environment, a general cooling trend is apparent over the 75 million year duration of the Cretaceous, particularly since about 90 Ma (Douglas & Savin, 1975; Boersma & Shackleton, 1981; Spicer & Corfield, 1992). This trend is shown by the oxygen isotope ($\delta^{18}O$) records of foraminifera from ocean sediments which reflect the temperature in which the organisms grew (i.e. as apparent in shell calcification). Planktonic

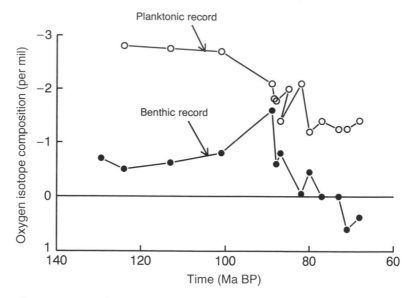

Figure 7.1. Oxygen isotope data from planktonic and benthic foraminifera from the low latitude Pacific Ocean spanning the Cretaceous (from Douglas & Savin, 1975 and Boersma & Shackleton, 1981).

and benthic foraminifera provide estimates of the temperature of surface and deep waters respectively, and the difference between the two can be used to interpret ocean circulation changes. Isotopic records for surface water and deep ocean foraminifera from the low latitude Pacific Ocean both show a marked trend towards more negative oxygen isotope values (Fig. 7.1).

The marine oxygen isotope data (Fig. 7.1) can be used to estimate palaeo-temperatures according to the equation:

$$T = 16.0 - 4.14(\delta_c - \delta_w) + 0.13(\delta_c - \delta_w)^2 \qquad (7.1)$$

where T is temperature (°C), δ_c is the $\delta^{18}O$ ratio of the carbonate and δ_w is the $\delta^{18}O$ ratio of seawater (Attendorn & Bowen, 1997). There are, however many uncertainties associated with the application of equation 7.1 for determining ocean palaeotemperatures. The isotopic composition of seawater in the past is unknown (Attendorn & Bowen, 1997), and for the Cretaceous it is assumed there was no influence of major ice caps, a value of $-1.2‰$ being typical (Sellwood et al., 1994), although some correction might be needed for surface ocean waters depleted in ^{16}O due to evaporation (Spicer & Corfield, 1992). There is also a possible bias in palaeotemperature estimates with equation 7.1 due to changes in salinity (Klein et al., 1996), resulting from freshwater–seawater mixing, and changes in seawater carbonate ion concentrations (Spero et al., 1997).

Calculated from equation 7.1, with δ_w equal to $-1.2‰$, isotopic evidence

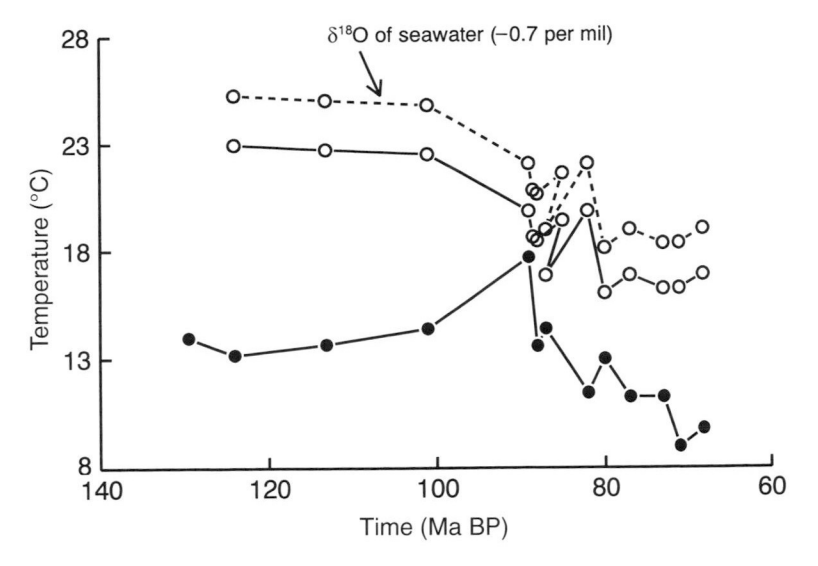

Figure 7.2. Temperature trends in surface and deep waters of the Pacific Ocean, estimated from oxygen isotope data (Fig. 7.1) and eq. 7.1. For the surface ocean record, a second set of palaeotemperatures was calculated with $\delta_w = -0.7$ ‰, as recommended by Spicer & Corfield (1992). Open and closed symbols represent planktonic and benthic foraminifera respectively.

from deep sea cores indicates that the temperature of the surface and deep ocean waters dropped by over 5 °C between 90 and 65 Ma (Fig. 7.2), i.e. during the second part of the Cretaceous. Examination of the oxygen isotope record for the next 10 Ma reveals a continued but less dramatic cooling trend, implying that the early Cretaceous was a significant time of anomalous warmth (Spicer & Corfield, 1992). Preliminary analyses indicate that the late Cretaceous temperature decline resulted from increased biological productivity, via enhanced photosynthesis in the surface ocean, leading to a draw-down in atmospheric CO_2 by increased carbon burial (Spicer & Corfield, 1992). There must also have been an impact of increased plant cover, with the continued evolution of higher plants, on rock weathering rates, as one of the long-term controls on the concentration of atmospheric CO_2 (Berner, 1994). Overall, the Cretaceous period can be regarded in two parts, the early and mid-Cretaceous being significantly warmer with a higher CO_2 concentration (*c.* 100–90 Pa) than the cooler and lower CO_2 concentration (*c.* 500–600 ppm) environment of the late Cretaceous. Mechanistic studies of leaf-scale modelling indicated, early on, the potential for the Cretaceous CO_2 and temperature trends to influence the terrestrial carbon cycle (Beerling, 1994) and the global-scale consequences are explored in this chapter.

In this chapter the productivity, distribution and biogeochemistry of terrestrial ecosystems have been investigated at different time intervals of the

Cretaceous to reflect the overall cooling trends represented by the marine isotopic data. This has been achieved through the use of GCM climate simulations for the mid-Cretaceous (100 Ma) (Price *et al.*, 1995, 1997, 1998) and the very end of Cretaceous (65 Ma) (Otto-Bliesner & Upchurch, 1997; Upchurch *et al.*, 1998). The close of the Cretaceous and beginning of the Tertiary period at 66 Ma (K/T boundary) was marked by the impact of a large (10–14 km) diameter bolide (Alvarez *et al.*, 1980), with an influence on climate and, presumably, terrestrial ecosystem function. The global effect of these influences on the world's biota is uncertain, as interpreted from the fossil record (Ward, 1995; Archibald, 1996) and their quantitative nature is largely unknown. Therefore we have attempted a global-scale study, quantifying the possible effects of short-term and long-term environmental change resulting from the impact event on terrestrial ecosystems (Lomax *et al.*, 2000, 2001). The approach has been to develop a range of both short-term (10^0–10^3 yr) and long-term (10^4–10^5 yr) post-impact climates by adjusting a late Cretaceous GCM global climate (Otto-Bliesner & Upchurch, 1997) in line with the palaeodata (Wolfe, 1990) and modelling studies (O'Keefe & Ahrens, 1989; Barron *et al.*, 1993; Covey *et al.*, 1994).

The Cretaceous was also noteworthy for the evolution and rapid diversification of angiosperms, a feature clearly shown in the fossil record (Lidgard & Crane, 1990), and much debate has centred on the controls (biotic vs. abiotic) of the floristic diversity within terrestrial ecosystems (Wing & DiMichele, 1995). These twin themes have been investigated with a simple model accounting for the family-level diversity of vegetation based on the importance of low temperature, accumulated growing season warmth and canopy structure (leaf area index, LAI) (Woodward & Rochefort, 1991) applied to the mid- and late Cretaceous. This assessment is extended to consider changes in the post-K/T boundary impact climate on the ability of the environment to support diverse assemblages of vegetation.

The global mid- and late Cretaceous environment

The global Cretaceous climates were generated by the UGAMP GCM mid-Cretaceous (100 Ma) simulations and the National Center for Atmospheric Research (NCAR) late Cretaceous (66 Ma) simulation. Both use close approximations to the continental geography and orography for each interval (Fig. 7.3) which, by this time, had begun to resemble the present-day configuration (Smith *et al.*, 1994). The UGAMP mid-Cretaceous simulation was made with the GCM in a 'greenhouse' mode, where sea surface temperatures are fixed using a simple zonally symmetric profile ranging from 28 °C in the tropics to 0 °C at the poles (Valdes *et al.*, 1996). The model includes an element of seasonality and was run at the University of Reading with an atmospheric CO_2 concentration of 1080 ppm and a spatial resolution of 3.75° × 3.75°. All other parameters, including the Earth's orbital characteristics and solar constant, were kept at their present-day values. Detailed descriptions of the model set-up and climate can be found elsewhere (Valdes *et al.*, 1996; Price *et al.*, 1995, 1997, 1998). The model was run for a 10-year period and the climate of the last four years averaged to produce the 'mid-Cretaceous climate'.

The late Cretaceous simulation was made with the NCAR GENESIS GCM (Thompson & Pollard, 1995) with a resolution of 4.5° lat. × 7.5° long. for the atmospheric model and 2° lat. × 2° long. for the land surface and was taken from the work of Upchurch *et al.* (1998). The prescribed boundary conditions for the simulation were atmospheric CO_2 concentration (580 ppm), latest Maastrichtian palaeogeography (Fig. 7.3b) and present-day orbital configurations, but with a slightly reduced solar constant (Crowley & Baum, 1991). Full climate model details are given elsewhere (Otto-Bliesner & Upchurch, 1997; Upchurch *et al.*, 1998). In this chapter, the 'best guess' simulation of Otto-Bliesner & Upchurch (1997) has been used, which includes some physiological and physical feedbacks of vegetation on climate, particularly important at high latitudes.

At the global scale, the GCM-derived mean annual temperatures (MATs) (Fig. 7.4) show that the cooling trend between the mid- and late Cretaceous represented in the $\delta^{18}O$ of foraminifera (Fig. 7.2) is expressed most strongly at the global scale as an expansion of cool high latitude regions and a contraction of the warm low latitude regions. This trend is clearly seen when the climates are viewed as latitudinal averages (Fig. 7.5), in which mid-Cretaceous MATs do not fall below zero even at latitudes above 60° N whereas those for the late Cretaceous fall to −10 °C in both northern and southern polar regions.

The GCM-derived global precipitation patterns for the mid- and late Cretaceous show quite similar amounts (in terms of mean monthly values), distributed in largely similar regions (Fig. 7.6). The similarity is surprising given that the precipitation fields were generated by two different GCMs, and that in both the grid sizes are much smaller than the convective element of the atmosphere, which can lead to poor representation of the seasonal cycle. Some differences do, however, emerge between the two intervals. In particular, the equatorial regions through central south America, central Africa, northern India, eastern North America and eastern Asia had all become wetter by the late Cretaceous (Fig. 7.6), a feature most strongly expressed in the latitudinal averages (Fig. 7.7).

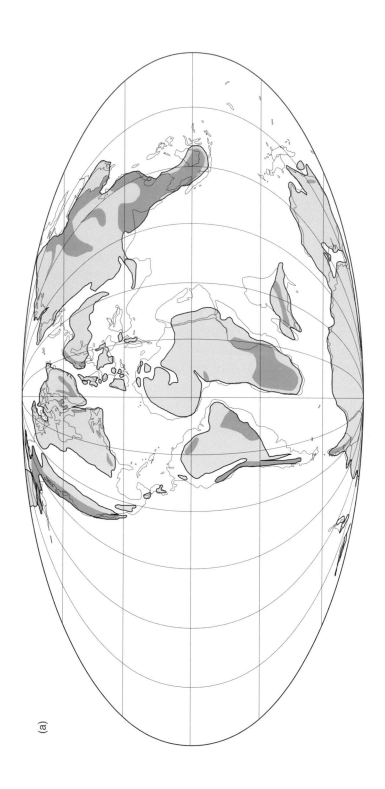

(a)

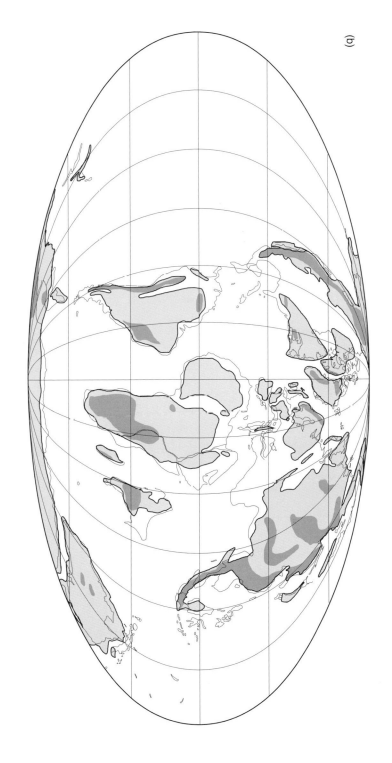

(b)

Figure 7.3. Reconstructed continental configurations for (a) the Cenomanian (95 Ma) and (b) the Maastrichtian (66 Ma) stages of the Cretaceous (from Smith *et al.*, 1994). Dark grey shading indicates uplands.

(a)

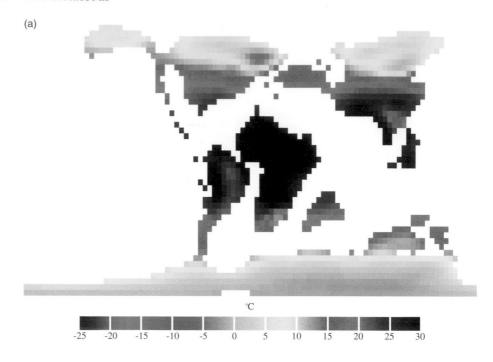

(b)

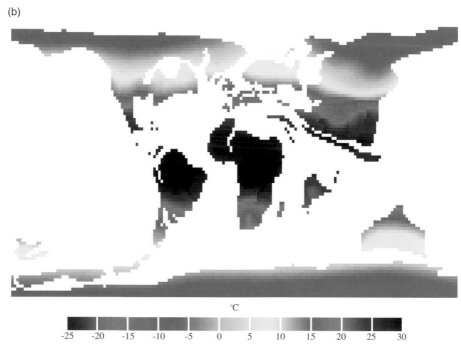

Figure 7.4. Mean annual temperature over the land in (a) the mid-Cretaceous (100 Ma) and (b) the late Cretaceous (66 Ma).

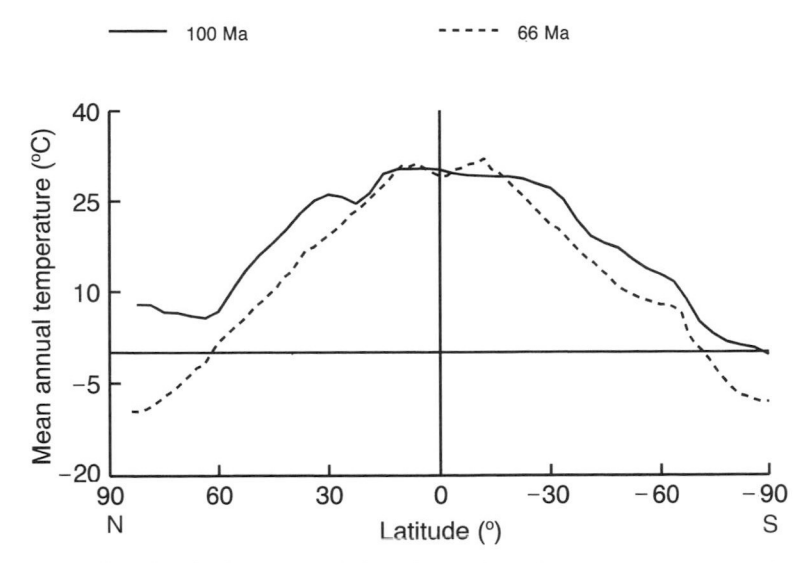

Figure 7.5. Latitudinal averages of the mid- and late-Cretaceous mean annual temperatures.

Both mid- and late Cretaceous climates have been compared and extensively validated against the fossil record of climatically sensitive indicators, although different approaches to testing were adopted for each era (Price *et al.*, 1995, 1997, 1998; Otto-Bliesner & Upchurch, 1997; Upchurch *et al.*, 1998). For the UGAMP mid-Cretaceous simulation, a quantitative approach to validation was taken whereby climatic requirements for modern bauxites and peatlands were applied to the Cretaceous output to predict the occurrence of these sediments. In all cases, the predictions showed good correspondence with the observed distribution of sediments, indicating that the GCM successfully replicated global patterns of precipitation and temperature in the mid-Cretaceous (Price *et al.*, 1997).

The NCAR-derived late Cretaceous climate has been tested against palaeodata using a different approach (Otto-Bliesner & Upchurch, 1997). The resulting climate was used in a correlative scheme, in which vegetation distribution is predicted by its modern-day climatic envelope (Köppen, 1936). The classification was then used to predict the distribution of vegetation in the late Cretaceous for comparison with a global reconstruction of vegetation based on over 300 records of fossil plant remains and lithological indicators (Otto-Bliesner & Upchurch, 1997; Upchurch *et al.*, 1998). The resulting match between the predicted and observed datasets was reasonably good, indicating that the GCM climate gave a close approximation to the 'real' late Cretaceous climates. Errors expected from the influence of high CO_2 on plant climatic ranges (Woodward & Beerling, 1997) cannot be excluded. Overall, the

(a)

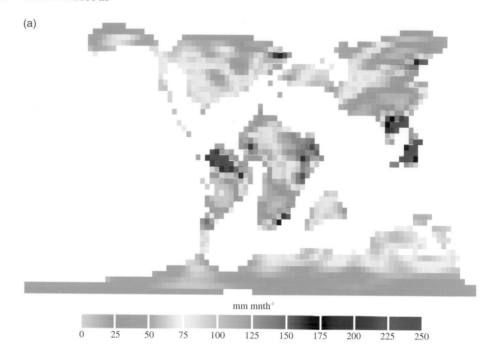

(b)

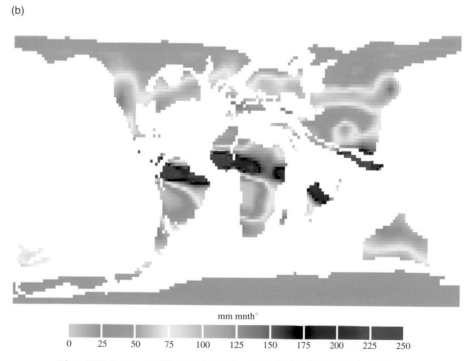

Figure 7.6 Mean monthly precipitation over the land in (a) the mid-Cretaceous and (b) the late Cretaceous.

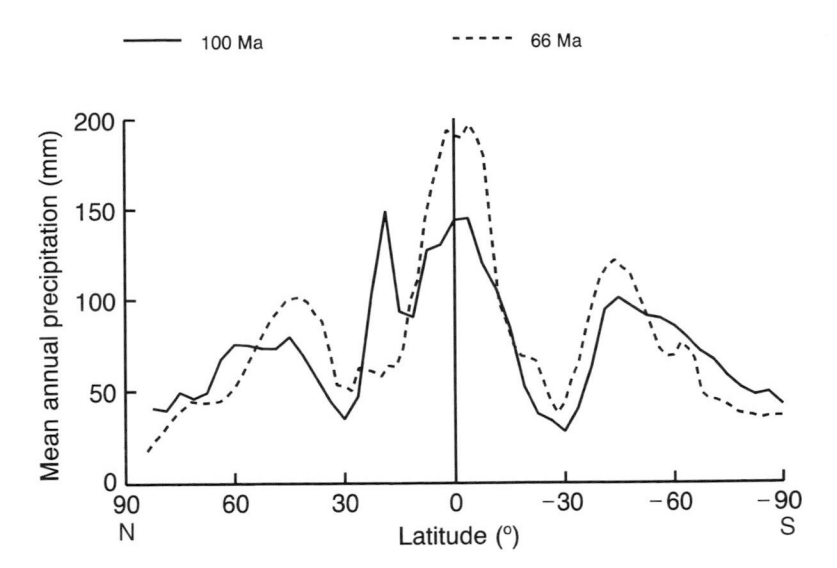

Figure 7.7. Latitudinal averages of mean monthly precipitation in mid- and late Cretaceous GCM climates.

validation of each Cretaceous GCM palaeoclimate indicates their utility for predicting the function of the terrestrial biosphere at these times.

Post-K/T boundary impact environments

The NCAR late Cretaceous climate has been adjusted to obtain a crude representation of the possible short-term (10^0–10^3 yr) and long-term (10^4–10^5 yr) effects of a bolide impact at the K/T boundary on terrestrial eco-system operation at the global scale. The two timescales were selected to be broadly consistent with climate modelling results for the duration of the reductions in both temperature and incoming solar radiation (Covey *et al.*, 1994; Pope *et al.*, 1994), and palaeobotanical evidence (Wolfe, 1990) and sea surface temperature reconstructions from sediments for post-K/T boundary warming (Brinkhuis *et al.*, 1998).

The Chicxulub impact crater (diameter 100 km) in Mexico (21° N) is gener-ally regarded as the most likely candidate for the terminal Cretaceous impact event, based on the age of infilled sediments and the underlying target rocks (Krogh *et al.*, 1993), as well as its size and morphology (Morgan *et al.*, 1997). From the transient size of the cavity, Morgan *et al.* (1997) predicted a diameter of *c.* 10–14 km for the impactor, depending on whether it was a comet or an asteroid, and an impact energy of 5×10^{23} J (equivalent to 1.2×10^8 megatons of TNT, where 1 megaton (Mt) $= 4.18 \times 10^{15}$ J). The mass of carbonate vaporised depends on whether the impactor was a comet or a meteorite, its size, and the depth of the carbonate marine terrace at the site of impact (O'Keefe & Ahrens, 1989). Geochemical and petrographic analyses of fossil meteorite fragments (Kyte, 1998), and isotopic studies of chromium at the K/T boundary (Shukolyukov & Lugmair, 1998), all indicate signatures consistent with a carbonaceous chondrite rather than porous cometary material, implying that the impactor was probably an asteroidal meteorite rather than a comet. In consequence, a 12 km diameter meteorite was predicted from the Chixculub crater dimensions (Morgan *et al.*, 1997). The expected short-term effects would be an initial cooling due to high dust loading in the atmosphere, the long-term effects being a climatic warming due to the large amounts of carbon rock vaporised and converted into atmospheric CO_2. The next two sections consider these changes in greater detail and the corresponding adjustments made to the late Cretaceous (66 Ma) global climate used to force the vegetation– biogeochemistry model.

Short-term post-impact environment, 10^0–10^3 years

The most obvious major effect of such a high energy impact is the vaporisation of target rock, creating and propelling a large quantity of fine-grain particles (dust, soot or sulphate aerosols) into the upper atmosphere (Fig. 7.8a). This would occur even where oceans were overlying the target rocks, since the depth of the oceans (4 km) is less than the estimated size of the impactor. Atmospheric opacity might also be further enhanced by sulphate aerosols (Pope *et al.*, 1994) and the soot from wildfires (Wolbach *et al.*, 1985, 1988, 1990a,b). The first short-term environmental influence of the K/T boundary impact therefore would be global reductions in the amount of incoming radiation received at the Earth's surface, with consequent influence on global temperatures and photosynthesis.

Reductions in surface temperature, accompanying an increased concentration of dust in the upper atmosphere, have been predicted by atmospheric GCMs to be rather small since any immediate changes would be offset by the heat reservoir of the oceans, thereby minimising the severity of the climatic disturbance (Covey *et al.*, 1994). These climate model results do not support earlier suggestions for a possible global freezing scenario after a K/T boundary impact event (Toon *et al.*, 1982; Pollack *et al.*, 1983; Wolfe, 1991). In their simulations with a globally-distributed dust cloud of small particles (1 μm diameter), Covey *et al.* (1994) reported a rapid drop in global surface temperature of 13 °C within the first few days and then a slow recovery to 6 °C below normal after one year. Later simulations (Pope *et al.*, 1994) suggest that cooling may have been more prolonged (8–13 yr) and more severe, whilst sea surface temperature reconstructions (Brinkhuis *et al.*, 1998) suggest a post-impact cooling phase of 10^4

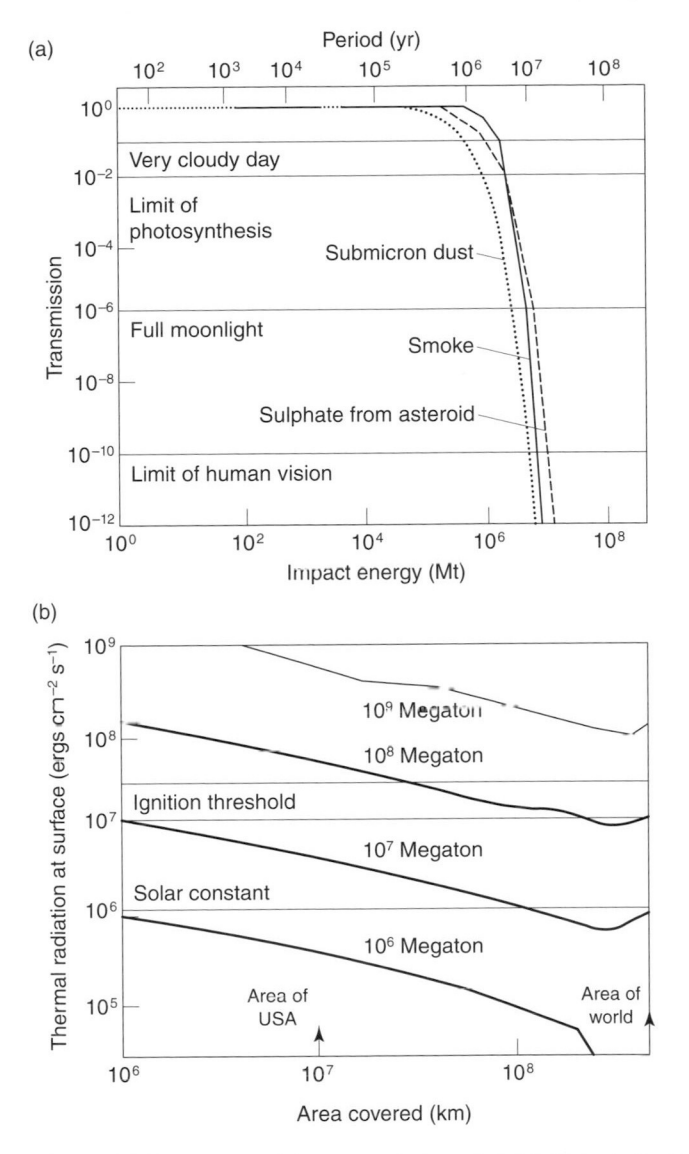

Figure 7.8. (a) Estimates of the transmission of visible light to the Earth's surface as it passes through dust, smoke and sulphate aerosols. Note that energies greater than 10^6 Mt are calculated to lead to global darkness once every *c.* 5–10 Ma. (b) The effect of ballistic ejector re-entering the atmosphere in terms of the radiative flux experienced on the Earth's surface. From Toon *et al.* (1997).

years. For the purposes of this study, the short-term post-impact climate has simply been created by first reducing the late Cretaceous mean annual temperatures by 13 °C for the impact year, and then by 6 °C for the next 100 years, in line with the GCM results of Covey *et al.* (1994). This ignores possible effects of the infalling debris releasing kinetic energy as radiant heat (Fig. 7.8b).

Quantifying reduction of incoming solar radiation associated with the dust cloud is more complex. The amount of radiation escaping absorption and passing through a given concentration of particles (value given for 1 μm diameter particles) is related to their specific extinction coefficients, the fraction of light scattered, rather than absorbed, by dust and an asymmetry factor measuring the degree of forward rather than backward scattering. Taking satellite monitoring observations of stratospheric SO_2 distribution injected by Mt Pinatubo as a guide (c. 15° N) (Graedel & Crutzen, 1997), the ejected dust would most likely be rapidly distributed between 25° N and 30° S of the equator. The slight difference in latitude between the impact site and Mt Pinatubo provides a convenient natural allowance for a possible bias due to an oblique impact (Morgan *et al.*, 1997). Assuming an initial dust loading of 2.5×10^{15} kg, but with the removal of 70% of this material after one year (Pollack *et al.*, 1983) due to settling, and its compression to a narrow latitudinal range, incoming solar radiation for this region would be reduced by 35%; accordingly, this adjustment was made to the model input. An independent climate impact modelling assessment (Pope *et al.*, 1994) supports this reduction and indicates that transmission was reduced by 10–20% compared with normal levels. A global dust cloud might also alter the hydrological cycle (Covey *et al.*, 1994) but, since this is the most uncertain feature of GCMs (see Chapter 4), it is presently regarded as rather speculative and the precipitation fields of the 66 Ma simulation were unchanged.

Due to the near-instantaneous vaporisation of the marine carbonate terrace in which the asteroid landed, the atmospheric carbon reservoir would have accumulated an extra 3000–10 000 Gt C, depending on the depth of the target carbonate terrace (1 km vs. 4 km, respectively) (O'Keefe & Ahrens, 1989). This could have raised the pre-impact CO_2 partial pressure by a factor of 3 to 10, assuming no rapid CO_2 uptake by the oceans. In the short term at least, the impact would have created a very unusual combination of conditions for terrestrial vegetation of high CO_2, low temperatures and low light. Possibly the only approximate modern analogue environment is the understorey of dense temperate rainforests where near-complete canopy closure reduces light and retains CO_2 emitted from soil respiration.

Besides the impact-related effects on climate there is also a direct effect of the impact on vegetation due to the associated blast wave, characterised by an abrupt pressure pulse followed by a substantial wind (Toon *et al.*, 1997), the strength of which is defined by the difference between ambient pressure and the pressure at the blast wave front. We consider the case of a 276 hPa overpressure, corresponding to a wind speed of 70 m s^{-1}, well above hurricane force. The maximum distance, r (km) of the overpressure contour from the point of detonation at a given altitude, h (km) for the K/T impact event

Table 7.1. *Summary of global short-term (10^0–10^3 yr) post-K/T boundary impact climates used to force the vegetation model*

Latitudinal reductions in irradiance by 35%
Reduction in mean annual temperature by 6 C
Increase in atmospheric CO_2 (4×580 ppm)

Note:
All of the above environmental changes were used to force the vegetation model after the destruction of vegetation biomass within the blast wave area.

can be estimated from an empirical relation derived from nuclear weapons testing:

$$r = ah - bh^2E^{-\frac{1}{3}} + cE^{\frac{1}{3}} \qquad (7.2)$$

where E is the energy of the explosion in megatons, $a = 2.09$, $b = 0.449$, $c = 5.08$. It has been estimated that 40% of the K/T impact energy eventually reached the atmosphere (O'Keefe & Ahrens, 1989), most of it going into long-term low-grade heating and only 3% into overpressure shocking of the air. Therefore, the maximum distance a 276 hPa overpressure blast wave could travel, based on an optimal detonation height, h_o (km) $= 2.3 \times E^{\frac{1}{3}}$), would be 1.2×10^3 km, with a total blast area of 4.2×10^6 km², centred at a palaeolatitude of c. 20° N (Morgan *et al.*, 1997). This represents an area of only a few per cent of the total Earth's surface but similar in size to the USA. Calculations of this nature are the only means of estimating the blast area since palaeoevidence is not sufficiently abundant to determine it directly. In addition to the impact of a blast wave, there is also evidence for widespread wildfire resulting from the impact (Wolbach *et al.*, 1985, 1988, 1990 a,b) releasing carbon into the atmosphere. The possible impacts of this global wildfire are considered in more detail below.

To simulate the effect of the short-term post-impact environment on terrestrial ecosystems, equilibrium vegetation and soil carbon pools were first established with the 66 Ma global climate. We then imposed reductions in irradiance and an increase in atmospheric CO_2 as given in Table 7.1, together with a 13°C drop in mean annual temperature for the impact year. Following this 'impact year' scenario, temperatures were reduced by 6 °C and the simulation run for 100 model years with reduced irradiance and high CO_2 atmosphere as before. In a separate sensitivity analysis, the same scenario was run again but with the effects of temperature and irradiance restricted to between 30 °S and 25 °N to account for a possible rapid loss of dust from the atmosphere and its concentration around equatorial regions.

Long-term post-impact environment, 10^4–10^5 years

The long-term (10^4–10^5 yr) environmental consequences of the K/T boundary impact event are generally considered the opposite of the short-term effects, and probably mimicked a global warming event (O'Keefe & Ahrens, 1989; Wolfe, 1990). The warming is thought to have occurred because dust would have been removed from the atmosphere more rapidly than the CO_2. Some influence of the oceans might have been exerted by this time since re-equilibrium of CO_2 by dissolution in the deep ocean water or dissolution of deep-sea sediments may occur on timescales of 10^3–10^4 years (Broecker & Peng, 1982). There might also have been some effect of weathering of carbonate and silicate crustal rocks after 10^5 years (Berner, 1994). However, we choose to allow CO_2 levels to remain at 4×580 ppm (2320 ppm) to investigate a possible upper value for the long-term post-impact effects on terrestrial ecosystems.

Besides atmospheric CO_2 increase, there would also have been the injection of large amounts of water vapour into the atmosphere (from the underlying oceans), an important contributor to post-impact global warming (through the 'greenhouse' effect) and, like CO_2, with a longer residence time than atmospheric dust. However, neither the sign nor magnitude of water vapour effects are clear cut, because although global-scale stratospheric water vapour injections would enhance the greenhouse effect, this warming would be countered to some extent by the increased albedo due to ice cloud formation and rapid horizontal transport processes carrying water-rich air to colder polar regions of the stratosphere (Toon et al., 1997). Uncertainties clearly exist in the driving mechanisms of global post-impact changes in temperature in the long term. Palaeobotanical evidence from close to the impact site supports expectation for a post-impact warming event persisting for 10^4–10^6 years (Wolfe, 1990). Therefore, this warming was simulated at the global scale by increasing monthly temperatures of the late Cretaceous climate by latitude and season based on CO_2 sensitivity studies with a similar version of the NCAR GCM but Cretaceous palaeogeography (Barron et al., 1993).

In addition to changes in temperature, palaeoenvironmental reconstructions from fossil leaf assemblages spanning the K/T boundary imply a change in the hydrological cycle some 10^4–10^6 years after the impact (Wolfe, 1990). These fossil leaf assemblages suggest a four-fold increase in the post-impact precipitation regime, particularly above $30°N$ (Wolfe, 1990). Consequently this was incorporated into the long-term post-impact climate by increasing the late Cretaceous monthly precipitation by 30% in the northern hemisphere

Table 7.2. *Summary of global long-term (10^4–10^5 yr) post-K/T boundary impact climates used to force the vegetation model*

Increase in atmospheric CO_2 concentration to 2320 ppm
Latitudinally-zoned 30% increase in mean annual precipitation
Latitudinally-zoned 4 °C increase in temperature

only, since insufficient information exists to justify extrapolation to the southern hemisphere.

The influence of the long-term post-impact environment on terrestrial ecosystems was assessed by adjusting the pre-impact climate as discussed above and summarised in Table 7.2. The model results from the short-term impact were then used as the starting point for the numerical simulations quantifying the long-term impacts with the newly adjusted climate and atmospheric CO_2 concentration.

Global vegetation productivity and structure in the Cretaceous

Global terrestrial NPP throughout the Cretaceous was generally high, about double the estimates of present-day primary production under a contemporary climate (c. Gt 50 C yr^{-1}), although global NPP fell between the mid- and the late Cretaceous (Table 7.3). Examination of the spatial patterns of NPP variations for both intervals indicates that NPP reductions in the late Cretaceous occur at high latitudes of the northern and southern hemispheres (Fig. 7.9) probably due to the lower polar temperatures simulated by the GCM at this time (Fig. 7.4). In contrast, the equatorial regions of the late Cretaceous were more productive than those of the mid-Cretaceous (Fig. 7.9) and, since mean annual temperatures in these regions were generally similar (Fig. 7.4), this is most likely due to higher amounts of precipitation (Fig. 7.6).

The global pattern of LAI follows similar trends to that of NPP, with areas of greatest canopy depth being associated with regions of highest productivity (Fig. 7.10). Where low precipitation occurs both LAI and NPP are severely restricted and these areas would be equivalent to deserts/semi-deserts. In the mid-Cretaceous, these 'desert' regions extend through southern parts of Asia, South America and Africa (Figs. 7.10a and 7.11a). By the late Cretaceous, the southern Asian deserts contracted but those in South America and Africa continued to remain a similar size (Figs. 7.10b and 7.11b). The location of deserts in the mid-Cretaceous shows some agreement with the global distribution of

Table 7.3. *Global terrestrial net primary production (NPP) and mean leaf area index (LAI) in the Cretaceous. See Tables 7.1 and 7.2, respectively, for more details*

	NPP (Gt C yr^{-1})	Average LAI
Mid-Cretaceous	100.7	5.6
Late-Cretaceous	78.9	4.8
With blast wave destruction of vegetation biomass	78.2	4.8
Short-term post-impact environment (10^0–10^3 yr)	73.9	4.1
Long-term post-impact environment (10^4–10^5 yr)	146.8	6.6

evaporites for this interval (Price *et al.*, 1997), except in the middle of Asia where bauxites occur. Bauxites are thought to represent a generally humid environment and the reason for this discrepancy is unclear. For the late Cretaceous, the location of deserts and semi-deserts shows very good correspondence with reconstructions from lithological indicators of arid conditions (Otto-Bliesner & Upchurch, 1997; Upchurch *et al.*, 1998).

The presence of polar forests represented by large fossilised tree trunks, often in quite high densities, in northern and southern hemispheres is obvious testament to a climate conducive to productive vegetation throughout the Cretaceous (Frakes *et al.*, 1992). Assuming wide tree ring widths to be indicative of high productivity, unlimited by light and water supply but with low temperature seasons (i.e. cool winters), then the modelled areas of high productivity should correspond with wide ring widths, at least in regions where the vegetation experienced some degree of seasonality. It emerges that growth ring widths measured from fossil woods of mid-Cretaceous and late Cretaceous age (Creber & Chaloner, 1985) are quite wide compared with modern high latitude arctic plants confirming, in part, the potential for forests at quite high latitudes to achieve substantial growth. In the southern hemisphere, analyses of the tree ring sequences of fossil forests preserved in Antarctica also show uniformly wide ring widths, indicating favourable conditions for tree growth, with fossil forests of these regions considered to be analogous to the Australian tropical forests of today (Francis, 1986a, b). The limited palaeobotanical observations are therefore consistent with the global pattern of NPP simulated here for the Cretaceous.

The imposition of the short-term post-impact environment led to dynamic responses of NPP that differed from those of carbon storage in vegetation biomass and soil organic matter (Fig. 7.12). Global NPP shows a dramatic collapse following the abrupt drop in irradiance and temperature after the impact and then a rapid recovery to above pre-impact levels within a decade

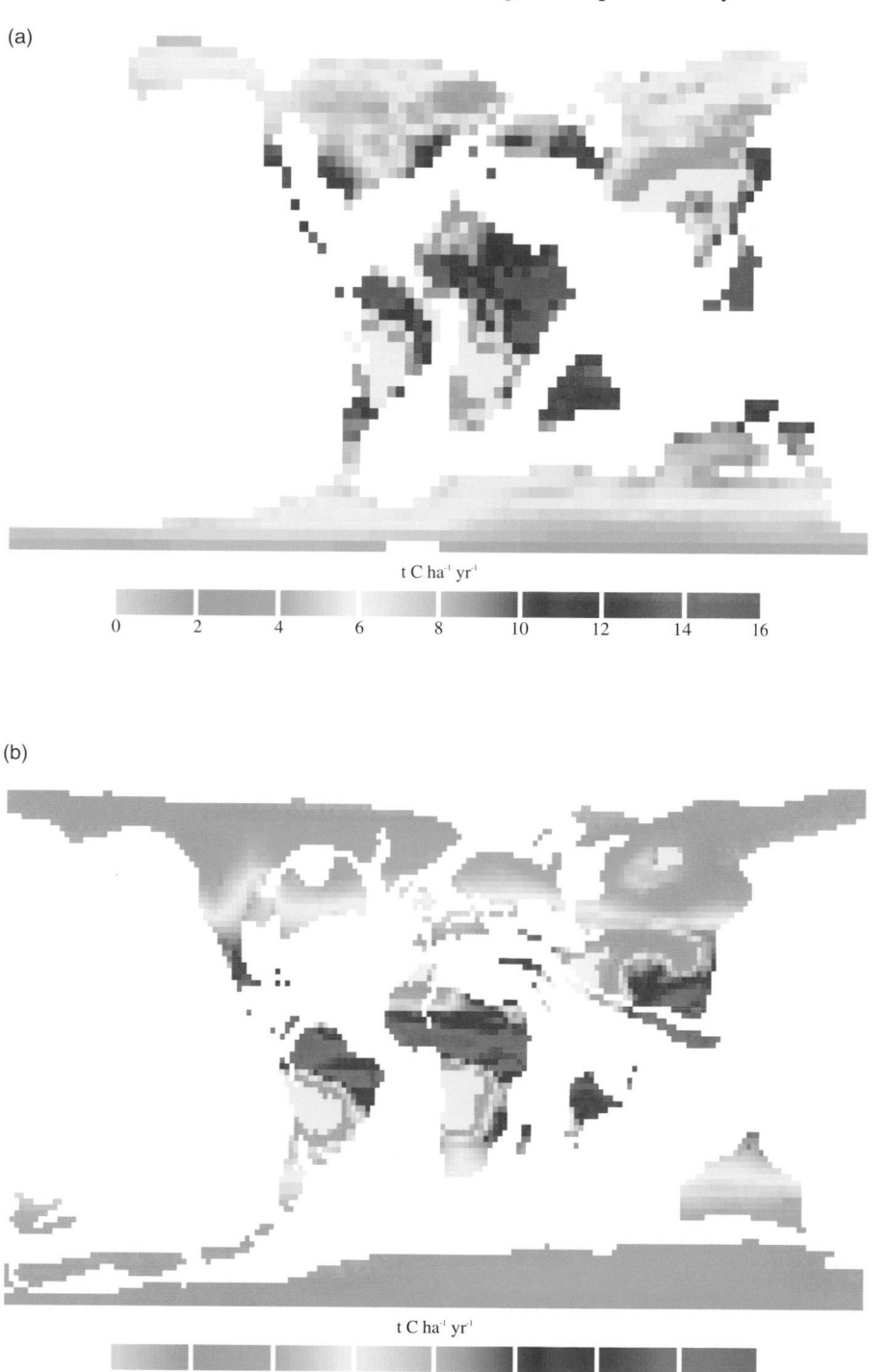

Figure 7.9. Global patterns of net primary productivity in (a) the mid-Cretaceous and (b) the late Cretaceous.

(a)

(b)

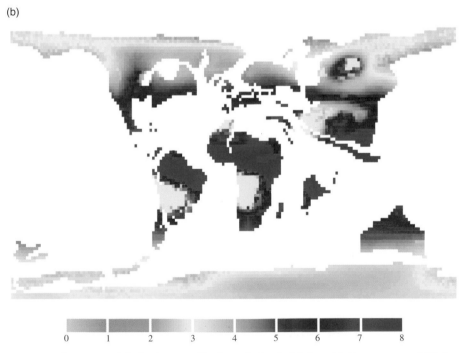

Figure 7.10. Global patterns of leaf area index in (a) the mid-Cretaceous and (b) the late Cretaceous.

(Fig. 7.12a) (Lomax *et al.*, 2001). Both features were consistently reproduced in the simulations regardless of whether the environmental effects were applied globally or restricted within a narrow latitudinal range. The recovery of global NPP to above pre-impact levels occurs because the relative benefit of the rise in CO_2 on canopy development and photosynthetic productivity offsets the costs of reductions in incoming solar energy. A rapid rebound of terrestrial primary production contrasts sharply with the situation in the marine realm where, following mass extinction at the K/T boundary, organic carbon fluxes to the deep ocean were not re-established for up to 3 million years (D'Hondt *et al.*, 1998).

Above-ground net primary production influences the accumulation of carbon in vegetation biomass (as the sum of leaf, stem and root NPPs × their respective carbon residence times) and carbon stored in soil organic matter. Both of these components of the global carbon cycle have long residence times and therefore exhibit a longer response time than NPP (Fig. 7.12b). Following the initial loss of vegetation biomass due to increased wildfire, forests become re-established and this allows the gradual accumulation of carbon in trunk biomass, as a result of their longevity and CO_2-stimulated NPP. This scenario is in agreement with observations on fossil pollen and cuticle analyses showing the replacement of low-biomass fern-colonisers with higher biomass woody angiosperms at least in the southern sites of North America (Fig. 7.28) (Beerling *et al.*, 2001). The soil organic matter carbon pool is generally less responsive but accumulates carbon because of increased litter (leaves and surface roots) production by forests in the higher CO_2 world, which under the cooler post-impact climate does not become respired away.

The longer-term effects post-K/T boundary impact environments on vegetation were generally unidirectional (Fig. 7.12). With the 'best guess' long-term post-impact environment (high atmospheric CO_2 concentration, climatic warming and redistribution of northern hemisphere precipitation; Table 7.2), global NPP nearly doubled over the pre-impact situation (Table 7.3). The most substantial increases in NPP and LAI occurred over large areas of the northern hemisphere (Fig. 7.12) but not generally at lower latitudes. The latitudinal differences occur through the dominating influence of temperature. At low latitudes, canopy LAI and NPP are close to the maximum achievable for the prevailing climate in the late Cretaceous and so showed only small increases. In contrast, the high latitude temperature limitations (Figs. 7.9 and 7.10) were alleviated by the warming with corresponding increases in growth and canopy development. A similar effect was noted in the CO_2 sensitivity analysis of Jurassic simulations discussed in Chapter 6.

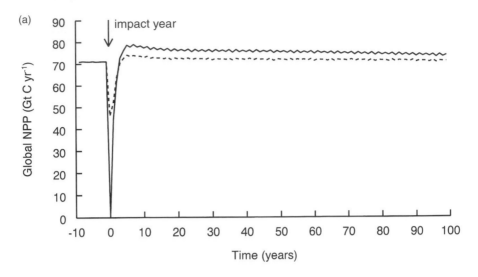

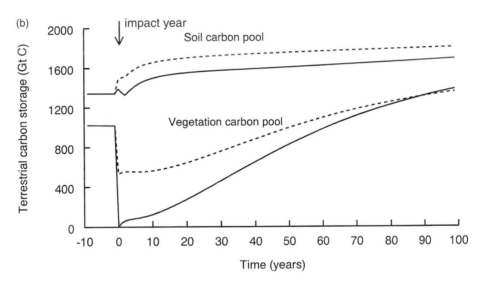

Figure 7.11. Time series response of (a) global NPP and (b) carbon storage in vegetation biomass and soil organic matter following the imposition of post-impact short-term changes in climate (see Table 7.1). The solid and broken lines indicate, respectively, environmental changes applied to latitudinally restricted regions, or globally. After Lomax *et al.* (2001).

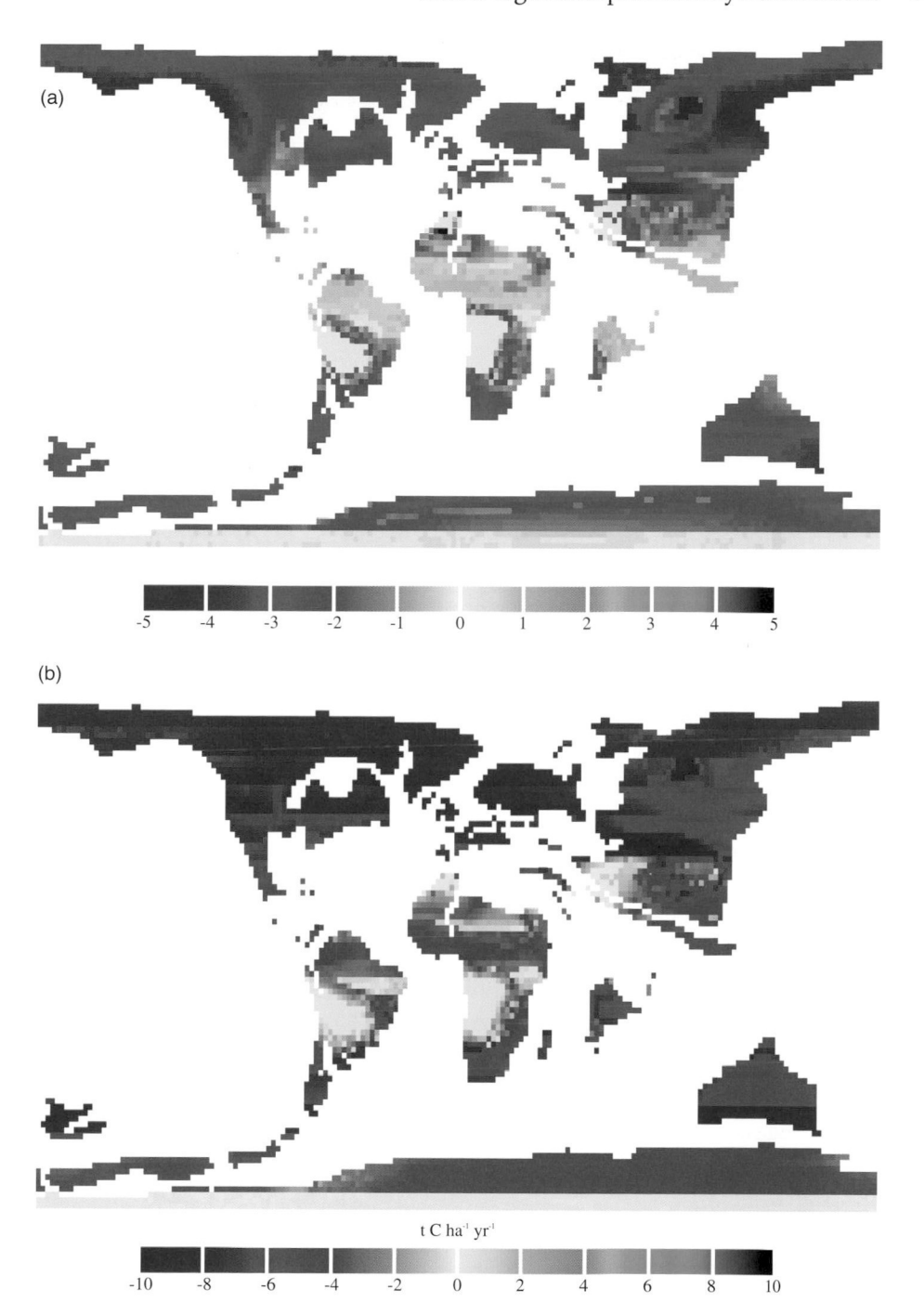

Figure 7.12. Effect of the long-term post-K/T boundary impact environment on global patterns of (a) LAI and (b) NPP. The maps show the difference between simulations with the imposed post-impact climate minus that modelled for the late Cretaceous.

Table 7.4. *Global terrestrial carbon storage in the Cretaceous. See Tables 7.1 and 7.2, respectively, for more details of the short-term and long-term post impact climates*

	Vegetation carbon (Gt C)	Soil carbon (Gt C)	Total (Gt C)
Mid-Cretaceous	1465.1	1344.4	2809.5
Late Cretaceous	1396.9	1568.6	2965.5
With blast wave destruction of vegetation biomass	1342.8	1553.5	2896.3
Short-term post-impact environment (10^0–10^3 yr)	1352.9	1900.9	3253.8
Long-term post-impact environment (10^4–10^5 yr)	3488.4	2232.8	5721.2

Global carbon storage by terrestrial ecosystems in the Cretaceous

Changes in vegetation productivity and structure, described previously, feed through and influence the size of the vegetation and soil carbon pools. Total carbon storage in vegetation and soils in the mid- and late Cretaceous was substantially greater than modelled for present-day potential vegetation, but was similar for both intervals (Table 7.4). The global patterns show high vegetation carbon accumulations at low latitudes (Fig. 7.13), and these are more extensive throughout South America, Africa and southern Asia in the late Cretaceous than in the mid-Cretaceous. In general, the highest vegetation biomass carbon reflects the dominance of long-lived, evergreen broad-leaved forests. Validation of the predicted global patterns of biomass carbon concentrations depends in part on confirming the distribution of the dominant functional types and considered later in this chapter. It is interesting to note at this stage, however, that for the late Cretaceous, high concentrations of vegetation biomass throughout South America, Africa, India and southern Asia closely correspond with the reconstructed distribution of tropical rainforests and semi-deciduous forests at this time (Otto-Blienser & Upchurch, 1997; Uphurch *et al.*, 1998).

The global pattern of soil carbon accumulation primarily reflects temperature constraints on rates of surface litter decomposition and consequently this accumulates most at cool high latitudes (Fig. 7.14). Conversely, at low latitudes, high temperature and high precipitation allow faster cycling of carbon through the soils. The overall soil carbon patterns in the mid- and late Cretaceous are similar, but some differences emerge. In the mid-Cretaceous, higher soil carbon accumulation is predicted throughout Australia compared with the late Cretaceous situation and lower values are predicted throughout eastern North America, Greenland and central Eurasia (Fig. 7.14). Some of these differences are borne out in the geological evidence (Fig. 7.15). Reconstructions of the global distribution of coals of appropriate ages

(a)

(b)

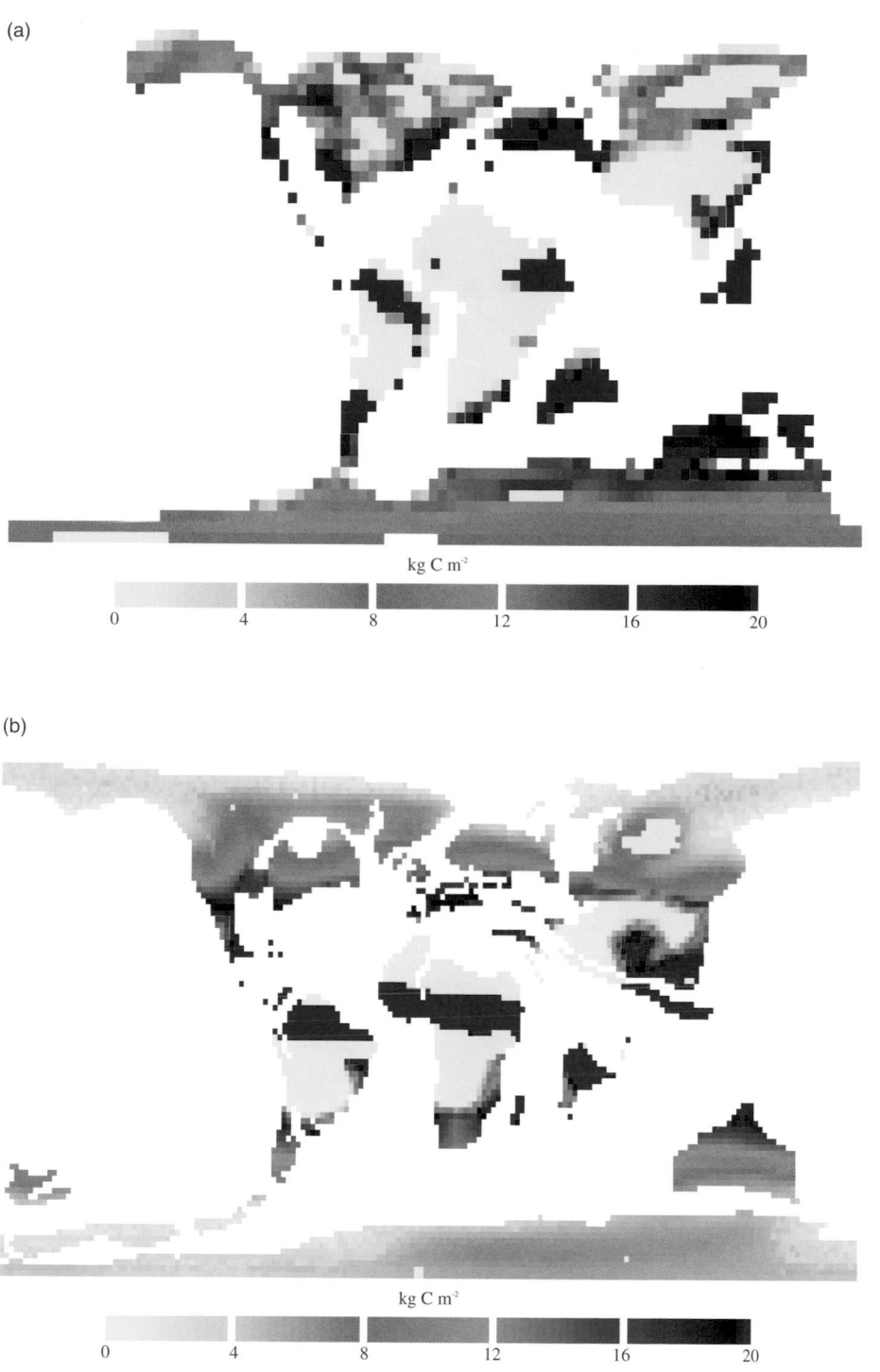

Figure 7.13. Global patterns of carbon stored in vegetation biomass during (a) the mid-Cretaceous and (b) the late Cretaceous.

(a)

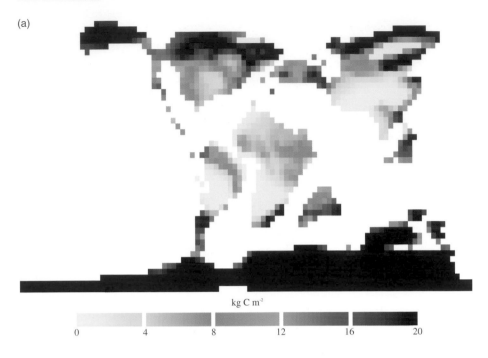

(b)

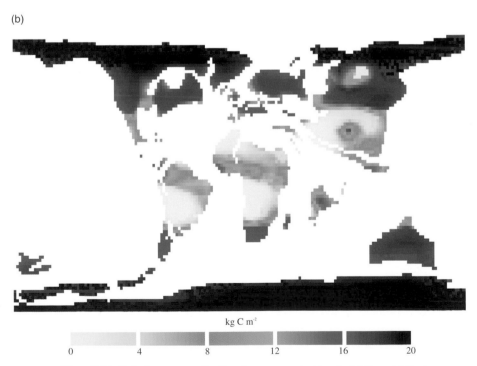

Figure 7.14. Global patterns of soil carbon concentration in (a) the mid-Cretaceous and (b) the late Cretaceous.

(McCabe & Parrish, 1992; Price *et al.*, 1997) show increased occurrence of mid-Cretaceous coals in Australia, and lower latitude coal formation throughout the eastern edge of North America. For the late Cretaceous, no soils with a particularly high (>16 kg C m^{-2}) carbon content are predicted for northern South America or central Africa, yet the geological data show the existence of coal deposits in these regions (Fig. 7.15b). The reasons for these differences between predictions and observations are unclear, but it may be that the requirements for coal deposition include other factors besides surface litter accumulation through, for example, waterlogging. In Alaska, however, high soil carbon concentrations are predicted, and significant mid-Cretaceous coal seams have been reported (Spicer & Parrish, 1986; Spicer *et al.*, 1992). This may reflect an overlap between high soil carbon concentrations and an excess of precipitation over evapotranspiration, a theme explored further later in this chapter.

The use of the UGAMP mid-Cretaceous dataset offers an interesting comparison between the predictions of possible sites of coal formation based on terrestrial biogeochemistry and predictions made on correlations with climate. Using a very similar mid-Cretaceous GCM climate simulation, Price *et al.* (1997) applied a correlative climate model of coal formation based on the criteria for modern peat occurrence [periods of drought (<40 mm month^{-1}) for one month of the year or more during warm months ($T>10\,^{\circ}$C)]. A comparison between soil carbon concentrations (Fig. 7.14a) and predicted peatland occurrence based on climate (Fig. 7.16) indicates substantial agreement (in terms of high soil carbon concentrations) throughout Antarctica, and all of the major land masses in the northern hemisphere, the most notable area of disagreement being Greenland. The agreement is encouraging because although both predictions rely on climatic data, those of soil carbon concentration depend on the combined responses of a suite of interrelated processes involved in the terrestrial cycling of carbon.

Interestingly, coal production is predicted in Antarctica in the mid- and late Cretaceous, as inferred from high soil carbon concentrations (Fig. 7.14), and, in the mid-Cretaceous, on the basis of climate (Fig. 7.16). No significant deposits of Cretaceous coals have, however, been reported for Antarctica, although very thin discontinuous coals have been reported from a scattered set of localities (Macdonald & Francis, 1992). Changes in the polar position of Antarctica are insufficient to explain the lack of organic matter accumulation since reasonable productivity in the mid-Cretaceous is modelled (Fig. 7.9a), and supported by the preservation of fossil forests (Francis, 1986a, b), and there appears to be no *a priori* reason why coal formation could not have occurred (Macdonald & Francis, 1992). It seems possible that volcanism and

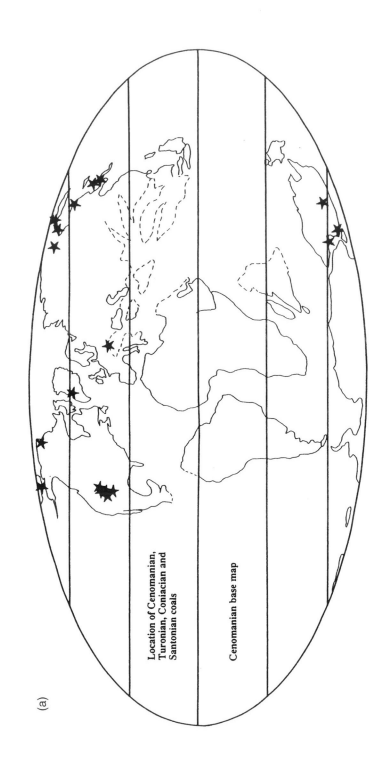

(a)

Location of Cenomanian,
Turonian, Coniacian and
Santonian coals

Cenomanian base map

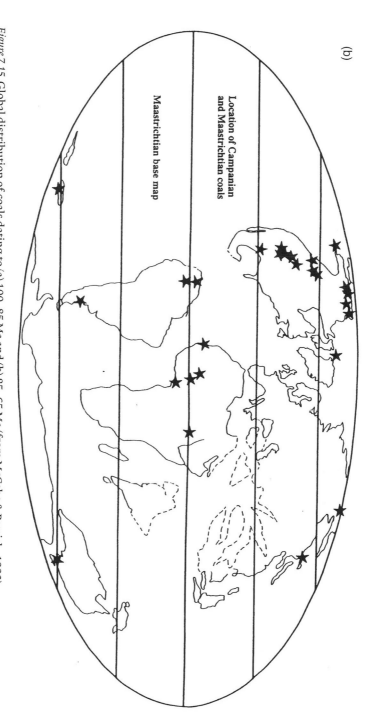

(b)

Location of Campanian
and Maastrichtian coals

Maastrichtian base map

Figure 7.15. Global distribution of coals dating to (a) 100–85 Ma and (b) 85–65 Ma (from McCabe & Parrish, 1992).

Figure 7.16. Mid-Cretaceous global distribution of climatically-sensitive sediments and predicted distribution of peatlands (shaded areas) based on climate (from Price *et al.*, 1997).

tectonic activity combined to limit sediment accumulation in basins on west Antarctica, as well as vegetation effects on site water balance (Beerling, 2000b), and that basins on the eastern edge have yet to be sufficiently well explored.

The direct obliteration of terrestrial vegetation biomass by the K/T boundary impact blast wave was rather small, reducing total biospheric carbon storage by c. 70 Gt C (Table 7.4), about 2% of the total vegetation biomass. The loss of ecosystem carbon by wildfire (quantified in the next section) and damage by the blast wave would be partially offset by increased soil carbon storage in the short term following a decreased global temperature and consequent slowing of the rate of surface litter decomposition (Table 7.4). Modelled changes in terrestrial ecosystem carbon storage due to impact-related changes in the environment, and their influence on the terrestrial carbon cycle, are used in the next section to draw up an inventory for net changes in terrestrial carbon storage resulting from the short-term effects of the K/T impact event.

In the long term, a warmer climate, high CO_2, high precipitation environment allowed dramatic increases in vegetation productivity and canopy structure (Table 7.3) and, since these conditions were thought to have persisted for several thousand years, this leads to the development of mature, long-lived forests with significant carbon storage in their biomass (Table 7.4). Soil carbon concentration also increased substantially because of the strong stimulation in vegetation productivity coupled with a rise in the C:N ratio of the vegetation and soil organic matter, the latter making it more recalcitrant. The increase in terrestrial biospheric carbon storage is about triple that modelled before the impact event, but is not matched by a similar increase in soil carbon storage and reflects the expansion of long-lived tropical forests.

Loss of carbon by global wildfire at the K/T boundary

The direct short-term effects of environmental changes resulting from an impact event on terrestrial ecosystem biogeochemistry may have led to a small increase in land carbon storage (Table 7.4). Set against this increase may have been a carbon loss by wildfire, as indicated by a global charcoal and soot layer (Wolbach et al., 1985, 1988, 1990a,b), coinciding with an iridium-enriched layer at the K/T boundary. Vegetation and soil carbon would have been ignited directly in the vicinity of the impact site by the heating of the atmosphere and elsewhere by the sub-orbital re-entry of burning impact ejector materials (Melosh et al., 1990) and increased incidence of lightning triggered by charge separation due to the settling of ejector material through the atmosphere (Wolbach et al., 1990a). Regardless of the ignition mechanism, the soot and charcoal enrichments recorded at a global set of sites have been taken at face value as evidence for wildfire coincident with the K/T boundary impact event.

The extent of vegetation burning at the K/T boundary is uncertain since it is difficult to reconstruct from layers of soot in ancient sediments. To estimate the extent of biomass burning an alternative approach has been developed based on an attempt at understanding changes in the global stable carbon isotope budget at this time. The isotopic composition of atmospheric CO_2 after the burning of terrestrial ecosystem carbon (δ_a'), and vaporisation of the carbonate rock platform by the impact, can be described by the mass-weighted isotopic composition of the three systems involved: the atmosphere, the vegetation biomass and marine carbonate:

$$\delta_a' = \frac{\delta_b m_b + \delta_a m_a + \delta_c m_c}{m_b + m_a + m_c} \tag{7.3}$$

where δ_b, δ_a and δ_c refer to carbon isotope composition of the terrestrial biospheric carbon released into the atmosphere by burning (δ_b), the atmospheric CO_2 before the burning (δ_a) and the carbonate rock platform vaporised by the impact (δ_a) and m_b, m_a and m_c are the respective masses of each carbon reservoir.

Most of the terms in equation 7.3 can be defined from earlier studies. The isotopic composition of the atmosphere, assuming it is regulated in the long term by marine inorganic carbon offset by 7‰ (Mora et al., 1996), can be taken from the marine benthic carbon record with a value of $+1‰$, so that $\delta_a = -6‰$. The mass of carbon in the atmosphere with a CO_2 concentration of 580 ppm would be equivalent to 1600 Gt C, assuming 10 ppm = 20 Gt C in the atmospheric reservoir (Siegenthaler & Sarmiento, 1993). The benthic $\delta^{13}C$ record is also an appropriate measure for the isotopic composition of the marine carbonate platform, giving $\delta_c = 1‰$ before the impact (Zachos et al., 1989; Stott & Kennett, 1989). According to the calculations of O'Keefe & Ahrens (1989), the mass of CO_2 released by a 6 km diameter asteroid would have been between 3000 and 10000 Gt C, depending on the thickness of the target marine terrace.

The final remaining unknown term in equation 7.3 is the isotopic composition of atmospheric CO_2 after combustion of the vegetation (δ_a'). As pointed out earlier (Chapter 3), the isotopic composition of fossilised terrestrial organic matter combines a physiological term, discrimination against ^{13}C during photosynthesis (Δ), and an atmospheric term (δ_a), which are related by (Farquhar et al., 1989):

Table 7.5. *Global and southern USA (all land area between 15 and 30° N and 66–110° W) GPP and area weighted mean annual discrimination against* ^{13}C *by vegetation. See Table 7.1 for further details*

Simulation	Discrimination (Δ, ‰)	
	Global	Southern USA
Late Cretaceous	18.9	16.9
Short-term post-impact environment	21.2	20.9

$$\Delta = \frac{\delta_a - \delta_b}{\left(1 + \dfrac{\delta_b}{1000}\right)} \qquad (7.4)$$

Therefore, by accounting for carbon isotope discrimination by terrestrial vegetation (Δ), and combining this estimate with measurements of δ_b after the K/T boundary, it becomes possible, by rearrangement of equation 7.4, to calculate δ_a as:

$$\delta_a = \Delta + 0.001\Delta\delta_b + \delta_b \qquad (7.5)$$

Here, Δ was calculated at the global scale using a standard model describing $^{13}CO_2$ discrimination in C_3 plant canopies during photosynthesis weighted by gross primary productivity (Lloyd & Farquhar, 1994) (Table 7.5).

An increase in Δ, without any changes in δ_a', should lead to a shift towards less negative δ_b values across the K/T boundary (eq. 7.4). However, measurements of δ_b made on fossil terrestrial organic carbon from sites in southern USA (Schimmelmann & DeNiro, 1984; Beerling *et al.*, 2001), palaeosol carbonates (Lopez-Martinez *et al.*, 1998) and elemental carbon (Wolbach *et al.*, 1990a,b) all imply a shift towards more negative values immediately after the K/T boundary. This measured shift is in the opposite direction to that expected from physiological considerations, indicating that terrestrial vegetation was utilising a source of CO_2 that had become isotopically more negative after the impact. Thus δ_a' must have become more negative.

To estimate δ_a', equation 7.5 was constrained with a mean measurement of post-impact δ_b, taken here from two southern USA sites as -27.6‰ (Schimmelmann & DeNiro, 1984; Beerling *et al.*, 2001) and a modelled value of Δ, averaged for vegetation in the same region (Table 7.5). This procedure yields δ_a' equal to -7.3‰, a negative shift of 1.3‰ after biomass burning, and assumes that changes towards more negative values were independent of changes in plant community structure and the accumulation of deathbed

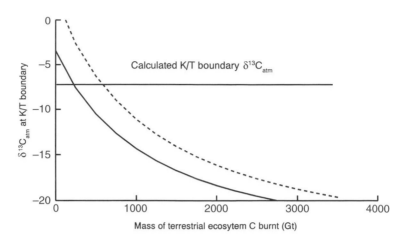

Figure 7.17. Relationship between the isotopic composition of atmospheric CO_2 after the K/T boundary impact (δ_a) and the amount of terrestrial carbon released into the atmosphere by burning from global wildfire (m_b), calculated using eq. 7.6. The two curves represent the effect of either 3000 Gt C or 10 000 Gt C release to the atmosphere, which represent the upper and lower depths of the target carbonate marine terrace.

organic carbon. One consequence of this result is that it predicts a negative isotopic excursion should be detectable in terrestrial sediments world-wide, assuming the isotopically negative CO_2 is rapidly mixed at the global scale.

The mass balance equation set up earlier (eq. 7.3) can now be solved after rearrangement to estimate m_b, the mass of CO_2 loss through burning as a function of δ_a', giving:

$$m_b = \frac{-(\delta_a m_a + \delta_c m_c - \delta_a' m_a - \delta_a' \delta_c)}{(\delta_b - \delta_a')} \tag{7.6}$$

The relationship between δ_a' and m_b (Fig. 7.17) shows that as more terrestrial carbon is burned, so δ_a' becomes more negative. If the mass of CO_2 vaporised increases, then the effect of biomass burning on δ_a is diluted (Fig. 7.17). Solving equation 7.6 with $\delta_a = -7.3$ yields two values for m_b, of 199 and 546 Gt C, depending on the mass of CO_2 released from the marine carbonate terrace (m_c). The mass balance approach is unable to distinguish between contributions from the surface soil organic carbon pool and vegetation because soil organic matter typically has an isotopic composition close to that of vegetation (Bird & Pousai, 1997). Data on contemporary forest fires suggest that the majority of the CO_2 was derived from vegetation rather than soils (Crutzen & Goldammer, 1993). A net rapid release of 199–546 Gt C into the atmosphere could have raised the atmospheric CO_2 partial pressure by 10–25 Pa, in addition to that from the vaporisation of the carbonate platform (O'Keefe & Ahrens, 1989), contributing 0.4–1.0 °C warming towards the temperature increase across the boundary as interpreted from palaeobotanical studies of fossil leaf assemblages (Wolfe, 1990).

The mass balance calculation ignores any influence of ocean chemistry and biology on atmospheric CO_2 and its isotopic composition, since re-equilibrium of CO_2 by dissolution in deep ocean water or dissolution of deep-sea sediments typically occurs on timescales of 10^3 to 10^4 years (Broecker & Peng, 1982). Box diffusion modelling of the global cycle at this time has indicated that the effect of biomass burning on δ_a' may have contributed to the carbon isotope spike at the K/T boundary (Ivany & Salawitch, 1993), together with the collapse of marine primary production (Stott & Kennett, 1989; Zachos *et al.*, 1989). However, uncertainties in sedimentary dating, mainly due to depositional hiatuses, limit this interpretation (Keller & MacLeod, 1993).

The new estimate of net carbon release to the atmosphere by wildfire from vegetation provides only an indication of the original mass of vegetation burned since combustion is usually incomplete, with much of the original biomass remaining as charcoal and dead unburned materials. An estimate of the original biomass burned can be obtained using constraints from sedimentary data. The approach has been to derive a simple theoretical relationship between 'burn efficiency' (b_e, 0–1) of global wildfire and the total biomass burned (m_{bb}), calculated as m_b / b_e (Fig. 7.18), yielding a power-law relationship of the form:

$$m_{bb} = a_o b_e^{-1} \tag{7.7}$$

where a_0 defines the placement of the curve and equals 25 340 and 61 500 for the 3000 and 10 000 Gt C release, respectively. The relationship shows that with an increase in burn efficiency, the proportion of the late Cretaceous terrestrial biosphere lost by fire at the K/T boundary decreases (Fig. 7.18) because perfectly efficient combustion is equivalent to total conversion of biomass into CO_2.

CO_2 emissions from vegetation average 80–85% of the fuel carbon (Lobert & Warnatz, 1993). Taking the lower value of 80%, equation 7.7 yields an original biomass burned of between 248 and 683 Gt C, i.e. 16–44% of the available carbon stored in the above-ground vegetation biomass. Whilst this does not constitute flagrant global forest fire, as sometimes proposed (e.g. Melosh *et al.*, 1990), it nevertheless represents a significant burning event especially when placed in the context of carbon emissions from modern forest fires. Global carbon emissions from wildfire, calculated from the worldwide extent of contemporary boreal peatlands, have been estimated at 29 Gt C (Morrissey *et al.*, 2000), an order of magnitude smaller than the extent of the fire here calculated to have followed the terminal Cretaceous impact event. We note in passing that

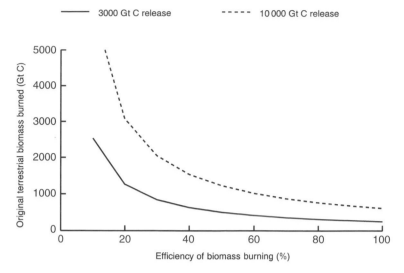

Figure 7.18. Relationship between the proportion of the late Cretaceous terrestrial carbon burnt and the efficiency of burning by global wildfire. Note that a highly efficient fire means the mass of CO_2 released to the atmosphere is equal to the mass of vegetation burned.

the repeated occurrence of fossil charcoal throughout much of the Mesozoic sedimentary record indicates that fires played an important role in vegetation development during this period of Earth history (e.g. Scott *et al.*, 2000), as it must have done with or without O_2-assistance during the Carboniferous. Ignition of wildfires relates to climate, and the warm, high-CO_2 environment of the Mesozoic and early Tertiary was probably conductive to triggering this agent of vegetation change. Land surface temperature is positively correlated to lightning flash (Williams, 1992) and intriguing results from a recent climate change modelling study in a high CO_2 world with modern geography show a 30% increase in cloud-to-ground lightning activity compared with the situation at ambient CO_2 (Price & Rind, 1994).

Assuming 4% soot (elemental carbon) production from a burning of this size, then globally-distributed, a K/T fire-related spike in elemental carbon concentration immediately after the boundary would be 2–5 mg cm^{-2}. Elemental carbon data from across 11 sites world-wide have been measured but many have been compromised by methodological shortcomings and/or poor definition of the iridium spike (Wolbach *et al.*, 1990b). The two best sites, at Woodside Creek, New Zealand and Sumbar, former USSR, yield values of 4.8 and 11 mg cm^{-2}, so the calculated values are close to the lower observed range. In practice, however, elemental carbon production from vegetation fires would not be distributed evenly across the surface of the land and sea but would be expected to exhibit marked spatial heterogeneity depending on particle size and atmospheric transport processes.

Table 7.6. *Changes in terrestrial ecosystem carbon storage before and shortly after the K/T boundary*

	Global terrestrial carbon storage (Gt C)
Before	2896
Carbon losses after K/T impact	
Impact-site obliteration of vegetation and soils	70
Global wildfire (mean of upper and lower estimate)	446
Carbon gains after K/T impact	
Environmental effects on ecosystem biogeochemistry	358
After	2738
Net change	−158

A global inventory for changes in land carbon storage arising from all of the many direct and indirect effects of a short-term post-K/T boundary impact (Table 7.6) shows that carbon losses from biomass burning and impact damage were virtually offset by the effects of environmental changes on the biogeo-chemical processes of terrestrial ecosystems. In consequence, a rather small short-term net C loss is predicted after the initial environmental effects of a K/T boundary impact event.

Post-K/T boundary changes in ecosystem properties and the geological record

Both the short-term and long-term changes in the global environment following an impact event at the K/T boundary have been shown to influence vegetation productivity and exert contrasting impacts in terrestrial ecosystem carbon storage. Relative changes in the amount of water lost by transpiration from plant canopies compared to incoming precipitation lead to potential waterlogging of soils – a feature increasing coal deposition (Beerling, 1997, 2000b; Beerling *et al.*, 1999) and recognisable in fossil soil characteristics (Fastovsky & McSweeney, 1987; Retallack *et al.*, 1987; Lehman, 1990). It follows that the potential for coal formation might be identified as the difference between precipitation and transpiration, as considered for the Carboniferous in Chapter 5.

For the late Cretaceous, it emerges that a map of the difference between precipitation and evapotranspiration (Fig. 7.19a) shows close correspondence with the global map of coal formation described earlier (Fig. 7.15b) (McCabe & Parrish, 1992). The agreement is closer than that with modelled soil carbon

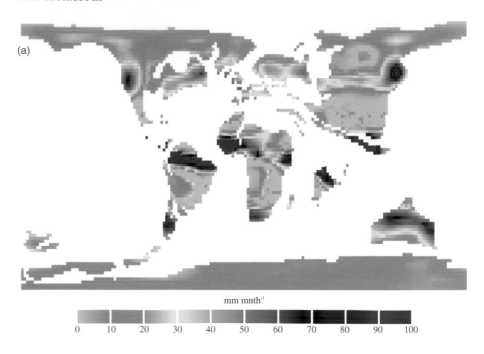

(a)

mm mnth^{-1}

0   10   20   30   40   50   60   70   80   90   100

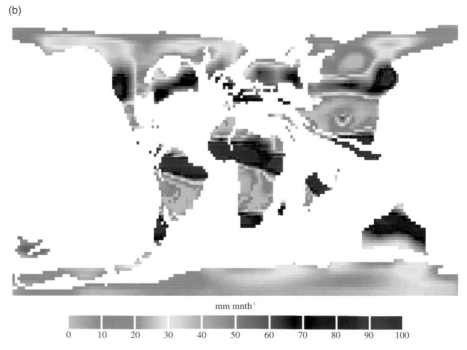

(b)

mm mnth^{-1}

0   10   20   30   40   50   60   70   80   90   100

Figure 7.19. Difference maps between annual precipitation and annual evapotranspiration for (a) the late Cretaceous, (b) 'best guess' short-term post-K/T boundary impact environment and (c) 'best guess' long-term post-K/T boundary impact environment.

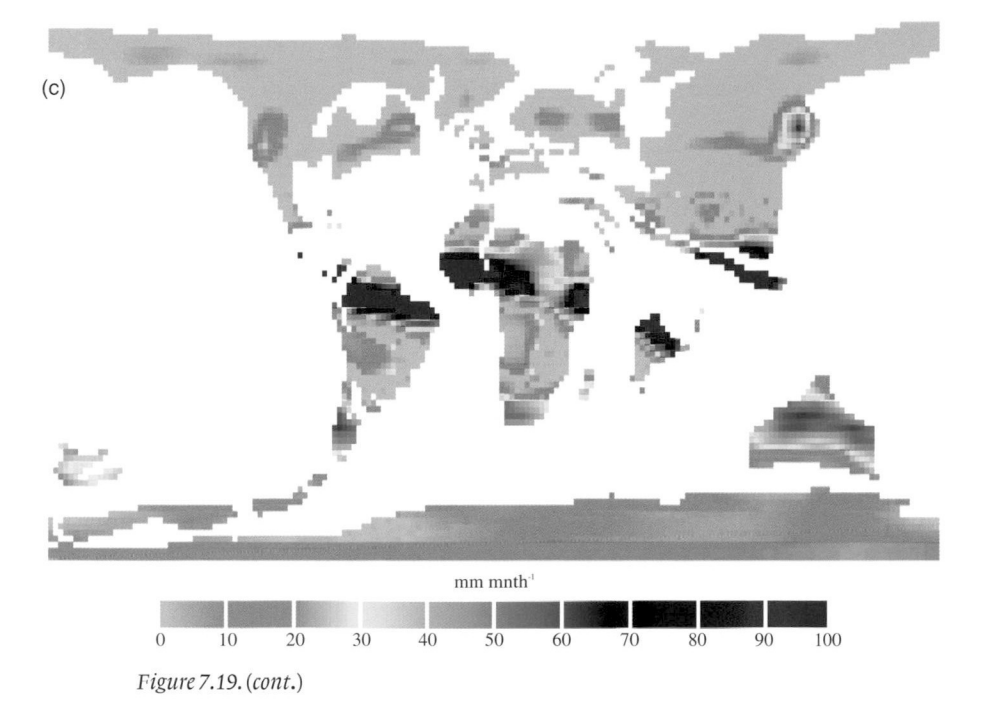

(c)

mm mnth^{-1}

| | | | | | | | | | | |
| 0 | 10 | 20 | 30 | 40 | 50 | 60 | 70 | 80 | 90 | 100 |

Figure 7.19. (cont.)

concentrations since the observed presence of low latitude coals directly corresponds with areas of high soil water accumulation. Similar areas of excellent agreement occur in southern South America, eastern North America and eastern Asia (Fig. 7.19a). This comparison provides strong support for the predicted difference between the delivery of water as precipitation and its loss by transpiration during plant growth. The difference map also suggests that extensive coal formation in Antarctica was unlikely because, despite high soil carbon concentrations, there was only a relatively small excess of precipitation over transpiration, indicating that anaerobic preservation was unlikely. Consequently, we next examine how the potential for coal formation might alter with short-term and long-term changes in climate after the K/T boundary impact event.

The short-term post-K/T boundary impact climate dramatically increased potential areas of waterlogging and hence the potential for coal formation. The localities of these regions remain unchanged but their geographical extent is extended beyond the areas delimited by the pre-impact situation. These increases in soil water occur because of marked reductions in plant transpiration under the high atmospheric CO_2 partial pressures, and lower temperatures. At the global scale, plant and soil transpiration was reduced to 78% of the pre-impact total (Table 7.7). In support of these predictions (Fig. 7.19b), sites in North America (Izett, 1990) and western Canada (Sweet *et al.*, 1990) show clear

Table 7.7. *Global vegetation water loss and water-use efficiency in the late-Cretaceous and early Tertiary. The water-use efficiency of the terrestrial biosphere was calculated by dividing global NPP (Table 7.3) by global transpiration*

	Total plant Transpiration (Gt H_2O yr^{-1})	Terrestrial biosphere water-use (Gt C/Gt H_2O yr^{-1}) ($\times 10^{-4}$)
Late Cretaceous	95 870	8.2
Short-term post-impact environment (10^0–10^3 yr)	75 110	9.8
Long-term post-impact environment (10^4–10^5 yr)	111 970	13.1

evidence for coal bed formation directly overlying the K/T boundary layer. Studies of predicted coal formation in the other regions (Fig. 7.19a) could usefully test the model results. Moreover, the contact between the impact layer and overlying boundary coal bed is sharp, implying rapid formation, as might be expected with sudden reductions in plant transpiration.

Studies of fossil soils from across the Cretaceous–Tertiary transition (Fastovsky & McSweeney, 1987; Retallack *et al.*, 1987; Lehman, 1990) have traditionally been interpreted as indicating increased rainfall and climatic cooling. We suggest on the basis of the modelled vegetation–climate-CO_2 interactions that evidence of waterlogging at the K/T boundary provides further support for a rise in atmospheric CO_2 and climatic cooling through its impact on plant ecosystem function, especially the depression of plant transpiration (Beerling, 1997).

The longer-term post-impact environment leads to a rather different set of responses, particularly in the northern hemisphere (Fig. 7.19c). In this case, global warmth and high CO_2 allow dramatic increases in mid- to high latitude vegetation productivity and canopy development (Fig. 7.12), such that nearly all of the annual precipitation is balanced by vegetation transpiration. This shift leads to a predicted switch from waterlogged soils to those characterising much drier conditions and this may, in turn, bring about differences in the types of terrestrial sediments that form in such regions. Clearly, sedimentary investigations of post-K/T boundary sites across a wide range of northern hemisphere sites might prove a useful test of these predictions.

Global changes in vegetation transpiration and net primary productivity under the different Cretaceous–early Tertiary environments also influence the annual water-use efficiency (WUE) of the whole terrestrial biosphere (Table 7.7). The short-term and long-term changes in climate both lead to an increase in the water use of the land biosphere but through contrasting responses of canopy transpiration. In the short term, global transpiration is reduced by high

CO_2 and global cooling, with only a small change in primary production so that biospheric WUE increases, whereas in the long term, the warmer, high CO_2 environment stimulates growth, so that canopies are generally more leafy (higher LAI), leading to greater water loss, a response further increased by higher temperatures. However, since NPP is also strongly stimulated by these conditions, the biospheric WUE nearly doubles relative to the pre-impact situation (Table 7.7).

Stable carbon isotope constraints on modelled Cretaceous vegetation activity

The geological record provides only an indirect indication of vegetation productivity in the form of fossil plant assemblages, usually interpreted in terms of vegetation types (e.g Spicer *et al.*, 1993). A direct test of modelled vegetation activity has been applied by comparing predictions and measurements of the stable carbon isotope composition ($\delta^{13}C$) of terrestrial organic matter. When the atmospheric component is removed from this signal, a biological-related ^{13}C discrimination (Δ) is isolated and this in turn depends upon the assimilation-weighted ratio of CO_2 concentration inside the leaf (C_i) relative to that in the atmosphere (C_a), after accounting for isotopic fractionations associated with the CO_2 fixing enzyme rubisco and diffusion through air and stomata (cf. Chapter 3). The value of Δ calculated from $\delta^{13}C$ measurements of terrestrial organic matter therefore relates to the mean annual C_i/C_a ratio during photosynthesis by foliage, a value equivalent to that modelled for each geological period and influenced by environmental impacts on photosynthetic CO_2 drawdown and stomatal limitation to CO_2 diffusion into leaves.

In this test, frequency histograms of modelled ^{13}C discrimination (Δ) for all pixels with terrestrial productivity in the mid- and late Cretaceous (Fig. 7.20 a,c) were compiled for comparison with observations. Observational datasets were obtained for the mid-Cretaceous (Bocherens *et al.*, 1994; Tu *et al.*, 1999; Hasegawa, 1997) and late Cretaceous (Bocherens *et al.*, 1994); $\delta^{13}C$ measurements were converted to Δ using $\delta^{13}C_a$ values of -6‰ in equation 7.4 from marine carbonates (Chapter 3) (Fig. 7.20 b,d).

The results for the mid-Cretaceous (Fig. 7.22a) show that the most frequently occurring modelled Δ values were 18–19‰ in agreement with observations (Fig. 7.22b). The modelled Δ values had a broader range than so far observed: this may reflect the fact that $\delta^{13}C$ measurements have been made on mid-Cretaceous fossil leaves from a limited set of sites. Inspection of the global pattern of mid-Cretaceous mean annual Δ values (Fig. 7.23) indicates they occur predominantly in the low latitudes of central Africa and in eastern Antarctica and Australia. Fossil materials from these particular localities remain to be investigated, although interestingly $\delta^{13}C$ measurements made on early Cretaceous fossil woods from plants in south-eastern Australia have had values as high as -16‰ (Gröcke, 1998), giving a corresponding Δ value of 10‰.

Interpreted from a physiological standpoint, low Δ values indicate low C_i/C_a ratios which can arise through high rates of photosynthesis and/or low stomatal conductances. Given the low mean annual temperature (Fig. 7.4a) and precipitation (Fig. 7.6a) regime, it most likely represents a stomatal limitation to CO_2 diffusion into the leaf. Clearly, more isotopic investigations are required on southern hemisphere plant fossils to elucidate physiological controls on plant productivity at high latitudes in the mid-Cretaceous.

For the late Cretaceous, a different frequency distribution of Δ values emerges (Fig. 7.20c), with the most common range being skewed towards 20–22 ‰ and a smaller range $c.$ 17–18‰. A similar pattern emerges from the observations (Fig. 7.20d), with the most frequent values at 16 –17‰ and 19 to 22‰. In this case a broader range of Δ values were recorded from observations in support of the wide range of values predicted (Fig. 7.15a).

Vegetation diversity in the Cretaceous

The final section of this chapter considers changing global patterns of vegetation through the Cretaceous era, and comparison with reconstructed palaeovegetation maps (Saward, 1992; Upchurch *et al.*, 1998) based on facies analysis of plant-bearing fossil sediments, palynological analysis and climatically-sensitive sediment. The post-K/T boundary impact results have also been used to assess possible changes in plant functional type distributions on different timescales. Consideration is given to the potential carrying capacity (in terms of flowering plant diversity) of the Cretaceous period, defined by its thermal environment (minimum temperatures and heat sum of the growing seasons) and the potential for canopy development. It has been assumed that Angiosperm evolution was occurring.

Global-scale distribution of plant functional types

The mid-Cretaceous (100 Ma) distribution of the five major vegetation types predicted by the model is not dissimilar (Fig. 7.22a) to the situation modelled for 50 million years earlier in the late Jurassic (Chapter 6). Globally at 100 Ma, mixed tropical evergreen forests and dry savannah-type shrublands dominated in the low latitudes around the equator. Vegetation in the high latitudes of the northern and southern hemispheres, however, shows contrasting patterns of functional type distribution due to differences in temperatures (Fig. 7.4a). The northern hemisphere is dominated by deciduous broad-leaved forests, interspersed with small amounts of evergreen needle-leaved trees, whereas the southern hemisphere is dominated by evergreen needle-leaved forests interspersed with small amounts of broad-leaved deciduous forests. Tropical evergreen forests dominate in parts of South America and Africa, in northern Australia and throughout India, all areas where the corresponding carbon concentrations in vegetation biomass (Fig. 7.13a) were highest. This arises because of the longevity of this type of forest and subsequent carbon accumulation in stem wood.

Efforts to validate the model predictions of vegetation distribution in the mid-Cretaceous are hampered by the lack of a detailed vegetation reconstruction. A global palaeovegetation map for the mid-Cretaceous has been derived (Saward, 1992) using data on dominance/subordinate elements of fossil floras from macrofossil and palynological studies. For the mid-Cretaceous three zones were recognised (Fig. 7.22b): 1i, tropical belts of lowered diversity; 1ii, para-tropical belts, experiencing little seasonality and dominated by savannah woodland-type vegetation; 2i, para-temperate belt, a transitional zone incorporating elements from temperate and para-tropical regions and 2ii, the temperate belts, characterised by seasonal variations in growth and extensive deciduous/semi-deciduous conifer-dominated forests. Reconstructed global-scale palaeovegetation maps are not without their problems, as indeed are reconstructions of maps of present-day vegetation (see Chapter 3 for further discussion). For example, the selective preservation of fossils may distort the true picture of vegetation at a particular site, and with only a few sites worldwide, the difficulty in accurately placing the boundaries between dominant vegetation types is obvious. In consequence the following data-model comparisons can only be qualitative.

Nevertheless, a comparison between the global palaeovegetation map for mid-Cretaceous vegetation (Fig. 7.22b) and model predictions (Fig. 7.22a) shows a fair degree of similarity. Fossil evidence for tropical vegetation is scarce, but within the reconstructed tropical belt, the model predicts a mixture of evergreen broad-leaved forests, deciduous broad-leaved forests and savannah-type shrublands. The distribution of tropical evergreen forests is limited by the low rates of precipitation predicted by the GCM. The fossil data provide evidence for all of these types of vegetation, except tropical rainforests.

The cooler, drier high latitudes of the late Cretaceous lead to an expansion of deciduous needle-leaved forests in both hemispheres and a considerable expansion of evergreen needle-leaved forests in the northern hemisphere (Fig. 7.23a). By the late Cretaceous, tropical rainforests have expanded considerably throughout the lower latitudes due to the greater precipitation predicted by the NCAR GCM simulations. The palaeovegetation map for the late Cretaceous

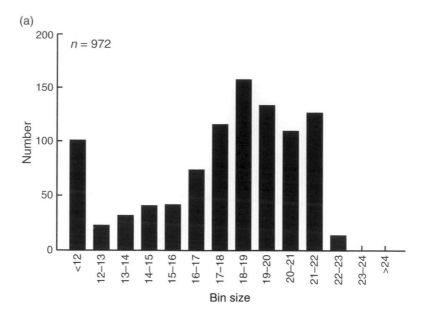

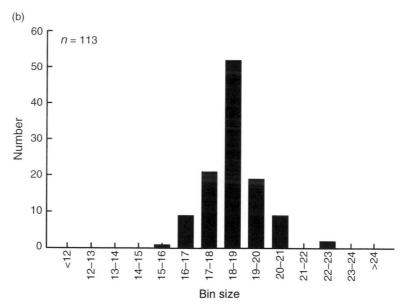

Figure 7.20. Histograms of ^{13}C discrimination values (bin sizes in ‰) constructed from modelled (a) and observed (b) mid-Cretaceous, and modelled (c) and observed (d) late Cretaceous. Observations from Bocherens *et al.* (1994), Tu *et al.* (1999) and Hasegawa (1997).

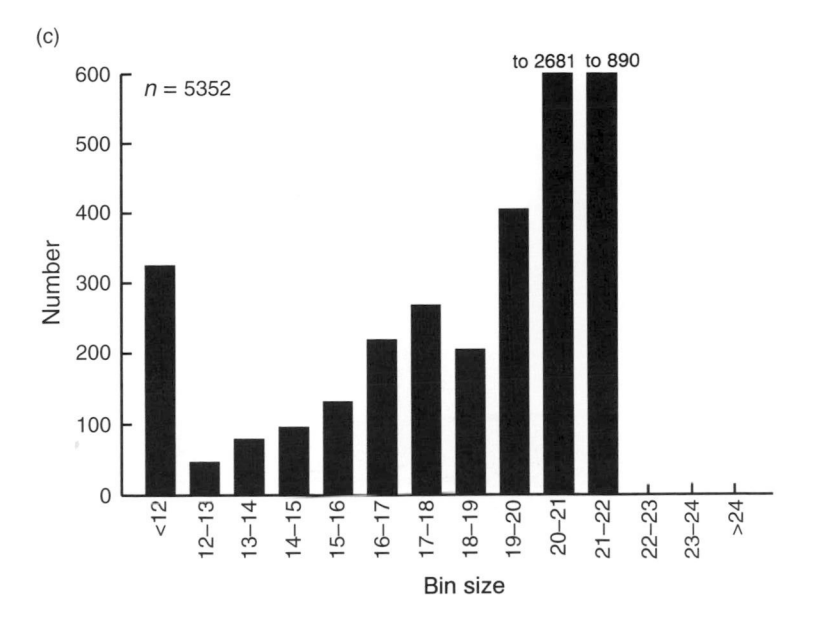

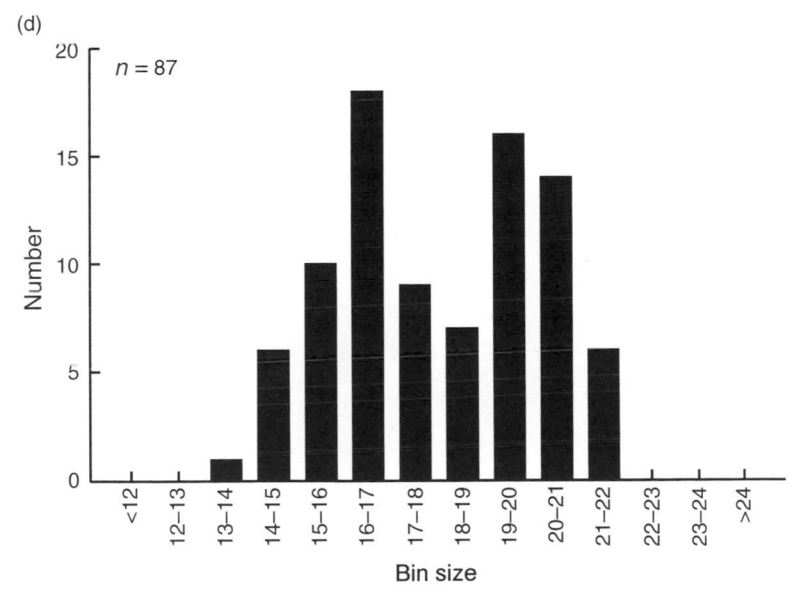

Figure 7.20. (cont.)

(a)

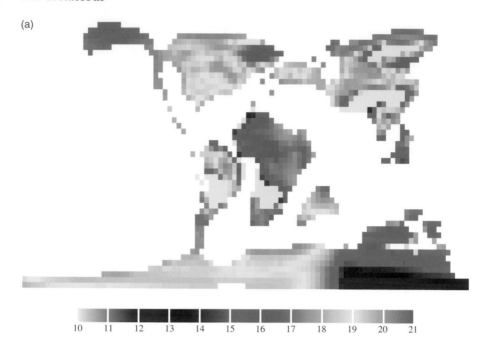

(b)

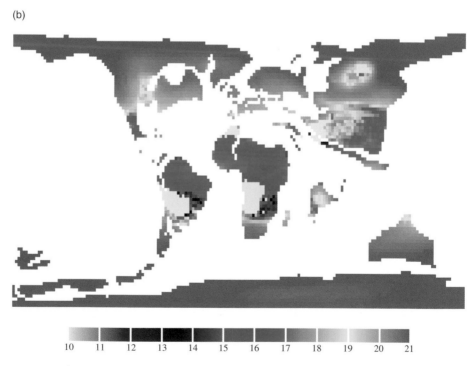

Figure 7.21. (a) Mid-Cretaceous and (b) late Cretaceous patterns of GPP-weighted mean annual ^{13}C discrimination (‰).

(Upchurch *et al.*, 1998), based on extensive lithological and palaeobotanical evidence, validates some features of the predicted distributions. In particular, the map of Upchurch *et al.* (1998) shows the high latitude dominance of polar deciduous forests in the northern and southern hemispheres, although the distinction between evergreen and deciduous conifers from the fossil record of needles and leaves is uncertain (Fig. 7.23b). The reconstruction also shows the low latitude occurrence of tropical rainforest and tropical semi-deciduous forests, in large regions corresponding to the model predictions (Fig. 7.23a).

The single largest discrepancy between model and data is for the extent of broad-leaved deciduous forests. Model prediction indicates these to be distributed throughout regions where subtropical broad-leaved evergreen forest and woodland have been reconstructed. Fossil evidence in this case is quite robust, being dependent upon the presence of small evergreen leaves, few or no drip-tips, and the presence of palms and gingers (fossil woods without growth rings) and thick angiosperm cuticles (Upchurch *et al.*, 1998). In the case of the model, broad-leaved deciduous woodlands are predicted because of a significant dry season at mid-latitudes or cold period at high latitudes, indicating possible evolutionary changes in the climatic tolerance of this group of plants over the past 65 Ma and/or problems with the seasonal cycle of the GCM climatic data. Similar errors might also be expected with the mid-Cretaceous simulations for deciduous broad-leaved forests. However, incorrect placement of this particular functional type instead of subtropical broad-leaved forests and woodlands is unlikely to introduce large errors into the amounts of carbon stored in vegetation biomass.

The effects of long-term (10^4–10^5 yr) changes in climate arising through an extraterrestrial impact event at the Cretaceous–Tertiary boundary, on the distribution of plant functional types has also been considered (Fig. 7.24), building on the construction of these climates from previous sections.

The long-term post-K/T boundary impact environments with higher temperatures, increased precipitation and high CO_2 lead to the considerable expansion of tropical evergreen broad-leaved forests from sites of the refugial areas after a short-term cooling (Fig. 7.24). This expansion leads, in part, to the considerable increase in terrestrial carbon storage over the same timescale. Evergreen needle-leaved forests become re-established in Antarctica but these are displaced further south by broad-leaved forests. In the northern hemisphere, their distribution contracts owing to competitive displacement by broad-leaved deciduous and evergreen forests, which can now tolerate the warmer temperatures in these regions.

(a)

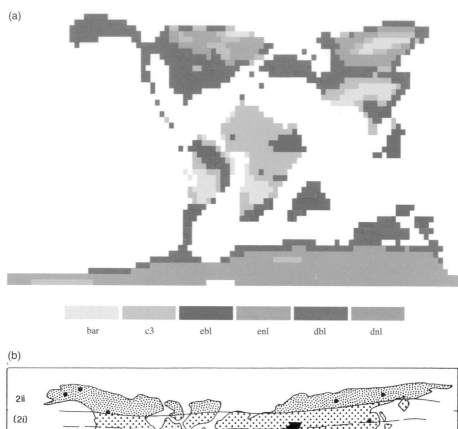

(b)

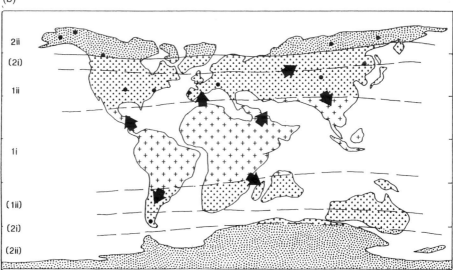

Figure 7.22. (a) Modelled distribution of the major functional type distributions in the mid-Cretaceous (100 Ma). Key: bar, bare ground; c3, shrubs and savannah-type grasslands; ebl, evergreen broad-leaved forest; enl, evergreen needle leaved forests; dbl, deciduous broadleaved forests; dnl, deciduous needle-leaved forest. (b) Palaeovegetation map for the mid-Cretaceous (from Saward, 1992). • indicates sites using megafloral point data and arrows show the direction of general angiosperm dispersal routes. Key: 1i, tropical vegetation including savannah woodland and desert; 1ii, 2i, paratropical vegetation, savannah woodland (cycadophytes, ferns and brachyphyllous conifers); 2ii, temperate vegetation, deciduous and semi-deciduous 'leafy' coniferous, ginkgophyte and fern forest.

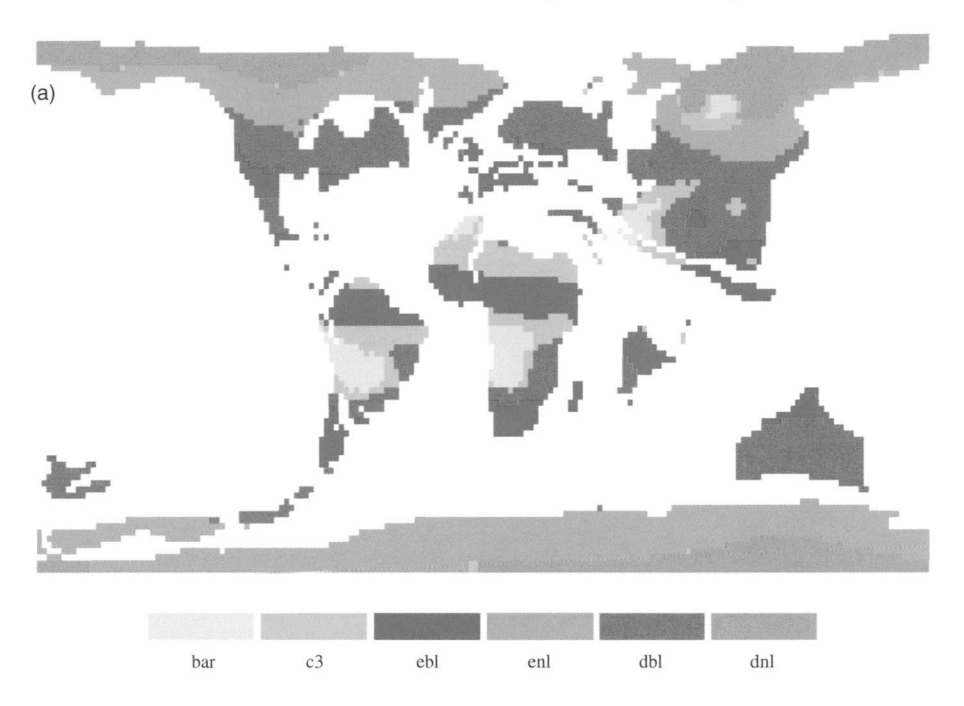

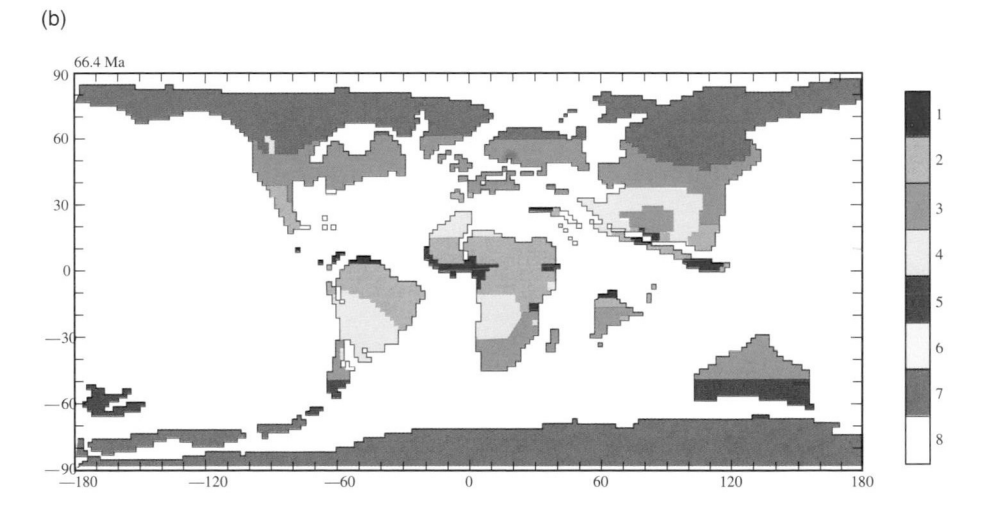

Figure 7.23. (a) Modelled distribution of the major functional type distributions. Key as in Fig. 7.22. (b) Reconstructed distribution of major vegetation types in the late Cretaceous (Maastrichtian) (from Upchurch *et al.*, 1998). Code: 1, tropical rainforest; 2, tropical semi-deciduous forest; 3, subtropical broad-leaved evergreen forest and woodland; 4, desert and semi-desert; 5, temperate evergreen broad-leaved and coniferous forest; 6, tropical savannah; 7, polar deciduous forest; 8, bare soil.

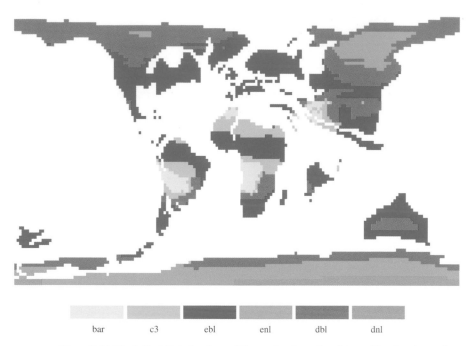

bar   c3   ebl   enl   dbl   dnl

Figure 7.24. Modelled distribution of the major functional type distributions after long-term changes in climate resulting from the K/T boundary impact event. Key as in Fig. 7.22a.

Changes in plant family diversity through the Cretaceous

The distribution of plant functional types is modelled based on the eco-physiological attributes described in Chapter 4. However, the maps (Figs. 7.22–7.24) provide no indication of the diversity of vegetation that the Cretaceous environment might support and how this might be influenced though impact-related changes in climate. Extensive analyses of the plant fossil record (mainly leaves, fruits, seeds and woods) provide clear evidence for the rapid diversification of angiosperms from the early Cretaceous onwards, but the driving force(s) for this radiation remains a matter of some debate and may be related to biotic and abiotic factors (Wing & Sues, 1992).

The Cretaceous therefore represents an intriguing interval to examine how changes in climate might affect the carrying capacity of the environment, in terms of species diversity. The approach has been to apply a very simple, but validated model describing the environmental controls on the diversity of gymnosperms and angiosperms at the level of family. Three features of environment exert a dominant degree of control on floristic diversity: absolute minimum temperatures, the length of the growing season, and water supply to the plants

(Woodward & Rochefort, 1991). Each component contributes to the total diversity of a given site, D (normalised to 100):

$$D = \frac{D_m D_d D_w}{10^6} \tag{7.8}$$

where D_m, D_d and D_w are the diversity components controlled by absolute minimum temperature, the length of the growing season and site water balance, respectively. Application of this model to ancient climates assumes controls on the diversity of vegetation derived from contemporary vegetation, applied to vegetation in the geological past.

Minimum temperatures limit diversity because different species have different capacities to endure low temperatures (Chapter 3), and this feature is often seen as a control on many current plant distributions (Woodward, 1987a). A linear relationship between family diversity and minimum temperatures, T_m, over the range 10 to $-90\,^{\circ}$C, emerges from analyses of observational data (Woodward & Rochefort, 1991) described by:

$$D_m = 90.9 + (0.909 T_m) \tag{7.9}$$

and constrained where $D_m = 100$ if $T_m > 10\,^{\circ}$C, and $D_m = 9$ if $T_m < -90\,^{\circ}$C.

The length of the growing season is important for allowing plants to complete their life cycles and is calculated as a heat sum, H, defined as the annual sum of the mean daily temperatures above a defined threshold value. Observations show that plants from cold climates, e.g. tundra, tolerate the smallest heat sum, around 200, whilst tropical vegetation experiences values $>10\,000$. A simple linear relationship describes how vegetation diversity increases over the heat sum range of 200–5000 day-degrees (Woodward & Rochefort, 1991):

$$D_d = 0.02 H \tag{7.10}$$

where $D_d = 100$ if $H > 5000$, and $D_d = 4$ if $H < 200$. The length of the growing season, H, was calculated by first recording the total number of days over the year that photosynthetic net primary production was positive and then calculating the temperature sum for days with a temperature over a $5\,^{\circ}$C threshold.

The third component exerting control on vegetation diversity is the balance between precipitation and transpiration, which in turn largely determines the leaf area index (LAI) of vegetation (Chapter 4). The maximum LAI of a particular vegetation type may typically occur when annual evapotranspiration equals precipitation. A linear formulation describes the relationship between increasing vegetation diversity and LAI (Woodward & Rochefort, 1991):

$$D_w = 11.1 LAI \tag{7.11}$$

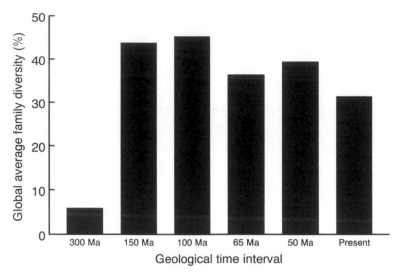

Figure 7.25. Global-average area weighted vegetation diversity calculated for five different geological eras compared with present-day (1988) climate.

Note that LAI as computed by the SDGVM is sensitive to climate and the CO_2 partial pressure, as well as edaphic conditions.

When the globally-averaged vegetation diversity values (D) for the five eras considered in this book are calculated, it emerges that each period within the Mesozoic and early Tertiary would have been capable of supporting a greater diversity of vegetation than the present-day climate (Fig. 7.25). The exception to this pattern was the cool climate of the late Carboniferous (300 Ma) (Fig. 7.25). However, careful analyses of the plant fossil record, taking into account sampling effort, appears to suggest similar diversity at Palaeozoic and Cenozoic sites (Wing & DiMichele, 1995), although the interpretation of global patterns of 'overall' diversity is considered by these authors to be dubious. In contrast to the Carboniferous, late Jurassic (100 Ma) and mid-Cretaceous environments, with globally averaged D values exceeding 40%, compared with 31% for the present, were predicted to be suitable for supporting highly diverse assemblages of plants. The predictions arise because land surface higher temperatures increase the absolute minimum temperature, T_m, and the heat sum, H, and so D_m and D_d also rise. Furthermore, at high CO_2 concentrations, LAI increases together with an accompanying rise in diversity controlled by this feature (D_w). These results support the notion that the environment at these times was highly suitable for supporting diverse assemblages of species and that it awaited evolutionary advancements by land plants for this environmental space to become filled (Lidgard & Crane, 1990).

When the same analysis is applied to the vegetation and climatic changes following the short-term and long-term consequences of a terminal Cretaceous impact event, contrasting effects emerge. In the short term, the global average family diversity of vegetation drops, relative to the pre-impact situation, by nearly 10% whereas with the longer-term effects it increases by 15%. The decline arises because the climatic cooling lowers minimum temperatures everywhere (eq. 7.9) and curtails the length of the growing season (eq. 7.10), effects that are not offset by changes in canopy LAI (eq. 7.11). The fossil record indicates that plant extinctions at the K/T boundary exhibited a distinct latitude-related degree of severity, with the greatest level of extinction being apparent at low to mid-latitudes of North America close to the bolide impact site (Wolfe & Upchurch, 1986; Spicer, 1989b; Nichols & Fleming, 1990). Collectively the patterns of plant extinction and model results suggest that besides local ecosystem devastation resulting from the impact blast wave, an environmental filter operated on a timescale of several hundred years to limit the recovery of plant diversity. Following a short-lived impact winter, a proposed mechanism for widespread extinction (Wolfe, 1991), the resulting environmental changes may have selected for only those taxa with the capacity to endure the seasonally lower temperatures and with an ability to grow and reproduce in a short growing season. Such tight constraints on survival, growth and reproduction would have suited relatively few taxa. This environmental filter or limitation was then apparently relaxed as the post-impact 'greenhouse' climate was established. However, despite this, detailed analyses of megafossil plant remains from across the Cretaceous–Tertiary boundary in New Mexico indicate that while productivity had recovered, biodiversity remained depressed (Fig. 7.26) (Beerling *et al.*, 2001), with full recovery taking as long as 1–2 million years (Wolfe & Upchurch, 1987). It would appear therefore that, as in the marine realm, biodiversity recovery in terrestrial ecosystems following an extinction event operates on a very long time scale (Kirchner & Weils, 2000).

Conclusions

The global-scale simulations described in this chapter indicate the highly productive nature of the Cretaceous environment. Changes in terrestrial vegetation primary production between the mid- and late Cretaceous paralleled changes in climate and CO_2 over this time. The values established for carbon storage by the terrestrial biosphere in the mid- and late Cretaceous are broadly in agreement with the available geological and palaeobotanical data and have allowed the use of the late Cretaceous simulations to provide a baseline case for analyses of a K/T boundary impact event.

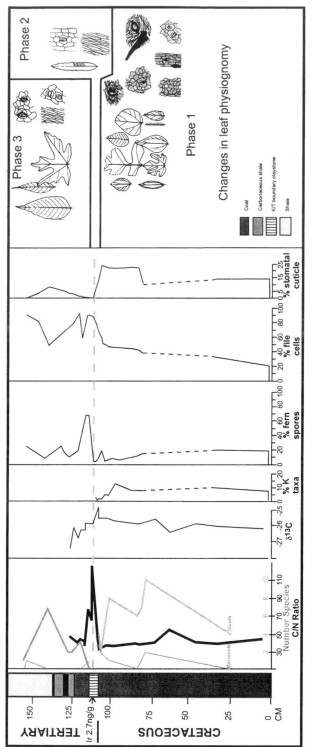

Figure 7.26. Changes in ecosystem structure and diversity reconstructed with palynological and fossil cuticle analysis from the Sugarite site in the Raton Basin, New Mexico, USA through the Cretaceous and into the Tertiary (from Beerling *et al.*, 2001). Note the loss of Cretaceous (K) pollen taxa, abundance of fern-spores at the K/T boundary, coincident with an iridium-rich layer, and the abrupt drop and recovery of cuticle abundance with file cells (representative of herbaceous stems, leaf petioles and leaf rachises. Ecosystem biodiversity, expressed as number of dicotyledonous cuticular species fails, to recover to Cretaceous levels following the crash at the K/T boundary. Leaf and cuticular morphotypes are illustrated for different vegetation phases. Redrawn from Wolfe & Upchurch (1987).

No attempts have been made to link impact-related changes in the environment with plant extinctions. Instead, analyses of the possible consequences of an extraterrestrial impact event at the K/T boundary have been confined to predictions of changes in ecosystem structure and biogeochemistry, and these results indicate markedly different effects, in terms of their sign and magnitude, depending on the timescale of interest. The short-term 'best guess' changes in climate (10^0–10^1 yr) were not predicted to result in a global devastation of terrestrial ecosystems based on three previously suggested fatal processes: the impact blast wave, global wildfire and global cooling. Additional mechanisms of mortality proposed earlier (Alvarez *et al.*, 1980), related to the impact event, particularly the production of acid rain arising from high loadings of SO_2 in the atmosphere and the impact of NO_x produced by wildfire, have not been considered because of the lack of mechanistic information relating to both their action on physiological processes. Possible effects of an atmospheric CO_2 rise (Caldeira & Rampino, 1990), following increased volcanic eruptions as evidenced by the production of the Deccan traps in India (Courtillot *et al.*, 1988) have not been considered explicitly but would be expected to contribute partially to the rise in CO_2 included in our analyses.

The global carbon isotope mass balance approach, combined with physiological modelling and stable isotope observations, indicates a relatively minor role of global wildfire in restructuring terrestrial ecosystems after the K/T impact. The longer-term (10^4–10^5 yr) environmental change resulting from the impact would have been highly suitable for the establishment of productive and diverse assemblages of vegetation. By taking this interdisciplinary approach we avoid problems associated with uncertainties in the timing of the impact (e.g. summer vs. winter) and the downstream effects of this uncertainty in estimating the extent of global wildfire (e.g. Davenport *et al.*, 1990).

If a longer-term post-impact climatic warming occurred as suggested here, through a sustained high CO_2 event, then terrestrial ecosystems could have substantially increased primary production and carbon storage. These predictions are qualitatively consistent with a change in ecosystem function recorded as increased coal deposition in the northern hemisphere after the K/T boundary. All of the analyses considered in this chapter strongly indicate that the dramatic changes in the environment resulting from an impact event at the K/T boundary would have led to a biotic response acting as a negative feedback on climate, thereby contributing to the re-establishment of pre-impact conditions. In addition, the calculated increase in primary production compared with the pre-impact situation may have accelerated rates of weathering of silicate rocks, a mechanism ultimately responsible for removing excess CO_2 from the atmosphere.

8

The Eocene

Introduction

The early/middle Eocene (55–50 Ma) was the warmest interval of the past 65 million years, and represents the last time the Earth operated in a strong 'greenhouse' mode with a configuration of the continental land masses close to that of the present day. Although the Miocene (15 Ma) was a more recent episode of non-glacial climate, it did not have the extreme warmth of the middle Eocene, particularly regarding the maintenance of warm, high latitude surface temperatures (Barron, 1987), as indicated by marine oxygen isotope data (Shackleton & Boersma, 1981; Zachos *et al.*, 1994). Climate modelling studies have shown that the overall Eocene warmth was compatible with a higher-than-present partial pressure of atmospheric CO_2 (Sloan & Rea, 1995). This suggestion is supported by modelling of the long-term carbon cycle which predicts values during the Eocene of 600–900 ppm CO_2 (Berner, 1994), and by geochemical estimates based on the isotopic composition of marine (700 ppm) (Freeman & Hayes, 1992) and terrestrial carbon (300–700 ppm) (Sinha & Stott, 1994) (Fig. 8.1). These studies therefore provide direct and indirect evidence for the operation of a high CO_2 greenhouse effect during the Eocene. However, further mechanisms are thought to have operated, causing increased polar warmth without significant warming of the tropics (e.g. Sloan *et al.*, 1995; Valdes, 2000).

The estimated range of atmospheric CO_2 concentrations during the Eocene is similar to that projected into the year 2100, based on the IS92a ('business-as-usual') emission scenario of the Intergovernmental Panel on Climate Change (790 ppm CO_2) (Wigley & Raper, 1992), which represents CO_2 increases, assuming a slow reduction in economic growth and a gradual increase in carbon fuel conservation measures (Mitchell *et al.*, 1995) (Fig. 8.1). The trend is predicted with a simple view of oceanic CO_2 uptake and no carbon uptake by the terrestrial biosphere (Wigley & Raper, 1992). As a conse-

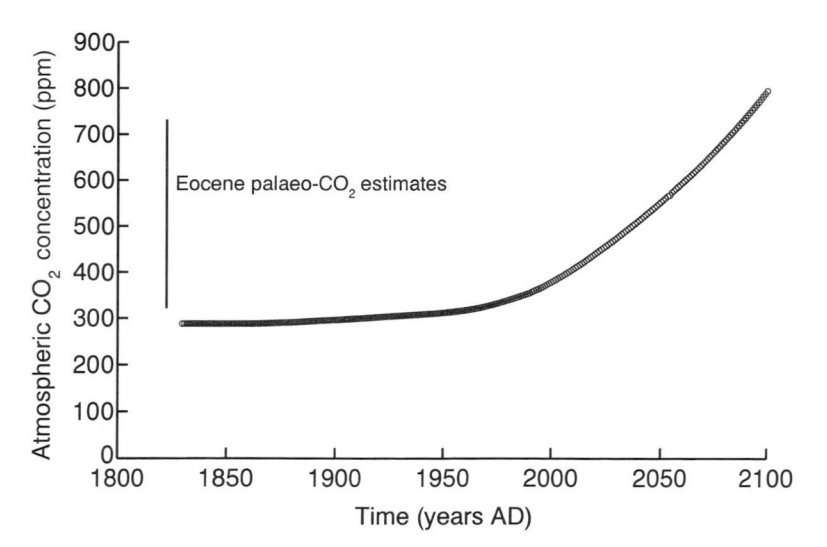

Figure 8.1. Trends in concentration of atmospheric CO₂ for 1830–2100 representing the IS92a CO₂ emission scenario (Wigley & Raper, 1992). Also shown is the range of CO₂ estimates for the Eocene from the geochemical model of Berner (1994), and from isotopic studies on fossil soils (Sinha & Stott, 1994) and marine organic carbon (Freeman & Hayes, 1992).

quence of the similarities between past and future atmospheric CO₂ concentrations, it is of interest to examine whether the warming of the Earth's climate in some future 'greenhouse' world will approach that of the ancient greenhouse world of the Eocene, some 50 million years ago.

The interest in such a possibility is two-fold. It may provide a suitable time interval for testing the ability of GCMs to simulate global climates in a high CO₂ world and a means of comparing the predicted consequences of future global change on terrestrial ecosystems with those of the geological past. In other words, as Chaloner (1998) pointed out, 'is the past the key to the future or has someone changed the lock?' In the case of the Eocene it is quite likely that the lock has changed, since a number of boundary conditions were significantly different from now; for example, the Earth was largely ice-free in the Eocene (Miller *et al.*, 1987) with a subsequent rise in sea level (by some 75 m) and altered oceanic circulation patterns. In a current global change context, this rise compares to the rather small increase due to global warming (up to 60 cm) predicted by 2100 (Wigley & Raper, 1992), and during Quaternary interglacials (90 cm). There is also the problem of explaining the very shallow pole–equator–pole temperature gradient of the Eocene that is thought to be unrelated to the concentration of atmospheric CO₂ (Barron, 1987; Sloan *et al.*, 1995; Sloan & Pollard, 1998).

Despite identifying these differences in boundary conditions, as a first analysis, it is of interest to compare Mesozoic and Cenozoic trends in global temperature change with those predicted by GCMs for a future greenhouse warming. If nothing else, this exercise serves to give a geological perspective on the scale of possible future global warming. Globally-averaged temperature trends for the past 100 Ma have been taken from Crowley & Kim (1995), who re-calculated palaeotemperatures from the oxygen isotope record of benthic foraminifera using a range of data, including revised estimates for the Eocene and the Cenomanian of the Cretaceous (90 Ma). The revisions allowed for latitudinal variations in the oxygen isotope composition of seawater (see Chapter 7), excluded from the original calculations of Shackleton & Boersma (1981) and Sellwood *et al.* (1994). The resulting geological temperature change curve has been compared with two estimates of future warming by the Hadley Centre coupled ocean–atmosphere GCM, the first using the IS92a CO_2 increases to the year 2050 only, and the second using the CO_2 increases together with projected increased loading of atmospheric aerosols for the same scenarios (Mitchell *et al.*, 1995). Sulphate aerosols, in this case of anthropogenic origin, cool the Earth by reflecting long-wave radiation back into space.

This simple first comparison of predicted short-term future global warming (Fig. 8.2) shows a strong sensitivity to sulphate loading in the atmosphere. Projected global temperature increases by a coupled ocean–atmosphere model for the next few decades are apparently greater than experienced on Earth over the past 10–15 Ma but not as great as reconstructed for the middle Miocene or the middle Eocene (Fig. 8.2). The short-term future influence of an increased CO_2 atmospheric content is therefore unlikely to yield a climatic warming outside the range experienced by the most recently-evolved groups of land plants.

Possible longer-term (centuries) warming trends beyond the year 2050 can also be considered, as achieved by Crowley & Kim (1995), using a simple one-dimensional (1-D) energy balance model (EBM) (see Chapter 2) coupled to an upwelling diffusion model. Despite the apparent simplicity of the approach, earlier work has shown the 1-D EBM to be capable of reproducing temperature changes in the short term closely compatible with those of more sophisticated coupled GCMs (Kim & Crowley, 1994). In this case a simple approach provides a cheap and quicker means of assessing possible century-scale climate responses to CO_2 increases.

The EBM was driven with two different CO_2 emission scenarios, one considering the effects of strict conservation measures limiting CO_2 emissions to present levels (5 Gt C yr^{-1}), cessation of deforestation and a simple negative

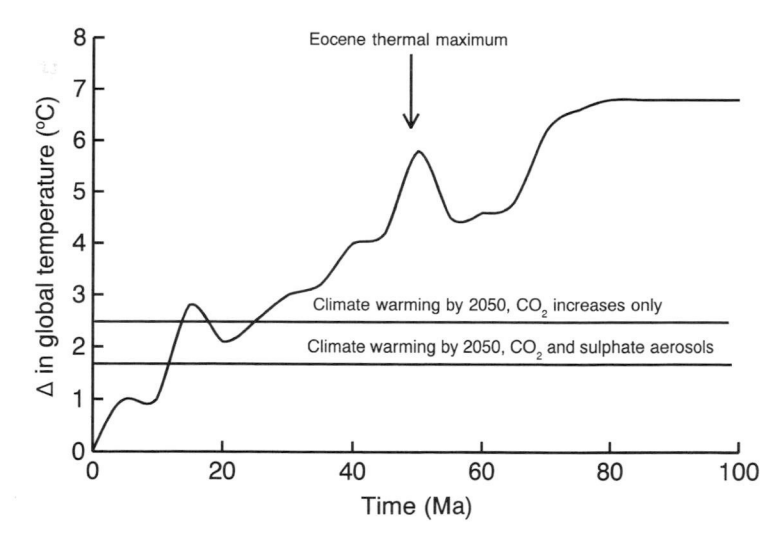

Figure 8.2. Reconstructed changes in global temperature (Δ) over the past 100 Ma, depicted as a change in global temperature relative to the present (after Crowley & Kim, 1995), and projected increases in global temperature by the Hadley Centre GCM for AD 2050, based on CO_2 emission scenario IS92a with and without the direct effects of sulphate aerosol forcing (from Mitchell *et al.*, 1995).

biospheric feedback on CO_2 concentrations (a so-called 'restricted' scenario) (Walker & Kasting, 1992). For comparison, the other scenario is 'unrestricted' and represents a high-end CO_2 emission situation (Fig. 8.3a). Both patterns of CO_2 accumulation in the atmosphere begin to decay after all of the fossil fuel reserves are combusted and as century-scale oceanic CO_2 uptake gradually depletes the atmospheric reservoir (Walker & Kasting, 1992). Conversion of these CO_2 patterns to radiative forcing for use in the EBM then permits an analysis of their likely impacts on the long-term temperature of the Earth. The final requirement for this modelling exercise is the temperature sensitivity of the EBM to a doubling of CO_2. This is an uncertain feature of all climate models and so three different estimates have been used (1.5 °C, 2.5 °C and 4.5 °C) (Crowley & Kim, 1995).

Calculated in this way, the predicted future range for maximal temperature increases over the next few hundred years, as a result of human activities, shows a warming largely unprecedented over the past 100 Ma (Fig. 8.3b). Even the restricted CO_2 scenario, with a low climate sensitivity to CO_2 change, results in climatic warming exceeding that of the Miocene (Fig. 8.3b). Uncertainties in the representation of cloud processes within GCMs limits their range of climate sensitivities to CO_2. However, since changes in global temperatures derived from palaeoclimatic records must inherently include

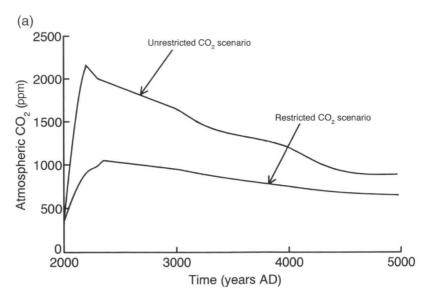

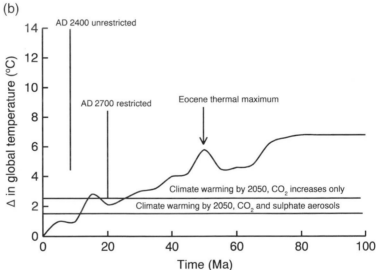

Figure 8.3. (a) CO_2 changes resulting from emission scenarios of fossil fuel burning and due to biomass destruction in the long term (after Walker & Kasting, 1992), and (b) resulting predictions of maximum future warming using a 1-dimensional EBM relative to the isotopic curve of global temperature change over the past 100 Ma (after Crowley & Kim, 1995). Note different time scales for (a) and (b).

the net effect of cloud feedback processes, it has been suggested that palaeoclimate reconstructions could narrow this area of uncertainty in climate modelling (Hoffert & Covey, 1992; Covey *et al.*, 1996). Taking the mid-Cretaceous and last glacial maximum as examples of climates warmer and cooler than present, respectively, Hoffert & Covey (1992) calculated a 'best estimate' for climate sensitivity to a doubling of CO_2 equal to $2.3 \pm 0.9\,°C$, within the range cited by the IPCC (Houghton *et al.*, 1995). The derivation of this 'best guess' estimate assumes a linear response in the climate system sensitivity to CO_2 increases that may not be robust when CO_2 concentrations extend beyond double the present-day value. However, taking the 'best guess' long-term temperature increase (i.e. in the mid-range presented in Fig. 8.3b) shows that projections of future warming in the next few hundred years will be greater than those recognised for the past 50–100 Ma. Furthermore, since Cretaceous temperatures are comparable to those of the lower Palaeozoic (Crowley & Baum, 1995), the potential effect of greenhouse increases will exceed those for much of the past 500 Ma.

A high CO_2 greenhouse-warmed world in the Eocene, and a high CO_2 greenhouse-warmed world at some point in the future could both have similar impacts on the functioning of terrestrial vegetation (Drake *et al.*, 1997). Under the current atmospheric CO_2 partial pressure, large quantities of rubisco are required to support light-saturating rates of photosynthesis, with a correspondingly large requirement for nitrogen. At higher CO_2 concentrations, close to those of the Eocene and the year 2100 (800 ppm), experiments using transgenic plants with reduced leaf content of rubisco have demonstrated that a decreased requirement for rubisco leads to no loss in carbon gain (Masle *et al.*, 1993). This feature of plant growth in a high CO_2 environment ultimately leads to more efficient use of nitrogen. With higher temperatures and a high CO_2 concentration the situation improves further (Woodrow, 1994) (Fig. 8.4), because rubisco operates more efficiently. Plant growth throughout much of the Mesozoic, and particularly between the Jurassic and the Eocene, was therefore probably less expensive in terms of nitrogen (and other nutrients) use than it is for vegetation under the current climate and CO_2 concentration.

Given the global warmth of the Eocene, and a future high CO_2 world, the aim of this chapter will be to compare modelled ecosystem responses of the past with those of the future, to tease out possible similarities and differences between the two intervals. Global climates representing the years 2060 and 2100 have been used as the climates of the future (Mitchell *et al.*, 1995) since these represent GCM simulations with CO_2 concentrations of 600 and 800 ppm respectively, within the likely range estimated for the Eocene (Fig. 8.1).

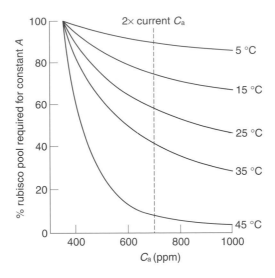

Figure 8.4. Proportion of rubisco required to support a constant rubisco-limited photosynthetic rate at 350 ppm CO_2 with an increase in CO_2 and leaf temperature (from Drake *et al.*, 1997).

The difficulty in simulating the observed sea surface temperature gradient in the Eocene by climate models (Zachos *et al.*, 1994) requires comparison against a variety of independent terrestrial palaeoclimate proxies data for reconstructing palaeotemperatures and palaeoprecipitation (Wing & Greenwood, 1993; Greenwood & Wing, 1995; Wilf *et al.*, 1998). The physiological basis for estimating palaeoprecipitation is examined in relation to evidence from contemporary CO_2 enrichment experiments with plants.

We first consider the impact of each of these three global climates on the productivity and structure of terrestrial vegetation. For the Eocene, consideration is given to the possible influence of vegetation on polar climate, via its influence on the albedo of the Earth's surface. The comparison between the past and the future is extended to consider the spatially-averaged productivity of different forest types. An attempt at testing the Eocene predictions of forest productivity has been made by comparing modelled high latitude productivities with those derived from the fossil record of tree growth, using the approach described in Chapter 6. Next, the potential for future greenhouse climates to alter the distribution of vegetation to reproduce that of the Eocene is considered. In this section, comparisons are first made between the predicted global distribution of the different functional types of vegetation in the Eocene and those based on the plant fossil record (Wolfe, 1985; Frakes *et al.*, 1992). The final section considers how carbon storage in the biomass of vegetation and soils of the Eocene compares with predictions for the future and their potential feedback on CO_2 accumulation in the atmosphere and global temperatures.

Global climates of the Eocene and the future

The early Eocene was marked by important changes in oceanic basin configuration, particularly the closure of Tethys, the opening of the Norwegian–Greenland sea and the initial isolation of Antarctica (Fig. 8.5). These tectonic changes had a subsequent impact on oceanic circulation patterns, that had weaker vertical ocean temperature gradients at high southern latitudes (Kennett & Stott, 1991) and warmer deep Atlantic waters (Miller *et al.*, 1987) compared with the present day.

The simulations used here to force the vegetation model have been made at the University of Reading using the UGAMP GCM. The simulations include many of the palaeogeographic differences between the past and present (Fig. 8.5) and were run with a $3.75° \times 3.75°$ spatial resolution and prescribed sea surface temperatures (SSTs), derived from the oxygen isotope composition of foraminifera (Zachos *et al.*, 1994). Prescription of SSTs based on observed estimates enables a more reliable simulation of palaeoclimates, particularly at high latitudes and circumvents the need for defining the mechanisms for producing high latitude SSTs. Therefore, the model is not really predicting temperatures over the oceans.

The global patterns of mean annual land temperatures (MAT) in the Eocene and for the year 2100 show similar values at mid- and low latitudes (Fig. 8.6). The more southerly location of Australia in the Eocene, compared with the present day, resulted in correspondingly cooler MATs. In comparing these past and future climates, it should be pointed out that the climates for 2060 and 2100 were not in equilibrium but part of a transient GCM simulation, in contrast to the Eocene. Warmer future climates would have resulted if Mitchell *et al.* (1995) had continued the simulations at the specified concentration of CO_2. Since their simulations were transient, the major northern hemisphere ice sheets persisted, with an influence on climate, whereas this feature was absent in the Eocene (although seasonal snow cover is predicted). If future warming simulations were run to equilibrium then it is possible that all of the ice sheets would melt, resulting in a world resembling, climatically, that of the Eocene. As throughout much of Earth history when the atmospheric CO_2 concentration was higher than now, the latitudinal gradient in MATs (Fig. 8.7) shows stable tropical temperatures (Crowley, 1991), but with higher polar temperatures in the Eocene. However, by the year 2100, MATs just north of the equator potentially exceed those of the Eocene (Fig. 8.7).

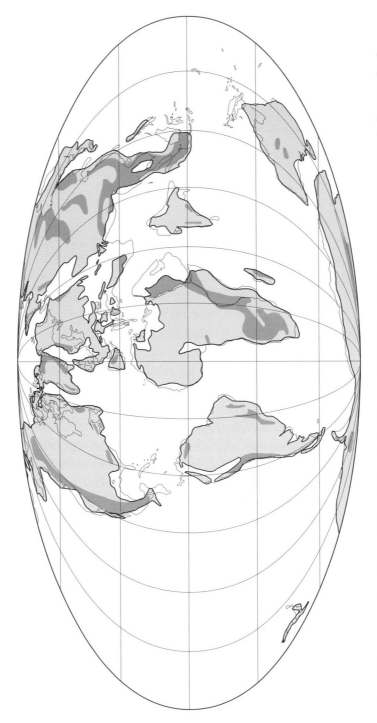

Figure 8.5. Reconstruction of the positions of the major landmasses at 50 Ma (from Smith *et al.*, 1994). Dark shading indicates uplands.

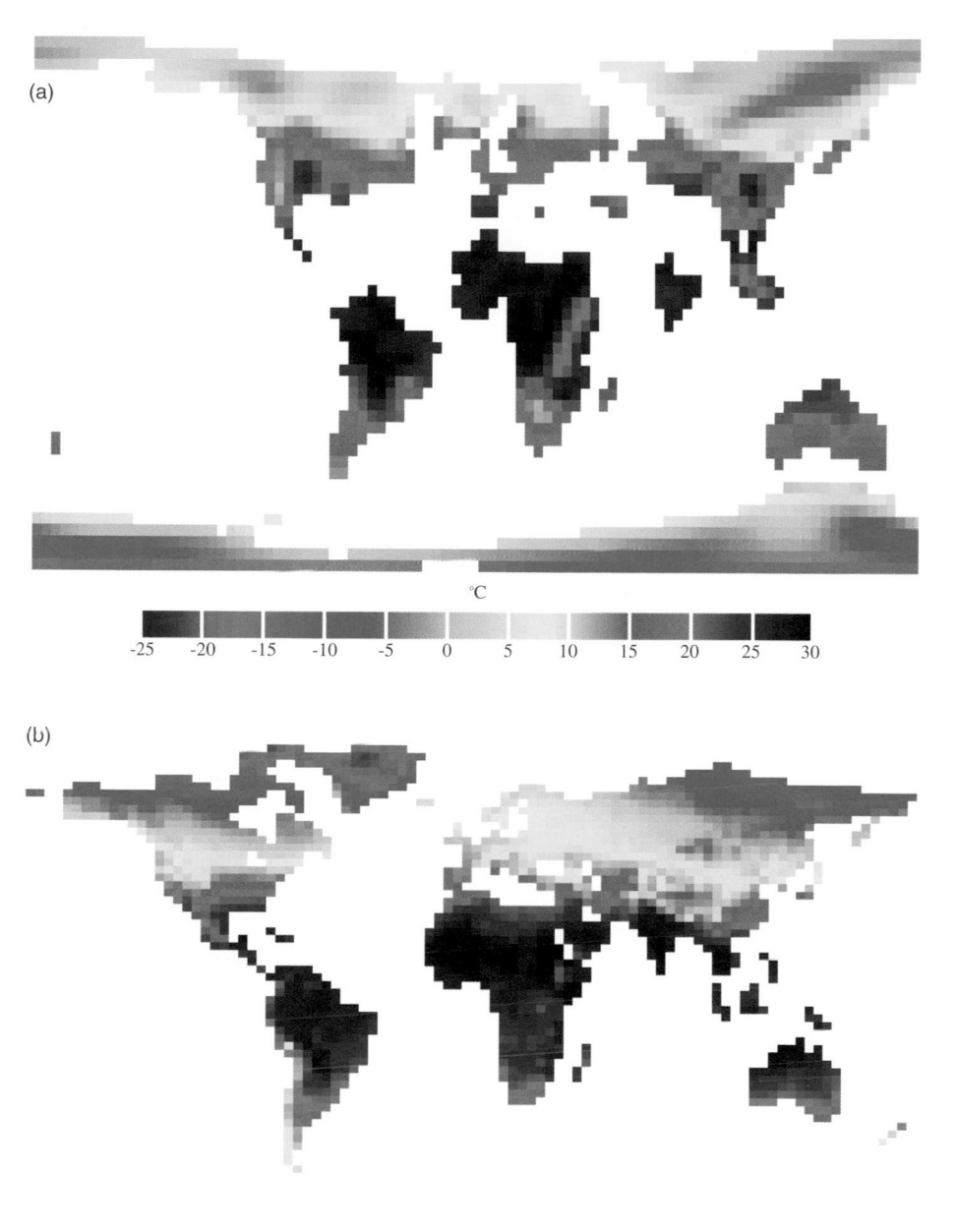

Figure 8.6. Global distribution of mean annual land temperatures in (a) the Eocene, (b) AD 2060 and (c) AD 2100.

(c)

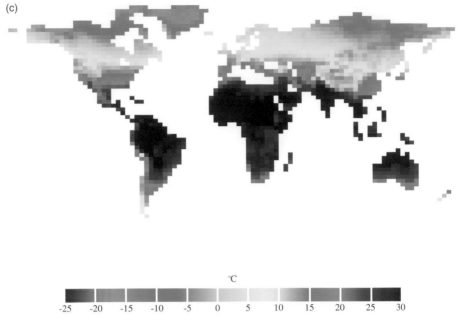

°C

| -25 | -20 | -15 | -10 | -5 | 0 | 5 | 10 | 15 | 20 | 25 | 30 |

Figure 8.6. (cont.)

The simulated global patterns of mean annual land surface precipitation (MAP) for the Eocene show greater differences in high latitudes from those predicted for 2060 and 2100 than those for MAT (Fig. 8.8). In the Eocene, the low and mid-latitudes are wetter over larger geographical areas than in the future, particularly around Greenland, the eastern USA, India and Australia. This pattern is reflected in the latitudinal averages, where MAP is generally higher in the Eocene than in the future (Fig. 8.9). The greater amount of precipitation over Greenland and Antarctica in the Eocene is probably related to the lack of ice sheets. For example, unpublished simulations for a present-day climate without permanent ice sheets results in much wetter high latitudes (P. J. Valdes, personal communication). It emerges that the GCM simulations of future climates show rather small changes in precipitation with the CO_2 increases but, again, this may be related to the transient nature of the GCM runs. However, as outlined earlier in Chapter 3, precipitation patterns are one of the most uncertain features of GCMs and should not be over-interpreted.

Overall, global land temperatures simulated for the Eocene could be attained somewhere between 2060 and 2100 (Table 8.1). The GCM simulations of future climates, however, indicate that these climates are unlikely to be as wet as in the Eocene (Table 8.1).

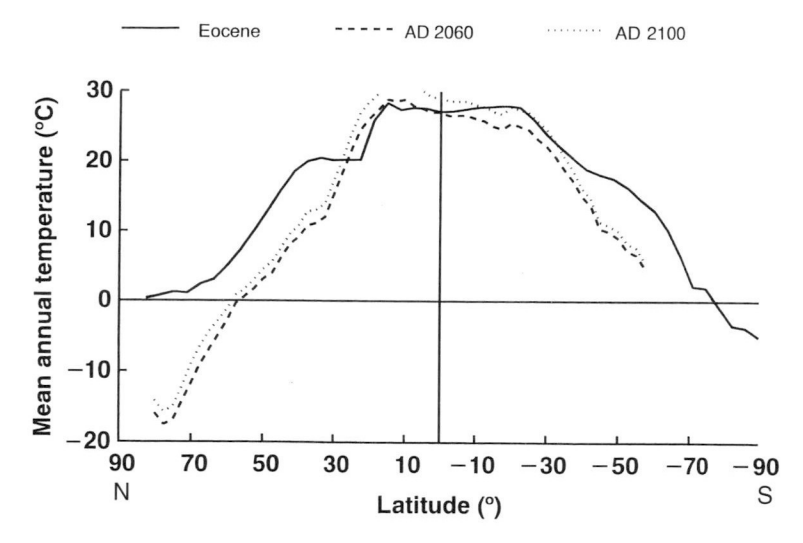

Figure 8.7. Area-weighted latitudinal averages of mean annual land temperatures in the Eocene, 2060 and 2100.

Comparison of Eocene GCM climate with geological data

There are difficulties in reproducing the polar warmth of the Eocene climate as reconstructed from fossil evidence (Barron, 1987; Sloan & Barron, 1992; Sloan *et al.*, 1995). Therefore comparison of the UGAMP simulations with geological data is required to indentify possible errors in the climate simulations.

The first comparison has been between the modelled terrestrial climates and proxy data from the plant fossil record. Attempts at reconstructing terrestrial Eocene climates (MATs and MAPs) have been largely based on analyses of the plant fossil record (Sloan & Barron, 1992; Wing & Greenwood, 1993; Greenwood & Wing, 1995; Wilf *et al.*, 1998). There are reservations about the use of floristic composition and leaf margin analyses of fossil floras for estimating past temperatures, not least because they assume that plant growth in the high CO_2 Mesozoic greenhouse world was the same as now. As emphasised in earlier chapters, this is most unlikely to have been the situation (cf. Beerling, 1998), and will particularly limit palaeoprecipitation estimates (Wilf *et al.*, 1998), because of reductions in canopy transpiration and increased efficiency of water-use during plant growth in a high CO_2 environment. In addition, temperature estimates from leaf margin analyses appear incompatible with the presence of frost-sensitive taxa such as palms, cycads and gingers, (Wing & Greenwood, 1993; Greenwood & Wing, 1995). Nevertheless, the results from these analyses of terrestrial fossil floras provide the only

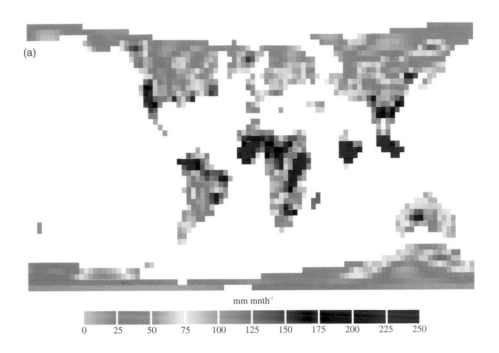

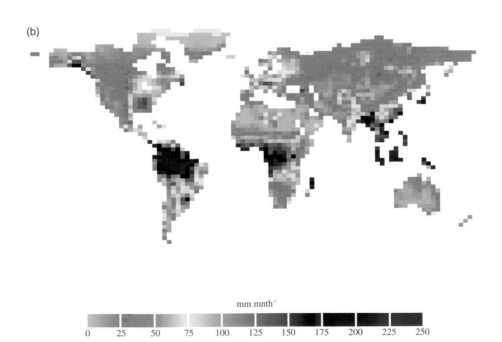

Figure 8.8. Global distribution of mean annual precipitation over land in (a) the Eocene, (b) AD 2060 and (c) AD 2100.

(c)

mm mnth⁻¹

0   25   50   75   100   125   150   175   200   225   250

Figure 8.8. (*cont.*)

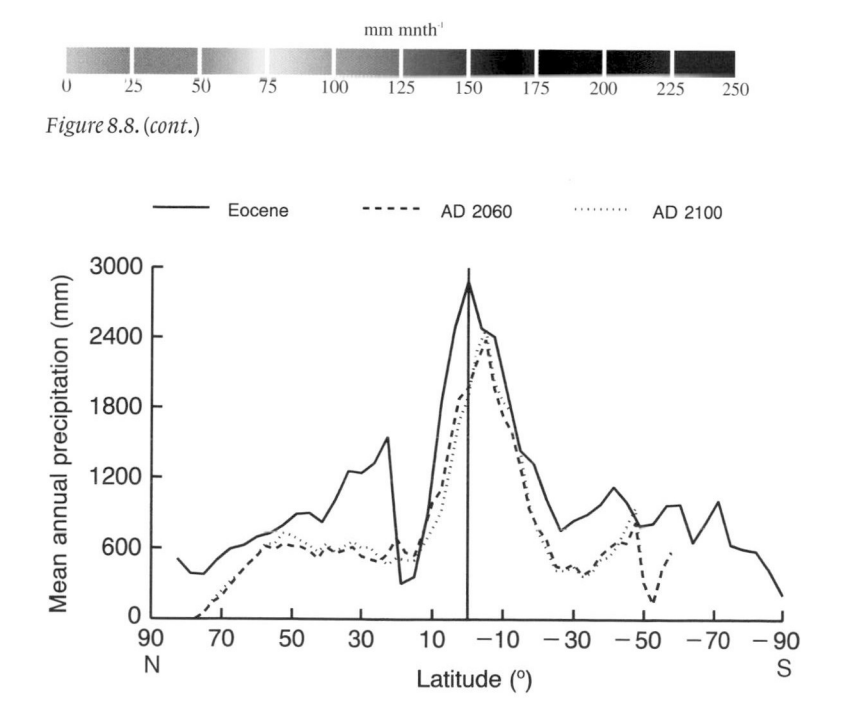

Figure 8.9. Area-weighted latitudinal averages of mean annual precipitation over land in the Eocene, 2060 and 2100.

Table 8.1. *Simulated land surface characteristics of the Eocene and future climates*

Time	Mean annual temperature (°C)	Mean annual precipitation (mm d^{-1})
Eocene	16.6	3.1
AD 2060	15.0	2.2
AD 2100	17.0	2.0

currently available means of comparing climate model results with the geological evidence and so have been used here.

The comparison shows that the modelled Eocene patterns of MATs across a wide latitudinal gradient are generally close to those obtained from analyses of fossil floras. Overall, the GCM predicted higher MATs than the fossil data in the southern hemisphere, and lower MATs than the fossil data in the northern hemisphere (Fig. 8.10a). Errors in both the climate model and palaeoclimate reconstructions from terrestrial floras therefore limit interpretation of the significance of these differences.

Comparison of modelled trends in precipitation with MAPs estimated from fossil floras of early to middle Eocene age is restricted mainly to North America and Alaska, spanning a rather narrow palaeolatitudinal range of 40–60° N (Sloan & Barron, 1992; Wing & Greenwood, 1993; Wilf *et al.*, 1998), and sites in southern Australia (Greenwood, 1996). In contrast to the temperature estimates, there are very marked differences in MAPs computed by the GCM and estimated from fossil floras (Fig. 8.10b). One set of estimates (Wing & Greenwood, 1993), based on multiple regression analyses between leaf margin characters of modern floras and MAP, explained only 50% of the relationship, indicating limitations in its application for precipitation reconstructions. Recognising these limitations, Wilf *et al.* (1998) attempted to improve the approach by regressing the mean leaf area of a vegetation sample against MAP. This approach explained 76% of the variance in a modern dataset collected from a range of sites, but also requires the use of modern analogue vegetation types to estimate leaf area (Wilf *et al.*, 1998), the implicit assumption being that plant growth in the high CO_2 Eocene environment has no impact on leaf area.

It is possible to test this assumption using published data from plant CO_2 enrichment experiments (Table 8.2). Data on total leaf area per plant were taken from studies on a wide range of plant types (trees, shrubs and grasses) and experimental treatments, including drought, irradiance, temperature and

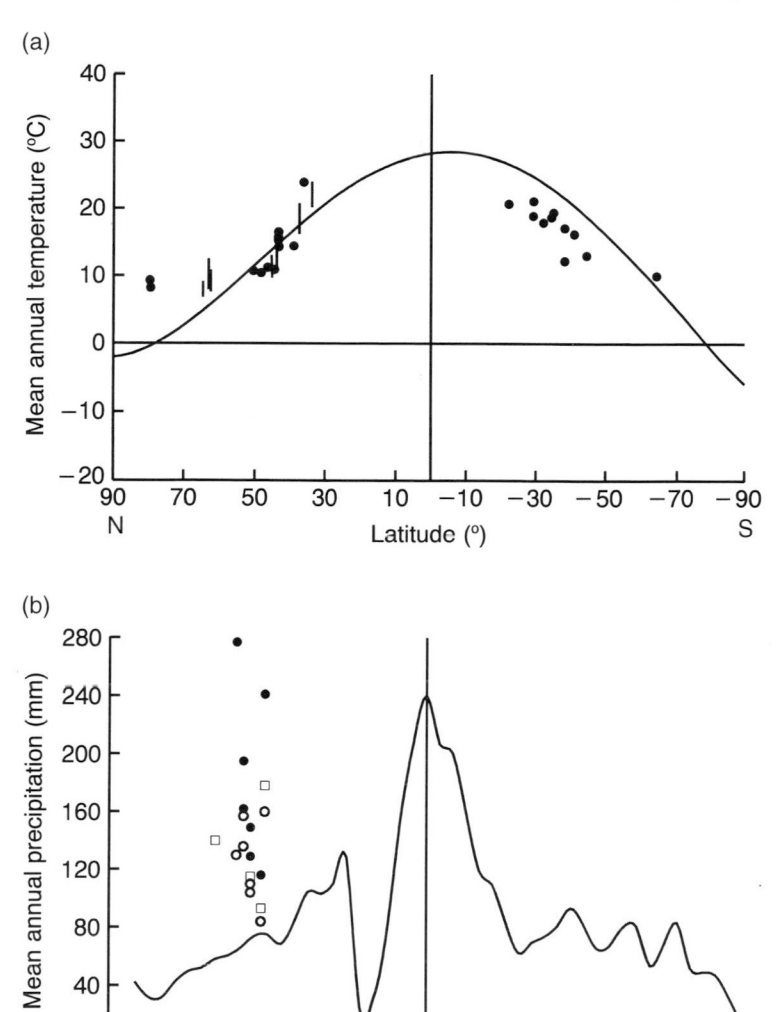

Figure 8.10. Latitudinal averages of (a) mean annual land temperature (MAT) and (b) mean annual land precipitation (MAP). The line in (a) is a 3rd-order polynomial fit to the area-weighted MAT from Fig. 8.7 and in (b) a spline fit to the MAP simulations by the GCM. In (a) the palaeo-estimates are from Greenwood & Wing (1995) (●) and Sloan & Barron (1992) (vertical bars). In (b), the palaeo-estimates are from Wing & Greenwood (1993) (●), Wilf *et al.* (1998) (○), Sloan & Barron (1992) (□), and Greenwood (1996) (■).

Table 8.2. *Species and studies used to examine the influence of CO$_2$ enrichment on leaf size*

Species	Authors	Species	Authors
Tropical trees		**Temperate trees**	
Acacia mangium	Ziska *et al.* (1991)	*Acer saccharum*	Tschaplinski *et al.* (1995)
Aechemea magdalena (CAM)		*Betula pendula*	Rey & Jarvis (1997)
Anana comsosus (CAM)		*B. populifolia*	Rochefort & Bazzaz (1992)
Ficus obtusifolia		*B. lenta*	
Paspallum conjugatum		*B. papyrifera*	
Pharus latifolius		*B. alleghaniensis*	
Manihot esculentum		*Castanea sativa*	Kohen *et al.* (1993)
Tabebuia rosea		*Fagus sylvatica*	Egli *et al.* (1998)
Eucalyptus acrorhyncha	Roden & Ball (1996)	*Liriodendron tulipifera*	Norby & O'Neill (1991)
		Liquidambar styraciflua	Tschainski *et al.* (1995)
E. camaldulensis	Wong *et al.* (1992)	*Picea abies*	Egli *et al.* (1998)
E. cypellocarpa		*Platanus occidentalis*	Tschainski *et al.* (1995)
E. miniata	Duff *et al.* (1994)	*Quercus robur*	Picon *et al.* (1996)
E. pauciflora	Wong *et al.* (1992)		Guehl *at al.* (1994)
E. pulverulenta			
E. rossii	Roden & Ball (1996)	**Grasses**	
E. tetrodonta	Duff *et al.* (1994)	*Panicum laxum*	Ghannoum *et al.* (1997)
Shrub		*P. antidole*	(C$_4$ photosynthetic pathway)
Linera benzoin	Cipollini *et al.* (1993)	*Dacytlis glomerata*	Ziska & Bunce (1994)
Herbs			
Anthyllis vulneraria	Ferris & Taylor (1993)		
Lotus corniculatus			
Medicago sativa			
Sanguisorba minor			
Plantago major	Ziska & Bunce (1994)		

nitrogen fertilisation. The results (Fig. 8.11) show convincingly that atmospheric CO$_2$ enrichment leads to a greater leaf area of vegetation in water-limited and non-limiting conditions. Across all 38 species, and a total of 68 measurements (Table 8.2), the mean increase in total leaf area was 70% with a doubling in CO$_2$ (Fig. 8.11). The increase occurs because of the potential for more growth in high CO$_2$ with a given water supply. This effect would lead to overestimates of the amount of precipitation required for a given observed leaf area in the fossil record, an expectation consistent for the Eocene where reconstructed MAPs are typically much greater than those of the GCM (Fig. 8.10b).

Comparisons of the UGAMP Eocene temperature with the geological data show close correspondence with the terrestrial MATs determined from some high latitude fossil floras. Larger discrepancies occur with the modelled and

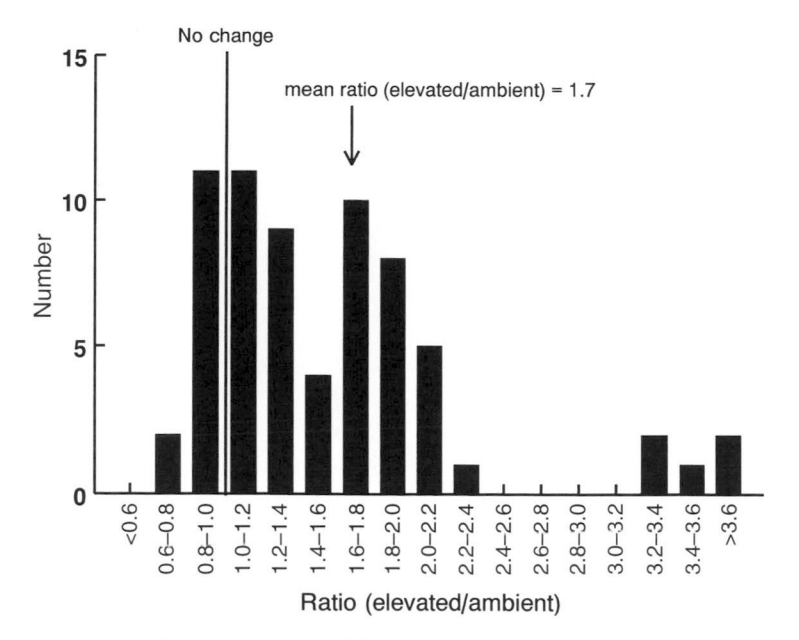

Figure 8.11. Histogram compiled from 68 measurements (from 38 species) of change in total plant leaf area with a doubling of the atmospheric CO_2 concentration during growth. All measurements are expressed as the ratio of leaf area at elevated CO_2 divided by that at ambient CO_2 and were taken from the published studies listed in Table 8.2.

reconstructed MAPs. However, the underlying assumption required for correlating a precipitation signal from the fossil record is flawed, and so this limits the validity of this test of model predictions. Concerns have also been raised about the influence of temperature on leaf size, and its interaction with other environmental factors which may further limit the approach (Wolfe & Uemura, 1999). The main contrasts between the ancient greenhouse climate of the Eocene and that simulated for a future greenhouse climate (AD 2100), when the atmospheric CO_2 concentration reaches a comparable value, are greater polar warmth and precipitation at 50 Ma.

It is also clear that testing the Eocene terrestrial climates derived by GCMs on the basis of the climatic tolerances of modern analogue vegetation types may not be robust and the development of alternative approaches is required. Application of isotopic studies of growth rings to marine and terrestrial organisms offers one possibility. Seasonal growth rings are evident in the shells of fossil marine gastropods and bivalves (Andreasson & Schmitz, 1996, 1998; Fricke *et al.*, 1998) and fossil herbivore teeth (Sharp & Cerling, 1998), both of which yield isotopic records with a strong seasonal cycle of temperature change. Estimates of seasonal changes in terrestrial temperatures might

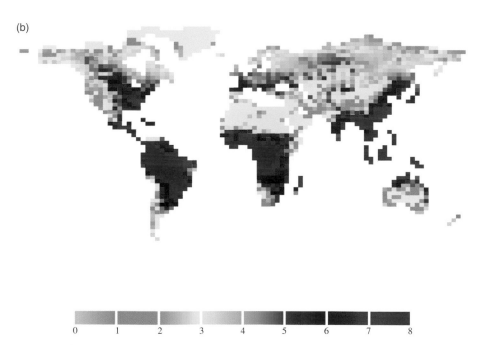

Figure 8.12. Global patterns of leaf area index for (a) the Eocene, (b) AD 2060 and (c) AD 2100.

(c)

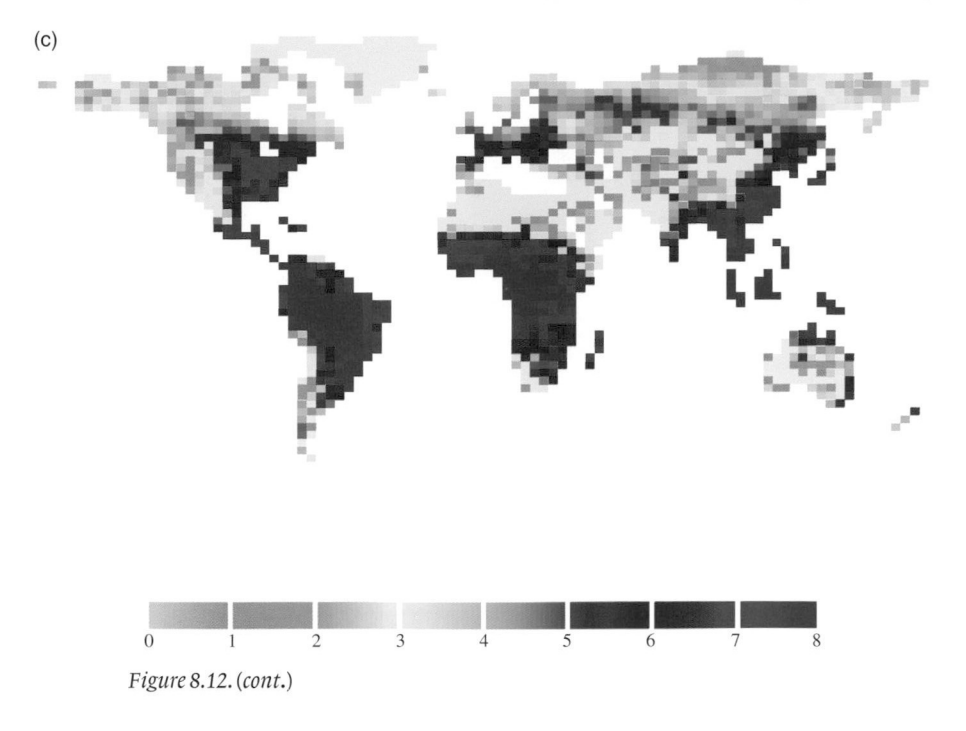

| 0 | 1 | 2 | 3 | 4 | 5 | 6 | 7 | 8 |

Figure 8.12. (cont.)

also be extracted from isotopic measurements of exceptionally well-preserved high latitude Eocene woods that have become 'mummified', rather than 'coalified' (i.e. the original organic material is preserved), and which show large distinct growth rings.

Structure and productivity of terrestrial vegetation in the Eocene

The global-scale impacts of Eocene and future climates on terrestrial ecosystems have been investigated by forcing the SDGVM with the Eocene climate and an atmospheric CO_2 concentration of 600 ppm, representing a 'best guess' value from geochemical studies. The modelled global warmth and high CO_2 environment of the Eocene allowed the widespread development of canopies of terrestrial vegetation with a high leaf area index (Fig. 8.12a). This prediction is supported by sedimentary evidence, at high northern latitudes of the Canadian Arctic, which indicates a warm moist environment with dense vegetation cover and extensive coal-forming swamps (Miall, 1984). In a future globally-warmed world with increases in atmospheric CO_2 concentration, geographical areas of high LAI also become quite widespread, but even by the

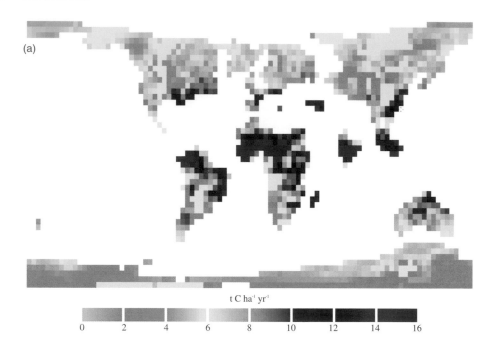

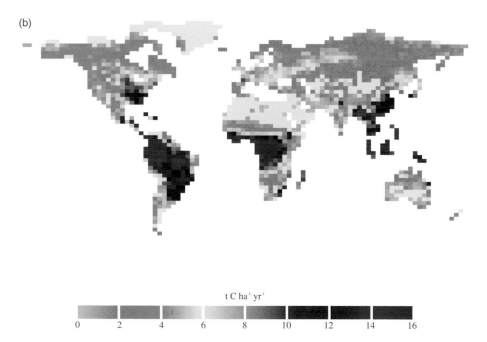

Figure 8.13. Global patterns of terrestrial net primary productivity for (a) the Eocene, (b) AD 2060 and (c) AD 2100.

(c)

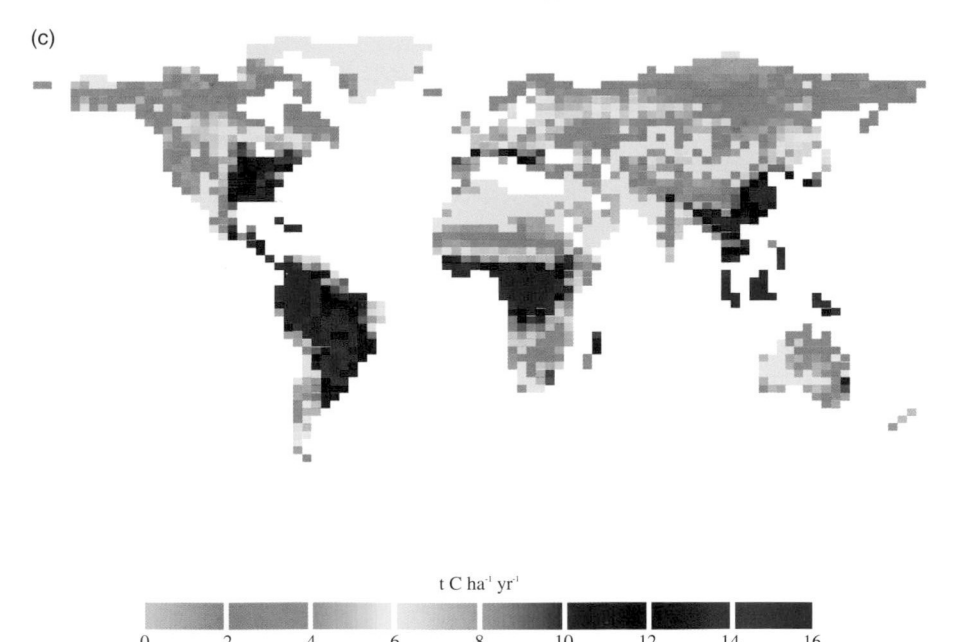

t C ha⁻¹ yr⁻¹

0   2   4   6   8   10   12   14   16

Figure 8.13. (cont.)

year 2100 fail to approach the situation in the Eocene (Fig. 8.12c), particularly
at high latitudes of both hemispheres.

The global patterns of terrestrial net primary productivity (NPP) generally
reflect those of LAI (Fig. 8.13). In the Eocene, the deep vegetation canopies
(Fig. 8.12a) are highly productive, even at high latitudes, but including some
large regions where NPP is restricted particularly through northern Russia,
parts of Asia and in a vertical band through Arctic Canada and North America
(Fig. 8.13a). The restrictions occur through reduced summer precipitation.
Several marked differences emerge between predictions of the global patterns
of LAI and NPP for the Eocene and those made with the future climates. For
the years 2060 and 2100, NPP in high latitude regions remains generally low
(Fig. 8.13b,c). Where productivity does approach that of the Eocene in middle
latitudes (AD 2100) throughout central Europe, the areal extent is quite
restricted, as with the pattern for LAI (Fig. 8.12c). At low latitudes, it is also
notable that although temperatures predicted for 2060 and 2100 exceed those
of the Eocene (between 30° N and 10° S), productivity is also greater, in some
parts by up to 4 t C ha⁻¹ yr⁻¹ (Fig. 8.13).

One of the most striking differences between the past and the present is the
productivity of the land masses of Antarctica and Australia. In the ice-free
world of the Eocene (Miller *et al.*, 1987), high NPP and LAI occur in Australia

because of the much greater precipitation compared with future climates (Fig. 8.8), rather than any marked changes in temperature (Fig. 8.6). Future climatic warming continues to allow the persistence of Australian deserts, thereby limiting the productivity of the continent as a whole. The presence of the ice sheet in Antarctica obviously precludes its extensive colonisation by terrestrial vegetation by the year 2100, but in the Eocene this land mass had a significant productivity, with an estimated total of 4.2 Gt C yr^{-1}. The location of India at lower latitudes in the Eocene resulted in a warmer and wetter climate than now, with a correspondingly higher LAI and NPP.

The most prominent region of similarity between patterns of NPP and LAI in the past and predicted for the future is the south-eastern USA. The region is modelled to have a high LAI and NPP (*c.* 12 t C ha^{-1} yr^{-1}) in the Eocene and this situation is predicted to return over the next 100 years of warming and CO_2 increase (Figs. 8.12 and 8.13). The return to a productive American southwest occurs through a gradual north-westerly extension in high rainfall patterns. Globally, total annual terrestrial productivity for the Eocene was 90.0 Gt C, and 78.1% and 86.9% lower, at 70.3 Gt C and 78.2 Gt C for 2060 and 2100, respectively.

The global pattern of terrestrial productivities can be combined with the modelled geographical extent of each plant functional type (see p. 273), to determine the spatially averaged productivity at different times. This analysis has been performed for the three dominant forest types (deciduous broad-leaved forests, evergreen broad-leaved forests and evergreen needle-leaved forests) for the Eocene, 2060 and 2100. The results (Fig. 8.14) show that evergreen needle-leaved and deciduous broad-leaved forests had similar average productivities in the Eocene and in future climates. The increase in temperature and CO_2 between the years 2060 and 2100 results in modest (<0.5 t C ha^{-1} yr^{-1}) increases in the growth of both forest types. For the more productive evergreen broad-leaved forests, equivalent to the contemporary tropical rainforests, productivity increases markedly beyond that of the Eocene value by 2060 and further still by 2100 (Fig. 8.14). This pattern results for two reasons: first, because the warmer low latitude temperatures of the future climates directly stimulate the expansion and productivity of tropical forests; second, the Eocene tropical forests are distributed across a wider latitudinal range and into higher latitudes (see next section) where the cooler climate limits productivity. Averaged over its entire distribution, therefore, the Eocene tropical forests have a lower productivity.

Calculated as area-weighted latitudinal averages, the LAI pattern shows the dominance of high values in equatorial regions for all three simulations (Fig. 8.15a). The values fall rapidly with increasing latitude in the future simula-

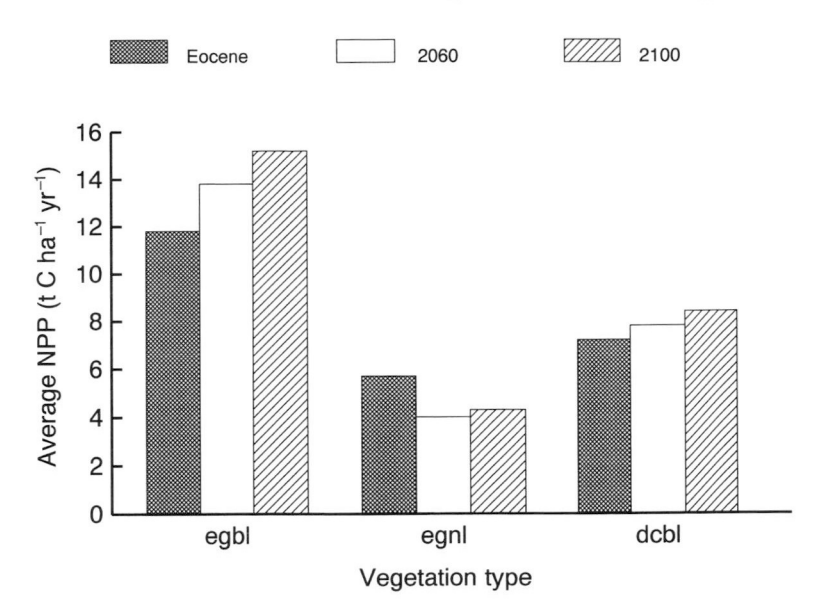

Figure 8.14. Spatially-averaged area-weighted changes in the productivity of three different forest types modelled for the Eocene, 2060 and 2100. Functional types: egbl, evergreen broad-leaved trees; egnl, evergreen needle-leaved trees; dcbl, deciduous broad-leaved trees.

tions but are maintained at higher values (4–6) in the Eocene. As with the global picture, the latitudinal changes in NPP show a similar pattern of change to those of LAI (Fig. 8.15b). The high values of both NPP and LAI, therefore, are due to higher temperatures in combination with high CO_2 concentrations rather than high CO_2 alone.

The model results suggest that the rate at which organic layers (e.g. litter mats) accumulate in fossiliferous sediments could have been faster than estimated from litter production by modern mid-latitude forests, because vegetation in the palaeoenvironments could have supported quite high LAIs. This rate is important since the modern analogue approach is frequently used to estimate sedimentation rates and hence the duration of time represented by a particular organic horizon (e.g. Greenwood & Basinger, 1994; Kojima *et al.*, 1998). The differences can be quantified. Kojima *et al.* (1998) calculated the accumulation rates, x (cm yr^{-1}), of Eocene lignites from the Canadian Arctic by assuming that the dominant taxon within the lignites (*Metasequoia occidentalis*) had an LAI equivalent to that of modern deciduous conifers:

$$x = \frac{LAI.S.D}{rW} \tag{8.1}$$

(a)

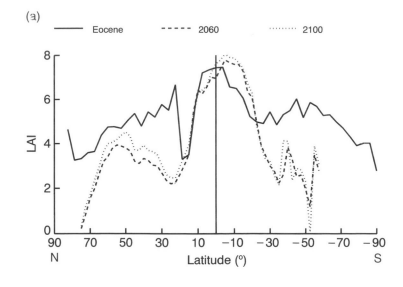

(b)

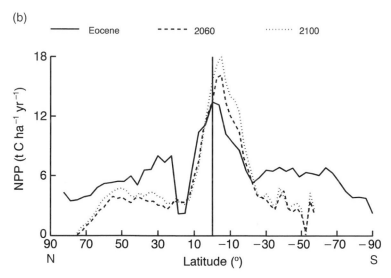

Figure 8.15. Area-weighted latitudinal averages of (a) leaf area index and (b) net primary productivity for the Eocene, 2060 and 2100.

where S is the ground area of the sample (cm^2), D is the thickness of the sample (cm), r is the surface area/weight ratio (typically 50 cm^2 g^{-1}) and W is the weight of the sample (g).

By assuming an LAI of 5, for modern deciduous conifers Kojima *et al.* (1998) calculated accumulation rates from equation 1 of 0.16 cm yr^{-1}. However, the high CO_2 world of the Eocene could probably have supported LAIs at 79° N closer to 7–8 (Fig. 8.13a), giving correspondingly higher accumulation rates of 0.22–0.26 cm yr^{-1}. Further corrections are required to account for compaction and loss of organic materials by decomposition. So, neglecting compaction for a moment, an Eocene lignite 100 cm thick, with an accumulation rate of 0.16 cm yr $^{-1}$, could represent a duration of 625 years. In contrast, with the duration calculated from a revised accumulation rate taken from the model simulations of LAI (0.26 cm yr^{-1}), the same thickness of lignite could represent 384 years, a difference in age of some 240 years. The example illustrates the potential errors inherent in extrapolating modern plant characters back to the past when plants grew in very different environments.

Feedbacks of Eocene vegetation on climate

A striking feature of the model results is the establishment of vegetation with a high LAI in the polar regions during the Eocene (Fig. 8.12 and Fig. 8.15a), due to the warmer temperatures, high CO_2 and higher precipitation, compared with future climate. The existence of these polar forests, in both the fossil record and model predictions, indicates their strong potential for feedback by altering land surface–atmosphere energy exchanges (see Chapter 6). In the Eocene, this feedback has direct implications for climate modelling studies attempting to explain the extreme polar warmth of the early middle Eocene (Sloan et al., 1992, 1995; Sloan & Rea, 1995; Sloan & Pollard, 1998). Numerous mechanisms relating to the physical climate system have been postulated as possible explanations for the shallow equator-to-pole temperature gradient of the Eocene (Table 8.3). Several are, however, inconsistent with the observed rates of climate system responses, or have not been found in climate modelling studies to reconcile models and data. High latitude type II (water vapour) polar stratospheric clouds (PSCs) can warm polar regions and their formation might be associated with high concentrations of atmospheric methane (Sloan & Pollard, 1998). The prescription of PSCs over high latitudes only, rather than allowing their formation through climatic and atmospheric chemistry processes within the climate model, reveals their potential to force land temperatures. Further work is required to identify the mechanism by which increased PSC formation might be brought about, although the role of methane production from terrestrial ecosystems is probably important (Sloan et al., 1992; Valdes, 2000).

The significance of the high LAI of Eocene vegetation is that it offers a further complication to the explanation of high polar temperatures. High values of LAI tend to warm the land surface by lowering its albedo but can also

Table 8.3. *Mechanisms investigated to explain the equator-to-pole temperature gradient in the early/middle Eocene*

Oceanic mechanisms
Double warm deep water formation (Sloan *et al.*, 1995)
Double warm surface water transport (Sloan *et al.*, 1995)
Increase (by a factor of 6) warm deep water production of warm saline water or increase
    thermohaline circulation (Barron *et al.*, 1993)

Atmospheric mechanisms
Decrease high latitude albedo by 45–65% by changes in atmospheric dynamics (Sloan *et al.*, 1995)
Increase high latitude polar stratospheric cloud cover (Sloan & Pollard, 1998)
Expanded Hadley Cell (Farrell 1990)
Increased atmospheric CO_2 concentrations (Sloan & Rea, 1995; Sloan *et al.*, 1995)
Increased methane concentrations (Sloan *et al.*, 1992)
Cool tropical sea surface temperatures through a 90% increase in cloud cover (Horrell, 1990)

cool it by enhancing evapotranspiration and, consequently, cloud cover (Betts *et al.*, 1997). Coupled vegetation–climate modelling studies have shown that at high CO_2 concentrations (640 ppm CO_2) and in regions of abundant vegetation cover, the evaporation effect dominates (Betts *et al.*, 1997) (Fig. 8.16). In general, with the modern configuration of lakes and land masses, the greater the increase in LAI, the greater the cooling effect on climate. Therefore, if vegetation–climate feedbacks were included in climate model simulations for the Eocene, polar regions might be even cooler than without these feedbacks (Fig. 8.16), increasing the discrepancy between models and data for these areas. We suggest this is an area worth further investigation with coupled climate–vegetation models.

Terrestrial productivity of early Tertiary fossil forests

The plant fossil record provides clear evidence for the presence of dense, high latitude forests in the form of fossil tree remains (usually stumps, logs and roots) buried in Eocene (*c.* 50 Ma) sediments of Ellesmere Island (78° N) (Francis, 1988; Kumagai *et al.*, 1995) and Axel Heiberg Island (Francis, 1991) in the Canadian Arctic. These fossils represent some of the most northerly forests yet recorded, although it should be noted that polar forests in the northern hemisphere are widespread today with some coniferous forests reaching 72° N in the Taimyr Peninsula in Siberia (Archibold, 1995). Fossil remains of plants from high latitudes of the southern hemisphere have been reported, see the review by Read & Francis (1992). The phenomenon of polar forests is therefore not confined to the distant past.

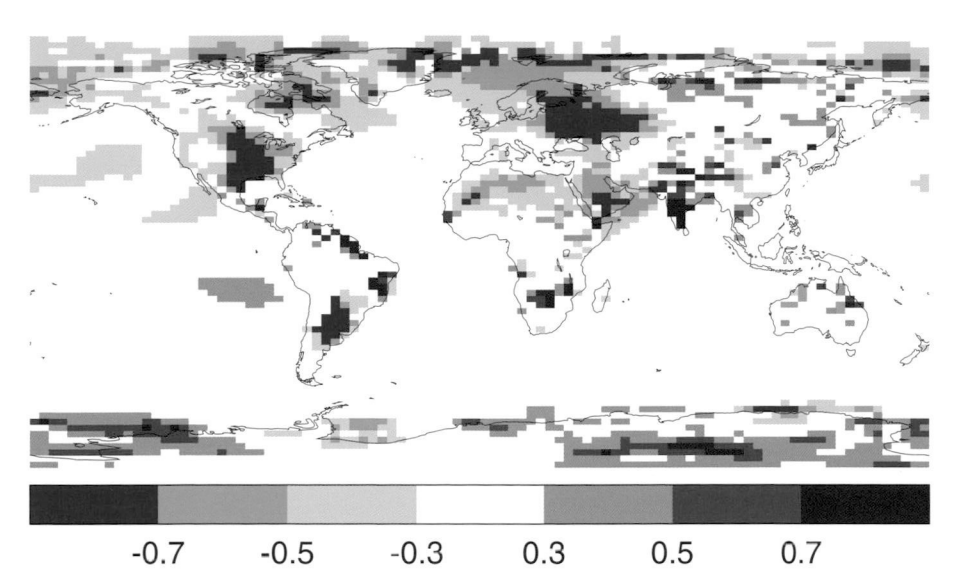

Figure 8.16. Changes in temperature (K) due to combined changes in leaf area index and stomatal conductance compared to those obtained from a change in stomatal conductance. Note that the majority of the land surface is cooled by vegetation feedbacks in a 2 × present CO_2 world (from Betts *et al.*, 1997).

The Eocene forest trees on Canadian islands were large, with *in situ* fossil stumps up to 5 m in diameter, quite closely spaced (367–325 ha^{-1}) and with wide growth rings, indicating the potential for high terrestrial productivity. The spacing of the stumps may not necessarily reflect the original tree density of the forest since tree death will have occurred over many hundreds of years. The fossils do, though, provide tangible evidence supporting the predicted distribution of a productive land surface in these regions (Fig. 8.13 and 8.14) and their morphological characters provide some qualitative support for the model simulations of significant high latitude terrestrial productivity.

Living trees at such latitudes would have endured long periods of darkness during the polar winters followed by rapid increases in day length to continuous light in the polar summers. Such conditions for tree growth are without parallel in the southern hemisphere of today's world and the mechanisms underlying the survival strategies of these forests remain to be investigated, although plant survival in prolonged darkness has been demonstrated (Read & Francis, 1992) and a high concentration of atmospheric CO_2 may also have played an important role (Beerling, 1998). Predictions of significant terrestrial productivity at high latitudes in the prevailing climate of both the northern and southern hemispheres are, however, achieved from temperature-dependent rates of physiological processes in contemporary vegetation, without the

Table 8.4. *Growth ring widths and estimated net primary productivities of fossil forests in the early Tertiary. Productivity is estimated using the empirical approach described in Chapter 6, with the same assumptions*

Age/locality	Palaeolatitude	Ring width (mm)	NPP ($t\,C\,ha^{-1}\,yr^{-1}$) Tree density (ha^{-1})			NPP model ($t\,C\,ha^{-1}\,yr^{-1}$)
			50	150	200	
Lower Tertiary						
King Charles Island, Spitzbergen[a]	61°N	4.4	10.8	21.6	32.3	6
Hare Island, West Greenland[a]	62°N	5.4	13.2	26.4	39.7	8
Cairo[a]	5 °N	faint or absent	n/a			
Palaeocene						
Ellesmere Island[c]	76°N	0.8 ± 0.3	1.9	5.9	7.8	7
Cross Valley formation, Seymour Island[d]	59–62°N	2.0	4.9	14.7	19.6	6
North slope, Alaska[e]	85°N	1.8	4.4	13.2	17.6	5
Early/middle Eocene						
Axel Heiberg Island[b]	76 °N	3–5	7–12	14–24	22–37	7
Ellesmere Island[b]	76°N	up to 10	24.6	73.7	98.3	7
Ellesmere Island[a]	76°N	3.0	7.3	22.0	29.3	7
Ellesmere Island[c]	76°N	1.6 ± 0.8	3.9	11.7	15.6	7
Late Eocene						
La Mesta formation, Seymour Island[d] (angiosperm wood)	59–62°N	3.5	8.6	25.7	34.3	n/a

Sources: From [a]Creber & Chaloner (1985), [b]Francis (1988, 1991), [c]Kumagai *et al.* (1995), [d]Francis (1986a,b), [e]Spicer & Parrish (1990).

need to invoke changes in the temperature sensitivity of plant respiration rates. This suggests there may be no need to invoke any strong trends in evolutionary adaptation to the conditions.

Quantitative comparisons of NPP have been made by first estimating the productivity of the conifer fossil forests on the basis of growth ring widths of the fossil woods (Table 8.4). To provide a temporal context for the Eocene values, additional studies of Palaeocene and late Eocene fossil tree ring widths have also been used in the calculations. Uncertainties about tree density in these ancient forests limit the utility of comparison. Nevertheless, based on the lower Tertiary and early/middle Eocene fossil materials, it can seen that the model estimates are close to or at the lower end of the range calculated using tree ring widths (Table 8.4).

A specific example can be examined for Eocene forest productivity in Alaska, where the model predicts NPP to be 6–7 t C ha^{-1} yr^{-1} (Fig. 8.13), compared with estimates based on fossil tree ring widths of 4.4–17.6 t C ha^{-1} yr^{-1}, depending on the density of the trees in the forests. Both estimates exceed the predicted productivity of this region in a future high CO_2 globally-warmed world (Fig. 8.14). All such comparisons between productivity estimates based on the biophysical and biogeochemical considerations of carbon cycling and those from empirical relationships should not be over-interpreted, because of the limitation of the different approaches. The two estimates overlap within the range of tree densities calculated here, and this is encouraging given the very different approaches to calculating terrestrial productivity. As in the Jurassic study (chapter 6), modelled NPP at high latitudes would not support the high densities recorded for polar fossil forests from Axel Heiberg Island (484 and 325 trees ha^{-1}) and Ellesmere Island (367 trees ha^{-1}) (Francis, 1991). Tree densities such as these are typically seen only in tropical/neotropical forests in the contemporary climate (Pole, 1999), indicating that this may not have been the absolute density of living trees.

Global vegetation distribution in the Eocene and in the future

The global pattern of plant functional types for the Eocene is quite distinct from the year 2100 (Fig. 8.17a). The predicted distribution of C_3 grasses in the Eocene (Fig. 8.17a) is equivalent to a mixture of grasslands and shrublands. Megafossil evidence shows modern tribes of grasses from the late Palaeocene/early Eocene onwards (Crepet & Feldman, 1988), but widespread grasslands did not appear until after the mid- to late Miocene (Potts & Behrensmeyer, 1992). C_4 grasses are thought to have evolved much later in the Miocene (Thomasson et al., 1988) and have not been considered in the Eocene simulations. The pattern of each dominant functional type indicates the high latitude occurrence of deciduous broad-leaved trees in the northern hemisphere, particularly throughout large parts of Greenland, the southern USA, Europe and in western Asia (Fig. 8.17a). In the southern hemisphere these forests extend throughout parts of South America, Africa, Australia and Antarctica (Fig. 8.17a). Evergreen broad-leaved trees attain substantial coverage through central Africa, parts of South America, India and parts of central Australia. Much of Antarctica and Alaska are dominated by evergreen needle-leaved forests (Fig. 8.17a). No deciduous needle-leaved forests dominate in the Eocene, reflecting its warmer winter climate.

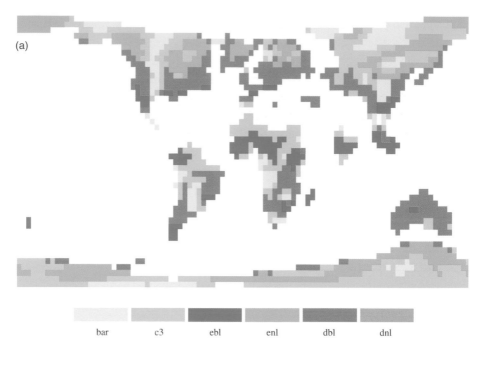

Figure 8.17. Global patterns of plant functional types in (a) the Eocene and (b) 2100. Key: bar, bare soil; C_3, grasslands with C_3 photosynthetic pathway; ebl, evergreen broad-leaved trees; enl, evergreen needle-leaved trees; dbl, deciduous broad-leaved trees; dnl, deciduous needle-leaved trees.

The global patterns of vegetation have been compared with palaeobotanical evidence for the early/middle Eocene. Such global reconstructions are necessarily based on a rather scattered set of localities with suitable fossil plant remains, as well as interpolation between widely differing localities. Despite the difficulties in predicting the distribution of vegetation types in the Eocene, some form of validation is needed, not only to test the reliability of future projections of vegetation change, but also for quantifying terrestrial aspects of the global carbon cycle at this time (Wolfe, 1985).

Wolfe (1985) first produced global maps of vegetation types for the late/middle Eocene, which have subsequently been re-mapped onto new palaeogeographic reconstructions by Frakes *et al.* (1992) (Fig. 8.18). Although Wolfe (1985) used available data from fossil floras, he relied on present-day correlations between vegetation type and temperature to fill in the 'gaps'. Despite these potential difficulties, a comparison of the reconstructed versus modelled vegetation types shows several areas of agreement (Figs. 8.17a and 8.18). At high latitudes in the northern hemisphere, the reconstructions indicate the dominance of mixed coniferous forest in agreement with more recent evidence considered earlier for the presence of Eocene conifer forests in the Canadian Arctic and in Antarctica (Francis, 1988, 1991; Spicer & Parish, 1990). At progressively lower latitudes, the coniferous forests are thought to have given way to broad-leaved evergreen paratropical rainforests. In the simulations, the evergreen needle-leaved forests give way to water-limited deciduous broad-leaved forests, with some evergreen broad-leaved forests also in evidence; both being broadly consistent with palaeobotanical data.

A further strong similarity exists between the simulated distribution of vegetation in Australia and that reconstructed from the fossil record. Based on palaeobotanical data, Australia is considered to have comprised of polar broad-leaved deciduous and evergreen forests (Fig. 8.18), as predicted (Fig. 8.17a). Following the study of Wolfe (1985), Greenwood (1996) has shown that central Australia during the Eocene was dominated by sclerophyllous communities of tropical rainforest plants.

The predictions show a particular dissimilarity with the vegetation reconstructions for Antarctica (Figs. 8.17a and 8.18), which is predicted to be dominated by coniferous woodlands. The reconstructions, however, suggest that Australia was colonised only at the highest latitudes by mixed coniferous woodlands and towards the edges of the continent by polar broad-leaved forests. Inspection of the original maps of Wolfe (1985) indicates that, unlike other areas, all of the vegetation zones for Antarctica, South America, southern Africa and Australia are reconstructed from the fossil material of just two

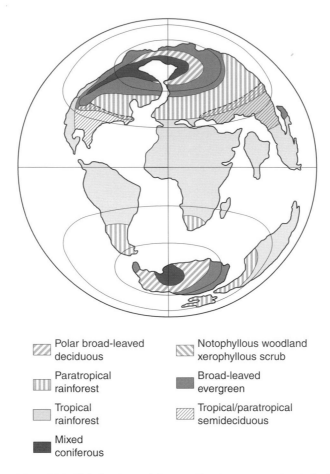

Polar broad-leaved
deciduous

Paratropical
rainforest

Tropical
rainforest

Mixed
coniferous

Notophyllous woodland
xerophyllous scrub

Broad-leaved
evergreen

Tropical/paratropical
semideciduous

Figure 8.18. Global patterns of vegetation types reconstructed with a mixture of palaeobotanical data and present-day climate–physiognomic relations. Redrawn by Frakes *et al.* (1992) from the original maps of Wolfe (1985).

sites. The comparison therefore is limiting for testing purposes since it is not based on extensive palaeobotanical analyses.

Although differences in detail emerge for the predicted and reconstructed global vegetation patterns of the middle Eocene, there remains a surprisingly high degree of similarity between the two maps. The surprise is because the results imply that the ecophysiological controls on plant distributions have not changed markedly over the last 50 million years of global climatic and CO_2 change. It also strongly implies that some of the essential processes required to capture vegetation dynamics under a high CO_2 concentration have been adequately represented in the SDGVM. There is, however, a need for greater spatial coverage for the reconstructions based on analyses of palaeobotanical data. This need is required not least to improve our appreciation of global vegetation patterns the last time the world experienced a 'greenhouse' climate without significant ice formation in polar regions (Miller *et al.*, 1987).

It is of interest to compare predicted future patterns of vegetation change with those of the greenhouse world of the Eocene. The changes in functional type distribution with future global change are discussed further in Chapter 10. There are, however, several similarities between the movement of vegetation types from the present day to 2100 and those of the Eocene. In particular, the northward spread of evergreen needle-leaved forests into high latitudes by 2100 (Fig. 8.17b), at the expense of the tundra, mimics the pattern in the Eocene. There is also an extension into higher latitudes of deciduous broad-leaved trees throughout central Europe, parts of Asia, South America and southern Africa by 2100, in a pattern similar to that of the Eocene (Fig. 8.17a,b).

Past and future distributions of vegetation in the southern hemisphere are forecast to be very different, with grasslands persisting in Australia in AD 2100 but which in the Eocene was dominated by evergreen and deciduous broad-leaved woodlands (Fig. 8.17). In the extreme south of South America and southern Africa tropical rainforests persisted in the Eocene, in regions predicted to be dominated by C_3 and C_4 grasslands by 2100. Despite continued warming by 2100, Greenland is unlikely to support the dense coniferous and deciduous forests as in the Eocene. The Eocene also sees the break-up of tropical rainforests rather than the simple expansion of their range predicted for 2100.

In short, therefore, the high latitude northern hemisphere rearrangement of vegetation types in a future greenhouse world begins to approximate that of the Eocene, but in low latitude regions and in areas of the southern hemisphere, a very different pattern of vegetation change is forecast for the future.

Carbon storage by terrestrial ecosystems in the Eocene and the future

Total carbon storage by the Eocene terrestrial biosphere is high (Table 8.5), but it differs markedly between the two periods because of their contrasting climates and palaeogeographies. The high CO_2 and warm climate of the Eocene, together with the extensive development of long-lived evergreen and deciduous broad-leaved forests at this time (Table 8.6) increased the potential for carbon storage in vegetation biomass relative to the Carboniferous. Much of the Eocene forest coverage shows agreement with the palaeobotanical

Table 8.5. *Total carbon stored in vegetation and soils in the Eocene, and the future climates of 2060 and 2100*

	Vegetation (Gt C)	Soils (Gt C)
Eocene (total)	1134.8	1295.0
Eocene (Antarctica)	46.3	150.0
AD 2060	883.9	724.0
AD 2100	911.1	825.1

reconstructions considered earlier, supporting the carbon storage figures. The land mass of Antarctica accounts for some 2.8% of the vegetation carbon and 12.8% of the soil carbon in the Eocene (Table 8.5).

The geology of the early/middle Eocene indicates the potential for substantial carbon storage in soils. Late Palaeocene coal beds, for example, are some of the thickest in the entire Phanerozoic record (Shearer *et al.*, 1995; Retallack *et al.*, 1996), extending in some localities to 150 m. Wetland soils probably also played an important role in terrestrial carbon storage during the Eocene. Sloan *et al.* (1992) estimated that early Eocene wetlands covered a total area of 5.6×10^6 km^2, some three times that of the present day, based on an analysis of Eocene 'coally' clastic sediments. Assuming a carbon storage figure for modern wetland soils of 723 t C ha^{-1} (Adams *et al.*, 1990), up to 400 Gt C, i.e. 34% of the total soil carbon storage (Tables 8.5 and 8.6) might have been accounted for by these systems.

The impact of future greenhouse environments increases carbon storage in terrestrial ecosystems through increases in both vegetation biomass and soil carbon components (Tables 8.5 and 8.6). Even with the northward extension of high latitude northern hemisphere deciduous and evergreen forests, carbon storage in the biomass of vegetation of the year 2100 is still half that of the Eocene. Models of future environments indicate quite large increases in carbon storage in evergreen broad-leaved and evergreen needle-leaved trees (Table 8.6).

The contrast between carbon storage by terrestrial ecosystems in the Eocene and in a future high CO$_2$ world is emphasised when the values are remapped globally (Figs. 8.19 and 8.20). With the establishment of Eocene forests in Greenland, North America and Australia, as well as parts of Antarctica, a significant amount of carbon is accumulated in vegetation biomass compared with simulations for 2060 and 2100 (Fig. 8.19; Table 8.6).

Table 8.6. *Area-weighted total carbon storage by terrestrial ecosystems broken down into different functional types of vegetation and their underlying soils for the Eocene, 2060 and 2100*

Age	Carbon storage by functional type (Gt C)					
	C_3 grasses	C_4 grasses	Evergreen broad-leaved trees	Evergreen needle-leaved trees	Deciduous broad-leaved trees	Deciduous needle-leaved trees
Eocene						
Vegetation	35.4	n/a	597.9	191.9	469.7	—
Soils	364.8	n/a	217.9	271.2	280.8	—
2060						
Vegetation	10.6	15.3	394.7	81.5	210.5	11.5
Soils	196.8	81.9	132.3	239.4	149.1	56.7
2100						
Vegetation	17.5	13.2	453.3	97.5	231.1	12.5
Soils	228.6	65.4	135.9	251.1	154.2	48.4

The global pattern of soil carbon storage is generally the inverse of that for vegetation biomass (Fig. 8.19b) and occurs because the low temperatures of the high latitudes slow decomposition rates, enhancing carbon accumulation in soils.

The carbon storage figures for the Eocene terrestrial biosphere imply quite large shifts in the carbon cycle relative to the mass of carbon in the atmosphere (Fig. 8.21), extra carbon presumably being derived from the oceans and/or the Earth's crust via volcanic activity. Biospheric carbon storage is not taken into account directly by long-term geochemical models of the carbon cycle, although vegetation is included indirectly through its impacts on the weathering rates of carbonate and silicate rocks (Berner, 1994). Nevertheless, the carbon storage estimates for the Eocene (Table 8.5) can be used as a first order constraint on the likely values predicted by the geochemical approach. Taking a figure for carbon storage by the terrestrial biosphere from late Cretaceous simulations (65 Ma; Chapter 7) of 2966 Gt C, the Eocene values represent a decrease of 536 Gt C, equivalent to a net release of 260 ppm of CO_2 to the atmosphere (assuming 1 ppm $CO_2 = 2$ Gt C in the atmosphere; Siegenthaler & Sarmiento, 1993). In consequence, the atmospheric concentration of CO_2 'corrected figure' for vegetation feedback on the carbon cycle could have been up to 260 ppm higher than estimated by Berner (1994). The calculation is a simplistic view since it ignores oceanic responses and assumes that the increases in carbon storage by the terrestrial biosphere occurred rapidly,

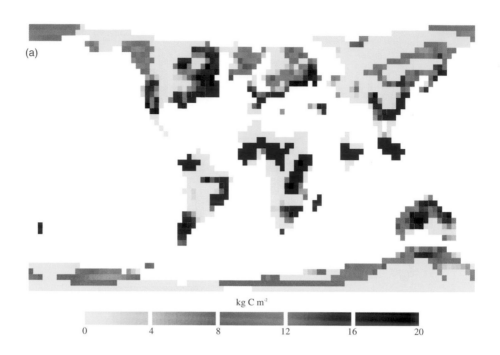

(a)

kg C m⁻²

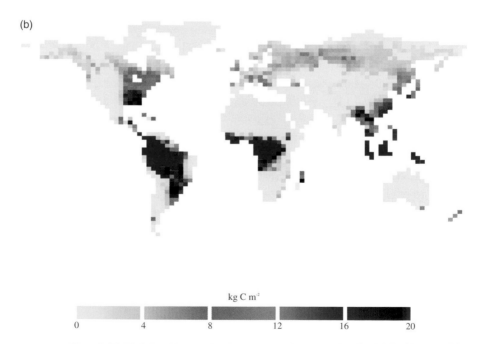

(b)

kg C m⁻²

Figure 8.19. Global patterns of carbon storage in vegetation for (a) the Eocene, (b) 2060 and (c) 2100.

(c)

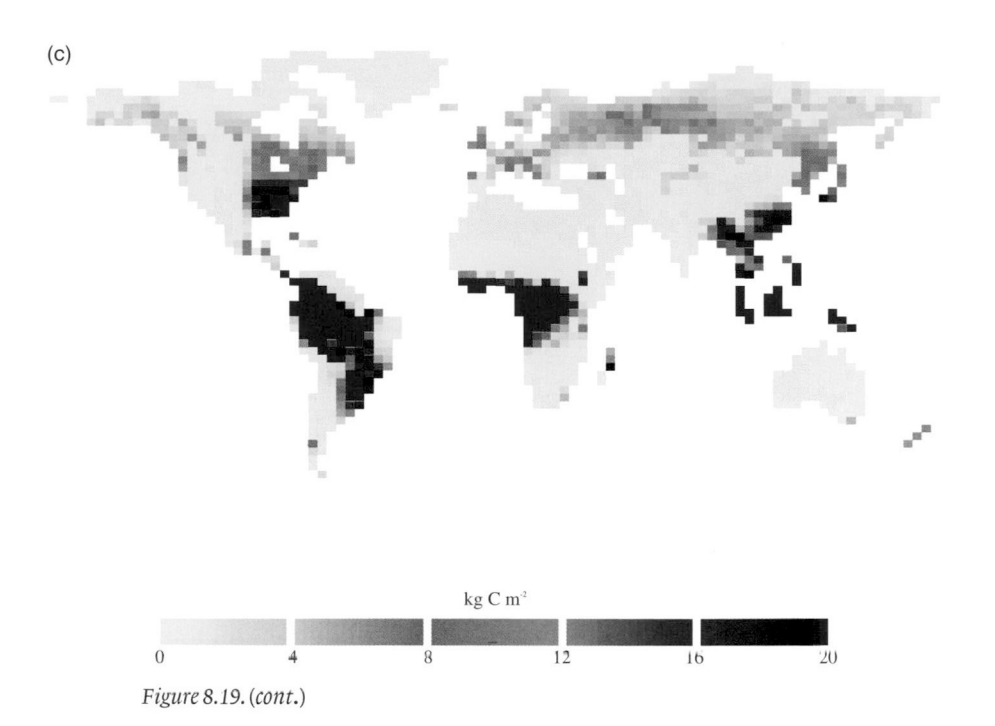

Figure 8.19. (cont.)

but it nevertheless illustrates the need for representing biospheric processes in geochemical models.

The impact of a biospheric release of 260 ppm CO_2 to the Eocene atmosphere on global temperature can be calculated from a simple CO_2-greenhouse effect formulation (Walker *et al.*, 1981; see Chapter 6), which calculates the influence of CO_2 on the greenhouse effect using the ratio of atmospheric CO_2 concentration at some time in the past, relative to the standard (300 ppm). According to this formulation, an increase from 600 ppm CO_2, the 'best guess' result of Berner's 1994 geochemical model, to 860 ppm CO_2 could have raised the global temperature by 0.6 °C (Fig. 8.22), indicating the potential of carbon release from the terrestrial biosphere to impact on global climatic conditions.

The strong potential for carbon sequestration by the terrestrial biosphere, in the early Eocene, has been recognised as a possible biotic feedback on climate during the close of the Palaeocene. High resolution carbon isotope records from marine and terrestrial sediments indicate that major changes in global climate occurred between the close of the Palaeocene and the early Eocene (*c.* 55.5 Ma), probably triggered by the release of large methane

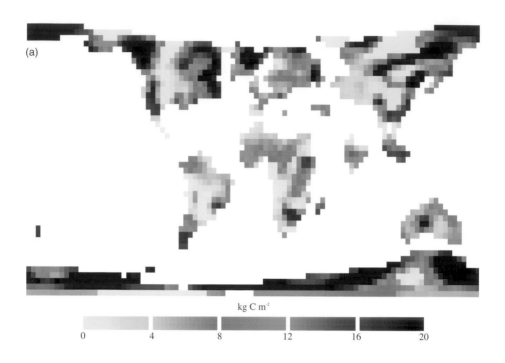

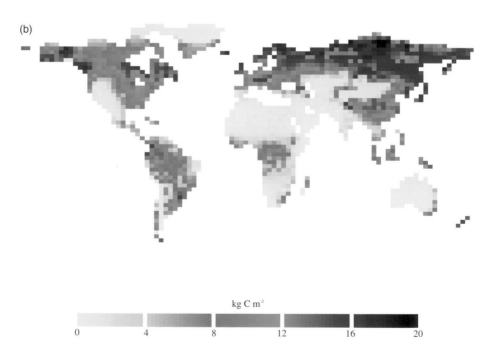

Figure 8.20. Global patterns of carbon storage in soils for (a) the Eocene, (b) 2060 and (c) 2100.

(c)

kg C m⁻²

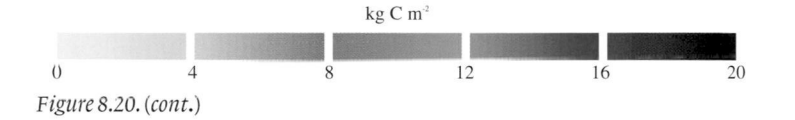

0   4   8   12   16   20

Figure 8.20. (cont.)

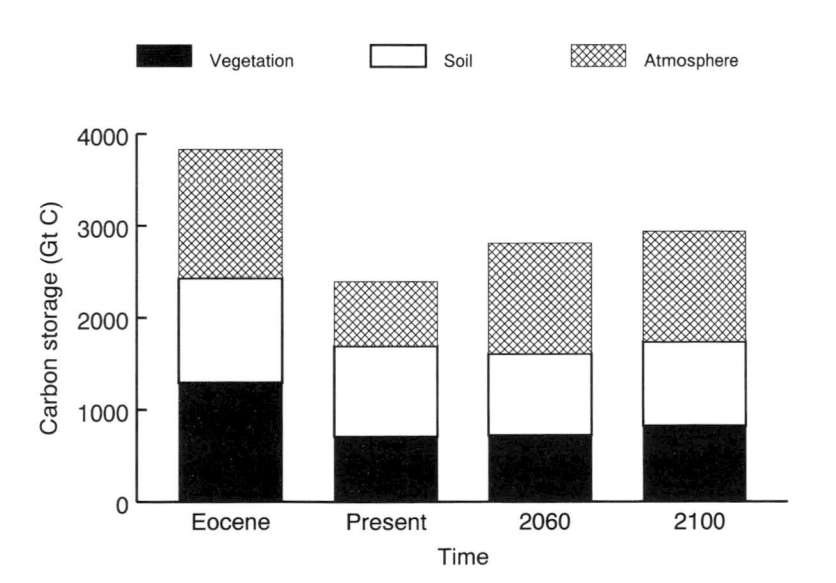

Figure 8.21. Changes in the mass of carbon in the atmosphere, vegetation and soils. Figures for the present-day biosphere from Chapter 9.

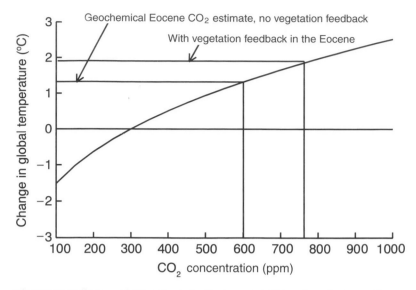

Figure 8.22. Influence of CO_2 release by the terrestrial biosphere, between the latest Cretaceous and the Eocene, on global temperature change, calculated using the CO_2-greenhouse formulation of Walker *et al.* (1981).

reserves from the sea floor (Dickens *et al.*, 1998). According to a carbon isotope mass balance analysis, based on the amount and isotopic composition of carbon in the three main reservoirs of the Earth (oceanic, atmospheric and terrestrial ecosystems), global climatic events at the Palaeocene/Eocene boundary markedly increased carbon storage by terrestrial ecosystems (Beerling, 2000a). The increase was potentially sufficient to sequester significant quantities of atmospheric CO_2 released originally from the ocean floor as methane, and hence decrease the extent of the 'greenhouse' effect at this time, thereby contributing a biotic feedback mechanism aiding climatic stabilisation (Beerling, 2000a).

Conclusions

The warm and ancient 'greenhouse' world of the Eocene is unlikely to be repeated over the next few centuries of warming associated with anthropogenic increases in greenhouse gases, despite the projected rise in atmospheric CO_2 concentration by the year 2100 equal to or exceeding that estimated for the Eocene. The main difference between the ancient and future greenhouse worlds appears to be the existence of a more shallow equator-to-pole temperature gradient at 55–50 Ma compared with the present. This, together with the largely ice-free situation of the Eocene, and the southward displacement of the Greenland and European land masses, allowed establishment of vegetation and substantial terrestrial productivity at high latitudes of both hemispheres. Despite these differences in boundary conditions, simulated global terrestrial net primary productivity and carbon storage by AD 2100 begin to approach the early Eocene situation.

Aspects of climate and vegetation modelling considered here strongly suggest that if vegetation in the Eocene grew in a higher-than-present CO_2 concentration, as seems likely, then estimates of past precipitation regimes from fossil floras relying on modern analogue approaches will be severely limited. Since this is one of the least reliable aspects of GCM predictions, the lack of a secure quantitative palaeoprecipitation indicator limits our testing of GCMs when operating with a high CO_2 concentration in both a palaeo- and a future context.

9

The Quaternary

Introduction

The Quaternary period, approximately the past two million years, is characterised by successive sequences of glacial–interglacial climatic oscillations, largely attributed to changes in the orbital parameters of the Earth's rotation around the sun and on its own axis through a variety of gravitational attractions, each varying with the temporal dynamics of the solar system (Imbrie & Imbrie, 1979; Berger, 1976, 1978). There is evidence that the orbital forcing of climate has prevailed throughout Earth history, with cyclical variations of the organic carbon and calcium carbonate components of sediments spanning much of the last 125 million years (Herbert, 1997) and, most famously, in the coal-bearing cyclothems of the Carboniferous (Pennsylvanian subperiod) (Broecker, 1997).

Orbital forcing of climate results from quasi-periodic variation in three main orbital parameters, each with a different periodicity; eccentricity, with a primary period of 100 ka, obliquity (axial tilt), with an average period of 41 ka and precession, every 19 ka. These 'predicted' periodicities are broadly in line with continuous ocean and ice core geochemical records (Hays et al., 1976; Barnola et al., 1987; Jouzel et al., 1987). Long oceanic records (730 ka) of the variations in oxygen isotope composition of marine foraminifera indicate rhythmic climatic variations, with strong cyclicity in the data at 106, 40–43, and 24 and 19.5 ka corresponding to the calculated return interval of each orbital parameter (Hays et al., 1976).

Analyses of air trapped in the major ice sheets of the world provide important records of past climatic changes in the late Quaternary environment, including changes in atmospheric CO_2 and temperature, both with important consequences for the terrestrial biosphere. The Vostok ice core from Antarctica provides the longest continuous record (>400 ka) of changes in the partial

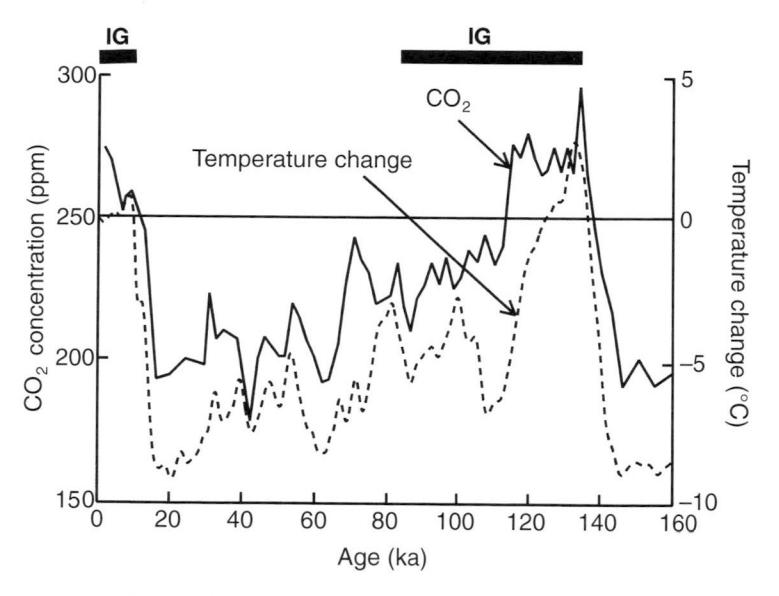

Figure 9.1. Changes in atmospheric CO_2 concentration and temperature (reconstructed from the deuterium composition) from the Vostok ice core. Solid horizontal bars IG indicate the age and duration of interglacial episodes; gaps indicate glacial episodes (Jouzel *et al.*, 1993). Data from Jouzel *et al.* (1987) and Barnola *et al.* (1987).

pressure of CO_2 and air temperature over the ice sheets (Barnola *et al.*, 1987; Jouzel *et al.*, 1987, 1993) (Fig. 9.1), covering the last glacial–interglacial cycle. The record shows a temperature amplitude of *c.* 11 °C over this time, and a strong covariance of fluctuations in atmospheric CO_2 and air temperature. Glacial periods are characterised by low atmospheric concentrations of CO_2 (*c.* 200 ppm) and methane (*c.* 0.4 ppm) and low temperatures, interglacials by higher partial pressures of both gases (280 ppm and 0.6 ppm, respectively) and higher temperatures (Fig. 9.1).

An interesting feature of the ice core studies is the repeated peak in dust concentrations (i.e. dust loading on the ice sheet) before the termination of glaciations, indicative of marked changes in the hydrological cycle, particularly increased aridity. These affect climate directly and indirectly. Global climate modelling suggests that a direct climatic consequence of the observed abrupt increases in atmospheric dust loading is an episodic regional warming of up to 5 °C through its absorption of thermal radiation and thus may represent a potential 'trigger' for past abrupt climatic warming events (Overpeck *et al.*, 1996). An indirect effect on climate may occur through iron fertilisation of the oceans and a subsequent increased draw-down of atmospheric CO_2 (Falkowski *et al.*, 1998). Simple box model calculations indicate this mechanism might account for 30% of the lowering of glacial CO_2 concentration (Falkowski *et al.*, 1998).

High amplitude variations in both temperature and CO_2 exert a strong controlling influence on plant photosynthesis, transpiration and respiration, and the imposition of the repeated climate, hydrologic and atmospheric changes must have had direct impacts on the function, structure and distribution of terrestrial ecosystems. Quantifying and describing the likely nature of these impacts is the central aim of this chapter. The analyses begin at the scale of individual leaves and are then extended to the global scale to describe the carbon and water fluxes through terrestrial vegetation, its distribution, carbon storage and influence on the biogeochemical cycling of atmospheric oxygen.

The global-scale analyses focus on the mid-Holocene, 6000 years before present (6 ka BP) and the last glacial maximum (LGM) (21 ka BP), using high resolution GCM palaeoclimate simulations with prescribed sea surface temperatures (Hall *et al.*, 1996 a,b; Hall & Valdes, 1997) and lower spatial resolution GCM simulations with interactive sea surface conditions (Kutzbach *et al.* 1998). These models enabled us to determine how sensitive the results of vegetation modelling were to the prescribed late Quaternary global climate. Further sensitivity analyses have been made to quantify the impact of the low concentrations of atmospheric CO_2 in the mid-Holocene and the LGM on several aspects of the plant–climate interactions described here.

The fossil record indicates the changing distribution of vegetation since the last ice age. Reproducing this pattern of change represents a challenge testing whether current climatic controls on vegetation translate to those of the mid-Holocene and the LGM with the associated changes in global climate and lower-than-present CO_2 partial pressures. The challenge is complementary to that described for the Jurassic (Chapter 6) and the Cretaceous (Chapter 7), when the global climate was warmer than now and the concentration of CO_2 higher. Of particular interest is how the low concentration of atmospheric CO_2 and increased aridity influenced the late Quaternary distribution of plants with the C_4 photosynthetic pathway (Cole & Monger, 1994; Robinson, 1994b; Ehleringer *et al.*, 1997; Collatz *et al.*, 1998), and is investigated here by measurements of the isotopic composition of terrestrial plant organic matter from lake sediments and peat bogs.

Carbon storage by the terrestrial biosphere during the LGM is an area of some uncertainty and controversy (Faure *et al.*, 1998), with significant differences between terrestrial and marine palaeodata (Adams *et al.*, 1990; Crowley, 1995; Adams & Faure, 1998), model simulations (Prentice *et al.*, 1993; Esser & Lautenschlager, 1994; Francois *et al.*, 1998) and theoretical estimates based on an isotope mass-balance approach (Bird *et al.*, 1994, 1996). The issue is an important one because it affects our ability to explain shifts in the global carbon cycle, in particular whether the terrestrial biosphere was a major sink for atmospheric CO_2 during the last deglaciation. Therefore, we describe two related approaches leading to revised estimates of increases in terrestrial carbon storage since the LGM: one based on modelling plant distributions and the biogeochemical cycling of carbon in vegetation and soils, the other based on carbon isotope discrimination (Δ_A) by the terrestrial biosphere. The value of Δ_A is important because it is used to partition net CO_2 fluxes between the ocean and the land (Tans *et al.*, 1993).

The final section considers the influence of late Quaternary environments on terrestrial vegetation activity and its consequences for the biogeochemical cycling of atmospheric oxygen. The isotope composition of atmospheric oxygen ($\delta^{18}O_2$) reflects the total biospheric exchange of O_2 and the fractionations associated with marine and terrestrial photosynthesis and respiration. The difference between $\delta^{18}O_2$ and the $\delta^{18}O$ of seawater defines the Dole effect (Dole *et al.*, 1954), currently 23.5‰ (Kroopnick & Craig, 1972). Vegetation influences $\delta^{18}O_2$ (Berry, 1992; Bender *et al.*, 1985, 1994), because over half the annual O_2 flux is derived from photosynthesis by terrestrial plants. This flux carries an isotopic signal reflecting evaporative enrichment in ^{18}O of leaf water over soil water, by the slower evaporation of $H_2^{18}O$ compared with $H_2^{16}O$ from the air–water interfaces of chloroplasts. However, to quantify past changes in partitioning of terrestrial and ocean productivities using the Dole effect requires quantifying the effects of terrestrial vegetation (Bender *et al.*, 1994).

Gas exchange responses of C3 plants to a glacial–interglacial cycle of environmental change

Possible changes in C_3 land plant function in the late Quaternary have first been estimated by considering the impacts of the last glacial–interglacial cycle of environmental change on gas exchange of individual leaves. Simulations of leaf CO_2 assimilation and stomatal conductance to water vapour have been made using the Vostok ice core CO_2 and temperature records as environmental data driving the biophysical leaf gas exchange–energy balance model described earlier (Chapter 3).

The results (Fig. 9.2) indicate that leaf gas exchange during interglacial conditions was characterised by high rates of photosynthesis and low stomatal conductances, and under glacial conditions by low photosynthetic rates but high stomatal conductances. These two sets of responses contribute to

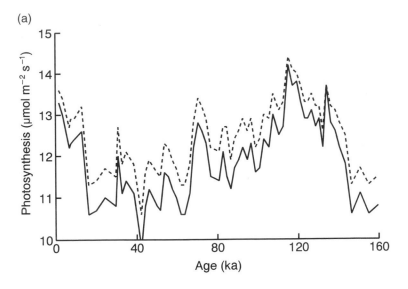

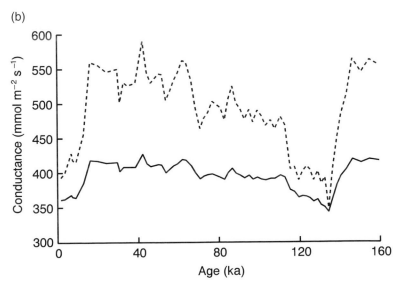

Figure 9.2. Predicted changes in (a) photosynthetic rates, (b) stomatal conductance and (c) instantaneous water-use efficiency of leaves over the past 160 ka, based on Vostok ice core CO_2 and temperature changes for the last glacial–interglacial climate oscillation. Solid lines indicate responses of a hypostomatous leaf with a fixed stomatal density (120 mm^{-2}); broken lines indicate responses with an effect of CO_2 concentration on stomatal density. Other environmental conditions were: relative humidity 70%, irradiance 700 μmol m^{-2} s^{-1}, $V_{max} = 105.0$ μmol m^{-2} s^{-1}, $J_{max} = 210.6$ μmol m^{-2} s^{-1}.

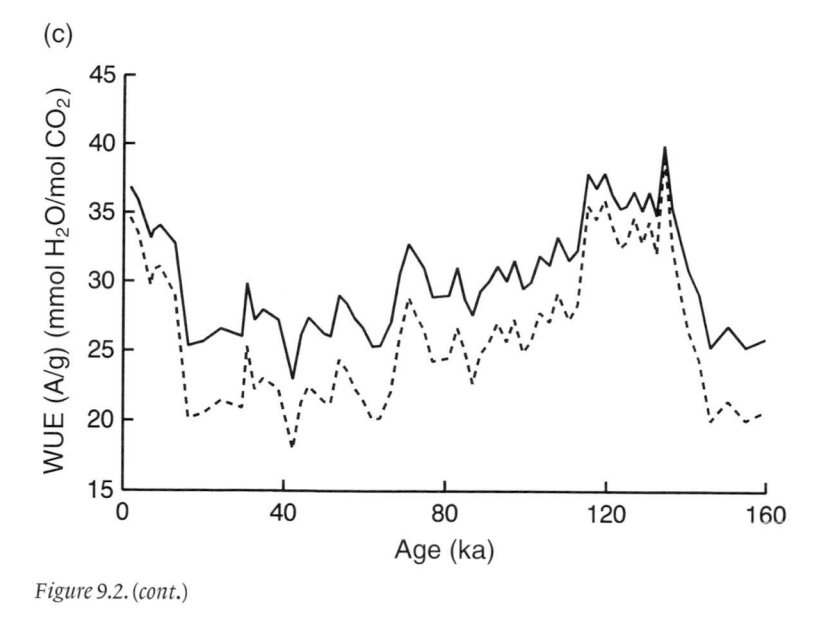

(c)

Figure 9.2. (cont.)

high instantaneous water-use efficiency (IWUE, ratio of photosynthesis to stomatal conductance) of plant growth during interglacials relative to glacials. Similar results have been reported for plants grown experimentally across a glacial-to-present CO_2 gradient (Polley *et al.*, 1992, 1993a,b; Sage & Reid, 1992). Moreover, these experiments showed that leaf gas exchange responses were translated into above-ground growth responses, with lower whole-plant WUE and nitrogen-use efficiency at glacial CO_2 concentrations (Polley *et al.*, 1995), a feature investigated at the global scale later in this chapter (p. 334).

In addition to CO_2 and temperature effects on leaf metabolism (Sage & Reid, 1992; Tissue *et al.*, 1995), there is also an effect of atmospheric CO_2 on stomatal development (Woodward, 1987b), with a corresponding impact on leaf gas exchange properties. Studies of fossil leaves of single species, extending back to the last glaciation, have shown an inverse correlation between stomatal density and the corresponding concentration of atmospheric CO_2 estimated from ice core records (Beerling *et al.*, 1993; Van der Water *et al.*, 1994). Therefore, a second set of gas exchange predictions was made, allowing stomatal density to change inversely with variations in the concentration of atmospheric CO_2 (Fig. 9.1) over the past 160 ka. This response was derived from observations on fossil leaves of the woody dwarf shrub *Salix herbacea* (Beerling *et al.*, 1993).

Inclusion of the responses of stomatal density to CO_2 concentration in the gas exchange modelling results shows differential effects on photosynthesis and stomatal conductance (Fig. 9.2), with the greatest effect on stomatal conductance. The net effect is markedly to reduce leaf IWUE, particularly during glacial periods, compared with the IWUE of a leaf with a 'fixed' stomatal density (Fig. 9.2c) operating under the same environmental conditions. For individual plants, water-use efficiency is almost directly proportional to the concentration of atmospheric CO_2 for a given temperature and humidity, so that growth under low CO_2 requires marked increased transpiration rates to achieve reasonable photosynthesis rates (Farquhar, 1997). Therefore, increasing stomatal conductances during the low CO_2 concentrations of glacials (as low as 180 ppm) enables plants to increase their net carbon gain when quite close to the functional limits of rubisco (Chapter 2).

The actual carbon gain may have been further amplified by selection of higher yielding genotypes during exposure of plants to a succession of glacial–interglacial climatic cycles over hundreds of thousands of years. For example, selective breeding has shown that tobacco plants can achieve increased capacity for total dry matter production under low CO_2 concentrations within a few generations (Delgado *et al.*, 1994). Similarly, experiments on populations of *Arabidopsis thaliana* originating from high elevation (up to 3400 m above sea level), and therefore exposed to reduced concentration of CO_2, provide clear evidence for adaptation to low concentrations of CO_2 (Ward & Strain, 1997), with the potential for evolutionary 'drift' in response to exposure to low CO_2 for thousands of years.

Experimental and theoretical studies indicate that plant growth was more expensive, in terms of water use, during glacials than interglacials (Polley *et al.*, 1992, 1993a,b, 1995; Dippery *et al.*, 1995), with consequences for correlative approaches taken for summarising palaeoclimate and palaeovegetation data (e.g. Webb *et al.*, 1998). One such approach interprets fossil plant and pollen data in terms of climate by using 'climate response surfaces'. These are constructed from presence/absence data on modern plant distributions and observational climatic datasets. Climatic variables selected are typically the temperature of the coldest month, length of the growing season in day-degrees, and the difference between annual precipitation and evapotranspiration, each providing crude representations of energy and moisture related controls on plant distributions. The problem with such an approach is that the concentration of CO_2 decreases and has the capacity to alter distribution limits under a given climate.

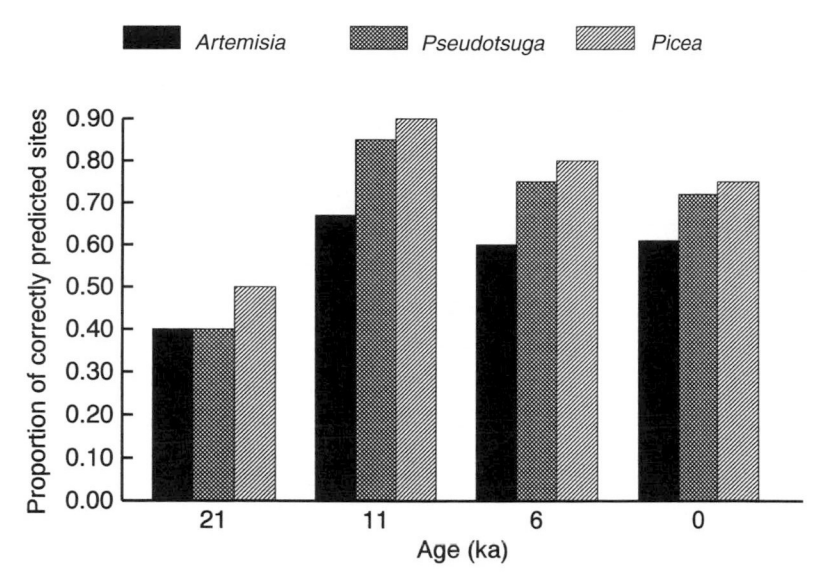

Figure 9.3. Proportion of sites for which the presence/absence of three woody taxa was correctly predicted with present-day plant–climate response surfaces applied to the past. Predictions were made using the global palaeoclimate datasets for each interval generated by the NCAR CCM1 climate model, redrawn from Bartlein *et al.* (1998).

A broad-scale test of whether CO_2 effects are important in the correlative approach has been derived from the work of Bartlein *et al.* (1998). These authors constructed North American climatic response surfaces for the conifers *Picea* spp. (spruce) and *Pseudotsuga menziesii* (Douglas-fir) and the woody herb *Artemisia tridenta* (sagebrush) from the present-day climate and presence/absence data. Distributions of the same taxa were then predicted with the response surface in the same region using the palaeoclimates simulated by NCAR GCM for 21, 16, 14, 11 and 6 ka BP and the resulting 'predicted' distributions compared with the reconstructions based on palaeoecological data, mainly fossil pollen.

If CO_2 effects on plant distributions are important they should be greatest at 21 ka, when the concentration of CO_2 was lowest. Comparison between predicted and observed distributions indicates the proportion of sites with correctly predicted presence/absence to be determined. The results (Fig. 9.3) indicate that the proportion of sites in which the presence or absence was correctly predicted was markedly lower for 21 ka than for the other intervals.

Global climate change since the LGM

The nature of vegetation–climate interactions in the late Quaternary has been extended to the global scale using two different GCM simulations of palaeoclimates for the mid-Holocene (6 ka) and the LGM (21 ka). The UGAMP GCM is based on the European Centre for Medium-Range Weather Forecasting (ECMWF) and is nearly identical to that described by Slingo *et al.* (1994). In the model, physical parameterisations are evaluated on a 2.8° lat. × 2.8° long. grid, with 19 levels in the vertical (Hall & Valdes, 1997). For the 6 ka runs, sea surface temperatures were prescribed to be the same as today with an atmospheric CO_2 concentration of 280 ppm; all other boundary conditions, including orbital parameters, are given by Hall & Valdes (1997). For the 21 ka simulation, the same version of the model has been run and climate averaged over the previous 5 years. Boundary conditions, sea surface temperatures (SSTs), sea ice extent and land areas were defined according to CLIMAP (CLIMAP, 1976) (Hall *et al.*, 1996a,b), but with a revised land surface elevation.

The second set of GCM palaeoclimate simulations was taken from the NCAR CCM version 1 GCM (available on the World Wide Web at: www://ftp.ngdc.noaa.gov/paleo/gcmoutput/) which has a low spatial resolution (4.4° lat. × 7.5° long.) but incorporates interactive sea surface conditions through the use of a mixed-layer (slab) ocean model (Kutzbach *et al.*, 1998). A consequence of interactive sea surface conditions is that SSTs are predicted and compared with palaeo-SST data. The boundary conditions for the 6 ka and 21 ka simulations are similar to those of the UGAMP model, with values and the rationale behind their choice discussed by Kutzbach *et al.* (1998).

The UGAMP GCM has the advantage that the higher spatial resolution allows better representation of mid-latitude depressions and storm tracks, but prescribes sea surface temperatures for 71% of the Earth's surface. To remove model bias, and facilitate comparison between the results, monthly mean climate anomalies for each grid point (the specified palaeosimulation minus the control run) were calculated and added to the 1988 monthly ISLSCP global datasets (selected as a 'typical' present-day example of global climate), with differences in spatial resolution being resolved through interpolation. The resulting vegetation maps are presented with the original spatial resolution of the GCMs, since interpolation at a higher spatial scale is unlikely to capture the 'real' palaeoclimates at these locations.

Calculated in this way, the mid-Holocene average yearly temperatures were very similar for both GCMs (Fig. 9.4a,b), with latitudinally-averaged patterns closely tracking those of 1988 (Fig. 9.5a). There was greater divergence between the GCM simulations of precipitation (Fig. 9.4c,d), with the NCAR model producing drier conditions in the equatorial regions and at high latitudes in the southern hemisphere than the UGAMP model (Fig. 9.5b). Detailed analyses of the UGAMP simulation indicated increased continental warmth in summer and cold in winter, and an altered position of the jet stream with associated changes in precipitation, particularly increased wetness of the Sahel (Hall *et al.*, 1996a,b; Hall & Valdes, 1997; Harrison *et al.*, 2000), comparable to fossil pollen and lake level data (Hall & Valdes, 1997). In contrast, some of the detailed features of the NCAR mid-Holocene simulation showed rather poor agreement with observations based on fossil plant remains (Prentice *et al.*, 1998), with winter temperatures too warm and summers too dry throughout Europe.

The global climate simulations for the LGM showed greater differences between the UGAMP and NCAR GCMs (Figs. 9.6 and 9.7). The NCAR model produced cooler climates (Fig. 9.6a,b) across a wide range of latitudes (Fig. 9.7a) and wetter climates than the UGAMP model (Fig. 9.6c,d), particularly in the low latitudes of the northern and southern hemispheres. Both GCMs show the expected increased extent of sub-zero mean monthly temperatures in the high latitudes of the northern hemisphere (Fig. 9.6).

Comparison of the GCM-derived glacial climates with palaeoecological data has been less extensive than with those of the mid-Holocene. Hall *et al.* (1996a,b) noted, however, that the UGAMP model produced sufficient snowfall to feed ice sheet growth, consistent with the maintenance of their observed extent. The NCAR 21 ka simulation has been used in extensive correlative modelling exercises to map plant functional types (Webb, 1988) for comparison with reconstructions based on the plant fossil record. Unfortunately, the entire set of papers devoted to biome reconstructions used a correlative vegetation model (BIOME 1) or correlative climate response surfaces without any explicit consideration of the impact of atmospheric CO_2 or soil nutrient effects on plant physiology. Consequently, discrepancies between modelled and observed distributions may have been due to errors in either the climate and/or vegetation models, so the results are somewhat inconclusive.

(a)

°C

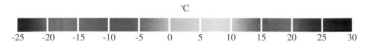

-25   -20   -15   -10   -5   0   5   10   15   20   25   30

(b)

°C

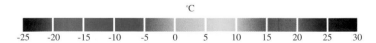

-25   -20   -15   -10   -5   0   5   10   15   20   25   30

Figure 9.4. Average annual land temperatures (a,b) and precipitation (c,d) of the mid-Holocene palaeoclimate simulations by the UGAMP (a,c) and NCAR (b,d) GCMs. Maps show the climates after the simulated anomalies have been added to the ISLSCP 1988 datasets.

(c)

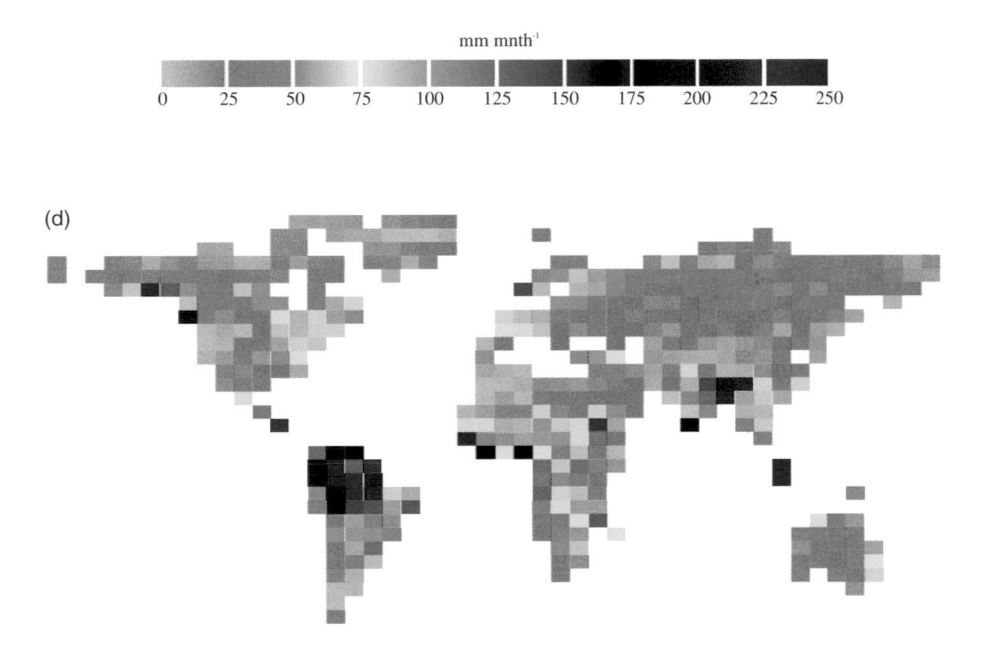

(d)

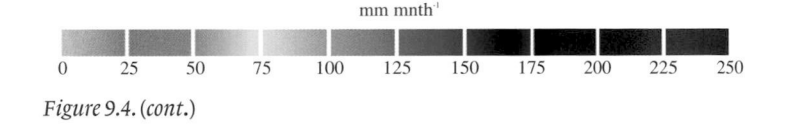

Figure 9.4. (cont.)

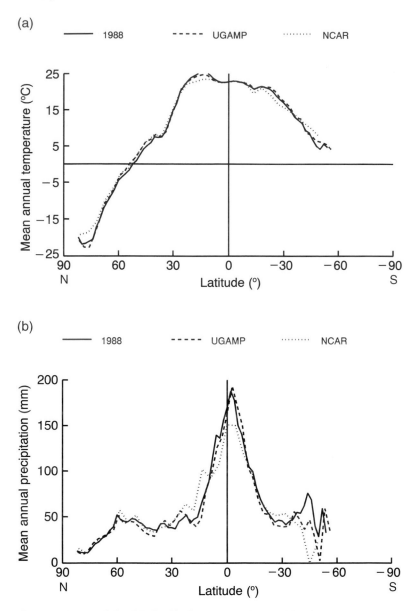

Figure 9.5. Area-weighted latitudinal averages of annual land (a) temperature and (b) precipitation for the mid-Holocene and, for comparison, the 1988 ISLSCP data.

Changes in global primary productivity and vegetation structure since the LGM

The global-scale study first considers the impact of the late Quaternary environment on the basic vegetation properties of leaf area index (LAI) and net primary productivity (NPP), using both the UGAMP and NCAR GCM palaeoclimates.

Global patterns of LAI (Fig. 9.8) indicate that even during the mid-Holocene the development of high LAIs is geographically restricted, with absolute values being lower in central Africa and South America relative to the present day (Fig. 9.8a,b). In most areas, LAI is modelled to be lower than present at low latitudes and similar to present at mid- to high latitudes (Fig. 9.9a). Under glacial climates and low concentration of CO_2, LAI is further restricted with the potential for a vegetated surface of the Earth being severely diminished (Fig. 9.8c). The cooler, wetter glacial climate of the NCAR model, compared with that of the UGAMP model (Fig. 9.7), leads to simulations of correspondingly higher predictions of LAI, at all latitudes, than those predicted using the UGAMP glacial climate (Fig. 9.9b). Low LAIs occur primarily because the low concentration of CO_2 restricts substrate availability for canopy construction and the low glacial temperatures limit growth and nutrient cycling, and hence nutrient availability, from the soils. Furthermore, the low water-use efficiency and lower precipitation regime means that canopies with a high LAI cannot be sustained. Given that LAI strongly influences regional and global climate by modifying the albedo and energy exchanges of the Earth's terrestrial surface, the marked differences in LAI between now and the LGM indicate the potential for large feedbacks between vegetation and climate at this time. Inclusion of such effects within GCMs could quantify the feedback, but at present, even the latest state-of-the-art simulations with coupled, intermediate complexity, ocean–atmosphere models continue to ignore this requirement (Weaver *et al.*, 1998).

The global patterns of NPP for the mid-Holocene and the LGM (Fig. 9.10) generally correspond to those modelled for LAI (Fig. 9.8). This close correspondence can be seen geographically, where regions of restricted LAI match those of low NPP (Fig. 9.10), and when expressed as latitudinal averages (Fig. 9.11). NPP is particularly low: even in tropical regions annual NPP is only *c.* 6 t C ha^{-1}, about half that recorded for tropical evergreen forests in the present climate. Low terrestrial primary productivity is a consequence of low CO_2, temperature and precipitation on the processes of plant growth and nutrient uptake. Additionally, low temperatures will also limit the turnover (i.e.

(a)

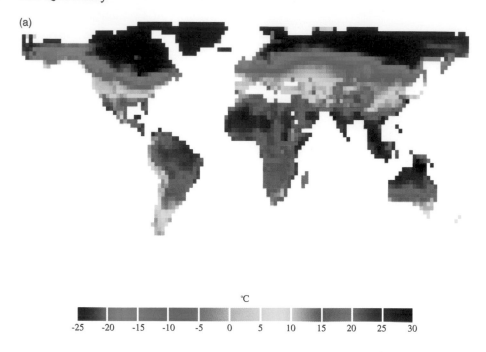

°C

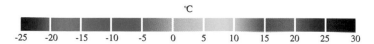

(b)

Figure 9.6. Average annual land temperatures (a,b) and precipitation (c,d) of the last glacial maximum palaeoclimate simulations by the UGAMP (a,c) and NCAR (b,d) GCMs. Maps show the climates after the simulated anomalies have been added to the ISLSCP 1988 datasets.

(c)

mm mnth^{-1}

0   25   50   75   100   125   150   175   200   225   250

(d)

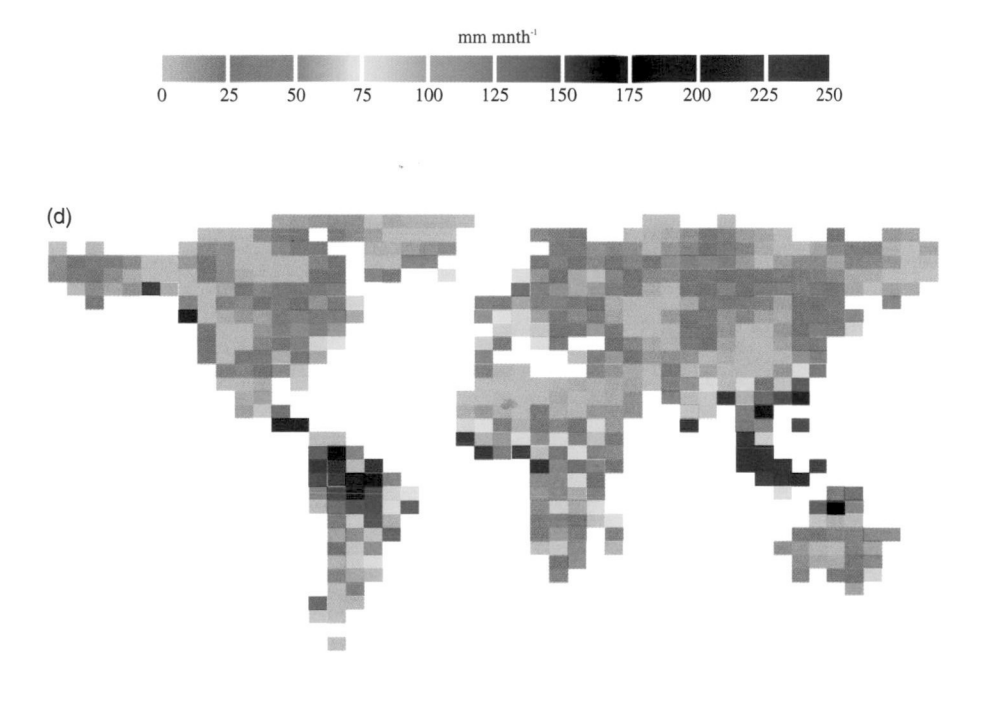

mm mnth^{-1}

0   25   50   75   100   125   150   175   200   225   250

Figure 9.6. (cont.)

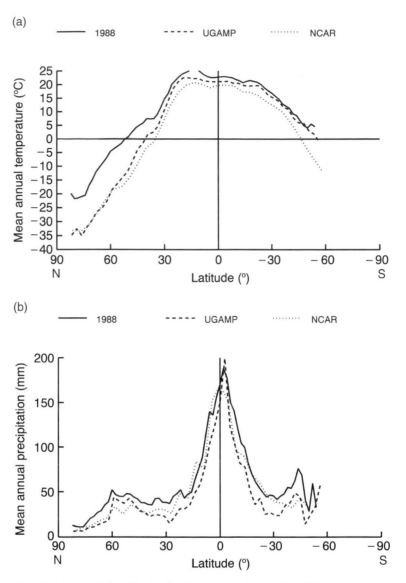

Figure 9.7. Area-weighted latitudinal averages of annual land (a) temperature and (b) precipitation for the last glacial maximum and, for comparison, the 1988 ISLSCP data.

(a)

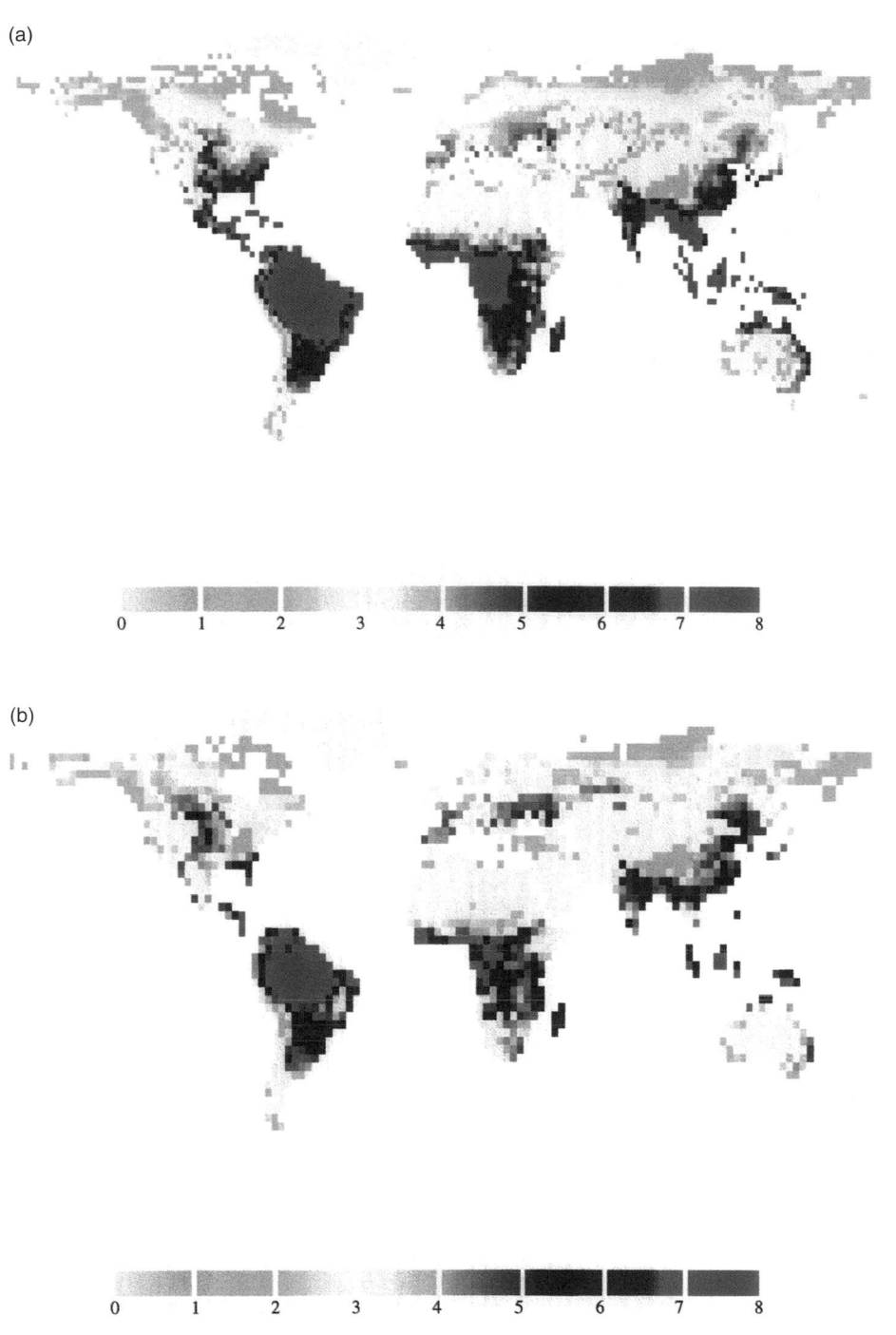

Figure 9.8. Modelled global patterns of leaf area index for (a) the present day (1988), (b) the mid-Holocene and (c) the LGM predicted using the UGAMP palaeoclimate simulations.

(c)

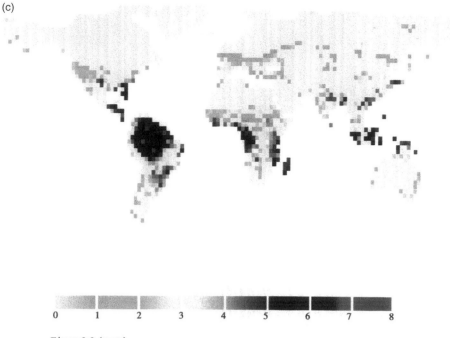

Figure 9.8. (*cont.*)

decomposition) of soil organic matter and nitrogen release, reducing nutrient availability to the plants.

The coverage of land surface by terrestrial vegetation is also severely reduced in glacial environments. Under the 1988 climate, *c.* 71% of the terrestrial land surface is suitable for the growth of vegetation (Table 9.1), with a similar value for the mid-Holocene. In the glacial environment, this figure is markedly reduced to 38–50% (Table 9.1), in part because of the development of large ice sheets over parts of North America and Europe.

Global NPP is reduced slightly in the mid-Holocene compared with 1988, a result consistent across both GCMs global climates (Table 9.1). Although there have been no other published studies of global terrestrial NPP for the mid-Holocene, a regional estimate based on the fossil record has been reported (Monserud *et al.*, 1995). Monserud *et al.* (1995) reconstructed changes in the NPP for the Siberian region of northern Russia, delineated between latitudes 50° and 80° N and longitudes 65 to 145° E, for the mid-Holocene (4600–6000 yr BP) from palaeovegetation records and showed a small increase in NPP. The model results for this region give values of 2.2 Gt C yr^{-1} for 1988, and 2.1–2.4 Gt C yr^{-1} for the mid-Holocene (NCAR and UGAMP climates respectively).

Global NPP for the LGM is predicted to be 40–56% lower than for 1988

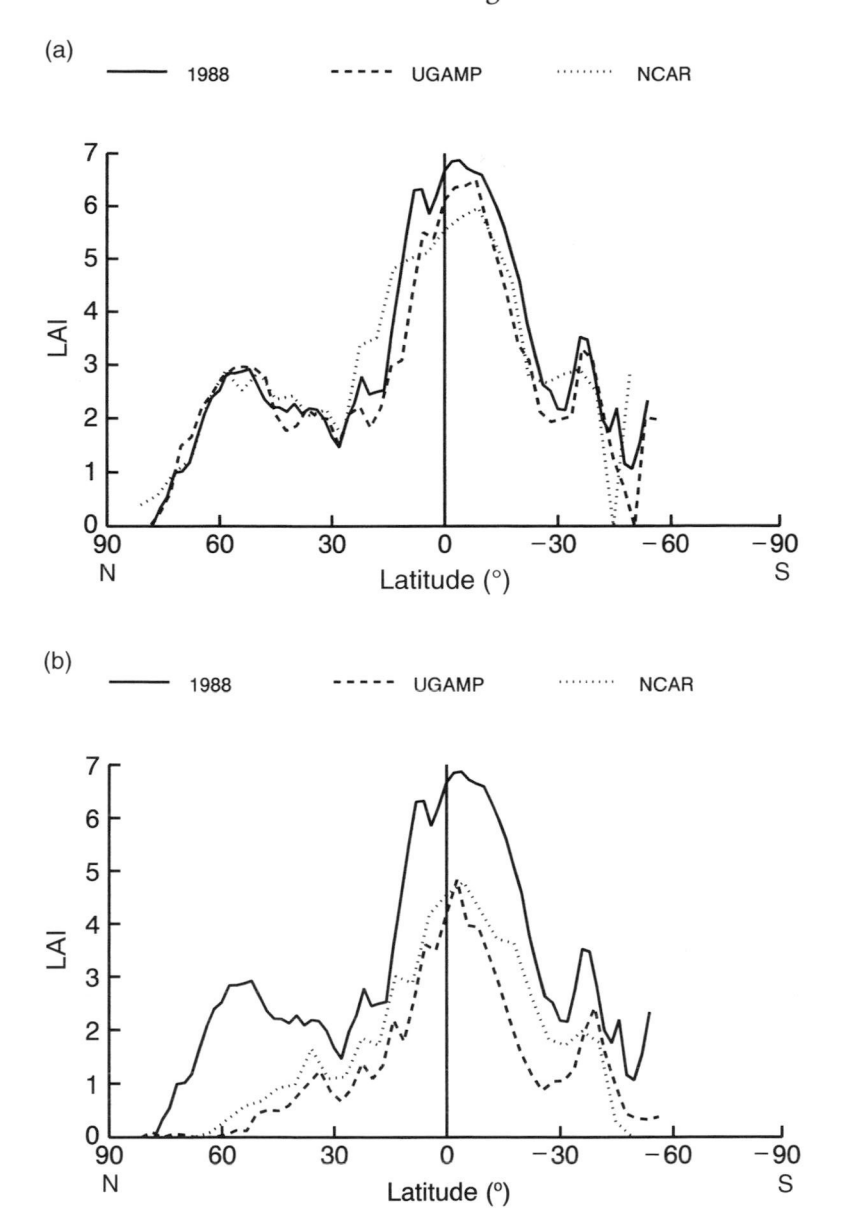

Figure 9.9. Area-weighted latitudinal averages of leaf area index for (a) the mid-Holocene and (b) the LGM, modelled using the UGAMP and NCAR palaeoclimate simulations. Also shown are the latitudinal patterns modelled using the 1988 global climate datasets.

(a)

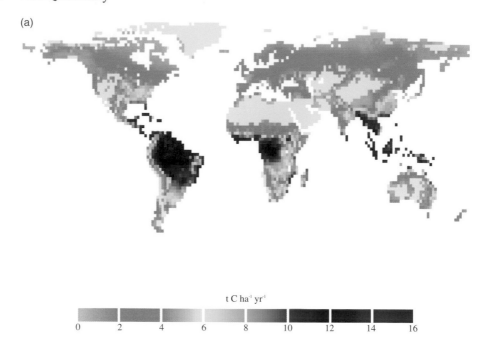

t C ha⁻¹ yr⁻¹

(b)

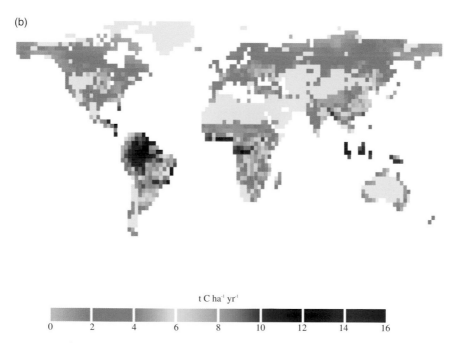

t C ha⁻¹ yr⁻¹

Figure 9.10. Modelled global patterns of net primary productivity for (a) the present day (1988), (b) the mid-Holocene and (c) the LGM predicted using the UGAMP palaeoclimate simulations.

(c)

t C ha^{-1} yr^{-1}

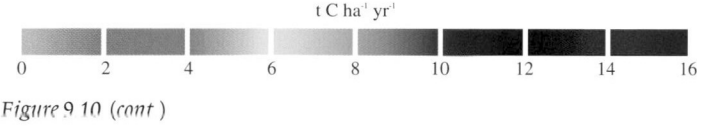

| 0 | 2 | 4 | 6 | 8 | 10 | 12 | 14 | 16 |

Figure 9.10 (cont.)

(Table 9.1). Other estimates of global terrestrial primary productivity during the last ice age (18 ka BP) are 75% of the present-day value (Meyer, 1988), and Esser & Lautenschlager (1994) reported a value of 27 Gt C yr^{-1} using the correlative Osnabruck biosphere model. This latter figure is lower than the range estimated here (Table 9.1). The global NPP totals can be divided by the global total of water lost through plant transpiration to estimate changes in WUE of the terrestrial biosphere through the late Quaternary (Table 9.1). Calculated in this way, the terrestrial biosphere as a whole fixes *c.* 8.2×10^{-4} Gt C yr^{-1}/ Gt of H$_2$O lost through transpiration under current climate; this decreases to 7.2 $\times 10^{-4}$ Gt C yr^{-1}/ Gt of H$_2$O for the mid-Holocene and to 5.4×10^{-4} Gt C yr^{-1}/ Gt of H$_2$O for the last ice age (Table 9.1).

Increases in the concentration of CO$_2$ could partly alleviate vegetation drought associated with growth in a cold, dry glacial environment. To quantify this potential, the SDGVM was re-run using the GCM glacial climate with the CO$_2$ increased to 350 ppm. The results (Table 9.1) support the expectations from physiological considerations with global NPP increasing by 42–52%, but with minimal reductions in global plant transpiration. Canopy transpiration is not reduced by the increased CO$_2$ because increases in LAI offset the small reductions in stomatal conductance. The WUE of the

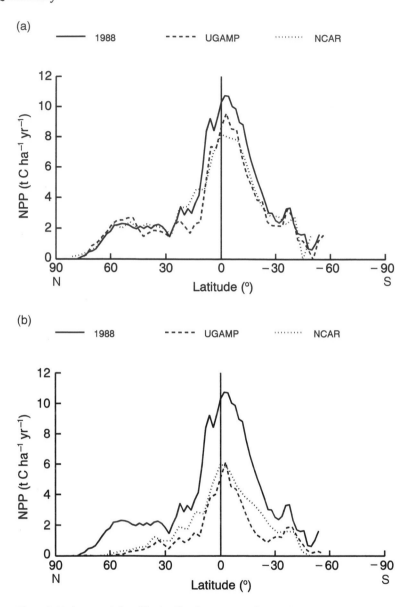

Figure 9.11. Area-weighted latitudinal averages of net primary productivity for (a) the mid-Holocene and (b) the last glacial maximum modelled using the UGAMP and NCAR palaeoclimate simulations. Also shown are the latitudinal patterns modelled using the 1988 global climate datasets.

Table 9.1. *Summary of terrestrial vegetation cover, productivity and water loss in the current climate and two intervals in the late Quaternary. Terrestrial biospheric water-use efficiency is defined as global NPP/global transpiration*

Age	Proportion of land surface vegetated (%)	NPP (Gt C yr^{-1})	GPP (Gt C yr^{-1})	Total plant transpiration (Gt H$_2$O yr^{-1})	Terrestrial biosphere WUE (Gt C/Gt H$_2$O yr^{-1})
1988	70.5	50.3	152.2	61 500	8.2×10^{-4}
Mid-Holocene (6 ka)					
NCAR	77.1	44.3	125.8	61 300	7.2×10^{-4}
UGAMP	71.2	41.0	116.8	56 300	7.3×10^{-4}
Last glacial maximum (21 ka)					
200 ppm CO$_2$					
NCAR	50.0	28.2	77.1	50 200	5.6×10^{-4}
UGAMP	37.7	19.9	56.9	37 000	5.3×10^{-4}
350 ppm CO$_2$					
NCAR	51.1	40.1	111.8	50 700	7.9×10^{-4}
UGAMP	39.0	30.2	89.2	39 900	7.6×10^{-4}

Note:
1 Gt = 10^{15} g.

terrestrial biosphere nevertheless increases, allowing increased canopy development and productivity for the same amount of precipitation and under the glacial climates as before (Fig. 9.12). Vegetation cover over the Earth's surface resulting from an increase in WUE (Table 9.1) is extended only marginally by 1–2%, implying that some additional constraint besides precipitation limits plant growth outside those areas colonised previously at 200 ppm CO$_2$, most probably low temperatures. Under a glacial climate, increases in LAI track those of NPP, becoming greater at lower latitudes. This occurs because LAI is already quite low (Fig. 9.8c) (up to 6–7) in equatorial regions, and so the addition of more layers in the canopy is supported because sufficient irradiance is received by these lower canopy layers to meet the costs of maintenance and construction respiration.

Distribution of plant functional types since the LGM

The predicted present-day distribution of plant functional types was compared with observational data on the distribution of different functional types in Chapter 4, with general agreement between the two datasets. The comparison is not, however, without complications associated with drawing up global maps of 'observed vegetation' classifications. Nevertheless, it was

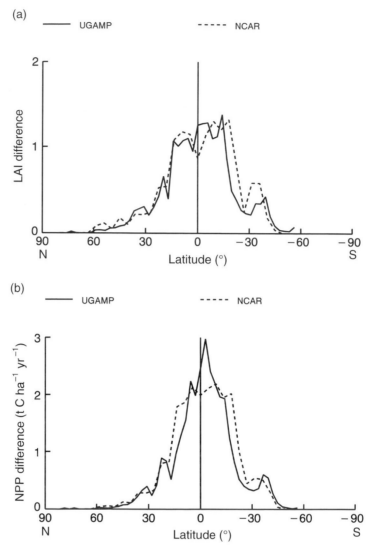

Figure 9.12. The effect of CO_2 partial pressure on the area-weighted latitudinal averages of (a) leaf area index and (b) net primary productivity predicted for the LGM using the UGAMP and NCAR palaeoclimate simulations. The figure shows the differences in latitudinal averages between runs with the vegetation model at 350 ppm minus 200 ppm CO_2.

concluded that the functional type model was adequate for capturing the broad global-scale distribution of the main types of the world's terrestrial vegetation.

Therefore, the SDGVM has been used to predict the distribution of the six functional types (evergreen broad-leaved and needle-leaved trees, deciduous broad-leaved and needle-leaved trees, C_3 and C_4 grasses) during the mid-Holocene and the LGM. These predictions, based on a largely mechanistic approach described in Chapter 4, require no underlying map of vegetation types, or correlations between the current climatic 'envelope' of a given vegetation type projected back into the past (Webb, 1998). Low temperature limits are included despite the possibility that these may be modified by the concentration of CO_2 (Beerling, 1998). As yet there is no consensus on the influence of atmospheric CO_2 concentration on the frost sensitivity of plants. Field-grown evergreen *Eucalyptus pauciflora* tree seedlings show increased susceptibility to frost damage at elevated CO_2, with higher ice nucleation temperatures than when grown at current ambient CO_2 (Lutze *et al.*, 1998; Beerling *et al.*, 2001), whilst for the deciduous birch *Betula alleghaniensis* elevated CO_2 increases its frost tolerance (Wayne *et al.*, 1998). Moreover, the likely impact of low CO_2 concentrations (180–280 ppm) on low temperature tolerances of plants have not yet been investigated. As a consequence we continue to use low temperature thresholds to differentiate the geographical ranges of different functional types of trees since no mechanistic information exists describing the action of CO_2 on low temperature tolerances in plants.

Testing the predictions of past vegetation distributions requires analysis of two components, the geographical extent and the actual distribution of a particular type of vegetation. We have attempted to test both components for the Quaternary simulations because a greater level of detail may be extracted from the fossil record compared with the much older studies of earlier chapters. For the mid-Holocene, the global distribution of the six functional types shows close similarities when the SDGVM is driven by the UGAMP and NCAR 6 ka palaeoclimates (Fig. 9.13). Most of the functional types are predicted to cover similar geographical extents at 6 ka as in 1988, the most striking expansion being the C_4 grasses (Table 9.2). A first test of these results has been to compare the areal extent of each functional type with the reconstructions of Adams & Faure (1998), since these are the most complete and up-to-date compilations of the palaeodata available. The test is, however, imperfect since the 8 ka and 5 ka time slices of Adams & Faure (1998) were averaged to represent the 'mid-Holocene' situation. There are two major differences between the modelled and reconstructed extent of each functional type: the model overestimates the extent of C_3 and C_4 grasses and underestimates the extent of evergreen broad-leaved trees (Fig. 9.14). The underestimates of evergreen broad-leaved trees occur because of low GCM predictions of precipitation, with consequent increases in the area of grasses and deciduous broad-leaved trees.

(a)

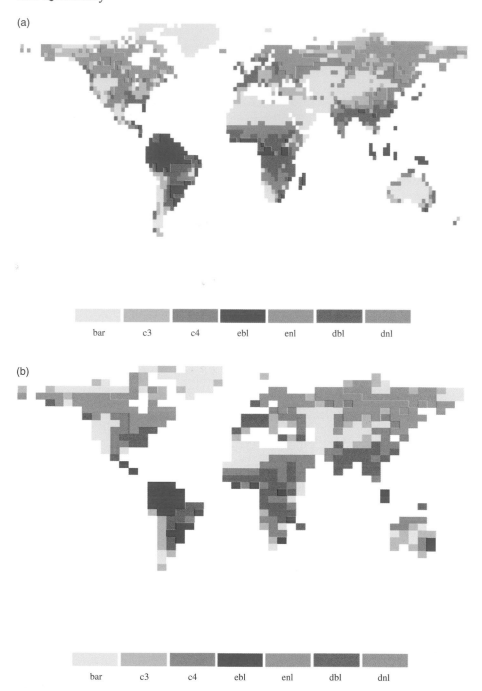

(b)

Figure 9.13. Modelled global distribution of plant functional types for the mid-Holocene using the SDGVM driven by (a) UGAMP and (b) NCAR GCM global palaeoclimate simulations. Key: bar, bare ground; c3, C₃ grasses; c4, C₄ grasses; ebl, evergreen broad-leaved trees; enl, evergreen needle-leaved trees; dbl, deciduous broad-leaved trees; dnl, deciduous needle-leaved trees.

Table 9.2. *Summary of the simulated global distribution of functional types for the present day (1988), the mid-Holocene (6 ka) and the LGM (21 ka)*

Age	Bare ground	Grasses C_3	C_4	Evergreen broad-leaved trees	Evergreen needle-leaved trees	Deciduous broad-leaved trees	Deciduous needle-leaved trees
		Area of functional type (10^6 km^2)					
1988	31.5	21.6	23.5	15.1	17.5	21.8	4.2
Palaeosimulations							
6 ka							
UGAMP	38.5	17.8	28.6	11.4	11.1	20.3	4.9
NCAR	30.9	18.2	31.6	11.1	17.1	23.3	3.9
21 ka (200 ppm CO$_2$)							
UGAMP	99.5	9.5	22.7	9.2	3.0	14.4	0.2
NCAR	81.2	19.6	20.4	12.4	6.1	20.0	2.6
21 ka (350 ppm CO$_2$)							
UGAMP	97.7	15.4	17.4	8.0	3.3	16.5	0.2
NCAR	79.6	25.4	14.9	11.9	6.6	21.0	2.7

Global-scale compilations of reconstructed vegetation types for the mid-Holocene, based on palaeoecological data (pollen and macrofossil remains) have not yet been constructed and those for north-west Europe are difficult to compare directly with our functional type maps because of their coarse spatial resolution. Instead, therefore, Figure 9.13 has been compared with the distribution of biomes reconstructed for Canada and the eastern USA from palaeoecological data (mainly pollen) since this covers a large spatial area (Williams *et al.*, 1998, 2000).

By applying a 'biomization' method for objectively summarising fossil pollen data, Williams *et al.* (1998, 2000) reconstructed the distribution of the major plant functional types for the mid-Holocene in North America and Canada (Fig. 9.15). The reconstruction shows several areas of agreement and disagreement with the model predictions (Fig. 9.16). The fossil evidence, for example, indicates the presence of warm mixed forests and temperate deciduous forests in the south-eastern USA (Fig. 9.15), in agreement with the modelled dominance of both evergreen and deciduous broad-leaved forests in these regions. In the central USA, the reconstructed 'steppe' vegetation (Fig. 9.15) corresponds to the dominance of modelled C$_4$ grasses (Fig. 9.16), although its predicted distribution through Canada is greater than recorded in the fossil record.

The most notable difference between the reconstructed and modelled distributions is the extent of taiga (equivalent to the evergreen needle-leaved

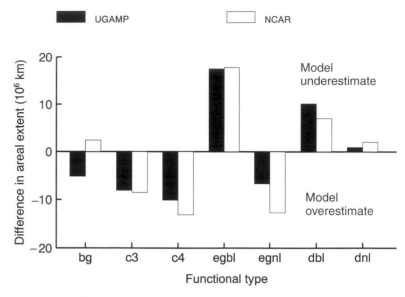

Figure 9.14. Difference between reconstructed and modelled areal extent of the main functional types for the mid-Holocene. To allow comparison of the modelled and reconstruction surface areas, reconstructions based on palaeoecological data (Adams & Faure, 1998) were re-grouped to correspond to the six functional types as follows, the abbreviations as reported in Table 1 of Adams & Faure (1998): bare ground (bg) = tropical semi-desert and desert, polar/Mediterranean desert, temperate desert, mediterranean/dry tundra, ice; C_3 grasses (c3), temperate semi-desert, moist tundra, steppic tundra, tundric tundra; C_4 grasses (c4), tropical savannah, moist steppe, dry steppe; evergreen broad-leaved trees (egbl), tropical rainforest, monsoon forest, tropical woodland, tropical scrub, tropical montane forests, mediterranean scrub; evergreen needle-leaved trees (egnl), open boreal; deciduous broad-leaved trees (dbl), warm temperate forests, temperate woodland, temperate scrub, forest steppe; deciduous needle-leaved trees (dnl), mid taiga.

functional type). The fossil data show that this biome was distributed throughout much of Canada (Fig. 9.16), but is predicted to be a mixture of evergreen needle-leaved forests and C_3 grasses that is probably a more open parkland. This result indicates that the growing-season temperatures were too cool and possibly too dry to allow the establishment of high forest.

Interest in changes of land carbon storage since the LGM has led to several global-scale reconstructions of palaeovegetation maps for this interval based on fossil pollen and sedimentary evidence (Adams *et al.*, 1990; Crowley, 1995; Adams & Faure, 1998), and these provide a useful basis for comparison with the predicted distribution of functional types (Fig. 9.17). As with the 6 ka global simulations, the modelled global extent of each functional type has

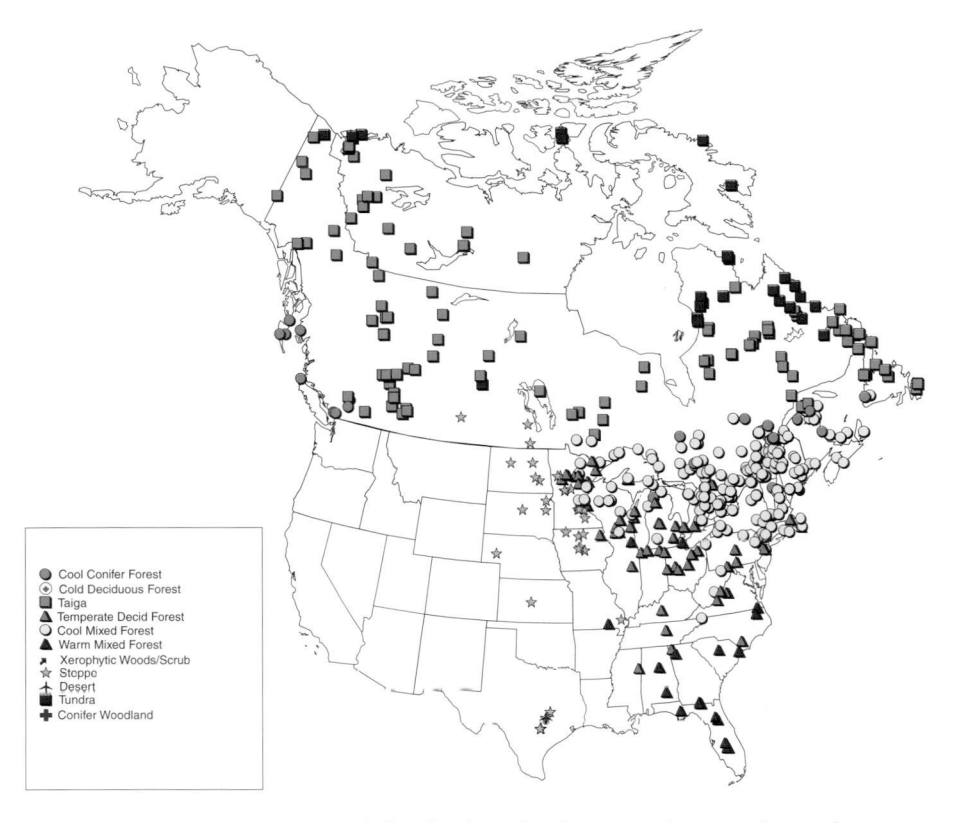

Figure 9.15. Reconstructed distribution of major vegetation types in North America, based on analysis of fossil pollen from a wide range of sites (from Williams *et al.*, 2000).

first been compared with the palaeovegetation reconstructions of Adams & Faure (1998). In this comparison, the main differences between the models and the data are overestimation of the extent of bare ground and underestimation of C$_3$ grasses, particularly when the SDGVM was driven with the UGAMP simulation (Fig. 9.18). Both GCM-derived palaeoclimates result in the SDGVM overestimating the extent of deciduous broad-leaved trees, as in the mid-Holocene simulations (Fig. 9.14), again probably as a result of limited precipitation in tropical areas.

The global predictions of functional type distributions for the last ice age (Fig. 9.17) have been compared with the palaeovegetation reconstruction of Crowley (1995) based on extensive work of the Co-operative Holocene Mapping Project (COHMAP, 1988) and supplemented with information from additional sites (Fig. 9.19). The reconstruction indicates greater vegetation cover than the vegetation model predicts, although the palaeovegetation map (Fig. 9.19) gives a visually misleading impression by classifying 'bare ground'

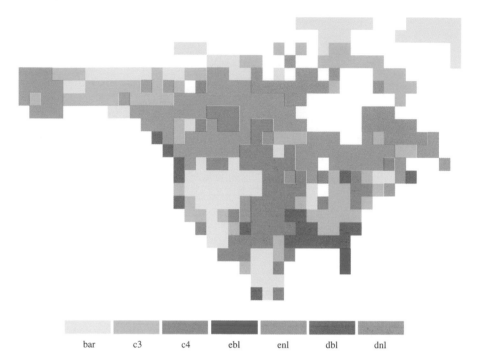

bar   c3   c4   ebl   enl   dbl   dnl

Figure 9.16. Modelled distribution of functional types for the mid-Holocene in the USA, Canada and Alaska using the SDGVM driven by UGAMP GCM palaeoclimate. Key as for Fig. 9.13.

with three colours representing desert, semi-desert and ice. Nevertheless, the modelled geographical extent of C_3 grasses in the northern hemisphere is markedly underestimated in this comparison using the UGAMP GCM simulation (Fig. 9.19). Another major area of discrepancy is the existence of a belt of conifer forest through the Asian sub-continent and the USA (Fig. 9.19), that is instead predicted to be confined to small regions of south-east Asia and eastern North America (Fig. 9.17). The modelled lack of vegetation cover reflects the extremely cold year-round conditions at mid- to high northern latitudes.

There are, however, a number of common features between the observed and predicted maps. In particular, predictions made with the NCAR simulations place the evergreen broad-leaved forests in the Amazonian basin, Indonesia and central Africa in near-identical locations to the reconstruction of Crowley (1995) (Figs. 9.17 and 9.19) and Adams & Faure (1998). The persistence of evergreen tropical rainforests in the Amazon during the LGM supports evidence from pollen data (Colinvaux *et al.*, 1996) that their presence in this area was continuous but reduced in extent. The predicted locations of deciduous broad-leaved forests show close correspondence with the

(a)

(b)

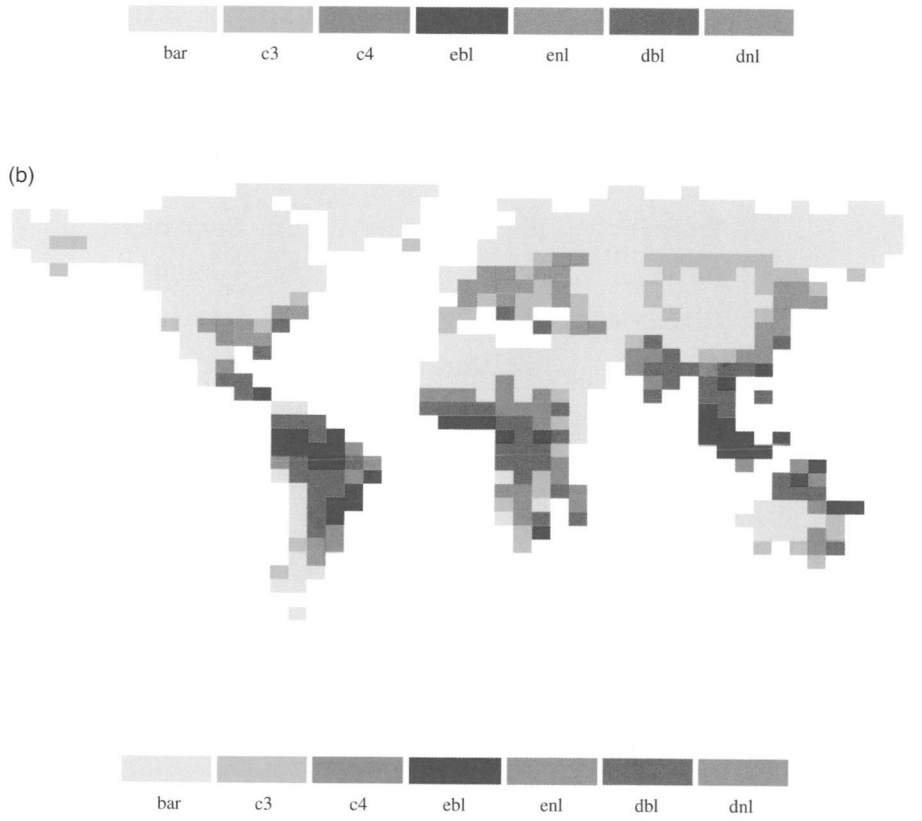

Figure 9.17. Modelled global distribution of plant functional types for the LGM using the SDGVM driven by the (a) UGAMP and (b) NCAR GCM global palaeoclimate simulations. Key as for Fig. 9.13.

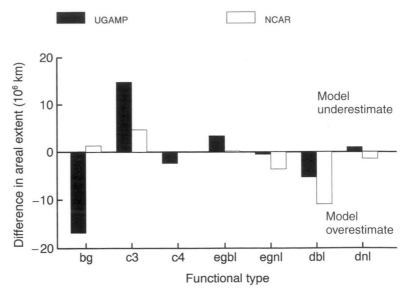

Figure 9.18. Difference in areal extent between palaeo-vegetation reconstructions of the six main functional types (Adams & Faure, 1998) minus the modelled values. UGAMP and NCAR are the distributions predicted using these two palaeoclimate simulations respectively. Vegetation types as in Fig. 9.14.

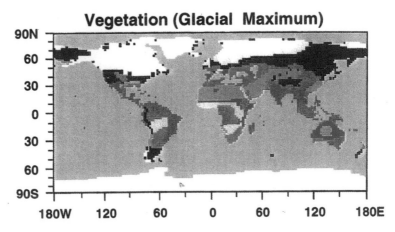

Figure 9.19. Global vegetation reconstruction for the LGM (from Crowley, 1995).

reconstructed distribution of savannah. If the palaeo-reconstructions are taken at face value, the overall impression is that the SDGVM has only moderate success in predicting the distribution of different vegetation types during the LGM, with the most 'realistic' predictions emerging from the use of NCAR glacial simulation. It is, however, not clear whether both the UGAMP and NCAR GCMs simulated glacial climates that were too cool and dry and/or that the physiological underpinning of the climatic controls on glacial vegetation types were different from those modelled to be governing current vegetation. The issue of how low CO_2 concentrations interact with low temperature tolerances of different plant groups, in this respect, is identified as an area for further experimental investigation.

As an additional comparison with the fossil data, but at a smaller spatial scale and with data independent of the COHMAP (1988) compilations used by Crowley (1995), the model results have been compared with the biome reconstructions for North America (Williams *et al.*, 1998, 2000). The dataset is not directly comparable since the pollen has been grouped for sites dating to 18 rather than 21 ka BP. It does, however, indicate the likely distribution of functional types during cold, low CO_2 glacial conditions (Fig. 9.20) and has the advantage over global-scale compilations of more representative regional detail. In this comparison, the predictions show an improved match, with similarities between the predicted and observed locations of evergreen broad-leaved forests in Florida, deciduous broad-leaved forests in the south-eastern USA, and evergreen needle-leaved forests in central southern USA (Fig. 9.21).

Differences in the match between modelled plant distributions and those reconstructed from the fossil record, may depend on the problems associated with scaling-up to the global scale from *c.* 200 pollen samples at individual sites over the entire global terrestrial surface (Crowley, 1995). The primary pollen database used to construct Figure 9.19 was extrapolated from these 200 sites to a $2° \times 2°$ grid box for mapping purposes, and this process led to inevitable compromises and subjective decisions in the grouping of samples into a given type of vegetation. Some areas are under-represented in pollen samples, e.g. tropical rainforest regions, and other areas, e.g. savannah, have been reconstructed elsewhere on the basis of interdisciplinary evidence to a much greater extent (Adams *et al.*, 1990; Adams & Faure, 1998). The marked reductions in the Australian desert area and the absence of the northern Argentinian deserts in the work of Crowley (1995) are, for example, contrary to the sedimentological data for the regions (Adams & Faure, 1998).

It is clear that many problems combine to make palaeovegetation reconstructions from data uncertain, particularly summarising pollen samples to obtain global coverage, and there are equal but different uncertainties in the

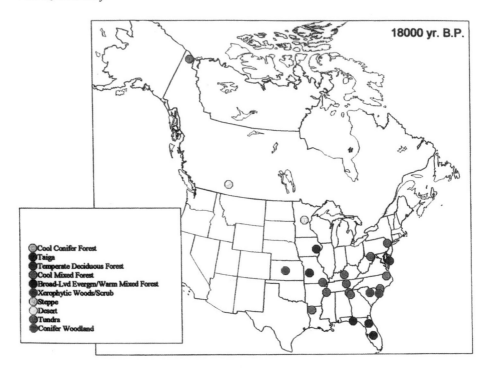

Figure 9.20. Reconstructed distribution of major vegetation types in north America and Canada *c.* 18 ka BP, based on analyses of fossil pollen from a wide range of full-glacial sites (from Williams *et al.*, 2000).

climate and vegetation models. These uncertainties preclude, to a certain extent, the rigorous testing of both vegetation and climate model simulations for the LGM. New methods of objectively summarising pollen data should, however, reduce some of the observational uncertainties and these are now beginning to be applied at the regional scale. Improvements in the observational databases will provide a more secure basis for testing our ability to describe the relevant plant physiological and climatic processes in a glacial environment.

The changing distribution of C_4 plants since the LGM

The global and regional-scale analyses of functional type distributions indicated that grasses with C_3 and C_4 photosynthetic physiologies had the largest responses (in terms of geographical extent) in the past relative to the present day (Table 9.2). C_4 plants are readily distinguished from C_3 plants in the fossil record by their high (less negative) carbon isotope composition $(\delta^{13}C)$ ($-7‰$ to $-15‰$ for C_4 plants vs. $-20‰$ to $-35‰$ for C_3 plants), a signal

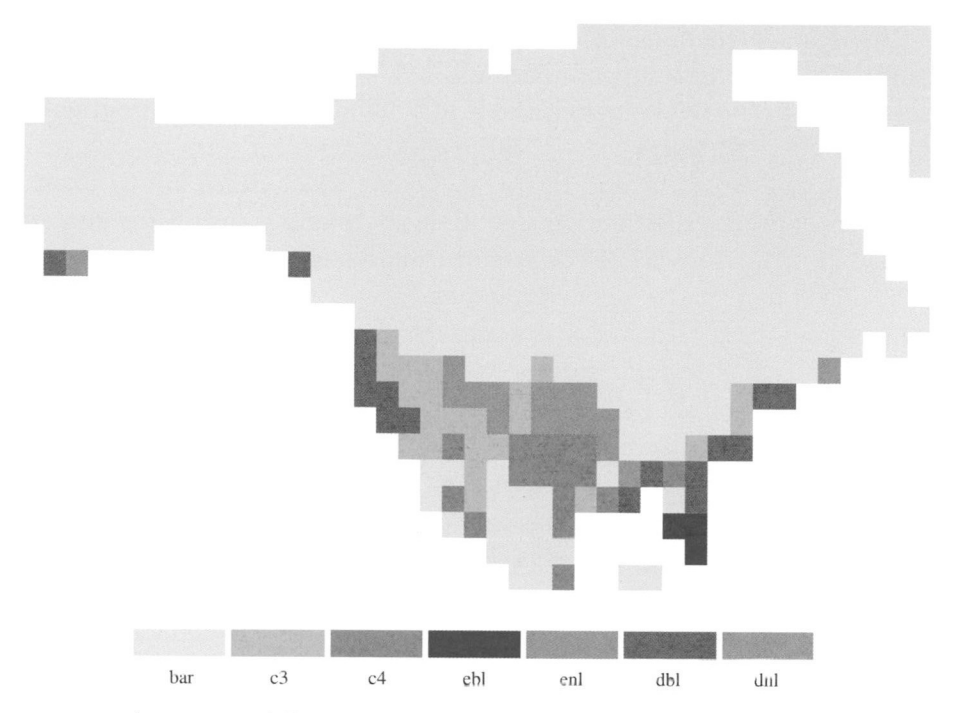

Figure 9.21. Modelled distribution of functional types for the mid-Holocene in the USA, Canada and Alaska using the SDGVM driven by UGAMP GCM palaeoclimate. Key as for Fig. 9.13.

retained by organic matter preserved in lake and bog sediments. Therefore, $\delta^{13}C$ measurements on well-dated terrestrial organic matter or particular bio-markers provide a means of comparing the modelled C_3/C_4 plant distributions with the predictions for specific sites on the Earth's surface. Such comparisons also provide a marker of our ability to forecast accurately possible changes in the distribution of C_4 plants in a future high CO_2 'greenhouse world' (Collatz *et al.*, 1998).

Globally, at the present day, C_4-dominated (>60%) grasslands are distributed across the southern boundary of the Sahel in northern Africa, areas of southern Africa, South America, India and northern Australia (Fig. 9.22), in general agreement with observations (extensive vegetation classification of these regions, based on observations, has been summarised from the literature by Collatz *et al.*, 1998). Several areas are predicted to have a more even mixture of C_3 and C_4 plants, particularly the Great Plains region of North America (Fig. 9.22). In the SDGVM, the occurrence of C_4 plants is predicted on the basis of the relative NPPs of C_3 and C_4 grasses. The approach therefore is a simplified version of that described by Collatz *et al.* (1998), although these authors predict near-pure C_3 plant stands through the middle of the Asian sub-continent rather than a predominance of C_4 plants (Fig. 9.22a). Overall, however, the results provide general support that our simplified approach captures the necessary climatic and physiological factors controlling the current distribution of C_4 plants.

In the mid-Holocene and the LGM, vegetation of near-pure C_4 plants shows an expanded distribution around those regions of their occurrence in 1988 (Fig. 9.22). However, the current distribution of C_4 plants is best viewed as a relict of these past wider distributions. Extensive $\delta^{13}C$ data on terrestrial bulk organic matter from all sites with expanded distributions are not available, but detailed isotopic studies extending back to the LGM have been reported for several sites in India and central Africa.

In southern India, the profiles of $\delta^{13}C$ in organic matter from peats provide convincing evidence for the occurrence of C_4 plants at this region during the mid-Holocene and the last glaciation (Sukumar *et al.*, 1993), with values of -14‰ for 4–6 ka and 20 ka. The modelled continued dominance of C_3 plants in Brazil during the Holocene is supported by $\delta^{13}C$ measurements on soil organic matter from a range of sites (Martinelli *et al.*, 1996) which show no evidence for the replacement of forests by C_4 savannah grasses in this region. In the Holocene, C_4 plants are predicted to encroach into the south-western USA (Fig. 9.22b), and $\delta^{13}C$ measurements on fossils of mid-Holocene age support this prediction (Toolin & Eastoe, 1993).

Carbon isotope data from three climatically-sensitive localities in central Africa (Fig. 9.23) provide an interesting set of comparisons within a narrow geographical range for the predictions of this region (Fig. 9.22). The predictions for Lake Bosumtwi (Fig. 9.23a) show a high proportion of C_4 plants for the LGM, with a switch to near-total C_3 plants by the mid-Holocene. This pattern of change is observed in the down-core $\delta^{13}C$ variations of organic matter from the sediments at this site (Fig. 9.23a), although large oscillations are recorded between -30 and -5‰ indicating rapid dynamic changes between C_3 and C_4 plants at this site. For Lake Barombi Mbo (Fig. 9.23b), the isotopic evidence shows organic matter of full-glacial age with values of -25 to -30‰, and a trend to more negative values over the past 10 ka. This chronological pattern indicates the likely dominance of C_3 plants in a C_3/C_4 mixture for the full-glacial with a shift to pure C_3 plant stands by the start of the Holocene. These are also consistent with the model predictions showing plant communities at this site in both the mid-Holocene and LGM comprising only 20% C_4 plants (Fig. 9.22c). At the third of the three African sites, the Kashiri peat bog, a more distinct pattern emerges from the $\delta^{13}C$ measurements, with evidence for C_4 plant dominance at 20 ka followed by a progressive removal until about 10 ka and then increasing dominance from 10 ka onwards (Fig. 9.23c). Such a pattern of change is mirrored by the model results for the LGM, with a strong (70%) dominance of C_4 plants at this time (Fig. 9.22c) but, in contrast to the isotopic evidence, a marked reduction is predicted for the mid-Holocene.

Cerling *et al.* (1998) plotted the corresponding changes in the concentration of atmospheric CO_2, inferred from ice core studies, and showed the dominance of C_4 plants reflected this trend (Fig. 9.23d). Ice core evidence used in this way provides independent support for the physiological importance of low CO_2 in promoting C_4 plant dominance in terrestrial ecosystems. However, a number of isotopic studies made on bulk organic matter from these tropical lakes and peat bogs have uncertainties attached to the source of the carbon measured for isotopic analyses. This requires the time-consuming and expensive isolation of specific biomarker molecules to separate terrestrial, aquatic and bacterial carbon sources to provide a more secure basis for palaeoecological and palaeoenvironmental interpretations. Careful isotopic work on organic carbon fractions isolated from sediments of high-altitude lakes on Mount Kenya and Mount Elgon, East Africa, provides direct evidence that carbon limitation during the low CO_2 concentration of glaciations limited the distribution of trees on these tropical mountains (Street-Perrott *et al.*, 1997). During the LGM, the $\delta^{13}C$ of total organic carbon was dominated by a mixture of C_4 grass and algal lipids, whereas during the start of the Holocene C_3 plant and algal lipids dominated, indicating that the increase in concentration of CO_2 over this time allowed trees to grow where previously the vegetation was characterised by grassy heathland.

The palaeoecological isotopic data and measurements of atmospheric CO_2 from ice core studies implicate low CO_2 concentrations as one of the key driving forces determining C_4 plant distributions in the late Quaternary. Therefore, the sensitivity of the predicted glacial-age C_4 distributions to CO_2 was examined by mapping SDGVM predictions at 350 ppm CO_2 instead of 200 ppm. The resulting global distributions (Fig. 9.24) show the expected clear reduction in extent of C_4 plants, particularly in India, Africa and southern South America. This occurs because C_4 plants utilise a carbon concentrating mechanism that is advantageous at low CO_2 concentrations but energetically more expensive than C_3 plant metabolism as CO_2 increases. These physiological and energetic considerations are included in the C_4 model of photosynthesis and so are translated into differences in plant distribution. The model predictions at 350 ppm CO_2 are difficult to reconcile with the carbon isotope data for the selected sites reviewed above, underscoring the

(a)

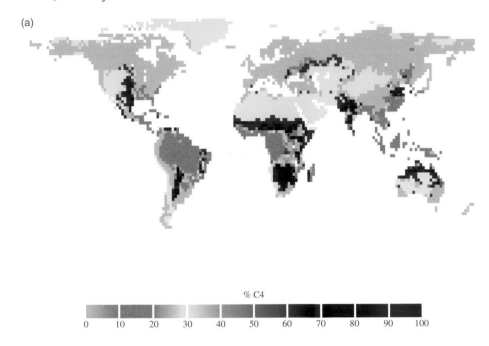

(b)

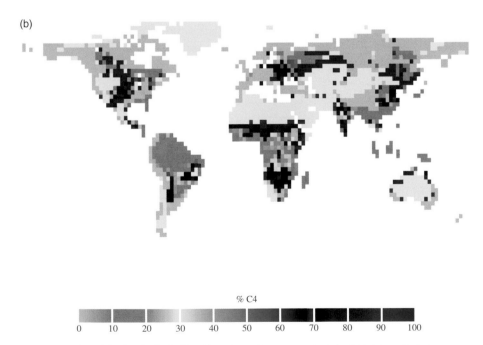

Figure 9.22. Modelled global fraction of C4 grasses in (a) 1988, (b) mid-Holocene and (c) the LGM, using the SDGVM driven by the UGAMP global palaeoclimatic simulations.

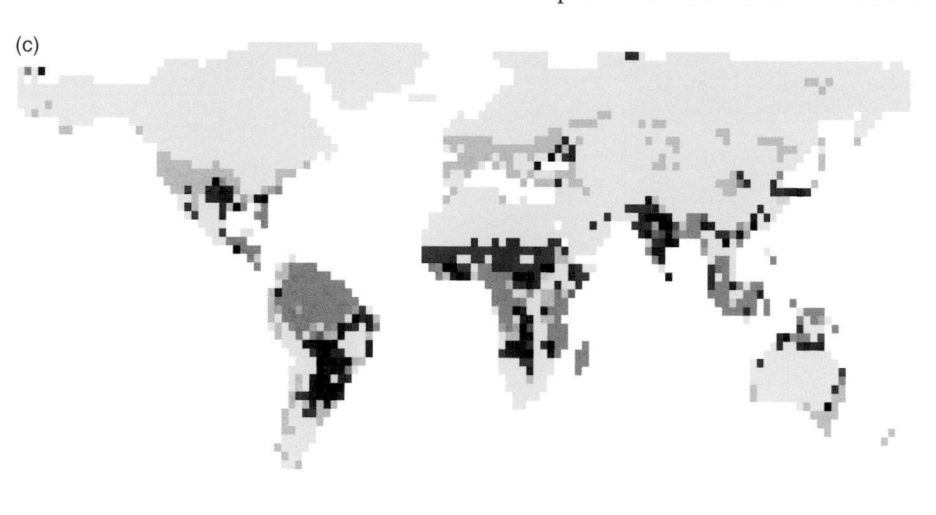

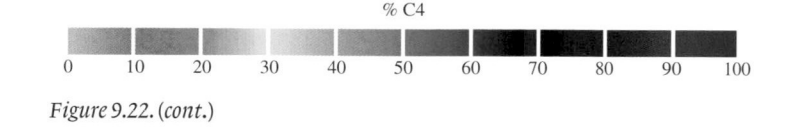

Figure 9.22. (cont.)

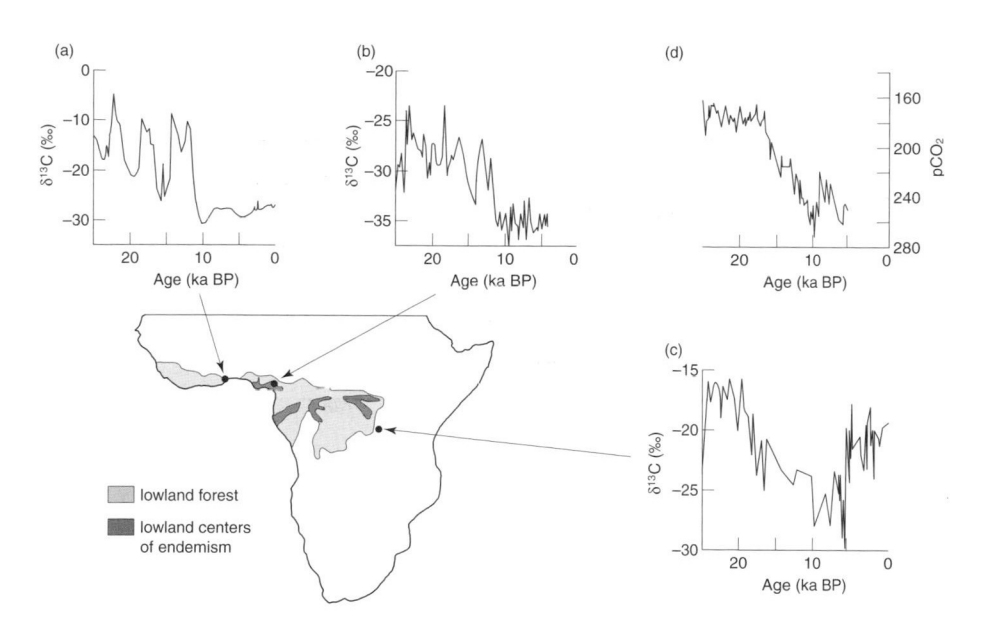

Figure 9.23. Shifts in the carbon isotope composition (δ^{13}C) of organic matter from (a) Lake Bosumtwi, (b) Lake Barombi Mbo and (c) Kashiri peat bog, in Africa; (d) illustrates shifts in atmospheric CO_2 over the same time interval from ice core studies (from Cerling *et al.*, 1998).

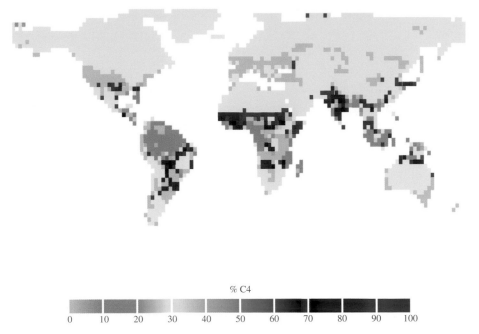

% C4

| 0 | 10 | 20 | 30 | 40 | 50 | 60 | 70 | 80 | 90 | 100 |

Figure 9.24. Modelled global fraction of C_4 grasses for 21 ka using the SDGVM driven by the UGAMP global palaeoclimatic simulations but at 350 ppm CO_2 instead of 200 ppm.

importance of a mechanistic representation of atmospheric CO_2 concentrations in the photosynthetic physiologies of C_3 and C_4 plants for accurate representation of vegetation distributions.

Given the reasonable success of the model at predicting late Quaternary changes in C_4 distributions it is interesting to speculate whether the mapped distributions for the mid-Holocene and LGM (Fig. 9.22) are potentially useful for targeting sites of future palaeoecological investigations. Most notably, sediments from sites yet to be explored in central north America and eastern Asia in the mid-Holocene may contain evidence of an abundance of C_4 plants. For the LGM, a similar set of 'C_3/C_4 sensitive' sites occur in central South America and northern Australia.

Changes in terrestrial carbon storage since the LGM

Understanding the controls on the increase in atmospheric CO_2 since the last glacial maximum is of widespread interest for improving the inventory of the global carbon cycle during the last glacial–interglacial climatic cycle (Faure *et al.*, 1998). During glacial periods the oceanic reservoirs are thought to have sequestered large amounts of carbon (Broecker & Peng, 1993) which was transferred to terrestrial biosphere via the atmosphere during the deglaciation. A more complete account requires a quantitative analysis of possible changes in terrestrial carbon storage on land, in vegetation and soils, as well. This section presents an analysis of such changes for comparison with previous modelling studies (Prentice *et al.*, 1993; François *et al.*, 1998), estimates based on palaeodata (Adams *et al.*, 1990; Adams & Faure, 1998), and approaches combining models and data (van Campo *et al.*, 1993; Peng *et al.*, 1998).

Our analysis is the first to use a fully coupled vegetation–biogeochemistry model, deriving soil nutrient status, and explicitly includes mechanistic models of the C_3 and C_4 photosynthetic pathways. This inclusion is important because C_4 species have a competitive advantage at low concentrations of CO_2 (see previous section), comprising a larger proportion of the total terrestrial biomass during the mid-Holocene and the LGM than now. Total carbon in the vegetation was determined from the NPP and ecosystem productivities (Chapter 4), and the simulated areal extent of each functional type using the ISLSCP 1988 climate datasets and both the UGAMP and NCAR 6 ka and 21 ka palaeoclimate simulations.

The resulting modelled carbon storage figure for the present-day terrestrial biosphere (1691 Gt C in 1988) (Table 9.3) is lower than figures reported by other modelling studies (2122-2217 Gt C) (Prentice *et al.*, 1993; François *et al.*, 1998). Neither modelling approach took account of soil nutrient status, or even attempted to derive it by coupling vegetation and biogeochemistry models. The most recent estimate for carbon storage in modern natural vegetation based on observational data (Adams & Faure, 1998) is, however, also higher than our model estimate (2639 Gt C), although compilations of carbon storage by modern vegetation and soils are not without their problems in terms of accounting for human activity on vegetation, assigning suitable carbon densities to different vegetation types and accounting for carbon in dead standing biomass. The model predictions for the present day do not include any agricultural types of vegetation. For 1988, *c.* 6.4% of the total biospheric carbon stock is in C_4 plant biomass and soils, much less than the 17.1% reported by François *et al.* (1998).

Total amount of carbon stored in terrestrial ecosystems (vegetation and soils) during the mid-Holocene (6 ka) was lower than the modern value by 431 Gt C (mean of both simulations) (Table 9.3). Based on a revised methodology for constructing the global distribution of palaeovegetation from analyses of palynological, pedological and sedimentological records, Adams & Faure (1998) reported virtually no change in land carbon storage for 5 ka and a 168

Gt reduction between now and 8 ka. Uncertainties in drawing up inventories of carbon stocks in vegetation and soils, as well as those in constructing climate and vegetation models, limit such comparisons as tests of either approach.

For the LGM, carbon storage by the terrestrial biosphere varied from 486 to 831 Gt C depending on the GCM climatic forcing dataset (Table 9.3). The higher value with the NCAR glacial climate results from the cooler, wetter glacial conditions compared with the UGAMP simulation. Taking a modern global total of carbon stocks on land of present-day potential vegetation (Table 9.3), the predicted increase in total carbon storage since the LGM based on carbon cycle modelling alone ranged from 661 to 1204 Gt C. As expected (Farquhar, 1997), the increase was sensitive to the concentration of atmospheric CO_2 during the last glaciation. With the glacial climates and 350 ppm CO_2, carbon storage in terrestrial ecosystems during the LGM increased by 296 Gt (UGAMP) and 388 Gt (NCAR) (Table 9.3), indicating quite severe CO_2 limitations on ecosystem function at this time. An increase in carbon storage by the terrestrial biosphere between the LGM and the present-day 'potential' vegetation of 750–1120 Gt C is greater than previous modelling efforts but close to the most recent estimated range based on palaeodata (Table 9.4).

Because of its importance in understanding glacial–interglacial dynamics of the global carbon cycle, numerous attempts have been made to estimate the magnitude of the change in carbon storage by the terrestrial biosphere since the LGM based on several different approaches, including vegetation modelling, palaeodata, and carbon isotope mass balance constraints (Table 9.4). In general, early vegetation modelling studies calculated the increase in terrestrial carbon storage between the LGM and the present day to be lower than that calculated from the palaeodata (Table 9.4). The new results presented here, however, agree most closely with the palaeodata, and are towards the upper range of estimates based on analyses of the carbon isotope mass balance (Table 9.4). Mass balance calculations are in themselves not without uncertainties associated with estimating the carbon isotope composition of bulk terrestrial carbon during the last glaciation (Bird *et al.* 1994, 1996), an issue considered in greater detail in the next section.

At this stage, it should be noted that estimated changes in land carbon storage based on palaeodata are generally higher than all other approaches (Table 9.4). One reason for this might be that carbon storage values reported for modern soils and modern vegetation types are related back to the glacial situation or some other Quaternary interval, on the assumption that they are directly analogous. To investigate this assumption, the equilibrium soil carbon concentrations for 1988, the mid-Holocene and the LGM were

Table 9.3. *Area-weighted carbon storage in different functional types and underlying soils for the present-day (1988), the mid-Holocene (6 ka) and the last glacial maximum (21 ka)*

Age	Carbon storage by functional type (Gt C)					
	C_3 grasses	C_4 grasses	Evergreen broad-leaved trees	Evergreen needle-leaved trees	Deciduous broad-leaved trees	Deciduous needle-leaved trees
1988						
Vegetation	4.7	13.9	377.4	62.6	240.8	9.4
Soils	208.1	107.3	159.7	256.9	169.3	66.4
Global total 1690.9 Gt C						
(Including bare ground soil carbon, 14.3)						
Palaeosimulations						
6 ka, UGAMP						
Vegetation	3.5	13.9	226.4	36.8	162.8	11.6
Soils	157.0	154.7	101.8	144.2	119.2	68.0
Global total 1200.2 Gt C						
(Including bare ground soil carbon, 0.3)						
6ka, NCAR						
Vegetation	3.2	15.9	227.6	65.2	160.0	10.3
Soils	157.8	142.8	106.0	231.9	138.0	58.4
Global total 1319.4 Gt C						
(Including bare ground soil carbon, 0.3)						
21 ka, UGAMP (200 ppm CO_2)						
Vegetation	1.2	7.4	106.1	3.5	71.3	0.1
Soils	78.0	57.3	61.1	33.8	68.5	2.2
Global total 486.0 Gt C						
(Including bare ground soil carbon, 0.2)						
21 ka, UGAMP (350 ppm CO_2)						
Vegetation	3.2	8.9	182.4	5.5	168.7	0.3
Soils	112.8	64.8	81.8	43.3	107.1	2.9
Global total 782.3 Gt C						
(Including bare ground soil carbon, 0.4)						
21 ka, NCAR (200 ppm CO_2)						
Vegetation	2.7	8.7	150.0	14.2	117.0	3.4
Soils	149.9	76.2	98.5	70.3	107.0	32.6
Global total 831.1 Gt C						
(Including bare ground soil carbon, 0.6)						
21 ka, NCAR (350 ppm CO_2)						
Vegetation	5.8	9.1	236.6	21.9	233.3	4.4
Soils	220.7	73.6	128.1	90.6	156.0	38.7
Global total 1219.0 Gt C						
(Including bare ground soil carbon, 0.2)						

Table 9.4. *Estimates of increased carbon storage by the terrestrial biosphere between the LGM and pre-industrial*

Estimate (Gt C)	Reference
Vegetation modelling	
200–400	Prentice *et al.* (1993)
213	Esser & Lautenschlager (1994)
118–590	François *et al.* (1998)
747–1117	this study (Table 9.2)
Palaeodata	
1350	Adams *et al.* (1990)
400–700	van Campo *et al.* (1993)
469–950	Peng *et al.* (1998)
900–1900	Adams & Faure (1998)
C-isotope mass balance budget	
450	Crowley (1991)
750–1050	Crowley (1995)
310–550	Bird *et al.* (1994)
300–700	Bird *et al.* (1996)

mapped, and the results (Fig. 9.25) show that in fact the assumption is most unlikely to be correct because during glacials the low CO_2 and temperatures curtail terrestrial NPP (Fig. 9.10c) and this, in turn, limits the input of carbon into soils as surface litter (leaves and fine roots). Therefore, even though there are slower rates of decomposition at low glacial temperatures, the soils do not attain a carbon concentration similar to that of the present day (Fig. 9.25a). A comparable situation applies to the mid-Holocene but with lesser impact resulting from the warmer climates (Fig. 25b).

Global ^{13}C discrimination by the terrestrial biosphere in the late Quaternary: implications for land carbon storage

The carbon-isotope mass balance analysis provides a means of estimating changes in carbon storage by utilising geochemical records of shifts in the isotopic composition of carbon in the oceanic, atmospheric and terrestrial reservoirs (Crowley, 1991, 1995; Bird *et al.*, 1994, 1996; Beerling, 1999c). Because of the difficulties of estimating changes in carbon stored in present-day potential vegetation it is most relevant to calculate the change in ecosystem carbon storage between the mid-Holocene and the LGM, since by the mid-Holocene the deglacial CO_2 increase had already occurred (Barnola *et al.*,

1987; Neftel *et al.*, 1988) and extensive land clearance by human activity was not yet under way (Houghton & Skole, 1990).

Assuming the conservation of mass, any change between these three reservoirs must be balanced, and can be defined by:

$$(\delta_a m_a) + (\delta_o m_o) + (\delta_b m_b) = (\delta_a' m_a') + (\delta_o' m_o') + (\delta_b' m_b') \tag{9.1}$$

where δ is the isotopic composition of the carbon (‰), m is the mass (Gt) and the subscripts a, o and b refer to the atmospheric, oceanic and terrestrial carbon reservoirs, respectively, at mid-Holocene (without primes) and at the LGM (with primes). Equation 9.1 can then be re-arranged to relate the isotopic composition of terrestrial carbon ice age (δ_b') to changes in total terrestrial carbon storage (Bird *et al.*, 1994, 1996):

$$\delta_b' = \frac{(\delta_a m_a) + (\delta_b m_b) + (\delta_o m_o) - (\delta_a' m_a') - \delta_o'[m_o + (m_a m_a') + (m_b m_b')]}{m_b'} \tag{9.2}$$

The advantage of re-expressing equation 9.1 in terms of δ_b' is that it enables the calculation of the difference between the terrestrial carbon storage in the pre-industrial atmosphere (m_b) and the LGM (m_b') relative to the isotopic composition of glacial age organic carbon (δ_b'). All of the remaining terms can be specified directly from the literature, and an updated version of the mass balance inventory is given in Table 9.5.

The solution to equation 9.2 requires an estimate of the isotopic composition of bulk terrestrial organic carbon in the mid-Holocene (δ_b) and the LGM (δ_b'). This value is difficult to determine solely by isotopic measurements on fossil plant remains because it should integrate and reflect the relative proportions of C_3 and C_4 plants, each with very different isotopic compositions. The breakdown of the global carbon cycle described by equations 9.1 and 9.2 is, however, most sensitive to the difference in the isotopic composition of bulk carbon rather than the absolute values. Here both δ_b and δ_b' have been calculated from physiological considerations linking discrimination against $^{13}CO_2$ during photosynthesis (Δ) (Lloyd & Farquhar, 1994).

The bulk Δ values of plants are most strongly dependent upon the photosynthetic pathway of the plant (Farquhar, 1983; Farquhar *et al.* 1989; Farquhar & Lloyd, 1993; Lloyd & Farquhar, 1994). For C_3 plants the extent of $^{13}CO_2$ discrimination is dependent upon both photosynthetic and stomatal activity (Chapter 2), but weighted by discriminations associated with the draw-down of CO_2 across the mesophyll and CO_2 fixation itself (i.e. it represents the net effect of a large number of leaf structural properties). Nevertheless, fractionation effects are relatively invariant across leaf types (Farquhar & Lloyd, 1993) and are largely a function of the differences in the ratio of concentrations of

(a)

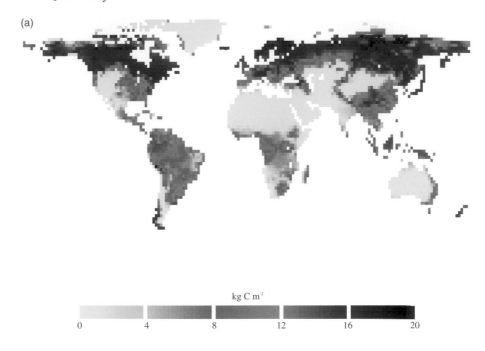

kg C m²

(b)

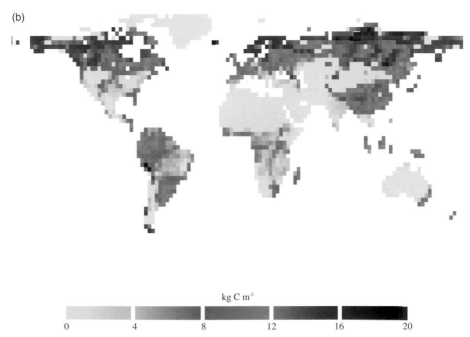

kg C m²

Figure 9.25. Modelled global distribution of soil carbon concentration in (a) 1988, (b) mid-Holocene and (c) 21 ka using the SDGVM driven by the UGAMP global palaeoclimatic simulations.

(c)

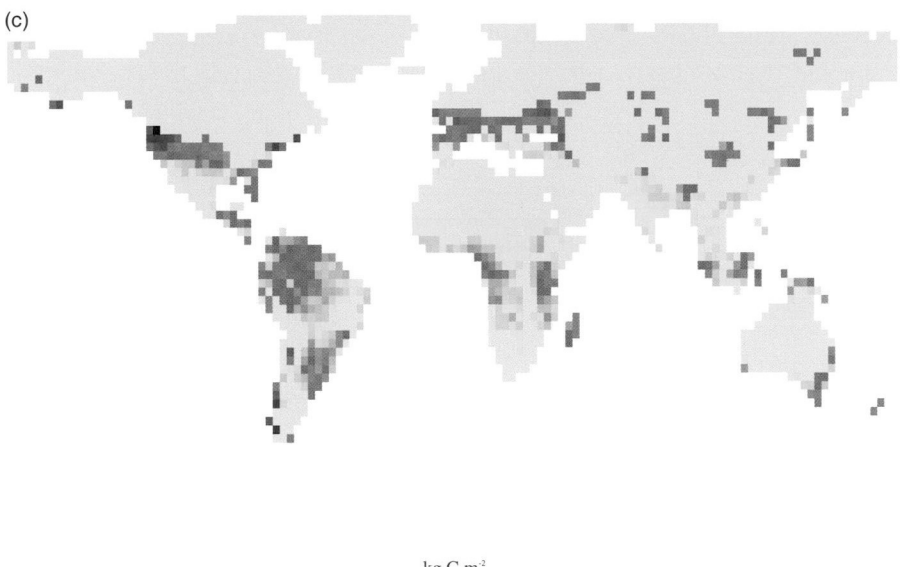

kg C m^{-2}

| 0 | 4 | 8 | 12 | 16 | 20 |

Figure 9.25. (cont.)

CO_2 within the leaf. A more complete expression for these effects, than that given in Chapters 2 and 3, is provided by Lloyd & Farquhar (1994):

$$\Delta(C_3) = a\left(1 - \frac{C_i}{C_a} + 0.025\right) + 0.075(e_s + a_s)$$

$$+ b\left(\frac{C_i}{C_a} - 0.1\right) - \frac{e\dfrac{R_d}{k} + f\Gamma^*}{C_a} \tag{9.3}$$

where a is the fractionation against $^{13}CO_2$ during diffusion in free air (4.4‰), e_s is the equilibrium fractionation for CO_2 in solution (1.1‰), a_s is the fractionation against $^{13}CO_2$ during diffusion in water (0.7‰), b is discrimination against $^{13}CO_2$ during photosynthetic fixation of CO_2 (27.5‰), e and f are the fractionations associated with respiration (0.0‰) and photorespiration (8.0‰) respectively, C_i is the intercellular CO_2 concentration, C_a is the external CO_2 concentration, R_d is the foliar respiration in the light, k is the carboxylation efficiency and Γ^* is the CO_2 photocompensation point, with a temperature sensitivity given by DePury & Farquhar (1997).

For C_4 plants a theoretical treatment for ^{13}C discrimination (Δ_A) has been described (Farquhar, 1983), capturing the enzymic and anatomical differences in this group of plants, and is given by:

Table 9.5. *Values of the isotopic composition and mass of carbon in the atmospheric, oceanic and terrestrial reservoirs for the mid-Holocene and at the LGM, from Beerling (1999c)*

Term	Symbol	Value	Reference
Mass of C in mid-Holocene atmosphere	m_a	530 Gt	Indermühle *et al.* (1999)
Mass of C in mid-Holocene biosphere	m_b	1415	Table 9.3
Mass of C in mid-Holocene oceans	m_o	38 000 Gt	Siegenthaler & Sarmiento (1993)
Mass of C in the LGM atmosphere	m_a'	400 Gt	Barnola *et al.* (1987)
Mass of C in the LGM biosphere	m_b'		this study
Mass of C in the LGM oceans	m_o'		$m_o + (m_a - m_a') + (m_b - m_b')$
$\delta^{13}C$ value of mid-Holocene atmospheric CO_2	δ_a	−6.3‰	Indermühle *et al.* (1999)
$\delta^{13}C$ value of mid-Holocene biospheric C	δ_b		this study
$\delta^{13}C$ value of mid-Holocene oceanic C	δ_o	0.0‰	
$\delta^{13}C$ value of the LGM atmospheric CO_2	δ_a'	−7.0‰	Leuenberger *et al.* (1992)
$\delta^{13}C$ value of the LGM biospheric C	δ_b'		this study
$\delta^{13}C$ value of the LGM oceanic C	δ_o'	−0.4‰	Crowley (1995)

$$\Delta(C_4) = a\left(1 - \frac{C_i}{C_a} + 0.0125\right) + 0.0375(e_s - a_s)$$

$$+ [b_4 + (b_3 - e_s - a_s)\phi]\left(\frac{C_i}{C_a} - 0.05\right) \qquad (9.4)$$

where b_4 is the temperature-sensitive discrimination by phosphoenolpyruvate carboxylase (PEP-c), b_3 is discrimination by rubisco and ϕ is the ratio of the rate of CO_2 leakage from the bundle sheath cells to the rate of PEP carboxylation (0.2) (Lloyd & Farquhar, 1994). All the other terms in equation 9.4 are as defined for equation 9.3.

To estimate δ_b globally, Δ was calculated on a monthly basis for C_3 and C_4 plants, depending on the functional type assigned earlier, and weighted according to monthly GPP. For the mid-Holocene, this procedure gave an average ^{13}C discrimination value of 14.9‰ for the terrestrial biosphere as a whole (Fig. 9.25a, Table 9.6), and 19.4‰ for one comprising only of C_3 plants. At the global scale the largest differences in Δ occur where C_4 plants (mostly grasses) are distributed (Fig. 9.25a).

During the mid-Holocene and the LGM, C_4 plants were more widely dis-

Table 9.6. *Average global discrimination against $^{13}CO_2$ by the terrestrial biosphere for 6 ka and 21 ka*

| Simulation | Discrimination (‰) | | $\delta^{13}C_a$ | $\delta^{13}C$ of bulk carbon | $\delta^{13}C$ of bulk carbon (corrected) |
	C$_3$ only biosphere	C$_3$ and C$_4$ plants			
6 ka					
UGAMP	19.4	14.9	−6.3	−20.9	−23.9
NCAR	19.6	15.4	−6.3	−21.4	−24.4
Mean	19.5	15.2		−21.2	−24.2
21 ka					
UGAMP	18.6	12.7	−7.0	−19.4	−22.4
NCAR	19.7	15.7	−7.0	−22.3	−25.3
Mean	19.2	14.2		−20.9	−23.9

(After Beerling, 1999c)

tributed at the expense of C$_3$ plants, so that the globally averaged Δ_A is reduced (Table 9.6), and this is reflected in the globally distributed patterns (Fig. 9.26a,b). In the mid-Holocene, this is most clearly seen in the northern African Sahel region, whereas for the LGM, reductions in Δ due to the expansion of C$_4$ plants occur mainly in northern Africa and throughout large regions of India (Fig. 9.26).

Modelled Δ values were corrected for the isotopic composition of atmospheric CO$_2$ assimilated by the plants, with values reported from ice core studies (Table 9.5) to obtain the isotopic composition of the bulk terrestrial carbon. The globally-averaged estimates (Table 9.6) are maximum values since the physiological modelling does not account for the re-utilisation of low δ^{13}C in respired CO$_2$. This effect reduces overall values by up to 3‰ (cf. Bird *et al.*, 1996), and so for the mass calculations this correction has been applied accordingly (Table 9.6).

According to the constraints of the global isotope mass balance, terrestrial carbon storage increased by 550–680 Gt C between the mid-Holocene and the LGM (Fig. 9.27). The upper estimate of this range is close to the increase predicted by direct modelling of the global terrestrial carbon cycle at this time, which gives 668 Gt C, as the mean across all of the mid-Holocene and glacial simulations (Table 9.3).

The combination of direct modelling of the terrestrial carbon cycle and a mass balance approach incorporating the isotopic composition and mass of the atmospheric and oceanic reservoirs yields very consistent results. The two approaches converge to suggest a 'best guess' range around 550–750 Gt C, a

(a)

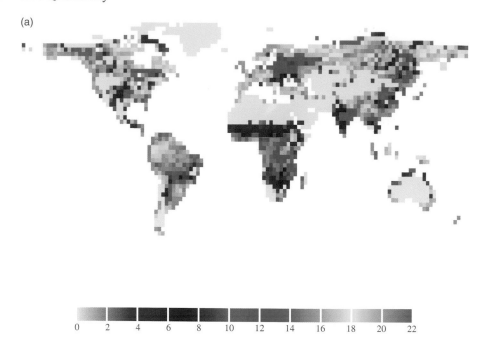

(b)

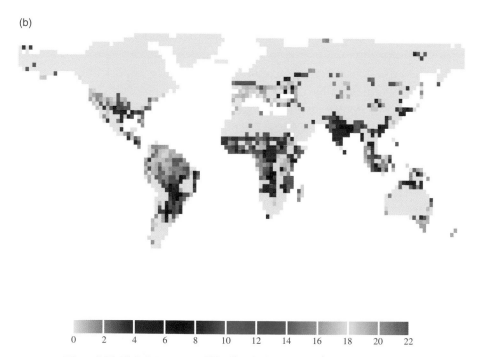

Figure 9.26. Global patterns of ^{13}C discrimination (Δ_A in ‰), weighted by gross primary productivity, for (a) mid-Holocene and (b) the last glacial maximum, predicted from the vegetation model using the UGAMP palaeoclimate simulations.

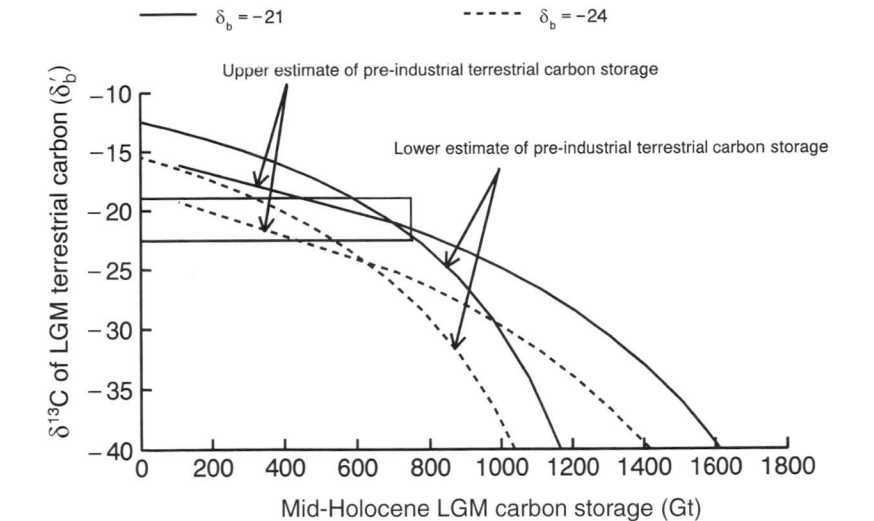

Figure 9.27. Relationship between carbon isotope composition of bulk terrestrial carbon during the last glacial maximum (LGM) and the increase in carbon storage between the LGM and the mid-Holocene, that satisfies the global carbon isotope mass balance constraints. The horizontal box indicates the modelled range of the isotopic composition of LGM carbon; the two curves depict the range of values that satisfy the isotopic mass balance constraints for the predicted isotopic composition of mid-Holocene terrestrial carbon (Table 9.3). The range of marine estimates are from Crowley (1995) and Maslin *et al.* (1995), the palaeodata-based estimates are: (1) Maslin *et al.* (1995), (2) Adams *et al.* (1990) and (3) Adams and Faure (1998).

value at the lower end of palaeodata. Although the two approaches described here are not entirely independent of each other, since both use output from the same simulations, the results go some way to reconciling mass balance calculations and carbon storage estimates from the terrestrial and marine palaeodata.

This new range of carbon storage figures can be used to quantify the role of vegetation in the increase in atmospheric CO_2 concentration recorded in ice cores since the LGM and the mid-Holocene (80 ppm). Assuming that 10 ppm CO_2 is equivalent to 20 Gt C in the atmosphere (Siegenthaler & Sarmiento, 1993), then the increased carbon storage by the terrestrial biosphere since 21 ka has the potential to sequester 350–400 ppm of atmospheric CO_2 released from the oceanic reservoirs. Even assuming that the expanding biomass kept pace with the CO_2 rise during deglaciation between 15 ka and 8 ka (Neftel *et al.*, 1988), the rate of sequestration by terrestrial vegetation must have been low (0.04–0.05 Gt C yr^{-1}). Inclusion of oceanic responses would diminish this potential event further, giving a rise of 35–40 ppm (Broecker & Peng, 1993;

Maslin *et al.*, 1995). It would seem unlikely that, contrary to earlier suggestions (Adams *et al.*, 1990), increased carbon storage by terrestrial vegetation and soils played an important role in 'damping' oceanically driven glacial-to-interglacial CO_2 variations. However, quantification of the absolute amount of carbon sequestered onto land during the most recent deglaciation remains important since it allows an estimate of the real rise in atmospheric CO_2 that may have occurred but would not have been recorded in ice cores. A rise of 30–40 ppm over and above the 80 ppm recorded in ice cores suggests that the total amount of carbon lost from the oceans, and which should be accounted for by ocean carbon cycle models, was greater than previously realised (Broecker & Peng, 1993; Maslin *et al.*, 1995).

Vegetation and the oxygen isotope composition of atmospheric O_2

This book is primarily concerned with quantifying and describing the operation of terrestrial vegetation in past environments. However, quantifying the influence of vegetation activity on the Dole effect, i.e. the difference in the $\delta^{18}O$ of atmospheric O_2 relative to that of seawater, provides a means of estimating changes in the relative variations in marine and terrestrial productivities (Bender *et al.*, 1985, 1994; Sowers *et al.*, 1991; Keeling, 1995) (note that all isotope ratios in this section are expressed relative to Standard Mean Ocean Water, SMOW). This is because $\delta^{18}O_2$ reflects the balance between the gross O_2 fluxes of marine and terrestrial systems and the isotopic fractionations associated with photosynthesis and respiration of both systems. Therefore, in this section the vegetation and climate model simulations have been used to develop an approach for reconstructing this ratio, by first quantifying the contribution of vegetation to the Dole effect and then constraining the mass balance of ^{18}O in O_2 using the late Quaternary palaeo-records of the Dole effect.

Vegetation influences $\delta^{18}O_2$ because the slower transpiration of $H_2^{18}O$ than $H_2^{16}O$ leads to an enrichment of leaf water with ^{18}O (δ_L). This enrichment is then passed to the O_2 produced by photosynthesis without further fractionation (Guy *et al.*, 1993). Despite this information, the impact of vegetation on $\delta^{18}O_2$ is one of the greatest uncertainties in fully accounting for the ^{18}O budget in the biogeochemical cycling of oxygen, and this limits attempts to reconstruct past changes in the ratio of terrestrial to marine productivity from the palaeo-record of the Dole effect (Beerling, 1999b). The uncertainty arises because previous estimates of a figure for the globally-averaged δ_L

(Farquhar *et al.*, 1993; Ciais *et al.*, 1997) were approximately half the theoretically expected value (Dongmann, 1974; Bender *et al.*, 1994).

One reason for the low δ_L values is the calculation of the isotopic composition of atmospheric water (δ_V) without inclusion of plant transpiration effects
(Beerling, 1999b). δ_V is required for describing leaf water enrichment relative
to soil water in the Craig–Gordon model of evaporative enrichment (Craig &
Gordon, 1965). Therefore, we first estimate δ_L at the global scale for 1988, the
mid-Holocene and the LGM to complement observations on the Dole effect
from ice core O$_2$ records and isotopic measurements on foraminifera which
reflect the isotopic composition of seawater.

Using the approach described previously (Beerling, 1999d), the Craig–
Gordon model has been used to calculate the $\delta^{18}O$ of water at the evaporative
sites in the chloroplasts (δ_E) under steady-state conditions (Farquhar *et al.*,
1993). The assumption leads to small differences between modelled leaf water
enrichment and observed values due to a range of temporal, spatial and physical variations within leaves (Yakir *et al.*, 1994; Farquhar & Lloyd, 1993).
However, at the global scale the Craig–Gordon model captures the required
detail (Farquhar *et al.*, 1993), so for modelling purposes, it is assumed that δ_E is
sufficiently close to δ_L.

The Craig–Gordon model of evaporative enrichment, originally derived for
a free surface, but subsequently modified for plant cells (Farquhar *et al.*, 1993),
predicts leaf water enrichment (δ_L) from:

$$\delta_L = \delta_S + \varepsilon_K + \varepsilon^* + \left(\delta_V - \delta_S - \varepsilon_K\right)\frac{e_a}{e_i} \tag{9.5}$$

where δ_S is the isotopic composition of the source water, δ_V is the isotopic composition of water vapour in the surrounding air, e_a and e_i are the vapour pressures of water in the atmosphere and intercellular spaces, ε^* is the
proportional depression of equilibrium vapour pressure by ^{18}O (9.2‰ at 25
°C), with a temperature sensitivity given by Bottinga & Craig (1969), and ε_K is
the kinetic fractionation factor accounting for the weighted diffusion
through stomata and the boundary layer (26‰) (Farquhar *et al.*, 1993). The isotopic composition of source water (soil water) reflects that of precipitation,
with an almost completely dampened seasonal variability, and is predicted
from annual mean temperature, precipitation and elevation. The palaeosimu-
lations include differences in elevation due to ice sheet loading during the
LGM and post-glacial isostatic rebound in the mid-Holocene. As previously, δ_V
was calculated as a constant $-10‰$ depletion everywhere (Ciais & Meijer,
1998), weighted by monthly canopy transpiration (Beerling, 1999d).

δ_L is weighted by the gross flux of O_2 produced by terrestrial vegetation (i.e. gross primary productivity (GPP) plus photorespiratory O_2 consumption). The photorespiratory O_2 production is described by GPP/ϕ, where ϕ is the ratio of photorespiration to carboxylation, given by (Farquhar *et al.*, 1980):

$$\phi = \left(\frac{V_{omax}}{V_{cmax}}\right)\left(\frac{O_i}{C_i}\right)\left(\frac{K_c}{K_o}\right) \times 10^{-3} \qquad (9.6)$$

where V_{omax} and V_{cmax} are the maximum rates of oxygenation and carboxylation respectively, O_i and C_i are the intercellular partial pressures of O_2 and CO_2, and K_C and K_O are the Michaelis–Menten constants for carboxylation and oxygenation respectively. GPP/ϕ was estimated on a monthly basis using canopy averages V_{cmax} and C_i (depending on LAI) calculated from the vegetation model, V_{omax} calculated as $0.21V_{cmax}$ (Farquhar *et al.*, 1980). Both C_i and V_{max} are dependent upon canopy structure as well as atmospheric CO_2, climate and edaphic conditions (Chapter 4).

To investigate the significance of the globally-averaged estimates of δ_L (Table 9.7) and their gross O_2 fluxes for changes in the Dole effect at corresponding times, it is first necessary to outline the components of the isotope mass balance for oxygen. This comprises three terms, defined as the terrestrial and marine Dole effects and the effects of stratigraphic diminution of the Dole effect (Bender *et al.*, 1994). The terrestrial Dole effect is described by:

$$F_{TGPP}\delta_L = F_{TR}(\delta_{ATM} - \delta_{TR}) \qquad (9.7)$$

where F_{TGPP} is the annual total O_2 flux produced by terrestrial vegetation (Table 9.7), F_{TR} is the annual total of O_2 consumed by terrestrial respiration processes and δ_{TR} is the net isotopic fractionation associated with these processes. The estimate of δ_{TR} is important since it has a large fractionation and reflects the climate in which the plants are growing.

For current climatic conditions, Bender *et al.* (1994) estimated δ_{TR} to be 18.0‰ as a composite flux-weighted value representing the different biochemical pathways involved in terrestrial plant respiration [(dark respiration) $0.59 \times 18.0‰ +$ (Mehler reaction) $0.1 \times 15.1‰ +$ (photorespiration) $0.31 \times 21.2‰ -0.7‰$ for equilibrium enrichment of leaf water in air]. For the mid-Holocene and the LGM the weighting for photorespiration increases because a greater proportion of GPP is lost as photorespiration under the lower partial pressure of atmospheric CO_2 at these times (Table 9.7). Using the values in Table 9.7, a constant 0.1 proportion for the Mehler reaction and the remainder as dark respiration, δ_{TR} for the mid-Holocene becomes 18.5‰ and for the LGM 19.4‰.

Table 9.7. *Global terrestrial gross primary productivity and gross O_2 weighted values of leaf water enrichment (δ_L) for the present (1988), the mid-Holocene (6 ka) and the LGM (21 ka). Value in parentheses is the percentage photorespiration*

Age	GPP (Pmol O_2 yr^{-1})	GPP (% photorespiration) (Pmol O_2 yr^{-1})	δ_L (‰)
Current climate (ISLSCP)			
1988	12.7	17.3 (34%)	8.3
Palaeosimulations			
6 ka			
UGAMP	9.7	14.2	9.2
NCAR	10.5	15.2	9.6
Mean	10.1	14.3 (45%)	9.4
21 ka			
UGAMP	4.7	8.2	8.0
NCAR	6.4	10.9	7.4
Mean	5.6	9.6 (74%)	7.7

Note:
1 Pmol $= 10^{15}$ mol.

The oceanic Dole effect can be defined by:

$$F_{MGPP}\delta_{ML} = F_{SOR}(\delta_{ATM} + \delta_{SE} - \delta_{SOR}) + F_{DOR}(\delta_{ATM} + \delta_{SE} - \delta_{DOR}) \qquad (9.8)$$

where F_{MGPP} is the total annual flux of O_2 produced by the oceans, δ_{ML} is the isotopic fractionation during this O_2 production (0.0‰), δ_{SE} is the fractionation which occurs when O_2 is dissolved in seawater (0.7‰), F_{SOR} is the total annual flux of O_2 consumed by respiration in the surface ocean ($=F_{MGPP} \times 0.95$) and δ_{SOR} its fractionation (20‰), F_{DOR} is the total annual flux of O_2 consumed by the deep ocean ($=F_{MGPP} \times 0.05$) and δ_{DOR} its net fractionation (12.0‰) (Bender *et al.*, 1994).

The third term required to complete the budget for $\delta^{18}O$ of O_2 is the stratospheric diminution effect. This occurs because exchange of O_2 between the troposphere and the stratosphere imparts a small fractionation effect on ^{18}O, estimated by Bender *et al.* (1994) to be 0.4‰. However, expressed on an annual basis, δ_S becomes (0.4‰ / the turnover time of O_2 in air (1200 yr) $\times$ 56 years), the residence time of the troposphere with respect to its exchange with the stratosphere, 0.018‰. The mass of O_2 involved in this exchange is 660×10^{15} mol (660 Pmol).

Combining the terrestrial, oceanic and tropospheric/stratospheric flux terms, the final mass balance equation is given by:

$$F_{TGPP}\delta_L + F_{MGPP}\,\delta_{ML} + F_O\,(\delta_{ATM} - 0.018) = F_{TR}(\delta_{ATM} - \delta_{TR}) + F_{SOR}$$
$$(\delta_{ATM} + \delta_{SE} - \delta_{SOR}) + F_{DOR}(\delta_{ATM} + \delta_{SE} - \delta_{DOR}) + F_O\,(\delta_{ATM} - 0.018) \qquad (9.9)$$

Under steady-state conditions, $F_{TGPP} = F_{TR}$, and $F_{MGPP} = F_{SOR} + F_{DOR}$, and since ocean GPP fractionation is zero (δ_{ML}), equation 9.9 can be simplified and solved to predict either δ_{ATM} or, when δ_{ATM} is known from ice core studies, solved for F_{MGPP}. When solved for F_{MGPP} it is desirable to calculate the equivalent marine NPP (F_{MNPP}), since this is the term correlated with sedimentary carbon fluxes. The scaling relationship between gross primary O_2 production and respiratory O_2 consumption by planktonic and benthic communities (Duarte & Agusti, 1998) is:

$$R = aF_{MGPP}{}^b \qquad (9.10)$$

where a and b are constants of 1.0 and 0.78, respectively. Therefore, taking an O_2:C ratio of marine organic matter of 1.4:1 (Laws, 1991) and converting to a weight basis gives global marine net primary production (F_{MNPP} in Pg C yr^{-1}) as:

$$F_{MNPP} = \left(\frac{F_{MGPP} - R}{1.4}\right) \times 12 \qquad (9.11)$$

Calculated from equation 9.9, the Dole effect (δ_{ATM}) for 1988 is estimated to be $+23.1‰$, implying that global marine gross productivity is lower than the 12 Pmol O_2 yr^{-1} estimated by Bender *et al.* (1994). Solving the mass balance for F_{MGPP}, using all of the values for the terms for the present day, gives a value of 8.0 Pmol O_2 yr^{-1}, and a net primary production (F_{MNPP}) of 25.0 Pg C yr^{-1}. This final value is lower than the range (36.5–45.6 Pg C yr^{-1}) calculated for the contemporary oceans from satellite measurements of chlorophyll concentration, and information on sea surface temperature, incident solar radiation and mixed layer depths (Antoine *et al.*, 1996; Behrenfield & Falkowski, 1997; Falkowski *et al.*, 1998).

Building on this analysis, an interpretation of the palaeo-record of the Dole effect has been made in terms of defining the implied ratio of marine to terrestrial gross productivities. The calculations have been constrained using the modelled leaf water enrichment and gross O_2 productions in Table 9.7, values of δ_{ATM} from ice cores, and δ_{ML} from the isotopic composition of foraminifera from fossiliferous ocean sediments (Bender *et al.*, 1994). The results from these calculations indicate that ocean productivity was higher than present during the mid-Holocene (6 ka) and the LGM (21 ka). However, the absolute magnitude of F_{MGPP} will vary depending on the GCM glacial climate simulations, particularly the relative humidity fields. Nevertheless, the results provide quantitative estimates of ocean GPP in the late Quaternary

Table 9.8. *Observed Dole effect, derived from ice core and foraminifera studies, and modelled gross* (F_{MGPP}) *and net marine productivity* (F_{MNPP}) *for the late Quaternary*

Age	Obs.[a] Dole effect (‰)	F_{MGPP} (Pmol O_2 yr^{-1})	F_{MNPP} (Pg C yr^{-1})
Palaeosimulations			
6 ka			
UGAMP	23.1	12.8	47.2
NCAR	23.1	15.0	57.8
Mean		13.9	52.5
21 ka			
UGAMP	23.5	5.7	15.6
NCAR CCM 1	23.5	7.5	23.4
Mean		6.6	38.0

Note:
[a]Dole effect data from Bender *et al.* (1994).

allowing some comparison with palaeo-productivity proxies from sediments of the equatorial Pacific (Herguera *et al.*, 1994) and southernmost Atlantic sector (Kumar *et al.*, 1995). These sedimentary proxies tend to predict a higher productivity for the glacial ocean relative to that of the mid-Holocene, but this is not observed in the calculation derived from the oxygen isotope mass balance analysis (Table 9.8). This may be in part because the isotopic fractionations associated with the different biochemical pathways of respiration in higher plants under glacial conditions have been underestimated. Although we have included the influence of the low glacial CO_2 concentration on the flux-weighted fractionation of photorespiration, it is possible that the relative roles of cyanide-sensitive and cyanide-insensitive pathways could also be different (Siedow & Umbach, 1995; Gonzalez-Meler *et al.*, 1996). This is because the cyanide-insensitive pathway appears unaffected by the concentration of CO_2, unlike the cyanide-sensitive pathway, with the possibility that the ratio of the two was very different under low CO_2 concentrations. Since each pathway has a different fractionation this could lead to an underestimation of isotopic fractionation due to plant respiration in a glacial environment. In addition, sedimentary proxies are typically only applicable to specific ocean basins and so may not necessarily be representative of global oceanic behaviour.

Nevertheless, a preliminary attempt can be made to interpret palaeo-shifts in the Dole effect reported by Bender *et al.* (1994), in terms of the changing ratio of terrestrial to marine productivity. For the present this ratio is calculated to be 1.7, for the mid-Holocene 1.0 and for the LGM 1.4. Ocean gross primary productivity is a difficult quantity to estimate because it requires information on O_2 production and consumption by phytoplankton and bacterial communities integrated over a wide range of spatial and temporal scales (Antoine *et al.*, 1996). Taking an isotope mass balance approach, and constraining the side of the equation dealing with fractionations and fluxes associated with terrestrial vegetation, permits the partitioning of biospheric productivity between the oceans and the land.

Conclusions

The ability of the current generation of GCMs to simulate changes in global climates since the LGM, and which have occurred repeatedly during the late Quaternary, is surprisingly limited, and there is some way to go before the climate fields of GCMs can be used in an uncorrected form (i.e. without the calculation of monthly climate anomalies and their addition to a climate representative of the 'present-day' situation). None of the GCM simulations used in this chapter has explicitly included any feedback between vegetation and climate, and this may represent a 'missing link' in the modelling of Quaternary palaeoclimates, as it probably does for older climates (Beerling *et al.*, 1998). Regional scale palaeo-studies focusing on the mid-Holocene, for example, in northern Africa (Kutzbach *et al.*, 1996; TEMPO, 1996; Hoelzmann *et al.*, 1998) and high latitudes of the northern hemisphere (Foley *et al.*, 1994; Gallimore & Kutzbach, 1996), confirm this suspicion, with discrepancies between palaeoenvironmental data and model results being considerably reduced by inclusion of biophysical feedbacks associated with vegetation.

Nevertheless, the GCM climate simulations when used in their corrected form reproduce general features of late Quaternary climate sufficiently well to be of use for modelling their impact on the functioning of the terrestrial biosphere. It is clear that the terrestrial biosphere was operating under extremely impoverished conditions of low CO_2, low temperature and low precipitation during glacial times, with global NPP *c.* 50% that of the present day and the vegetated proportion of the Earth's surface being severely restricted. These restrictions limited carbon storage on land in terrestrial vegetation and soils. Estimates of changes in land carbon storage since the LGM, based on combining the geographical distribution of plant functional types and a mass balance approach, produced figures overlapping those obtained from scaled-up reconstructions of global palaeovegetation maps. We note, however, that neither approach is free from methodological problems but suggest the most likely increase is 700–800 Gt C.

The global-scale approach, with an emphasis on terrestrial vegetation, has enabled us to attempt an interpretation of palaeo-changes in the Dole effect in terms of the ratio of terrestrial and marine productivities. The approach may also be of use further back in time where oxygen isotope records of seawater are available (e.g. Beerling, 1999e). This modelling work has the potential to be further refined as a means of summarising GCM climates, particularly the humidity fields, by predicting the oxygen isotope composition of fossil plant cellulose for comparison with measurements on fossil leaves and woods.

10

Climate and terrestrial vegetation in the future

Introduction

This chapter moves on to using the vegetation model to simulate likely changes of vegetation in the future. The scenario of future and transient climatic and CO_2 change is from the 2nd Hadley Centre Coupled Model (HadCM2; Johns *et al.*, 1997). The GCM output has been adjusted (W. Cramer) to a tight spatial and quantitative match with observed climatic data between 1931 and 1960 (Chapter 3; Cramer, *et al.*, 2001). These same corrections are applied throughout the transient changes in climate from 1830 to the year 2100. These changes occur in response to a business-as-usual scenario of future increase in atmospheric CO_2 and are themselves the results of economic models, such as for future fossil fuel use (Wigley, 1997). The period of simulation is extended from 2100 to 2200 by using a period of constant, or stabilised, conditions to provide a method for investigating the presence and nature of any delayed or inertial responses by vegetation to transients of climate and CO_2.

The climatic scenarios

The major, driving variables for the vegetation model are atmospheric CO_2 concentration (Fig. 10.1), terrestrial temperature (Fig. 10.2) and terrestrial precipitation (Fig. 10.3). Changes in sunshine hours, or cloudiness and atmospheric humidity are also derived by HadCM2 and used to force the vegetation model. Atmospheric CO_2 concentration, plus other greenhouse gases, are the drivers of climatic change in the HadCM2; consequently there is a close relationship between atmospheric CO_2 concentration and temperature, with a 0.94 °C increase in temperature for every 100 ppm increase in CO_2 concentration. This relationship is linear ($r^2 = 0.99$, $n = 380$). The relationship

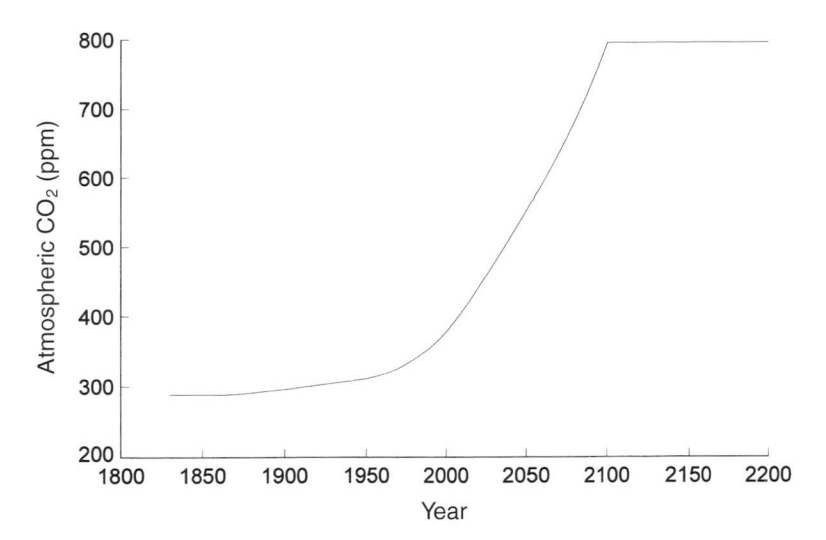

Figure 10.1. Scenario of change in atmospheric CO_2 concentration, 1830–2200, from modified HadCM2 GCM simulation.

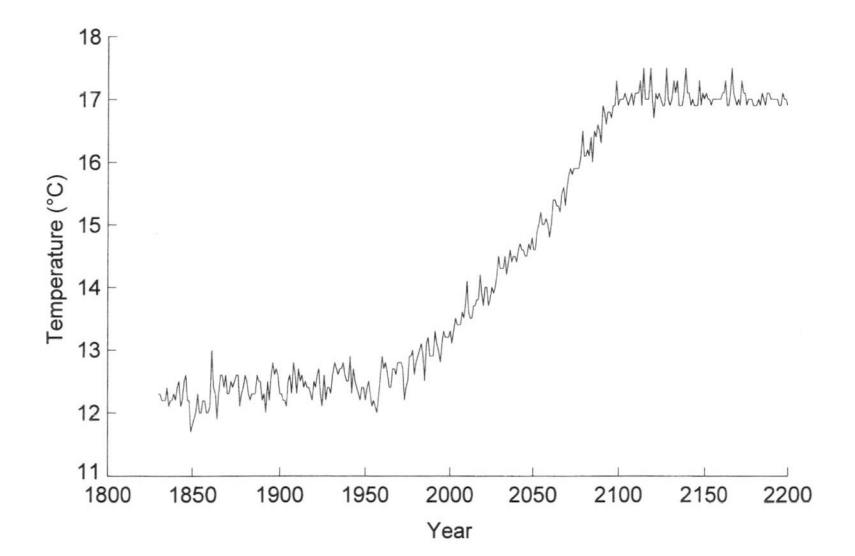

Figure 10.2. Terrestrial temperature (details as for Fig. 10.1).

between atmospheric CO_2 concentration and precipitation is much weaker than temperature ($r^2 = 0.17$ for a linear regression), with a 5.4 mm yr^{-1} increase in precipitation for a 100 ppm increase in atmospheric CO_2 concentration.

The poor correlation between CO_2 and precipitation indicates that the GCM simulates a range of interactive processes, such as between land and

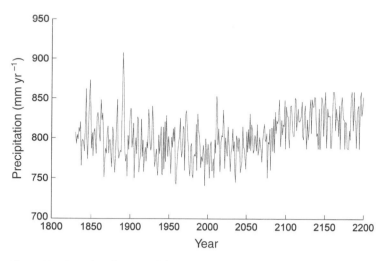

Figure 10.3. Simulated terrestrial precipitation (details as for Fig. 10.1).

ocean which erode any close and simple relationship between CO_2, temperature and precipitation (Dickinson, 1992).

Global totals of terrestrial responses

The simulated responses of vegetation to the transient changes in climate will be considered in two parts. The first will investigate global-scale totals of productivity and runoff responses and the second global-scale spatial responses of functional types. The global-scale totals will also be used to investigate the differing strength of vegetation responses to three different climatic treatments, defined as follows:

- the full treatment of changes in atmospheric CO_2 (Fig. 10.1), temperature and precipitation (Figs. 10.2 and 10.3) and designated as treatment C + T;
- changes in temperature (Fig. 10.2) and precipitation (Fig. 10.3) but with no changes in atmospheric CO_2 concentration, treatment T;
- a change in CO_2 alone (Fig. 10.1) but with a constant cycle of climate from the years 1861 to 1890, treatment C.

Net primary productivity

Terrestrial net primary productivity (NPP) increases dramatically (Fig. 10.4) in those treatments with an increase in atmospheric CO_2 concentration (C + T and C) but hardly changes with a constant CO_2 concentration (treatment T). The combined treatment, C + T, stimulates NPP more than the

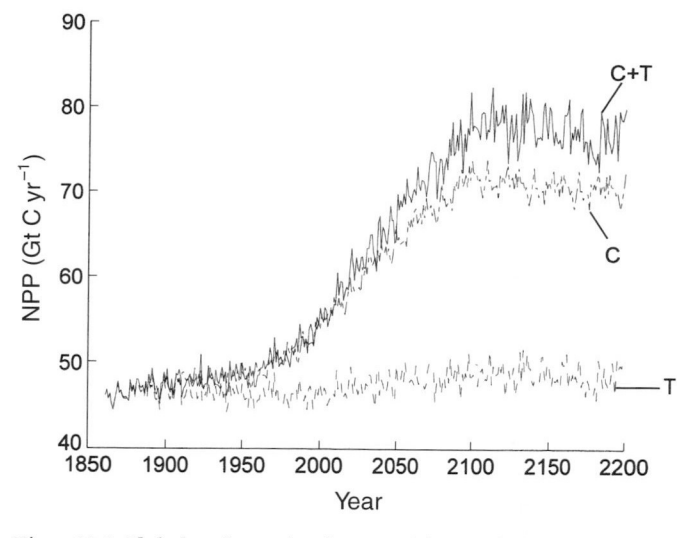

Figure 10.4. Global-scale totals of terrestrial net primary productivity under three treatments: C + T, changes in CO_2 and climate; T, changes in climate; C, changes in CO_2.

CO_2 only treatment, C, indicating an interaction between changes in climate and CO_2. In particular this interaction reflects increases in NPP at high latitudes which are, under the present-day climate, temperature-limited (Chapter 3; Cao & Woodward, 1998).

The increasing stimulation of NPP by CO_2 is also entirely dependent on the continuing rise in CO_2 and as soon as constant concentrations are reached (2100) then NPP stabilises and starts to decline slowly to the year 2200. This declining CO_2 sensitivity of NPP is observed by other dynamic global vegetation models (DGVMs) running with the same treatments (Cramer *et al.*, 2001) and reflects changes in vegetation and declining rates of nitrogen mineralisation.

Net ecosystem production

The global carbon cycle is directly sensitive to net ecosystem productivity (NEP), the net CO_2 flux from vegetation, fire and the underlying soil. NEP is also very sensitive to interannual variations in climate (Cao & Woodward, 1998) but these have been removed by taking 10-year running mean averages of predicted NEP (Fig. 10.5).

When global climate, terrestrial vegetation and soils are at equilibrium NEP will be zero, with carbon sinks, in particular living vegetation, in exact balance with carbon sources such as dead and decaying vegetation and soils.

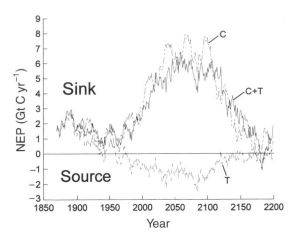

Figure 10.5. 10-year running mean averages of net ecosystem productivity (NEP). Positive values indicate the carbon sink capacity of terrestrial vegetation; negative values indicate source capacity.

Over the period of these experimental simulations neither climate nor vegetation or soils are in equilibrium and so NEP is not zero, unlike other chapters in this book investigating palaeoclimates. Those treatments which include changing atmospheric CO_2 concentration maintain positive NEPs for most of the simulation. Under the treatments C + T and C, NEP increases markedly from the 1980s but saturates at about the year 2050, even though CO_2 continues to increase. This is important when considering the economics and politics of anthropogenic CO_2 emission stabilisation. The terrestrial biosphere will not continue to absorb human-controlled emissions of CO_2 at a constant rate, rather a declining rate with time (Cao & Woodward, 1998), a feature which has not yet been accounted for in some IPCC and related projections (Wigley *et al.* 1996; Wigley, 1997; Schimel, 1998). Over the period 1990 to 2100, the terrestrial biosphere is predicted to sequester *c.* 30% of carbon emissions under treatment C and *c.* 25% under treatment C + T. With climate change alone (treatment T) the terrestrial biosphere is a carbon source adding *c.* 6% to total emissions.

The saturation of NEP by the year 2050 indicates that the continuing increase in vegetation NPP (Fig. 10.4) is now matched by more slowly increasing rates of litter accumulation and decay in the soil. Stabilising climate and CO_2, as from 2100 in these simulations, will not support a continued rise in NPP, but the increasing rate of litter decay is expected to be maintained for longer, therefore NEP should drop rapidly. This response is clearly seen from treatments C + T and T (Fig. 10.5) and by 2180 NEP reaches a new equilibrium value close to zero. There is inertia in the responses of NEP, through slower

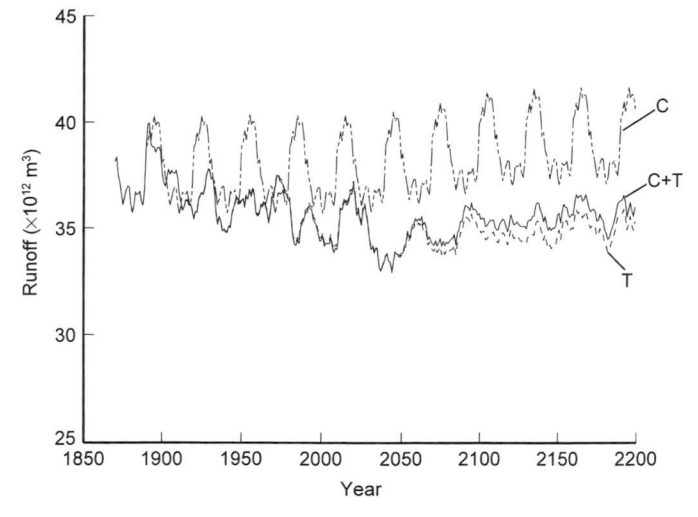

Figure 10.6. Total global runoff, shown as the 10-year running mean average under the three climate treatments.

rates of litter accumulation and decay as already indicated, but also through slow changes in vegetation distribution and structure (Woodward *et al.*, 1998). The response for the climate-only treatment T is more rapid than for the other treatments, reaching the equilibrium zero value after *c.* 30 years. Therefore increasing CO_2 concentrations also increase the inertia of the system, primarily through reductions in the rate and amount of litter decay. Litter quality is not influenced strongly by treatment T, but vegetation is, and responds more rapidly than soil.

Future simulations of NEP cannot be tested, but present-day ranges from *c.* 0.5 to 2.0 Gt C yr^{-1}, are in the same range as estimates of terrestrial NEP extracted from time trends of atmospheric CO_2 and $\delta^{13}C$ (Keeling *et al.*, 1995) and O_2 (Keeling *et al.*, 1996).

Runoff

Terrestrial vegetation influences the runoff of precipitation into streams and pools and, thereby, also influences water supplies for human and other terrestrial animal populations. As a consequence of human use the present-day estimate of runoff is quite well quantified at 36×10^{12} m^3 yr^{-1} (Chahine, 1992). Like NEP, runoff is very responsive to interannual changes in climate and so the 10-year running mean average has been extracted from the simulations (Fig. 10.6). Both treatments C + T and T simulate contemporary runoff values close to the observed, indicating the effective joint operation of the vegetation model and the modified HadCM2 predictions of precipitation for the present day.

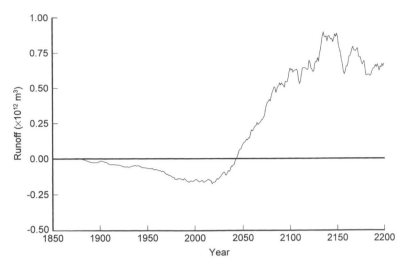

Figure 10.7. Difference in runoff between the climate plus CO_2 change treatment (C + T) and the climate change treatment (T).

The CO_2-only treatment causes a marked periodicity of runoff, because of the 25-year repeat climate cycle (1866–1890) and so is an artefact of the treatment design. The other treatments show gradual declines in runoff to about the year 2075, followed by stabilisation to 2200 (Fig. 10.6). The decline in runoff parallels a reduction in the ratio of runoff to precipitation, indicating that the change is not directly due to climate but to greater water use by vegetation under warmer conditions. Increasing CO_2 and climate change (C + T) do not completely offset this primarily climate-driven response. The saturation of the runoff response at about 2075 also coincides with an increase in precipitation (Fig. 10.3) and a restoration of contemporary runoff values.

The anti-transpirant effect of CO_2 (Chapter 2) is shown by the gradual increase in runoff in treatment C (Fig. 10.6), although at this global scale the effects are small. This effect of CO_2 concentration has been investigated in the full treatment (changes in climate and CO_2, C + T) by subtracting the trend in runoff from the climate-only treatment, T (Fig. 10.7). The effect of CO_2 is small, reaching a maximum increase of 2% of the global runoff for the period of stabilised conditions from 2100 to 2200. This effect of CO_2 becomes noticeable after 2050, the time when global NEP begins to saturate (Fig. 10.5), and indicates that the response is only appreciable when vegetation growth and expansion slows under the new climatic treatments.

Carbon sequestration

Carbon is sequestered from the atmosphere into two pools, soil carbon (Fig. 10.8) and vegetation biomass (Fig. 10.9).

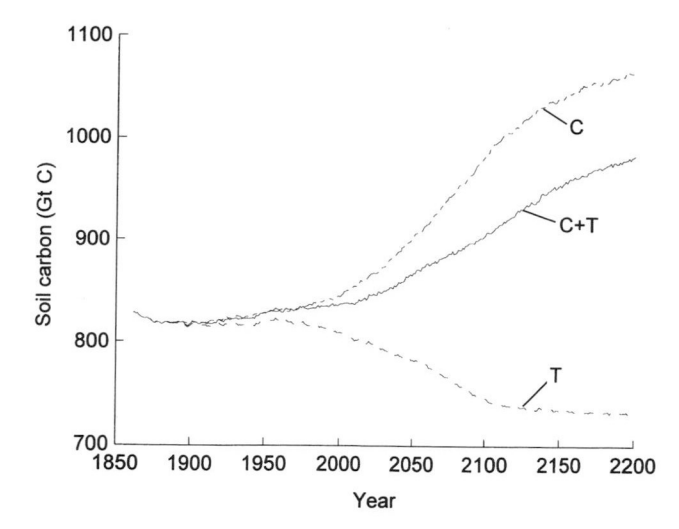

Figure 10.8. Accumulation of soil carbon under the three climate treatments.

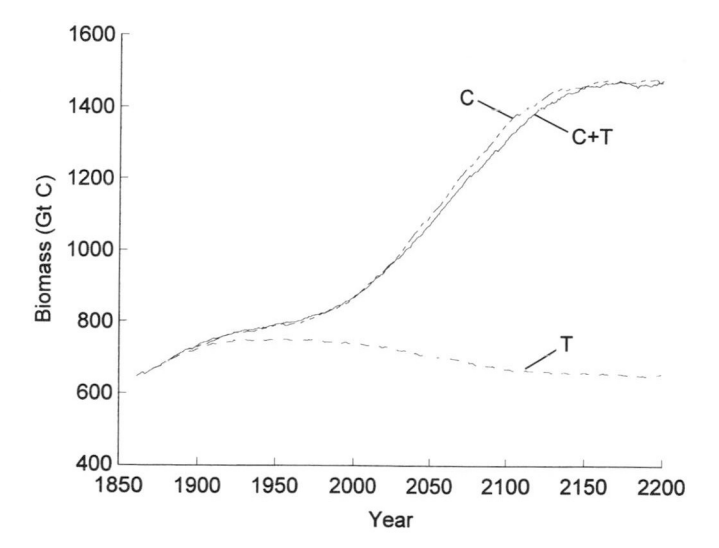

Figure 10.9. Accumulation of vegetation biomass, measured as carbon, under the three treatments.

In the vegetation model (Chapter 4), soil carbon is essentially reactive carbon (McGuire *et al.* 1995), which is accumulated completely during the model spin-up and subsequent climate and CO_2 transients, by the vegetation model. This approach underestimates the likely global total of soil carbon (1500 Gt C; Schlesinger, 1977; Post *et al.*, 1982), itself a number of high uncertainty, because older soils originating from before the last 200 years of the model spin-up period, which are included in the global total, are not included in the model simulations. McGuire *et al* (1995) simulate the contemporary reactive pool of soil carbon to be 707 Gt C, using a different soil and vegetation model, and this is quite close to the current estimate (Fig. 10.8) of 820 Gt C.

The three different treatments exert distinct impacts on soil carbon, from reductions under the climate-only treatment, T, to the largest accumulation under the CO_2-only treatment C. Both of the accumulating treatments (C + T and C) indicate that, even after 100 years of stable conditions, soil carbon continues to accumulate. By contrast, the loss of soil carbon under the climate-only treatment is rapidly terminated after the onset of stable conditions.

Vegetation biomass continues to increase (treatments C + T and C) throughout the period of transient change (Fig. 10.9) but exhibits inertia, less than soil carbon, finally stabilising after *c.* 50 years of uniform conditions. The decline in vegetation carbon under the climate-only treatment rapidly halts after the imposition of the period of stable conditions. The C + T and C treatments have indistinguishable effects on vegetation biomass, indicating that increasing CO_2 concentration is the dominant controller of biomass accumulation.

Changes in the distributions of dominant functional types

Discussions about the effects of future transient climatic changes on vegetation distribution are confined to the full treatment (C + T) of changing climate and CO_2 concentration. Further analyses of the impacts of all treatments, using a suite of different models, can be found elsewhere (Cramer *et al.*, 2001).

In this chapter the predicted dominant functional types are based on biomass, which is slightly different from predictions based on cover used in Chapter 4. Chapter 4 includes predictions of dominant functional types for potential vegetation and averaged for the whole of the 1990s; the first simulation for this chapter is for 1995 (Fig. 10.10). The simulations for 1995 will be compared with those for 2055 (Fig. 10.11) and 2105 (Fig. 10.12), respectively mid-way and at the end of the transient climatic change from the present day.

The changes in functional types between 1995 and 2055 (Figs. 10.10 and 10.11) are primarily due to the responses of the most rapidly responding functional types, the C_3 and C_4 non-arboreal vegetation types. The Sahel region of Africa is predicted to change from C_4 grassland to an area probably consisting of C_3 shrubs and grasses. Small westward extensions of the deciduous forest of the USA into the prairies are also predicted. A much larger change of functional types is simulated from 2055 to 2105 (Figs. 10.11 and 10.12).

bar   c3   c4   ebl   enl   dbl   dnl

Figure 10.10. Dominant plant functional types, based on biomass, for 1995. Key: bar, bare ground; c3, grasses, herbs and shrubs with C$_3$ photosynthetic metabolism; c4, grasses, herbs and shrubs with C$_4$ photosynthetic metabolism; ebl, evergreen broad-leaved trees; enl, evergreen needle-leaved trees; dbl, deciduous broad-leaved trees; dnl, deciduous needle-leaved trees.

Particularly noticeable are the reduction in the area of deciduous needle-leaved forest in Siberia, the eastward extension of the European broad-leaved deciduous forest and an increase in desertification for Australia, India, the Middle East and the western USA.

The inertia of vegetation change is simulated to continue throughout the period of climatic stabilisation (Figs. 10.13 and 10.14). The evergreen needle-leaved forest continues to engulf former areas of tundra and deciduous needle-leaved forest, and the deciduous forests of Europe and North America also continue to spread eastwards into the evergreen needle-leaved forests of Russia and North America, respectively. The northern coastline of the South American broad-leaved forest is predicted to become more arid throughout the whole series of predictions (Figs. 10.10 to 10.14), ending with predominantly C$_4$ vegetation. This feature is a characteristic of the HadCM2 GCM simulation (Betts *et al.* 1997) and may not be shown by other future transient model simulations, either at the Hadley Centre or elsewhere.

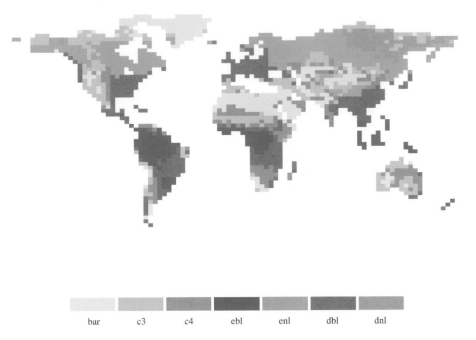

bar	c3	c4	ebl	enl	dbl	dnl

Figure 10.11. Dominant plant functional types, based on biomass, for AD 2055. Key as for Fig. 10.10.

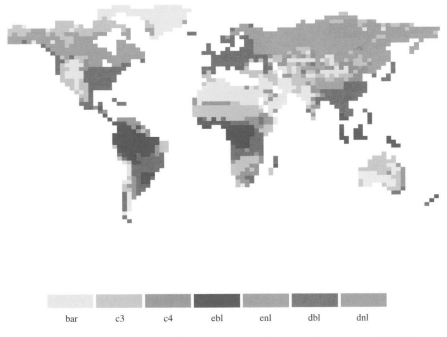

bar	c3	c4	ebl	enl	dbl	dnl

Figure 10.12. Dominant plant functional types, based on biomass, for 2105. Key as for Fig. 10.10.

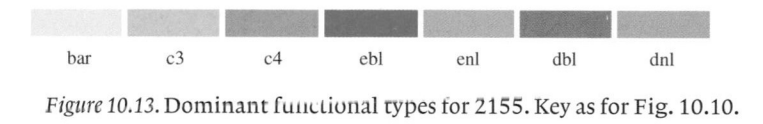

bar   c3   c4   ebl   enl   dbl   dnl

Figure 10.13. Dominant functional types for 2155. Key as for Fig. 10.10.

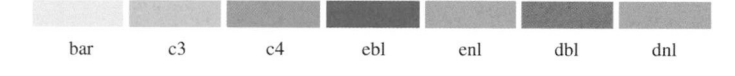

bar   c3   c4   ebl   enl   dbl   dnl

Figure 10.14. Dominant functional types for 2200. Key as for Fig. 10.10.

Conclusions

The problem of GCM inaccuracies, for present-day simulations, has already been discussed (Chapter 4). GCM-specific simulations, perhaps like that for South America, indicate that these simulations should not be taken to be anything other than good estimate simulations for a potential future world. The future change in atmospheric CO_2 concentration is uncertain because it is sensitive to human intervention and, although we understand many of the processes of vegetation responses to climate and atmospheric CO_2 concentrations, we have little knowledge about interactive responses to parallel changes in climate and CO_2, or even about the potential of species or functional types to move around the landscape (Woodward, 1987a). However, there is little doubt (Houghton *et al.* 1996) that the Earth is being subjected to a new human experiment of environmental modification and it is critical that ecologists address future possibilities for the terrestrial biosphere, because only then can the findings, such as those presented in this chapter, be used to formulate new environmental policies.

11

The end view

General issues

This book has achieved what might be considered an idiosyncratic view of terrestrial plant life since its first appearance in the Silurian period, over 400 million years ago. Particular eras have been selected for examination, primarily because GCMs have already been run for these eras and so climate fields are available for driving a vegetation model. However, as indicated in the Introduction, these eras have been selected for good geological and investigative reasons. Over the period of 400 million years many geological pro cesses, which seem too slow for contemporary investigation, have exerted very large influences on the Earth and its terrestrial vegetation. In particular, plate tectonics have changed the geography of the continents and movements of the Earth's crust have created mountains. In combination, these major processes have also caused massive outgassing of greenhouse gases (Marzoli *et al.*, 1999), with attendant changes in climate and vegetation (McElwain *et al.*, 1999). The timescales of these events are familiar in the realm of geology, yet this book has emphasised biology, in which the familiar timescales are much shorter. The integration of these timescales can be most readily achieved by considering the carbon cycle, which is central to the whole theme of this book.

The carbon cycle

A familiar representation of the contemporary carbon cycle (Fig. 11.1, from Houghton *et al.* 1996) indicates the pools of carbon in the atmosphere, vegetation and soil, the oceans and an estimate of fossil fuels. The burning of fossil fuels, and the oceanic and terrestrial pools of carbon, exchange fluxes of carbon with the atmosphere. The ratio of pool size to flux rate indicates the average residence or turnover times for carbon in these reservoirs (Fig. 11.2).

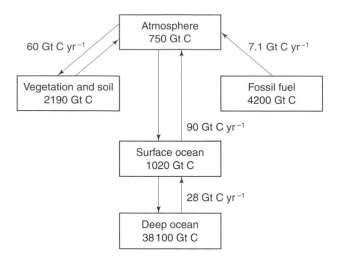

Figure 11.1. Contemporary pool sizes and fluxes from pools to the atmosphere (from Houghton *et al.*, 1996).

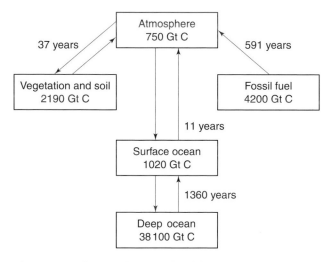

Figure 11.2. Carbon pool sizes and residence times for transfer of carbon to and from the atmosphere.

The longest residence time, of over 1000 years, is in the oceans. The large pool size and long residence time of carbon in the oceans indicate that on a time-scale of thousands of years the oceans will be the primary determinants of these components of the carbon cycle. So very large changes in the activity of the terrestrial biosphere would have rather little effect on either the atmospheric or the oceanic pool sizes, on the timescale of thousands of years.

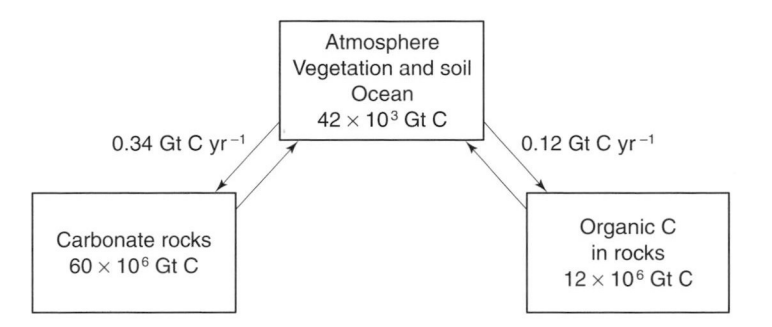

Figure 11.3. Carbon pools and fluxes for long term reservoirs (from Walker, 1994).

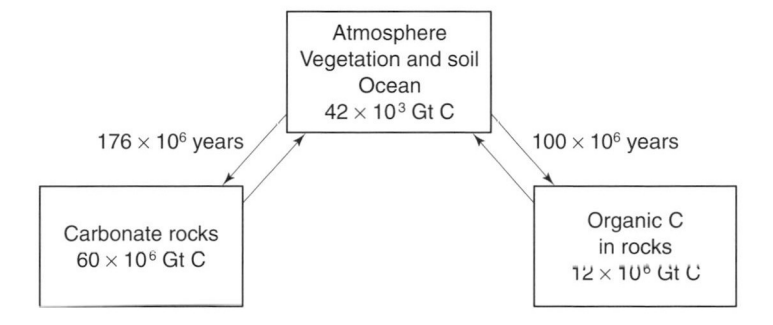

Figure 11.4. Residence times of carbon in the long-term carbon pools.

On short timescales, in the order of decades, net carbon fixation by the terrestrial biosphere and by oceanic photosynthesis, and the solution of CO_2 in seawater, will exert the dominant effects on the atmospheric CO_2 concentration. The estimated reserves of fossil fuels are much greater than the amount of carbon stored in either vegetation and soil or the atmosphere, and so there is considerable potential for humans to influence atmospheric CO_2 concentrations over a long time period, at least in human terms.

On the million-year timescales of this book it becomes important to consider additional pools of carbon which might affect the atmosphere and, in turn, influence the climate. Figure 11.3 shows the addition of two very large carbon pools: carbonate rocks, and organic carbon (coal, hydrocarbons and kerogen) in sedimentary rocks (Walker, 1994). The fluxes of carbon from these large reservoirs are very small compared with the active photosynthetic fluxes (Fig. 11.1). However, the very large residence times of these pools (Fig. 11.4) indicate that on the timescale of millions of years these pools and fluxes dominate the carbon cycle and the atmospheric pool of carbon.

The very slow fluxes which drive the exchange of carbon from rocks to the

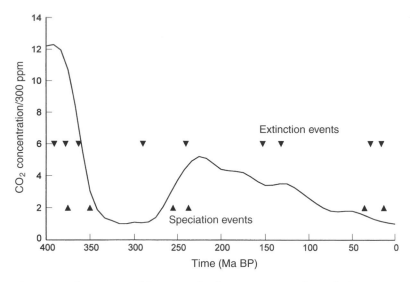

Figure 11.5. Time course of the atmospheric CO_2 concentration, relative to 300 ppm and over the last 400 million years (from Berner, 1998). The timing of significant plant species extinction events (▼) and speciation events (▲) are from Niklas (1997).

atmosphere on the timescale of millions of years result from three major processes (Berner, 1998):

1. The weathering of calcium and magnesium silicates and carbonates, whereby atmospheric CO_2 is converted to bicarbonate at the Earth's surface and then precipitated as carbonate.
2. The weathering of ancient and burial of contemporary organic matter.
3. The thermal breakdown of carbonate minerals and organic matter by diagenesis, metamorphism and magmatism.

Terrestrial vegetation plays a part in some of these slow processes. Experimental studies indicate the potential for two- to five-fold increases in the rate of weathering of calcium and magnesium moving from unvegetated to vegetated areas (Moulton & Berner, 1998). The secretion of acids from plant roots exerts a large influence on the weatherability and weathering rates of rocks (Volk, 1987). An increase in these capacities would tend to reduce the rate at which CO_2 increased in the atmosphere. The burial of dead plant organic matter was a clear feature of the Carboniferous and Permian periods (330 to 260 Ma) and this burial would, again, have exerted a negative feedback on the atmospheric CO_2 concentration.

The simulated time course of atmospheric CO_2 concentration over the last 400 million years (Berner, 1998) indicates significant deviations from the contemporary situation (a ratio of 1.2 on Fig. 11.5) to >12 in the Devonian period (400 Ma). The most marked dynamic is the rapid fall of the atmospheric CO_2 concentration in the Devonian, in which the rapidly diversifying terrestrial vegetation (Beerling *et al.*, 2001) probably played a major role in increasing the weatherability, but not necessarily the weathering rate (Berner, 1998), of silicate rocks. The increasing stature of vegetation, with an associated requirement for greater structural strength, also led to large increases in the burial of woody plant material which was, at least initially, probably very resistant to fungal breakdown (Robinson, 1990a).

It appears that on these long timescales, terrestrial vegetation exerts a primarily negative effect on atmospheric CO_2 concentration. The most rapid change occurred about 325 million years ago. However, a long-term downward trend to the present was initiated from *c.* 225 Ma and has only been reversed, currently, through the burning of fossil fuels. The positive effects, which will cause atmospheric CO_2 to rise, are primarily geochemical, e.g. volcanism, plate tectonics and climate change. The climatic effects which would reduce the negative feedback of vegetation on atmospheric CO_2 are low temperatures, which would reduce rates of weathering and the amount of woody material to be buried; and also extremely low temperatures, as experienced in ice ages, which will reduce the vegetated area of the Earth's surface, thus the area of weathering. However, long-term ice ages would be required to counter long-term geochemical effects.

Plant species

Traditional palaeobotany is concerned with the timing and location of fossil plant material and the interpretation of this material, in terms of evolution and ecology. This approach has not been taken here, where the emphasis has been on vegetation and vegetation processes. The emphasis on vegetation follows from the emphasis on the carbon cycle, the major life process. Whereas fossil remains are scattered and the record incomplete, the simulated fields of vegetation and vegetation processes are complete, but dependent on the climatic fields derived from GCMs. The palaeo-GCMs depend on initial climatic constraints, which are in turn defined by relatively sparse, but usually marine, fossils. It must be expected, therefore, that GCMs are, at best, limited in their accuracy to simulate specific climates. GCM simulations aim to define an average climate through the whole of a selected geological era, perhaps as much as a million years or greater. A major feature of this approach using simulations of a vegetation model is that the outcomes of the modelling exercise are objective, in that there has been no subjective interpretation of particular distributions and no adjustment of the vegetation model to run in individual cases.

The discussion of residence times in the carbon cycle indicates, for all of the geological eras so far investigated (Carboniferous to Eocene), that the short-term carbon cycle (Figs. 11.1 and 11.2) is both at equilibrium and therefore also not directly significant in controlling the atmospheric CO_2 concentration. An exception to the considerations of equilibrium situations concerns extinction events, as at the K/T boundary. In geological terms, and particularly in terms of the long-term carbon cycle (Fig. 11.3), the pools and fluxes were not at equilibrium. The specific interest in these instances is how the carbon cycle responded to large changes in carbon inputs to the atmosphere (Beerling, 2000a). Similarly, because vegetation change is also rapid, compared with the time frames of the geological eras, short-term feedbacks of an equilibrium distribution of vegetation on climate are negligible. The simulations therefore indicate the best that can be determined, based on the contemporary understanding of plant processes, of the influences of these palaeo-climates on vegetation processes. It should not be expected that these simulations will relate well to the occurrences of particular species of fossils, with their own peculiar ecologies and histories. However the simulations can relate, for example, the end products of basic vegetation processes, such as carbon burial, to the distribution of coals. Even this correlation is not certain, as in certain situations the presence of vegetation minimises the anaerobic preservation of organic carbon in the soil, and so significant coal deposits may be unlikely (Beerling, 2000b).

Figure 11.5 indicates that major plant extinction and speciation events are not uniformly distributed through time. The steep decline in atmospheric CO_2, and associated changes in climate during the Devonian, were associated with both major extinction and speciation events. A major feature of the whole of the Phanerozoic is the evolution of the gymnosperms at about 350 million years ago and the extensive radiation of angiosperms about 40 Ma. The sporadic extinction events between 240 and 130 Ma were characterised, primarily, by pteridophyte extinctions, while gymnosperms were the major losses over the last 30 Ma.

Further investigation of the timing of the evolution of a wide range of plant groups, notably horsetails, ferns, pteridosperms, conifers and angiosperms, indicates that they evolved at times when atmospheric CO_2 concentration was falling, or low (Woodward, 1998). Such a situation would have led to low water-use efficiencies, because of a high potential for water loss but associated with a low potential for carbon gain. This would have led to a highly selective situation favouring new physiological characteristics for enduring the environmental constraints (Raven, 1993).

These considerations of plant evolution through time indicate a quite intimate link with estimates of the atmospheric CO_2 concentration and the operation of the global carbon cycle. Overall it seems that, on these long timescales, vegetation as a whole acts as a negative feedback on atmospheric CO_2 concentration, through carbon burial and impacts on the weatherability and weathering rates of rocks. It is also noticeable that, in spite of contemporary human impacts, species richness is currently at its highest for the whole of the Phanerozoic. This represents the current status of a remarkable period of terrestrial evolution. It is interesting to note, again, that this increase in richness appears to be related to a continuing decline in atmospheric CO_2 (Fig. 11.5). Assuming that the geological-scale reconstructions and simulations of atmospheric CO_2 concentration by Berner (1998) are about correct, then the timescale of this decline suggests a continually improving capacity by plant species to influence silicate rock weatherability and weathering rate and also carbon burial. On average (Niklas, 1997) a new plant species appears about every 0.38 million years and survives, again on average, for about 3.5 Ma. This timescale of evolution is similar to the estimated turnover times of vegetation and soil carbon to carbonate rocks (0.12 Ma, based on the relative contributions of the atmospheric, vegetation plus soil and oceanic carbon pools to the flux shown on Figure 11.3) and to organic carbon in sedimentary rocks (0.35 million years). This should follow if changes in atmospheric CO_2 and related changes in climate are influenced by the slow capture of plant carbon into rock reservoirs, and if evolution leads to species with an increased capacity to carry through this process.

Contemporary and future timescales

As indicated earlier, ecologists concerned with the contemporary state are primarily motivated to investigate processes on short timescales, from years to nearly decades. These timescales (Fig. 11.2) do not integrate well with geological timescales. As a consequence there is often limited contact between contemporary ecologists and palaeoecologists. The aim in writing this book has been to emphasise the relatively seamless connection between the carbon cycles at all timescales and that there is no artificial divide between contemporary and historical understanding. Slow rates of weathering influence atmospheric CO_2 on timescales of millions of years, rates of terrestrial carbon burial and capture into rocks occur on a slightly faster timescale of 0.1–0.4 Ma, oceans influence the carbon cycle on a 1000–2000 year timescale, and vegetation and soil on $c.$ 10–40 year timescale. Of major interest for the contemporary and future (next century) cycle is the degree of feedback on vegetation processes resulting from increases in atmospheric CO_2 concentration. Such a response has been simulated (Chapter 9) but it is a moderately short-term effect, saturating within about 50 years. This is extremely short term for either geological or oceanic timescales but it is central when devising political and economic strategies for mitigating the effects of fossil fuel emissions. Clearly in the long term (1000 years and greater) this effect will just be a small 'blip' for a long-lived biosphere and atmosphere, but it is currently a crucial issue because it addresses human management of the biosphere and the whole Earth system – our current wardenship of the Earth. Current plans fail to consider the impacts of natural vegetation on the carbon cycle, yet the fluxes involved can be 25% or more of fossil fuel emissions.

Conclusions

This book outlines a simulation approach to understanding how vegetation has responded to the average climate of different geological eras. Such an approach is possible because the basic processes involved – photosynthesis, respiration, transpiration, nutrient dynamics – are universal now and, all the evidence indicates, in the past. The approach avoids the direct use of identifiable species as these would be too short-lived for the timescale of the Phanerozoic and too little would be known about their responses to unusual environmental conditions. However, measurements on fossils of stable isotopes of carbon and stomatal density have proved to be important and useful constraints in testing the applicability of results obtained by the vegetation simulations.

References

Adams, J.M. & Faure, H. 1998. A new estimate of changing carbon storage on the land since the last glacial maximum, based on global land ecosystem reconstructions. *Global and Planetary Change*, **16–17**, 3–24.

Adams, J.M., Faure, H., Faure-Denard, L., McGlade, J.M. & Woodward, F.I. 1990. Increases in terrestrial carbon storage from the last glacial maximum to the present. *Nature*, **348**, 711–714.

Algeo, T.J. & Scheckler, S.E. 1998. Terrestrial–marine teleconnections in the Devonian links between the evolution of lands, weathering processes, and marine anoxic events. *Philosophical Transactions of the Royal Society*, **B353**, 113–130.

Alvarez, L.W., Alvarez, W., Azaro, F. & Michel, H.V. 1980. Extraterrestrial cause for the Cretaceous–Tertiary extinction. *Science*, **208**, 1095–1108.

Alvin, K.L., Fraser, C.J. & Spicer, R.A. 1981. Anatomy and palaeoecology of *Pseudofrenelopsis*. *Palaeontology*, **24**, 169–176.

Andreasson, F.P. & Schmitz, B. 1996. Winter and summer temperatures of the early middle Eocene of France from *Turritella* $\delta^{18}O$ profiles. *Geology*, **24**, 1067–1070.

Andreasson, F.P. & Schmitz, B. 1998. Tropical Atlantic seasonal dynamics in the early middle Eocene from stable oxygen and carbon isotope profiles of mollusk shells. *Paleoceanography*, **13**, 183–192.

Antoine, D., Andre, J-M. & Morel, A. 1996. Ocean primary production. 2. Estimation at the global scale from satellite (coastal zone color scanner) chlorophyll. *Global Biogeochemical Cycles*, **10**, 57–69.

Aphalo, P.J. & Jarvis, P.G. 1993. An analysis of Ball's empirical model of stomatal conductance. *Annals of Botany*, **72**, 321–327.

Archibald, J.D. 1996. *Dinosaur extinction and the end of an era. What the fossils say*. Columbia Press, New York.

Archibold, O.W. 1995. *Ecology of world vegetation*. Chapman & Hall, London.

Attendorn, H.G. & Bowen, R.N.C. 1997. *Radioactive and stable isotope geology*. Chapman & Hall, London.

Badger, M.R. & Andrews, T.J. 1987. Co-evolution of rubisco and CO_2 concentrating mechanisms. In *Progress in Photosynthesis Research*, **3**, ed. J. Biggins, pp. 601–609. Martinus Nijhoff, Dordrecht.

Ball, J.T., Woodrow, I.E. & Berry, J.A. 1987. A model predicting stomatal conductance and its contribution to the control of photosynthesis under different environmental conditions. In *Progress in Photosynthesis Research*, ed. I. Biggins, pp. 221–224. Proceedings of the VIIth International Congress on Photosynthesis, Vol. IV. Matrinus Nijhoff, Dordrecht.

Banks, H. P. 1981. Time of appearance of some plant biocharacters during Siluro-Devonian time. *Canadian Journal of Botany*, **59**, 1292–1296.

Barnola, J. M., Raynaud, D., Korotkevich, Y. S. & Lorius, C. 1987. Vostok ice core provides 160,000-year record of atmospheric CO_2. *Nature*, **329**, 408–414.

Barron, E. J. 1982. Cretaceous climate: a comparison of atmospheric simulations with the geological data. *Palaeogeography, Palaeoclimatology, Palaeoecology*, **40**, 103–133.

Barron, E. J. 1983. A warm, equable Cretaceous: the nature of the problem. *Earth Science Reviews*, **19**, 305–338.

Barron, E. J. 1987. Eocene equator-to-pole surface ocean temperatures: a significant climate problem? *Paleoceanography*, **2**, 729–739.

Barron, E. J. 1994. Chill over the Cretaceous. *Nature*, **370**, 415.

Barron, E. J., Fawcett, P. J., Peterson, W. H., Pollard, D. & Thompson, S. L. 1995. A 'simulation' of mid-Cretaceous climate. *Paleoceanography*, **10**, 953–962.

Barron, E. J., Fawcett, P. J., Pollard, D. & Thompson, D. 1993. Model simulations of Cretaceous climates: the role of geography and carbon dioxide. *Philosophical Transactions of the Royal Society*, **B341**, 307–316.

Barron, E. J. & Peterson, W. H. 1990. Mid-Cretaceous ocean circulation: results from model sensitivity studies. *Paleoceanography*, **5**, 319–337.

Barron, E. J., Peterson, W. H., Pollard, D. & Thompson, S. L. 1993. Past climate and the role of ocean heat transport: model simulations for the Cretaceous. *Paleoceanography*, **8**, 785–798.

Barron, E. J. & Washington, W. M. 1985. Warm Cretaceous climates: high atmospheric CO_2 as a plausible mechanism. In *The carbon cycle and atmospheric CO_2: natural variations Archean to present*, ed. E. T. Sundquist & W. S. Broecker. *Geophysical Monographs Series*, 546–553, American Geophysical Union, Washington, DC.

Bartlein, P. J., Anderson, K. H., Anderson, P. M. *et al.* 1998. Palaeoclimate simulations for North America over the past 21,000 years: features of the simulated climate and comparisons with palaeoenvironmental data. *Quaternary Science Reviews*, **17**, 549–585.

Beerling, D. J. 1993. Changes in the stomatal density of *Betula nana* leaves in response to increases in the atmospheric carbon dioxide concentration since the late-glacial. *Special Papers in Palaeontology*, **49**, 181–187.

Beerling, D. J. 1994. Modelling palaeophotosynthesis: late Cretaceous to present. *Philosophical Transactions of the Royal Society*, **B346**, 421–432.

Beerling, D. J. 1997. The net primary productivity and water use of forests in the geological past. *Advances in Botanical Research*, **26**, 193–227.

Beerling, D. J. 1998. The future as the key to the past for palaeobotany? *Trends in Ecology and Evolution*, **13**, 311–316.

Beerling, D. J. 1999a. Long-term responses of boreal vegetation to global change: an experimental and modelling investigation. *Global Change Biology*, **5**, 55–74.

Beerling, D. J. 1999b. Atmospheric carbon dioxide, past climates and the plant fossil record. *Botanical Journal of Scotland*, **51**, 49–68.

Beerling, D. J. 1999c. New estimates of carbon transfer to terrestrial ecosystems between the last glacial maximum and the Holocene. *Terra Nova*, **11**, 162–167.

Beerling, D. J. 1999d. The influence of vegetation activity on the Dole effect and its implications for changes in biospheric productivity in the mid-Holocene. *Proceedings of the Royal Society*, **B266**, 627–632.

Beerling, D. J. 1999e. Quantitative estimates of changes in marine and terrestrial primary productivity over the past 300 million years. *Proceedings of the Royal Society*, **B266**, 1821–1827.

Beerling, D. J. 2000a. Increased terrestrial carbon storage across the Paleocene–Eocene boundary. *Paleogeography, Paleoclimatology, Paleoecology*, **161**, 395–405.

Beerling, D. J. 2000b. The influence of vegetation cover on soil organic matter preservation in Antarctica during the Mesozoic. *Geophysical Research Letters*, **27**, 253–256.

Beerling, D. J. & Berner, R. A. 2000. Impact of a Permo-Carboniferous high O_2 event on the terrestrial carbon cycle. *Proceedings of the National Academy of Sciences, USA*, **97**, 12428–12432.

Beerling, D. J. & Chaloner, W. G. 1993. Evolutionary responses of stomatal density to global CO_2 change. *Biological Journal of the Linnean Society*, **48**, 343–353.

Beerling, D. J., Chaloner, W. G., Huntley, B., Pearson, A. & Tooley, M. J. 1993. Stomatal density responds to the glacial cycle of environmental change. *Proceedings of the Royal Society*, **B251**, 133–138.

Beerling, D. J., Heath, J., Woodward, F. I. & Mansfield, T. A. 1996. Drought-CO_2 interactions in trees: observations and mechanisms. *New Phytologist*, **134**, 235–242.

Beerling, D. J., Lomax, B. H., Upchurch, G. R., Nichols, D. J., Pillmore, C. L., Handley, L. L. & Scrimgeour, C. M. 2001. Coordinated isotopic and palaeobotanical evidence for the recovery of terrestrial ecosystems ahead of marine primary production following a biotic crisis at the Cretaceous–Tertiary boundary. *Journal of the Geological Society of London* (in press).

Beerling, D. J., Osborne, C. P. & Chaloner, W. G. 2001. Evolution of leaf-form in land plants linked to atmospheric CO_2 decline in the Late Palaeozoic era. *Nature*, **410**, 352–354.

Beerling, D. J. & Quick, W. P. 1995. A new technique for estimating rates of carboxylation and electron transport in leaves of C_3 plants for use in dynamic global vegetation models. *Global Change Biology*, **1**, 289–294.

Beerling, D. J., Terry, A. C., Hopwood, C. & Osborne, C. P. 2001. Feeling the cold: atmospheric CO_2 enrichment and the frost sensitivity of terrestrial plant foliage. *Palaeogeography, Palaeoclimatology, Palaeoecology* (in press).

Beerling, D. J. & Woodward, F. I. 1993. Ecophysiological responses of plants to global environmental change since the last glacial maximum. *New Phytologist*, **125**, 641–648.

Beerling, D. J. & Woodward, F. I. 1995. Leaf stable carbon isotope composition records increased water use efficiency of C_3 plants in response to atmospheric CO_2 enrichment. *Functional Ecology*, **9**, 394–401.

Beerling, D. J. & Woodward, F. I. 1996. Palaeo-ecophysiological perspectives on plant responses to global change. *Trends in Ecology and Evolution*, **11**, 20–23.

Beerling, D. J. & Woodward, F. I. 1997. Changes in land plant function over the Phanerozoic: reconstructions based on the fossil record. *Botanical Journal of the Linnean Society*, **124**, 137–153.

Beerling, D.J. & Woodward, F.I. 1998. Modelling changes in land plant function over the Phanerozoic. In *Stable isotopes and the integration of biological, ecological and geochemical processes*, ed. H. Griffiths, pp. 347–361. Bios, Oxford.

Beerling, D.J., Woodward, F.I., Lomas, M. & Jenkins, A.J. 1997. Testing the responses of a dynamic global vegetation model to environmental change: a comparison of observations and predictions. *Global Ecology and Biogeography Letters*, **6**, 439–450.

Beerling, D.J, Woodward, F.I., Lomas, M.R., Wills, M.A., Quick, W.P. & Valdes, P.J. 1998. The influence of Carboniferous palaeoatmospheres on plant function: an experimental and modelling assessment. *Philosophical Transactions of the Royal Society*, **B353**, 131–140.

Beerling, D.J., Woodward, F.I. & Valdes, P.J. 1999. Global terrestrial productivity in the mid-Cretaceous (100 Ma): model simulations and data. *Geological Society of America Special Publication*, **323**, 385–390.

Behrehenfeld, M.J. & Falkowski, P.G. 1997. Photosynthetic rates derived from satellite-based chlorophyll concentrations. *Limnology and Oceanography*, **42**, 1–20.

Bender, M., Labeyrie, L.D., Raynaud, D. & Lorius, C. 1985. Isotopic composition of atmospheric O_2 in ice linked with deglaciation and global primary productivity. *Nature*, **318**, 349–353.

Bender, M., Sowers, T. & Labeyrie, L. 1994. The Dole effect and its variations during the last 130,000 years as measured in the Vostok ice core. *Global Biogeochemical Cycles*, **8**, 363–376.

Berger, A.L. 1976. Obliquity and precession for the last 5,000,000 years. *Astronomy and Astrophysics*, **51**, 127–135.

Berger, A.L. 1978. Long-term variations of daily insolation and Quaternary climatic changes. *Journal of Atmospheric Sciences*, **35**, 2362–2367.

Berger, A.L., Gallee, H., Fichefet, T., Marsiat, I. & Tricot, C. 1990. Testing the astronomical theory with a coupled climate-ice-sheets model. *Global and Planetary Change*, **3**, 113–124.

Berner, R.A. 1987. Models for carbon and sulfur cycles and atmospheric oxygen: application to Paleozoic geologic history. *American Journal of Science*, **287**, 177–196.

Berner, R.A. 1993. Paleozoic atmospheric CO_2: importance of solar radiation and plant evolution. *Science*, **261**, 68–70.

Berner, R.A. 1994. Geocarb II: a revised model of atmospheric CO_2 over Phanerozoic time. *American Journal of Science*, **294**, 56–91.

Berner, R.A. 1997. The rise of land plants and their effect on weathering and atmospheric CO_2. *Science*, **276**, 544–546.

Berner, R.A. 1998. The carbon cycle and CO_2 over Phanerozoic time: the role of land plants. *Philosophical Transactions of the Royal Society*, **B353**, 75–82.

Berner, R.A. & Canfield 1989. A new model for atmospheric oxygen over Phanerozoic time. *American Journal of Science*, **289**, 333–361.

Berry, J.A. 1992. Biosphere, atmosphere, ocean interactions: a plant physiologist's perspective. In *Primary productivity and biogeochemical cycles in the sea*, ed. P.G. Falkowski & A.D. Woodhead, pp. 441–454. Plenum, New York.

Betts, A.K., Ball, J.H. & Beljaars, A.C.M. 1993. Comparison between the land surface response of the ECMWF model and the FIFE-1987 data. *Quarterly Journal of the Royal Meteorological Society*, **119**, 975–1001.

Betts, R.A., Cox, P.M., Lee, S.E. & Woodward, F.I. 1997. Contrasting physiological and structural vegetation feedbacks in climate change simulations. *Nature*, **387**, 796–799.

Bird, M.I., Lloyd, J. & Farquhar, G.D. 1994. Terrestrial carbon storage at the LGM. *Nature*, **371**, 566.

Bird, M.I., Lloyd, J. & Farquhar, G.D. 1996. Terrestrial carbon storage from the last glacial maximum to the present. *Chemosphere*, **33**, 1675–1685.

Bird, M.I. & Pousai, P. 1997. Variations of $\delta^{13}C$ in the surface soil organic carbon pool. *Global Biogeochemical Cycles*, **11**, 313–322.

Bocherens, H., Friis, E.M., Mariotti, A. & Pedersen, K.R. 1994. Carbon isotopic abundances in Mesozoic and Cenozoic fossil plants: palaeoecological implications. *Lethaia*, **26**, 347–358.

Boersma, A. & Shackleton, N.J. 1981. Oxygen and carbon isotope variations and planktonic foraminifera depth habitats, late Cretaceous to Paleocene, Central Pacific. *Initial Reports of the Deep Sea Drilling Project*, **62**, 513–526.

Bonan, G.B., Pollard, D. & Thompson, S.I. 1992. Effects of boreal forest vegetation on global climate. *Nature*, **359**, 716–718.

Bottinga, Y. & Craig, H. 1969 Oxygen isotope fractionation between CO_2 and water, and the isotopic composition of marine atmospheric CO_2. *Earth and Planetary Science Letters*, **5**, 285–295.

Bousquet, J., Straus, S.H., Doerksen, A.H. & Price, R.A. 1992. Extensive variation in evolutionary rate of *rbc*L gene sequences among seed plants. *Proceedings of the National Academy of Sciences, USA*, **89**, 7844–7848.

Bowes, G. 1993. Facing the inevitable: plants and increasing atmospheric CO_2. *Annual Review of Plant Physiology and Plant Molecular Biology*, **44**, 309–332.

Bowes, G. 1996. Photosynthetic responses to changing atmospheric carbon dioxide concentration. In *Photosynthesis and the environment*, ed. N.R. Baker, pp. 387–407. Kluwer Academic, The Netherlands.

Box, E.O. 1996. Plant functional types and climate at the global scale. *Journal of Vegetation Science*, **7**, 309–320.

Brankovic, C. & Van Maanen, J. 1985. *The ECMWF Climate System*. ECMWF research memorandum, No. 109, 51 pp. ECMWF Operations Department, Shinfield Park, Reading, Berks., RGE 9AX, UK.

Brinkhuis, H., Bujak, J.P., Smit, J., Versteegh, G.J.M. & Visscher, H. 1998. Dinoflagellate-based sea surface temperature reconstructions across the Cretaceous–Tertiary boundary. *Palaeogeography, Palaeoclimatology, Palaeoecology*, **141**, 67–83.

Broecker, W.S. 1989. The salinity contrast between the Atlantic and Pacific Oceans during glacial time. *Paleoceanography*, **4**, 207–212.

Broecker, W.S. 1997. Thermohaline circulation, the achilles heel of our climate system: will man-made CO_2 upset the current balance? *Science*, **278**, 1582–1588.

Broecker, W.S. & Peng, T.H. 1982. *Tracers in the sea*. Eldigo, New York.

Broecker, W.S. & Peng, T.H. 1993. What caused the glacial-to-interglacial CO_2 change? In *The global carbon cycle*, ed. M. Heimann, pp. 95–115. NATO ASI Series, Vol. 15.

Budyko, M.I., Ronov, A.B. & Yanshin, A.L. 1987. *History of the Earth's atmosphere*. Springer-Verlag, New York.

Bustin, R.M. & Dunlop, R.L. 1992. Sedimentologic factors affecting mining, quality, and geometry of coal seams of the late Jurassic–early Cretaceous Mist Mountain Formation, southern Canadian Rocky Mountains. *Geological Society of America Special Paper*, **267**, 117–138.

Caldeira, K. & Kasting, J. F. 1992. The life-span of the biosphere revisited. *Nature*, **360**, 721–723.

Caldeira, K. & Rampino, M. R. 1990. Carbon dioxide emissions from Deccan volcanism and a K/T boundary greenhouse effect. *Geophysical Research Letters*, **17**, 1299–1302.

Campbell, G. S. 1977. *An introduction to environmental physics*. Springer-Verlag, New York.

Campbell, W. J., Allen, L. H. & Bowes, G. 1990. Response of soybean canopy photosynthesis to CO_2 concentration, light and temperature. *Journal of Experimental Botany*, **41**, 427–433.

Cannell, M. G. R. 1982. *World forest biomass and primary production data*. Academic Press, New York.

Cao, M. & Woodward, F. I. 1998. Dynamic responses of terrestrial ecosystem carbon cycling to global climate change. *Nature*, **393**, 249–252.

Cerling, T. E., Ehleringer, J. R. & Harris, J. M. 1998. Carbon dioxide starvation, the development of C4 ecosystems, and mammalian evolution. *Philosophical Transactions of the Royal Society*, **B353**, 159–171.

Ceulemans, R., Shao, B. Y., Jiang, X. N. & Kalina, J. 1996. First- and second-year aboveground growth and productivity of two *Populus* hybrids grown at ambient and elevated CO_2. *Tree Physiology*, **16**, 61–68.

Chahine, M. T. 1992. The hydrological cycle and its influence on climate. *Nature*, **359**, 373–380.

Chaloner, W. G. 1989. Fossil charcoal as an indicator of palaeoatmospheric oxygen level. *Journal of the Geological Society*, **146**, 171–174.

Chaloner, W. G. 1998. Book review: Past and future rapid environmental changes: the spatial and evolutionary responses of terrestrial biota, ed. B. Huntley *et al. Journal of Ecology*, **86**, 896–897.

Chaloner, W. G. & Creber, G. T. 1989. The phenomenon of forest in Antarctica: a review. In *Origins and evolution of the Antarctic Biota*, ed. A. J. Crame, pp. 85–89. Special Publication No. 47, Geological Society of London.

Chaloner, W. G. & Lacey, W. S. 1973. The distribution of late Palaeozoic floras. *Special Papers in Palaeontology*, **12**, 271–289.

Chaloner, W. G. & Sheerin, A. 1979. Devonian macrofloras. In *The Devonian System*, pp. 145–161. Special Papers in Palaeontology 23. Palaeontological Association, London.

Chen, J. L., Reynolds, J. F., Harley, P. C. & Tenhunen, J. D. 1993. Co-ordination theory of leaf nitrogen distribution in a canopy. *Oecologia*, **93**, 63–69.

Chen, S. H., Moore, B. D. & Seeman, J. R. 1998. Effects of short- and long-term elevated CO_2 on the expression of ribulose-1,5-bisphosphate carboxylase/oxygenase genes and carbohydrate accumulation in leaves of *Arabidopsis thaliana* (L.) Heynh. *Plant Physiology*, **116**, 715–723.

Chen, T. H. and 42 other authors 1997. Cabauw experimental results from the project of intercomparison of land-surface schemes. *Journal of Climate*, **10**, 1194–1215.

Ciais, P., Denning, A. S, Tans, P. P. *et al*. 1997. A three-dimensional synthesis study of $\delta^{18}O$ in atmospheric CO_2. I. Surface fluxes. *Journal of Geophysical Research*, **102**, 5857–5872.

Ciais, P. & Meijer, H.A.J. 1998. The $^{18}O/^{16}O$ isotope ratio of atmospheric CO_2 and its role in global carbon cycle research. In *Stable isotopes: integration of biological, ecological and geochemical processes*, ed. H. Griffiths, pp. 409–431. Bios, Oxford.

Cichan, M.A. 1986. Conductance of the woods of selected Carboniferous plants. *Paleobiology*, **12**, 302–310.

Cipollini, M.I., Drake, B.G. & Whigman, D. 1993. Effects of elevated CO_2 on growth and carbon/nutrient balance in the deciduous woody shrub *Lindera benzoin* (L.) Blume (Lauraceae). *Oecologia*, **96**, 339–346.

CLIMAP 1976. The surface of the ice age Earth. *Science*, **191**, 1131–1136.

Cobb, J.C. & Cecil, C.B. (eds.) 1993. *Modern and ancient coal-forming environments*. Geological Society of America Special Paper, 286, Boulder, Colorado.

COHMAP members 1988. Climatic changes of the last 18,000 years: observations and model simulations. *Science*, **241**, 1043–1052.

Cole, D.R. & Monger, H.C. 1994. Influence of atmospheric CO_2 on the decline of C_4 plants during the last glaciation. *Nature*, **368**, 533–536.

Colinvaux, P.A., De Oliveira, P.E., Moreno, J.E., Miller, M.C. & Bush, M.B. 1996. A long pollen record from lowland Amazonia: forest and cooling in glacial times. *Science*, **274**, 85–88.

Collatz, G.J., Berry, J.A. & Clark, J.S. 1998. Effects of climate and atmospheric CO_2 partial pressure on the global distribution of C_4 grasses: present, past and future. *Oecologia*, **114**, 441–454.

Collatz, G.J., Ribas-Carbo, M. & Berry, J.A. 1992. Coupled photosynthesis–stomatal conductance model for leaves of C4 plants. *Australian Journal of Plant Physiology*, **19**, 519–538.

Cope, M.J. & Chaloner, W.G. 1980. Fossil charcoal as evidence of past atmospheric composition. *Nature*, **283**, 647–649.

Courtillot, V., Feraud, G., Maluski, H., Vandamme, D., Moreau, M.G. & Besse, J. 1988. Deccan flood basalts and the Cretaceous/Tertiary boundary. *Nature*, **333**, 843–846.

Covey, C., Sloan, L.C. & Hoffert, M.I. 1996. Paleoclimate data constraints on climate sensitivity: the paleocalibration method. *Climatic Change*, **32**, 165–184.

Covey, C., Thompson, S.L., Weissman, P.R. & MacCracken, M.C. 1994. Global climatic effects of atmospheric dust from an asteroid or comet impact on Earth. *Global and Planetary Change*, **9**, 263–273.

Craig, H. 1953. The geochemistry of the stable carbon isotopes. *Geochimica et Cosmochimica Acta*, **3**, 53–92.

Craig, H. 1957. Isotopic standards for carbon and oxygen and correction factors for mass-spectrometric analysis of carbon dioxide. *Geochimica et Cosmochimicha Acta*, **12**, 133–149.

Craig, H. & Gordon, L.I. 1965. Deuterium and oxygen-18 variation in the ocean and marine atmosphere. In *Proceedings of Conference on Stable Isotopes in Oceanographic Studies and Paleotemperatures*, ed. T. Tongiorgi, pp. 9–130. Laboratory of Geology and Nuclear Sciences, Pisa, Italy.

Cramer, W., Bondeau, A., Woodward, F.I. *et al*. 2001. Global terrestrial vegetation and carbon dynamic responses to transient changes in CO_2 and climate. *Global Change Biology* (in press).

Crane, P.R. 1987 Vegetation consequences of angiosperm diversification. In *The origins of angiosperms and their biological consequences*, pp. 107–144. Cambridge University Press, New York.

Creber, G. T. & Chaloner, W. G. 1985. Tree growth in the Mesozoic and early Tertiary and the reconstruction of palaeoclimates. *Palaeogeography, Palaeoclimatology, Palaeoecology*, **52**, 35–60.

Creber, G. T. & Francis, J. E. 1987. Productivity in fossil forests. In *Proceedings of the International Conference on Ecological aspects of tree ring analysis*, pp. 319–326. Department of Energy, USA.

Crepet, W. L. & G. D. Feldman 1988. Paleocene/Eocene grasses from the south-western USA. *American Journal of Botany*, **76**, 161.

Crowell, J. C. 1982. Continental glaciation through geologic times. In *Climate in Earth history*, ed. W. H. Berger & J. C. Crowell, pp. 77–82. National Academy Press, Washington DC.

Crowley, T. J. 1990. Are there any satisfactory geologic analogues for a future greenhouse warming? *Journal of Climate*, **3**, 1282–1292.

Crowley, T. J. 1991. Ice age carbon. *Nature*, **352**, 575–576.

Crowley, T. J. 1993. Geological assessment of the greenhouse effect. *Bulletin of the American Meteorological Society*, **74**, 2363–2373.

Crowley, T. J. 1995. Ice age terrestrial carbon changes revisited. *Global Biogeochemical Cycles*, **9**, 377–389.

Crowley, T. J. & Baum, S. K. 1991. Estimating Carboniferous sea level fluctuations from Gondwana ice extent. *Geology*, **19**, 975–977.

Crowley, T. J. & Baum, S. K. 1994. General circulation model study of late Carboniferous interglacial climates. *Palaeoclimates*, **1**, 3–21.

Crowley, T. J. & Baum, S. K. 1995. Reconciling late Ordovician (440 Ma) glaciations with very high ($14\times$) CO_2 levels. *Journal of Geophysical Research*, **100**, 1093–1101.

Crowley, T. J., Baum, S. K. & Kim, K. Y. 1993. General circulation model sensitivity experiments with pole-centered supercontinents. *Journal of Geophysical Research*, **98**, 8793–8800.

Crowley, T. J. & Kim, K. Y. 1995. Comparison of longterm greenhouse projections with the geologic record. *Geophysical Research Letters*, **22**, 933–936.

Crowley, T. J. & North, G. R. 1991. *Paleoclimatology*. Oxford University Press.

Crutzen, P. J. & Goldhammer, J. G. 1993. *Fire in the environment. The ecological, atmospheric, and climatic importance of vegetation fires*. John Wiley, Chichester.

Davenport, S. A., Wdowiak, T. J., Jones, D. D. & Wdowiak, P. 1990. Chrondritic metal toxicity as a seed stock kill mechanism in impact-caused mass extinctions. *Geological Society of America Special Paper*, **247**, 71–86.

DeBoer, P. L. 1986. Changes in organic carbon burial during the early Cretaceous. In *North Atlantic palaeooceanography*, ed. C. P. Summerhayes & N. J. Shackleton, pp. 321–331. Special Publication No. 21, Geological Society of London.

DeFries, R. S. & Townshend, J. R. G. 1994. NDVI-derived land cover classification at global scales. *International Journal of Remote Sensing*, **15**, 3567–3586.

Delgado, E., Vedell, J. & Medrano, H. 1994. Photosynthesis during leaf ontogeny of field-grown *Nicotiana tabacum* L. lines selected by survival at low CO_2 concentrations. *Journal of Experimental Botany*, **45**, 547–552.

DePury, D.G.G. & Farquhar, G.D. 1997. Simple scaling of photosynthesis from leaves to canopies without the errors of big-leaf models. *Plant, Cell and Environment*, **20**, 537–557.

D'Hondt, S., Donaghay, P., Zachos, J.C., Luttenberg, D. & Lindinger, M. 1998. Organic carbon fluxes and ecological recovery from the Cretaceous–Tertiary mass extinction. *Science*, **282**, 276–279.

Diaz, H.F. & Markgraf, V. (eds.) 1992. *El Niño: historical and paleoclimatic aspects of the Southern Oscillation*. Cambridge University Press.

Dickens, G.R., Castillo, M.M. & Walker, J.C.G. 1998. A blast of gas in the latest Paleocene: simulating first-order effects of massive dissociation of organic methane hydrate. *Geology*, **25**, 259–262.

Dickinson, R.E. 1992. Land surface. In *Climate system modeling*, ed. K.E. Trenberth, pp. 149–171. Cambridge University Press.

DiMichele, W.A. & DeMaris, P.J. 1987. Structure and dynamics of a Pennsylvanian-age *Lepidodendron* forest: colonizers of a disturbed swamp habitat in the Herrin (No. 6) coal of Illinois. *Palaios*, **2**, 146–157.

DiMichele, W.A. & Hook, R.W. 1992. Paleozoic terrestrial ecosystems. *In Terrestrial ecosystems through time.*, ed. A.K. Behrensmeyer *et al.*, pp. 205–325. University of Chicago Press.

DiMichele, W.A. & Phillips, T.L. 1994. Paleobotanical and paleoecological constraints on models of peat formation in the Late Carboniferous of Euramerica. *Palaeogeography, Palaeoclimatology, Palaeoecology*, **106**, 39–90.

Dippery, J.K., Tissue, D.T., Thomas, R.B. & Strain, B.R. 1995. Effects of low and elevated CO_2 on C_3 and C_4 annuals. I. Growth and biomass allocation. *Oecologia*, **101**, 13–20.

Dole, M., Lane, G., Rudd, D. & Zaukelies, D.A. 1954. Isotopic composition of atmospheric oxygen and nitrogen. *Geochimica et Cosmochimica Acta*, **6**, 65–78.

Dongmann, G. 1974. The contribution of land photosynthesis to the stationary enrichment of ^{18}O in the atmosphere. *Radiative and Environmental Biophysics*, **11**, 219–225.

Douglas, R.G. & Savin, S.M. 1975. Oxygen and carbon isotope analyses of Tertiary and Cretaceous microfossils from Shatsky Rise and other sites in the North Pacific Ocean. *Initial Reports of the Deep Sea Drilling Project*, **32**, 509–521.

Downs, C.A., Heckathorn, S.A., Bryan, J.K. & Coleman, J.S. 1998. The methionine-rich low-molecular-weight chloroplast heat-shock protein: evolutionary conservation and accumulation in relation to thermotolerance. *American Journal of Botany*, **85**, 175–183.

Drake, B.G., González-Meler, M.A. & Long, S.P. 1997. More efficient plants: a consequence of rising atmospheric CO_2? *Annual Review of Plant Physiology and Plant Molecular Biology*, **48**, 609–639.

Duarte, C.M. & Agusti, S. 1998. The CO_2 balance of unproductive aquatic ecosystems. *Science*, **281**, 234–236.

Duff, G.A., Berryman, C.A. & Eamus, D. 1994. Growth, biomass allocation and foliar nutrient contents of two *Eucalyptus* species of the wet–dry tropics of Australia grown under CO_2 enrichment. *Functional Ecology*, **8**, 502–508.

Edwards, D. 1993. Cells and tissues in the vegetative sporophytes of early land plants. *New Phytologist*, **125**, 225–247.

Edwards, D. 1996. New insights into early land plant ecosystems: a glimpse of a Lilliputian world. *Review of Palaeobotany and Palynology*, **90**, 159–174.

Edwards, D., Feehan, J. & Smith, D.G. 1983. A late Wenlock flora from Co. Tipperary, Ireland. *Botanical Journal of the Linnean Society*, **86**, 19–36.

Egli, P., Maurer, S., Günthardt-Goerg, M.S. & Körner, C. 1998. Effects of elevated CO_2 and soil quality on leaf gas exchange and above-ground growth in beech–spruce model ecosystems. *New Phytologist*, **140**, 185–196.

Ehleringer, J.R., Cerling, T.E. & Helliker, B.R. 1997. C_4 photosynthesis, atmospheric CO_2, and climate. *Oecologia*, **112**, 285–299.

Ehleringer, J.R., Sage, R.F., Flanagan, L.B. & Pearcy, R.W. 1991. Climate change and the evolution of C_4 photosynthesis. *Trends in Ecology and Evolution*, **6**, 95–99.

Elick, J.M., Driese, S.G. & Mora, C.I. 1998. Very large plant and root traces from the early to middle Devonian: implications for early terrestrial ecosystems and atmospheric $p(CO_2)$. *Geology*, **26**, 143–146.

Ellis, R.J. (1984). *Chloroplast biogenesis*, ed. R.J. Ellis. Cambridge University Press.

Ellsworth, D.S., Oren, R., Huangm, C., Phillips, N. & Hendrey, G.R. 1995. Leaf and canopy responses to elevated CO_2 in a pine forest under free-air CO_2 enrichment. *Oecologia*, **104**, 139–146.

Esser, G. & Lautenschlager, M. 1994. Estimating the change of carbon in the terrestrial biosphere from 18 000 BP to present using a carbon cycle model. *Environmental Pollution*, **83**, 45–52.

Esser, G., Lieth, H.F.H., Scurlock, J.M.O. & Olson, R.J. 1997. *Worldwide Estimates and Bibliography of Net Primary Productivity derived from Pre-1982 Publications*. ORNL Technical Memorandum TM-13485, Oak Ridge National Laboratory, Tennessee.

Evans, J.R. & Terashima, I. 1988. Photosynthetic characteristics of spinach leaves grown with different nitrogen treatments. *Plant and Cell Physiology*, **29**, 157–165.

Falcon-Lang, H. 1998. The impact of wildfire on an early Carboniferous coastal environment, North Mayo, Ireland. *Palaeogeography, Palaeoclimatology, Palaeoecology*, **139**, 121–138.

Falcon-Lang, H.J. 2000. Fire ecology of the Carboniferous tropical zone. *Palaeogeography, Palaeoclimatology, Palaeoecology*, **164**, 339–355.

Falcon-Lang, H.J. & Scott, A.C. 2000. Upland ecology of some Late Carboniferous cordaitalean trees from Nova Scotia and England. *Palaeogeography, Palaeoclimatology, Palaeoecology*, **156**, 225–242.

Falkowski, P.G., Barber, R.T. & Smetacek, V. 1998. Biogeochemical controls and feedbacks on ocean primary productivity. *Science*, **281**, 200–206.

Farquhar, G.D. 1983. On the nature of carbon isotope discrimination in C_4 species. *Australian Journal of Plant Physiology*, **10**, 205–226.

Farquhar, G.D. 1997. Carbon dioxide and vegetation. *Science*, **278**, 1411.

Farquhar, G.D., Ehleringer, J.R. & Hubick, K.T. 1989. Carbon isotope discrimination and photosynthesis. *Annual Reviews of Plant Physiology and Plant Molecular Biology*, **40**, 503–537.

Farquhar, G.D. & Lloyd, J. 1993. Carbon and oxygen isotope effects in the exchange of carbon dioxide between terrestrial plants and the atmosphere. In *Stable isotopes and plant carbon-water relations*, ed. J. R. Ehleringer, A. E. Hall & G. D. Farquhar, pp. 47–70. Academic Press, San Diego.

Farquhar, G. D., Lloyd, J., Taylor, J. A. *et al.* 1993. Vegetation effects on the isotope composition of oxygen in atmospheric CO_2. *Nature*, **363**, 439–443.

Farquhar, G. D., O'Leary, M. H. & Berry, J. A. 1982. On the relationship between carbon isotope discrimination and the intercellular carbon dioxide concentration in leaves. *Australian Journal of Plant Physiology*, **9**, 121–137.

Farquhar, G. D. & Richards, R. A. 1984. Isotopic composition of plant carbon correlates with water-use efficiency of wheat genotypes. *Australian Journal of Plant Physiology*, **11**, 539–552.

Farquhar, G. D., Von Caemmerer, S. & Berry, J. A. 1980. A biochemical model of photosynthetic CO_2 assimilation in leaves of C_3 species. *Planta*, **149**, 78–90.

Farquhar, G. D. & Wong, S. C. 1984. An empirical model of stomatal conductance. *Australian Journal of Plant Physiology*, **11**, 191–210.

Farrell, B. F. 1990. Equable climate dynamics. *Journal of Atmospheric Science*, **47**, 2986–2995.

Fastovsky, D. E. & McSweeney, K. 1987. Paleosols spanning the Cretaceous–Paleogene transition, eastern Montana and western Dakota. *Geological Society of America Bulletin*, **99**, 66–77.

Faure, H., Faure-Denard, L. F. & Adams, J. M. (eds) 1998. Quaternary carbon cycle change. Special Issue. *Global and Planetary Change*, **16–17**, 1–198.

Fawcett, P. J., Barron, E. J., Robison, V. D. & Katz, B. J. 1994. The climatic evolution of India and Australia from the late Permian to mid Jurassic: a comparison of climate model results with the geologic record. *Geological Society of America Special Paper*, **288**, 139–157.

Ferris, R. & Taylor, G. 1993. Contrasting effects of elevated CO_2 on the root and shoot growth of four native herbs commonly found in chalk grassland. *New Phytologist*, **125**, 855–866.

Field, C. B., Behrenfeld, M. J., Randerson, J. T. & Falkowski, P. 1998. Primary production of the biosphere: integrating terrestrial and oceanic components. *Science*, **281**, 237–240.

Foley, J. A., Kutzbach, J. E., Coe, M. T. & Levis, S. 1994. Feedbacks between climate and boreal forests during the Holocene epoch. *Nature*, **371**, 52–54.

Fordham, M., Barnes, J. D., Bettarini, I. *et al.* 1997. The impact of elevated CO_2 on growth and photosynthesis in *Agrostis canina* L. ssp. *monteluccii* adapted to contrasting atmospheric CO_2 concentrations. *Oecologia*, **110**, 169–197.

Frakes, L. A., Francis, J. E. & Syktus, J. I. 1992. *Climate modes of the Phanerozoic*. Cambridge University Press.

Francis, J. E. 1983. The dominant conifer of the Jurassic Purbeck formation, England. *Palaeontology*, **26**, 277–294.

Francis, J. E. 1986a. The dynamics of polar fossil forests: Tertiary fossil forests of Axel Heiberg Island, Canadian Arctic Archipelago. *Geological Survey of Canada*, **403**, 29–38.

Francis, J. E. 1986b. Growth rings in Cretaceous and Tertiary wood from Antarctica and their palaeoclimatic significance. *Palaeontology*, **29**, 665–684.

Francis, J. E. 1988. A 50 million-year-old fossil forest from Strathcone Fiord, Ellesmere Island, Arctic Canada: evidence for a warm polar climate. *Arctic*, **41**, 314–318.

Francis, J. E. 1991. The dynamics of polar fossil forests: tertiary fossil forests of Axel Heiberg Island, Canadian Arctic archipelago. In *Tertiary fossil forests of the Geodetic Hills, Axel Heiberg Island, Arctic Archipelago*, ed. R. L. Christie & N. J. McMillan, pp. 29–38. Geological Survey of Canada Bulletin 403.

François, L. M., Delire, C., Warnant, P. & Munhoven, G. 1998. Modelling the glacial–interglacial changes in the continental biosphere. *Global and Planetary Change*, **16–17**, 37–52.

François, L. M., Walker, J. C. G. & Opdyke, B. N. 1993. The history of global weathering and the chemical evolution of the ocean–atmosphere system. *Geophysical Monograph*, **74**, 143–159.

Freeman, K. H. & Hayes, J. M. 1992. Fractionation of carbon isotopes by phytoplankton and estimates of ancient CO_2 levels. *Global Biogeochemical Cycles*, **6**, 185–198.

Fricke *et al.* 1998. Evidence for rapid climate change in North America during the latest Paleocene thermal maximum: oxygen isotope composition of biogenic phosphate from the Bighorn Basin (Wyoming). *Earth and Planetary Science Letters*, **160**, 193–208.

Friedli, H. H., Lötscher, H., Oeschger, H., Siegenthaler, U. & Stauffer, B. 1986. Ice core record of $^{13}C/^{12}C$ ratio of atmospheric CO_2 in the past two centuries. *Nature*, **324**, 237–238.

Gallimore, R. G. & Kutzbach, J. E. 1996. Role of orbitally induced changes in tundra area in the onset of glaciation. *Nature*, **381**, 503–505.

Gates, W. L., Henderson-Sellers, A., Boer, G. J. *et al.* 1996. Climate models – evaluation. In *Climate Change 1995. The Science of Climate Change*, ed. J. T. Houghton *et al.*, pp. 233–284. Cambridge University Press.

Gauslaa, Y. 1984. Heat resistance and energy budget in different Scandinavian plants. *Holarctic Ecology*, **7**, 1–78.

Ghannoum, O., von Caemmerer, S., Barlow, E. W. R. & Conroy, J. P. 1997. The effect of CO_2 enrichment and irradiance on the growth, morphology and gas exchange of a C_3 (*Panicum laxum*) and a C_4 (*Panicum antidotale*) grass. *Australian Journal of Plant Physiology*, **24**, 227–237.

Golenberg, E. M., Giannasi, D. E., Clegg, M. T., Smiley, C. J., Durbin, M., Henderson, D. & Zurawski, G. 1990. Chloroplast DNA sequence from a Miocene Magnolia species. *Nature*, **344**, 656–658.

Gonzalez-Meler, M. A., Ribas-Carbo, M., Siedow, J. N. & Drake, B. G. 1996. Direct inhibition of plant mitochondrial respiration by elevated CO_2. *Plant Physiology*, **112**, 1349–1355.

Goward, S. N., Tucker, C. J. & Dye, N. G. 1985. North American vegetation patterns observed with the NOAA-7 advanced very high resolution radiometer. *Vegetatio*, **64**, 3–14.

Graedel, T. E. & Crutzen, P. J. 1997. *Atmosphere, climate and change*. Scientific American, New York.

Graham, J. B., Dudley, R., Aguilar, N. M. & Gans, C. 1995. Implications of the late Palaeozoic oxygen pulse for physiology and evolution. *Nature*, **375**, 117–120.

Gray, H. R. 1956. *The form and taper of forest tree stems*. Imperial Forestry Institute Paper no. 2, University of Oxford.

Greenwood, D. R. 1996. Eocene monsoon forests in central Australia? *Australian Systematic Botany*, **9**, 95–112.

Greenwood, D. R. & Basinger, J. F. 1994. The palaeoecology of high-latitude Eocene swamp forests from Axel Heiberg Island, Canadian High Arctic. *Review Palaeobotany and Palynology*, **81**, 83–97.

Greenwood, D.R. & Wing, S.L. 1995. Eocene continental climates and latitudinal temperature gradients. *Geology*, **23**, 1044–1048.

Grocke, D.R. 1998. Carbon-isotope analyses of fossil plants as a chemostratigraphic and palaeoenvironmental tool. *Lethia*, **31**, 1–13.

Guehl, J.M., Picon, C., Aussenac, G. & Gross, P. 1994. Interactive effects of elevated CO_2 and soil drought on growth and transpiration efficiency and its determination in two European forest tree species. *Tree Physiology*, **14**, 707–724.

Gunderson, C.A. & Wullschleger, S.D. 1994. Photosynthetic acclimation in trees to rising atmospheric CO_2: a broader perspective. *Photosynthesis Research*, **39**, 369–388.

Guy, R.D., Fogel, M.L. & Berry, J.A. 1993. Photosynthetic fractionation of the stable isotopes of oxygen and carbon. *Plant Physiology*, **101**, 37–47.

Hall, D.O. & Scurlock, J.M.O. 1991. Climate change and the productivity of natural grasslands. *Annals of Botany*, **67** (Supplement 1), 49–55.

Hall, N.M.J., Dong, B. & Valdes, P.J. 1996a. Atmospheric equilibrium, instability and energy transport at the last glacial maximum. *Climate Dynamics*, **12**, 497–511.

Hall, N.M.J. & Valdes, P.J. 1997. A GCM simulation of climate 6000 years ago. *Journal of Climate*, **10**, 3–17.

Hall, N.M.J., Valdes, P.J. & Dong, B. 1996b. The maintenance of the last great ice sheets: a UGAMP GCM study. *Journal of Climate*, **9**, 1004–1019.

Hallam, A. 1984. Continental humid and arid zones during the Jurassic and Cretaceous. *Palaeogeography, Palaeoclimatology, Palaeoecology*, **47**, 195–223.

Hallam, A. 1985. A review of Mesozoic climates. *Journal of the Geological Society of London*, **142**, 433–445.

Hallam, A. 1992. *Phanerozoic sea-level changes*. Columbia University Press, New York.

Hallam, A. 1993. Jurassic climates as inferred from the sedimentary and fossil record. *Philosophical Transactions of the Royal Society of London*, **B341**, 287–296.

Hallam, A. 1997. Estimates of the amount and rate of sea-level change across the Rhaetian–Hettangian and Pliensbachian–Toarcian boundaries (latest Triassic to early Jurassic). *Journal of the Geological Society of London*, **154**, 773–779.

Hallam, A. & Wignall, P.B. 1997. *Mass extinctions and their aftermath*. Oxford University Press.

Hansen, J., Fung, I., Lacis, A. *et al.* 1988. Global climate changes as forecast by Goddard Institute for Space Studies three-dimensional model. *Journal of Geophysical Research*, **93**, 9341–9364.

Haq, B.U. & van Eysinga, F.W.B. 1998. *Geological timetable*. Fifth revised enlarged and updated edition. Elsevier Science, Netherlands.

Harley, P.C., Thomas, R.B., Reynolds, J.F. & Strain, B.R. 1992. Modelling photosynthesis of cotton grown in elevated CO_2. *Plant, Cell and Environment*, **15**, 271–282.

Harrison, S.P. and 11 other authors 2000. Intercomparison of simulated global vegetation distributions in response to 6 kyr B.P. orbital forcing. *Journal of Climate* (in press).

Hasegawa, T. 1997. Cenomanian–Turonian carbon isotope events recorded in terrestrial organic matter from northern Japan. *Palaeogeography, Palaeoclimatology, Palaeoecology*, **130**, 251–273.

Hatch, M.D. 1992. C_4 photosynthesis: an unlikely process full of surprises. *Plant and Cell Physiology*, **33**, 333–342.

Hättenschwiler, S. & Körner, C. 1996. System-level adjustments to elevated CO_2 in model spruce ecosystems. *Global Change Biology*, **2**, 377–387.

Hättenschwiler, S. & Körner, C. 1998. Biomass allocation and canopy development in spruce model ecosystems under elevated CO_2 and increased N deposition. *Oecologia*, **113**, 104–114.

Hättenschwiler, S., Miglietta, F., Raschi, A. & Körner, C. 1997. Thirty years of *in situ* tree growth under elevated CO_2: a model for future forest responses? *Global Change Biology*, **3**, 463–471.

Haxeltine, A. & Prentice, I.C. 1996. BIOME3: an equilibrium terrestrial biosphere model based on ecophysiological constraints, resource availability, and competition among plant functional types. *Global Biogeochemical Cycles*, **10**, 693–709.

Haxeltine, A., Prentice, I.C. & Creswell, I.D. 1996. A coupled carbon and water flux model to predict vegetation structure. *Journal of Vegetation Science*, **7**, 651–666.

Hays, J.D., Imbrie, J. & Shackleton, N.J. 1976. Variations in the Earth's orbit: pacemaker of the ice ages. *Science*, **194**, 1121–1132.

Herbert, T.D. 1997. A long marine history of carbon cycle modulation by orbital–climatic changes. *Proceedings of the National Academy of Sciences, USA*, **94**, 8362–8369.

Herguera, J.C. & Berger, W.H. 1994. Glacial to postglacial drop in productivity in the western equatorial Pacific: mixing rate vs. nutrient concentrations. *Geology*, **22**, 629–632.

Herman, A.B. & Spicer, R.A. 1996. Palaeobotanical evidence for a warm Cretaceous arctic ocean. *Nature*, **380**, 330–333.

Hirose, T., Ackerly, D.D., Traw, M.B. & Bazzaz, F.A. 1996. Effects of CO_2 elevation on canopy development in the stands of two co-occurring annuals. *Oecologia*, **108**, 215–223.

Hirose, T. & Werger, M.J.A. 1987. Maximizing daily canopy photosynthesis with respect to the leaf nitrogen allocation pattern in the canopy. *Oecologia*, **72**, 520–526.

Hoelzmann, P., Jolly, D., Harrison, S.P., Laarif, F., Bonnefille, R. & Pachur, H.J. 1998. Mid-Holocene land-surface conditions in northern Africa and the Arabian peninsula: a data set for the analysis of biogeophysical feedbacks in the climate system. *Global Biogeochemical Cycles*, **12**, 35–51.

Hoffert, M.I. & Covey, C. 1992. Deriving global climate sensitivity from palaeoclimate reconstructions. *Nature*, **360**, 573–576.

Holmes, C.W. & Brownfield, M.E. 1992. Distribution of carbon and sulfur isotopes in Upper Cretaceous coal of northwestern Colorado. In *Controls on the distribution and quality of cretaceous coals.*, ed. P.J. McCabe & J.T. Parrish, pp. 57–68. Geological Society of America.

Horrell, M.A. 1990. Energy balance constraints on ^{18}O based paleo-sea surface temperature estimates. *Paleoceanography*, **5**, 339–348.

Houghton, J.T., Meira Filho, L.G., Bruce, J. *et al.* (eds.) 1995. *Climate Change 1994. Radiative forcing of climate change and an evaluation of the IPCC IS92 emission scenarios.* Cambridge University Press.

Houghton, J.T., Meira Filho, L.G., Callander, B.A., Harris, N., Kattenberg, A. & Maskell, K. (eds.) 1996. *Climate Change 1995 The Science of Climate Change*. IPCC, Cambridge University Press.

Houghton, R.A. & Skole, D.L. 1990. Carbon. In *The Earth as transformed by human action.*

Global and regional changes in the biosphere over the past 300 years, ed. B. L. Turner, pp. 393–408. Cambridge University Press.

Hunt, E. R., Piper, S. C., Nemani, R., Keeling, C. D., Otto, R. D. & Running, S. W. 1996. Global net carbon exchange and intra-annual atmospheric CO_2 concentrations predicted by an ecosystem process model and three-dimensional atmospheric transport model. *Global Biogeochemical Cycles*, **10**, 431–456.

Hyde, W. T., Crowley, T. J., Tarasov, L. & Peltier, W. R. 1999. The Pangean ice age: studies of a coupled climate-ice sheet model. *Climate Dynamics*, **15**, 619–629.

Imbrie, J. & Imbrie, K. P. 1979. *Ice Ages: solving the mystery*. Macmillan, London.

Ivany, L. C. & Salawitch, R. J. 1993. Carbon isotopic evidence for biomass burning at the K–T boundary. *Geology*, **21**, 487–490.

Izett, G. A. 1990. The Cretaceous–Tertiary boundary interval, Raton Basin, Colorado and New Mexico. *Geological Society of America Special Paper*, **249**, 1–100.

Johns, T. C., Carnell, R. E., Crossley, J. F., Gregory, J. M., Mitchell, J. F. B., Senior, C. A., Tett, S. F. B. & Wood, R. A. 1997. The second Hadley Centre coupled ocean–atmosphere GCM: model description, spinup and validation. *Climate Dynamics*, **13**, 103–134.

Johnson, E. A. & Gutsell, S. L. 1994. Fire frequency models, methods and interpretations. *Advances in Ecological Research*, **25**, 239–287.

Jones, H. G. 1992. *Plants and microclimate. A quantitative approach to environmental plant physiology*, 2nd edition. Cambridge University Press.

Jones, T. P. 1994. ^{13}C enriched Lower Carboniferous fossil plants from Donegal, Ireland: carbon isotope constraints on taphonomy, diagenesis and palaeoenvironment. *Review of Palaeobotany and Palynology*, **81**, 53–64.

Jones, T. P. & Chaloner, W. G. 1991. Fossil charcoal, its recognition and palaeoatmospheric significance. *Palaeogeography, Palaeoclimatology, Palaeoecology*, **97**, 39–50.

Jordan, D. B. & Ogren, W. L. 1983. Species variation in kinetic properties of ribulose 1,5-bisphosphate carboxylase/oxygenase. *Archives of Biochemistry and Biophysics*, **227**, 425–433.

Jouzel, J., Barkov, N. I., Barnola, J. M. *et al*. 1993. Extending the Vostok ice-core record of palaeoclimate to the penultimate glacial period. *Nature*, **364**, 407–412.

Jouzel, J., Lorius, C., Petit, J. R. *et al*. 1987. Vostok ice core: a continuous isotope temperature record of the last climatic cycle (160,000 years). *Nature*, **329**, 403–408.

Justice, C. O., Townshend, J. R. G., Holben, B. N. & Tucker, C. J. 1985. Analysis of the phenology of global vegetation using meteorological satellite data. *International Journal of Remote Sensing*, **6**, 1271–1318.

Kasting, J. F. & Grinspoon, D. H. 1991. The faint young sun problem. In *The Sun in time*, ed. C. P. Sonett, M. S. Giampapa & M. S. Matthews, pp. 447–462. University of Arizona.

Keeling, C. D., Whorf, T. P., Wahlen, M. & van der Plicht, J. 1995. Interannual extremes in the rate of rise of atmospheric carbon dioxide since 1980. *Nature*, **375**, 666–670.

Keeling, R. F. 1995. The atmospheric oxygen cycle: the oxygen isotopes of atmospheric CO_2 and O_2 and the O_2/N_2 ratio. *Reviews of Geophysics Supplement*, 1253–1262.

Keeling, R. F., Piper, S. C. & Heimann, M. 1996. Global and atmospheric CO_2 sinks deduced from changes in atmospheric O_2 concentration. *Nature*, **381**, 218–221.

Keller, G. & MacLeod, N. 1993. Carbon isotopic evidence for biomass burning at the K–T boundary: comment and reply. *Geology*, **21**, 1149–1150.

Kennett, J.P., Stott, L.D. 1991. Abrupt deep sea warming, paleoceanographic changes and benthic extinctions at the end of the Paleocene. *Nature*, **353**, 319–322.

Kerr, A.C. 1998. Oceanic plateau formation: a cause of mass extinction and black shale deposition around the Cenomanian–Turonian boundary? *Journal of the Geological Society of London*, **155**, 619–626.

Keys, A.K. 1986. Rubisco: its role in photorespiration. *Philosophical Transactions of the Royal Society of London*, **B313**, 325–336.

Kiehl, J.T. 1992. Atmospheric general circulation modeling. In *Climate system modeling*, ed. K.E. Trenberth, pp. 319–369. Cambridge University Press.

Kim, K.Y. & Crowley, T.J. 1994. Modelling the climate effect of unrestricted greenhouse emissions over the next 10,000 years. *Geophysical Research Letters*, **21**, 681–684.

Kirchner, J.W. & Wells, A. 2000. Delayed recovery from extinctions throughout the fossil record. *Nature*, **404**, 177–180.

Klein, R.T. Lohmann, K.G. & Thayer, C.W. 1996. Bivalve skeletons record sea-surface temperature and $\delta^{18}O$ via Mg/Ca and $^{18}O/^{16}O$ ratios. *Geology*, **24**, 415–418.

Knoll, A.H. & Niklas, K.J. 1987. Adaptation, plant evolution, and the fossil record. *Review of Palaeobotany and Palynology*, **50**, 127–149.

Kohen, E.A., Venet, L. & Mousseau, M. 1993. Growth and photosynthesis of two deciduous forest species at elevated carbon dioxide. *Functional Ecology*, **7**, 480–486.

Kojima, S., Sweda, T., LaPage, B.A. & Basinger, J.F. 1998. A new method to estimate accumulation rates of lignites in the Eocene Buchanan Lake Formation, Canadian Arctic. *Palaeogeography, Palaeoclimatology, Palaeoecology*, **141**, 115–122.

Köppen, W. 1936. Das geographische system der klimate. In *Handbuch der Klimatologie*, ed. W. Köppen & R. Geiger, pp. 1–44. Gebrüder Borntraeger, Berlin.

Körner, C., Diemer, M., Schäppi, B., Niklaus, P. & Arnone, J. 1997. The responses of alpine grasslands to four seasons of CO_2 enrichment: a synthesis. *Acta Œcologica*, **18**, 165–175.

Körner, C., Farquhar, G.D. & Wong, S.C. 1991. Carbon isotope discrimination by plants follows latitudinal and altitudinal trends. *Oecologia*, **88**, 30–40.

Körner, C. & Miglietta, F. 1994. Long-term effects of naturally elevated CO_2 on mediterranean grassland and forest trees. *Oecologia*, **99**, 343–351.

Kothavala, Z., Oglesby, R.J. & Saltzman, B. 1999. Sensitivity of equilibrium surface temperature of CCM3 to systematic changes in atmospheric CO_2. *Geophysical Research Letters*, **26**, 209–212.

Krogh, T.E., Kamo, S.L., Sharpton, V.L., Marín, L.E. & Hildebrand, A.R. 1993. U-Pb ages of single shocked quartz zircons linking distal ejecta to the Chicxulub crater. *Nature*, **366**, 731–734.

Kroopnick, P. & Craig, H. 1972. Atmospheric oxygen: isotopic composition and solubility fractionation. *Science*, **175**, 54–55.

Küchler, A.W. 1983. World map of natural vegetation. In *Goode's World Atlas*, pp. 16–17. Rand McNally.

Kuhn, W.R., Walker, J.C.G. & Marshall, H.G. 1989. The effect on earth's surface temperature from variations in rotation rate, continent formation, solar luminosity and carbon dioxide. *Journal of Geophysical Research*, **94**, 11129–11136.

Kumagai, H., Sweda, T., Hayashi, K. *et al.* 1995. Growth-ring analysis of early Tertiary conifer woods from the Canadian high arctic and its palaeoclimatic interpretation. *Palaeogeography, Palaeoclimatology, Palaeoecology*, **116**, 247–262.

Kumar, N., Anderson, R. F., Mortlock, R. A. *et al.* 1995. Increased biological productivity and export production in the glacial Southern Ocean. *Nature*, **378**, 675–680.

Kutzbach, J. E. 1992. Modeling large climatic changes of the past. In *Climate system modeling*, ed. K. E. Trenberth, pp. 669–688. Cambridge University Press.

Kutzbach, J. E., Bonan, G., Foley, J. & Harrison, S. P. 1996. Vegetation/soil feedbacks and African monsoon response to orbital forcing in the Holocene. *Nature*, **384**, 623–626.

Kutzbach, J. E., Gallimore, R., Harrison, S., Behling, P., Selin, R. & Laarif, F. 1998 Climate and biome simulations for the past 21,000 years. *Quaternary Science Reviews*, **17**, 473–506.

Kutzbach, J. E. & Ziegler, A. M. 1993. Simulation of Late Permian climate and biomes with an atmospheric–ocean model: comparisons with observations. *Philosophical Transactions of the Royal Society*, **B341**, 000–000.

Kyte, F. T. 1998. A meteorite from the Cretaceous/Tertiary boundary. *Nature*, **396**, 237–239.

Larcher, W. 1994. Photosynthesis as a tool for indicating temperature stress events. In: *Ecophysiology of photosynthesis*, ed. E. D. Schultze & M. M. Caldwell, pp. 261–277. Springer-Verlag, Berlin.

Larcher, W. 1995. *Physiological plant ecology. Ecophysiology and stress physiology of functional groups*, 3rd edition. Springer-Verlag, Berlin.

Lawlor, D. W. 1993. *Photosynthesis: molecular, physiological and environmental processes*. 2nd edition. Longman, Harlow, Essex.

Laws, E. A. 1991. Photosynthetic quotients, new production and net community production in the open ocean. *Deep Sea Research*, **38**, 143 167.

Lean, J. & Rowntree, P. R. 1993. A GCM simulation of the impact of Amazonian deforestation on climate using an improved canopy representation. *Quarterly Journal of the Royal Meteorological Society*, **119**, 509–530.

Leemans, R. & Cramer, W. P. 1991. *The IIASA data base for mean monthly values of temperature, precipitation, and cloudiness on a global terrestrial grid*. The International Institute for Applied Systems Analysis (IIASA), Laxenburg, Austria. RR-91–18.

Lehman, T. M. 1990. Paleosols and the Cretaceous–Tertiary boundary transition in the Big Bend region of Texas. *Geology*, **18**, 362–364.

Lenton, T. M. & Watson, A. J. 2000. Redfield revisited: 2. What regulates the oxygen content of the atmosphere? *Global Biogeochemical Cycles*, **14**, 249–268.

Leuenberger, M., Siegenthaler, U. & Langway, C. C. 1992. Carbon isotope composition of atmospheric CO_2 during the last ice age from an Antarctic ice core. *Nature*, **357**, 488–490.

Li, H., Taylor, E. L. & Taylor, T. N. 1996. Permian vessel elements. *Science*, **271**, 188–189.

Lidgard, S. & Crane, P. R. 1990. Angiosperm diversification and Cretaceous floristic trends: a comparison of palynofloras and leaf macrofloras. *Paleobiology*, **16**, 77–93.

Lloyd, J. & Farquhar, G. D. 1994. ^{13}C discrimination during CO_2 assimilation by the terrestrial biosphere. *Oecologia*, **99**, 201–215.

Lloyd, J. & Farquhar, G. D. 1996. The CO_2 dependence of photosynthesis, plant growth responses to elevated CO_2 concentrations and their interaction with soil nutrient status. I. General principles and forest ecosystems. *Functional Ecology*, **10**, 4–32.

Lobert, J. M. & Warnatz, J. 1993. Emissions from combustion process in vegetation. In *Fire in the environment. The ecological, atmospheric, and climatic importance of vegetation fires*, ed. P. J. Crutzen & J. G. Goldhammer, pp. 15–37. John Wiley, Chichester.

Lomax, B. H., Beerling, D. J., Upchurch, G. R. & Otto-Bliesner, B. L. 2000. Terrestrial ecosystem responses to global environmental change across the Cretaceous–Tertiary boundary. *Geophysical Research Letters*, **27**, 2149–2152.

Lomax, B. H., Beerling, D. J., Upchurch, G. R. & Otto-Bliesner, B. L. 2001. Rapid recovery of terrestrial productivity in a simulation study of the terminal Cretaceous impact event. *Earth and Planetary Science Letters*, (in press).

Long, S. P. 1991. Modification of the response of photosynthetic productivity to rising temperature by atmospheric CO_2 concentrations: has its importance been underestimated? *Plant, Cell and Environment*, **14**, 729–740.

Long, S. P. & Drake, B. D. 1991. Effect of the long-term elevation of CO_2 concentration in the field on the quantum yield of photosynthesis in the C_3 sedge, *Scirpus olneyi*. *Plant Physiology*, **96**, 221–226.

Long, S. P., Humphries, S. & Falkowski, P. G. 1994. Photoinhibition of photosynthesis in nature. *Annual Review of Plant Physiology and Plant Molecular Biology*, **45**, 633–662.

Long, S. P., Jones, M. B. & Roberts, M. J. (eds.) 1992. *Primary productivity of grass ecosystems of the tropics and sub-tropics*. Chapman & Hall, London.

Lopez-Martinez, N., Ardevol, L., Arribas, M. E., Civis, J. & Gonzalez-Delgado, A. 1998. The geological record in non-marine environments around the K/T boundary (Tremp formation, Spain). *Bulletin Societe Geologie France*, **169**, 11–20.

Los, S. O., Justice, C. O. & Tucker, C. J. 1994. A global 1 degree by 1 degree NDVI data set for climate studies derived from the GIMMS continental NDVI data. *International Journal of Remote Sensing*, **15**, 3493–3518.

Lottes, A. L. & Ziegler, A. M. 1994. World peat occurrence and the seasonality of climate and vegetation. *Palaeogeography, Palaeoclimatology, Palaeoecology*, **106**, 23–37.

Lovelock, J. E. 1979. *Gaia – a new look at life on Earth*. Oxford University Press.

Lutze, L. J., Roden, J. S., Holly, C. J., Wolfe, J., Egerton, J. J. G. & Ball, M. C. 1998. Elevated atmospheric [CO_2] promotes frost damage in evergreen tree seedlings. *Plant, Cell and Environment*, **21**, 631–635.

McCabe, P. J. & Parrish, J. T. 1992. Tectonic and climatic controls on the distribution and quality of Cretaceous coals. *Geological Society of America Special Paper*, **267**, 1–15.

Macdonald, D. L. M. & Francis, J. E. 1992. The potential for Cretaceous coal in Antarctica. *Geological Society of America Special Paper*, **267**, 385–395.

McElwain, J. C., Beerling, D. J. & Woodward, F. I. 1999. Fossil plants and global warming at the Triassic–Jurassic boundary. *Science*, **285**, 1386–1390.

McElwain, J. C. & Chaloner, W. G. 1995. Stomatal density and index of fossil plants track atmospheric carbon dioxide in the Palaeozoic. *Annals of Botany*, **76**, 389–395.

McFadden, B. A. & Tabita, F. R. 1974. D-ribulose 1,5-diphosphate carboxylase and the evolution of autotrophy. *BioSystems*, **6**, 93–112.

McFadden, B. A., Torres-Ruiz, J., Daniell, H. & Sarojini. 1986. Interaction, functional relations and evolution of large and small subunits in Rubisco from Prokaryota and Eukaryota. *Philosophical Transactions of the Royal Society of London*, **B313**, 347–358.

McGuffie, K. & Henderson-Sellers, A. 1997. *A climate modelling primer*, 2nd edition. John Wiley, Chichester.

McGuire, A. D., Melillo, J. M., Joyce, L. A. *et al.* 1992. Interactions between carbon and nitrogen dynamics in estimating net primary productivity for potential vegetation in North America. *Global Biogeochemical Cycles*, **6**, 101–124.

McGuire, A.D., Melillo, J.M., Kicklighter, D.W. & Joyce, L.A. 1995. Equilibrium responses of soil carbon to climate change: empirical and process-based estimates. *Journal of Biogeography*, **22**, 785–796.

McKnight, C.L., Graham, S.A., Carrol, A.R. *et al.* 1990. Fluvial sedimentology of an Upper Jurassic petrified forest assemblage, Shishu Formation, Junggar Basin, Xinjiang, China. *Palaeogeography, Palaeoclimatology, Palaeoecology*, **79**, 1–9.

McMurtrie, R.E. & Wang, Y.P. 1993. Mathematical models of the photosynthetic response of tree stands to rising CO_2 concentrations and temperature. *Plant, Cell & Environment*, **16**, 1–13.

McRoberts, C.A., Furrer, H. & Jones, D.S. 1997. Palaeoenvironmental interpretation of a Triassic-Jurassic boundary section from Western Austria based on palaeoecological and geochemical data. *Palaeogeography, Palaeoclimatology, Palaeoecology*, **136**, 79–95.

Manabe, S., Stouffer, R.J., Spelman, M.J. & Bryan, K. 1991. Transient responses of a coupled ocean-atmosphere model to gradual changes of atmospheric CO_2. Part 1. Annual mean response. *Journal of Climate*, **4**, 785–818.

Martinelli, L.A., Pessenda, L.C.R., Espinoza, E. *et al.* 1996. Carbon-13 variation with depth in soils of Brazil and climate change during the Quaternary. *Oecologia*, **106**, 376–381.

Marzoli, A., Renne, P.R., Piccirillo, E.M., Ernesto, M., Bellicni, G. & De Min, A. 1999. Extensive 200-million-year-old continental flood basalts of the central Atlantic magmatic province. *Science*; **284**, 616–618.

Masle, J., Farquhar, G.D. & Gifford, R.M. 1990. Growth and carbon economy of wheat seedlings as affected by soil resistance to penetration and ambient partial pressure of CO_2. *Australian Journal of Plant Physiology*, **17**, 465–487.

Masle, J., Hudson, G.S. & Badger, M.R. 1993. Effects of ambient CO_2 concentration on growth and nitrogen use in tobacco (*Nicotiana tabacum*) plants transformed with an antisense gene to the small subunit of ribulose-1,5-bisphosphate carboxylase/oxygenase. *Plant Physiology*, **103**, 1075–1088.

Maslin, M.A., Adams, J., Thomas, E., Faure, H. & Haines-Young, R. 1995. Estimating carbon transfer between the ocean, atmosphere and the terrestrial biosphere since the last glacial maximum. *Terra Nova*, **7**, 358–366.

Matthews, E. 1983. Global vegetation and land use: new high resolution data bases for climate studies. *Journal of Climate and Applied Meteorology*, **22**, 474–487.

Medlyn, B.E., Badeck, F.W., De Pury, D.G.G. *et al.* 1999. Effects of elevated [CO_2] on photosynthesis in European forest species: a meta-analysis of model parameters. *Plant, Cell and Environment*, **22**, 1475–1495.

Meehl, G.A. 1989. The coupled ocean–atmosphere modeling problem in the tropical Pacific and Asian monsoon regions. *Journal of Climate*, **2**, 1146–1163.

Meehl, G.A. 1992. Global coupled models: atmosphere, ocean, sea ice. In *Climate system modeling*, ed. K.E. Trenberth, pp. 555–581. Cambridge University Press.

Meeson, B.W., Corprew, F.E., McManus, J.M.P. *et al.* 1995. *ISLSCP Initiative I – Global Data Sets for Land–Atmosphere Models, 1987–1988*. Volumes 1–5, published on CD by NASA.

Melosh, H.J., Schneider, N.M., Zahnle, K.J. & Latham, D. 1990. Ignition of global wildfires at the Cretaceous/Tertiary boundary. *Nature*, **343**, 251–254.

Meyer, M.K. 1988. *Net primary productivity estimates for the last 18,000 years evaluated from simulations by a global climate model*. MS dissertation, University of Wisconsin, Madison.

Miall, A.D. 1984. Variations in fluvial style in the lower Cenozoic synorogenic sediments of the Canadian Arctic Islands. *Sedimentary Geology*, **38**, 499–523.

Miglietta, F., Magliulo, V., Bindi, M. *et al.* 1998. Free air CO_2 enrichment of potato (*Solanum tuberosum* L.): development, growth and yield. *Global Change Biology*, **4**, 163–172.

Miglietta, F., Raschi, A., Bettarini, I., Resti, R. & Selvi, F. 1993. Natural springs in Italy: a resource for examining the long-term response of vegetation to rising CO_2 concentrations. *Plant, Cell and Environment*, **16**, 873–878.

Miller, K.G., Fairbanks, R.G. & Mountain, G.S. 1987. Tertiary oxygen isotope synthesis, sea level history, and continental margin erosion. *Paleoceanography*, **2**, 1–19.

Mitchell, J.F.B., Johns, T.C., Gregory, J.M. & Tett, S.F.B. 1995. Climate response to increasing levels of greenhouse gases and aerosols. *Nature*, **376**, 501–504.

Mitchell, P.L. 1997. Misuse of regression for empirical validation of models. *Agricultural Systems*, **54**, 313–326.

Monserud, R.A., Denissenko, O.V., Kolchugina, T.P. & Tchebakova, N.M. 1995. Changes in phytomass and net primary productivity for Siberia from the mid-Holocene to the present. *Global Biogeochemical Cycles*, **9**, 213–226.

Monserud, R.A. & Leemans, R. 1992. Comparing global vegetation maps with the kappa-statistic. *Ecological Modelling*, **62**, 275–293.

Monteith, J.L. 1981. Evaporation and environment. In *The state and movement of water in living organisms*, ed. C.E. Fogg. SEB Symposium, Vol. 19, pp. 205–234. Cambridge University Press.

Monteith, J.L. & Unsworth, M.H. 1990. *Principles of environmental physics*, 2nd edition. Edward Arnold, London.

Moore, G.T., Hayashida, D.N., Ross, C.A. & Jacobsen, S.R. 1992a. The palaeoclimate of the Kimmeridgian/Tithonian (Late Jurassic) world. I. Results using a general circulation model. *Palaeogeography, Palaeoclimatology, Palaeoecology*, **93**, 113–150.

Moore, G.T., Sloan, L.C., Hayashida, D.N. & Umigar 1992b. The palaeoclimate of the Kimmeridgian/Tithonian (Late Jurassic) world. II. Sensitivity tests comparing three different palaeotopographic settings. *Palaeogeography, Palaeoclimatology, Palaeoecology*, **95**, 229–252.

Moore, P.D. 1983. Plants and the palaeoatmosphere. *Journal of the Geological Society of London*, **140**, 13–25.

Moore, P.D. 1995. Biological processes controlling the development of modern peat-forming ecosystems. *Coal Geology*, **28**, 99–110.

Mora, C.I., Driese, S.G. & Colarusso, L. 1996. Middle to late Paleozoic atmospheric CO_2 levels from soil carbonate and organic matter. *Science*, **271**, 1105–1107.

Morante, R. & Hallam, A. 1996. Organic carbon isotopic record across the Triassic-Jurassic boundary in Austria and its bearing on the cause of mass extinction. *Geology*, **24**, 391–394.

Morgan, J., Warner, M., Brittan, J. *et al.* 1997. Size and morphology of the Chicxulub impact crater. *Nature*, **390**, 472–476.

Morrisey, L.A., Livingston, G.P. & Zoltai, S.C. 2000. Influences of fire and climate on patterns of carbon emissions in boreal peatlands. In *Fire, climate and carbon cycling in the boreal forest*, eds. E.S. Kasischke & B.J. Stocks, pp. 423–439. Ecological Studies 138. Springer-Verlag, Berlin.

Moulton, K.L. & Berner, R.A. 1998. Quantification of the effect of plants on weathering: studies in Iceland. *Geology*, **26**, 895–898.

Mulholland, B.J., Craigon, J., Black, C.R., Colls, J.J., Atherton, J. & London, G. 1998. Growth, light interception and yield responses of spring wheat (*Triticum aestivum* L.) grown under elevated CO_2 and O_2 in open-top chambers. *Global Change Biology*, **4**, 121–130.

Müller, M.J. 1982. *Selected climatic data for a global set of standard stations for vegetation science*. Dr W. Junk, The Hague.

Neftel, A., Oeschger, H., Staffelbach, T. & Stauffer, B. 1988. CO_2 record in the Byrd ice core 50,000–5,000 years BP. *Nature*, **331**, 609–611.

Neilson, R.P. 1995. A model for predicting continental-scale vegetation distribution and water balance. *Ecological Applications*, **5**, 362–385.

Neilson, R.P., King, G.A. & Koerper, G. 1992. Towards a rule-based biome model. *Landscape Ecology*, **7**, 27–43.

Nemani, R. & Running, S.W. 1996. Implementation of a hierarchical global vegetation classification in ecosystem function models. *Journal of Vegetation Science*, **7**, 337 346.

Nichols, D.J. & Fleming, R.F. 1990. Plant microfossil record of the terminal Cretaceous event in the western United States and Canada. *Geological Society of America Special Paper*, **247**, 445–455.

Nie, G.Y., Long, S.P., Garcia, R.L. *et al.* 1995. Effects of free-air CO_2 enrichment on the development of the photosynthetic apparatus in wheat, as indicated by changes in leaf proteins. *Plant, Cell and Environment*, **18**, 855–864.

Niklas, K.J. 1985. The evolution of tracheid diameter in early vascular plants and its implications on the hydraulic conductance of the primary xylem strand. *Evolution*, **39**, 1110–1122.

Niklas, K.J. 1992. *Plant biomechanics: an engineering approach to plant form and function*. University of Chicago Press.

Niklas, K.J. 1993. Scaling of plant height: a comparison among major plant clades and anatomical grades. *Annals of Botany*, **72**, 165–172.

Niklas, K.J. 1997. *The evolutionary biology of plants*. University of Chicago Press.

Niklas, K.J., Tiffney, B.H. & Knoll, A.H. 1983. Patterns in vascular land plant diversification. *Nature*, **303**, 614–616.

Nobel, P.S. 1988. *Environmental biology of Agaves and Cacti*. Cambridge University Press.

Norby, R.J. & O'Neill, E.G. 1991. Leaf area compensation and nutrient interactions of CO_2-enriched seedlings of yellow-poplar (*Liriodendron tulipifera* L.). *New Phytologist*, **117**, 515–528.

Norby, R.J., Wullschleger, S.D., Gunderson, C.A., Johnson, D.W. & Ceulemans, R. 1999. Tree responses to rising CO_2 in field experiments: implications for the future forests. *Plant, Cell and Environment*, **22**, 683–714.

North, G.R. 1975. Theory of energy-balance climate models. *Journal of Atmospheric Science*, **32**, 2033–2043.

North, G.R. 1988. Lessons from energy balance models. In *Physically-based modelling and simulation of climate and climatic change*, ed. M.E. Schlesinger, pp. 627–651. Kluwer, Dordrecht.

North, G.R., Cahalan, R.F. & Coakley, J.A. 1981. Energy balance climate models. *Review of Geophysics and Space Physics*, **19**, 91–121.

North, G.R., Mengel, J.G. & Short, D.A. 1983. Simple energy balance model resolving the seasons and the continents: application to the astronomical theory of the ice ages. *Journal of Geophysical Research*, **88**, 6576–6586.

Ogren, W. 1994. Energy utilization by photorespiration. In *Regulation of atmospheric CO_2 and O_2 by photosynthetic carbon metabolism*, ed. N.E. Tolbert & J. Preis, pp. 115–125. Oxford University Press

O'Keefe, J.D. & Ahrens, T.J. 1989. Impact production of CO_2 by the Cretaceous/Tertiary extinction bolide and the resultant heating of the Earth. *Nature*, **338**, 247–249.

Olson, J. 1981. Carbon balance in relation to fire regimes. In *Fire regimes and ecosystem properties*, ed. H.A. Mooney, T.M. Bonnicksen, N.L. Christensen & W.A. Reiners, pp. 327–378. USDA Forest Service Technical Report WO-26, Washington, DC.

Olson, J.S., Watts, J. & Allison, L. 1983. *Carbon in Live vegetation of major world ecosystems*. W-7405-ENG-26, US Department of Energy. Oak Ridge National Laboratory, Tennessee.

Osborne, C.P. & Beerling, D.J. 2001. Sensitivity of tree growth to a high CO_2 environment – consequences for interpreting the characteristics of fossil woods from ancient 'greenhouse' worlds. *Palaeogeography, Palaeoclimatology, Palaeoecology* (in press).

Osborne, C.P., Drake, B.G., LaRoche, J. & Long, S.P. 1997. Does long-term elevation of CO_2 concentration increase photosynthesis in forest floor vegetation? Indian strawberry in a Maryland forest. *Plant Physiology*, **114**, 337–344.

Otto-Bliesner, B.L. & Upchurch, G.R. 1997. Vegetation-induced warming of high-latitude regions during the Late Cretaceous period. *Nature*, **385**, 804–807.

Overpeck, J., Rind, D., Lacis, A. & Healy, R. 1996. Possible role of dust-induced regional warming in abrupt climate change during the last glacial period. *Nature*, **384**, 447–449.

Owensby, C.E., Coyne, P.I., Ham, J.M., Auen, L.M. & Knapp, A.K. 1993. Biomass production in a tallgrass prairie ecosystem exposed to ambient and elevated CO_2. *Ecological Applications*, **3**, 644–653.

Parrish, J.M., Parrish, J.T. & Ziegler, A.M. 1986. Permian–Triassic paleography and paleoclimatology and implications for Therapsid distribution. In *The ecology and biology of mammal-like reptiles*, ed. N. Hotton II, P.D. MacLean, J.J. Roth & E.C. Roth, pp. 109–131. Smithsonian Institution Press, Washington, DC.

Parrish, J.T. 1993. Climate of the supercontinent Pangea. *Journal of Geology*, **101**, 215–233.

Parrish, J.T., Ziegler, A.M. & Scotese, C.R. 1982. Rainfall patterns and the distribution of coals and evaporites in the Mesozoic and Cenozoic. *Palaeogeography, Palaeoclimatology, Palaeoecology*, **40**, 67–101.

Parton, W.J., Scurlock, J.M.O., Ojima, D.S. *et al.* 1993. Observations and modeling of biomass and soil organic matter dynamics for the grassland biome worldwide. *Global Biogeochemical Cycles*, **7**, 785–809.

Peixoto, J.P & Oort, A.H. 1992. *Physics of Climate*. American Institute of Physics, New York.

Peng, C.H., Guiot, J. & van Campo, E. 1998. Estimating changes in terrestrial vegetation and carbon storage: using palaeoecological data and models. *Quaternary Science Reviews*, **17**, 719–735.

Penning de Vries, F.W.T. 1975. The use of assimilates in higher plants. In *Photosynthesis in different environments*, ed. J.P. Cooper, pp. 459–480. Cambridge University Press.

Peterson, A.G., Ball, J.T., Luo, Y. *et al.* and CMEAL participants. 1999. The photosynthesis–leaf nitrogen relationship at ambient and elevated carbon dioxide: a meta-analysis. *Global Change Biology*, **5**, 331–346.

Picon, C., Guehl, J.M. & Aussenac, G. 1996. Growth dynamics, transpiration and water-use efficiency of *Quercus robur* plants submitted to elevated CO_2 and drought. *Annales Science Forestry*, **53**, 431–446.

Pole, M. 1999. Structure of a near-polar latitude forest from the New Zealand Jurassic. *Palaeogeography, Palaeoclimatology, Palaeoecology*, **147**, 121–139.

Pollack, J.B., Toon, O.B., Ackerman, T.P., McKay, C.P. & Turco, R.P. 1983. Environmental effects of an impact-generated dust cloud: implications for the Cretaceous–Tertiary extinctions. *Science*, **219**, 287–289.

Pollard, D. & Shulz, M. 1994. A model for the potential locations of Triassic evaporite basins driven by palaeoclimatic GCM simulations. *Global and Planetary Change*, **9**, 233–249.

Polley, H.W., Johnson, H.B., Marino, B.D. & Mayeux, H.S. 1993a. Increase in plant water use efficiency and biomass over glacial to present CO_2 concentrations. *Nature*, **361**, 61–64.

Polley, H.W., Johnson, H.B. & Mayeux, H.S. 1992. Carbon dioxide and water fluxes of C_3 annuals and C_3 and C_4 perennials at subambient CO_2 concentrations. *Functional Ecology*, **6**, 693–703.

Polley, H.W., Johnson, H.B. & Mayeux, H.S. 1995. Nitrogen and water requirements of C_3 plants grown at glacial to present carbon dioxide concentrations. *Functional Ecology*, **9**, 86–96.

Polley, H.W., Johnson, H.B., Mayeux, H.S. & Malone, S.R. 1993b. Physiology and growth of wheat across a subambient carbon dioxide gradient. *Annals of Botany*, **71**, 347–356.

Pope, K.O., Baines, K.H., Ocampo, A.C. & Ivanov, B.A. 1994. Impact winter and the Cretaceous/Tertiary extinctions: results of a Chicxulub asteroid impact model. *Earth and Planetary Science Letters*, **128**, 719–725.

Post, W.M., Emanuel, W.R., Zinke, P.J. & Stangenberger, A.G. 1982. Soil carbon pools and world life zones. *Nature*, **298**, 156–159.

Potts, R. & Behrensmeyer, A.K. 1992. Late Cenozoic terrestrial ecosystems. In *Terrestrial ecosystems through time. Evolutionary paleoecology of terrestrial plants and animals*, ed. A.D. Behrensmeyer *et al.*, pp. 419–541. University of Chicago Press.

Prentice, I.C., Cramer, W., Harrison, S.P., Leemans, R., Monserud, R.A. & Solomon, A.M. 1992. A global biome model based on plant physiology and dominance. *Journal of Biogeography*, **19**, 117–134.

Prentice, I.C., Harrison, S.P., Jolly, D. & Guiot, J. 1998. The climate and biomes of Europe at 6000 yr BP: comparisons of model simulations and pollen-based reconstructions. *Quaternary Science Reviews*, **17**, 659–668.

Prentice, I.C., Sykes, M.T., Lautenschlager, M., Harrison, S.P., Denissenko, O. & Bartlein,

P.J. 1993. Modelling vegetation patterns and terrestrial carbon storage at the last glacial maximum. *Global Ecology and Biogeography Letters*, **3**, 67–76.

Price, C. & Rind, D. 1994. The impact of a $2 \times CO_2$ climate on lightning-caused fires. *Journal of Climate*, **7**, 1484–1494.

Price, G.D., Sellwood, B.W. & Valdes, P.J. 1995. Sedimentological evaluation of general circulation model simulations for the 'greenhouse' earth: Cretaceous and Jurassic case studies. *Sedimentary Geology*, **100**, 159–180.

Price, G.D., Valdes, P.J. & Sellwood, B.W. 1997. Quantitative palaeoclimate GCM validation: late Jurassic and mid-Cretaceous case studies. *Journal of the Geological Society*, **154**, 769–772.

Price, G.D., Valdes, P.J. & Sellwood, B.W. 1998. A comparison of GCM simulated Cretaceous 'greenhouse' and 'icehouse' climates: implications for the sedimentary record. *Palaeogeography, Palaeoclimatology, Palaeoecology*, **142**, 123–138.

Quebedaux, B. & Chollet, R. 1977. Comparative growth analyses of *Panicum* species with different rates of photorespiration. *Plant Physiology*, **59**, 42–44.

Ramanathan, V. & Coakley, J.A. 1978. Climate modeling through radiative-convective models. *Review of Geophysics and Space Physics*, **16**, 465–489.

Ramanathan, V. & Collins, W. 1991. Thermodynamic regulation of ocean warming by cirrus clouds deduced from observations of the 1987 El Niño. *Nature*, **351**, 27–32.

Raup, D.M. & Sepkoski, J.J. 1982. Mass extinctions in the marine fossil record: testing for periodicity of extinction. *Science*, **215**, 1501–1503.

Raval, A. & Ramanathan, V. 1989. Observational determination of the greenhouse effect. *Nature*, **342**, 758.

Raven, J.A. 1993. The evolution of vascular land plants in relation to quantitative function of dead water-conducting cells and of stomata. *Biological Reviews*, **68**, 337–363.

Raven, J.A. 1996. Inorganic carbon assimilation by marine biota. *Journal of Experimental Marine Biology and Ecology*, **203**, 39–47.

Raven, J.A., Johnston, A.M., Parsons, R. & Kübler, J. 1994. The influence of natural and experimental high O_2 concentrations on O_2-evolving phototrophs. *Biological Reviews*, **69**, 61–94.

Raven, J.A. & Spicer, R.A. 1996. The evolution of crassulacean acid metabolism. In *Crassulacean acid metabolism*, ed. Winter & Smith, pp. 360–385. Springer-Verlag, Berlin.

Read, D.J. 1991. Mycorrhizas in ecosystems. *Experientia*, **47**, 376–391.

Read, J. & Francis, J. 1992. Responses of some southern Hemisphere tree species to a prolonged dark period and their implications for high-latitude Cretaceous and Tertiary floras. *Palaeogeography, Palaeoclimatology, Palaeoecology*, **99**, 271–290.

Rees, P.M., Ziegler, A.M. & Valdes, P.J. 2000. Jurassic phytogeography and climates: new data and model comparisons. In *Warm climates in Earth history*, ed. B.T. Huber, K.G. Macleod & S.L. Wing, pp. 297–318. Cambridge University Press.

Retallack, G.J. 1995. Permian–Triassic crisis on land. *Science*, **267**, 77–80.

Retallack, G.J., Leahy, G.D., Spoon, M.D. 1987. Evidence from paleosols for ecosystem changes across the Cretaceous/Tertiary boundary in eastern Montana. *Geology*, 15, 1090–1093.

Retallack, G.J., Veevers, J.J. & Morante, R. 1996. Global coal gap between Permian–Triassic extinction and middle Triassic recovery of peat-forming plants. *Geological Society of America Bulletin*, **108**, 195–207.

Rey, A. & Jarvis, P.G. 1997. Growth response of young birch trees (*Betula pendula* Roth.) after four and a half years of CO_2 exposure. *Annals of Botany*, **80**, 809–816.

Robinson, J.M. 1989. Phanerozoic O_2 variation, fire, and terrestrial ecology. *Palaeogeography, Palaeoclimatology, Palaeoecology*, **75**, 223–240.

Robinson, J.M. 1990a. Lignin, land plants, and fungi. Biological evolution affecting Phanerozoic oxygen balance. *Geology*, **15**, 607–610.

Robinson, J.M. 1990b. The burial of organic carbon as affected by the evolution of land plants. *Historical Biology*, **3**, 189–201.

Robinson, J.M. 1991. Phanerozoic atmospheric reconstructions: a terrestrial perspective. *Palaeogeography, Palaeoclimatology, Palaeoecology*, **97**, 51–62.

Robinson, J.M. 1994a. Speculations on carbon dioxide starvation, Late Tertiary evolution of stomatal regulation and floristic modernization. *Plant, Cell and Environment*, **17**, 345–354.

Robinson, J.M. 1994b. Atmospheric CO_2 and plants. *Nature*, **368**, 105–106.

Rochefort, L. & Bazzaz, F.A. 1992. Growth response to elevated CO_2 in seedlings of four co-occurring birch species. *Canadian Journal of Forest Research*, **22**, 1583–1587.

Roden, J.S. & Ball, M.C. 1996. Growth and photosynthesis of two eucalyptus species during high temperature stress under ambient and elevated CO_2. *Global Change Biology*, **2**, 115–128.

Roy, H. & Nierzwicki-Bauer, S.A. 1991. Rubisco: genes, structure assembly and evolution. In *The Photosynthetic apparatus: molecular biology and operation*, ed. L. Bogorad & I.K. Vasil, pp. 347–364. Academic Press, San Diego.

Ryan, M.G. & Yoder, B.J. 1997. Hydraulic limits to tree height and tree growth. *Bioscience*, **47**, 235–242.

Sage, R.F. 1994. Acclimation of photosynthesis to increasing atmospheric CO_2: the gas exchange perspective. *Photosynthesis Research*, **39**, 351–368.

Sage, R.F. & Reid, C.D. 1992. Photosynthetic acclimation to sub-ambient CO_2 (20 Pa) in the C_3 annual *Phaseolus vulgaris*. *Photosynthetica*, **27**, 605–617.

Sage, R.F., Sharkey, T.D. & Seeman, J.R. 1989. Acclimation of photosynthesis to elevated CO_2 in five C_3 species. *Plant Physiology*, **89**, 590–596.

Sakai, A. & Larcher, W. 1987. *Frost survival of plants. Responses and adaptation to freezing stress*. Springer-Verlag, Berlin.

Saltzman, B. 1983. *Theory of climate*, ed. B. Saltzman. *Advances in Geophysics*, Vol. 25. Academic Press, New York.

Savard, L., Li, P., Strauss, S.H., Chase, M.W., Michaud, M., & Bousquet, J. 1994. Chloroplast and nuclear gene sequences indicate Late Pennsylvanian time for the last common ancestor of extant seed plants. *Proceedings of the National Academy of Sciences, USA*, **B91**, 5163–5167.

Saward, S.A. 1992. A global view of Cretaceous vegetation patterns. *Geological Society of America Special Paper*, **267**, 17–35.

Schapendonk, A.H.C.M., Dijkstra, P., Groenworld, J., Pot, C.S. & van de Geijn, S.C. 1997. Carbon balance and water use efficiency of frequently cut *Lolium perenne* L. swards at elevated carbon dioxide. *Global Change Biology*, **3**, 207–216.

Schenk, U., Manderscheid, R., Hugen, J. & Weigel, H.J. 1995. Effects of CO_2 enrichment and intraspecific competition on biomass partitioning, nitrogen content and microbial carbon in soil of perennial ryegrass and white clover. *Journal of Experimental Botany*, **46**, 987–993.

Schimel, D.S. 1998. The carbon equation. *Nature*, **393**, 208–209.

Schimmelmann, A. & DeNiro, M.J. 1984. Elemental and stable isotope variations of organic matter from a terrestrial sequence containing the Cretaceous/Tertiary boundary at York Canyon, New Mexico. *Earth and Planetary Science Letters*, **68**, 392–398.

Schlesinger, W.H. 1977. Carbon balance in terrestrial detritus. *Annual Review of Ecology and Systematics*, **8**, 51–81.

Schlesinger, W.H. 1997. *Biogeochemistry: an analysis of change*, 2nd edition. Academic Press, San Diego.

Schneider, S.H. 1992. Introduction to climate modeling. In *Climate system modeling*, ed. K.E. Trenberth, pp. 3–26. Cambridge University Press.

Scotese, C.R. & McKerrow, W.S. 1990. Revised world maps and introduction. In *Palaeozoic Palaeogeography and Biogeography*, ed. W.S. McKerrow & C.R. Scotese, *Geological Society Memoir*, **12**, 1–21.

Scott, A.C. 1978. Sedimentological and ecological control of Westphalian b plant assemblages from West Yorkshire. *Proceedings of the Yorkshire Geological Society*, **41**, 461–508.

Scott, A.C. 1979. The ecology of coal measure floras from northern Britain. *Proceedings of the Geological Association*, **90**, 97–116.

Scott, A.C. & Jones, T.P. 1994. The nature and influence of fire in Carboniferous ecosystems. *Palaeogeography, Palaeoclimatology, Palaeoecology*, **106**, 91–112.

Scott, A.C., Lomax, B.H., Collinson, M.E., Upchurch, G.R. & Beerling, D.J. 2000. Fire across the K–T boundary: initial results from the Sugarite coals, New Mexico, USA. *Palaeogeography, Palaeoclimatology, Palaeoecology*, **164**, 381–395.

Sellers, P.J. 1985. Canopy reflectance, photosynthesis and transpiration. *International Journal of Remote Sensing*, **6**, 1335–1372.

Sellers, P.J., Bounoua, L., Collatz, G.J. *et al.* 1996. Comparison of radiative and physiological effects of doubled atmospheric CO_2 on climate. *Science*, **271**, 1402–1406.

Sellers, P.J., Los, S.O., Tucker, C.J. *et al.* 1994. A global 1*1 degree NDVI data set for climate studies. Part 2: the generation of global fields of terrestrial biophysical parameters from the NDVI. *International Journal of Remote Sensing*, **15**, 3519–3545.

Sellers, P.J., Los, S.O., Tucker, C.J. *et al.* 1996. A revised land surface parameterization (SiB2) for atmospheric GCMs. Part II: the generation of global fields of terrestrial biophysical parameters from satellite data. *Journal of Climate*, **9**, 706–737.

Sellwood, B.W. & Price, G.D. 1994. Sedimentary facies as indicators of Mesozoic climate. *Philosophical Transactions of the Royal Society*, **B341**, 225–233.

Sellwood, B.W., Price, G.D. & Valdes, P.J. 1994. Cooler estimates of Cretaceous temperatures. *Nature*, **370**, 453–455.

Shackleton, N.J. & Boersma, A. 1981. The climate of the Eocene ocean. *Journal of the Geological Society*, **138**, 153–157.

Sharkey, T.D. 1988. Estimating the rate of photorespiration in leaves. *Physiologia Plantarum*, **73**, 147–152.

Sharp, Z.D. & Cerling, T.E. 1998. Fossil isotope records of seasonal climate and ecology: straight from the horse's mouth. *Geology*, **26**, 219–222.

Shaw, R.H. & Pereira, A.R. 1982. Aerodynamic roughness of a plant canopy: a numerical experiment. *Agricultural Meteorology*, **26**, 51–65.

Shearer, J.C., Moore, T.A. & Demchuk, T.T. 1995. Delineation of the distinctive nature of Tertiary coal beds. *International Journal of Coal Geology*, **28**, 71–98.

Sheen, J. 1990. Metabolic repression of transcription in higher plants. *Plant Cell*, **2**, 1027–1038.

Shugart, H.H. 1984. *A theory of forest dynamics. The ecological implications of forest succession models*. Springer-Verlag, New York.

Shukolyukov, A. & Lugmair, G.W. 1998. Isotopic evidence for the Cretaceous–Tertiary impactor and its type. *Science*, **282**, 927–929.

Shuttleworth, W.J. & Gurney, R.J. 1990. The theoretical relationship between foliage temperature and canopy resistance in sparse crops. *Quarterly Journal of the Meteorological Society*, **116**, 497–519.

Siedow, J.N. & Umbach, A.L. 1995. Plant mitochondrial electron transfer and molecular biology. *The Plant Cell*, **7**, 821–831.

Siegenthaler, U. & Sarmiento, J.L. 1993. Atmospheric carbon dioxide and the ocean. *Nature*, **365**, 119–125.

Singsaas, E.L., Lerdau, M., Winter, K. & Sharkey, T.D. 1997. Isoprene increases thermotolerance of isoprene-emitting species. *Plant Physiology*, **115**, 1413–1420.

Sinha, A. & Stott, L.D. 1994. New atmospheric pCO_2 estimates from paleosols during the Paleocene/early Eocene global warming interval. *Global and Planetary Change*, **9**, 297–307.

Slingo, J.M., Blackburn, M., Betts, A., *et al.* 1994. Mean climate and transience in the tropics of the UGAMP GCM: sensitivity to convective parameterisation. *Quarterly Journal of the Royal Meteorological Society*, **120**, 881–922.

Sloan, L.C. & Barron, E.J. 1992. A comparison of Eocene climate model results to quantified paleoclimate interpretations. *Palaeogeography, Palaeoclimatology, Palaeoecology*, **93**, 183–202.

Sloan, L.C. & Pollard, D. 1998. Polar stratispheric clouds: a high latitude warming mechanism in an ancient greenhouse world. *Geophysical Research Letters*, **25**, 3517–3520.

Sloan, L.C. & Rea, D.K. 1995. Atmospheric carbon dioxide and early Eocene climate: a general circulation modelling sensitivity study. *Palaeogeography, Palaeoclimatology, Palaeoecology*, **119**, 275–292.

Sloan, L.C., Walker, J.C.G. & Moore, T.C. 1995. Possible role of oceanic heat transport in early Eocene climate. *Paleoceanography*, **10**, 347–356.

Sloan, L.C., Walker, J.C.G., Moore, T.C., Rea, D.K. & Zachos, J.C. 1992. Possible methane induced polar warming in the early Eocene. *Nature*, **357**, 320–322.

Smith, A.G., Smith, D.G. & Funnell, B.M. 1994. *Atlas of Mesozoic and Cenozoic coastlines*. Cambridge University Press, Cambridge.

Smith, T.M., Shugart, H.H. & Woodward, F.I. (eds.) 1997. *Plant functional types: their relevance to ecosystem properties and global change*. Cambridge University Press.

Soltis, P.S., Soltis, D.E. & Smiley, C.J. 1993. An *rbcL* sequence from a Miocene *Taxodium* (bald cypress). *Proceedings of the National Academy of Sciences, USA*, **89**, 449–451.

Sowers, T., Bender, M., Raynaud, D., Korotkevich, Y.S. & Orchado, J. 1991. The $\delta^{18}O$ of atmospheric O_2 from air inclusions in the Vostok ice core: timing of CO_2 and ice volume changes during the penultimate deglaciation. *Paleoceanography*, **6**, 679–696.

Spero, H.J., Lea, D.W. & Bemis, B.E. 1997. Effect of seawater carbonate concentration on foraminiferal carbon and oxygen isotopes. *Nature*, **390**, 497–500.

Spicer, R.A. 1989a. Physiological characteristics of land plants in relation to environment through time. *Transactions of the Royal Society of Edinburgh: Earth Sciences*, **80**, 321–329.

Spicer, R.A. 1989b. Plants at the Cretaceous Tertiary boundary. *Philosophical Transactions of the Royal Society*, **B325**, 291–305.

Spicer, R.A. & Corfield, R.M. 1992. A review of terrestrial and marine climates in the Cretaceous with implications for modelling the 'greenhouse Earth'. *Geological Magazine*, **129**, 169–180.

Spicer, R.A. & Parrish, J.T. 1986. Paleobotanical evidence for cool north polar climates in the middle Cretaceous (Albian–Cenomanian). *Geology*, **14**, 703–706.

Spicer, R.A. & Parrish, J.T. 1990. Late Cretaceous–early Tertiary palaeoclimates of northern high latitudes: a quantitative view. *Journal of the Geological Society, London*, **147**, 329–341.

Spicer, R.A., Parrish, J.T. & Grant, P.R. 1992. Evolution of vegetation and coal-forming environments in the Late Cretaceous of the North slope of Alaska. *Geological Society of America Special Paper*, **267**, 177–192.

Spicer, R.A., Rees, P. & Chapman, J.L. 1993. Cretaceous phytogeography and climate signals. *Philosophical Transactions of the Royal Society*, **B341**, 277–286.

Stanley, S.M. 1986. *Earth and life through time*. Freeman, New York.

Steffen, W.L., Walker, B.H., Ingram, J.S. & Koch, G.W. (eds.) 1992. *Global Change and terrestrial ecosystems: the operational plan*. International Geosphere Biosphere Programme. Global Change Report No. 21, IGBP, Stockholm.

Stirling, C.M., Davey, P.A., Williams, T.G. & Long, S.P. 1997. Acclimation of photosynthesis to elevated CO_2 and temperature in five British native species of contrasting functional type. *Global Change Biology*, **3**, 237–246.

Stock, J.B., Stock, A.M. & Mottonen, J.M. 1990. Signal transduction in bacteria. *Nature*, **344**, 395–400.

Stott, L.D. & Kennett, J.P. 1989. New constraints on early Tertiary palaeoproductivity from carbon isotopes in foraminifera. *Nature*, **342**, 526–529.

Street-Perrott, F.A., Haung, Y., Perrott, R.A. *et al.* 1997. Impact of lower atmospheric carbon dioxide on tropical mountain ecosystems. *Science*, **278**, 1422–1426.

Stubblefield, S. & Banks, H.P. 1978. The cuticle of *Drepanophycus spinaformis*, long ranging Devonian lycopod from New York and Edstern, Canada. *American Journal of Botany*, **65**, 110–118.

Sukumar, R., Ramesh, R., Pant, R.K., Rajagopalan, G. 1993. A $\delta^{13}C$ record of late Quaternary climate change from tropical peats in southern India. *Nature*, **364**, 703–706.

Sweet, A.R., Braman, D.R. & Lerbekmo, J.F. 1990. Palynofloral response to K/T boundary events: a transitory interruption within a dynamic system. *Geological Society of America Special Paper*, **247**, 457–469.

Tans, P., Keeling, R.F. & Berry, J.A. 1993. Oceanic ^{13}C data. A new window on CO_2 uptake by the oceans. *Global Biogeochemical Cycles*, **7**, 353–368.

TEMPO 1996. Potential role of vegetation feedback in the climate sensitivity of high-latitude regions: a case study at 6000 years B.P. *Global Biogeochemical Cycles*, **10**, 727–736.

Thomasson, J. R., Nelson, M. E. & Zakrezewski, R. J. 1988. A fossil grass (Gramineae: Chloridoideae) from the Miocene with Krantz anatomy. *Science*, **233**, 876–878.

Thompson, S. J. & Pollard, D. (1995) A global climate model (GENESIS) with a land-surface-transfer scheme (LSX). Part 1: present climate simulation. *Journal of Climate*, **8**, 732–761.

Tingey, D. T., Johnson, M. G., Phillips, D. L., Johnson, D. W. & Ball, J. T. 1996. Effects of elevated CO_2 and nitrogen on the synchrony of shoot and root growth in ponderosa pine. *Tree Physiology*, **16**, 905–916.

Tissue, D. T., Griffin, K. L., Thomas, R. B. & Strain, B. R. 1995. Effects of low and elevated CO_2 on C_3 and C_4 annuals. II. Photosynthesis and leaf biochemistry. *Oecologia*, **101**, 21–28.

Toolin, L. J. & Eastoe, C. J. 1993. Late Pleistocene–recent atmospheric $\delta^{13}C_a$ records of C_4 grasses. *Radiocarbon*, **35**, 1–7.

Toon, O. B., Pollack, J. B., Ackerman, T. P., Turco, R. P., McKay, C. P. & Liu, M. S. 1982. Evolution of an impact-generated dust cloud and its effects on the atmosphere. *Geological Society of America Special Paper*, **190**, 215–221.

Toon, O. B., Zahnle, K., Morison, D., Turco, R. P. & Covey, C. 1997. Environmental perturbations caused by impacts of asteroids and comets. *Review of Geophysics*, **35**, 41–78.

Trenberth, K. E. (ed.) 1992. *Climate System Modeling*. Cambridge University Press.

Tschaplinksi, T. J., Stewart, D. B., Hanson, P. J. & Norby, R. J. 1995. Interactions between drought and elevated CO_2 on growth and gas exchange of seedlings of three deciduous tree species. *New Phytologist*, **129**, 63–71.

Tu, N. T. T., Bocherens, H., Mariotti, A. *et al.* 1999. Ecological distribution of Cenomanian terrestrial plants based on $^{13}C/^{12}C$ ratios. *Palaeogeography, Palaeoclimatology, Palaeoecology*, **145**, 79–93.

Tyree, M. T. & Sperry, J. S. 1989. Vulnerability of xylem to cavitation and embolism. *Annual Review of Plant Physiology and Molecular Biology*, **40**, 19–38.

Upchurch, G. R., Otto-Bliesner, B. L. & Scotese, C. 1998. Vegetation-atmosphere interactions and their role in global warming during the latest Cretaceous. *Philosophical Transactions of the Royal Society*, **B353**, 97–112.

Urey, H. C. 1952. *The Planets, their origins and development*. Yale University Press.

Vakhrameev, V. A. 1991. *Jurassic and Cretaceous floras and climates of the Earth*. Cambridge University Press.

Valdes, P. J. 1993. Atmospheric general circulation models of the Jurassic. *Philosophical Transactions of the Royal Society*, **B341**, 317–326.

Valdes, P. J. 2000. Warm climate forcing mechanisms. In *Warm climates in Earth history*, ed. B. T. Huber, K. G. MacLeod & S. L. Wing, pp. 3–20. Cambridge University Press.

Valdes, P. J. & Crowley, T. J. 1998. A climate model intercomparison for the Carboniferous. *Palaeoclimates: Data and Modelling*, **2**, 219–238.

Valdes, P. J. & Sellwood, B. W. 1992. A palaeoclimate model for the Kimmeridgian. *Palaeogeography, Palaeoclimatology, Palaeoecology*, **95**, 47–72.

Valdes, P. J., Sellwood, B. W. & Price, G. D. 1996. Evaluating concepts of Cretaceous equability. *Palaeoclimates: Data and Modelling*, **2**, 139–158.

Van Campo, E., Guiot, J. & Peng, C. 1993. A data-based re-appraisal of the terrestrial carbon budget at the last glacial maximum. *Global and Planetary Change*, **8**, 189–201.

Van de Water, P. K., Leavitt, S. W. & Betancourt, J. L. 1994. Trends in the stomatal density and

$^{13}C/^{12}C$ ratios of *Pinus flexilis* needles during the last glacial–interglacial cycle. *Science*, **264**, 239–243.

Van Gardingen, P.R., Jeffree, C.E. & Grace, J. 1989. Variation in stomatal aperture in leaves of *Avena fatua* L. observed by low-temperature electron microscopy. *Plant, Cell and Environment*, **12**, 887–898.

VEMAP members, 1995. Vegetation/ecosystem modeling and analysis project: Comparing biogeography and biogeochemistry models in a continental-scale study of terrestrial ecosystem responses to climate change and CO_2 doubling. *Global Biogeochemical Cycles*, **9**, 407–437.

Visscher, H., Brinkhuis, H., Dilcher, D.L. *et al.* 1996. The terminal Paleozoic fungal event: evidence of terrestrial ecosystem destabilization and collapse. *Proceedings of the National Academy of Sciences, USA*, **93**, 2155–2158.

Volk, T. 1987. Feedbacks between weathering and atmospheric CO_2 over the last 100 million years. *American Journal of Science*, **287**, 763–779.

Volk, T. 1989. Rise of angiosperms as a factor in long-term climatic cooling. *Geology*, **17**, 107–110.

von Caemmerer, S. & Evans, J.R. 1991. Determination of the average partial pressure of CO_2 in chloroplasts from leaves of several C_3 plants. *Australian Journal of Plant Physiology*, **18**, 287–305.

von Caemmerer, S. & Farquhar, G.D. 1981. Some relationships between the biochemistry of photosynthesis and the gas exchange of leaves. *Planta*, **153**, 376–387.

Walker, D.A., Leegood, R.C. & Sivak, M.N. 1986. Ribulose bisphosphate carboxylase-oxygenase: its role in photosynthesis. *Philosophical Transactions of the Royal Society of London*, **B313**, 305–324.

Walker, J.C.G. 1994. Global geochemical cycles of carbon. In *Regulation of atmospheric CO_2 and O_2 by photosynthetic carbon metabolism*, ed. N.E. Tolbert & J. Preis. pp. 75–89. Oxford University Press.

Walker, J.C.G., Hays, P.B. & Kasting, J.F. 1981. A negative feedback mechanism for the long-term stabilization of Earth's surface temperature. *Journal of Geophysical Research*, **86**, 9776–9782.

Walker, J.C.G. & Kasting, J.F. 1992. Effects of fuel and forest conservation on future levels of atmospheric carbon dioxide. *Global and Planetary Change*, **97**, 151–189.

Wanless, H.R. & Shepard, F.P. 1936. Sea level and climatic changes related to Late Paleozoic cycles. *Geological Society of America Bulletin*, **47**, 1177–1206.

Ward, P.D. 1995. After the fall: lessons and directions from the K/T debate. *Palaios*, **10**, 530–538.

Ward, J.K. & Strain, B.R. 1997. Effects of low and elevated CO_2 partial pressures on growth and reproduction of *Arabidopsis thaliana* from different elevations. *Plant, Cell and Environment*, **20**, 254–260.

Washington, W.M. & Meehl, G.A. 1989. Climate sensitivity due to increased CO_2: experiments with a coupled atmosphere and ocean general circulation model. *Climate Dynamics*, **4**, 1–38.

Washington, W.M. & Parkinson, C.L. 1986. *An Introduction to three-dimensional climate modeling*. University Science Books and Oxford University Press.

Watson, A.J., Lovelock, J.E. & Margulis, L. 1978. Methanogenesis, fires and the regulation of atmospheric oxygen. *Biosystems*, **10**, 293–298.

Watson, R.T., Zinyowera, M.C. & Moss, R.H. (eds.) 1995. *Climate Change 1995: Impacts,*

Adaptation and Mitigation. Contribution of Working Group II to the Second Assessment Report of the Intergovernmental Panel on Climate Change. Cambridge University Press.

Wayne, P.M., Reekie, E.G. & Bazzaz, F.A. 1998. Elevated CO_2 ameliorates birch response to high temperature and frost stress: implications for modelling climate-induced geographic range shifts. *Oecologia*, **114**, 335–342.

Weaver, A.J., Eby, M., Fanning, A.F. & Wiebe, E.C. 1998. Simulated influence of carbon dioxide, orbital forcing and ice sheets on the climate of the last glacial maximum. *Nature*, **394**, 847–853.

Webb, T. (ed.) 1998. Late Quaternary climates: data synthesis and model experiments. *Quaternary Science Reviews*, **17**, 1–688.

Webb, T., Anderson, K.H., Bartlein, P.J. & Webb, R.S. 1998. Late Quaternary climate change in Eastern North America: a comparison of pollen-derived estimates with climate model results. *Quaternary Science Reviews*, **17**, 587–606.

Webber, A.N., Nie, G.Y. & Long, S.P. 1994. Acclimation of the photosynthetic proteins to rising atmospheric CO_2. *Photosynthesis Research*, **39**, 413–425.

Whitten, D.G.A. & Brooks, J.R.V. 1972. *Dictionary of geology*. Penguin, London.

Wigley, T.M.L. 1997. Implications of recent CO_2 emission-limitation proposals for stabilization of atmospheric concentrations. *Nature*, **390**, 267–270.

Wigley, T.M.L. & Raper, S.C.B. 1992. Implications for climate and sea level of revised IPCC emission scenarios. *Nature*, **357**, 293–300.

Wigley, T.M.L., Richels, R. & Edmonds, J.A. 1996. Economic and environmental choices in the stabilization of atmospheric CO_2 concentrations. *Nature*, **379**, 240–243.

Wilf, P., Wing, S.L., Greenwood, D.R. & Greenwood, C.L. 1998. Using fossil leaves as palaeoprecipitation indicators: an Eocene example. *Geology*, **26**, 203–206.

Williams, E.R. 1992. The Schumann resonance – a global tropical thermometer. *Science*, **256**, 1184–1187.

Williams, J.W., Summers, R.L., Webb, T. 1998. Applying plant functional types to construct biome maps from Eastern North American pollen data: comparisons with model results. *Quaternary Science Reviews*, **17**, 607–627.

Williams, J.W., Webb, T., Richard, P.J.H. & Newby, P. 2000. Late Quaternary biomes of Canada and the Eastern United States. *Journal of Biogeography* **27**, 585–607.

Wilson, K.M., Pollard, D., Hay, W.W., Thompson, S.L. & Wold, C.N. 1994 General circulation model simulations of Triassic climates: preliminary results. *Geological Society of America Special Paper*, **288**, 91–116.

Wilson, M.F. & Henderson-Sellers, A. 1985. A global archive of land cover and soils data for use in general circulation models. *Journal of Climatology*, **5**, 119–143.

Wing, S.L. & DiMichele, W.A. 1995. Conflict between local and global changes in plant diversity through geological time. *Palaios*, **10**, 551–564.

Wing, S.L. & Greenwood, D.R. 1993. Fossils and fossil climate: the case for equable Eocene continental interiors in the Eocene. *Philosophical Transactions of the Royal Society*, **B341**, 243–252.

Wing, S.L. & Sues, H.D. 1992. Mesozoic and early Cenozoic terrestrial ecosystems. In *Terrestrial ecosystems through time*, ed. A.K. Behrensmeyer *et al.*, pp. 327–416. University of Chicago Press, Chicago.

Witzke, B.J. 1990. Palaeoclimatic constraints for Palaeozoic palaeolatitudes of Laurentia and Euramerica. In *Palaeozoic Palaeogeography and Biogeography*, ed. W.S. McKerrow & C.R. Scotese, *Geological Society Memoir*, **12**, 57–73.

Wolbach, W.S., Anders, E. & Nazarov, M.A. 1990b. Fires at the K/T boundary: carbon in Sumbar, Turkmenia, site. *Geochimica et Cosmochimica Acta*, **54**, 1133–1146.

Wolbach, W.S., Gilmour, I. & Anders, E. 1990a. Major wildfires at the Cretaceous/Tertiary boundary. *Geological Society of America*, **247**, 391–400.

Wolbach, W.S., Gilmour, I., Anders, E., Orth, C.J. & Brooks, R.R. 1988. Global wildfire at the Cretaceous–Tertiary boundary. *Nature*, **334**, 665–669.

Wolbach, W.S., Lewis, R.S. & Anders, E. 1985. Cretaceous extinctions: evidence for wildfires and search for meteoritic material. *Science*, **230**, 167–170.

Wolfe, J.A. 1985. Distribution of major vegetation types during the Tertiary. In *The global carbon cycle and atmospheric CO$_2$: natural variations Archean to Present*, eds E.T. Sundquist & W.S. Broecker, pp. 357–375. American Geophysical Union Research Monographs No. 32, Washington, DC.

Wolfe, J.A. 1990. Palaeobotanical evidence for a marked temperature increase following the Cretaceous/Tertiary boundary. *Nature*, **343**, 153–156.

Wolfe, J.A. 1991. Palaeobotanical evidence for a June 'impact winter' at the Cretaceous/Tertiary boundary. *Nature*, **352**, 420–422.

Wolfe, J.A. & Uemura, K. 1999. Using fossil leaves as paleoprecipitation indicators: an Eocene example: comment and reply. *Geology*, **27**, 91–92.

Wolfe, J.A. & Upchurch, G.R. 1986. Vegetation, climatic and floral changes at the Cretaceous–Tertiary boundary. *Nature*, **324**, 148–152.

Wolfe, J.A. & Upchurch, G.R. 1987. Leaf assemblages across the Cretaceous–Tertiary boundary in the Raton Basin, New Mexico and Colorado. *Proceedings of the National Academy of Sciences, USA*, **84**, 5096–5100.

Wong, S.C., Cowan, I.R. & Farquhar, G.D. 1979. Stomatal conductance correlates with photosynthetic capacity. *Nature*, **282**, 424–426.

Wong, S.C., Kriedemann, P.E. & Farquhar, G.D. 1992. CO$_2$ × nitrogen interaction on seedling growth of four species of Eucalypt. *Australian Journal of Botany*, **40**, 457–472.

Woodrow, I.E. 1994. Optimal acclimation of the C$_3$ photosynthetic system under enhanced CO$_2$. *Photosynthesis Research*, **39**, 401–412.

Woodward, F.I. 1987a. *Climate and plant distribution.* Cambridge University Press.

Woodward, F.I. 1987b. Stomatal numbers are sensitive to increases in CO$_2$ from pre-industrial levels. *Nature*, **327**, 617–618.

Woodward, F.I. 1988. Temperature and the distribution of plant species. In *Plants and temperature*, ed. S.P. Long & F.I. Woodward. SEB Symposium, Vol. 42, pp. 59–75. Company of Biologists, Cambridge.

Woodward, F.I. 1996. Developing the potential for describing the terrestrial biosphere's response to a changing climate. In *Global change and terrestrial ecosystems*, ed. B.H. Walker & W.L. Steffen, pp. 511–528. Cambridge University Press.

Woodward, F.I. 1998. Do plants really need stomata? *Journal of Experimental Botany*, **49**, 471–480.

Woodward, F.I. & Bazzaz, F.A. 1988. The response of stomatal density to CO$_2$ partial pressure. *Journal of Experimental Botany* **39**, 1771–1781.

Woodward, F.I. & Beerling, D.J. 1997. The dynamics of vegetation change: health warnings for equilibrium 'dodo' models. *Global Ecology and Biogeography Letters*, **6**, 413–418.

Woodward, F. I. & Cramer, W. 1996. Plant functional types and climatic changes: Introduction. *Journal of Vegetation Science*, **7**, 306–308.

Woodward, F. I., Lomas, M. R. & Lee, S. E. 2001. Predicting the future production and distribution of global terrestrial vegetation. In *Terrestrial Global Productivity*, ed. R. Jacques, B. Saugier & H. Mooney, pp. 521–541. Academic Press.

Woodward, F. I. & Rochefort, L. 1991. Sensitivity analysis of vegetation diversity to environmental change. *Global Ecology and Biogeography Letters*, **1**, 7–23.

Woodward, F. I. & Sheehy, J. E. 1983. *Principles and measurements in environmental biology*. Butterworths, London.

Woodward, F. I. & Smith, T. M. 1994a. Global photosynthesis and stomatal conductance: modelling the controls by soils and climate. *Advances in Botanical Research*, **20**, 1–41.

Woodward, F. I. & Smith, T. M. 1994b. Predictions and measurements of the maximum photosynthetic rate at the global scale. In *Ecophysiology of photosynthesis*, ed. E. D. Schulze & M. M. Caldwell. Ecological Studies, Vol. 100, pp. 491–509. Springer-Verlag, New York.

Woodward, F. I., Smith, T. M. & Emanuel, W. R. 1995. A global land primary productivity and phytogeography model. *Global Biogeochemical Cycles*, **9**, 471–490.

Wright, V. P. & Vanstone, S. D. 1991. Assessing the carbon dioxide content of ancient atmospheres using palaeo-calcretes: theoretical and empirical constraints. *Journal of the Geological Society of London*, **148**, 945–947.

Wullschleger, S. D. 1993. Biochemical limitations to carbon assimilation in C_3 plants – a retrospective analysis of the A/C_i curves from 109 species. *Journal of Experimental Botany*, **44**, 907–920.

Yakir, D., Berry, J. A., Giles, L. & Osmond, C. B. 1994. Isotopic heterogeneity of water in transpiring leaves: identification of the component that controls the $\delta^{18}O$ of atmospheric O_2 and CO_2. *Plant, Cell and Environment*, **17**, 73–80.

Yapp, C. J. & Poths, H. 1992. Ancient atmospheric CO_2 pressures inferred from natural geothites. *Nature*, **355**, 342–344.

Yapp, C. J. & Poths, H. 1996. Carbon isotopes in continental weathering environments and variations in ancient CO_2 partial pressure. *Earth and Planetary Science Letters*, **137**, 71–82.

Zachos, J. C., Arthur, M. A. & Dean, W. E. 1989. Geochemical records for suppression of pelagic marine productivity at the Cretaceous–Tertiary boundary. *Nature*, **337**, 61–64.

Zachos, J. C., Stott, L. D. & Lohmann, K. C. 1994. Evolution of early Cenozoic marine temperatures. *Paleoceanography*, **9**, 353–387.

Ziegler, A. M., Raymond, A. L., Gierlowski, T. C., Horrell, M. A. Rowley, D. B. & Lottes, A. L. 1987. Coal, climate, and terrestrial productivity: the present and early Cretaceous compared. In *Coal and coal-bearing strata: recent advances*. Geological Society Special Publication No. 32, pp. 25–49.

Ziska, L. H. & Bunce, J. A. 1994. Increasing growth temperature reduces the stimulatory effect of elevated CO_2 on photosynthesis or biomass in two perennial species. *Physiologia Plantarum*, **91**, 183–190.

Ziska, L. H. & Bunce, J. A. 1997. The role of temperature in determining the stimulation of CO_2 assimilation at elevated carbon dioxide concentration in soybean seedlings. *Physiologia Plantarum*, **100**, 126–132.

Ziska, L.H., Hogan, K.P., Smith, A.P. & Drake, B.G. 1991. Growth and photosynthetic response of nine tropical species with long-term exposure to elevated carbon dioxide. *Oecologia*, **86**, 383–389.

Ziska, L.H., Weerakoon, W., Namuco, O.S. & Pamplona, R. 1996. The influence of nitrogen on the elevated CO_2 response in field-grown rice. *Australian Journal of Plant Physiology*, **23**, 45–52.

Index

Note: Page numbers in **bold** denote figures; those in *italics* tables or boxed material.